# INTERNATIONAL CORPORATE GOVERNANCE

*International Corporate Governance* analyses the escalating crisis in corporate governance, and the growing interest in corporate governance reform around the world. This important new textbook:

- investigates the reasons for the failure of Enron, WorldCom, Tyco, Parmalat and other major international corporations;
- examines the role of international standards of corporate governance, with the intervention of the OECD, World Bank and IMF;
- explores the continuing cultural diversity in corporate and institutional forms in the United States and United Kingdom, Europe and Asia Pacific.

The text considers the development of the institutional elements of corporate governance with the separation of ownership and control and the diffusion of share ownership, and records the transformation of corporate governance in the main markets of the world, the further internationalisation of financial markets and the increasing salience of institutional share ownership. Illustrated with a wealth of up-to-the-minute case studies and excellent illustrative material to guide the student reader through this complex subject, *International Corporate Governance* will be an essential text for anybody studying corporate governance today. The accompanying website can be found at www.routledge.com/textbooks/9780415323109.

**Thomas Clarke** is Director of the Centre for Corporate Governance and Professor of Management at the University of Technology, Sydney. Formerly DBM Professor of Corporate Governance at Leeds Business School and Visiting Professor at CEIBS, Shanghai, he was a member of the RSA Tomorrow's Company inquiry that influenced the review of UK company law. At the OECD in Paris he helped develop the international corporate governance code adopted by governments throughout the world.

# International Corporate Governance

## A comparative approach

Thomas Clarke

Routledge
Taylor & Francis Group

LONDON AND NEW YORK

First published 2007 by Routledge
2 Park Square, Milton Park, Abingdon, Oxon OX14 4RN

Simultaneously published in the USA and Canada
by Routledge
270 Madison Ave, New York, NY 10016

*Routledge is an imprint of the Taylor & Francis Group, an informa business*

© 2007 Thomas Clarke

Typeset in Amasis MT Lt by CEPHA Imaging Pvt. Ltd., INDIA
Printed and bound in Great Britain by MPG Books Ltd, Bodmin

*British Library Cataloguing in Publication Data*
A catalogue record for this book is available from the British Library

*Library of Congress Cataloging in Publication Data*
Clarke, Thomas, 1950–
International corporate governance: a comparative approach / Thomas Clarke.
p. cm.
Includes bibliographical references and index.
1. Corporate governance.   2. Comparative management–Case Studies. I. Title.
HD2741.C57 2007
658′.049–dc22
2006039140

ISBN10: 0-415-32309-6 (hbk)
ISBN10: 0-415-32310-X (pbk)
ISBN10: 0-203-30072-6 (ebk)

ISBN13: 978-0-415-32309-3 (hbk)
ISBN13: 978-0-415-32310-9 (pbk)
ISBN13: 978-0-203-30072-5 (ebk)

# Contents

List of Figures                                                         xii
List of Tables                                                          xv
Acknowledgements                                                        xviii

**Foreword by Sir Adrian Cadbury**                                      **xx**

**1  CYCLES OF GOVERNANCE**                                             **1**

Definitions                                                             1
Genesis of corporate governance                                        3
  *The South Sea Bubble*                                                3
  *Splitting the atom of ownership*                                     4
Forms of business associations                                         6
  *Corporate governance lifecycles*                                    7
Diversity in corporate governance                                      8
Globalisation of corporate governance                                  11
Cycles of governance                                                   11
Crisis in corporate governance                                         14
  *The US stock market bubble*                                         14
  *Enron and WorldCom*                                                 16
Reform of corporate governance                                         17
  *Sarbanes–Oxley Act*                                                 17
Continuing crisis in corporate governance                             18
  *CEO pay*                                                            18
  *Earnings misstatements*                                            21
Governance and corporate performance                                  22
Corporate governance and sustainability                               23
Agency and double agency dilemmas                                     23
Theoretical perspectives on boards and governance                     25
  *Multiple theoretical lenses*                                       29
Approach of this book                                                 30

**2  BOARDS AND DIRECTORS: THE POLITICAL MECHANISMS OF CORPORATE
GOVERNANCE**                                                          **33**

Introduction                                                          33
What do boards do?                                                    33
Directors' duties                                                     36
  *Business judgement rule*                                          36

Board duties and functions 37
Board and CEO relationship 38
Active and passive boards 40
*Active boards* 40
*Passive boards* 41
The Enron board: asleep at the wheel? 42
The WorldCom board: going through the motions 44
Boards and performance: accountability and value creation? 45
Changing roles of boards and directors 48
*Types of boards: unitary and supervisory boards* 48
*Elements of board design* 49
The reform of boards 50
*Audit committee* 51
*Remunerations committee* 51
*Nomination committee* 52
The effective chair 53
The role of non-executive directors 55
*Independence?* 56
Board best practices 56
Investigating board processes 58
Board roles in monitoring and strategy? 59
Accountability and risk management 60
*Internal controls* 62
*Identifying risks* 63
*Conflicts of interest* 63
Disclosure 64
The strategic role of the board 65
To whom is the board responsible? 67
*Shareholder primacy* 69
CEO power and capability 69
*Management vision* 69
*CEO power* 70
*Esprit de corps* 70
Management and board defences 71
CEO and executive compensation 72
Executive remuneration guidelines 79
The decline and fall of the emperor CEO? 80
Conclusions 82

**3 FINANCE, LAW AND MARKETS: THE INSTITUTIONAL ELEMENTS OF
CORPORATE GOVERNANCE 83**

Introduction 83
Corporate governance regimes 83
Institutional origins of corporate governance 85
*The separation of ownership and control* 87
The development of law and regulation 88
*The peculiarities of the Anglo-American institutions* 91
Bank, majority and market based finance 93
*Direct control via debt* 93

Market control via equity                                                        94
Market control via debt                                                          94
Direct control via equity                                                        94
Majority group control                                                           95
The market for corporate control                                                 98
Alternative corporate governance systems                                        100
Control mechanisms in corporate governance                                      104
Crises in corporate governance                                                  106
The increasing importance of institutional investors                            109
Increasing scale and activity                                                   110
Patient capital?                                                                112
Hedge funds: the wolf in shareholder's clothing?                                113
Private equity                                                                  116
Breaking the short-term cycle                                                   117
A new era for institutional investors?                                          118
Corporate governance and corporate performance                                  119
The reluctance of the institutions to exercise governance oversight             120
How institutions get involved in corporate governance                           122
The governance of investment institutions                                       124
Conclusions                                                                     128

**4  ANGLO-AMERICAN CORPORATE GOVERNANCE                                         129**

Introduction                                                                    129
Market based systems of corporate governance                                    129
US corporation regulation                                                       131
Delaware                                                                        133
Corporate failure and the reform of corporate governance                        135
Further efforts at reform                                                        138
United Kingdom                                                                   139
Cadbury reforms                                                                 140
Further UK reform                                                               142
Australia and New Zealand                                                        144
Shareholder value orientation                                                   149
The new economy                                                                 151
The Enron shock                                                                 152
Wider implications of Enron and the Sarbanes–Oxley Act                          154
New York Stock Exchange: Grasso's fall                                          156
Big on marketing light on regulation                                            157
Advancing inequality in the United States                                       157
Corporate governance reform around the world                                    158
Corporate failure in other countries: the One-Tel and HIH collapse              158
US company earnings misstatements                                               160
Sarbanes–Oxley costs of implementation                                          161
Rules-based and principles-based approaches                                      162
The myth of Anglo-American corporate governance                                 162
Further corporate governance reform in the UK                                   165
Further corporate governance reform in Australia: CLERP 9                        167
ASX corporate governance principles                                             168
Conclusions                                                                     169

## 5 EUROPEAN CORPORATE GOVERNANCE — 170

Introduction — 170
European relationship based approaches — 170
Bank finance and business networks — 171
Regional variations — 173
Different political, legal and regulatory structures — 173
The development of European corporate governance codes — 175
    *European Commission* — 176
    *France* — 176
    *Recomandations Sur Le Gouvernment D'Enterprise (1998, 2001, 2004)* — 176
    *Italy* — 176
    *Spain* — 178
    *Denmark* — 178
    *Germany* — 178
    *Switzerland* — 178
    *Sweden* — 179
    *Norway* — 179
    *Netherlands* — 179
    *Belgium* — 179
    *Code convergence?* — 179
The transformation of corporate governance systems — 181
    *Germany* — 181
    *France* — 185
    *Italy* — 186
Corporate governance failure in Europe — 187
The reform of European corporate governance institutions and practices — 188
    *FEE Report on European Corporate Governance* — 190
Modernising company law and enhancing corporate
    governance — 190
Convergence or harmonisation? — 192
The impact of shareholder value — 193
Reassessing the international role of Europe — 196
    *Isolationism/protectionism will not work* — 196
    *EU dominates global FDI* — 196
    *Euronext* — 197
Corporate governance in transitional economies — 197
    *Russia* — 198
Conclusions — 199

## 6 ASIA PACIFIC CORPORATE GOVERNANCE — 200

Introduction — 200
Asia Pacific relationship-based approaches — 200
Family controlled companies and business networks — 201
Weak governance mechanisms and institutions — 202
    *Boards* — 203
    *Finance* — 203
Economic growth and corporate governance — 204
East Asian financial crisis — 205

The beginning of reform 207
   *Japan* 209
   *China* 214
   *India* 217
The development of Asia Pacific corporate governance codes 219
   *Thailand* 219
   *Malaysia* 219
   *Indonesia* 219
   *China* 221
   *India* 221
   *Philippines* 221
   *Hong Kong* 221
   *Japan* 221
   *Singapore* 221
Continuing reform 221
   *Due diligence of directors* 221
Conclusions 227

**7 THE GLOBALISATION OF CORPORATE GOVERNANCE** **228**

Introduction 228
A universal corporate governance system? 228
The premium for corporate governance 229
What globalisation means 231
   *Deregulation of finance* 233
Globalisation of capital markets 234
The growth of equity markets 236
   *New York Stock Exchange* 238
Globalisation of regulation 242
   *OECD Principles of Corporate Governance (1999)* 244
   *OECD Principles (2004)* 246
   *International development of corporate governance standards* 251
Convergence of corporate governance 255
   *History and politics* 256
   *Law and regulation* 257
   *Culture: deep causation* 258
   *Institutional complementarities* 259
   *Rushing towards convergence?* 260
Diversity in corporate governance 262
Future trends 265
   *Complexity of corporate governance forms* 265
Conclusions 266

**8 CORPORATE SOCIAL RESPONSIBILITY** **267**

Introduction 267
The significance and impact of corporate social responsibility 267
The integrity of corporate social responsibility 269
Defining social and environmental sustainability 271

Tomorrow's markets 273
    People 273
    Innovation 273
    Natural capital 273
    Connection 274
    Roles and responsibilities 274
From the margins to the mainstream? 276
The legitimacy of CSR from a governance perspective 279
    Corporations enlightened shareholder value? The duty to promote the
        success of the company 279
The legitimacy of CSR from a governance perspective 285
    Investment institutions' effective portfolio management: the duty to address
        ESG issues? 285
Socially responsible investment and corporate social responsibility 288
Socially responsible investment strategies 291
    United States 291
    United Kingdom 295
    Australia 298
Social and environmental investment indices 299
SRI impact upon corporate environmental and social responsibility 302
Corporate reporting of CSR 303
Future developments: the redesign of the corporation 304

**CASE STUDIES   CORPORATE GOVERNANCE IN CRISIS** 307

Anglo-American Corporations 313

1   **Enron** 315

2   **WorldCom** 331

3   **Tyco** 354

European Corporations 363

4   **Royal Ahold** 365

5   **Parmalat** 374

6   **DaimlerChrysler** 388

7   **Vodafone–Mannesmann** 402

Asia Pacific Corporations                                                    419

8    James Hardie                                                           421

9    HIH Insurance Group                                                    434

10   Nomura                                                                 452

Appendix 1   Corporate Governance Websites                                 467

Appendix 2   Regional and Country Codes and Reports                        477

References                                                                  481
Index                                                                       511

# List of Figures

| | | |
|---|---|---|
| 1.1 | The forms of business association | 6 |
| 1.2 | Corporate governance lifecycle | 8 |
| 1.3 | Domestic market capitalisation, 1990–2004 | 12 |
| 1.4 | Value of share trading, 1990–2004 | 12 |
| 1.5 | Six months in the life of WorldCom, Enron, Tyco and Parmalat | 16 |
| 1.6 | Average top US CEOs annual remuneration vs. top rest of world CEOs ($ million) | 20 |
| 1.7 | Top five US CEOs annual remuneration vs. top five US fund managers CEOs, 2005 | 21 |
| 1.8 | Total number of US corporation earnings restatements, 1997–2005 | 22 |
| 1.9 | From owner entrepreneur to double agency dilemma | 25 |
| | | |
| 2.1 | Framework analysing board activities | 34 |
| 2.2 | Size and composition of boards in the UK | 35 |
| 2.3 | Red flags known to Enron's board | 43 |
| 2.4 | The transformation from management control to independent boards | 52 |
| 2.5 | The learning board model | 61 |
| 2.6 | Composition of median CEO pay in the US, 1980–2001 | 75 |
| 2.7 | Executive pay as a multiple of worker pay in the US, 1990–2005 | 76 |
| 2.8 | Comparison of CEO and worker pay in the US, 1990–2002 (in 2005 dollars) | 77 |
| | | |
| 3.1 | Trends in financial assets of institutional investors | 86 |
| 3.2 | Berle and Means adapted ownership model | 89 |
| 3.3 | Pension fund allocation around the world, 2003 | 111 |
| 3.4 | Institutional investor concern for corporate governance | 112 |
| 3.5 | Monitoring activities by institutional investors | 120 |
| 3.6 | Investment fund managers' role in corporate governance | 121 |
| 3.7 | Number of corporate governance proposals | 123 |
| 3.8 | Resolutions not supported by AMP Capital Investors, July–December 2005 | 124 |
| 3.9 | The complex governance and regulatory relationships of the institutional investors | 128 |
| | | |
| 4.1 | US reform of corporate governance regulation, 1932–2002 | 132 |
| 4.2 | US corporate governance legislation and the Standard and Poor index, 1990–2002 | 136 |
| 4.3 | UK reform of corporate governance regulation, 1992–2005 | 141 |
| 4.4 | UK corporate governance regulation and FTSE 100 index, 1992–2002 | 143 |
| 4.5 | Australian reform of corporate governance regulation, 1992–2004 | 147 |
| 4.6 | Corporate governance and regulation in Australia | 148 |

| 4.7 | Enron's rise and fall | 153 |
|---|---|---|
| 4.8 | The rise and fall of WorldCom | 154 |
| 4.9 | NYSE's annual profit vs. CEO Dick Grasso's annual compensation | 156 |
| 4.10 | Distribution of stock market holdings, by wealth class, 2004 | 158 |
| 4.11 | Comparison of CEO and worker pay in the US, 1990–2002 | 158 |
| 5.1 | Weight of pension funds in the economy and financial markets, 2001 | 172 |
| 5.2 | Recent flurry of new corporate governance codes in Europe | 175 |
| 5.3 | Multiple corporate governance reform processes in Europe | 177 |
| 5.4 | The dual system (1): segregation of duties | 183 |
| 5.5 | The dual system (2): equal representation of employee and shareholder representatives | 184 |
| 5.6 | Activities of supervisory board | 184 |
| 5.7 | Parmalat share price collapse | 188 |
| 5.8 | Ahold share price collapse | 189 |
| 5.9 | What shareholders' democracy? Companies applying 'one share/one vote' principle | 191 |
| 5.10 | Dividends, number of employees and personnel expenditure per employee | 195 |
| 6.1 | Concentration of family control of corporate assets in East Asia | 202 |
| 6.2 | Change in share indexes of East Asia region, 1997–1998 | 206 |
| 6.3 | Market capitalisation of stock exchanges in Asia Pacific, 1998 | 207 |
| 6.4 | The Japanese model transformation | 213 |
| 6.5 | Transitions of Japanese corporate governance, 1960s–2000 | 215 |
| 6.6 | Asia Pacific reform of corporate governance regulation | 220 |
| 6.7 | Countries with higher concentration of wealth show less progress in institutional reforms | 223 |
| 7.1 | Recent evolution of domestic equity market capitalisation | 236 |
| 7.2 | Evolution of share trading, by region | 237 |
| 7.3 | Market capitalisation of NYSE listed companies, 1996–2005 | 239 |
| 7.4 | Investor holdings of non-US equities | 240 |
| 7.5 | New listings in major markets, 1998–2005 | 242 |
| 7.6 | Development of international principles of corporate governance guidelines | 252 |
| 7.7 | Corporate governance objectives | 263 |
| 7.8 | Multiple convergence of governance institutions and relationships | 264 |
| 7.9 | Corporate governance convergence: alternative directions | 266 |
| 8.1 | The economics of climate change | 268 |
| 8.2 | Key stakeholders according to corporate executives | 278 |
| 8.3 | CSR stakeholder model driving enlightened shareholder value | 280 |
| 8.4 | Legal and moral liability are converging | 285 |
| 8.5 | Fund trustees' fiduciary duties | 287 |
| 8.6 | Institutional investor voting, 2000–2003 | 288 |
| 8.7 | Growth of SRI investment assets in Australia, 2000–2006 | 289 |
| 8.8 | Growth of SRI investments in the US, 1995–2005 | 290 |
| 8.9 | Screens most commonly used in screened portfolios in the US, 2005 | 292 |
| 8.10 | Proportion of UK funds taking SRI concerns into account to differing degrees | 299 |
| 8.11 | Corporate strategies to deliver value to society | 304 |

| C1.1 | Timeline of Enron's collapse | 319 |
|------|------|------|
| C1.2 | How Enron buys power: Enron's political contributions | 321 |
| C1.3 | How Enron buys power: Ken Lay's contributions | 321 |
| | | |
| C2.1 | WorldCom's rise and fall | 335 |
| C2.2 | Top 250 ICT firms' net income, by sector | 336 |
| C2.3 | Ebbers' loan balance vs. current stock price | 339 |
| C2.4 | Arthur Andersen fees | 343 |
| C2.5 | Pension fund losses due to WorldCom collapse | 346 |
| | | |
| C3.1 | Tyco's share price and share trading, 2001–2006 | 355 |
| | | |
| C4.1 | Ahold overstatement of net income according to the Dutch GAAP | 368 |
| C4.2 | Ahold share price collapse | 370 |
| | | |
| C5.1 | The Tanzi pyramid holding I: the family holdings | 376 |
| C5.2 | The Tanzi pyramid holding II: the finance companies | 377 |
| C5.3 | Parmalat's six subsidiaries involved in the fraud | 379 |
| C5.4 | Parmalat stock price collapse | 380 |
| | | |
| C6.1 | Top ten global car manufacturers' rank, by volume of sales | 399 |
| | | |
| C7.1 | Structure of Mannesmann, pre-takeover | 412 |
| C7.2 | Ownership structure of former Mannesmann units | 412 |
| C7.3 | Vodafone–Mannesman historical stock prices, 1998–2006 | 415 |
| | | |
| C8.1 | The transfer of the assets of James Hardie & Coy and Jsekarb Pty | 425 |
| C8.2 | James Hardie & Coy and Jsekarb Pty renamed and separated from James Hardie Group | 426 |
| C8.3 | Dutch Company JHI NV becomes holding company of group | 427 |
| C8.4 | JHIL removed from James Hardie group into ABN 60 Foundation | 428 |
| C8.5 | James Hardie's share price | 430 |
| | | |
| C9.1 | HIH's share price rise and decline, June 1992 to February 2001 | 440 |
| C9.2 | Sale of HIH principal assets, 2001 | 440 |
| C9.3 | Causes of business exits in Australia | 441 |
| C9.4 | Causes of bankruptcies in Australia | 442 |
| C9.5 | Conflicted auditing of HIH | 445 |
| C9.6 | Andersen's increasing non-audit fees | 447 |
| | | |
| C10.1 | Nomura share price | 464 |

# List of Tables

| | | |
|---|---|---|
| 1.1 | Properties of insider and outsider systems of corporate governance | 10 |
| 1.2 | US top ten highest paid CEOs, 2005 | 19 |
| 1.3 | Rest of the world highest paid CEOs, 2004 | 20 |
| 1.4 | Theoretical perspectives on corporate governance | 27 |
| 2.1 | Specialised board committees | 50 |
| 2.2 | Comparative analysis of board structure, 2003 | 53 |
| 2.3 | ISS corporate governance quotient | 54 |
| 2.4 | Key risk areas | 62 |
| 2.5 | Typology of directors | 66 |
| 2.6 | Studies on strategic involvement of the board | 67 |
| 2.7 | Board defences | 73 |
| 2.8 | The incidence of board entrenchment and related provisions in US corporations | 74 |
| 2.9 | Adverse effects of approaches to controlling managers | 80 |
| 2.10 | Changes in executive pay composition: international comparisons | 81 |
| 3.1 | The distribution of outstanding listed equity among different categories of shareholders | 84 |
| 3.2 | The evolution of corporate governance forms and democratic governance | 86 |
| 3.3 | Number of takeovers, by region | 99 |
| 3.4 | Corporate governance regimes | 100 |
| 3.5 | Corporate governance alternative systems | 102 |
| 3.6 | Reputational intermediaries for sound corporate governance | 105 |
| 3.7 | How efficient are the various methods of controlling managers? | 107 |
| 3.8 | Pension funds and life insurance assets in selected OECD economies, 2003–2004 | 110 |
| 4.1 | US institutional ownership equities, 1990 and 2004 | 130 |
| 4.2 | Share ownership in the UK | 139 |
| 4.3 | Key differences between UK and US reporting frameworks and shareholder rights | 163 |
| 5.1 | Distribution of share ownership in German publicly traded companies | 171 |
| 5.2 | Summary of recent changes to company law and regulation | 180 |
| 5.3 | The distribution of net value added in large German firms, 1992–1994 and 1996–1998 | 195 |
| 5.4 | Penetration of active share ownership in some European countries | 198 |

| | | |
|---|---|---|
| 6.1 | Dimensions of the East Asian crisis, 1997–1998 | 206 |
| 6.2 | The distribution of share ownership in Japan, by type of shareholder | 210 |
| 6.3 | The corporate governance mechanisms in developing and transition countries | 224 |
| 6.4 | Corporate governance in selected countries of Asia Pacific, 2000–2005 | 226 |
| 6.5 | Market capitalisation of selected Asia Pacific countries, 2005 | 226 |
| 7.1 | Evolution of income, exports and capital flows, 1985–2002 | 233 |
| 7.2 | Largest stock exchanges in market capitalisation, year-end 2006 | 238 |
| 7.3 | Largest exchanges in share trading value, 2005–2006 | 238 |
| 7.4 | Global comparison of market capitalisation of domestic listed companies 1980–2005 | 240 |
| 7.5 | Global comparison of annualised trading | 241 |
| 8.1 | The range of environmental costs | 275 |
| 8.2 | KPMG CSR surveys, 1993–2005 | 276 |
| 8.3 | Drivers for corporate social responsibility | 277 |
| 8.4 | US shareholder actions planned for 2003–2004, including key resolutions | 293 |
| 8.5 | US companies' highest votes on social policy resolution | 294 |
| CI.1 | Corporate governance matrix of cases and issues | 311 |
| C1.1 | The impact of deregulation in the transformation of the US energy industry | 316 |
| C1.2 | Example of an SPE descendancy: the descendants of LJM2 | 318 |
| C1.3 | How Enron employees in Fastow's division reached spectacular returns on investment into the SPEs | 318 |
| C2.1 | WorldCom acquisitions, December 1996 to July 2001 | 333 |
| C2.2 | Shares sold by board members, 1996–2002 | 336 |
| C2.3 | Ebbers' personal loans | 338 |
| C2.4 | What Ebbers bought with WorldCom company loans | 338 |
| C2.5 | Creative accounting | 339 |
| C2.6 | Possible WorldCom conspiracies | 340 |
| C2.7 | Grubman's recommendations | 342 |
| Appendix C2.1 | Events in WorldCom history | 349 |
| Appendix C2.2 | The fate of former WorldCom actors | 351 |
| C3.1 | Kozlowski's misappropriations | 357 |
| C3.2 | Tyco trial timeline | 358 |
| C6.1 | The DaimlerChrysler merger timeline | 391 |
| C6.2 | Merging DaimlerChrysler: product models | 394 |
| C6.3 | Daimler–Benz vs. Chrysler | 397 |
| C6.4 | DaimlerChrysler shareholding, by region | 399 |
| C7.1 | German and Anglo-American corporate governance models | 404 |
| C7.2 | History of Mannesmann AG | 405 |
| C7.3 | Mannesmann AG, 1998: sales, earnings and employment, by division | 406 |
| C7.4 | Largest shareholders, 1999 | 408 |
| C7.5 | The banks involved in the takeover bid | 410 |
| C7.6 | Takeover of UK companies by German companies, 1986–2006 | 413 |

| C8.1 | James Hardie timeline | 423 |
|------|------------------------|-----|
| C9.1 | HIH reported contributions to total assets, 1994–2000 | 435 |
| C9.2 | HIH reported contributions to consolidated revenue, 1994–2000 | 435 |
| C9.3 | HIH reported contributions to operating profit before income tax | 439 |
| C9.4 | Symptoms of business decline | 443 |
| C9.5 | The influence of ex-Andersen auditors on HIH board | 447 |
| C10.1 | The top five investment firms in the world, as per May 2005 | 453 |
| C10.2 | Major commercial code amendments, 1993–2002 | 459 |
| C10.3 | The underworld players and the Nomura players | 462 |
| C10.4 | The board structure of Nomura Holdings | 465 |

# Acknowledgements

The author and the publisher would like to thank the following publishers, organisations and individuals:

Aglietta, M. and Breton, R. (2001), Financial Systems, Corporate Control and Capital Accumulation, *Economy and Society*, 30(4): 433-466 (Table 3.4).

Agosto, MariaKatia de Stato (2004), *Il Caso Parmalat*, CERADI, http://www.archivioceradi.luiss.it/bancaemercati/index.php?catid=19 (Figures C5.1, C5.2).

AMP Capital Investors (2006), *AMP Capital Investors Corporate Governance Mid-Year Update* (August 2006) (Figure 3.8).

Apreda, R. (2003), *The Semantics of Governance*, Working Paper Series, no. 245, University of Cema, Buenos Aires (Table 3.6).

Bebchuk, L., Cohen, A. and Ferrel, A. (2004), *What Matters in Corporate Governance?*, Harvard Law School Working Paper, no. 491, November (Table 2.8).

Becht, M., Bolton, P., and Röell, A. (2003), *Corporate governance and control*, in G.M. Constantinides, M. Harris and R. Stulz (eds), Handbook of Finance, 2003, Elsevier (Table 3.3).

Berglof, E. and Claessens, S. (2004), *Corporate Governance and Enforcement*, World Bank Working Paper, no. 3409 (Table 6.3).

Beyer, J. and Hassel, A. (2001), The Effects of Convergence, *Economy and Society*, 31(3): 309–332, Taylor and Francis (Figure 5.10; Table 5.3).

Claessens, S., Djankov, S. and Lang, L. (1999), Figure 10 reproduced from Corporate Governance and Development, *Focus*, 1 by Stijn Claessens, International Bank for Reconstruction/The World Bank (Figure 6.7).

Economic Policy Institute (2006–2007), *State of Working America*, www.epi.org (Figure 4.10).

Ethical Investment Association (EIA) (2006), Ethical Investment Association (EIA) *2006 SRI Benchmarking Survey* (Figure 8.7).

Eurosif (2006), *Active Share Ownership in Europe: 2006 European Handbook*, Eurosif/Deutsche Bank, *Corporate Governance Research* (Figure 5.2; Table 5.4); Eurosif/OECD, *Financial Market Trends*, no. 87 (2004) (Figure 5.1).

FTSE ISS (2005), *Measuring the Impact of Corporate Governance on Global Portfolios*, Corporate Governance Rating and Index Series, http://www.issproxy.com/pdf/CGIResearchStudy2005pdf (Figure 1.5); http://www.isscgq.com/CGQratings.htm (Table 2.3).

Garrat, R. (2003), *Thin on Top*, Nicholas Brealey (Figure 2.5).

Gomez, P.-Y. and Korine, H. (2003), *Democracy in Corporatia: Tocqueville and the Evolution of Corporate Governance*, Working Paper, no. 9, October, European Entrepreneurial Learning Ecole de Management (Table 3.2).

Goyer, M. (2001), Corporate Governance and the Innovation System in France, *Industry and Innovation*, 8(2): 132–158, Taylor and Francis (Table 2.1).

Heins-Bunde, J. (2006) Working Paper, Henley Management CG Conference, 4 October (Figures 5.4, 5.5, 5.6).

HIH Royal Commission (2003), *Failure of HIH Insurance, Volume 1: A Corporate Collapse and its Lessons*, © Commonwealth of Australia reproduced by permission (Figure C9.1; Tables C9.1, C9.2, C9.3).

Institute of Chartered Accountants in England and Wales (2005), Table 4.3 reproduced from *Divided by Common Language: Where Economics Meets the Law* by Tim Bush, with the kind permission of the Institute of Chartered Accountants of England & Wales (Table 4.3).

Institute for Policy Studies/United States for a Fair Economy (2006), *Executive Excess*, http://www.faireconomy.org/reports/2006/ExecutiveExcess2006.pdf (Figures 2.7, 2.8).

International Labour Office (ILO) (2004), Gunter, B. and Hoeven, R., *The Social Dimension of Globalisation: A Review of the Literature*, Working Paper, no. 24, Policy Integration Department, World Commission on the Social Dimension of Globalisation, International Labour Office, Geneva, June, p. 3. Copyright © 2004 International Labour Organization (Table 7.1).

Kirkpatrick, G. (2004), *Typology of Directors' Policy Dialogue on Corporate Governance in China*, Shanghai, 25 February, © OECD 2004 (Table 2.5).

KPMG (2005), International Surveys of Corporate Responsibility Reporting, KPMG International, Sidney (Tables 8.2, 8.3).

Mays Report (2003), Department of Environment and Heritage, Commonwealth of Australia and ABN AMRO Morgans (Figure 8.3); AMP Henderson Global Investors, Fund Managers and Governance, Diagram 5 (Figure 3.6).

Monks, R., Miller, A. and Cook, J. (2004), Shareholder Activism on Environmental Issues: A Study of Proposals at Large US Corporations (2000–2003), *Natural Resources Forum*, Blackwell Publishing (Figures 3.7, 8.6).

Morley Fund Management (2003) (Figure 3.4).

Nelson, J. (2004), *The Public Role of Private Enterprise*, Working Paper, 1, Corporate Social Responsibility Initiative (Figure 8.11).

OECD (2001), *Corporate Governance Patterns in OECD Economies*, © OECD 2001 (Table 3.1).

OECD (2001), *Institutional Investors Statistical Yearbook 2001*, © OECD 2001 (Figure 3.1).

OECD (2004), *Corporate Governance: A Survey of OECD Countries*, © OECD 2004 (Table 5.2).

OECD (2004), Corporate Governance in Japan, OECD Policy Dialogue in Corporate Governance, Beijing, 25–26 February, © OECD 2004 (Figure 6.5).

Office of Public Sector Information (OPSI) (2006), PSI licence no. C2006010940, OPSI, Norwich (Higgs Report; Stern Review) (Figures 2.2, 8.1).

Redmond, P. (2005), *Companies and Securities Law*, Thompson Lawbook, Fourth Edition, LBC (Figure 1.1).

Seki, T. and Tokyo Stock Exchange (2005), http://www.tse.or.jp/English/data/research/shareownership.html (Table 6.2).

Social Investment Forum (SIF) (2005), *2005 Report on Socially Responsible Investing Trends in the United States*, SIF (Figures 8.8, 8.9; Tables 8.4, 8.5).

Taylor, Bernard (2004), Leading the Boardroom Revolution, *Corporate Governance: An International Review*, 12(4): 423 (Figure 2.4).

Tricker, R.I. (2004), *The Economist Essential Director*, Profile Books. London (Figure 2.1).

UK National Statistics (2004), PSI licence no. C2007001109, UK National Statistics (Table 4.2).

UK SIF (2000), Response of UK Pension Funds to SRI Disclosure Regulation, paper by Eugenie Mathieu, UK SIF, London (Figure 8.10).

UNEPFI (2005), *A Legal Framework for the Integration of Environmental, Social and Governance Issues into Institutional Investment*, Freshfields, Bruckhaus and Derringer, UNEPFI, Geneva, http://www.unepfi.org/fileadmin/documents/freshfields_legal_resp_20051123pdf (Figure 8.5).

USS/Just Pensions (2002), Do UK Pension Funds Invest Responsibly?, Universities Superannuation Scheme/Just Pensions, www.usshq.co.uk, www.justpensions.org (Box 8.1).

Vitols, Sigurt (2005), Changes in Germany's Bank-Based Financial System, *Corporate Governance: An International Review*, 13(3): 386–396, Blackwell Publishing (Table 5.1).

Watson Wyatt (2005), *The Role of Equities in Pension Funds*, Watson Wyatt, Sidney, www.watsonwyatt.com (Figure 3.3).

World Federation of Exchanges (2005), *Annual Report*, World Federation of Exchanges (Figures 1.3, 1.4, 7.1, 7.2; Tables 6.5, 7.2, 7.3, 7.4).

Every effort has been made to contact copyright holders for their permission to reprint tables and figures in the book. The publishers would be grateful to hear from any copyright holder who is not here acknowledged and will undertake to rectify any errors or omissions in future editions of this book.

# Foreword

This is a justifiably ambitious treatise. Professor Clarke sets out to cover every aspect of the theory and practice of corporate governance across the world and succeeds in doing so, adding a set of relevant and riveting case studies for good measure. Taking account of the astonishing rapidity of developments in this field internationally, his book represents a remarkable achievement. Given the pace with which the study of corporate governance has burgeoned, the chance of capturing its global reach again in a single volume is fast receding. In all this, the importance of advances in understanding the governance structures and processes of companies extends beyond the corporate world. Governance is of universal importance: all institutions need to be governed and the findings and conclusions contained in Professor Clarke's groundbreaking work overflow their corporate banks.

A strength of the book lies in the author's selection of appropriate research evidence and of authoritative academic comment. His choice illuminates the wide range of issues raised by his study and is notable for its balance, leaving readers to form their own conclusions, but to do so with an understanding of the nature and origins of differences in points of view. It is not only that these excerpts clarify the corporate governance arguments and hypotheses which Professor Clarke guides us through, but they also form a treasure house of apt quotations, which will be lucratively mined by those writing on the subject. He points out that where research findings show apparently contrary results, as with the relationship between governance and performance, it may well be because the wrong measure has been chosen or because a single proxy has been taken to represent a complex variable. The effectiveness of boards turns on the quality and breadth of experience of board members and on the skill of their chairs in getting the best out of them. Governance issues are inevitably complex and the evidence required to address them has to be equally many-faceted.

What comes across clearly from the broad sweep of Professor Clarke's survey of international corporate governance is first the variety of forms which it takes around the world and second the degree to which amoeba-like they adapt to their rapidly changing environments. Markets, sources of finance, consumer demands and the expectations of society are continuously evolving. There can be no steady state of corporate governance and no one right answer. This is why the OECD is quoted as encouraging diversity and a market for governance arrangements. For systems and processes, it is survival of the fittest within any given framework, with no certainty over how fitness will continue to be defined.

There are forces for conformity in some aspects of corporate governance, notably the increasing reach of international institutional investors and the discipline of capital markets. But as Professor Clarke writes: 'while capital markets have acquired an apparently irresistible force in the world economy, it still appears that institutional complementarities at the national and regional level represent immovable objects'. Corporate structures around the world have developed from

local roots and are shaped by their legal, historical and cultural backgrounds. International companies recognise that in management terms they need to respect such differences. In addition, it is only those companies that tap world markets for capital, which have to meet their governance requirements. However, while diversity of corporate governance forms will continue to have its place, certain standards of governance have a universal significance. What matters are corporate governance outcomes, rather than the particular nature of the structures and processes which lead to those outcomes. The essential outcome is trust and funds will flow to those companies and countries which inspire trust. This is why disclosure is the basis of codes of corporate governance.

Looking more widely at the world picture which Professor Clarke presents, what changes in the corporate scene stand out as having future significance and what major challenges does he identify? Perhaps the greatest single change has been in the mobilisation of financial resources and in their concentration in the hands of institutional investors; the book describes this development clearly and thoroughly. Private finance has overtaken public finance as the engine of economic development worldwide. Corporate governance is about power and accountability for the use of power. The balance of power has swung towards institutional investors and the issue is how they will use that power and on whose behalf. Their accountability is blurred by conflicts of interest and the ability of those whose money they are investing to influence their governance decisions is slight. That ability could be enhanced as we move into a wired world, where all information will be available on line. Members of pension funds, for example, could then have direct contact with those who invest their savings for them, rendering those who manage their money more accountable for their actions.

The move around the world to providing financial and corporate information electronically is surely one of the significant forces for change which is emerging. This is particularly so when allied to another force for change, which is the increasing impact of public opinion on companies. When a major international enterprise has to reverse a scientifically arrived at decision, because of an internet mounted protest, it foreshadows another shift in the balance of power. Advances in information technology enable individual shareholders, consumers and concerned members of the public to organise collectively and speedily behind a common cause. This is against a background of greater sensitivity by companies to the consequences of risks to reputation.

When it comes to corporate governance challenges, Professor Clarke identifies a number. One relates to the governance role of boards of directors. He writes: 'Whether boards can be effectively reformed remains an open question'. On this point there is growing support for regular board evaluation, the pursuance of which is likely to influence board development. The degree to which this proposal has been taken seriously in Britain can be judged by the 1998 corporate governance report referring to it simply as 'an interesting development'. This was turned shortly afterwards into the strict Combined Code recommendation that: 'The board should undertake a formal and rigorous annual evaluation'. It remains to be seen how widely this proposal will be accepted internationally and the degree of rigour with which it will be carried out.

He foresees another challenge in whether the increasing hold of the investing institutions will lengthen financial and economic time horizons or shorten them. He sums the issue up as follows: 'As the power of the institutions expands further they could either become an irresistible force for further economic instability induced by short-termism, or they could impress upon markets and companies longer-term horizons, and the pursuit of sustainability'.

The fundamental challenge, however, which Professor Clarke poses picks up that point about sustainability and relates to whether the pressures on companies to give a higher priority to their responsibilities to society will elicit what he regards as an adequate response. He argues that shareholders, stakeholders and governments will require companies to act with greater responsibility in their use of resources and in recognising their impact on communities and on the

environment. His conclusion is that: 'only a fundamental redesign of corporate forms, objectives and value measures can fully meet the realities of responsibility'.

I commend Professor Clarke's comprehensive review of the international state of corporate governance for the ground it covers and for its clarity of expression. It will set a benchmark against which to evaluate and measure progress in the field of corporate governance as companies respond in their individual ways to society's changing values.

Sir Adrian Cadbury

# 1

# Cycles of Governance

Cycles of crisis and reform in corporate governance are becoming a worldwide phenomenon. Contemporary concerns, originating in market and corporate failures in the United States and United Kingdom, have extended to Europe, the Asia Pacific, and beyond. The vital significance of corporate governance for accountability and performance is now fully recognised in the industrial world, and perhaps even more acutely in the transitional economies of Eastern Europe, East Asia and Latin America. What used to occur quietly behind closed boardroom doors is now a matter of considerable public interest. Successive recent controversies have highlighted some of the dilemmas of corporate governance, but since the origins of industry there were deep apprehensions regarding the ownership and control of businesses 'Corporate governance has only recently emerged as a discipline in its own right, although the strands of political economy it embraces stretch back through centuries' (World Bank 2000: 1).

There are many explanations for the recent sustained and intense interest in corporate governance:

- the vast growth of deregulated international capital markets, with highly mobile capital exploring investment opportunities globally;
- a developing realisation of the importance of the massively increasing scale and activity of multinational corporations in determining the prosperity of national economies;
- the rapidly growing proportion of individual wealth held in securities due to the phenomenal development of investment institutions, particularly pension funds and insurance companies;

- the dawning awareness that if these investments are to be secure there must be more effective monitoring and improved standards of corporate governance;
- a general trend in society, facilitated by new technology and driven by social awareness, towards developing greater openness, transparency and disclosure.

Yet the most widespread reason for the heightened interest in corporate governance is the now general sense that corporations cast a long shadow, and they must be governed responsibly if they are to benefit the economy and society. It is likely the present significance will continue to develop, as James Wolfensohn, the former President of the World Bank, put it, 'The proper governance of companies will become as crucial to the world economy as the proper governing of countries' (*The Economist*, 2 January 1999: 38).

## DEFINITIONS

The etymology of the words *corporate governance* is derived from ancient Greek and Latin (though there are similar words in most languages). The word *corporate* derives from the Latin word *corpus* meaning *body*, and comes from the Latin verb *corporare* to form into one body, hence a *corporation* represents a body of people, that is a *group of people authorised to act as an individual*. The word *governance* is from the Latinised Greek *gubernatio* meaning management or government, and this comes from the ancient Greek *kybernao* to steer, to drive, to guide, to act as a pilot.

This etymological origin of the concept of corporate governance captures a creative meaning of collective endeavour that defies the contemporary inclination to place a passive and regulatory emphasis on the phrase. Adrian Cadbury cites Cicero in conveying the original meaning of this contested concept:

> Governance is a word with a pedigree that dates back to Chaucer and in his day the word carried with it the connotation wise and responsible, which is appropriate. It means either the action of governing or the method of governing and it is in the latter sense it is used with reference to companies ... A quotation which is worth keeping in mind in this context is: 'He that governs sits quietly at the stern and scarce is seen to stir'.
>
> It appeals to me, because it suggests that governance need not be heavy-handed. The governor should be able to keep the corporate ship on course with a minimum use of the tiller.
>
> (Cadbury 2002: 1)

The most direct and useful definition of corporate governance is that employed in the UK *Report of the Committee on the Financial Aspects of Corporate Governance*: 'Corporate governance is the system by which companies are directed and controlled' (Cadbury 1992: 15), which has also the benefit of being the shortest definition. The OECD in its 1999 *Principles of Corporate Governance* elaborated the definition by referring to corporate governance structures and objectives:

> Corporate governance is the system by which business corporations are directed and controlled. The corporate governance structure specifies the distribution of rights and responsibilities among different participants in the corporation, such as the board, managers, shareholders and other stakeholders, and spells out the rules and procedures for making decisions on corporate affairs. By doing this, it also provides the structure through which the company objectives are set, and the means of attaining those objectives and monitoring performance.

With the revised *Principles* published in 2004 the OECD develops the definition to include the relationships, context and benefits of good governance:

> Corporate governance involves a set of relationships between a company's management, its board, its shareholders and other stakeholders. Corporate governance also provides the structure through which the objectives of the company are set, and the means of attaining those objectives and monitoring performance are determined. Good corporate governance should provide proper incentives for the board and management to pursue objectives that are in the interests of the company and its shareholders and should facilitate effective monitoring. The presence of an effective corporate governance system, within an individual company and across an economy as a whole, helps to provide a degree of confidence that is necessary for the proper functioning of a market economy. As a result, the cost of capital is lower and firms are encouraged to use resources more efficiently, thereby underpinning growth.
>
> (OECD 2004a: 11)

However corporate governance has wider implications and is critical to economic and social well being, firstly in providing the incentives and performance measures to achieve business success, and secondly in providing the accountability and transparency to ensure the equitable distribution of the resulting wealth. The significance of corporate governance for the stability and equity of society is captured in the broader definition of the concept offered by Cadbury (2000):

> Corporate governance is concerned with holding the balance between economic and social goals and between individual and communal goals. The governance framework is there to encourage the efficient use of resources and equally to require accountability for the stewardship of those resources. The aim is to align as nearly as possible the interests of individuals, corporations and society.

## GENESIS OF CORPORATE GOVERNANCE

Though the business corporation emerged as the dominant form for business association only in the early twentieth century, its antecedents lie eight hundred years earlier in the notion of the corporate entity developed to resolve problems of group relations in religious and social communities. These medieval elements were transformed by the application of corporate ideas and practices of the business enterprises that came later (Redmond 2005: 28). Among these devices was the idea of the 'incorporate person' – the interpretation of companies as legal persons with rights and duties.

In many ancient and modern organisations legal transactions have to be carried out and duties incurred by a succession of joint holders of an office on behalf of a number of people who are interested in carrying out a common purpose or object.

> This being the case, it is necessary from the point of view both of private and of public law to replace the vague group by something more definite. The law knows the natural person. Its rules and its process are fitted to deal with him. They are not fitted to deal with indeterminate groups which exist, and yet show a tendency to crumble when an attempt is made to apply legal rules and principles in detail to themselves and their activities. It is for this reason that the law adopts the device of 'constituting the official character of the holders for the time being of the same office, or the common interest of the persons who for the time being are adventurers in the same undertaking into an artificial person or ideal subject of legal capacities and duties'. Thus we get the distinction between 'persons natural created by God', and 'persons incorporate or politick created by the policy of man ... either sole or aggregate of many'... This conception was received by the common lawyers because it supplied a useful explanation of certain associations which frequently appeared in the law courts as the owners of property or franchises, a useful theory for the regulation of their activities, and a useful mode of checking

the too frequent multiplication of these bodies'.

> (Holdsworth 1908: 469; cited in Redmond 2005: 30)

### The South Sea Bubble

Such corporate bodies recognised by common law were applied to business organisations in England and Holland when charters were granted to incorporate trading companies which became joint stock companies. These attracted considerable public interest 'it seemed suddenly to become a widely held belief that to subscribe to a capital fund was to become rich' (Cooke 1950: 81). Speculative excesses quickly followed the formation of the early trading companies, disillusioning investors in the Dutch East India Company in 1609 as they found their capital locked into a company only publishing its accounts every *ten years*, and which insisted on paying dividends in spices (pepper, mace and nutmeg) (Frentrop 2003: 75–76). A century later in England the South Sea Company after a euphoric rise in its share price discovered it had fanned a boom far beyond its own stocks, and persuaded friends in government to pass the 1720 Bubble Act. When this legislation failed to work, the directors of South Sea attempted to bring legal proceedings to forfeit the charters of other companies, precipitating a collapse in the market which burst the speculative bubble, and sunk their own company (Redmond 2005: 36).

The resulting reluctance on the part of Parliament to grant charters for private incorporation, led companies to be formed essentially as partnerships, with rules deriving from the law of partnership, contract and trusts (Redmond 2005: 40). This created an enduring distinction between legal interpretations in the UK and the US:

> The modern English business corporation has evolved from the unincorporated partnership based on mutual agreement, rather than from the corporation, based on a grant from the state, and owes more to partnership principles

than to rules based on corporate personality. Thus we in England still do not talk about business corporations or about corporate law, but about companies and company law ... Hence modern American corporation law owes less to partnership and contractual principles than does British.

(Gower 1956: 1371)

However, the principle of people managing companies being responsible for the investments of others was now well established in business organisations. The resulting concerns regarding corporate governance are not a new thing, and Adam Smith in 1776 in *The Wealth of Nations* made a comment on company management that would echo through the ages: 'Being managers of other people's money than their own, it cannot well be expected that they should watch over it with the same anxious vigilance with which the partners in a private co-partner frequently watch over their own ... Negligence and profusion, therefore, must always prevail more or less in the management of the affairs of a joint stock company' (Smith 1976: 264–265).

## Splitting the atom of ownership

As technological change advanced with the industrial revolution, there occurred a wider diffusion of ownership of many large companies as no individual, family or group of managers could provide sufficient capital to sustain growth. Berle and Means chronicled the profound implications of this *separation of ownership and control:* 'the dissolution of the old atom of ownership into its component parts, control and beneficial ownership' (1933: 8). For Berle and Means it was axiomatic that as the number of shareholders increased, their influence upon corporate enterprise diminished as professional managers took control. As corporations became the dominant vehicles of the US economy, their legal instruments of incorporation – particularly in the state of Delaware which became the most popular jurisdiction in which to incorporate – increasingly reflected the interests not of stockholders, but of the executive management who intended to run the corporation. Berle and Means identify two

distinct functions of the corporate entity, firstly the commercial operations, and secondly the business of raising capital, and distributing risks, losses and gains. Whilst managers may reasonably insist on as free a hand as possible in running commercial business activities, it is quite a different thing to allow management power to determine how the financial surplus of the corporation is distributed.

The separation of ownership and control occurs as the ownership of corporations is progressively diluted from complete ownership to minority control, and though there are many devices for working control of a corporation to be retained by those with only a minority of the shares, eventually the situation is reached when ownership is so widely distributed that no minority interest is large enough to dominate the affairs of the company. At this point even the largest single interest amounts to just a small percentage of the total shareholdings, insufficient to place irresistible pressure upon management. Means (1931) recognises a range of potential forms of dilution of ownership control:

1 control through almost complete ownership;
2 majority control;
3 control through a legal device without majority ownership;
4 minority control;
5 management control.

Different mechanisms are outlined by Means by which managers are able to shift the enterprise profits, and to a considerable degree the underlying assets, among groups of stockholders (including themselves). There are countervailing forces including the need to maintain a reputation for probity if new sources of funds are to be accessed, the influence of the law and state regulation, and the intervention of the financial community. However, vigilance is required to prevent managers acquiring absolute power. Determining who has the power to select the directors indicates who has control of the corporation in the view of Means. The management appoint the proxy committee who are responsible for the election of directors. 'Since this committee is appointed by the existing management, the latter can virtually dictate their own successors. Where ownership is sufficiently sub-divided, the management can thus

become a self-perpetuating body even though its share in the ownership is negligible'. Though there is always the possibility of a shareholder revolt, under normal conditions the shareholder has little influence over the enterprise and there is little contest to managerial control. 'Thus in the management controlled company the separation of ownership and control has become virtually complete. The bulk of the owners have in fact almost no control over the enterprise, while those in control hold only a negligible proportion of the total ownership' (Means 1931: 80).

In what became the most influential work on corporate governance in the twentieth century *The Modern Corporation and Private Property* (1933) Berle and Means anticipate the emergence of a new form of social organisation, citing Walther Rathenau who commented on similar developments in German corporate life: 'The depersonalisation of ownership, the objectification of enterprise, the detachment of property from the possessor, leads to a point where the enterprise becomes transformed into an institution' (1933: 304). Berle and Means acknowledge that potentially there are three forms that might emerge to govern this new corporation:

1   The first is without regard for the change of character from *active* ownership to *passive* property ownership, to maintain the doctrine of strict property rights, by which the management are placed in a position of trusteeship for the *sole* benefit of the shareholders, despite the fact that the latter have ceased to have power or accept responsibility for the *active* property in which they have an interest.
2   In direct opposition to the doctrine of strict property rights, is the view that corporate developments have created a new set of relationships, giving to the management powers which are absolute and not limited by any implied obligation with respect to their use. This would reflect a significant modification of the principle of private property.
3   A third possibility exists however, that passive property rights should yield before the larger interests of society. The management of corporations should develop into a neutral technocracy, balancing the claims of various groups, employees, customers, shareholders and the

community, and assigning to each according to a transparent policy (1933: 306).

In the most passionate argument in favour of the merits of the third alternative as the right course for the future development of corporate governance Berle and Means declare:

> Eliminating the sole interest of the passive owner, however, does not necessarily lay a basis for the alternative claim that the new powers should be used in the interest of the controlling groups. The latter have not presented, in acts or words any acceptable defence of the proposition that these powers should be so used. No tradition supports this proposition. The control groups have, rather, cleared the way for the claims of a group far wider than either the owners or the control. They have placed the community in a position to demand that the modern corporation serve not alone the owners or the control but all society. This third alternative offers a wholly new concept of corporate activity. Neither the claims of ownership nor those of control can stand against the paramount interests of the community … It only remains for the claims of the community to be put forward with clarity and force.
>
> (1933: 309)

Some seven decades after Berle and Means expressed these hopes for a different concept of the corporation with much wider accountability to the community, the issue remains one of the most alive and highly contentious dilemmas for corporate governance. The call of Berle and Means for an increase in the recognition and scope of fiduciary duties of those who controlled corporations influenced legal thinking for much of the century. If this view fell from favour in the rampant opportunism of the 1980s and 1990s, the importance of the principle of fiduciary duty has re-emerged with a vengeance in the reaction to the revelations of managerial irresponsibility that were exposed in the US after the major corporate bankruptcies and the fall of the NASDAQ in 2001. Berle and Means left an enduring legacy in their work written during the depths of the 1930s Great Depression, concerning the need to enforce accountability and the responsible management

ONE

of corporations, arguments that shaped the US Securities Acts of the 1930s that remain the basis for federal securities law today (Holderness 2003).

## FORMS OF BUSINESS ASSOCIATIONS

The dominance of the corporation as the universal form of business association has never remain unchallenged. Redmond (2005: 99) illustrates the wide variety of legal structures through which people can pursue profit making objectives (Figure 1.1). The diversity of the forms of association is accompanied by a freedom of choice between them, and the principal restriction is that partnerships above a certain size should incorporate, as indicated in a judgement of 1880 that there was a need 'to prevent the mischief arising from large trading undertakings being carried on by large fluctuating bodies, so that persons dealing with them did not know with whom they were contracting' (Redmond 2005: 99). Different forms of business association can serve the same purpose, and the selection of business form requires careful consideration:

> While the principal forms of association have evolved or been fashioned to meet specific functions, there is no neat symmetry between the forms and functions of association. For any particular purpose for which individuals might wish to associate, there will generally be one or more incorporated and unincorporated forms available. The functions of associations are, of course, as diverse as the forms ... There is, therefore, a complex calculus involved in the choice of form of association. Generally, however, for large enterprises the advantages of incorporation, the transferability of corporate securities and the existence of organised securities markets will compel registration under the *Corporations Act* ... For small business the choice will not be clear-cut and will turn upon a complex of factors, legal and personal, which defy easy prediction.
>
> (Redmond 2005: 100, 107)

What are the determining factors influencing the decision to incorporate? Given the diversity of business forms and objectives generalisation is not possible, but the following are the major considerations:

1 *Limited liability*: A primary motive for incorporating a business is the desire to limit individual liability for the obligations of the enterprise. In contrast partners are personally liable for the firms' debts.

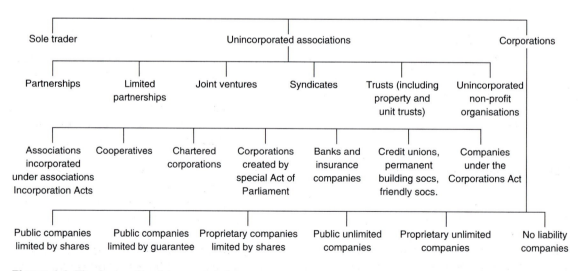

Figure 1.1 The forms of business association.

Source: Redmond P. (2005), *Companies and Securities Law*, Thomson Lawbook, 4th edn, Sydney: LBC, 99.

2 *Perpetual succession*: The company has perpetual succession since it is invested with the legal capacity and powers of an individual. The company is an entity distinct from the individuals comprising its membership. Its status is unaffected by the death or bankruptcy of a member, or the transfer of ownership interests.

3 *Financing*: Corporations are entitled to make a public issue of shares, or debt interests, and have the power to create a floating charge over the assets of the business. Unincorporated business forms are denied these means of raising finance.

4 *Cost, formality and continuing obligations*: Corporations have continuing obligations to disclose information for the benefit of creditors, members and the wider community (for example the address of its registered office, and details of its directors and secretary). Accounts disclosing the company's financial position need to be maintained, and for some companies audited and reported in summary form on a public register. There are penalties for directors and officers for non-compliance with duties of diligence and loyalty. This burden of formality is a major cost of incorporation, and in contrast partnerships are a remarkably flexible business form. With partnerships no formality is required for its internal structure, and there are no registration or reporting obligations.

5 *Taxation*: In the past in some jurisdictions there were double taxation consequences of incorporation as both the company's profits and the dividends distributed to individuals were taxable, though measure have been introduced towards restoring the tax neutrality of the choice of business form (Redmond 2005: 106–107).

## Corporate governance lifecycles

The main characteristics of pure business organisation forms attract different kinds of business formation. For the small business the *sole tradership* is often preferred, as the owners who are managing the enterprise wish to retain control, and claim the right to any surplus. This form carries the weaknesses of limited access to capital for growth, and little, if any, monitoring of management. The *partnership* provides a collegial form of business association, where the partners share the surplus, and with self-selection of managers and mutual monitoring, though again with the drawback of limited access to funds unless they are internally generated. The private or *proprietary company* allows the owners to control the enterprise through a board of directors they have direct representation on. The private company has the benefit of limited liability, and shareholders' assets are not subject to the claims of corporate creditors. Many business ventures commence with one or two entrepreneurs acting as sole traders, who establish a private company as the business gets larger with greater commitments, resources and responsibilities. Many private businesses remain at this stage in the corporate development lifecycle because it suits the proprietors, the business can grow through generating capital internally, and in some countries private companies may grow very large and prove dynamic and influential (often as long as the original proprietor survives). However many small companies become impatient to pursue the opportunities for more rapid growth and development that the market presents, and take on the greater corporate governance challenge of creating a public company (Figure 1.2).

The excitement of the initial public offering (IPO) of shares to the public as a company is listed on the stock exchange can be considerable for the founders, and sometimes for the general public. But when the excitement of raising perhaps millions of additional capital is over, it is often hard for the founding owners to come to terms with the fact that they no longer own the entire company. In the nascent state of a newly formed public company from a private concern, the original owners of the private company may still be the majority owners of the public company, and have a controlling interest, perhaps with membership of the board. But the board of directors must assume a new wider accountability to the minority public shareholders of the company. The *public corporation* separates ownership and management, has elaborate monitoring arrangements, the board of directors selects and monitors the managers, and there is internal and external auditing,

**Figure 1.2** Corporate governance lifecycle.

and external market and regulatory monitoring (Allen and Sherer 1995: 187). The public corporation has a continuity of existence, and new disclosure obligations. Finally with the mature public corporation the shareholdings become more numerous and dispersed, who delegate control to an independent board of directors, who hire and monitor management. This fully public form has the advantages of ready transferability of ownership and increased access to capital, without necessarily changing the incumbent management. It is this public corporation business form that has prevailed for the financing and management of large enterprises universally, however not without recurrent concerns concerning corporate governance:

> During the same period that the governance issue was gaining prominence, the corporate structure became universally accepted, with local variations in form, as the most efficient means of organising financial and human capital to produce goods and services. The corporation, with its classic attributes of perpetual life, limited liability, unrestricted purpose and transferability of ownership, has prevailed over competing systems internationally ... as a superior method of aggregating capital. The emergence of the corporation, as the dominant form of economic organisation across the world, was due to its proven competitive advantage. But in this, the focus on governance played its part. The theoretical model

of the publicly-quoted corporation was based on the shareholders electing the directors, the directors appointing the managers to carry out the activities of the corporation to satisfy the aims of the shareholders, and directors being held to account in the general meeting. The gaps between theory and practice are all too evident, particularly in the United States.

> (Cadbury and Millstein 2005: 8, 10)

This dissonance between the theory and practice of corporate governance is a lingering problem, which is rarely finally resolved:

> Experience around the world shows that although the powerful concept of a listed joint stock company has been successfully introduced in many countries, the accompanying legal and regulatory system has often lagged, leading in some cases to abuse of minority shareholders and to reduced growth prospects when financial markets lose credibility – or fail to achieve it in the first place.

> (Jesovar and Kirkpatrick 2005: 130)

## DIVERSITY IN CORPORATE GOVERNANCE

Different approaches to business formation and the accompanying corporate governance structures and regulations have evolved in different

social and economic contexts. Among the more important contextual and industrial variables that influence the business form and system of corporate governance adopted are:

- national, regional and cultural differences;
- ownership structure and dispersion;
- the industry and market environment of the corporation;
- firm size and structure;
- lifecycle variations, including origin and development, technology, and periodic crises and new directions;
- CEO tenure, attributes and background (Huse 2005: 68).

In the historical evolution of corporate governance in different regional cultures and countries, different choices were made about the most efficient company structures to adopt, and the appropriate forms of regulation. At the time of formation fundamental questions were posed, which by now have been largely forgotten: 'What should be the purpose of the corporation? Is it a community of human beings, a nexus of contracts, or the possession of its shareholders? Do corporations incur social obligations in return for the privileges that society grants to them? What constitutes a fair distribution of rewards from economic activity?' Jacoby (2002: 27). In the study of comparative corporate governance it is important to return to these fundamental questions in explaining the divergence and convergence of governance approaches: 'Why did corporate governance systems develop differently in these different countries? Which system does a better job at solving the problems of corporate governance? Will corporations in different countries converge to a similar system of corporate governance?' (McDonnell 2002: 2).

In the rich diversity of corporate governance forms internationally, there is a clear divergence between *outsider* systems found in Anglo-American countries with dispersed equity markets, separation of ownership and control and disclosure-based regulation; and the *insider* systems which predominates in Europe, Asia Pacific, and other regions of the world, with concentrated ownership, bank finance and the representation of majority interests on the board of directors.

While Berle and Means had assumed that all large public corporations would mature to an end-stage capital structure characterized by the separation of ownership and control, the contemporary empirical evidence is decidedly to the contrary. Instead of convergence toward a single capital structure, the twentieth Century saw the polarization of corporate structure between two rival systems of corporate governance.

(Coffee 2001: 3)

As important as the different ownership and regulatory structures adopted in the divergent governance systems, are the distinctive relationships forged and objectives pursued (Table 1.1). The outsider system is oriented very strongly towards shareholders, and perceives the major corporate objective as the delivery of shareholder value (often in the short term). In contrast the insider system is built on close relationships with a wide range of stakeholders, and conceives of the corporate mission as the creation of values for all stakeholders in perpetuity. With the increasing ascendancy of capital markets, the dominance of the Anglo-American approach to corporate governance over other systems is often assumed, though the strengths and weaknesses of all approaches need to be considered: 'Anglo-American finance economists are fond of touting the efficiency advantages of shareholder governance; they are convinced of the superiority of institutional arrangements in their home countries. But the fact of the matter is, each corporate governance system has attached to it a complex set of costs and benefits. Accurately toting up and comparing these sets is difficult if not impossible; claims of superiority are wishful thinking' (Jacoby 2002: 18). For those who think there will be a ready global convergence towards a uniform Anglo-American system of corporate governance, the rich diversity of political forms of governance in the developed world is a useful reminder of the institutional diversity that has survived and is valued (and represents the different political arenas in which corporate governance legal and regulatory reform will take place):

The 30 member countries of the OECD share core governance elements. These have

| Properties | Outsider systems | Insider systems |
| --- | --- | --- |
| **Ownership** | Dispersed ownership | Concentrated ownership |
| **Control** | Separation of ownership and control | Association of ownership with control |
|  | Little incentive for outside investors to participate in corporate control | Control by interested parties (banks, related firms, and employees) |
| **Finance** | Low debt/equity ratio and low ratio of bank credits to total liabilities | High debt/equity ratio and high ratio of bank credits to total liabilities |
|  | Highly sophisticated and diversified financial markets | Low level of sophistication and low opportunities for diversification of financial markets |
| **Growth** | Merger and acquisition | Organic growth |
| **Takeovers** | Hostile takeovers that are costly and antagonistic | Absence of hostile takeovers |
| **Orientation** | Short term | Long term |
| **Management mission** | Performance of assets to release shareholder value | Stewardship of business institution to achieve long term stakeholder values |
| **Business strategy** | Low commitment of outsider investors to long-term strategies of firms | Interested parties contribute to strategy, intervention by outside investors limited to periods of clear financial failure |
|  | Competitive strategy, marketing and profitability priorities | Production strategy, operations, quality and sales volume priorities |
| **Stakeholders** | Interests of other stakeholders are not represented | Other stakeholders are represented |
| **Weaknesses** | Takeovers may create monopolies | Insider systems may encourage collusion |
|  | Managers may become self-interested | Social obligations may slow necessary restructuring |

**Table 1.1** Properties of insider and outsider systems of corporate governance.

Source: Corbett, J. and Mayer, C. (1991), 'Financial Reform in Eastern Europe: Progress with the Wrong Model', *Oxford Review of Economic Policy*, 7, 57–75. Charkham, J. (1992), 'Corporate Governance: Lessons from Abroad', *European Business Journal*, 4, 2, 8–16. Ebster-Grusz, D. and Pugh, D.S. (1992), Anglo-German Business Collaboration, *British Academy of Management Conference*, Bradford University. Nunnenkampf, P. (1996), 'The German Model of Corporate Governance: Basic Features, Critical Issues, and Applicability to Transition Economies', Working Paper, 713, Kiel Institute of World Economics.

emerged with the evolution of the modern state and include: democracy and citizenship; representation; a constitution; the rule of law; competitive party and electoral systems; a permanent civil service; separation of powers between the executive, the legislature and the judiciary; judicial review; and secularity. Most of these elements are common to all OECD countries, but are combined in different ways. There are republics and constitutional monarchies, unitary or federal states, prime ministerial, presidential and semi-presidential systems. Legislatures may be bicameral or unicameral and possess features of the Westminster or congressional systems. Governments may operate under administrative law or common law, with a strong executive or a strong parliament, under close or distant judicial scrutiny, with a court of accounts or an auditor general.

Constitutional arrangements may be set out in a written constitution or embodied in

the accumulation of legislation, precedent and practice bearing on the constitutional structure. Heads of government may be directly or indirectly elected; ministers may be elected or appointed. Electoral systems may use forms of proportional representation or 'first past the post' voting. Powers are differently separated, and each branch of government is differently organised. These formal differences reflect the history of individual nations. More importantly, they signify that nations are animated and distinguished by cultural forces rooted in their past.

(OECD 2005e: 15)

## GLOBALISATION OF CORPORATE GOVERNANCE

There is a sense though that corporations and their governance could have burst the boundaries of any national jurisdiction. Multinational corporations are at the forefront of the drive towards globalisation and only international regulation might contain them. As the growth of foreign direct investment exceeds the growth in world trade, the centrality of corporations' internationalisation strategies to the evolving pattern of the industrial and investment processes of globalisation becomes increasingly apparent. Corporations have assumed this role of the compelling force in the transformation of the world economy 'the engine, worldwide, for private sector participation in the global market – to raise capital, create jobs, earn profits and divide the value added among those contributing to its success' (OECD 1998: 13). The realisation of the profound impact of corporations on the economies and societies of all countries of the world has focused attention on the growing importance of corporate governance. 'The importance of how corporations are *governed* – their ownership and control, the objectives they pursue, the rights they respect, the responsibilities they recognize, and how they distribute the value they create – has become a matter of the greatest significance, not simply for their directors and shareholders, but for the wider communities they serve' (Clarke and dela Rama 2006: xix).

Greater still than the impact of the multinational enterprises upon the globalising economy, has been the explosive growth of the international financial system that has often appeared to dwarf domestic economies. An important component of this financialisation of the world economy is the growth of capital markets, and the vast growth of equity markets from 1990 to 2004 (World Federation 2005: 55) (Figure 1.3). The ascendancy of Anglo-American equity markets is clear relative to the European and Asia Pacific markets (where in the past equity markets were marginal as other sources of capital investment predominated) (Figure 1.3). The centrality of equity markets for the Anglo-American world are revealed by the value of share trading between 1990 and 2004, as the disparity is even greater with Europe and the Asia Pacific where typically investments are for the longer term (Figure 1.4). The question is whether the increasing power of international capital markets will act like some giant financial tsunami sweeping away institutional differences throughout the rest of the world. The offer of deeper, liquid capital markets is extremely tempting to corporations around the world bent on international expansion; however, this new dependence on equity markets does come at price.

## CYCLES OF GOVERNANCE

Since the origins of industrial capitalism the business cycle of periodic booms and slumps has prevailed, and though macro-economic management may have reduced the impact of recessions, somehow in recent decades the violence of the oscillation of equity markets appears undiminished. The Anglo-American corporate governance system is much more oriented towards equity markets, and therefore the impact of shocks in the market is much greater. Business cycles in recent decades have appeared more volatile in the United States and UK. Though the longest bull market in history in the 1990s prompted assertions of 'the end of history', the crash when it occurred in the NASDAQ and NYSE in 2001 was in aggregate terms the greatest ever. Though equity markets have recovered since then to the level they were in 2000, it is

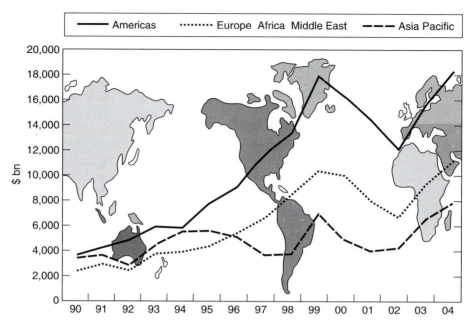

**Figure 1.3** Domestic market capitalisation, 1990–2004.

Source: World Federation of Exchanges (2005), Annual Report and Statistics, Paris: WFE/FIBV, 51.

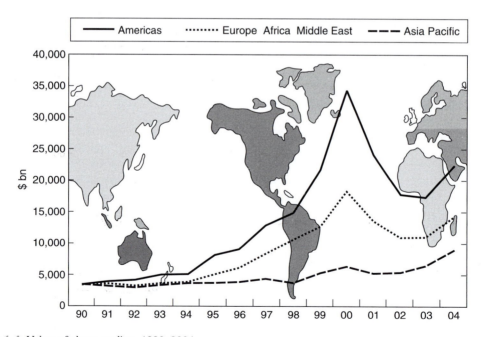

**Figure 1.4** Value of share trading, 1990–2004.

Source: World Federation of Exchanges (2005), Annual Report and Statistics, Paris: WFE/FIBV, 55.

evident that the business cycle will resume. Cyclicality may be compounded by many factors including technological innovation, market maturity, and economic and natural disasters. However the historical inclination of managers to mislead themselves and then manipulate the equity market is well documented, and investors have been known to delude themselves without too much assistance.

John Maynard Keynes in an early exploration into behavioural finance was prophetic: 'A conventional valuation [of stocks] which is established [by] the mass psychology of a large number of ignorant individuals is liable to change violently as the result of a sudden fluctuation of opinion due to factors which do not really matter to the prospective yield, since there will be no strong roots of conviction to hold it steady'. The resulting 'waves of optimism and pessimistic sentiment are unreasoning, and yet in a sense legitimate where no solid base exists for a reasonable calculation'. This trend would intensify as 'even expert professionals, possessing judgment and knowledge beyond that of the average private investor who, one might have supposed, would correct these vagaries ... would be concerned, not with making superior long term forecasts of the probable yield on an investment over its entire life, but with forecasting changes in the conventional valuation a short time ahead of the general public'. As a consequence Keynes warned stock markets become 'a battle of wits to anticipate the basis of conventional valuation a few months hence rather than the prospective yield of an investment over a long term of years' (1936: 154–155; cited in Bogle 2005: 97).

In response to the business cycle, corporate governance crisis and reform is essentially cyclical. Waves of corporate governance reform and increased regulation occur during periods of recession, corporate collapse and re-examination of the viability of regulatory systems. 'History shows that the boundaries of governance evolve in response to events in the corporate world and as business mores change. These boundaries – specific laws, regulations, recommendations and best practices – tend to shrink in latitude, and become more restrictive, whenever there is a crisis' (Cadbury and Millstein 2005: 28). During long periods of expansion, active interest in governance diminishes, as companies and shareholders become again more concerned with the generation of wealth, rather than in ensuring governance mechanisms are working appropriately for the retention of wealth, and its use for agreed purposes.

This cyclical historical saga revolves around the enduring agency and stewardship dilemmas of governance. Such dilemmas are universal in market systems, though internationally with different systems of corporate governance the unwinding of this saga has occurred at different times, for different reasons, and with different consequences.

The cyclical pattern of stock market booms encouraging and concealing corporate excesses is recurrent. Complacency concerning corporate governance during confident times compounds ensuing crises. When recession highlights corporate collapses, statutory intervention invariably occurs. Avoiding mandatory restrictive over-regulation requires active voluntary self-regulation, particularly in times of expansion (Clarke 2004).

There will never be a 'perfect' system of corporate governance. Market systems are competitive and volatile and dynamic systems of governance will reflect this. But corporate governance is about risk management. The continuous raising of standards of disclosure will be critical to effective corporate governance. The reason corporate governance standards and reforms will remain of public concern is that more of the public will have their wealth invested in companies that they will insist should behave responsibly. The drive to make corporate governance both improve corporate performance and enhance corporate responsibility will continue.

The current international wave of reform of corporate governance commenced with the Cadbury Code of Practice published by the London Stock Exchange in 1992 called in response to a series of corporate failures in the UK; the reform programme proceeded with an OECD inquiry in 1997–1999, and the publication of OECD guidelines on corporate governance that have been adopted since in national codes by all of the industrial countries, and with the assistance of the World Bank and

Asian development bank, by many developing countries. The urgency of this endeavour was increased by the Asian financial crisis of 1997–1998 that revealed the danger of *systemic* corporate governance failure. These codes have been reinforced by the influence of the market through investment institutions, and national regulators. Even with the efforts towards comprehensive reform serious weaknesses in corporate governance still occur, most spectacularly in the dot.com crash and then the dramatic failure of a series of major corporations in the United States in 2001/2002 commencing with Enron and WorldCom. It is likely interest in creating more robust institutions of corporate governance will remain an important social and economic priority for some time to come.

In an international survey of corporate governance developments conducted at the time of the publication of the revised corporate governance guidelines the OECD (2004b) commented:

> Policy concern with corporate governance has been driven in recent years primarily by a series of corporate scandals and failures in a number of countries. Although bankruptcies are to some extent a cyclical phenomenon, and especially so following an asset price bubble, systemic weaknesses have also been evident. This was particularly true with respect to financial disclosure and audit integrity but at a deeper level such weaknesses do raise serious questions about whether boards have been able to exercise independent judgement with respect to the oversight of management. The importance of preventing such weaknesses is already a key element of the OECD Principles which were widely accepted in member countries. This raises the question as to why the weaknesses were not foreseen and how implementation might have been better organised.

## CRISIS IN CORPORATE GOVERNANCE

William J. McDonough, Chairman of the Public Company Accounting Oversight Board, speaking at the Federal Reserve Bank of New York had this to say about the causes of the 2001/2002 US stock market crash:

> For 10 years, the United States enjoyed the longest economic expansion in the country's history. What could go wrong? Morality went wrong. In the mid-1990s, it became fashionable for companies in America to guide allegedly independent investment analysts to a view of the company's forthcoming quarterly earnings. We know that all numbers on a financial statement are estimates, including cash if the company operates in more than one currency. As a result, there is a certain amount of room for those estimates to be shaded to make the forecast. And then it became fashionable to expect and forecast ever-rising earnings, meaning, essentially, that product cycles and unexpected shocks and even the law of gravity no longer applied. It was a formula for cooking the books – and the books got cooked. There was another motive to cook the books. If earnings are good and always moving upward, the equity market loves it, and the stock multiple improves. That is really great if you are a senior executive, and your remuneration is related to the stock price. And that was the case. In 1993, the U.S. Congress passed a law limiting the expensing for tax purposes of the remuneration of any individual to $1 million per year, unless that remuneration is incentive-based. That law was the fairy godmother of stock options, which of course are incentive-based. And total remuneration grew spectacularly: in 1980, the average CEO of a Fortune 500 company made 40 times more than the average employee of the company. By 2000, that multiple had leaped by a factor of 10 to 400 times. I find it grotesquely immoral – explainable by no economic theory or principle other than greed.
> (2005: 1)

## The US stock market bubble

Bubbles have permeated stock markets from their beginnings, but the vast scale of the unprecedented US stock market bubble is hard to imagine: 'American stock price behaviour at the turn of the millennium had all the characteristics of a classic

bubble: prices climbed much faster than dividends or earnings ... Between January 1980 and August 2000 American stock prices as measured by the S&P500 index rose by 1239 per cent; over the same period the dividends on the shares underlying the index rose by only 188 per cent, while the earnings rose by 254 per cent' (Brennan 2004: 1). The precipitous rise of share prices was followed by a calamitous fall:

> In the period 2000–2002 the New York market suffered the biggest stock market crash in US history compared with GNP. Since early 2000 when it peaked at $15,000 billion, market capitalisation fell by $7,000 billion i.e. 46 per cent, and those who invested at the top of the market lost half of their investments'
> (Taylor 2003: 158; *The Economist*, 7 September 2002).

Leading corporations at the head of the new economy lost more than half their market value during this period including Microsoft, Cisco and Intel, many smaller new technology companies came close to bankruptcy, and even established corporations such as General Electric and Pfizer lost 40 per cent of their market capitalization. (*Financial Times*, 17 November 2005)

This enormous collapse in market value was not without its consequences: the people who made fortunes when the market was on the way up, are not the same people who lost much of what they thought they had when the market was on the way down. As Robert Shiller presciently forecast in his book *Irrational Exuberance* (2000: 203) which was published when the NASDAQ and NYSE stock markets were at an all time high:

> It is a serious mistake for public figures to acquiesce in the stock market valuations we have seen recently, to remain silent about the implications of such high valuations, and to leave all commentary to the market analysts who specialise in the nearly impossible task of forecasting the market over the short term and who share interests with investment banks or brokerage firms. The valuation of the stock market is an important national – indeed international – issue. All of our plans for the future,

as individuals and as a society, hinge on our perceived wealth, and plans can be thrown into disarray if much of that wealth evaporates tomorrow. It may even cause many of us to question the very viability of our capitalist and free market institutions.

The dramatic rise and shocking fall of the stock market had resulted not from some natural or economic disaster, but from the massive manipulative behaviour of corporate executives, investment banks, market analysts and many other professionals invested with the responsibility to maintain the probity of the market, but who chose instead the path of naked self-interest. As the crisis broke Alan Greenspan the Chairman of the US Federal Reserve Bank, offered his sage analysis of the mass earnings manipulation that was the underlying cause of the recent corporate crashes:

> Not surprisingly then, with the longer-term outlook increasingly amorphous, the level and recent growth of short-term earnings have taken on especial significance in stock price evaluation, with quarterly earnings reports subject to anticipation, rumor, and 'spin'. Such tactics, presumably, attempt to induce investors to extrapolate short-term trends into a favorable long-term view that would raise the current stock price. CEOs, under increasing pressure from the investment community to meet short-term elevated expectations, in too many instances have been drawn to accounting devices whose sole purpose is arguably to obscure potential adverse results. Outside auditors, on several well-publicized occasions, have sanctioned such devices, allegedly for fear of losing valued corporate clients. Thus, it is not surprising that since 1998 earnings restatements have proliferated. This situation is a far cry from earlier decades when, if my recollection serves me correctly, firms competed on the basis of which one had the most conservative set of books. Short-term stock price values then seemed less of a focus than maintaining unquestioned credit worthiness.
> (2002)

The consequences of hyper-inflated markets and under-governed companies arrived with the most

**Figure 1.5** Six months in the life of WorldCom, Enron, Tyco and Parmalat.
Source: FTSE (2005), *Research Report*, ISS CGI Series.

dramatic series of corporate crashes imaginable. Enron, WordCom, Tyco and Parmalat all experienced a total collapse in their share price with the first revelations of misstated accounts and irresponsible management (Figure 1.5).

## Enron and WorldCom

The greatest exponent of earnings manipulation ever was Enron. A company which began life in the gas pipeline business morphed during the financially driven new economy of the 1990s in the US into a virtual trading company. It loudly described itself as 'America's Greatest Corporation' a title widely accepted in the adoring business media.

At the time of Enron's collapse in December 2001, Enron Corporation was listed as the seventh largest company in the United States, with over $100 billion in gross revenues and more than 20,000 employees worldwide. It had received widespread recognition for its transition from an old-line energy company with pipelines and power plants, to a high tech global enterprise that traded energy contracts like commodities, launched into new industries

like broadband communications, and oversaw a multi-billion-dollar international investment portfolio.

(US Senate 2002: 6)

Enron sustained its meteoric rise through its ability to attract low-cost financing and investment, and for this Enron needed a high credit rating. To achieve this credit-rating and sustain the ever-rising share price that was giving Enron an iconic status in the marketplace (and enriching its executives beyond their dreams), Enron began developing off balance sheet entities to conceal debt and inflate earnings. All of this financial deceit unraveled when an SEC Inquiry began in October 2001, shortly followed by revelations of the huge related party transactions of the CFO, and the announcement of a series of major earnings restatements, with the largest bankruptcy ever experienced in America occurring almost immediately after.

WorldCom rapidly became in the late 1990s one of the largest telecoms companies in the United States, a growth fuelled by massive acquisitions made possible by maintaining a constantly rising share price. In November 1997 WorldCom and MCI Communications announced their $37 billion merger, the largest in US history. Utilising stock to pay for acquisitions required consistently

good financial results. WorldCom achieved this by exaggerating internet traffic, capitalising operating expenses claiming costs could be spread over several years, and inflating earnings. However WorldCom reached the limit of its ambitions when the $129 billion merger announced with Sprint Corporation to create the largest communications company in the US, was opposed by both the US Department of Justice and the European Union on the grounds of monopoly. Meanwhile 'WorldCom allowed lavish compensation, far beyond any rational calculation of value added by senior executives' (Breedon 2003: 2), and leading executives were permitted to ransack the finances of the company with loans and grants amounting to hundreds of millions of dollars. In June 2002 the internal audit department uncovered $3.8 billion of fraud, and the SEC began an investigation, with WorldCom filing for Chapter 11 bankruptcy in July 2002. By the end of 2002 WorldCom needed to restate $9 billion of reporting errors, including false reporting of expenses, and company loans made to executives. WorldCom was in the words of one official investigator 'the largest accounting fraud in history' (Breedon 2003: 1).

The excesses of this period when many corporations and investors were overwhelmed by uncontrollable and irresponsible acquisitiveness were put into perspective by one commentator:

> Over the 1990s, top managers diverted staggering wealth from shareholders to themselves. The biggest stock market bubble in US history explained much. But long-standing defects in corporate governance were also at work. The challenge is to find workable remedies. Irrational exuberance breeds excess. When the public is prepared to believe anything, management gets away with almost everything. It is far more difficult now that disillusioned investors believe almost nothing. For a while, at least, managers, accountants and even investment bankers have reason to be on their best behaviour. Yet this correction is not enough. What happened reflected more than the bull market, important though that was. And it was not just a case of a few bad apples. The behaviour reflected long-standing failings in corporate governance.
>
> (Wolf 2002)

## REFORM OF CORPORATE GOVERNANCE

### Sarbanes–Oxley Act

The response of the US Congress to what appeared at the time as the opening of a major fault line in corporate governance and the undermining of US equity markets, was to rush through the passage of the Sarbanes–Oxley Act. This legislation attempted to place a new regime of internal controls in US corporations, but reverberated in business regulation around the world. Congressman Michael G. Oxley, chair of the Financial Services Committee, author with Senator Paul Sarbanes of the Sarbanes–Oxley Act, described the background to the intense Congressional discussions of the dramatic events that gave rise to the urgent passing of the Act:

> 'There was a perception that American capitalism was in crisis. We faced numerous problems in corporate America ranging from bankruptcy to failures of investor protection to fraud. Shareholders were losing money fast, and that general trend was punctuated by the news of Enron, WorldCom, and Global Crossing. In addition to the hardships of these bankruptcies on employees and retirees, the energy and telecommunications sectors bore triple losses as the ripple effects continued. With losses of trillions of dollars in market capitalization, it's no wonder investors lost their nerve. Clearly this disparate set of problems was far outside the bounds of any normal economic trough or recession'.
>
> (House Committee on Financial Services 2003: 1, 2)

The sense of urgency was critical already in the Congressional Committee with the Enron collapse, when suddenly another corporate crisis occurred, 'WorldCom *took all the oxygen out of the room because it was so huge* – four or five times larger in bankruptcy terms than Enron. It really did change the debate, particularly in the Senate'. (ibid.)

Sarbanes–Oxley was welcomed by the wider public as a necessary restraint on corporate executives engaging in staggering financial misdemeanours without detection. But parts of the

Act were regarded as unduly restrictive in many US business circles, and overseas companies listed in the United States found themselves caught up in its rules based approach. William H. Donaldson Chair of the US Securities and Exchange Commission at a roundtable meeting in 2005 with Chief Financial Officers of corporations concerned about the workload that section 404 of the Act on reporting on internal controls was generating, defended Sarbanes–Oxley as:

> A necessary and understandable response to an unprecedented string of corporate scandals, which were rooted in intolerable governance, accounting and audit failures. Section 404 of the Act requires that management assess and report on the ineffectiveness of our internal controls over financial reporting, and that the company's external auditor report on both the internal controls and management's assessment of these controls. As I've said before, all of the provisions of the Sarbanes–Oxley Act, the internal control requirements of Section 404, may have the greatest potential to improve the accuracy and reliability of financial reporting. Strong controls are an important part of this goal, because our capital markets run on the basic premise that companies will present reliable and complete financial data for investment and policy decision-making.
>
> (SEC 2005: 6)

However, while business executives continued to complain about the developing over-regulation of their activity, that they claimed was imposing unnecessary costs, and undermining efficiency and entrepreneurship, a few outspoken lawyers and politicians claimed that regulation of corporate misdeeds did not go far enough. At the forefront of these was Eliot Spitzer the Attorney General of New York State, who embarrassed the SEC in launching a series of successful campaigns against a string of establishment Wall Street entities including legal actions in 2002 against ten leading investment banks and brokerage houses for offering biased investment advice through in-house analysts which resulted in fines and compensation of $1.4 billion, and separation of the analysts from the investment banks. Following on from this Spitzer investigated mutual fund brokers

who allowed special clients including hedge funds late trading after the market had closed, and secured more than $1 billion in fines and remuneration for investors. Spitzer concluded, 'A key lesson from the recent scandals is that the checks on the system have not worked. The honour code among CEOs didn't work. Board oversight didn't work. Self-regulation was a complete failure. But one thing has worked – law enforcement' (*Wall St Journal*, 5 April 2005).

## CONTINUING CRISIS IN CORPORATE GOVERNANCE

Despite the international effort to reform and improve corporate governance, and the considerable effort focused on achieving higher standards by companies, and better monitoring by regulators, the reality is that recurrent crises keep on occurring in corporate governance. This suggests there is a long way to go yet on the path to reform, certainly in the United States, and in many other countries. For example two important instances of corporate governance failure indicate ongoing problems in US corporate governance, the continuing excessive inflation in executive reward, and the widening extent of corporate earnings misstatements.

### CEO pay

During the boom years of the 1990s there was a rapid and sustained escalation in CEO salaries in the United States, and any expected adjustment downwards in executive reward with the market crash of 2001, and the halving of the market capitalisation of many large corporations, did not occur. Though there were more stringent efforts to link CEO compensation to performance, CEO reward remained at incredibly high levels whether the companies they managed did well or not. Extremely lucrative share option schemes continued, and if the options packages became more sophisticated, there were many devices such as backdating widely employed to ensure executives extracted the best possible reward from their options.

| Rank | Company | CEO | Pay (USD) | Market capitalisation ($ billions) |
|------|---------|-----|-----------|-----------------------------------|
| 1 | IAC/Interactive | Barry Diller | 295 000 000 | 14 |
| 2 | Capital One Financial | Richard D. Fairbank | 249 000 000 | 18 |
| 3 | Yahoo | Terry S. Semel | 230 000 000 | 47 |
| 4 | Nabors Industries | Eugene M. Isenberg | 203 000 000 | 11 |
| 5 | Colgate Palmolive | Reuben Mark | 147 970 000 | 27 |
| 6 | Country Wide Financial | Angelo R. Mozilo | 142 000 000 | 22 |
| 7 | Cendant | Henry R. Silverman | 139 960 000 | 21 |
| 8 | KB Home | Bruce E. Karatz | 135 560 000 | 6 |
| 9 | Lehman Brothers Holdings | Richard S. Fuld | 122 670 000 | 26 |
| 10 | Abercrombie & Fitch | Michael S. Jeffries | 114 000 000 | 6 |

Table 1.2 US top ten highest paid CEOs, 2005.

Source: Compiled from Sahadi, J. (2006), 'CEO Pay Up But Not Performance', CNNMoney (October 4, 2006). http://money.cnn.com/2006/10/04/news/companies/ceo_pay_survey/. Forbes (2006), Executive Compensation, 'Executive Pay What the Boss Makes', Forbes.com http://www.forbes.com/2006/04/17/06ceo_ceo-compensation_land.html. FT Global 500 Report (2005), http://www.ft.com/reports/ft5002006.

Table 1.2 indicates the total remuneration of the ten highest paid CEOs in the US in 2005, and the total remuneration of the ten highest paid CEOs from the rest of the world in 2004 is given in Table 1.3. Included in the compensation figures are base salary, bonuses, benefits, long term incentive plans, and profits from cashing out on stock options where this information was accessible. The rampant inflation of US CEO salaries relative to their colleague CEOs in the rest of the world, is demonstrated by the remarkable fact that the US average top CEO salary is more than 50 times greater than their counterparts in other countries, and that the *lowest* US CEO salary in this league is 17 times greater than the *highest* non-US CEO salary (Figure 1.6). What is more the overseas companies have on average 5 times the market capitalisation of the US companies, and the *lowest* paid non-US CEO's company has a market capitalisation over 14 times *higher* than the highest paid US CEO's company. While these comparisons are inevitably crude since much compensation of different forms is hidden in the US, and probably more so in other countries, these astonishing disparities are a measure of how out of control US CEOs' reward has been for a long time.

Claims that such extravagant salaries are required to incentivise US CEOs and create greater alignment between their interests and those of the shareholders scarcely stand scrutiny. As *CNN.Money* (4 October 2006) comments

In the 10 companies with the most highly paid CEOs, the pay-for-performance link is hard to find in seven of them, given that they had underperformed their peer group even as their CEOs banked somewhere between $95 million and $295 million ... Only three companies Yahoo, Valero Energy and Countrywide outperformed their peers in the past five years ... And in fact, two companies IAC/Interactive and Cendant created a negative shareholder return, which factors in reinvested dividends. Had the underperforming CEOs been linked to an index of their company peer's performance rather than to the stock's market price, their options that ran into millions of dollars would have been wiped out altogether.

Of course CEO salaries are only a part of wider structures of inequality that have become more extreme in recent years, and rewards for

| Rank | Company | CEO | Pay (USD) | Market capitalisation ($ billions) |
|------|---------|-----|-----------|-----------------------------------|
| 1 | UBS | Peter Wuffli | 6 820 000 | 95 |
| 2 | Roche Group | Franz Humer | 5 569 000 | 96 |
| 3 | Banco Santander Central | Alfredo Saenz | 5 448 000 | 76 |
| 4 | BP | Lord Browne of Madingley | 5 356 000 | 221 |
| 5 | Nestlé | Peter Brabeck-Letmathe | 5 165 000 | 110 |
| 6 | Glaxo SmithKline | Jean-Pierre Garnier | 4 688 000 | 134 |
| 7 | Nokia | Jorma Olilla | 4 292 000 | 72 |
| 8 | Siemens Group | Heinrich von Pierer | 3 804 000 | 70 |
| 9 | BHP Billiton | Charles Goodyear | 3 544 000 | 82 |
| 10 | Novartis Group | Daniel Vasella | 3 290 000 | 124 |

**Table 1.3** Rest of the world highest paid CEOs, 2004.

Source: Compiled from Kitchens Susan (2004), '*Executive Pay: What the Bosses Make*', Manifest The Proxy Voting Agency. Manifest Information Services. http://www.manifest.co.uk/news/2004/20040510Forbes.htm. Forbes (2006), Executive Compensation, '*Executive Pay What the Boss Makes*', Forbes.com http://www.forbes.com/2006/04/17/06ceo_ceo-compensation_land.html. FT Global 500 Report (2005), http://www.ft.com/reports/ft5002006.
Note: Figures on market capitalisation are based on reports as per 31 March 2005.

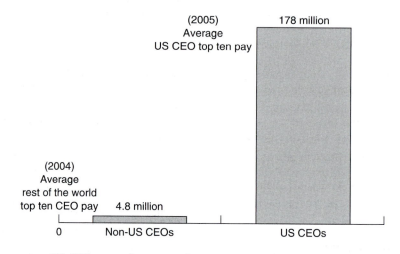

**Figure 1.6** Average top US CEOs annual remuneration vs. top rest of world CEOs ($ million).

Source: Sahadi, J. (2006), *CEO Pay Up But Not Performance*, CNNMoney, 4 October, http://money.cnn.com/2006/10/04/news/companies/ceo_pay_survey/. Forbes (2006), Executive Compensation, *Executive Pay What the Boss Makes*, Forbes.com, http://www.forbes.com/2006/04/17/06ceo_ceo-compensation_land.html.
FT Global 500 Report (2005), http://www.ft.com/reports/ft5002006. Kitchens, Susan (2004), *Executive Pay: What the Bosses Make*, Manifest: The Proxy Voting Agency, Manifest Information Services, http://www.manifest.co.uk/news/2004/20040510Forbes.htm.

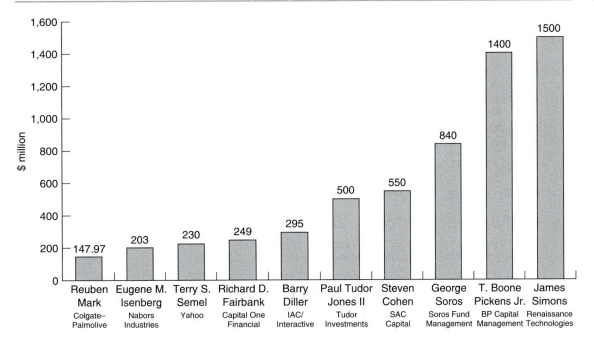

**Figure 1.7** Top five US CEOs annual remuneration vs. top five US fund managers CEOs, 2005.

Source: Sahadi, J. (2006), *CEO Pay Up But Not Performance*, CNNMoney, 4 October, http://money.cnn.com/ 2006/10/04/news/companies/ceo_pay_survey/. Forbes (2006), CEOCompensation, *Executive Pay What the Boss Makes*, Forbes.com, http://www.forbes.com/2006/04/17/06ceo_ceo-compensation_ land.html. FT Global 500 Report (2005), http://www.ft.com/reports/ft5002006. Schurr, S. (2006), Top Fund Managers Smash $1bn barrier, *Financial Times*, 26 May.

executives in the finance sector have become even more astronomically inflated (Figure 1.7). Whatever loss occurs to shareholder funds due to excessive CEO salaries in US corporations the wider implications of this extravagance are more serious, in terms of how the corporations are managed, as illustrated in the ongoing scandal of recurrent earnings misstatements in the United States.

## Earnings misstatements

Investors depend on the financial reports of companies in order to make their investment decisions, and capital can only be allocated efficiently if corporate financial reports are reliable. It is management's responsibility to ensure the accuracy of financial reporting, and that all material matters are fully disclosed. Accounting for complex transactions and determining the

exact moment when revenue is realised is a difficult task; however, investors have a right to expect financial reporting will be carried out with competence, diligence, honesty and transparency. While financial reporting internationally may be challenged reaching these high standards, the soaring number of corporate earnings statements in the United States in recent years does not encourage confidence in the veracity or efficiency of accounting standards or internal controls in many companies. Year by year the number of earnings restatements in the US listed companies has increased from 92 in 1997, to 225 in 2001, and 1,195 in 2005 (Figure 1.8). The 2005 figure of 1,195 earnings restatements represented one in every 12 public companies, nearly double the 613 earnings restatements in 2004 which represented one in every 24 companies: 'When so many companies produce inaccurate financial statements it seriously calls into question the quality of information that investors relied upon to

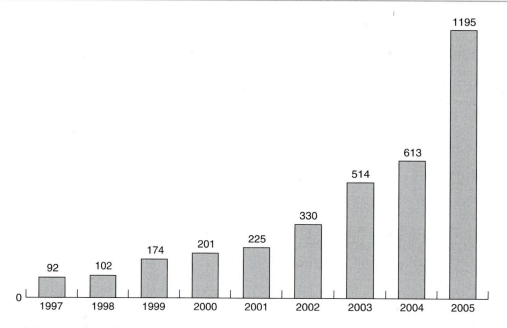

**Figure 1.8** Total number of US corporation earnings restatements, 1997–2005.

Source: Adapted from Coffee, Jr, J.C. (2002), 'Racing Towards the Top: The Impact of Cross-listings and Stock MarketCompetition on International Corporate Governance', *Columbia Law Review*, 107(7): 1757–1831. Glass Lewis and Co. (2006), Company website.

make capital allocation decisions. Investors need unbiased, competently prepared financial statements to make these decisions efficiently' (Glass, Lewis & Co. 2006: 1).

## GOVERNANCE AND CORPORATE PERFORMANCE

Good governance has always been intuitively associated not just with sound, but with successful companies. Countries known for their robust governance institutions attract investment capital. This was central to the understanding of corporate governance that informed the work of the Cadbury Committee which insisted: 'The country's economy depends on the drive and efficiency of its companies. Thus the effectiveness with which boards discharge their responsibilities determines Britain's competitive position. They must be free to drive their companies forward, but exercise that freedom within a framework of effective accountability. This is the essence of any system of good corporate governance' (1992: 1.1).

There is an increasing realisation the higher standards of corporate governance are not only necessary to ensure accountability, but also to positively improve corporate performance.

Though the evidence relating governance reforms to performance improvement in the past has proved mixed, more sophisticated methodologies are now being applied with more promising results, with 'an increasing body of finance literature suggesting companies with superior governance offer better relative investment performance or lower investment risk' (Goldman Sachs 2006: 4). As institutional investors increasingly become the majority shareholders in listed corporations across the world their interest in pursuing the link between governance and performance has heightened considerably. Hermes a leading UK investment activist suggests 'ensuring compliance with certain governance standards and active ownership based on a larger set of standards *in itself* will improve the performance of investee companies. A body of research, which is beginning to evolve principally in the US, seeking to establish which governance standards are

directly related to the performance of companies supports this view' (2006: 6).

The UNEP Finance Initiative in 2005 commissioned 22 different financial services firms internationally, including sell side research houses, asset management firms and an investment consultancy to investigate the most salient factors linking environmental, social and governance (ESG) issues to company value, which amounted to substantial evidence of a significant relationship (UNEP 2006). There is a strong sense emerging among both the general public and investment community that the wealth generating activities of corporations do need to be enhanced within a wider framework of social and environmental responsibility.

## CORPORATE GOVERNANCE AND SUSTAINABILITY

The definition and appreciation of what constitutes wealth creation is changing in radical ways which corporations and their governance are only just beginning to contemplate (Benn and Dunphy 2006). In the past it was all to easy for corporations to simply externalise their social and environmental costs. 'Just as evolution has made the shark a perfect eating machine, the device of limited liability has allowed the corporation to perfect its function ... The function perfected by limited liability is that of permitting corporations to externalize the costs of stock price maximization, that is to push those costs onto others. The corporation is the perfect externalizing machine' (Mitchell 2001).

However the realisation that social integration and ecological integrity represent values as material and valuable as any monetary values, suggests the next great challenge for companies is to bridge the divide between corporate governance and corporate social and environmental responsibility. Corporations increasingly will be held to account for their social and environmental impact. In social terms they will need to demonstrate a commitment to their employees, community and wider society that ensures they do no harm to the health and well-being of people, and do everything they can to improve the quality of life. In environmental terms corporations will be made to bear the cost of any impact on the environment, and there will be incentive structures to enable better responses and solutions to environmental problems. This widening of the responsibilities of companies, will demand a new conception of corporate governance and business objectives, a new understanding of the corporate mission.

There is some doubt as to whether existing explanations of corporate existence, activities and objectives are adequate to the task of examining or explaining this new corporate horizon. A great deal of legal and academic thinking on corporate governance remains trapped within the tight parameters of agency theory, assuming the only real issue is principal/agent relations, and that delivering shareholder value will resolve all problems. The understanding of the responsibilities and objectives of corporate governance needs to be developed to encompass wider concerns and deeper relationships. The corporate *licence to operate* needs to be negotiated not only with shareholders, but with a much wider constituency of stakeholders representing social and environmental interests. This argument will be developed in detail in Chapter 8 of this work, but for the present it is useful to briefly survey the present state of corporate governance theory.

## AGENCY AND DOUBLE AGENCY DILEMMAS

The dominant theoretical framework for understanding corporate governance is undoubtedly agency theory, whatever its evident limitations. Rampant executives running out of control at the shareholders expense is a sharp reminder of the significant and enduring agency dilemmas in corporate governance. Agency theory conceives of the firm as a nexus of constantly re-negotiated contracts by individuals each aiming to maximise their own utility (Alchian and Demsetz 1972). Jensen and Meckling (1976) suggest the essence of the agency problem is the separation of finance and management. Investors (principals) need the managers' (agents) specialised human capital to generate returns on their funds. The principals and agents effectively have a contract that specifies what managers can do with the funds, and how the returns will be divided between them and

the shareholders. A problem is that as future contingencies cannot be anticipated, complete contracts are not feasible. The principals and agents have to allocate residual control rights: the rights to make decisions not foreseen in the contract. Managers inevitably acquire considerable residual control rights, providing discretion over how to allocate investors' funds. From this point of view the subject of corporate governance concerns the constraints principals can put on agents to reduce misallocation of investor's funds.

Agency theory claims shareholders have the right to residual claims since they are the residual risk bearers: the only economic actors who make an investment in the corporation without a contractual guarantee of a specific return. As the *residual claimants* shareholders bear the risk of the company making a profit or a loss, and they have a direct interest in the allocation of corporate resources to make the largest residual possible. As the basis of agency theory is the self-interested utility-maximising motivation of individual actors, it is assumed the relationship between shareholders and managers will be problematic, and there is a single-minded focus on how the principal is able to prevent the agent from maxmising his own utility (Jensen 1994). For agency theorists efficient markets in corporate control, management, and information are the means that militate against the agency problem. However as agency dilemmas are so inherent in the corporate form, the universality of the publicly listed corporation is a phenomenon of enduring concern: 'Why, given the existence of positive costs of the agency relationship, do we find the usual corporate form of organisation with widely diffuse ownership so widely prevalent. If one takes seriously much of the literature regarding the "discretionary" power held by management of large corporations, it is difficult to understand the historical fact of enormous growth in equity in such organisations not only in the United States, but throughout the world' (Jensen and Meckling 1976: 330).

The way agency theory has come to dominate so completely the corporate governance literature is explained by Daily, Dalton and Cannella (2003: 372) as due to two factors:

First, it is an extremely simple theory, in which large corporations are reduced to two participants – managers and shareholders – and the interests of each are assumed to be both clear and consistent. Second, the notion of humans as self-interested and generally unwilling to sacrifice personal interests for the interests of others is both age old and widespread ... Economists struggled with this problem for centuries until Jensen and Meckling (1976) provided their convincing rationale for how the public corporation could survive and prosper despite the self-interested proclivities of managers. In nearly all modern governance research governance mechanisms are conceptualised as deterrents to managerial self-interest.

Agency theory does address some of the central dilemmas associated with the transformation of the simple control structures of the owner entrepreneur company (Figure 1.9), to the more complex controls required following the separation of ownership and control. However agency theory underestimates the complexity of what is in effect a double agency dilemma, firstly in the relationship between shareholders and board of directors, and secondly in the relationship between board of directors and management. Yet it is the fundamental tenets of agency theory that have informed much of corporate governance policy and practice in recent decades:

The dominant view of boards, a view that had underpinned the majority of reform activity, is that the board acts as a control mechanism to reduce the potential divergence of interests between corporate management and shareholders. Non-executive directors, because of their supposed independence and objectivity, provide an important check and balance to the power of the chief executive and his or her executive team. The notion of 'contestability' in the boardroom has become central, and the model for boards is unmistakably adversarial.

(Stiles and Taylor 2002: 1)

The translation of the complexities of the corporate world into a set of control relationships neglects the political, organisational and technical

**Figure 1.9** From owner entrepreneur to double agency dilemma.

Source: Adapted from Blake, Allan (1999), *Dynamic Directors*, London: Macmillan Business, 21, Fig. 1.1.

dimensions of business activity, that make it less predictable and controllable than it might appear.

> Agency theorists need to assume not only that people are self-seeking economic utility maximisers, but that they are fully competent self-seeking utility maximisers. In other words, they need to assume that, faced with particular choices, people will in fact make the decisions that maximise their utility ... Nobody with any knowledge of business would suggest that all managers are equally competent or that any

manager can infallibly achieve their objectives, whether these are the objectives set by their shareholders or those dictated by their own self-interest. The world of business is simply not like that. On the contrary, it is confused, uncertain and unpredictable. The information on which decisions have to be based is both insufficient and overwhelming, and can be full of contradictions. Implementation of a decision can be wrecked by a host of technical, personal and interpersonal factors quite outside a chief executive's control. The most carefully and competently constructed judgements, whether they be executive judgements of how to run the business, or non-executive judgements of how the executives are performing, can with hindsight appear fatally flawed.

(Hendy 2005: 58)

This is not to suggest that the effort to exercise effective control and coherent direction in corporate enterprise is futile, but it does imply that the application of simple rules or the assumption of crude interpretations of motivation is likely to be inappropriate. The effort to understand and to bring into some alignment the interests of shareholders, the activities and aspirations of managers, and the concerns of wider stakeholders, requires more careful analysis and application than agency theory might offer. As Pye and Pettigrew (2005: 30) argue 'The idea that all managers are self-interested agents who do not bear the full financial effects of their decisions (Jensen and Meckling 1976) has provided an extraordinary edifice around which three decades of agency research has been built, even though these assumptions are simplistic and lead to a reductionist view of business, that is, comprising two participants – managers (agents) and shareholders (principals)'. Attempting a deeper understanding of corporate governance relationships requires consideration of wider theoretical perspectives.

## THEORETICAL PERSPECTIVES ON BOARDS AND GOVERNANCE

For too long corporate governance has been observed through a single analytical lens that offers partial insights, but cannot begin to examine

the full dimensions of the problem, or offer convincing explanations. The complexity and richness of the dynamic phenomena involved in corporate governance requires the application of a range of theoretical critiques to understand more fully the dilemmas involved:

> A multitheoretic approach to corporate governance is essential for recognising the many mechanisms and structures that might reasonably enhance organisational functioning. For example, the board of directors is perhaps the most central internal governance mechanism. Whereas agency theory is appropriate for conceptualising the control/monitoring role of directors, additional (and perhaps contrasting) theoretical perspectives are needed to explain director's resource, service and strategy roles.
> (Daily, Dalton and Cannella 2003: 372)

Existing theoretical approaches to corporate governance follow a continuum from the narrow focus of agency theory and transaction cost theory inspired by financial economics, through approaches including stewardship, resource dependency, stakeholder and managerialist theories developed by organisational theorists, to more critical analysis originating in sociological and political critiques (Clarke 2004). Each theoretical approach has its own logic and limitations, and though a number of the approaches represent opposing interpretations of the same problem, in some cases the theories serve to illuminate different dimensions of the governance problem (Table 1.4).

After agency theory the most established theoretical approach is transaction cost economics. Ronald Coase (1937) insisted notwithstanding the assumption of neoclassical theory that the allocation of resources is coordinated through a series of exchange transactions on the market, that in the real world a considerable proportion of economic activity is organised in firms. Coase examines the economic explanation for the existence of firms, and why economic activities take place within firms rather than through markets. He explains the nature of firms in terms of the imperfections of markets, and in terms of the transaction costs of market exchange. New institutional economics differs from agency theory in that the

corporate governance problems of firms are perceived to proceed from a number of contractual hazards. This approach is concerned with discovering internal measures and mechanisms which reduce costs associated with contractual hazards to an efficient level: the external discipline of the market cannot be relied on to mitigate these problems, as it has only 'limited constitutional powers to conduct audits and has limited access to the firm's incentive and resource allocation machinery' (Williamson 1975: 143). Like-neo classical economics though, the locus of attention remains the shareholder-manager relationship, but in this case it is because shareholders are perceived to 'face a diffuse but significant risk of expropriation because the assets in question are numerous and ill-defined, and cannot be protected in a well-focused, transaction specific way' (Williamson 1984: 1210; Learmount 2002: 5). As with agency theory the narrowness of the focus limits the explanatory power of this analysis.

In contrast to agency theory, stewardship theory acknowledges a larger range of human motives of managers including orientations towards achievement, altruism, and the commitment to meaningful work. Stewardship theory maintains there is no inherent conflict of interest between managers and owners, and that optimum governance structures allow coordination of the enterprise to be achieved most effectively. Managers should be authorised to act since according to stewardship theory they are not opportunistic agents but good stewards who will act in the best interests of owners. Stewardship theory recognises a strong relationship between managers' pursuit of the objectives of the enterprise, the owners' satisfaction, and other participants in the enterprise reward. Davis, Schoorman and Donaldson (1997) suggest that as managers maximise shareholders' wealth through raising the performance of the firm, they serve their own purposes. Managers balance competing shareholder and stakeholder objectives, making decisions in the best interests of all. However there is an element of choice in corporate governance arrangements, both managers and owners can choose to have either agency or steward relationships, contingent upon their assessment of the motivations of each other, and the situation of the enterprise. Stewardship theory rescues the integrity of management as

ONE

| Dimension | Theoretical perspective | | | | | | |
|---|---|---|---|---|---|---|---|
| | Agency | Transaction costs economics | Stewardship | Resource dependency | Stakeholder | Managerial hegemony | Class hegemony |
| **Corporate governance and board role** | Self-interested utility maximising motivation of individual actors. Ensure match between managers ('agents') and shareholders ('principals') | Focus on governance needs of exchange relations. Concerned with mechanisms which reduce costs associated with contractual hazards | Ensure the stewardship of corporate assets. Maintains no inherent conflict of interest between managers and owners, and that optimum governance structures allow coordination of the enterprise to be achieved | Reduce uncertainty; boundary spanning; highlights the interdependence of firms rather than viewing them simply in terms of management intentions. Connecting firm with external resources helps to reduce uncertainty | Defines firms as inclusive multilateral agreements between the enterprise and multiple stakeholders. These relationships constrain and create the strategic possibilities of the company. | The board as a 'legal fiction'; managerial control. Need to understand the relationship between owners, managers and the board of directors | Perpetuate elite and class power; corporations as exploitative vehicle for accumulation of wealth and power |
| **Theoretical origin** | Economics and finance | Economics and finance | Organisation studies | Organisation studies | Politics, law and management organisation studies | Management organisation studies | Sociology and politics |
| **Unit of analysis** | Individual | Transaction | Coordination | Resources | Stakeholders | Management | Corporations |
| **Focal dimension** | Agency costs | Asset specificity | Stewardship | Interdependence | Relationships | Control | Exploitation |

Table 1.4 Theoretical perspectives on corporate governance.

| Dimension | Theoretical perspective | | | | | | |
|---|---|---|---|---|---|---|---|
| | Agency | Transaction costs economics | Stewardship | Resource dependency | Stakeholder | Managerial hegemony | Class hegemony |
| **Focal cost concern** | Residual loss | Maladaptation | n/a | n/a | n/a | n/a | n/a |
| **Contractual focus** | Ex ante alignment | Ex post governance | n/a | n/a | n/a | n/a | n/a |
| **Detail on board activity** | Low | Low | Low | Low | Low | Moderate | Low |
| **Empirical support** | Equivocal | Equivocal | Limited | Moderate | Moderate | Moderate | Moderate |
| **Limitations of theory** | Assumptions too narrow; ignores the complexity of organisations | Assumptions too narrow; ignores the complexity of organisations | Largely untested | Focus on resource attainment, not resource use; Interlocks not shown to influence behaviours | Multi-stakeholder relationships difficult to prioritise | Problems over definition of 'control'; owner networks underestimated | Partial view of board motivation and impact of corporations |
| **Representative studies** | Fama and Jensen (1985); Jensen and Meckling (1976); Kosnik (1987) | Coase (1937); Williamson (1975, 1984, 1985, 1998) | Donaldson and Davis (1991) | Pfeffer (1972); Pfeffer and Salanick (1978) | RSA (1995); Blair (1995); Clarke (1998) | Freeman (1984); Mace (1971); Lorsch & MacIver (1989) | Mills (1971); Useem (1980) |

Table 1.4—Cont'd

Source: Adapted from Zahra and Pearce (1989); Stiles and Taylor (2001).

a profession, something many managers would recognise and aspire towards.

There is a stream of theoretical approaches that widen the focus beyond internal monitoring, to explore the external challenges of corporate governance in terms of building relationships and securing resources. Resource dependence theory, institutional theory, and network theory all are interested in the external relations of corporations. Resource dependency theory highlights the interdependencies of organisations rather than viewing them simply in terms of management intentions. Hillman, Cannella and Paetzold (2000) for example examine how company directors may serve to connect the firm with external resources that help to overcome uncertainty, and provide access to relationships with suppliers, buyers, public policy makers and other social groups. Resource dependency approaches add a vital external dimension to corporate governance relationships.

Stakeholder theory defines organisations as multilateral agreements between the enterprise and its multiple stakeholders. The relationship between the company and its *internal* stakeholders (employees, managers, owners) is framed by formal and informal rules developed through the history of the relationship. This institutional setting constrains and creates the strategic possibilities for the company. While management may receive finance from shareholders, they depend upon employees to fulfil the productive purpose and strategic intentions of the company. *External* stakeholders (customers, suppliers, competitors, special interest groups and the community) are equally important, and also are constrained by formal and informal rules that businesses must respect.

Rather than conceiving of the company as a bundle of assets that belong to shareholders, Blair (1995) argues corporations may be conceived as institutional arrangements for governing the relationships between all of the parties that contribute firm-specific assets. This includes not only shareholders, but also long-term employees who develop specialised skills of value to the corporation, and suppliers, customers and others who make specialised investments. If the job of management is to maximise the total wealth of the enterprise rather than just the value of the shareholders' stake, then management must take into account the effect of corporate decisions on all stakeholders in the firm.

Stakeholder theory has an intellectual appeal and practical application, however it is argued that multiple stakeholder responsibilities can leave management with too much freedom of manoeuvre.

Managerialist theory focuses on the distinctions between the myth and the reality of the relative powers of managers and boards. Mace (1971) for example examines the 1960s ascendancy of corporate executives, when powerful CEOs selected and controlled the boards of directors of the companies they ran. He outlines how CEOs in the US were able to determine board membership, to decide what boards could and could not do, controlled the information and professional advice the board received, and determined the compensation of senior executives, including often themselves. When corporations fail, the question always arises, 'Where were the board of directors?' However there is a wide gap between what directors are supposed to do, what people generally assume directors do, and what they are actually allowed to do in practice. Mace catalogues how dysfunctional boards rather than being exceptional, became normal in the United States, as executives took control. Finally there are more radical theoretical critiques which suggest that corporations perpetuate the power of an elite, serving to exploit others in the interests of accumulating wealth and power (Mills 1971). Though radical analysis faded after the 1960s, it has enjoyed a new lease of life in the widespread critique of the impact of globalisation which corporations have spearheaded (Clarke and dela Rama 2006).

## Multiple theoretical lenses

Adopting and synthesising different theoretical perspectives may begin to provide a fuller understanding of the mechanisms and processes of corporate governance. In a recent survey of board practice Philip Stiles and Bernard Taylor recommend the explanatory power of a series of theoretical perspectives. The structure of the board, its monitoring of budgets and plans, and its address to performance and targets, all reflect

the assumptions of agency theory and transaction cost theory underpinning the control role of the board:

> Consistent with this theme, however, is the finding that boards may actively help companies to unlearn organisational practices that have become dysfunctional (Nystrom and Starbuck 1984). That is, boards may diagnose new opportunities, select new performance measures, and emphasise certain control systems at the expense of others, in order to bring the organisation to a new focus. This supports the stewardship theory of board activity and suggests that, in certain circumstances, both organisational economics and stewardship theories may be complementary. The combination of what Tricker (1994) calls the conformance and performance roles suggests that multiple theoretical lenses are appropriate. Reinforcing the case for complementary theoretical perspectives is the evidence of boundary-spanning activity on the part of non-executive directors but also of the executive directors, providing support for the resource-dependence view of board activity. Our approach is, therefore, in line with greater calls for reconciliation between economic and organisational perspectives (Kosnik 1987; Eisenhardt 1989; Judge and Zeithaml 1992) and shows that seemingly contradictory approaches can coexist as theoretical explanations' (Stiles and Taylor 2002: 122–123).

There are many other established and emerging theoretical tools that may enhance the understanding of corporate governance however, and they may prove increasingly necessary given the decisive challenges ahead. The essential and eternal concept of *trust* is a good place to commence. Trust is a vital component of corporate governance, and the absence of trust is deeply corrosive. As Stiles and Taylor (2002: 23) note, much of the activity of corporate governance revolves around the building of trust: 'A series of studies by Westphal and Zajac has highlighted how the interpersonal influence processes in the board/chief executive relationship can help trust and cooperation develop within the board and help problem-solving and decision-making activity (Westphal

and Zajac 1995, 1997; Zajac and Westphal 1996)'. In their own research on boards Stiles and Taylor (2001: 123–124) indicate how trust and control are not mutually exclusive,

> Underpinning the discussion has been the central role of trust in enhancing both board task performance and board cohesiveness. The model of trust argued for has not been the traditional one of trust and control conceptualised as opposite ends of a continuum. Rather trust and control are interdependent. Because the board operates in complex and uncertain conditions and is often characterised by role conflict the potential for both trust and control to coexist is apparent. Control mechanisms serve to focus members' attention on organisational goals, while trust mechanisms promote decision-making and enhance cohesiveness.

Other theoretical perspectives may well contribute to a radical reconceptualisation of corporate governance around theories such as social capital that conceives of value creation arising in social relationships; the knowledge based theory of the firm which acknowledges the increasing importance of intellectual capital; theories that see the firm as a complex adaptive system; theories of creativity and innovation; and most important of all the theory of sustainability, and whether the corporation can become a sustainable form of economic activity. These approaches all demand that corporate governance can only be understood by going beyond the shareholder/manager relationship, and the immediate mechanisms and institutions of governance, to a deeper understanding of the relationships between corporations and the economies and societies they serve (Clarke 2004).

## APPROACH OF THIS BOOK

This work aims to provide a critical and comparative view of the international development of corporate governance. The diversity and richness of corporate governance systems and practices will be emphasised, and ongoing viability and vitality of different approaches. The focus will be upon the contest between *outsider* and

*insider* systems of governance, and the degree to which convergence may be occurring as a result of the insistent pressure of capital markets and other forces of globalisation. The analysis concentrates on the Anglo-American, European and Asia Pacific regions as presently the most powerful centres of economic activity which are likely to determine the future direction of the development of corporate governance. Other developing regions of the world have corporate governance dilemmas to contend with also, many originating in the developed world (Clarke and dela Rama 2006).

The analysis employed will extend beyond the one-dimensional focus of agency theory that sees the problems of corporate governance wrapped up in the principal/agency relationship in which the only players are the shareholders, board and managers. The significance of the cultural and institutional arrangements of different corporate governance systems will be emphasised, a second dimension of governance which helps to explain the distribution of control, the allocation of rewards, and the exercise of regulation. As B. Minoru Makihara, the Chief Executive of Mitsubishi Corporation once said:

> The phrase corporate governance is often applied narrowly to questions about the structure and functioning of boards of directors, or the rights and prerogatives of shareholders in boardroom decision-making ... (but) a broader view of corporate governance, (is) one that refers to the whole set of legal, cultural, and institutional arrangements that determine what publicly traded corporations can do, who controls them, how that control is exercised, and how the risks and returns from the activities they undertake are allocated.
>
> (Monks and Minow 2001: xv)

However, a third dimension of corporate governance needs to be explored, and that is the impact of the governance of corporations on the wider international political economy, and whether corporations are capable of social and environmental responsibility.

The essential political mechanisms of corporate governance are examined in Chapter 2: focusing on the board of directors as the epicentre of governance activity. How boards work with CEOs to provide guidance and leadership to the company is considered. The tensions between the board's duty to monitor management and to commit to strategic direction are investigated. How CEOs have accumulated power is questioned, and whether more independent boards can regain authority. Chapter 3 explores the institutional elements of corporate governance, looking at different governance regimes with contrasting approaches to finance and legal and market regulation. The wide range of potential monitoring controls that exist in corporate governance are examined, and the question posed of whether the increasing concentration of ownership in the investment institutions will make for a fundamental change in how corporations are governed.

The following three chapters analyse the nature and development of governance in the Anglo-American, European and Asia Pacific regions. Each region has a distinctive culture and history of institutional development, which has resulted in very different corporate structures and business philosophies, and distinctive legal and regulatory approaches. The strengths and weaknesses of the three regional approaches are examined, and the trajectories of their corporate governance reform. If the European and Asia Pacific models are learning to come to terms with the performance demands of equity markets, the challenge is just as great for the Anglo-American model to come to terms with the increasing demand for greater corporate social responsibility.

The factors contributing to the advancing globalisation of corporate governance are investigated in Chapter 7 addressing the controversial question of whether one system of governance will become universal. The drive towards international standards of fairness, transparency, accountability and responsibility will be insistent; however, this may occur within countries committed to distinct cultures, legal systems and economic and social priorities. These differences will often constitute an important part of the cultural integrity and economic dynamism of the economies concerned. Finally Chapter 8 examines the growing materiality of corporate social and environmental responsibility. The greatest test of the governance of corporations in the future will be the challenge of sustainability. This will involve the redesign

of the corporation and of the institutions of the market around new principles and objectives to deliver sustainable values to the economy and society.

The work is supported by a series of case studies investigating critical aspects of corporate governance. Ironically the documentary evidence to call upon is much richer when corporate governance fails. At this point, analysts, media commentators, academics and lawyers focus upon what went wrong, often in voluminous studies. It is valuable to carry out forensic analyses of corporate governance failure, if only to learn what to look for in future if a company is going off the rails. Therefore the majority of the cases do cover the experience of the recent corporate governance disasters (Enron, WorldCom, Tyco, Parmalat, HIH). However in some of the cases the most fascinating part is how boards and executives confronted disaster, and somehow managed to recover the fortunes of the company (Royal Ahold, Tyco). To add some further international dimensions of corporate governance there is a case study on the challenge of constructing a successful company from the merger of two large corporations from different cultures (Daimler-Chrysler); and the tensions arising from a hostile takeover (Vodafone-Mannesmann). The James Hardie case illustrates the tragic consequences when a company fails to live up to its responsibilities to its employees and the community; and the Nomura case sheds light on the dark areas of corruption that are sometimes concealed by the public face of successful corporations. Case studies of successful corporate governance are not included, however in Appendix 1 are listed the websites of many companies in different regions of the world well regarded for their robust approach to corporate governance, and how well this is progressing may be investigated in company sources.

# 2
# Boards and Directors: The Political Mechanisms of Corporate Governance

## INTRODUCTION

This chapter examines the political mechanisms of corporate governance: how the essential processes fit together and operate. What boards of directors actually do is considered, their duties and functions and how they work with the CEO to provide leadership and guidance to the company. The agency dilemmas in corporate governance are explored, together with other theoretical interpretations of corporate governance. Whether boards can simultaneously provide accountability and stimulate value creation is considered. Different types of boards, and different approaches to board design are compared. The growing importance of non-executive directors in the reform of boards is debated, together with the question of independence of directors. The inner workings of board processes are investigated, and the tensions concerning the board's duties to monitor internal controls and take a lead in strategic direction. The growing power of chief executives and how this impacts upon the board is discussed in the context of the rapid inflation in executive reward, and how the board of directors may regain its authority is considered. The basic internal mechanisms of corporate governance that operate at board level need be made to work effectively, if the external market and regulatory institutions of corporate governance are to be able to properly fulfil their roles.

## WHAT DO BOARDS DO?

The board of directors is the fulcrum of corporate governance: the critical nexus in which the fortunes of the company are decided. At the beginning of a company's life the board often represents the DNA from which the company will grow and succeed. In maturity the board represents the source of values and objectives that will sustain the vigour of the company. The board is therefore responsible *internally* for the leadership and guidance of the corporate entity. However, the board has a wider set of *external* responsibilities, firstly towards investors, 'The board is the link between the shareholders of the firm and the managers entrusted with undertaking the day-to-day operations of the organisation' (Stiles and Taylor 2001: 4); and secondly towards the wider stakeholders who are the essential partners of the entity.

In fulfilling these duties boards have to balance the strategy and accountability elements of their duties in ways that encourage performance while maintaining effective control. According to Carter and Lorsch (2004: 67) boards are essentially involved in three distinct activities: monitoring the company and management performance; making major decisions; and offering advice and counsel to management, especially the CEO. Therefore the key roles of the board can be conceived as:

1 *Control*: Monitoring the management of the company and ensuring accountability.
2 *Strategy*: Approving and monitoring the strategic direction of the company.
3 *Counsel*: Providing advice and counsel to the company executives on critical matters.
4 *Institutional*: Building institutional relationships with investors, stakeholders and the community (Zahra and Pearce 1989; Johnson *et al.* 1996; Daily *et al.* 2003).

| | Outward looking | Providing accountability | Strategy formulation |

Figure 2.1 Framework analysing board activities.

Source: Hilmer, F. and Tricker, R.I. (1991), An Effective Board, *Company Director's Manual*, Sydney: Athol Yeomans, Pearson/Prentice Hall.

A framework for analysing board activities and functions, first elaborated by Fred Hilmer and Bob Tricker (1994), has proved its use in helping to develop the approach of generations of company directors (Figure 2.1). This framework clearly illustrates the competing demands and continual tensions upon boards of directors to balance conformance and performance, to monitor the present while preparing for the future, to provide monitoring and endorse strategy formulation. The framework is a reminder of the multidimensional roles and responsibilities of boards and directors, and of the need to avoid placing the entire emphasis on single functions.

How demanding it is to carry the burden of duties of a board with integrity, and complete the challenging functions with capability and positive outcomes should not be underestimated. Sarah Hogg the chair of 3i in the UK (at the time the only woman chair of a FTSE 100 company) emphasised 'The patience, skill, and sheer preparation needed to assemble, lead, motivate, monitor, and refresh a fully functioning board … A committee is not a natural decision-making machine, and the chairman's job is to see the board reaches not merely a consensus but a good decision' (Cadbury 2002: xii).

Though in the recent efforts to reform boards great attention has focused on the size, composition and structure of boards as the basis for achieving better boards (Figure 2.2), this often misses the importance of the essential individual and social characteristics of the board: 'Board structure and composition condition but cannot determine board effectiveness. Instead, board effectiveness depends upon the experience, skill and judgement of individual executive and non-executive directors and the ways in which these are combined to shape board conduct and relationships' (McNulty, Roberts and Stiles 2003: 2). The one element that is absolutely essential in the armoury of directors and boards is *judgement:*

Legally, the board is the highest authority in the company, the 'fountain of power,' yet top management naturally tends to exercise that power … Board members are expected to provide critical judgement on management performance – which requires an in-depth knowledge of, and intimacy with the affairs of the corporation – and at the same time to assure that this judgement is independent – which requires detachment and distance … The working style of the board must build its collective strength: the board needs the trusting familiarity of a close-knit group, yet members must be independent personalities who can resist 'groupthink' and raise critical questions of colleagues.

(Demb and Neubauer 1992: 13–16)

When companies fail it is inevitable that attention is focused on the role of the board of directors. Too often in these circumstances, it is

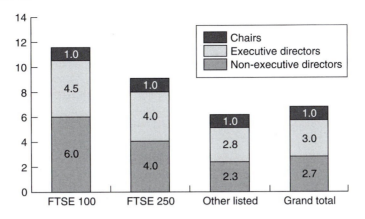

Figure 2.2 Size and composition of boards in the UK.

Source: Higgs, D. (2003), *Review of the Role and Effectiveness of Non-Executive Directors*, London: Department of Trade and Industry, 18. Also cited in the London Stock Exchange: *A Practical Guide to Corporate Governance*, http://www.londonstockexchange.com/NR/rdonlyres/C450E4FC-89C2-4042-804A-685855FF217B/0/PracticalGuidetoCorporateGovernance.pdf.

discovered that boards have not exercised judgement, have failed to exercise any meaningful form of accountability, and have clearly lost any sense of the strategic direction of the company they were invested with responsibility for. Cadbury and Millstein state:

It is clear why the board is firmly for shareholders and the market system the focal point. While boards in general have improved over the last 20 years, failures, some catastrophes, continue to occur. Enron, WorldCom and the rest are examples, as are the hundreds of 'restatements' following the Sarbanes–Oxley Act of 2002. Now, whole industries are coming under intense scrutiny, for example, insurance. Many of the failures can be attributed to boards being unaware of management's operational failures, as well as to boards being inattentive to the need to assure the rights of their shareholders: to be treated equitably (including minority and foreign shareholders); to obtain timely and accurate disclosure of all material information including the true financial situation, performance, ownership and governance of the company; and to be free of self-dealing and entrenchment by both board members and management.

(2005: 15)

The most fierce and enduring controversy involving the exercise of a board's responsibilities remains the issue of executive compensation. Executive reward is perceived widely to be out of control in the United States, and other countries that adopt a market based approach to corporate governance. More than anything, this suggests that companies are not being responsibly directed in the interests of their shareholders and wider stakeholders, but have become inwardly focused on the self-interest of company management. Will Hutton commented on the continuing apparently uncontrollable inflation in executive pay: 'I don't think directors understand how corrosive it is to pay themselves so much ... and that's the thing in today's boardroom culture: they don't really get it, why their behaviour is regarded as bad by their stakeholders' (2005: 52).

Is too much expected of company directors? Schrage contends performed properly the job of company board director is extremely demanding, and can become impossible if the focus on essentials is replaced by an ever-expanding brief. It is optimistic and often counter-productive to expect non-executive directors on a part-time basis to 'simultaneously and successfully formulate strategy, hire and fire senior executives, ensure rigid compliance with myriad global procedures, detect fraud, appropriately incentivise

managerial performance, and oversee metrics for organisational performance, all without any actionable conflicts of interest' (2004). Yet however complex and challenging the task, governments, investors, employees and the wider public are demanding much higher standards in the competence and performance of boards and directors, and will continue to insist that these are achieved.

## DIRECTORS' DUTIES

In the United States directors' duties are generally governed by the laws of the state the company is incorporated in, and there is no federal codification of directors' duties. 'The US legal tradition defines directors as the fiduciary agents of the corporation – those designated to hold assets in trust or to exercise authority on behalf of someone else – and, as such, they have two main legal duties: care and loyalty'. The duty of care asks directors 'to make informed and reasonable decisions, and to exercise reasonable supervision of the business'. The duty of loyalty requires them 'to act in good faith and in what they believe to be the best interest of the corporation, subordinating their personal interests to the welfare of the corporation' (Bagley 2002: 780). Many large US corporations are incorporated in the state of Delaware where under common law directors owe duties of care, loyalty and good faith to their company. (By statute Delaware corporations can include in their certificate of incorporation provisions limiting or excluding the liability of directors for breaches of their duty of care, though not of loyalty or good faith) (Linklaters 2005: 1). An influential association of US chief executives in the Business Roundtable (1997: 3) offered a general interpretation of directors' duties:

> Three broad duties stem from the fiduciary status of corporate directors: namely, the duties of obedience, loyalty, and due care. The duty of obedience requires a director to avoid committing ... acts beyond the scope of the powers of a corporation as defined by its charter or the laws of the state of incorporation ... The duty of loyalty dictates that a director must act in good faith and must not allow his personal

interest to prevail over the interests of the corporation ... The duty of care requires a director to be diligent and prudent in managing the corporation's affairs.

In the UK directors' duties are largely embedded in the common law established over time, with some statutory interpretative overlay. The Company Law Reform Bill (2005) which has taken many years to prepare does contain a statutory statement of directors' duties that would be owed to the company in place of the corresponding equitable and common law rules. The seven duties referred to are:

- to act within the powers conferred;
- to promote the success of the company for the benefit of its members. Directors must have regard to the long term and wider factors such as relationships with employees, suppliers, customers and the impact of the company's operations on the community and environment;
- to exercise independent judgement;
- to exercise reasonable care, skill and diligence;
- to avoid conflicts of interest;
- not to accept benefits from third parties;
- to declare an interest in a proposed transaction with the company.

Under this legislation shareholders will enjoy a statutory right to pursue a claim on behalf of the company against a director for negligence, default, breach of duty or breach of trust. (Companies are permitted to indemnify directors in respect of proceedings brought by third parties, and to pay directors legal costs as they are incurred, and the UK government is considering the question of companies limiting directors' liability for negligence with the prior consent of shareholders (Linklaters 2005: 2).

### Business judgement rule

In recognition of the complexity of business decision-making, and in order to allow the essential element of risk-taking in business activity, case law in the United States and in many other jurisdictions recognises the *business judgement rule*

that provides directors broad discretion to make decisions in good faith. As long as there is not evidence of fraud, gross negligence or other misconduct, directors will not be held responsible for a business judgement if it proves to be mistaken. In Delaware directors are presumed to have acted on an informed basis, in good faith and with no personal interest in the matter. Unless there is evidence of fraud or negligence a court will not second-guess directors by holding them liable for any action attributable to a rational business purpose. Recently however, Delaware courts have focused on instances of violations of directors' duty of care so egregious that they rise to the level of bad faith, a serious matter as directors cannot be indemnified from liabilities arising out of breaches of good faith (Linklaters 2005: 2). In other countries the investment institutions and general public are developing higher expectations of the competence and commitments of directors, and are becoming less forgiving of directors' failures. It is likely that the courts will increasingly reflect these higher expectations of directors' alertness and performance.

## BOARD DUTIES AND FUNCTIONS

The UK *Combined Code* concentrates on the mechanisms of independence and objectivity by which boards of directors may fulfil their duties, but does begin with a broad statements of the essential duties of the board:

> The board's role is to provide entrepreneurial leadership of the company within a framework of prudent and effective controls which enables risk to be assessed and managed. The board should set the company's strategic aims, ensure that the necessary financial and human resources are in place for the company to meet its objectives and review management performance. The board should set the company's values and standards to ensure that its obligations to its shareholders and others are understood and met.
>
> (Financial Reporting Council 2006: 1)

Established corporate governance wisdom suggests there must be a clear separation of the roles

of the board of directors and the role of executive management: it is the board's job to *direct*, and the management's job to *manage*. In practice the division of powers and distinction of roles is not so straightforward, and boards and executives have to find an acceptable *modus vivendi* that works for the company they are leading. Usually accepted understandings are reached and efficient practices are developed, though these can become unsettled at challenging times for the company before a new order is restored. Generally the company board is confined to a supervisory and strategic role, and the company executives are concerned with operational control and performance. The OECD *Principles of Corporate Governance* (2004) specifies the board's key functions as:

- Reviewing and guiding corporate strategy, major plans of action, risk policy, annual budgets and business plans; setting performance objectives, monitoring and implementation and corporate performance; and overseeing major capital expenditure, acquisitions and other divestitures.
- Monitoring the effectiveness of the company's governance practices and making changes as needed.
- Selecting, compensating, monitoring and, when necessary, replacing key executives and overseeing succession planning.
- Aligning key executives and board remuneration with the longer term interests of the company and its shareholders.
- Ensuring a formal and transparent board nomination and election process.
- Monitoring and managing potential conflicts of interest of management, board members and shareholders, including misuse of corporate assets and abuse of related party transactions.
- Ensuring the integrity of the corporation's accounting and financial reporting systems, including the independent audit and appropriate systems of control are in place, in particular systems for risk management, financial and operational control, and compliance with the law and relevant standards.
- Overseeing the process of disclosure and communications.

(2004: 24–25)

The American Law Institute's (1994) model of directors' duties indicates an evaluating and reviewing role, with the duty to appoint the senior executives who are responsible for managing the business, and then to review their progress:

- select, regularly evaluate, fix the compensation of, and, where appropriate, replace the principal senior executives;
- oversee the conduct of the corporation's business to evaluate whether the business is being properly managed;
- review, and, where appropriate, approve the corporation's financial objectives and major corporate plans and actions;
- review and, where appropriate, approve major changes in, and determinations of other major questions of choice respecting the appropriate auditing and accounting principles and practices to be used in the preparation of the corporation's financial statements; and
- perform such other functions as are prescribed by law, or assigned to the board under a standard of the corporation.

(3.01–3.02)

The Australian Stock Exchange (ASX) *Principles of Good Corporate Governance* (2003: 16) adopts the Cadbury formulation obliging companies to comply or explain non-compliance, and requires listed companies to 'recognise and publish the respective roles and responsibilities of board and management'. The company's governance framework should 'enable the board to provide strategic guidance for the company and effective oversight of management; the respective roles and responsibilities of board and senior executives are intended to facilitate board and management accountability'. The principles do not specify an exact distribution of functions, but suggest the board will usually be responsible for:

- oversight of the company including its control and accountability systems;
- appointing or removing the chief executive;
- ratifying the appointment and removal of the chief financial officer and the company secretary;
- input and final approval of management's development of corporate strategy and performance objectives;
- reviewing and ratifying systems of risk management and internal compliance and control, codes of conduct and legal compliance;
- monitoring senior management's performance and implementation strategy;
- approving and monitoring the progress of major capital expenditure, capital management, and acquisition and divestitures; and
- approving and monitoring financial and other reporting.

## BOARD AND CEO RELATIONSHIP

Though the various national and international corporate governance principles on the role of the board are a helpful guide to the essential duties of boards, they do not explain how the relationship between the CEO and the board is to be arranged and managed. This is of critical importance since this relationship has often proved an uneasy frontier in which boards have often consciously or unconsciously crossed into (often unhelpful) involvement in the operational detail of management. More worryingly, CEOs particularly in the United States, but occasionally in all jurisdictions, have been known to usurp the powers of the board of directors, leaving an enfeebled board with an entirely nominal role. In this context it is interesting to examine the experience of the resources group BHP Billiton, which was formed from a merger of BHP and Billiton in 2001. Brian Gilbertson the former CEO of Billiton became the abrasive and entrepreneurial CEO of the merged company, and proved too much for the board and chairman Don Argus to handle. The board quickly replaced Gilbertson with Chip Goodyear as CEO, and now has articulated a clear governance protocol regarding the board and CEO's relationship (in the meantime becoming Australia's largest and most successful company). The board protocol established processes relating to matters specifically reserved for board decision-making, and the authority delegated to the CEO:

In appointing the Board, shareholders vest the management and control of the business and

affairs of the Group in the Board. The Board has reserved some matters to itself for decision and, save for those matters, has delegated authority for all other matters to the CEO.

## Powers reserved for the board

The Board has reserved the following matters for its decision:

- Appointments to the position of CEO and approval of the appointment of executives reporting to the CEO
- Approval of strategy and annual budgets
- Determination of capital and non-capital items in accordance with the Approvals Framework
- Determinations and adoption of documents (including the publication of reports and statements to shareholders) that are required by the Group's constitutional documents, by statute or by other external regulation.

Subject to the limitations imposed by the group's constitutional documents, statute and other external regulation, the Board remains free to alter the matters reserved for its decision.

## Delegation

Beyond the items above the Board delegates to the CEO all authority to achieve the Corporate Objective. The CEO is free to take all decisions and actions which further the Corporate Objective, and which in his or her judgement are reasonable having regard to the CEO Limits.

## Accountability and monitoring

- The CEO is accountable to the Board for the authority that is delegated to the CEO, and the performance of the Group.
- The Board will monitor the decisions and actions of the CEO and the performance of the Group to gain assurance that progress is being made towards the Corporate Objective within the spirit of the CEO Limits.
- Throughout the annual Board cycle, the CEO will report systematically in a spirit of openness and trust on the progress being made by the Group's businesses towards the Corporate Objective and towards shorter and medium-term plans.

- The CEO will determine the format and system of reporting, which will address material developments in the following areas, and will describe for each of them the potential impact on the achievement of the Corporate Objective:
  - the development and implementation of strategy, and the annual plan;
  - the business and financial performance of the Group, and material events in markets which are critical to the achievement of the Corporate Objective;
  - the activities covered by the CEO Limits.
- The CEO will keep the Board informed in writing of decisions and actions that the CEO reasonably interprets to exceed the CEO Limits but are necessary and appropriate for the achievement of the Corporate Objective and the medium and short-term plans of the Group.
- The Board will also monitor performance through the Board committees where it is more effective to do so, or necessary to avoid potential conflicts of interest. The Committees will focus on gaining assurance that the conduct and performance of the CEO and the Group comply with the CEO Limits.
- The Board and its committees will determine the information required. They may make direct requests for information including from the CEO, any employee of the Group, the external auditor or any third party.
- The CEO (and his or her nominees) will supply the Board and its Committees with the information in a form that is appropriate to enable the Board and committees to make assessments and judgements, to conduct inquiries, and to gain assurance that the decisions and actions of the CEO, and the performance of the Group, are directed toward the Corporate Objective and fall within the CEO Limits.
- The Chairman of the Board, the chairmen of Committees, the CEO and the Company Secretary will strive collaboratively to ensure that effective systems are in place for the production and transmission of information and reports.

TWO

■ Relationships and dialogue between individual members of the Board and the CEO and senior executives that focuses on gaining a better understanding of the Group's business will be encouraged but will not alter the roles, accountabilities and divisions of authority in this Board Governance Document.

(BHP Billiton 2006)

This protocol was backed up by an evaluation and reward policy that emphasised the remuneration of executives including the CEO was linked to the achievement of corporate objectives with transparent systems of evaluation, and that the Chairman of the board will lead the non-executives in an annual formal evaluation of the performance of the CEO. However it is unlikely that many boards will have articulated clearly the division of power and responsibility with the CEO; indeed if boards are becoming more active generally, there are other indications of a rather more passive existence for boards continuing beyond the recent reforms.

## ACTIVE AND PASSIVE BOARDS

### Active boards

The ideal portrayal of the board is as an active, deliberative and decisive forum for the business: 'Boards of directors collectively determine, through the decisions they make, the fate of the corporation … The principal work of a board of directors is to make decisions' (Leblanc and Gillies 2005). Certainly the extensive portfolio of significant board activities encompassing succession planning, budgeting, strategy, risk management, compliance, disclosure, and corporate social and environmental responsibility suggest a very full agenda. However, boards are inevitably part-time, (due firstly to the necessary extensive external other commitments of directors that enhance the potential contribution they may make to the company; and to the fact that boards that begin to become nearly full-time inevitably stray into operational management, often losing their sense of objectivity and detachment in the process). Therefore board work tends to be concentrated in very intensive short periods of time. (Since board papers will normally be circulated well in advance of meetings though, the amount of time spent on individual preparation by directors may far exceed the time actually spent at board meetings.)

However Carter and Lorsch (2004: 22) citing an Egon Zhender (2000) survey suggest 'The "average" directors in North America and Europe dedicate around 100 hours or even less to their task (including time spent outside meetings on their own, gathering and reviewing information), with an average seven meetings a year'. Other consultancy surveys suggest slightly more hours of engagement on the part of the typical non-executive, though the tradition in most countries in the majority of companies is that being a non-executive board director is a very part-time commitment (which explains why some non-executives felt free to acquire a string of company directorships, together with an even larger number of board positions on public, educational, voluntary or artistic bodies).

The weight of recent legislation is beginning to change these practices somewhat. The growing importance attributed to the work of board committees, the increasing emphasis on internal financial controls and risk management, the heightened sense of legal liability, the more conscious expectation for non-executives to at least be knowledgeable about the company strategy, and the new emphasis on director development, performance and assessment will have all taken their toll on any inclination on the part of non-executive directors towards a minimal commitment. It is likely today that being a non-executive member of an active and engaged board of directors might involve at least double the amount of time formerly thought necessary (which explains the emphasis in most codes of practice, and often also in large company director contracts, on a reasonable limit to the number of other non-executive director positions an individual may hold).

Of course the extent of non-executive involvement, and the intensity of the commitment called for, together with the resulting stress, is greatly amplified when the responsibilities of the position are put to the test in times of crisis. Such periods of corporate crisis may last a few days, or can

stretch into months or years. (One large company in Australia reported 83 board meetings in a single year during a prolonged crisis which involved corporate restructuring, divestment, adopting a new financial structure, and setting out on an entirely new strategic direction. In this case the company was conveyed from the brink of disaster (a humiliating takeover by a rival of the shell of the company), to a renewed growth and respect in the market.)

## Passive boards

There is much evidence that in the past boards of directors enjoyed a fairly passive existence, carrying out their duties, if at all, in a largely nominal way (Mace 1971; Lorsch and MacIver 1989). In the United States for example for much of the twentieth century it was accepted in many companies that the CEO would select and control the board: even if new directors wish to make an independent contribution, over time they learn passivity is what is expected: 'To initiate discussions where the boardroom culture has historically involved directors listening to management presentations, reacting primarily for the purposes of approving management initiatives, risks being viewed as obstructionist. The director who questions management and disrupts the carefully scheduled agenda will almost certainly receive feedback, either directly or non-verbally, that such interruptions are unwelcome' (Dalton and Dalton 2005: 96).

The growing prosperity of the US economy in the middle decades of the twentieth century encouraged the sense that all was well in the corporate world, and the best thing boards could do was offer unqualified support to their management. But this complacency was briefly dispelled when Penn Central the largest railway company in the country collapsed in 1970. Louis Cabot, a Harvard Professor gave a graphic account of the role of the board in the doomed company:

I served for one fateful year on the board of Penn Central. The education was fast, brutal and highly practical. Even today the lawsuits are not settled and that education has cost me several times more than the price of a Harvard Business School tuition. At each Penn Central directors' meeting, which only lasted one and a half hours, we were presented with long lists of relatively small capital expenditures to approve, we were shown sketchy financial reports which were rarely discussed in any detail. The reports were not designed to be revealing, and we were asked not to take them away from the meeting. We always had an oral report by the Chief Executive Officer promising better results next month which never came true.

As Cadbury (2002: 7) indicates Cabot 'did all the right things as an outside director, including writing a letter to the chairman to say that this was no way to run a business. But before any of the letters had even been answered, Penn Central had collapsed and Louis Cabot was being sued along with the other directors. What is clear from his vivid description of board meetings at Penn Central is that the board simply failed to do its job. It was both uninformed and misinformed and it exercised no control over the CEO'. The ensuing SEC inquiry into the misreporting of earnings and collapse of Penn State company, published an official report fiercely critical of the board's shortcomings and emphasised the need for board independence and for vigilant outside directors 'the somnolent Penn Central board … was typical of most giant corporations' boards in the post-war period' (Millstein 1998: 14).

The fact that even the most prestigious companies had dysfunctional boards is illustrated by Bill Wyman's sense as a long serving board member of General Motors until 1999 of the 'inactivity and passivity that had plagued GM board for many years'. Wyman insisted 'I was proud to serve on the GM board but we operated in a very passive manner. We were invited to join the board by the CEO, and rarely met alone to share our thoughts on the company's progress and, more particularly, on the performance of the CEO and management. The board endorsed the annual plans and long range strategies, but any role in developing or refining those plans was small. Board meetings were crowded with presentations, but with little time allotted for discussion' Carter and Lorsch (2004: 6).

The consistent attempt to marginalise boards by management, and the underestimation of the significance of their duties, was shattered by the fallout from the Enron debacle, and the new zeal associated with the enforcement of the Sarbanes–Oxley Act. Replacing rank complacency was the zealous enforcement of compliance. The sea change affecting one director was reported in the *Wall Street Journal* (21 June 2004). 'Having served on the board of public companies since 1993, she has watched the culture of boardrooms change from golf games, cigars and fancy dinners, to meetings that begin at 6am and intense pressure to submerge oneself in ever-changing accounting and governance regulations'.

There was certainly good reason for a dramatic change in board behaviour, since whatever may have gone before, the most spectacular case of a passive board was undoubtedly Enron with the most appalling consequences.

## THE ENRON BOARD: ASLEEP AT THE WHEEL?

On 2 December 2001, Enron Corporation, the seventh largest publicly traded corporation in the United States declared bankruptcy. The shock waves caused by this catastrophic corporate collapse transformed the corporate governance environment not simply in America, but throughout the rest of the world. It took many years of Congressional inquiry, SEC investigation and courtroom trials to bring the senior Enron executives, chair Kenneth Lay, CEO Jeffrey Skilling and CFO Andrew Fastow to justice (see Case Study 1). But the Enron board of directors were also directly responsible for this disaster.

The Special Investigation Committee set up by the Enron board itself under the chairmanship of William Powers issued a report on 1 February 2002 concluding 'The Board of Directors of Enron failed … in its oversight duties … with … serious consequences for Enron, its employees and shareholders … While the primary responsibility for the financial reporting abuses lies with Management … those abuses could and should have been prevented or detected at an earlier time had the Board been more aggressive and vigilant' (2002: 22, 24). The US Senate Committee on Governmental Affairs report on *The Role of Directors in Enron's Collapse* (2002) is more damning:

All of the Board members interviewed … were well aware of and supported Enron's intense focus on its credit rating, cash flow, and debt burden. All were familiar with the company's 'asset-lite' strategy and actions taken by Enron to move billions of dollars in assets off its balance sheet to separate but affiliated companies. All knew that, to accomplish its objectives, Enron has been relying increasingly on complicated transactions with multiple special purpose entities, hedges, derivatives, swaps, forward contracts, prepared contracts, and other forms of structured finance. While there is no empirical data on the extent to which US public companies use these devices it appears that few companies outside of investment banks use them as extensively as Enron. At Enron, they became dominant: at its peak, the company apparently had between $15 and $20 billion involved in hundreds of structured finance transaction.

(2002: 8)

The Senate investigation could not substantiate claims from Enron directors that they challenged management or asked tough questions, 'Instead the investigation found a Board that routinely relied on Enron management and Andersen representations with little or no effort to verify the information provided, that readily approved new business ventures and complex transactions, and that exercised weak oversight of company operations. The investigations also identified a number of financial ties between Board members and Enron which, collectively, raise questions about Board members' independence and willingness to challenge management' (2002: 14). The Senate inquiry identified more than a dozen red flags that should have caused the Enron Board to ask hard questions (Figure 2.3). 'Those red flags were not heeded. In too many instances, by going along with questionable practices, and relying on management and auditor representations' (2002: 59).

The US Senate investigations made the following findings with respect to the role of the

**Red flags known to Enron's board**

1  Audit committee told Enron accounting practices 'push limits'
2  Board approves Fastow's code of waiver for LJM1
3  Whitewing moved off-balance sheet with $1.5 billion
4  Board approves second Fastow waiver for LJM2
5  LJM2 update: 'Q41999: 8 days/6 deals/$125 million'
6  Executive committee approves third Raptor II
7  'Project Summer' to sell $6 billion in assets fails.
   Board approves Raptor III/IV
8  Board approves third Fastow waiver for LJM3.
   Board told $27 billion in assets off-balance sheet
9  Board told total revenues jump from $40 billion in 1999 to
   $100 billion in 2000: audit and finance committees review
   LJM procedures and for Y2000 transactions
10  *Fortune* article questions Enron's earnings and accounting
11  Board told 64% of asset portfolio 'troubled' or 'not performing';
    45 million Enron shares at risk in Raptors and Whitewing
12  Board told of $2.3 billion deficit in market values of Enron's
    international assets
13  Fastow sells interests in LJM to Kopper
14  Skilling resigns; finance committee told of $6.6 billion in
    prepays and FAS 125 transactions
15  Lay defends use of SPEs in online session with employees
16  Finance committee told of $800 million earnings write-down
    from Raptors; audit committee told of closed investigation
    into the Watkins letter

**Figure 2.3** Red flags known to Enron's board.

Source: US Senate Permanent Sub-committee on Investigations, May 2002.

Enron Board of Directors in Enron's collapse and bankruptcy:

1  ***Fiduciary failure***: The Enron board failed to safeguard Enron shareholders ... by allowing Enron to engage in high risk accounting, inappropriate conflict of interest transactions, extensive undisclosed off-the-books activities, and excessive executive compensation.
2  ***High risk accounting***: The board of directors knowingly allowed Enron to engage in high risk accounting practices.
3  ***Inappropriate conflicts of interest***: Despite clear conflicts of interest, the Enron board of directors approved an unprecedented arrangement allowing Enron's chief financial officer to establish and operate the LJM private equity funds which transacted business with Enron and profited at Enron's expense.

4  ***Extensive undisclosed off-the-books activity***: The Enron board of directors knowingly allowed Enron to conduct billions of dollars in off-the-books activity to make its financial condition appear better than it was and failed to ensure adequate public disclosure of material off-the-books liabilities that contributed to Enron's collapse.
5  ***Excessive compensation***: The Enron board approved excessive compensation for company executives, failed to monitor the cumulative cash drain caused by Enron's 2000 annual bonus and performance unit pans, and failed to monitor or halt abuse by board chair and chief executive officer Kenneth Lay of a company-financed, multi-million dollar, personal credit line.
6  ***Lack of independence***: The independence of the Enron board was compromised by financial ties between the company and certain

board members. The board also failed to ensure the independence of the company's auditor, allowing Andersen to provide internal audit and consulting services while serving as Enron's outside auditor (2002: 3).

The conclusion of the Senate Inquiry's investigation into the Enron board's complicity in the downfall of the company was withering:

> The failure of any Enron Board member to accept any degree of personal responsibility for Enron's collapse is a telling indicator of the Board's failure to recognize its fiduciary obligations to set the company's overall strategic direction, oversee management, and ensure responsible financial reporting … The Enron Board failed to provide the prudent oversight and checks and balances that its fiduciary obligation required and a company like Enron needed. By failing to provide sufficient oversight and restraint to stop management excess, the Enron Board contributed to the company's collapse and bears a share of the responsibility for it.
>
> (2002: 14, 59)

## THE WORLDCOM BOARD: GOING THROUGH THE MOTIONS

If the stance of the Enron board could best be described as supine, the performance of the board of WorldCom, the even larger bankruptcy that immediately followed Enron, was just as abysmal in the apparent failure to fulfil competently any of the duties that the board was supposed to carry out (see Case Study 2). As the report prepared for the District Court of New York stated:

> While it is not clear that the independent directors could have discovered the fraud, WorldCom's board didn't do many things that might have prevented or limited the tragedy. For example, the board does not appear to have been adequately involved with the Company and its personnel. On average the board met quarterly, and the meetings were largely filled with formal presentations to the directors and other routine exercises, including

CEO Ebber's opening prayer. These relatively infrequent meetings did not involve substantial amounts of time. Even meetings that were intended to review significant issues such as multibillion dollar acquisitions seem to have been concluded in a perfunctory manner. This was sufficient for blind ratification of actions, but not sufficient for informed, independent decision-making. The Audit Committee most vividly exemplified the board's inadequate time commitment … The Audit Committee spent as little as six hours *per year* in overseeing the activities of a company with more than $30 billion in revenue, while the WorldCom Compensation Committee met as often as 17 times per year. This level of activity was consistent with 'going through the motions' rather than developing a thorough understanding of the accounting policies, internal controls and audit programs in use by the Company … It does not appear that either the Company's internal audit department or the Audit Committee perceived the widespread serious weaknesses in the Company's internal controls over external financial reporting.

(Breeden 2003: 30–32)

The WorldCom Board did nothing to restrain CEO Bernie Ebber's wildest commercial adventures, even though by all accounts Ebbers did not have the background, experience or training to lead such a large corporation:

> The lack of time commitment was not the board's worst failing. Despite having a separate Chairman of the Board and independent members, the board did not act like it was in control of the Company's overall direction. Rather than making clear that Ebbers served at the pleasure of the Board, and establishing reasonable standards of oversight and accountability, the board deferred at every turn to Ebbers. Ebbers controlled the board's agenda, the timing and scope of board review of transactions, awards of compensation, and the structure of management. He ran the Company with an iron control, and the board did not establish itself as an independent force within the Company. The Chairman of the Board did not have a defined role of substance, did not have control

of the board's agenda, did not run the meetings and did not act as a meaningful restraint on Ebbers ... WorldCom met the formal standards, and yet the board did not take action to limit Ebbers' power. Formalities were usually observed, and yet no director said 'no' when the Ebers loans of $408 million came before the Board, no director said 'no' to grants of massive volumes of stock options, and no director appears to have questioned Ebbers' competence and fitness to serve as CEO until the disaster was unavoidable.

(Breeden 2003: 33–35)

The WorldCom board was dazzled by the meteoric growth of the company, and seduced by the apparent wealth this strategy generated, and did not perform the most minimal duties of accountability as a result.

## BOARDS AND PERFORMANCE: ACCOUNTABILITY AND VALUE CREATION?

The most profound theoretical and practical question regarding boards is whether they can do their fundamental tasks of accountability and value creation – which often seem to be in tension – with any degree of effectiveness and consistency. Research on boards' and directors' impact on company performance reflects the wider concerns of corporate governance. How do boards effect performance? How is performance defined in terms of accountability or profitability? What enhances board accountability? Does board size and composition influence performance? What influences board independence? What contributes to board authority? How important are board committees? How can boards contribute to company strategy? What contributes to board dynamics? How is board selection and development achieved? What is the relationship between the board and shareholders? Though intensively researched for some years the academic evidence on these critical issues remains inconclusive.

Inevitably, each board operates in a unique environment comprising different pressures,

in which decisions and actions taken at a particular time, against a particular historical legacy and set of future strategic ambitions, and which will lead to different indicators of performance being given priority, hence different drivers and constraints on action and evaluation of board performance ... In studies of board dynamics ... much like classic group process theory, there is great difficulty in disentangling individual and collective inputs, outcomes and effects ... Without the simplistic framework of agency theory assumptions, the job of an empirical researcher trying to tackle this amoeba-like situation becomes immensely more complex.

(Pye and Pettigrew 2005: 32–33)

However, there is a widespread intuitive belief that higher standards of corporate governance are associated with enhanced accountability and performance. There is a powerful sense that corporate governance accountability and value creation are inextricably bound together, and that the board can make a considerable contribution to getting this right. The ASX incorporates this confidence in the definition of corporate governance:

Corporate governance is the system by which companies are directed and managed. It influences how the objectives of the company are set and achieved, how risk is monitored and assessed, and how performance is optimised. Good corporate governance structures encourage companies to create value (through entrepreneurialism, innovation, development and exploration) and provide accountability and control systems commensurate with the risks involved.

(2003: 3)

In attempting to ascertain the contribution of corporate governance to performance, there are problems of definition, methodology and evidence. If corporate governance as a concept refers to the system of ownership and control, and to the structure of the board and its operations, this can be interpreted widely in terms of relations with a range of stakeholders, or narrowly in terms of compliance with the provisions of corporate governance codes.

The problem that researchers face is not only to define what is meant by 'corporate governance' but also what amounts to 'good' or 'bad' corporate governance. Similarly, the term 'performance' may refer to rather different concepts such as the development of share price, profitability or the present valuation of a company. As such the body of research into the link between corporate governance and performance contains studies that seek to correlate rather different concepts of corporate governance and measures of performance.

(Hermes 2005: 1)

Hermes (2005) identifies three categories of research on corporate governance and performance:

1  opinion-based research;
2  focus list research and performance of shareholder engagement funds; and
3  governance ranking research.

The drive for improved corporate governance has been led by the advanced industrial countries, and in the opinion-based research the widely publicised McKinsey surveys demonstrated the considerable premium investors were prepared to pay for better corporate governance. The OECD and other international institutions have emphasised the importance of improving corporate governance to increase access to international capital markets. Similarly there is a sense that at the company level, high performing boards are attractive to investors.

In the evidence submitted to the UK Modern Company Law Review (DTI 2000) the association of good corporate governance with higher performance was often made without necessarily suggesting a direct link: 'A robust governance framework, which includes assessing which risks are acceptable and the probability of their materialising, leads to value creation for shareholders and other stakeholders' (CIMA). 'The implementation of systems of corporate governance and risk evaluation and control can produce tangible benefits for businesses, both in terms of efficiency and, in the medium term, cost savings, but also in enhancing the confidence of investors in the company, which – all things being equal – may be beneficial to the share price and can greatly facilitate access to the capital markets' (Law Society).

Corporate governance codes … have helped to prevent abuse by dominant chief executives, have given more power to non-executive directors, and enabled audit committees to become effective. Growth in company share price has been significant over the period in which the corporate governance codes have been effective but it is difficult to infer a tangible link between those codes and such an increase. We suggest that the question as to whether the corporate governance codes have been beneficial in assisting wealth generation misses the point.

(Institute of Chartered Accountants of Scotland)

Turning to the evidence in the second category of research linking corporate governance and performance the work of focus and engagement investor funds. The California Pension Fund (CalPERs) has used an active approach in its focus fund for some years. In the five years to 2001 the CalPERS list outperformed by 14 per cent in the 2001 update, however by 2004 with the reversal that occurred in the market generally in 2001–2002, the CalPERS fund showed excess returns of just 8 per cent, with two-thirds of the sample under-performing (presumably because the high growth stocks of the 1990s, were the most affected in the 2001 downturn). Further evidence that active ownership may improve performance is demonstrated by shareholder engagement funds which identify under-performing companies with the potential for improvement. Hermes original UK Focus Fund outperformed the FTSE All Share Total Return Index by 4.5 per cent on an annualised basis since 1998. In the United States the Relational Investors LLC focus fund outperformed its benchmark by 10.1 per cent since its inception (Hermes 2005: 3). As more investment institutions develop active focus and engagement funds, the impact upon corporate governance and corporate performance will become clearer.

The third category of governance ranking research seeks to establish a link between one or more governance standards that measure the quality of a company's governance, and any

impact on company performance. There are significant problems associated with this approach identified by Hermes (2005: 3):

> The focus on certain standards by reference to which the quality of corporate governance can to some extent be objectively measured has obvious attractions. However, it also causes problems and distortions in the finding of the research. To begin with, for a variety of reasons any *single* governance standard may for a number of reasons be unrelated to the performance of companies in a particular market during a given period of time. Research that focuses on a single standard, such as the composition of boards, in isolation, may thus lead to incorrect conclusions. Moreover, such research does not effectively capture the general benefits that may result from active ownership involving engagement regarding a larger set of standards. More complex research considers a range of governance standards against which the corporate governance qualities of the companies investigated are assessed. The selection of a *set* of governance standards introduces a subjective element into governance ranking research. In addition researchers may attach different weight to them for the purposes of the ranking that underlies the studies, introducing further subjectivity. Many of the studies that suggest there is no link between corporate governance and performance focus on a *single* governance standard ... Similarly research involving a ranking based on *too many* potentially insignificant governance standards may distort the finding of a link between certain 'core' standards and performance. We therefore believe that the most valuable research focuses on a relatively small set of governance standards and seeks to identify which standards are directly related to performance.

Since much of the academic research on corporate governance and performance has either concentrated on a single standard, or attempted to examine a large number of variables, the studies have demonstrated methodological problems. 'Great inferential leaps are made from input variables such as board composition to output variables such as board performance with no direct evidence on the processes and mechanisms which presumably link the inputs to the outputs' (Pettigrew 1992: 171). For these reasons academic research focusing on boards' and directors' contribution to corporate governance remains tentative. 'The recent literature has not changed the overall balance of research evidence that still seems to indicate that the link between board composition and either firm performance or board control over the CEO and executive management is either not significant, or at least not straightforward' (DTI 2000b: 2). For example in the Dalton *et al.* 1998 meta-analysis of 159 studies over a 40-year time-frame they found 'no evidence of a systematic relationship between board composition – in its many manifestations – and firm financial performance. Not only were independent directors not associated with firm performance, but inside, outside and affiliated directors were not associated with higher or lower firm financial performance either' (Dalton and Dalton 2005: 92).

The most extensive governance ranking study supporting a link between the quality of corporate governance measured in terms of shareholder rights and corporate performance was completed by Gompers *et al.* (2003). An assessment of governance at 1,500 US corporations using 24 governance provisions analysed by the Institutional Investors Research Centre in the 1990s. The study found that if a fund had taken long positions in the top decile of the governance ranking, and short positions in the companies in the bottom decile, it would have outperformed the market by 8.5 per cent through the 1990s. Research conducted by Millstein and MacAvoy (1998) and by Governance Metrics International which does regular surveys of 1,600 companies worldwide also supported a link between good governance and shareholder returns. Bebchuk *et al.* (2004) investigated which of the 24 governance provisions of the IRRC correlated with company value and shareholder returns, and identified six provisions. These concerned the extent to which a majority of shareholders can impose their will on management, and mechanisms that facilitate the defence against hostile takeover. From this Bebchuk *et al.* constructed what they called an *entrenchment index* (the entrenchment of management in relation to investors), and found that increases in the level of entrenchment were associated with significant

reductions in the valuation of companies. Finally in research sponsored by the UNEP Finance Initiative Deutsche Bank discovered there was a positive relationship between the historic governance assessment of the companies and their profitability. The return on equity of the top 20 per cent companies (average 2002 15.9 per cent) was significantly higher than the bottom 20 per cent of companies (1.5 per cent).

## CHANGING ROLES OF BOARDS AND DIRECTORS

It is clear that boards of directors have evolved over time in response to internal dynamics, changes in the market environment, and developments in company law. In every company the board goes through a lifecycle paralleling the life of the company from the early imperative at inception to find capital, build product markets, and establish operating principles; and later to the more considered tasks of maintaining the values and viability of the mature organisation. Stiles and Taylor present a view of the board negotiating order through their different experiences:

> In broad terms, what we have seen through the empirical data is a view of boards whose members, through a complex interplay of context, individual abilities, and structural conditions, actively negotiate over time their respective roles and the social order of the board as a whole. With the legal duties of the board under-describing the de facto operations of board running, and regulations and codes of practice covering only part of board endeavour, ultimately the board's mandate will mean different things to different people, and 'negotiation is needed to achieve order in the context of change'.
>
> (Hosking 1996: 342)

### Types of boards: unitary and supervisory boards

Although in virtually all systems a board of directors is included as an essential mechanism of corporate governance, there are many varieties

of board structure and function that nonetheless serve similar purposes. The OECD corporate governance principles accept there are different models of corporate governance:

> For example, they do not advocate any particular board structure and the term 'board' … is meant to embrace the different national models of board structures found in OECD and non-OECD countries. In the typical two tier system, found in some countries, 'board' as used in the Principles refers to the 'supervisory board' while 'key executives' refers to the 'management board'. In systems where the unitary board is overseen by an internal auditor's body, the principles applicable to the board are also, *mutatis mutandis*, applicable. The terms 'corporation' and 'company' are used interchangeably.
>
> (OECD 2004b: 15)

Some of the different approaches to boards in the different regional corporate governance systems include:

- *US boards*: US boards are unitary and tend to be larger, and typically combine the roles of chair and CEO; there is a predominance of non-executives many of whom traditionally were CEOs of other companies.
- *UK boards*: UK boards are unitary, and separate the roles of chair and CEO; non-executives are in a majority; boards are often small particularly in smaller companies.
- *European boards (Germanic)*: European boards as in the north European German model tend to have two tiers, with stakeholder representation on supervisory boards, but preclude the face to face accountability of executives on the management board to board members from outside the company.
- *European boards (Latin)*: European boards of the Latin variety tend to have a large representation of owners and related interests on boards, with little separation of ownership and control.
- *Asian boards*: Asian boards tend to represent dominant family interests, or other majority shareholders, and there is no separation of ownership and control.

■ *Japanese boards*: Japanese boards traditionally were large nominal boards composed of executives and former executives of the company; the board performed largely ritualistic procedures to order and was based on long established relationships.

Debate continues in all systems concerning the ideal size, structure, operation and ultimate purpose of boards of directors. Whether the essential role of the board is monitoring management or offering strategic leadership, and the interests the board should reflect is often contested. The OECD attempts to tread diplomatically between the alternative views:

> With unitary board systems a tension is sometimes observed between the view that the board should contribute contacts, resources and skills to the operation of the company, and the position that the board is primarily in place to monitor the management. The two views have different implications for the structure of the board, the former arguing for a greater share of insiders relative to outsiders. The Principles make a more nuanced case by specifying that the board is chiefly responsible for monitoring managerial performance and achieving an adequate rate of return for shareholders, while preventing conflicts of interest and balancing competing demands on the company. Most important of all, the board is responsible for guiding corporate strategy. In two tier board systems, the question of composition does not arise (i.e. the supervisory board is by law non-executive) although the degree to which it can and should guide corporate strategy and balance interests is often debated. Also debated is whether the absence of executives limits their access to information and restrains informed debate, and at the end of the day could lead to ineffective monitoring. This is an issue in Germany, leading the authorities to introduce a self-check system for supervisory boards. (One can accept the presence of serious weaknesses without going as far as Paul Davies who concluded that 'the German supervisory board continues to be a rather ineffective monitor, whereas the UK board has not only taken on the monitoring task formally but

is better placed to discharge it effectively in practice'.) However, the unwieldy size of supervisory boards also needs to be addressed. With the EU now offering companies the choice of one or two tier systems for companies registering under European statutes, (*societas europeaea*) the advantages and disadvantages of the two systems is once more open to debate. France is the first to give companies such a choice and Italy is following suit with three choices.

(OECD 2004; Davies 2000)

## Elements of board design

Board design and operation remains clearly a work in progress, though Carter and Lorsch (2004: 8) identify the fundamental elements as:

■ *Board structure*: Board size, leadership, and the committees required to accomplish its role.
■ *Board composition*: The mix of experience, skills and other necessary attributes of board members.
■ *Board processes*: How the board gathers information, builds knowledge, and makes decisions.

Together these elements form a system that requires balance and coherence to perform effectively: 'A board like any other organization is a *system* in which the behaviour of the directors is shaped by the design elements and the board's culture. The more effective the elements in the board's design are aligned with each other and with the board's role, and the more deliberate the board is in defining the behaviours it wants to encourage, the more likely the system is to produce behaviours that will make the board effective' (Carter and Lorsch 2004: 9).

The importance of considering how the behavioural elements of boards work in practice is emphasised by Finkelstein and Mooney (2003), who indicate that the structural elements of boards including the number of outside directors, director shareholdings, board size and the separation of CEO and chair roles (all of which were considered vital in promoting board effectiveness) did not in themselves provide the

capability of boards to act in some of the recent corporate governance disasters in the United States. Enron, WorldCom, Global Crossing, Qwest, and Tyco all had a majority of outside directors, all directors had extensive shareholdings, they all had large boards, and all had split the role of chair and CEO with the exception of Tyco. This suggests in any consideration of the reform of boards there must be closer attention to board *processes*, the dynamic capabilities and behaviour boards may apply to the challenges they face.

## THE REFORM OF BOARDS

The recurrent chorus of 'Where was the Board?' at each successive company failure has tested the faith of those who had an idealistic sense of the power and role of the board of directors in corporate governance, and made others place greater reliance on the external mechanisms of governance. However McNulty, Roberts and Stiles (2005: 100) counsel against abandoning the board, which may still serve as a more direct encounter with accountability:

> As is suggested by some elements of the Sarbanes–Oxley Act, there is a risk that we lose faith entirely in boards as a central mechanism of governance and instead fall back on uncertain legal or external market mechanisms ... The wisdom of the

seminal Cadbury Committee (1992) was that it interpreted its brief to report on the financial aspects of corporate governance not just through seeking to improve external transparency, but by also seeking to improve the quality of local board accountability ... The potential of face-to-face accountability on a regular and continual basis between executives and non-executives on a board of a particular company is very different to what can be achieved through remote disclosure and transparency to shareholders.

In this spirit of enhancing direct accountability much of the thrust of corporate reform in the last two decades in the Anglo-American world at least, has been to establish and increase the independence and powers of non-executive directors, and a range of board committees which are composed of non-executives (Table 2.1). The audit and compensation committee are well established in the United States, and the nomination committee is becoming so, as central components of the drive to make boards more independent of executive management. Similarly in the UK the Combined Code represent a renewed belief in the salience of the board's role: 'The provisions of the code are intended to make boards more independent and more effective in controlling the chief executive and the executive team' (Taylor 2004: 421). The key requirements for more effective corporate governance as set out in

| Country | Audit (1995) (%) | Audit (1998) (%) | Remuneration (1985) (%) | Remuneration (1998) (%) | Nomination (1985) (%) | Nomination (1998) (%) |
|---|---|---|---|---|---|---|
| France – CAC 40 | 0 | 90 | 0 | 70 | 0 | 43 |
| France – privatised firms | — | 100 | — | 75 | — | 66 |
| Germany – Dax 30 | 0 | 7 | 0 | 3 | 0 | 7 |
| Japan – Top 1,300 | 0 | 0 | 0 | 0 | 0 | 0 |
| UK – FTSE 350 | 21 | 100 | 23 | 100 | 7 | 73 |
| USA – S&P 500 | 34 | 100 | 30 | 97 | 5 | 87 |

Table 2.1 Specialised board committees.

Source: Goyer, Michael (2001), 'Corporate Governance and the Innovation System in France 1985–2000,' *Industry and Innovation*, 8(2): 135–58.

the code are:

1  to increase the number of non-executive directors;
2  to expand the non-executive directors' role in board committees;
3  to establish closer links with shareholders;
4  to introduce more transparent appointment procedures;
5  to extend training and development of directors;
6  to implement review of board performance (Taylor 2004: 421–422).

Potentially what this can amount to is a transfer of power from the formerly omnipotent combined president/chair/CEO of the US system in the mid-twentieth century, to a board exercising real independence and authority. This could prove a quiet revolution in the boardroom: firstly independent non-executive directors form a majority of the board, secondly they compose the key board committees which advise the board on critical issues. Of course chairs and CEOs would still exercise great authority and persuasive influence even in this new board structure, but they no longer would have direct control of the levers of power controlling board appointments, executive remuneration, and the audit process (Figure 2.4).

If this transfer of power is to have any substance the terms of reference of the board sub-committees are critical, and the vigour with which non-executives complete these duties even more important. The Financial Reporting Council (FRC) responsible for defining and implementing the UK *Combined Code on Corporate Governance* (2003) includes the following in the duties of the respective board sub-committees:

## Audit committee

The main role and responsibilities of the audit committee should be set out in written terms of reference and should include the following:

- to monitor the integrity of the financial statements of the company and any formal announcements relating to the company's financial performance, reviewing significant financial reporting judgements contained in them;
- to review the company's internal financial controls and, unless expressly addressed by a separate board risk committee composed of independent directors or by the board itself, the company's internal control and risk management systems;
- to monitor and review the effectiveness of the company's internal audit function;
- to make recommendations to the board, for it to put to the shareholders for their approval in general meeting, in relation to the appointment of the external auditor and to approve the remuneration and terms of engagement of the external auditor;
- to review and monitor the external auditor's independence and objectivity and the effectiveness of the audit process, taking into consideration relevant UK professional and regulatory requirements;
- to develop and implement policy on the engagement of the external auditor to supply non-audit services, taking into account relevant ethical guidance regarding the provision of non-audit services by the external audit firm (2003: 47).

## Remunerations committee

The committee should:

- determine and agree with the board the framework or broad policy for the remuneration of the chief executive, the chair of the company and such other members of the executive management as it is designated to consider. At a minimum, the committee should have delegated responsibility for setting remuneration for all executive directors, the chair and, to maintain and assure their independence, the company secretary. The remuneration of non-executive directors shall be a matter for the chair and executive members of the board. No director or manager should be involved in any decisions as to their own remuneration;
- determine targets for any performance-related pay schemes operated by the company;
- determine the policy for and scope of pension arrangements for each executive director (2003: 67).

Management controlling the levers of power

The board controlling the levers of power

**Figure 2.4** The transformation from management control to independent boards.

Source: Taylor, Bernard (2004), Leading The Boardroom Revolution, *Corporate Governance: An International Review*, 12(4): 423.

## Nomination committee

The committee should:

■ be responsible for identifying and nominating for the approval of the board, candidates to fill board vacancies as and when they arise;

■ before making an appointment, evaluate the balance of skills, knowledge and experience on the board and, in the light of this evaluation, prepare a description of the role and capabilities required for a particular appointment;

■ review annually the time required from a non-executive director. Performance evaluation

should be used to assess whether the non-executive director is spending enough time to fulfil their duties;

▩ consider candidates from a wide range of backgrounds and look beyond the 'usual suspects';

▩ keep under review the leadership needs of the organisation, both executive and non-executive, with a view to ensuring the continued ability of the organisation to compete effectively in the marketplace (2003: 69).

The effective use of these board sub-committees is extending beyond the Anglo-American countries to other jurisdictions (Table 2.2), as part of the effort to make boards more active and independent. Whether corporations have adopted these reforms or not has become a matter of some significance in terms of international corporate governance indices. For example the Institutional Shareholder Services Corporate Governance Quotient index devotes attention to this in rating companies for proxy voting purposes (Table 2.3).

## THE EFFECTIVE CHAIR

Whether the board of directors really makes an impact or not on the company's affairs, has a

great deal to do with the effectiveness of the chair of the board. A good chair may inspire collegial aspiration to do the right thing, a poor chair may cause disorientation. The practice of combining the roles of chair and chief executive has been under notice since the Cadbury Report on *The Financial Aspects of Corporate Governance*, which stated convincingly:

> Given the importance and particular nature of the chairman's role, it should in principle be separate from that of the chief executive. If the two roles are combined in one person, it represents a considerable concentration of power. We recommend, therefore, that there should be a clearly accepted division of responsibilities at the head of a company, which will ensure a balance of power and authority, such that no one individual has unfettered powers of decision. Where the chairman is also a chief executive, it is essential that there should be a strong and independent element on the board.
>
> (1992: 5)

This proposal promoted a widespread move towards separation of the roles of chair not only in the UK but in many other countries of the world, as they adopted similar codes (though in the United States CEOs clung to their joint roles of

|  | USA S&P 500 | UK | NL | ITALY | SPAIN |
|---|---|---|---|---|---|
| Average board size | 11 | 10.8 | 5.1 | 14 | 12.6 |
| Average annual board meetings | 7.8 | >8 | 6.8 | 12 | 9.4 |
| Outside directors (%) | 80 | 52.1 | 91 | 57 | 36 |
| Separation of ceo and chair (%) | 23 | 83.3 | 98 | Low | 68 |
| Average outside director's age | 60 | 58 | 60.7 | 57.9 | 56 |
| Have three key committees (%) | 80 | 91.3 | 89 | Low | 85 |
| Director's retirement age | 70/72 | — | — | 80 | 70 |
| Fully independent audit committee (%) | 98 | — | 94 | 100 | 100 |
| Fully independent compensation committee (%) | 96 | 86.7 | 73 | 16.7 | 67 |
| Fully independent nominating committee (%) | 91 | — | Low | Low | 67 |
| Average annual director's pay (cash retainer) | $43,667 | GBP 35K | €32K | €41.4K | €45.5K |
| Lead/senior director | 36 | 83 | — | 0 | — |
| Formal annual board evaluation (%) | 87 | 43 | — | — | — |

Table 2.2 Comparative analysis of board structure, 2003 (selected countries).

Source: Adapted company proxy filings; Spencer Stuart Board Indexes (2003).

**Board**

1 Board composition
2 Nominating committee
3 Compensation committee
4 Governance committee
5 Board structure
6 Board size
7 Changes in board size
8 Cumulative voting
9 Boards served on – CEO
10 Boards served on – other than CEO
11 Former CEOs
12 Chairman/CEO separation
13 Governance guidelines
14 Response to shareholder proposals
15 Board attendance
16 Board vacancies
17 Related party transactions – CEO
18 Related party transactions – other than CEO

**Audit**

19 Audit committee
20 Audit fees
21 Auditor ratification
22 Financial expert

**Charter/by-laws**

23 Poison pill adoption
24 Poison pill – shareholder approval
25 Poison pill – TIDE provision
26 Poison pill – sunset provision
27 Poison pill – qualified offer clause
28 Poison pill – trigger
29 Vote requirements – charter/by-law amendments
30 Vote requirements – mergers and business combinations
31 Written consent
32 Special meetings
33 Board amendments
34 Capital structure – Dual class
35 Capital structure – Blank cheque preferred

**State of incorporation**

36 State anti-takeover provisions
37 Control share acquisition provision
38 Control share cash-out provision
39 Freeze-out provision
40 Fair price provision
41 Stakeholder law
42 Poison pill endorsement

**Executive and director compensation**

43 Cost of option plans
44 Option repricing
45 Shareholder approval of option plans
46 Compensation committee interlocks
47 Director compensation
48 Option burn rate
49 Performance-based compensation
50 Option expensing
51 Board performance reviews
52 Individual director performance reviews
53 Meetings of outside directors
54 CEO succession plan
55 Outside advisers available to board
57 Director ownership
58 Executive stock ownership guidelines
59 Director stock ownership guidelines
60 Officer and director stock ownership
61 Mandatory holding period for options
62 Mandatory holding periods for restricted stock

**Director education**

63 Director education

Table 2.3 ISS corporate governance quotient.

Source: ISS 'Corporate Governance Quotient', Rockville, MD: Institutional Shareholder Services, http://www.isscgq.com/CGQratings.htm.

chair and CEO, as 'part of the American way of life'. ('It's only part of the US CEOs' way of life', a group of American investors once dryly commented). Separating the roles also focused attention on the significance of the distinctive duties of the chair (Cadbury 2002). According to the *Combined Code* the effective chair:

■ upholds the highest standards of integrity and probity;

- sets the agenda, style and tone of board discussions to promote effective decision-making and constructive debate;
- promotes effective relationships and open communication, both inside and outside the boardroom, between non-executive directors and executive team;
- builds an effective and complementary board, initiating change and planning succession in board appointments, subject to board and shareholders' approval;
- promotes the highest standards of corporate governance and seeks compliance with the provisions of the code wherever possible;
- ensures clear structure for and the effective running of board committees;
- ensures effective implementation of board decisions;
- establishes a close relationship of trust with the chief executive, providing support and advice while respecting executive responsibility; and
- provides coherent leadership of the company, including representing the company and understanding the views of shareholders (FRC 2003: 63).

Fulfilling these duties calls for special qualities that distinguish chairs from chief executives, as Adrian Cadbury who had a sterling career successively as both managing director and later chair of Cadbury Schweppes comments:

> Both the chairman and the chief executive need to have the capacity to lead, but leadership of the board is not the same as the leadership required to turn the board's decisions into action. Given that the board's job is to define the purpose of the company and how it is to be achieved, its chairman needs to have strategic sense, the ability to analyse the competitive environment and the capacity to stand back from the business of today. There is an understandable difference in time horizons between a chairman, who assumes a responsibility for the long-term survival of the enterprise, and a chief executive who appreciates that, unless the year's budget is delivered, there may be no long term-future for the chairman to consider.
>
> (2002: 108)

## THE ROLE OF NON-EXECUTIVE DIRECTORS

Non-executive directors in the past have tended not to have a very prominent profile in corporate governance, however since the publication of the Cadbury Report in 1992, they have acquired increasing significance as the key members of the board who can deliver both objectivity and expertise. Yet as the work of boards occurs behind closed doors, often the emphasis of reform proposals regarding the role of non-executives has emphasised their number and independence rather than other aspects of their ability and contribution: 'The work of the non-executive is almost completely invisible to all but fellow board members. It is perhaps for this reason that investors, working at a distance, have focused on issues of board structure and composition, particularly non-executive independence as proxies for board effectiveness' (McNulty, Roberts and Stiles 2003: 9).

Roberts, McNulty and Stiles (2005) argue non-executives should be:

- 'engaged but non-executive';
- 'challenging but supportive';
- 'independent but involved'.

Actually maintaining this delicate balance between helpfulness and intrusion is likely to challenge the most diplomatic of directors in difficult corporate situations.

> The role of the non-executive is to both support executives in their leadership of the business and to monitor and control their conduct; both aspects of the role can be achieved through strong and rigorous processes of accountability with the board. In practice, such accountability is achieved through a wide range of different behaviours – challenging, questioning, probing, discussing, testing, informing, debating and exploring that are at the very heart of how non-executives seek to be effective across the spectrum of different board relationships and their strategic and monitoring roles ... Questioning, challenge, explanation and debate form part of an ongoing dialogue that draws upon non-executive experience in

TWO

support of executive performance. Within such processes of accountability non-executives are constantly seeking to establish and maintain their own confidence in the conduct of the company; the performance and behaviour of the executives, the development of strategy, the adequacy of financial reporting and risk assessment, the appropriateness of remuneration, and the appointment and replacement of key personnel.

(McNulty, Roberts and Stiles 2003: 10)

In the new context of reformed corporate governance, non-executives are vital for enhancing the actual effectiveness of boards, and as a source of confidence to investors as to the effectiveness of boards. There are though dangers of reform undermining the condition for actual effectiveness for the sake of external perceptions of effectiveness, particularly as effectiveness requires 'a culture of openness and constructive dialogue in an environment of trust and mutual respect … as prerequisite for an effective board' (Higgs 2003: 33).

## Independence?

Great attention has been focused on the *independence* of non-executive directors as an essential element of board effectiveness. Given that many non-executive directors in the past owed their position to some close relationship with the company or CEO, this new insistence on independence is understandable. The UK *Combined Code* (2003: 7) suggests, 'A non-executive director is considered independent when the board determines that the director is independent in character and judgement and there are no relationships or circumstances which could affect, or appear to affect, the director's judgement'. Such relationships or circumstances would include where the director:

- is a former employee of the company or group until five years after employment (or any other material connection) has ended;
- has, or has had within the last three years, a material business relationship with the company either directly, or as a partner, shareholder,

director or senior employee of a body that has such a relationship with the company;
- has received or receives additional remuneration from the company apart from a director's fee, participates in the company's share option or a performance-related pay scheme, or is a member of the company's pension scheme;
- has close family ties with any of the company's advisers, directors or senior employees;
- holds cross-directorships or has significant links with other directors through involvement in other companies or bodies;
- represents a significant shareholder; or
- has served on the board for more than ten years.

Simular stipulations on independence of non-executive directors which have been adopted widely, have frequently provoked arguments that it is difficult to find people with no connection whatsoever with a company, particularly in small business communities, and that single minded adherence to this principle appears to be putting independence before competence. However the exercise in which the board identifies in its annual report the non-executive directors it determines to be independent has proved salutary, and made boards state the reasons it considers 'a director to be independent notwithstanding the existence of relationships or circumstances which may appear relevant to its determination' (FRC 2003: 7).

## BOARD BEST PRACTICES

Accepting the greater demands made upon boards and directors, the intensification of regulation, and the heightened public interest in what happens in the boardroom, it is inevitable that there has been a considerable effort in recent years to establish corporate governance best practices. For example the ASX essential corporate governance principles include:

1 *Lay solid foundations for management and oversight*: Recognise and publish the respective roles and responsibilities of board and management.
2 *Structure the board to add value*: Have a board of an effective composition, size

and commitment to adequately discharge its responsibilities and duties.

3 ***Promote ethical and responsible decision-making***: Actively promote ethical and responsible decision-making.

4 ***Safeguard integrity in financial reporting***: Have a structure to independently verify and safeguard the integrity of the company's financial reporting.

5 ***Make timely and balanced disclosure***: Promote timely and balanced disclosure of all material matters concerning the company.

6 ***Respect the rights of shareholders***: Respect the rights of shareholders and facilitate the effective exercise of those rights.

7 ***Recognise and manage risk***: Establish a sound system of risk oversight and management and internal control.

8 ***Encourage enhanced performance***: Fairly review and actively encourage enhanced board and management effectiveness.

9 ***Remunerate fairly and responsibly***: Ensure that the level and composition of remuneration is sufficient and reasonable and that its relationship to corporate and individual performance is defined.

10 ***Recognise the legitimate interests of stakeholders:*** Recognise legal and other obligations to all legitimate stakeholders (ASX 2003: 11).

Principles such as this are often extremely helpful to practitioners, however if they are translated into detailed best practices, and begin to be imposed as a set of rigid rules, they can become very constricting. This was never the intention of the principles based approach of which the Australian Stock Exchange principles and the UK *Combined Code* are examples: they were intended as a guide to engagement with integrity and intelligence, not a template for unthinking compliance:

> While most investors appear willing to accept explanations where the company has a good case, the review has identified a continuing concern that the Combined Code is viewed in some quarters as a rigid set of rules. This is not how the Code should be applied. The principle of '*comply or explain*' – for which the review found strong support – recognises that one size does not fit all, and that there will be circumstances where it is in the interests of the company and its owners to adopt practices that differ from those set out in the provisions of the Code. In those circumstances companies can comply with their obligations under the Listing Rules by explaining why they have taken that course of action. For 'comply or explain' to be effective companies need to provide meaningful explanations and investors need to consider them on their merits.
>
> (FRC 2006: 1)

Nevertheless, there is some evidence that a box-ticking, compliance driven mindset is becoming widespread in corporate governance, driven by many factors including the over-prescription of regulators, the governance templates of investment institutions and ratings agencies, the commercial interests of consultants and accounting firms selling compliance systems, and the resulting conformity of companies. Yet as Carter and Lorsch highlight, there are many contradictions in conventional approaches:

> Assumptions about board effectiveness have considerable impact on composition of boards, how directors approach their duties, and how they are compensated. But assumptions are flawed and unintended consequences can cause problems for boards that diminish their effectiveness. Contradictions of conventional board assumptions include:
>
> 1 ***Most directors should be independent.***
>   Directors with no relationship to the company are not likely to know very much about its business, and will have to learn, and will be dependent on the management for this.
> 2 ***Directors need to be financially aligned with shareholders.***
>   Making directors shareholders paradoxically can erode the director's independence, as the directors think about their personal financial interest rather than all shareholders' interests.
> 3 ***Directors must monitor management performance vigorously.***
>   While boards monitor and evaluate management's performance, they must participate in key decisions and offer advice,

and ultimately end up sitting in judgement on management decisions they have participated in, confusing accountability and making the working relationship with management more difficult.

4  **Directors should be generalists with a focus on the company as a whole.**

Generalist directors who have only a little time to monitor complex companies, are likely to have a superficial understanding of the business. In order to get the job completed effectively directors divide their labour and do much of the work in specific committees.

5  **The primary task of the board is to create shareholder value.**

In reality boards are responsible to a diverse set of interests. Shareholders themselves have different investment objectives and time horizons, and achieving long term shareholder value involves meeting the expectation of other stakeholders who contribute to the success of the company including employees, customers, suppliers, and creditors.

(2004: 42–3)

## INVESTIGATING BOARD PROCESSES

Although boards and directors have attracted considerable attention as they are the crucible of corporate governance, little is known about the melding processes that take place during board meetings to contribute effective corporate outcomes. Pye and Pettigrew (2005: 30) comment: 'We have a well-established and widely researched body of research into corporate governance based on the assumptions of agency theory, yet in comparison, we still know relatively little about how boards and directors *actually* behave or conduct their roles effectively'. They argue more substantive research is required which aims to link board characteristics to board outcome, discovering more about the behavioural processes involved. Dalton and Dalton identify themes common to Sarbanes–Oxley and Higgs of independence in board composition and structure, when structural independence must be accompanied by effective

board processes: 'In sum, structural independence does not equal performance independence. No amount of structure can overcome a failure in process. All too often, however, boardroom critics and shareholder activists focus on structural governance issues as a panacea for ineffective corporate governance' (2005: 95).

Hermalin and Weisbach (2003) highlight the issues that make empirical research on boards and directors such a complex task. Board activities and independence are usually not observable; there is an ongoing dynamic relationship between the board and CEO, which changes in the board membership can alter significantly; moreover boards are not monolithic structures, but composed of individuals who will not normally share a common agenda on all matters, even if there are identifiable groups on the board. Finally boards themselves are constantly interpreting and negotiating competitive environments subject to increasingly rapid change. Even if the board succeeds in mastering oversight and control of the company, the volatility and complexity of the market can prove demanding. Essentially boards dynamically evolve and develop over time in response to the many demands made upon them.

In US research into boards:

The usual board measures employed in these studies, that most often are archival-data based, are CEO duality, insider-outsider ratio, the number of board members and the directors' share ownership (Finkelstein and Mooney 2003; Johnson, Daily and Ellstrand 1996). Actual board behaviour is not explored in these studies, even though some of them use proxies for actual board behaviour. Fewer than one out of eight of the empirical board articles published in the leading scientific management journals is about actual board behaviour.

(Huse 2005: 66; Huse and Gabrielsson 2004)

Research on company boards and directors has traditionally been difficult to accomplish effectively. Whether due to confidentiality, pressure of work, or disinterest, often access has been difficult to secure. On the occasions where access has been achieved, researchers have sometimes been subject to capture in the charismatic world of

the powerful. However, recently more substantial research has been completed both in the UK (Johnson, Daily and Ellestrand 1996; Pettigrew and McNulty 1998; Stiles and Taylor 2002) and in North America (Davis and Useem 2002; Carver 2002; Dimma 2002). The remoteness of top executives, boards and directors is being replaced with a greater willingness to engage with the objectives of research (Pettigrew 1992; Johnson, Daily, and Ellestrand 1996). Partly this may be due to the increasing emphasis on openness in many organisations, it may be due also to an interest in exploring ideas and experiences about best practice in corporate governance at a time when there is increasing emphasis on getting this right.

The lack of knowledge of actual board processes and behaviour fuels mistaken assumptions regarding board motivations and actions, and undermines the efficacy of policy prescriptions:

> Inevitably, each board operates in a unique environment comprising different pressures, in which decisions and actions taken at a particular time, against a particular historical legacy and set of future strategic ambitions, and which will lead to different indicators of performance being given priority, hence different drivers and constraints on action and evaluation of board performance … In studies of board dynamics … much like classic group process theory, there is great difficulty in disentangling individual and collective inputs, outcomes and effects. Without the simplistic framework of agency theory assumptions, the job of an empirical researcher trying to tackle this amoeba-like situation becomes immensely more complex.
>
> (Pye and Pettigrew 2005: 33)

If studies are to successfully capture the subtleties of different board behaviour in different contexts, the portals of boardrooms of major corporations will need to become more accessible to researchers than is presently the case. Though it may seem a remote prospect, the opening up of boards to board assessment and development seemed unlikely until recently, and it has now become universal in large corporations. What would be the point of direct observation of board behaviour by board researchers? 'The major contribution of process research … is to catch reality in flight, to explore the dynamic qualities of human conduct and organisational life and to embed such dynamics over time in the various layers of context in which streams of activity occur' (Pettigrew 1997: 342). The theoretical and methodological assumptions of board process studies outlined by Pettigrew (1997: 340) would include:

- *embeddedness*, studying processes across a number of levels of analysis;
- *temporal interconnectedness*, studying processes in past, present and future time;
- a role in explanation for *context and actions*;
- a search for *holistic* rather than linear explanation of process; and
- a need to link process analysis to the location and explanation of *outcomes*.

The picture we presently have of board activity is that it is continually a quest for achieving balance and momentum simultaneously, attempting to ensure the company maintains its stability and integrity, while driving forward towards the new opportunities that are discovered.

## BOARD ROLES IN MONITORING AND STRATEGY?

Returning to the question central to an understanding of board practice and policy – can boards effectively exercise monitoring control and drive energetic strategic initiatives at the same time? 'These two aspects of the role, strategy and monitoring, that non-executive directors are expected to perform demonstrates the difficulties inherent in the position. Overemphasis on monitoring and non-executives can be perceived as mere policemen by the executives, setting up problematic divisions within the board, driving out trust; overemphasis on the strategy role risks accusations by distant investors of cosiness and collusion, the diminishing of independence, and capture' (McNulty, Roberts and Stiles 2003: 9).

While apparently difficult, this is the work that boards of directors set about accomplishing

involving careful consideration of the issues and measured judgement of the appropriate action:

> While there might be a tension, there was no essential contradiction between the monitoring and strategic aspects of the role of the non-executive director. Polarized conceptions of the role ... bear little relation to the actual conditions for non-executive effectiveness. An overemphasis on monitoring and control risks non-executive directors seeing themselves, and being seen, as an alien policing influence detached from the rest of the board. An overemphasis on strategy risks non-executive directors becoming too close to executive management, undermining shareholder confidence in the effectiveness of board governance.
>
> (Higgs Report 2003: 27)

Though in the past this careful negotiation of the board role might have been based on the intuition of experienced non-executive directors, today it is more likely that principles and processes will be applied that make a conscious effort to ensure all directors apply themselves professionally to the responsibilities of their role. This will include an explanatory letter of appointment, induction procedures, and regular director and board development and assessment. The commitment of an increasing number of boards is to learning, development and continuous improvement in their professional duties. In this way the governance review cycle can be accomplished with a strategy review cycle in what Bob Garratt (2003: 177) terms a 'learning board model' (Figure 2.5).

## ACCOUNTABILITY AND RISK MANAGEMENT

Accountability and risk management are among the most fundamental duties for the board of any company to perform. When companies fail, too often it is discovered that boards were satisfied with minimal formal procedures of accountability, possessed little information regarding internal controls, and had never seriously contemplated any risk assessment. The UK *Combined Code* offers the following advice on adopting a system of internal control:

> In determining its policies with regard to internal control, and thereby assessing what constitutes a sound system of internal control in the particular circumstances of the company, the board's deliberations should include consideration of the following factors:
>
> - the nature and extent of the risks facing the company;
> - the extent and categories of risk which it regards as acceptable for the company to bear;
> - the likelihood of the risks concerned materialising;
> - the company's ability to reduce the incidence and impact on the business of risks that do materialise; and
> - the costs of operating particular controls relative to the benefit thereby obtained in managing the related risks.
>
> The system of internal control should:
>
> - be embedded in the operations of the company and form part of its culture;
> - be capable of responding quickly to evolving risks to the business arising from factors within the company and to changes in the business environment; and
> - include procedures for reporting immediately to appropriate levels of management any significant control failings or weaknesses that are identified together with details of corrective action being undertaken.
>
> A sound system of internal control reduces, but cannot eliminate, the possibility of poor judgement in decision-making; human error; control processes being deliberately circumvented by employees and others; management overriding controls; and the occurrence of unforeseeable circumstances.
>
> (2003: 34–35)

Risks exist at all stages in the business cycle (Table 2.4), but in good times companies often become more relaxed about potential risks as

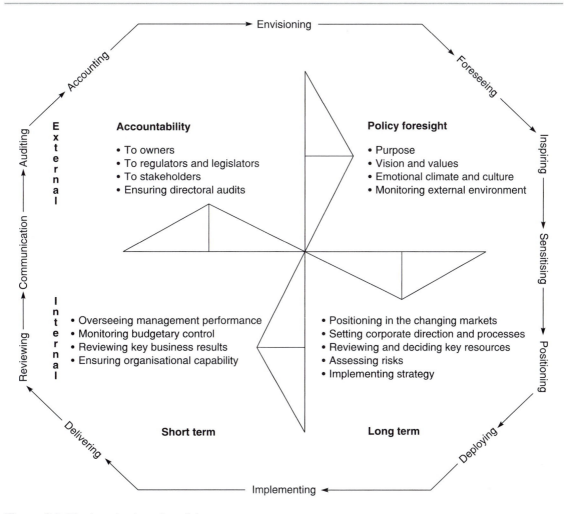

**Figure 2.5** The learning board model.

Source: Garratt, Bob (2003), *The Learning Board*, Henley International Corporate Governance. Henley Management College.

confidence grows. The abandonment of risk management in the euphoria of apparently easy money making was the characteristic board approach that led to the downfall of Enron, WorldCom, and many other US corporations in the seismic 2001–2002 accounting frauds. As the financial and accounting manoeuvres of the their companies became more complex and fraudulent, their boards of directors became more detached and ignorant about the finances of the companies they were supposedly supervising, to the point where as in the case of WorldCom what 'was strikingly absent on the Board was a meaningful

involvement in risk assessment'. Breedon (2003: 34–37) reported:

As WorldCom did acquisition after acquisition, its risk posture became more complicated and required more careful attention. For example, liquidity risks expanded as the Company's debt burden grew higher and as revenues ultimately weakened. There is no indication that the Board analysed how the enormous debts being accumulated by the Company in acquisitions would be carried and ultimately retired. Control risks also grew

| Business risk | Legislative risk | People risk | Disaster risk |
|---|---|---|---|
| ▪ Asset management and resource planning<br>▪ Business interruption<br>▪ Change: organisational/technical/political<br>▪ Construction activity<br>▪ Feasibility studies<br>▪ Foreign exchange operations<br>▪ Information systems/computer networks<br>▪ Investments<br>▪ Operations and maintenance systems<br>▪ Transport (air, sea, road, rail)<br>▪ Project management<br>▪ Purchasing contract management<br>▪ Treasury and finance | ▪ Design and product liability<br>▪ Directors' and officers' liability<br>▪ Employment procedures, training, discrimination and harassment<br>▪ Environmental issues<br>▪ Fraud prevention/detection/management<br>▪ Legislative requirements<br>▪ Occupational health and safety<br>▪ Public risk and general liability | ▪ Ethics and probity issues<br>▪ Human, animal and plant health<br>▪ Professional advice<br>▪ Reputation and image issues<br>▪ Security | ▪ Contingency, disaster and emergency planning<br>▪ Fire detection/fire prevention |

Table 2.4  Key risk areas.

Source: Adapted from data in Standards Australia (1999), *Risk Management: Australian/New Zealand Standard*, Sydney: Standards Australia.

exponentially as new companies were acquired and management failed to integrate systems, networks, commission plans or other areas of operations. Long range assessments of risks and review of management's plans for controlling risk did not seem to exist in either traditional telephony or data markets. Internet planning in particular appears to have failed to address cost issues or the possibility of slower than expected growth, though the company was betting tens of billions in investment predicated on executives' wild guesses about internet growth. Though wireless substitution was then and is today one of the most serious risks for WorldCom, even this was not the subject of serious analysis by the board ... The board failed to understand WorldCom's risks – including Ebbers' character and competence issues – or to design adequate risk control policies. Beyond that the corporate culture under Ebbers did not reward efforts to reinforce legal compliance, ethics, internal

controls, transparency, diversity or individual responsibility. Revenue growth and personal compensation were the exalted elements in the Ebbers corporate culture, and he demanded obedience above all other things.

**Internal controls**

Successive corporate collapses occurring without any warning from the internal control system or external audit, the consequent introduction of the Sarbanes–Oxley Act (2002) with the strenuous imposition of CEO and CFO sign off on the system of internal controls, and the adoption of similar practices throughout the rest of the world have attached a wholly different order of significance to the implementation of effective internal controls. As the UK Financial Reporting Council (2005: 3) insists:

Establishing an effective system of internal control is not a one-off exercise. No such

system remains effective unless it develops to take account of new and emerging risks, control failures, market expectations or changes in the company's circumstances or business objectives. The Review Group reiterates the view of the vast majority of respondents in emphasising the importance of regular and systematic assessment of the risks facing the business and the value of embedding risk management and internal control systems within business processes. It is the board's responsibility to make sure this happens.

The FRC explains why a sound system of internal controls are essential for reporting and risk management:

1 A company's system of internal control has a key role in the management of risks that are significant to the fulfilment of its business objectives. A sound system of internal control contributes to safeguarding the shareholders' investment and the company's assets.
2 Internal control facilitates the effectiveness and efficiency of operations, helps ensure the reliability of internal and external reporting and assists compliance with laws and regulations.
3 Effective financial controls, including the maintenance of proper accounting records, are an important element of internal control. They help ensure that the company is not unnecessarily exposed to avoidable financial risks and that financial information used within the business and for publication is reliable. They also contribute to the safeguarding of assets, including the prevention and detection of fraud.
4 A company's objectives, its internal organisation and the environment in which it operates are continually evolving and, as a result, the risks it faces are continually changing. A sound system of internal control therefore depends on a thorough and regular evaluation of the nature and extent of the risks to which the company is exposed. Since profits are, in part, the reward for successful risk-taking in business, the purpose of internal control is to help manage and control

risk appropriately rather than to eliminate it (2005: 3).

## Identifying risks

Because of the constantly changing business environment and the continuous development of new business ideas and practices, there is an imperative to be alert to emerging risks. In the very pressurised atmosphere induced by the growing demand for high returns by investors, managers are inclined to seek ways to satisfy this, which in the 1990s gave rise to the widespread practice of *creative accounting* including advancing the moment of revenue recognition by bringing forward sales recognition, and deferring expenses. Misstatements of earnings for these reasons have become a widespread problem in the Anglo-American system of corporate governance particularly, though in other corporate governance systems assets and earnings may be exaggerated or concealed for different reasons. There are many red flags for identifying business risks, many now appear self-evident, but passed unnoticed in the euphoria of the NASDAQ boom in the late 1990s for example:

- when money is easy to raise, be alert for companies doomed to fail;
- when the CEO leaves without adequate explanation;
- CEOs known as serial acquirers rather than builders;
- when companies reward failure by repricing stock options;
- when net profit is rising, but cash flow is declining, or negative;
- when the senior management includes the companies' former auditor;
- when cross-board memberships lead to conflicts of interest (Howell 2003: 14).

## Conflicts of interest

One important risk that directly involves the board directors themselves, is conflict of interest. In company law conflicts of interest are treated

very seriously. For example in Australia the *Corporations Act* (2001: s. 191 (1)) states 'A director of a company who has a material interest in a matter that relates to the affairs of a company must give the other directors notice of the interest. Disclosure is required for interests in contracts or proposed contracts, offices and property but the duty of disclosure may extend more widely'. The Act offers the following mechanism for dealing with a declared conflict at a board meeting: 'A director of a public company who has a material personal interest in a matter that is being considered at a directors' meeting must not be present while the matter is being considered at the meeting or vote on the matter' (2001: s. 195 (1)). This exclusion does not apply if the directors who do not have a personal interest in the matter pass a resolution that:

i. identifies the director, the nature and extent of the directors' interest in the matter and its relation to the affairs of the company; and
ii. states that those directors are satisfied that the interest should not disqualify the director from voting or being present.

(2001: s. 195 (2))

This is a vital function for the board which must consistently regulate and avoid conflicts of interest. Conflicts of interest are bound to occur from time to time with busy directors and executives engaged in complex business lives. However the prevalence of conflicts of interest is a persistent and worrying feature of corporate governance, particularly in developing countries. As directors are in possession of all the information regarding the plans and intentions of the company, any trading they complete in their own company shares could be considered *insider trading*, which is why it must be strictly regulated by the board. Almost all codes of conduct including that of the OECD emphasise the illegality of insider-trading, and the importance of members of the board and managers disclosing any material interest in transactions or matters affecting the company. However the OECD (2004a: 96) notes: 'In dealing with the most egregious abuses, insider-trading laws have been implemented in all OECD countries mainly during the 1990s but the indicators are that their

enforcement appears to have been quite modest. In some countries such as Germany, voluntary codes were first implemented but proved ineffective'.

In Germany stronger codes of conduct covering conflicts of interest have now been developed, and the Berlin Initiative Group devised the following code for supervisory boards operating in German corporations:

Members of the Management Board (the lower board in a two tier system) must always remain personally loyal to their company.

- Members of the Management Board in particular may neither directly nor indirectly through persons connected with them, take advantage of the company's business chances, assist competitors or undertake commercial transactions with the company which do not correspond with normal market conditions.
- Participation by members of the Management Board in other companies must be revealed to the Chairman of the Supervisory Board and has to be examined for any possible conflict of interest.
- The chairman of the Supervisory Board must approve acceptance of a seat on the supervisory board of another company, as well as engaging in significant ancillary activities.
- The Management Board will appoint a representative who issues guidelines for the sale and purchase of shares in the company and who supervises their operation. All members of the Management Board will acknowledge in writing the rules applicable for insider dealings as well as these guidelines.

## DISCLOSURE

A major responsibility of the board of directors is to ensure shareholders and stakeholders are provided with high quality disclosures on the financial and operating results of the company, and on company objectives, so that they may make informed and accurate assessments of the progress of the company. Almost all of

the corporate governance codes around the world including the OCED (2004a) principles, Sarbanes–Oxley Act (2002), Combined Code (2003) and EU Transparency Directive (2004) emphasise the importance of full disclosure as the vital basis for the effective working of all of the other mechanisms of corporate governance. UNCTAD (2006) has distilled these collected guidelines into requirements on financial disclosures, and on company objectives. With regard to financial disclosures UNCTAD (2006: 3) states:

> The quality of financial disclosures depends significantly on the robustness of the financial reporting standards on the basis of which the financial information is prepared and reported. In most circumstances, the financial reporting standards required for corporate reporting are contained in the generally accepted principles recognised in the country where the entity is domiciled. Over the last few decades, there has been increasing convergence towards a set of non-jurisdiction specific, widely recognised financial reporting standards. The International Financial Reporting Standards (IFRSs) issued by the International Accounting Standards Board provide a widely recognised benchmark in this respect. Furthermore, the board of directors could enrich the usefulness of the disclosures on the financial and operating results of a company by providing further explanation for example in the Management's Discussion and Analysis section of the company in addition to the disclosure required by the applicable financial reporting standards. The board could clearly identify inherent risks and estimates used in the preparation and reporting of the financial and operating results of the company in order to give investors a better understanding of the risks they are taking in relying on the judgement of management.

With reference to disclosure of company objectives UNCTAD recognises two general categories of company objectives: fundamental objectives that seek to answer the basic question of 'why does the company exist?' and secondly more basic commercial objectives. Included among the

essential non-financial disclosures of company objectives are:

1 ownership and shareholder rights;
2 changes in control and transactions involving significant assets;
3 governance structures and policies;
4 members of the board and key executives;
5 material issues regarding stakeholders, and environmental and social stewardship;
6 material foreseeable risk factors;
7 independence of external auditors;
8 internal audit function.

The traditional practice of including all of this disclosure in annual company reports, has now been largely superseded by the imperative for continuous disclosure, demanded by both markets and regulators. Today boards of directors of major corporations are required to continually consider carefully their responsibilities for disclosure of any significant matters that come before the board, for example of anticipated merger and takeover activity, even if this may involve a temporary suspension of trading in the company shares. At such junctures the board's responsibilities for accountability and for strategy may collide.

## THE STRATEGIC ROLE OF THE BOARD

Inevitably boards of directors will be involved in strategy, as Harvey-Jones rhetorically asks 'If the board is not taking the company purposefully into the future who is?' (1988: 162). But it is difficult to ascertain what is an appropriate level of involvement. Sarah Hogg chair of 3i, one of the most strategically innovative companies in the FTSE 100 commented 'Indisputably, this is a board function, but how is strategy set? Where do strategic discussions end and management responsibilities begin'? and argues 'The need to see the board's strategic responsibilities as long-term, aspirational, and qualitative, in contrast to short term budget-setting or competitive strategies' (Cadbury 2002: xii). There is here a distinction between the long term oversight of strategy that is rightly the board's responsibility, and the creation and implementation of strategies

| Executive directors | Knowledge of day-to-day operations; communicate and implement decisions | Management nexus focused |
| Non-executive ('outside') directors | Strategy; continuity; expertise | Long-term planning; oversight of key risk areas |
| 'Independent' directors | Perspective; objectivity | Conflict-sensitive functions |

Table 2.5 Typology of directors.

Source: Kirkpatrick Grant (2004), '*Typology of Directors' Policy Dialogue on Corporate Governance in China*,' presentation Shanghai, 25 February, Paris: OECD.

which is the role of executive management (Table 2.5).

It is the formulation and endorsement of strategy that the board can be at its most cohesive, as Stiles and Taylor argue:

> Close working between the executive and non-executive cadres promotes enhanced strategic discussion, greater information flow between members, and a lack of dominance of any one individual or sub-group over the board as a whole. One major problem with the adversarial view is that it downplays the role boards can play in the strategy process and in shaping the identity of the organization … Board involvement in the strategy process entails a much higher degree of collaboration between executives and non-executives and in a real sense a relaxing of the constraints of independence in order for trust to be generated and social cohesion to be established.
>
> (2002: 2)

As with the conduct of other board duties however, there is a gradation of engagement in strategic involvement, from passive boards that adopt a minimalist approach to their statutory duties, to boards that adopt a review and approve stance, to boards that do seek an active partnership with executive management in establishing the strategic direction of the enterprise (Table 2.6).

A strategic board is one that contributes to the leadership and direction of the business through a mix of monitoring and supportive behaviours vis-à-vis executives. Non-executives need to be continuously active in respect of both strategy process (how strategy is developed) and strategy content (the substance of choice, change and risk involved in corporate strategy). There is a strong consensus that responsibility for developing strategy rests with the chief executive, in concert with his/her executive committee. Non-executives then make an important contribution by bringing to bear experience and knowledge gained outside the organization, to challenge and test both the overarching strategic framework of the business as well as specific proposals for strategic investment, divestment and change.

(McNulty, Roberts and Stiles 2003: 2)

There is a frequent concern that too great an involvement in developing and monitoring strategy will lead inevitably to the board attempting to second-guess executives as they strive to implement strategies and make them succeed. Cadbury and Millstein advise:

> Perhaps boards should focus on a narrower band of responsibilities. For example, it has been suggested that boards focus primarily on strategies to maximise the long-term sustainable value of the company, with oversight of operational decision-making becoming less of a focus. This would allow the board to look beyond financial results and enable it to instead look to sustainable performance indicators such as product or service quality, customer satisfaction, innovation, employee commitment and relationships with outside stakeholders. Boards should be urged to assure themselves

| Strength of involvement | Description | Studies |
| --- | --- | --- |
| Passive | Statutory boards | Pro-forma (Pahl and Winkler 1974)<br>Minimalist (Pettigrew and McNulty 1995)<br>Statutory (Aram and Cowan 1986)<br>Managerial control (Molz 1985)<br>Ratifying (Wood 1983)<br>Legalistic (Zahra and Pearce 1989)<br>First-level board (Ferlie *et al.* 1994) |
| | Review boards | Review and approve (Molz 1985)<br>Review and analysis (Zahra 1990)<br>Second stage board (Ferlie *et al.* 1994)<br>Third party (Herman 1981) |
| Active | Partnership | Collegial (Vance 1983)<br>Shared leadership (Herman 1981)<br>Participative (Wood 1983)<br>Normative/strategic (Molz 1985)<br>Maximalist (Pettigrew and McNulty 1995)<br>Partnership (Zahra 1990) |

**Table 2.6** Studies on strategic involvement of the board.

Source: Stiles, Phillip and Taylor, Bernard (2001), *Boards at Work: How Directors View their Roles and Responsibilities*, Oxford: Oxford University Press.

that their responsibilities are realistic and capable of being fulfilled, not just enumerated. Investor and management expectations should be managed, so that boards are held accountable for those matters within their remit'.

(2005: 27)

This projects a better working relationship for board's involvement in strategy, rather than continually intruding on management's implementation, or challenging management in open confrontation, the board works consistently to shape the sustainable future of the enterprise:

The board's engagement in gatekeeping activity, screening strategic options and revising and in some case rejecting strategic proposals, provides a strong means to shape the direction of the organization. Though research had identified the board's role in reviewing and assessing proposals as an important element in adding value to the organization (Pettigrew 1992; Ferlie *et al.* 1996), the lack of evidence for boards overturning proposals has been used to support the managerialist claim. However, in teasing out the detail of this process, it is clear that boards set standards, for the quality and nature of proposals that are eventually presented before it; they set the boundaries of what is acceptable in a proposal and what is not.

(Stiles and Taylor 2002: 119)

## TO WHOM IS THE BOARD RESPONSIBLE?

If the board is to play a central role in the strategic direction of the company the underlying question is 'for what purpose'? It is not possible to answer this question fully without addressing the more fundamental question of 'to whom is the board responsible'? Adrian Cadbury states:

The simple answer to this question is that boards owe their duty to their shareholders. The precise and legal answer is that directors, and therefore the boards of whom they are made up, owe their duty to the company.

How real is the difference between these two concepts and does the difference matter? While serving the shareholder interest is a useful working definition of a board's duty, there are situations when it may cease to hold good ... First, it is clear that a company as a body corporate has a legal personality distinct from its members. A company is not, therefore, the same as its shareholders. The company is neither the agent of the shareholders nor their trustee ... In effect, the shareholders of a company elect its directors and entrust them with the control of the company' affairs. From there on, the directors owe their duty to the company and in following that course they may take decisions which some or all of the shareholders consider not to be in their best interests. The recourse which the shareholders have in that situation is to exercise their powers in the general meeting to vote in a new board of directors whom they consider will look after their interests more faithfully.

(2002: 41–42)

Recognition of the distinct personality of the company is a pre-condition to the legal structure for the limited liability of the members. 'The logic of separate personality and limited liability doctrines favours the externalisation of the social costs of corporate behaviour, shifting the risk of the enterprise operations away from shareholders and onto stakeholders or wider society, whether those with firm-specific investments such as employees, suppliers and local communities or the wider community' (Redmond 2005: 156). The corporation has a legal personality of a different character to a natural person, since though invested with the legal capacity and powers of an individual, its incorporate nature ensures that it has perpetual succession, unaffected by change in its membership. Further differences relating to the artificial character of the corporate personality exist, as in the comment attributed to the English Lord Chancellor Thurlow in the eighteenth century: 'Did you ever expect a corporation to have a conscience, when it has no soul to be damned, and no body to be kicked?' (Redmond 2005: 157).

But the corporate personality and limited liability of the public company place definite limits on the rights and powers of shareholders, as Cadbury comments:

> The distinction between a company and its shareholders was clearly drawn by Lord Evershed in 1947 in a case concerning compensation for the shareholders of Short Brothers on the compulsory acquisition of their shares in 1943: 'Shareholders are not in the eye of the law, part owners of the undertaking. The undertaking is something different from the totality of the shareholdings' ... What shareholders own are *shares*. These shares acknowledge the investment which their holders have made in a company carrying on a business and confer certain rights and responsibilities on their owners. The owners are entitled to whatever dividends are declared and they have some security against the assets of the company should it be wound up. Owning shares in a company is not strictly the same as owning the business carried on by the company.

(2002: 42)

Somehow though, a conventional wisdom has been broadcast in the US, and the UK that shareholders enjoy property rights over companies, and that therefore the purpose of companies is to exclusively serve shareholder interests. The fact this claim is *not* supported in law in either the US or UK, has not prevented its energetic propagation to many other jurisdictions, as Blair and Stout (2001: 9) argue:

> Commentators who use the rhetoric of property rights to justify shareholder primacy bring a strong moral overtone to their arguments, implying that any use of corporate assets that does not directly enhance shareholder wealth is a form of theft. Yet from a logical perspective, the naked claim that shareholders own the corporation is just that – a naked claim. As a legal matter, shareholders neither control how the firm's assets are used, nor are they entitled to receive dividends or make any other direct claim on the firm's earnings ... Contemporary corporate law treats corporations as separate and autonomous legal persons whose boards of directors have authority to make decisions and take action without

shareholder approval ... Shareholders do not own corporate assets nor have the right to control them. *Bryan v. Aikin* 10 Del. Ch. 466, 86 A. 674 (1913) ('The stockholder does not, and cannot, own the property of the corporation, or even the earnings, until they are declared in the form of dividends'.) Moreover, the legal rights shareholders do enjoy (e.g., the right to elect directors, to veto certain corporate transactions by majority voting, to offer proposals that the directors are often free to ignore, to receive dividends if and when the directors declare them) look very different from the rights enjoyed by those who 'own' physical assets such as land or jewelry. As a result the assertion that shareholders are 'owners' of corporations functions primarily as a rhetorical device designed to trump all other arguments. It is not, by itself, a serious legal or economic argument.

## Shareholder primacy

Yet the concept of shareholder primacy, and the concomitant insistence that the only real purpose of the corporation is to deliver shareholder value has become an almost universal principal of corporate governance, and often goes unchallenged. This self-interested, tenacious and simplistic belief is corrosive of any effort to realise the deeper values companies are built upon, the wider purposes they serve, and the broader set of relationships they depend upon for their success.

> For nearly as long as the public corporation has existed, the job description and legal obligations of corporate directors has been the subject of debate among scholars, practitioners, and policymakers. But to anyone who entered the debate in the last decade, and read only the dominant academic commentary or informal discussions in the business press, the issue might appear to have been conclusively settled in favor of the following two propositions. First, the board's only job is to faithfully serve the interests of the firm's shareholders. Second, the best way to do this is to maximize the value of the company's shares ... The idea that shareholders alone are the *raison d'être* of the corporation has come to dominate contemporary discussion

of corporate governance, both outside and (in many cases) inside the boardroom. Yet the 'shareholder primacy' claim seems at odds with a variety of important characteristics of US corporate law. Despite the emphasis legal theorists have given shareholder primacy in recent years, corporate law itself does not obligate directors to do what the shareholders tell them to do. Nor does it compel the board to maximize share value. To the contrary, directors of public corporations enjoy a remarkable degree of freedom from shareholder command and control. Similarly, the law grants them wide discretion to consider the interests of other corporate participants in their decision-making – even when this adversely affects the value of the stockholders' shares.

> (Blair and Stout 2001: 5)

The obsessive emphasis on shareholder value is an ideology that is constricting and misleading in business enterprise, and is intended to crowd out other relevant and viable strategies for business success:

> Shareholder primacy is both positively and normatively incorrect – at least in the extreme rhetorical form in which it is most commonly expressed. Corporate law does not (nor should it) require directors to maximize the value of the company's common stock. To the contrary, it grants (and should grant) the directors of public companies enormous freedom to decide where and how the firm ought to allocate its scarce resources. This arrangement does not *preclude* corporate directors from using their autonomy to pursue a higher stock price. However, it also does not prevent them from using the firm's resources instead to benefit managers, employees, or even the local community'.

> (Blair and Stout 2001: 6)

## CEO POWER AND CAPABILITY

### Management vision

The person increasingly at the centre of defining and projecting the responsibilities and objectives

of the corporation is the chief executive officer (CEO). The position of CEO has grown in status and public recognition as corporations have become larger and more powerful and extended their reach globally. The leadership qualities of CEOs are celebrated in business bookshops in the way once reserved for statesmen, generals or explorers. Among the qualities expected of CEOs is the *vision* to see a new future for the corporation (a sage CEO once said there is a hair's breadth difference between a vision and a hallucination), and as John Harvey-Jones the former CEO of ICI described it the capacity to *make things happen.* He also believed in the usefulness of dreams that could serve as stretch goals:

> Dreams do not have to be demonstrably achievable, although it helps if there is some broad indication of scale. They must not be precise, but they have to be ambitious far beyond the capabilities of day-to-day operations. They have to have the quality of credibility, but they have to attract the heart and minds of the people who will have to accomplish them and they have to have a long and in some cases imprecise time horizon ... the dreams have to be, by definition ... so far outside the horizons you have set for yourselves that they remove constraints in thinking and open up new horizons.
>
> (Demb and Neubauer 1992: 199)

## CEO power

Though the board of directors is invested with the responsibility for the company in law, the practical reality is often that the CEO is very much in charge. In the United States CEOs accumulated power to themselves as their corporations began to dominate world markets in the middle decades of the twentieth century, and the role of the board was marginalised:

> Corporate boards, assert legal tradition, are the sovereigns of their realm. But until they began to flex their muscles during the 1990s, boards rarely behaved that way, leaving most decisions in the hands of management (Lorsch and MacIver 1989; Useem 1996). State corporation

laws that assign ultimate responsibility for company affairs to the governing body permit directors to delegate the running of the company to management. The problem is that, until recently, management's power in large American companies reflected less a deliberate delegation of authority by a sovereign body than a de facto reality in which management had become dominant, effectively controlling the agenda of the board to which it was only nominally subordinate.

> (Useem and Zelleke 2006: 2)

Chief executives used their control of boards not only to prevent any challenge to their position, but to aggregate to themselves an increasing share of the wealth generated by the company, both in terms of rapidly inflating salaries, and massively growing stock options.

> A comparative perspective underscores the immense power, charisma and leadership given in the US corporate governance system to the chief executive officer (CEO), who usually also exercises the role of chairman of the board. In fact, in the USA, the split of these two roles is generally perceived as a transitional arrangement or a sign of weakness, particularly in the case of new outside CEOs. The over-centralisation of power in the CEO is evident in the gap between the CEO's salary and that of other executives.
>
> (Aguilera 2005: 45; Khurana 2002)

## *Esprit de corps*

An all-embracing *esprit de corp* is often encouraged in boards, and may well assist in maintaining collegiality and commitment among board members, but this can be misused by over-powerful CEOs who manipulate boards to prevent any challenge to their power or autonomy:

> Among large US corporations there are strong disincentives, rather than incentives, for non-executive directors to challenge executives or to adopt corporate governance reforms that will limit managerial autonomy. These disincentives come from the social pressure to maintain

managerial autonomy and authority for the elite of corporate leaders. Qualitative studies suggest that senior managers and directors of large established corporations have a shared group consciousness as members of a unified corporate leader elite.

(Wei Shen (2005: 84; Useem 1984)

The Westphal and Khanna (2003: 387) survey of Forbes 500 companies in the US discovered evidence that non-executive directors experience social sanctions by their peer directors if they are perceived to threaten the elite position by advocating:

- the separation of CEO and chair positions;
- the creation of independent nominating committees;
- the repeal of poison pill protection;
- the dismissal of the CEO.

One director said 'There's a strong feeling among most of the experienced directors I know those kinds of actions are inappropriate; they are politically correct, but that's not what directors should be doing – directors shouldn't get in the way of managers – directors are not managers' (Wei Shen 2005: 85).

Similarly in the UK the sway of CEOs means that executive directors at least are unlikely to express policy disagreements with their boss at board meetings, as one non-executive director commented:

> The executive directors of boards have very little awareness of their responsibilities under company law or any other law, and the reason for that is quite understandable: they owe their jobs, careers and futures to the chief executive. He appoints them. That doesn't mean they are necessarily a pushover, but let's put it this way – it makes their position quite difficult on the board, that is they cannot have an argument with the chief executive on the board because they are going to be fired; if they are going to have an argument with the chief executive or differences of opinion on policy, which occur all the time, that has to be off board.

> (McNulty, Roberts and Stiles 2003: 11)

## MANAGEMENT AND BOARD DEFENCES

The commitment to a resolute *espirit de corps* may readily develop into a determined *entrenchment* of management and boards in the face of a potential hostile takeover. Managerialist theory argues that though shareholders should make the ultimate decision regarding takeovers (with the management and board confined to recommending support or rejection), control is effectively in the hands of top management who dominate the board of directors and proxy voting machinery to ensure their continued rule (Herman 1981). While this control may be used to simply protect the entrenchment of management, Davis suggests the freedom from direct shareholder control often releases managers to make more balanced decisions: 'Because the dispersed stockholders have no effective mechanism to constrain or throw out management teams that don't serve their interests, managers are afforded a great deal of discretion in determining the actions of the firm. Thus, the organisation's managers are able to balance commitments to various stakeholders, buffer the organisation, co-opt or absorb elements of the environment, and otherwise serve the interests of the organisation as an ongoing entity even if it comes at the expense of the stockholders' interest in profitability' (Davis 1991: 583).

However in the 1980s in the United States a confluence of factors including the availability of large amounts of loan capital, and new financial instruments such as *junk bonds* (bonds with low credit ratings), and relaxed regulation of the anti-trust laws, suddenly large corporations that previously thought themselves invulnerable became takeover targets. This reinvigorated market for corporate control, it was thought provided a means to re-establish the link between ownership and control. Hostile takeovers it was argued, played a role in corporate governance by bringing purportedly efficient market pressures to bear on poorly performing managers (Goldstein 2000: 381). In fact managers themselves had found merger and takeover activity an easier route to growing their companies, but now this method of acquisition came back to bite them in the assault of hostile takeovers.

In historical perspective the corporate raiders of the 1980s were capitalizing on a transformation of the relation between finance and industry in the United States that had been going on since the 1950s. Paving the way for the financial revolution of the 1980s was the growing tendency of strategic managers of the US industrial corporations to reap their own personal rewards through participation if the market for corporate control rather than through enhancing the value creating capabilities of the companies that they were entrusted to manage.

(Lazonick 1992: 473)

But for top managers hostile takeovers presented the stigma of unemployment, and for workers and surrounding communities the consequences of takeover battles can be devastating as both sides expend enormous resources on investment bank and advisers' fees, and can often only recover from the debt accumulated in any restructuring activity intended to impress financial markets by slashing costs including employment. Yet for shareholders such takeovers offer the prospect of windfall gains. 'Thus, the bustling market for corporate control in the 1980s threatened the autonomy previously enjoyed by top managers of large corporations as well as the relationships such firms had developed with their employees and communities, and it exacerbated the potential for conflict between shareholders and managers' (Davis 1991: 584).

Responding to this threat top management and boards took protective action to make takeovers difficult without their consent. An ingenious array of *shark repellents* was created as barriers to hostile takeover (Table 2.7). Corporate charter amendments to protect against takeover take many forms but among the most common are the classified board provision; the supermajority provision; and the fair price provision. The classified board provision introduces staggered board elections, making it impossible for a new majority shareholder ousting the board and replacing it entirely in a single election. The supermajority provision raises the minimum number of shareholder votes necessary for a takeover or merger approval to two-thirds or three-quarters. The fair price provision requires board approval of a takeover or the

acquirer pays a minimum price for all remaining shares. The *poison pill* or shareholder rights plan is a security issued as a dividend to existing shareholders that entitles the holder to purchase shares in the firm at a deep discount if a takeover attempt occurs without board approval, dramatically increasing the cost a potential acquirer would have to pay to get control of the company. When the Delaware Supreme Court in November 1985 legitimated the adoption of a poison pill by boards, without shareholder approval, when the firm was not at the time threatened by a takeover attempt the adoption of poison pills rocketed (Davis 1991: 589).

As Table 2.8 indicates the adoption of a variety of shark repellents has become very widespread throughout US corporations.

## CEO AND EXECUTIVE COMPENSATION

A far more insidious indicator of the extent of management entrenchment in US corporations is the rapid escalation of CEO and executive remuneration, regardless of performance, that suggests in this respect management of is out of control of either boards or shareholders (Figure 2.7). William McDonough, the then President of the New York Federal Reserve Board in a speech in 2002 captured the sentiments of many regarding this reckless inflation of executive reward:

I believe there is one issue in particular which requires corrective action. A recent study shows that, 20 years ago, the average Chief Executive Officer of a publicly-traded company made 42 times more than the average production worker. Perhaps, one could justify that by the additional education required, the greater dedication, perhaps even the harder work. The same study shows that the average present day CEO makes over 400 times the average employee's income. It is hard to find somebody more convinced than I of the superiority of the American economic system, but I can find nothing in economic theory that justifies this development. I am old enough to have known both the CEO's of 20 years ago and those of today. I can assure you that we CEO's

| Provision | Description |
|---|---|
| Anti-greenmail | To prevent that a company could agree with a large shareholder to buy back his stock at a high price for the shareholder's promise not to seek control for a period of time |
| Blank cheque | Preferred stock over which the board determine voting, dividend, conversion and rights |
| Business combination | Laws that impose a delay of certain transactions (asset sales, mergers) |
| By-laws | They are amendment limitations to change governing documents of the corporation |
| Charter | See by-laws |
| Classified board | The directors are placed into different classes and serve overlapping terms. It prevents an outsider from gaining control of a board in a short-term horizon |
| Compensation plans | Allowing participants to cash out options or accelerate the payout of the bonuses should there be a change in control |
| Contracts | Indemnification contracts from legal expenses and lawsuits pertaining their conduct |
| Control – share cash out | Laws that enable shareholders to sell their stakes to a controlling shareholder at a fair price |
| Cumulative voting | A shareholder can allocate his total votes in a manner desired, to elect favoured directors |
| Directors' duties | They allow directors to consider constituencies other than shareholders when considering a merger (employees, host communities, suppliers) |
| Fair price | These requirements limit the range of prices a bidder can play in two-tier offers |
| Golden parachutes | Severance agreements which provide cash and non-cash compensation to senior executives upon a triggering event such as termination, demotion or resignation following a change in control |
| Director indemnification | To indemnify directors and executives from legal expenses and lawsuits pertaining their conduct. This provision uses the by-laws and charter of the company |
| Liability | It limits the director's personal liability, mainly for breaches of the duties of care but not for breaches of the duty of loyalty or for intentional misconduct |
| Pension parachutes | Surplus funds are required to remain the property of the pension fund and this prevents an acquirer from using these funds to finance an acquisition |
| Poison pills | Securities that provide their holders with special rights in the case of a triggering event such as a hostile takeover bid |
| Secret ballot | Independent third party or employees sworn to secrecy are used to proxy votes and the management agrees not to look at individual proxy cards |
| Executives severance | Agreements to assure executives of their positions or some compensation, but they are not contingent upon a change in control |
| Silver parachutes | Similar to golden parachutes but on behalf of employees |
| Special meeting | They increase or decrease the level of shareholder support required to call a special meeting |
| Supermajority | Charter provision for approval of mergers |
| Unequal voting | They limit the voting rights of some shareholders and expand those of others |
| Written consent | Limitations of action by written consent, for establishment of majority thresholders, unanimous consent, elimination of the right to take action |

Table 2.7 Board defences.

Source: Gompers, P.A., Ishii, J.L. and Metrick, A. (2001), 'Corporate Governance and Equity Prices', NBER Working Paper 8849, Cambridge, MA: NBER.

| Entrenchment index provisions | Year | | | | | |
|---|---|---|---|---|---|---|
| | 1990 | 1993 | 1995 | 1998 | 2000 | 2002 |
| Staggered board | 59.2 | 60.5 | 61.8 | 59.5 | 60.5 | 61.9 |
| Limits to amend by-laws | 14.5 | 16.2 | 16.1 | 18.2 | 20.2 | 23.2 |
| Limits to amend charter | 3.3 | 3.4 | 3.1 | 3.0 | 3.3 | 2.5 |
| Supermajority | 39 | 39.5 | 38.4 | 34.1 | 34.1 | 32.3 |
| Golden parachutes | 53.3 | 55.7 | 55.2 | 56.9 | 67.4 | 70.2 |
| Poison pill | 54.4 | 57.6 | 56.6 | 55.4 | 59.9 | 59 |
| All other provisions | | | | | | |
| Limits to special meeting | 24.8 | 30 | 32 | 34.8 | 38.3 | 61.9 |
| Limits to written consent | 24.8 | 29.3 | 32.1 | 33.3 | 36.2 | 46.4 |
| No cumulative vote | 81.6 | 83.6 | 85 | 87.8 | 89 | 90.4 |
| No secret ballot | 97.1 | 90.5 | 87.8 | 90.4 | 89.1 | 88.8 |
| Director indemnification | 40.8 | 39.5 | 38.55 | 24.5 | 23.6 | 19.1 |
| Director indemnification contracts | 16.6 | 15.3 | 12.6 | 11.2 | 9.1 | 8.1 |
| Director liability | 72.7 | 69.2 | 65.5 | 47.2 | 43.1 | 33.9 |
| Compensation plans | 45.3 | 66.1 | 72.8 | 63.2 | 72.6 | 74 |
| Severance agreements | 13.1 | 5.5 | 10.2 | 11.2 | 9.2 | 6.1 |
| Unequal vote | 2.4 | 2 | 1.9 | 1.7 | 1.5 | 1.6 |
| Blank cheque | 76.7 | 80.1 | 85.9 | 88 | 89.45 | 90.8 |
| Fair price | 58 | 59.1 | 57.6 | 49.4 | 48.5 | 44 |
| Cash out law | 4.1 | 3.7 | 3.6 | 3.1 | 2.7 | 2.5 |
| Directors' duties | 10.4 | 11.1 | 10.9 | 9.9 | 10.2 | 10.8 |
| Business combination law | 84.1 | 87.5 | 87.4 | 88.4 | 89 | 90.8 |
| Anti-green mail | 19.7 | 20.8 | 20.1 | 17.1 | 15.8 | 15 |
| Pension parachutes | 4 | 5.3 | 4 | 2.2 | 1.5 | 1 |
| Silver parachutes | 4.1 | 4.9 | 3.5 | 2.4 | 2 | 1.7 |

Table 2.8 The incidence of board entrenchment and related provisions in US corporations (%).

Source: Bebchuk, L., Cohen, A. and Ferrell, A. (2004), 'What Matters in Corporate Governance?', Harvard Law School, Working Paper 491, November.
Note: This sample is from data gathered by the Investor Responsibility Research Centre (IRRC) and covers 1,400 to 1,800 US corporations, including all the S&P 500 firms. The sample covers 90% of the total US stock market capitalisation.

of today are not 10 times better than those of 20 years ago.

The job of CEO is a very demanding one and needs to be generously rewarded to attract talented people and to offer them material incentives for staying committed to a tough role. However as McDonough argues this was always the case, long before the current excessive rewards were offered. The essential problem is not the absolute growth in CEO reward, it is firstly how the arrogation of an increasing share of the wealth of the corporations by the CEO impacts upon *relationships* with other employees, shareholders and the wider community. The second concern is how excessive and unrestrained CEO compensation displaces the CEOs' *objectives* from the development and success of the company to individual strategies of how to maximise their personal earnings.

This displacement of CEO goals is not a recent problem but occurred in earlier periods in different forms, for example in earlier periods of merger and takeover activity, often the most

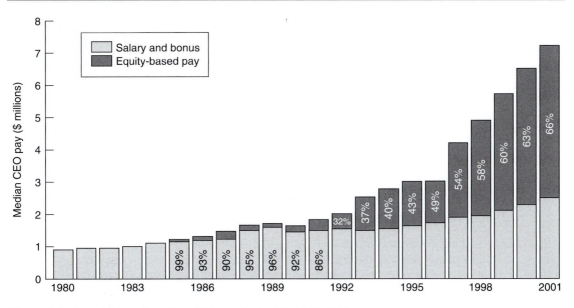

**Figure 2.6** Composition of median CEO pay in the US, 1980–2001.

Source: Hall, Brian J. (2003), Six Challenges in Designing Equity-Based Pay, *Journal of Applied Corporate Finance*, 15(3): 21–23.

insistent driver was CEOs' ambition, since they associated acquisitions with higher rewards for themselves. Similarly the sustained lack of capital investment in US and UK industry in the 1970s and 1980s was partly due to the self-interest of management: 'The problem was not only the high cost and mobility of capital. The problem was also the willingness of many top managers of industrial corporations to take advantage of the permissive financial environment to appropriate huge levels of compensation for themselves while neglecting to build organizational capabilities in the companies they were supposed to lead' (Lazonick 1992: 476).

There is much evidence to support the view that presently in large corporations in the US:

1 Executive compensation has been completely out of control for some time.
2 The disparity created with the rewards of other company workers is both morally unconscionable and functionally damaging.
3 Executives are taking an increasing share of the earnings of corporations, and are becoming significant shareholders in their own right.

4 Executive compensation in the past has often not been due to achieving results but has amounted to rewards for failure.
5 The elaborate structures designed to link executive reward to performance has often compounded the problems rather than alleviating them.
6 There is a real danger that the excessive compensation secured by US executives will become the benchmark for executive reward in other regions of the world where up till now executive rewards have remained modest in comparison.

Excessive executive compensation in US corporations is not an isolated problem, it is endemic, and it has occurred because executives seized control of their own reward structures, as Bebchuk and Fried argue

> Managerial power has played a key role in shaping executive pay. The pervasive role of managerial power can explain much of the contemporary landscape of executive compensation, including practices and patterns that

have long puzzled financial economists ... Managerial influence over the design of pay arrangements has produced considerable distortions in the arrangements, resulting in costs to investors and the economy. The influence has led to compensation schemes that weaken managers' incentives to increase firm value and even create incentives to take actions that reduce long-term value ... Flawed compensation arrangements have not been limited to a small number of 'bad apples'; they have been widespread, persistent and systemic. Furthermore, the problems have not resulted from temporary mistakes or lapses of judgement that boards can be expected to correct on their own; rather they have stemmed from structural defects in the underlying governance structure that enables executives to exert considerable influence over their boards. The absence of effective arm's-length dealing under today's system of corporate governance has been the primary source of problematic compensation arrangements. Finally, while recent reforms that seek to increase board independence will likely improve matters, they will not be sufficient to make boards adequately accountable; much more needs to be done.

(2005: 1–2)

More critical than the detachment of US executives from their shareholders' interests that occurred in the 1990s, was the distance that grew between the rewards and lifestyle of executives and their employees. In 1980 the ratio of CEO and worker compensation in the US was approximately 50:1, and by 1990 this had risen to a ratio of 109:1. With the meteoric rise in executive pay in the 1990s the ratio expanded to an unprecedented 525:1 (Erturk *et al.* 2004) (Figure 2.8). Though there was productivity growth during this era almost all the benefits went to top management: as Dew-Becker and Gordon who examined the distribution of the benefits of growth in the US comment 'Our results show the dominant share of real income gains accruing to the top 10 per cent and top 1 per cent is almost as large for labour income as total income ... It is not that all gains went to capital and none to labour; rather, our finding is that the share of gains that went to labour went to the very top of the distribution of wage and salary incomes' (2005: 77). In two decades US workers saw no measurable improvement in their wages, while US executives enjoyed the experience of becoming multi-millionaires en masse. This is hardly a recipe for a well integrated and orderly economy and society, and it is not surprising that the US now has among the worst social and health problems of any advanced industrial country (Figure 2.9).

Among the arguments used to justify the enormous increases in US CEO reward are the effects of the bull market and the greater demands made upon executives, when it could be argued greater

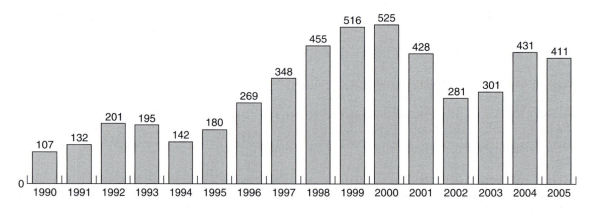

**Figure 2.7** Executive pay as a multiple of worker pay in the US, 1990–2005.

Source: Institute For a Fair Economy (2006), *Executive Excess*, Washington, DC: Institute for Policy Studies/United for a Fair Economy, 30, http://www.ips-dc.org/

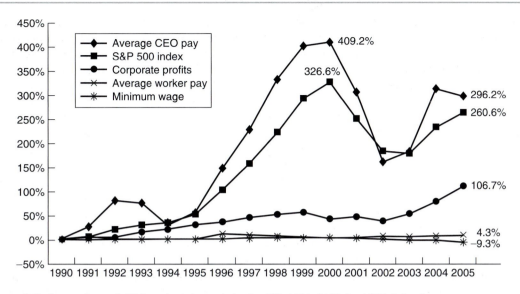

**Figure 2.8** Comparison of CEO and worker pay in the US, 1990–2002 (in 2005 dollars).

Source: Institute For a Fair Economy (2006), *Executive Excess*, Washington, DC: Institute for Policy Studies/United for a Fair Economy.

demands are actually made upon executives when the market is falling (Bebchuk and Grinstein 2005a: 299). A further argument put is that in these competitive times greater rewards are required as an incentive to executives, when there is little evidence that reward has been effectively linked to CEOs' own performance. It appears that neither boards nor shareholders have been able to prevent an unprecedented inflation in US executive reward which Bebchuck and Grinstein calculate cost $250 billion for the top five executives in all US listed corporations between 1993 and 2002, and saw the earnings of the top five executives as a proportion of aggregate firm earnings rise from 5 per cent in 1993 to 12.8 per cent in 2000–2002 (Bebchuk and Grinstein 2005: 297). When shareholder returns collapsed dramatically in 2001/2002, lavish CEO compensation in the S&P 500 continued regardless; and CEO compensation per dollar of net profit between 1960 and 2000 increased exponentially (*The Economist*, 25 October 2003).

Furthermore given the extensive opportunities for executives to translate earnings into stock they have become major shareowners in their own companies. Holderness *et al.* (1999) compared a cross-section of 1,500 US public companies in

1935 with a modern benchmark of 4,200 listed firms in 1995. They discovered that managerial ownership of common stock rose from 13 per cent in 1935 to 21 per cent in 1995. It seems the separation of ownership and control is now in reverse, and Core *et al.* (2003: 53) estimate the current levels of inside ownership at US public corporations at 20 per cent. A large proportion of these shares are owned by CEOs, and Mehran (1995) records average ownership by the CEO and his immediate family of 5.9 per cent for 153 randomly selected manufacturing firms, which in many cases would make them one of the largest shareholders.

One of the intellectual inspirations for the new incentive pay structures for management was a paper by Jensen and Murphy (1990) that insisted executives needed to see more alignment between their performance and reward. Yet most of the consequent movement to incentivise management has achieved the opposite of the intended effect. In their research on the growth in executive pay Bebchuk and Grinstein (2005a) conclude that executive pay during 1993–2003 grew by far more than could be explained by changes in firm size, performance and industry mix. In a further paper they discover 'an asymmetry between increase

and decreases in size: while increases in firm size are followed by higher CEO pay, decreases in firm size are not followed by reduction in such pay' (Bebchuk and Grinstein 2005b: 1).

Essentially the extraordinary elevation in executive reward that occurred in the 1990s in the United States had little to do with the productive efforts of the executives themselves, and was fuelled by the longest running bull market in history. The sustained rise in share prices in this period reflected institutional savings flows and momentum investing, together with falling interest rates. Stock options became an accelerator mechanism providing risk free bonuses to senior management.

> Corporate governance in the 1990s operated against a background of rising share prices, the capital market was not an agent of discipline but a facilitator of painless general enrichment through rising share prices; amidst increasing confusion about what management could do in a world whose stock market was running on narratives (not discounted cash flows) and encouraging CEOs to pose as heroes … Many CEOs in the decade of the 1990s profited personally from using the language of value creation to cover the practice of value skimming. Right at the end of the 1990s, just before the collapse of the Tyco share price and his personal disgrace, Denis Kozlowski, the Tyco CEO publicly defended his 1999 pay by claiming 'while I gained $139 million (in stock options) I created $37 billion in wealth for our shareholders'.
>
> (Erturk *et al.* 2004: 690)

While 'a rising tide lifts all boats' they surely fall again when the tide goes out, but this did not happen to executive salaries. Though the collapsing share market in 2001/2 exposed acute problems of corporate governance and strategy, and raised serious questions regarding the performance and reward of corporate executives, most bloated executive pay packets escaped largely unscathed. Indeed on the occasions when executives were dismissed for poor performance, it was often discovered that they had gilt edged pension entitlements that rewarded them massively for their failure, *stealth compensation* that

may include hidden pension entitlements, deferred compensation arrangements, and post-retirement consulting. This prompted the UK Department of Trade and Industry to publish its document on *Rewards for Failure* (2003) on director's remuneration, contracts, performance and severance, and alerted institutional investors to start checking the small print of executive's contracts more closely.

Among the many reasons why executive compensation packages have not delivered performance improvement, but often exacerbated the provision of increasing amounts of corporate earnings regardless of the contribution of the CEO, include the fact that behind the appearance of independence of compensation committees and the employment of external consultants, company directors have formed positive beliefs about types of pay arrangements from which they themselves have benefited during their management career (similarly compensation consultants enjoyed higher fees to the degree they can justify higher pay for the executives of the companies they are advising). Executive pay inflation has consistently been driven by boards seeking to pay their CEO more than the industry average, thus serving to progressively ratchet up the average. 'A review of reports of compensation committees in large companies indicates that a large majority of them used peer groups to determine pay and set compensation at or above the $50^{th}$ percentile of the peer group. Such ratcheting is consistent with a picture of boards that do not seek to get the best deal for their shareholders, but are happy to go along with whatever can be justified as consistent with prevailing practices' (Bebchuk and Fried 2005: 13).

When companies do use objective criteria these criteria are not designed to reward managers for their *own* contribution to the firm's performance, as bonuses are typically not based on the firm's operating performance or earnings increases relative to its industrial peers, but on metrics that cannot distinguish the contribution of industry wide or market wide movements. In fact conventional stock options allowed executives to gain from any increase in stock price above the grant-date market value, even when their company's performance might have significantly lagged that of their peers. Towards the end

of the 1990s CEOs became adept at achieving temporary spikes in the company's stock price to release the maximum benefit from stock options, even when their companies' long term stock performance was poor (Bebchuk and Fried 2005: 23–24). In addition a panoply of ways have been learned to further boost executive unearned reward through stock options including: *backdating* (the widespread practice of adjusting stock option grant dates to an earlier time than they were actually granted in order to provide a windfall to the option holder); *spring-loading*, the practice of scheduling an option grant before the release of positive corporate news, anticipating a rise in the stock price and attempting a maximum boost to the value of the stock option; and *bullet-dodging*, the practice of delaying a grant until after negative news is released and a company's stock price has declined. The problem with all of these tricks is that they are 'bound up with concepts of insider trading' as Christopher Cox, the chair of the Securities and Exchange Commission referred to spring-loading in testimony before a Senate Committee on 6 September 2006.

The out of control inflation in executive pay in the United States threatens to impact upon executive reward internationally. In the past there was some resistance to this: when the first President Bush took a large party of US executives to Japan to examine the reasons why US industry had failed to compete in the 1980s, the first suggestion of the Japanese executives to their American counterparts was, 'why don't you try paying yourselves less money'? (At the time Japanese executive salaries in manufacturing industries were a small fraction of US salaries.) Today many European and Asian executives look upon swollen US executive salaries more as a benchmark to aspire towards. Already a higher proportion of executive pay is being offered in equity-based compensation and in incentive payments in other parts of the world, which were significant stages in the acceleration of the inflation of US executive pay.

## Executive remuneration guidelines

In 2006 a survey of 768 directors in the 2,000 largest US corporations by Heidrick and Struggles and the USC Marshall School of Business, nearly 40 per cent of directors said CEO pay was 'too high in most cases', and yet 64 per cent of directors expected to see continued increases in cash compensation, and 58 per cent expected an increase in stock-based compensation (2006: 1). Nevertheless efforts continue to be made to make executive reward systems more rigorous and to eliminate fundamental problems such as mismatched time horizons and the gaming that can lead to fraudulent accounting (Hall 2003). Bebchuk and Fried (2005) recommend a series of measures to increase the transparency of executive pay arrangements including placing a dollar value on all forms of compensation, and to include these amounts in compensation reports; expensing options to make the costs more visible to investors; and reporting how much executive remuneration results from general market and industry movements. They recommend strengthening the link between pay and performance by reducing windfalls in equity-based compensation, filtering out gains in stock price due to general market movements; attaching bonuses to long term performance rather than short term accounting results, and including 'clawback' provisions if accounting numbers are subsequently restated; not paying for simply expanding the company through acquisition; and avoiding soft landing for executives where generous exit packages eliminates any gap between the rewards of good and poor performance.

However executive reward will remain an issue when there are questions regarding boards' accountability, and CEOs' dominating influence over boards. More fundamentally it may be questioned whether executive performance pay should be in the form of stock options at all, since these create an incentive for management to manage performance of financial results in order to maximise share price. Pay for performance might better be linked to the underlying drivers of performance that impact on the financials, and to non-financial performance indicators in a more balanced scorecard. The focus could then be upon management for sustainability, rather than short term performance management aimed at the stock price.

## THE DECLINE AND FALL OF THE EMPEROR CEO?

Much has been written about the culture of CEO dominance of the corporate paradigm which, combined with the mistaken theory that management ownership would align their interests with shareholders, led to options and 'numbers games'; and, ultimately to very 'managed' earnings and a burst bubble. As Bob Garratt's book title suggests, *The Fish Rots from the Head*. Too many business schools still follow the Harvard model of managerial capitalism and an emphasis on 'scientific' analysis of business practices, resulting in few governance courses at the business schools and the mantra of CEO dominance being perpetuated.

(Cadbury and Millstein 2005: 15)

However the efforts to restrain CEO power (including incentive pay systems and stock options) have often led to adverse effects, as each new control method is effectively subverted (Table 2.9).

A danger is that as US CEO pay runs further out of control it will continue to act as a powerful force to inflate CEO pay in other regions of the world. Though presently CEO pay in the rest of the world may be far lower than in the US, CEOs everywhere are actively utilising US CEO remuneration levels as a comparator, without considering the consequences of this top managerial responsibility for the feelings of the wider workforce who routinely face tightly restrained pay increases (Table 2.10).

However, reversing of the trend towards the Emperor CEO is one of the supreme challenges for corporate governance if further corporate catastrophes are to be averted.

As the report prepared by Richard C. Breeden for the District Court of New York on what needed to be done to learn from the WorldCom disaster to reform the governance of the MCI Inc company that was to continue graphically illustrated, WorldCom's governance was imperial rather than corporate:

Overarching the accounting issues at the Company was a series of deep-rooted failures

| Optimal contracting | Managerial power |
|---|---|
| *Diagnosis* | |
| 1  Opportunistic behaviour | Minimise outrage via camouflage |
| 2  Market for capital, labour and corporate control are not sufficient | Enthusiasm about equity based compensation benefits to managers[1] |
| *Solution* | |
| 3  Design incentive pay systems. Managers' behaviour optimises value creation and/or shareholder wealth | Compensation consultants justify *executive pay* CEOs control the board in charge of their remuneration |
| *Adverse effects* | |
| 4  Managers reap windfall income via stock price Increase independent of their actions | Options plans that filter out windfalls are not in the interests of managers. Therefore they are not used[2] |
| 5  The threat of takeover should discipline CEOs | Mergers and acquisitions justify higher compensation of managers but do not always increase shareholder value |

Table 2.9 Adverse effects of approaches to controlling managers.

Source: Adapted from Bebchuk and Fried (2003).
Notes
[1] 2000: CEO compensation was an average 7.89% of corporate profits in firms making up the 1,500 company exe comp sata (Balsam 2002).
[2] 2001: 5% of 250 largest US public firms used some form of reduced windfall options (Levinstone 2001).

| | Share of equity-based pay (%) | | | Share of at-risk pay (%) | | |
|---|---|---|---|---|---|---|
| | 1996 | 2001 | Change | 1996 | 2001 | Change |
| Europe (9) | 6 | 18 | 12 | 24 | 37 | 13 |
| Asia (6) | 6 | 24 | 18 | 23 | 39 | 16 |
| Latin America (4) | 0 | 21 | 21 | 26 | 45 | 19 |
| Commonwealth (3) | 8 | 20 | 12 | 27 | 46 | 19 |
| US (1) | 32 | 52 | 19 | 51 | 68 | 17 |
| Average (of 23 countries) | 6 | 22 | 16 | 26 | 42 | 16 |

**Table 2.10** Changes in executive pay composition: international comparisons.

Source: Hall, B. J. (2003), 'Six Challenges in Designing Equity-based Pay', *Journal of Applied Corporate Finance*, 15(3), 21–33, Table p. 24.
Notes: The data are for industrial companies with at least $500 million in sales. The Commonwealth countries are: Australia, New Zealand and Canada. The share of equity-based pay includes the present value of the 'long-term' incentives which primarily consist of stock, options and other equity like pay. The number in parentheses indicates the number of countries.

with the mechanisms of governance. One cannot say that the checks and balances against excessive power within the old WorldCom didn't work adequately. Rather, the sad fact is that there were no checks and balances. The failures of governance allowed the reckless pursuit of wealth by the CEO, and hid determination of compensation decisions throughout the Company. Indeed, Ebbers as CEO was allowed nearly imperial reign over the affairs of the Company, without the board of directors exercising any apparent restraint on his actions, even though he did not appear to possess the experience or training to be remotely qualified for his position. Within the Company, senior executives knew that wealth primarily through stock options and 'retention' grants flowed solely from the dictates of Ebbers, who was allowed to run the Company as if he were running a private family business. Ebbers became an unrestrained force capable of decreeing virtually everything that happened within WorldCom. The Compensation Committee of the board seemed to spend most of its efforts finding ways to enrich Ebbers, and it certainly did not act as a serious outside watchdog against excessive payments or dangerous incentives. As Lord Acton noted in 1887, 'power tends to corrupt and absolute power corrupts absolutely'. This phenomenon

certainly seemed to occur in the case of Ebbers and his tenure at WorldCom. There was an arrogance of power that limitless amounts of money could be spent on whatever Ebbers decided to do, whether it was acquisitions at profligate prices or payments to himself and a relatively small circle of senior associates … Indeed, it was executive compensation decisions more than anything else that seemed to lay the foundations for the fraud that ultimately transpired, and that represented the worst manifestation of WorldCom's governance failures.

(2003: 25)

The legal fallout from Enron, WorldCom, Tyco and other major corporate failures left a significant number of the former executives of these companies serving exceptionally long jail sentences, which might have made US executives examine the probity of all of their corporate dealings with some care (as witnessed in a dramatic increase in earnings restatements in 2002 and 2003). Despite the rigours of Sarbanes–Oxley though, it appears some things have not changed. In October 2006 a small flood of CEO resignations and firings was announced as the result of the discovery of extensive backdating of stock option grants in order to maximise executive compensation. More than 140 companies disclosed

internal or external regulatory probes into their option practices, and 60 companies said they have restated or plan to restate earnings as a result. In the most celebrated case William W. McGuire was forced to resign as chief executive of UnitedHealth Group one of the US's two largest health insurers, and to give up a portion of the $1.1 billion dollars he held in stock options. Investigating lawyers discovered that options were backdated for employees at all levels of the company between 1994 and 2002 but the most substantial and egregious were awarded to McGuire the long time company chair and CEO (*New York Times*, 16 October 2006).

Too great executive power and autonomy not only has led to some notable corporate failures, but even in more successful companies can impair the decision-making process. In companies with more active boards, executive autonomy is replaced by group based processes of learning through which executive decision-making is challenged and refined. As McNulty, Roberts and Stiles (2005: 102) suggest 'Autonomy can be seen as a dangerous fantasy that encourages people to believe they are above the law. Being held to account by our peers promotes not just performance, but also serves to keep us sane by reminding us of our limitations and dependence upon others'. CEOs can be afflicted by a 'dangerous assumption of perfect competence [that] … haunts the imagination of inflated executive egos' to which the experienced challenges by non-executives serves as a guard against such tendencies, and a timely reminder of the changing demands upon the business (McNulty, Roberts and Stiles 2005: 102). Ultimately the effective working of these checks and balances are essential to prevent corporate governance coming to resemble the dark moments of Shakespearian tragedy (Boyer 2005).

## CONCLUSIONS

The analysis of the political mechanisms of boards and directors reveals a great divide between the legal duties and functions of the board, and the actual performance of those duties and functions. Passive boards were prevalent in the past, and the more recent failures at Enron, WorldCom, Tyco and other major corporations, indicate boards completing the formalities rather than the substance of their office. Whether boards can be effectively reformed remains an open question: greater effort is now being made to achieve board independence and best practices but fundamental tensions still exist. Can boards adequately fulfil both the monitoring role and the strategic leadership role that is expected of them? To whom is the board ultimately responsible – simply shareholders or a wider constituency of stakeholders? How can boards offer support for CEOs at the same time as ensuring they do not run out of control? In the Anglo-American world boards have patently failed to restrain the inflation in executive remuneration which poses a serious question regarding the authority and integrity of boards. Perhaps though, the era of the all-powerful CEO was a temporary phase born out of the longest bull market in history. The institutions are now playing a more pivotal role in corporate governance, and the implications for corporate governance of this new development are presently playing out.

# 3

# Finance, Law and Markets: The Institutional Elements of Corporate Governance

## INTRODUCTION

This chapter explores the institutional elements of governance that form the environment in which companies and boards must operate. The different regional institutional regimes are examined, developing from contrasting historical and cultural experiences. The impact of the institutions of law and regulation, and financial and market institutions in shaping alternative corporate governance systems is considered. The range of control mechanisms that exist in corporate governance is outlined, and the cyclical crises in corporate governance systems is investigated. Finally, the emerging role of the institutional investors is analysed, posing the question of whether the increasing concentration of share ownership in the investment institutions will contribute towards more robust corporate governance. The conclusion reached is that as the power of the institutions expands further they could either become an irresistible force for further economic instability induced by short-termism, and the demand for immediate returns, or they could impress upon markets' and companies' longer-term horizons, improved governance and the pursuit of sustainability.

## CORPORATE GOVERNANCE REGIMES

The institutional elements of corporate governance provide the vital forces for the formation, growth and development of corporate life in any economy. The financial and legal institutions allow the means of finance, offer guidance and monitoring, and are the source of regulation and control. The governance structures of companies are constructed around these institutions, remain closely involved in meeting their requirements, and are ultimately constrained by the surrounding institutional structures. The role and significance of market institutions varies among governance systems. Historically it is clear that different corporate governance regimes in different regions and countries of the world helped to provide durable advantages that were not available elsewhere. Table 3.1 demonstrates the different equity ownership structures in the regions of the world, with institutional investors playing a dominant role in the US and UK, and cross-holding of shares in industrial groups by non-financial enterprises still prevalent in Germany and France.

Corporate governance regimes are often distinguished between the outsider systems of market based economies such as the USA and UK, and insider systems of relationship based economies such as practised in European or Asian countries. Each of these systems of corporate governance has inherent strengths and weaknesses as demonstrated in recent times. The outsider system of market based corporate governance that prevails in the United States and United Kingdom characterised by dispersed ownership and the primacy of shareholder value is the dominant force in international corporate governance. Here the principal/agent problems are assumed to be paramount. The market based approach has contributed to the dynamism and growth of the US and other economies that have adopted it, but recently experienced a major reversal in the failure of Enron and a number of other large corporations, that led to the Sarbanes–Oxley Act which

| | United States (1996) | Japan (2001) | Germany (1996) | France (1994) | United Kingdom (1994) | Italy (1994) | Sweden (1996) | Australia (1996) | Korea (1996) |
|---|---|---|---|---|---|---|---|---|---|
| **_Financial sector_** | 46 | 40 | 39 | 8 | 68 | 8 | 30 | 37 | 26 |
| Of which | | | | | | | | | |
| Banks + financial institutions | 7 | 30 | 10 | 4 | 10 | 5 | 1 | 4 | 12 |
| Insurance + pension funds | 28 | 10 | 12 | 2 | 50 | 3 | 14 | 25 | 6 |
| Investment funds | 12 | 0 | 8 | 2 | 8 | 0 | 15 | 8 | 8 |
| **_Non-financial sector_** | 54 | 60 | 70 | 92 | 32 | 92 | 70 | 63 | 74 |
| Of which | | | | | | | | | |
| Non-financial enterprises | 0 | 22 | 42 | 58 | 1 | 25 | 11 | 11 | 21 |
| Individuals | 49 | 20 | 15 | 19 | 21 | 50 | 19 | 20 | 34 |
| Public authorities | 0 | 1 | 4 | 4 | 1 | 8 | 8 | 0 | 7 |
| Foreign | 5 | 18 | 9 | 11 | 9 | 9 | 32 | 32 | 12 |
| _Total_ | _100_ | _100_ | _100_ | _100_ | _100_ | _100_ | _100_ | _100_ | _100_ |

**Table 3.1** The distribution of outstanding listed equity among different categories of shareholders.

Source: OECD Financial Accounts, The Conference Board International Patterns of Institutional Investment (New York 1997), Banque de France, G. P. Stapleton Ownership of the Australian Share Market and Implications for Securities Regulation, and OECD Secretariat Estimates, reproduced in _Corporate Governance Patterns in OECD Economies: Is Convergence Underway?_. © OECD 2001.

Note: Due to rounding, these figures may not add up to the total. Pension funds in Japan are managed by trust banks and Insurance companies. Division between banks and insurance companies are estimated. No data available on the extent to which mutual funds own shares. Security Australian figures are for the end of September 1996.

reinforced the commitment to transparency and disclosure.

In Europe a relationship based system of corporate governance has prevailed, reflecting the rich cultural diversity of the continent, and different corporate history and values. These insider systems are more dependent on loans from banks than the equity market, and tend to have the support of close business networks, that have sometimes been accused of being self-serving. Finally there are the family-based corporate structures of the Asia Pacific, again reflecting different cultural traditions and aspirations. A period of exceptionally strong economic growth ended with the East Asian financial crisis of 1997/1998, and since then attention has focused on strengthening the institutional foundations of corporate governance in the region.

Though there is much evidence of convergence of the regional corporate governance systems around some common international principles, there remains a widespread commitment to diversity of approach in practice. Differences in approach do reflect fundamental differences in how the values and objectives of corporations are interpreted, whether it is simply sufficient to focus on shareholder returns, or whether the firm is there to serve a much wider set of stakeholder interests? This leads to a questioning of the ultimate goals of business corporations, for example in the light of the increasing demand worldwide for business to be more socially responsible and environmentally sustainable. Corporate governance involves balancing complex interests in the pursuit of value creation for the benefit of a wide constituency.

In the past the focus of corporate governance in the Anglo-American countries was on the relationship of corporations to widely dispersed shareholders through the stock market; in the European system the emphasis concerned the relationship of corporations with the banks and major shareholders; and in Asia the interest was in the connection between dominant family shareholdings and corporations. There is increasing evidence emerging that a new corporate governance environment is developing in all of the regions with the dramatic increase in the scale and impact of equity markets and other financial markets, and the burgeoning growth, activity

and influence of the institutional investors. The investment institutions have been around for a long time, but for some years the phenomenal and sustained growth of the institutions has placed them at the forefront of the responsibility to ensure corporate governance is working. With the capacity to own the majority of listed company shares in all of the markets of the world, and to have a substantial presence in bond and credit markets also, their objectives and values will have a critical bearing on how the corporate governance system develops internationally (Figure 3.1).

## INSTITUTIONAL ORIGINS OF CORPORATE GOVERNANCE

The historical evolution of the regional governance systems has proved very different in orientation and outcome. Contrasting systems of corporate governance are largely built around different sources of funding and methods of monitoring. This different approach to financing and regulating corporations in the regions of the world has prevailed since the separate origins of capitalism in those places. The evolution of the corporate form can be traced from the common origin in the family and closely held capitalism of the early nineteenth century with the protection of ownership rights; through to the managerial capitalism of the early twentieth century with further protection for listed corporations and limited liability, and the refinement of the basic mechanisms of governance in the general meeting of shareholders and the board of directors. Finally the popular capitalism of the late twentieth century developed with protection of minority interests, the reassertion of increasing board control over managers and the arrival of mass ownership in the institutional investors (Table 3.2).

Different routes were followed in this contrasting evolution of corporate governance in the regions of the world. As a result different destinations were reached in corporate practice, company law, and associated institutional development in Anglo-American, European and Asian forms of corporate enterprise. In the Asian system of corporate governance significant elements of family ownership survive intact, and in the

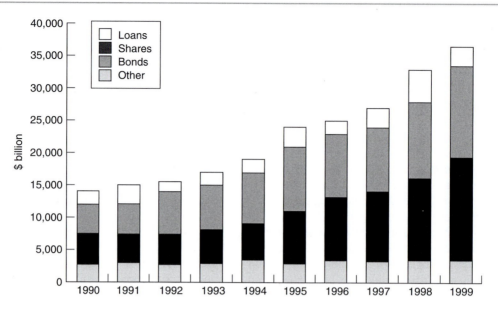

**Figure 3.1** Trends in financial assets of institutional investors.

Source: OECD, *Institutional Investors Statistical Yearbook 2001*, reproduced in *Financial Market Trends*: 80, September 2001, © OECD 2001.

| | Era | Nineteenth century–1920 | 1920–1970 | 1970–twenty-first century |
|---|---|---|---|---|
| | *Form of capitalism* | *Family capitalism* | *Managerial capitalism* | *Popular capitalism* |
| Elements of Democratic Governance | **Equality of rights to ownership** | *Implementation:* creation of rights to ownership independent of social standing | *Reinforcement:* strengthened by corporate law; protection for quoted corporation | *Reinforcement:* strengthened by new rules on the right to vote; protection of minority interests |
| | **Separation of ownership/ control** | No | *Implementation:* generalisation of the limited liability corporation, with general meetings, boards, executives | *Reinforcement:* increasing board control over managers |
| | **Representation with public debate** | No | No | *Implementation:* mass ownership; stakeholder activism |

**Table 3.2** The evolution of corporate governance forms and democratic governance.

Source: Gomez, Pierre-Yves and Korine and Harry (2003), 'Democracy in Corporatia: Tocqueville and the Evolution of Corporate Governance', Working Paper 2003/09, EM Lyon/European Entrepreneurial Learning.

European system managerial forms have survived in a robust form.

From this contrasting trajectory two parallel universes of corporate governance have emerged:

- a *dispersed* ownership model characterised by strong and liquid securities markets, high disclosure standards, high market transparency, and where the market for corporate control is the ultimate disciplining mechanism; and,
- a *concentrated* ownership model characterised by controlling shareholders, weak securities markets, low transparency and disclosure standards and often a central monitoring role for large banks who have a stake in the company. (Coffee 2002; Clarke 2005)

Though each of these systems has been widely adopted, and each could claim a significant measure of economic achievement in the growth and durability of national and regional economies, traditionally much of the attention has been focused on developments in the market based Anglo-American system. This is due to the international salience of Anglo-American equity markets, the prominence in world markets of US corporations, and the vast scale of the investment institutions originating in the US and UK. Since the early work of Berle and Means, much of the analysis of corporate governance has focused upon the apparent separation of ownership and control in the Anglo-American system of corporate governance, and the resulting perceived principal-agent problems. The focus of a great deal of financial economics and legal analysis for many years has been upon the agency issues which are a particular result of the institutional and corporate structure of the Anglo-American variant of corporate governance, though it is usually presented as if it is of universal applicability.

## The separation of ownership and control

The work of Berle and Means examined the profound implications of the separation of ownership and control in a series of publications which had a major impact on corporate governance theory and practice for generations to come. For them it was axiomatic that as the number of shareholders increased, their influence upon corporate enterprise diminished as professional managers took control. As corporations became the dominant vehicles of the US economy, their legal instruments of incorporation – particularly in the state of Delaware which became the most popular jurisdiction in which to incorporate – increasingly reflected the concerns not of stockholders, but of the executive management who intended to run the corporation. Berle and Means (1933) identify two distinct functions of the corporate entity, firstly the commercial operations, and secondly the business of raising capital, and distributing risks, losses and gains. Whilst managers may reasonably insist on as free a hand as possible in running commercial business activities, it is quite a different thing to allow management power to determine how the financial risk and surplus of the corporation is distributed.

The methods by which management is able to shift both the enterprise profits – and to a considerable degree the underlying assets – among groups of stockholders, including themselves, is outlined by Berle and Means. There are countervailing forces including the need to maintain a reputation for probity if new sources of funds are to be accessed, the influence of the law and state regulation, and the intervention of the financial community. However, vigilance is required to prevent management acquiring absolute power. Determining who has the power to select the directors indicates who has control of the corporation in the view of Berle and Means, who recognise a range of potential forms:

1 control through almost complete ownership;
2 majority control;
3 control through a legal device without majority ownership;
4 minority control;
5 management control.

The separation of ownership and control occurs as the ownership of corporations is progressively diluted from complete ownership to minority control, and though there are many devices for working control of a corporation to be retained by those with only a minority of the shares, eventually the situation is reached when ownership is so widely distributed that no minority interest is large

enough to dominate the affairs of the company. At this point even the largest single interest amounts to just a small percentage of the total share-holdings, insufficient to place irresistible pressure upon management. The management appoints the proxy committee who are responsible for the election of directors. 'Since this committee is appointed by the existing management, the latter can virtually dictate their own successors. Where ownership is sufficiently sub-divided, the management can thus become a self-perpetuating body even though its share in the ownership is negli-gible … Such control though resting on no legal foundation, appears to be comparatively secure where the stock is widely distributed'. Though there is always the possibility of a shareholder revolt, under normal conditions the shareholder has little influence over the enterprise and there is little contest to managerial control. 'Thus in the management controlled company the separation of ownership and control has become virtually complete. The bulk of the owners have in fact almost no control over the enterprise, while those in control hold only a negligible proportion of the total ownership' (Means 1931: 86–89).

In other ways Berle and Means left an endur-ing legacy in policy and practice concerning the economic, political and legal identity and activ-ity of the corporation (Clarke 2005). The basic model they proposed for conceiving of the mod-ern corporation still holds considerable descrip-tive and analytical validity, though it needs to be adapted for the new significance of the role of institutional investors as vital intermediaries of shareholder interests (Figure 3.2). The call of Berle and Means for an increase in the inten-sity and scope of the exercise of fiduciary duties of those who controlled corporations influenced legal thinking for much of the century. If this view fell from favour in the rampant opportunism of the 1980s and 1990s, the importance of the principle of fiduciary duty has re-emerged with a vengeance in the reaction to the revelations of managerial irresponsibility that were exposed in the US after the major corporate bankruptcies and the fall of the NASDAQ in 2001. As Bratton (2001) contends, within Anglo-American systems at least, the separation of ownership and con-trol remains corporate law's principal source of unsolved problems.

## THE DEVELOPMENT OF LAW AND REGULATION

As corporations developed within market econo-mies, a framework of law and regulation has evolved to bring order to their activities, to main-tain competition, and to ensure fair treatment of those who interact with corporations. In each country and region a set of laws, regulations, stock exchange listing requirements, and voluntary prac-tices together provides the basis for corporate governance. These institutions and relations are derived from the history, culture and economic circumstances of particular societies (Frentrop 2003). Three legal fields are relevant to the exis-tence and operation of corporate governance according to Aglietta and Reberioux (2005):

1 *Financial market regulation*: Comprises all regulations covering share issues (primary capital markets) and subsequent transactions (secondary capital markets), which aim to reduce information asymmetries between inves-tors and insiders of the company, to prevent misappropriation of value by inside players (Black 2001). Firstly regulation aims to increase financial transparency, and ensure disclosure of information, and secondly insider trading and internal transactions are prohibited.

2 *Corporate law*: Comprises the legal rules defining the relationships between different constituents of the company including share-holders, directors, managers and employees. Company law deals with the rights of share-holdings including voting rights, the power of general meetings of shareholders, the com-position and functioning of the board, the accountability of managers and directors, and the legitimate objectives and purposes of the company.

3 *Labour law*: Labour law directly affects corpo-rate governance when it legislates for worker involvement in decision-making processes. This can range from negotiated involvement in the firm through its supervisory body or collective bargaining processes, to consulta-tive involvement. Codetermination as prac-tised in Germany may be part of positive rights which induce managers to take the interests of employees into account when

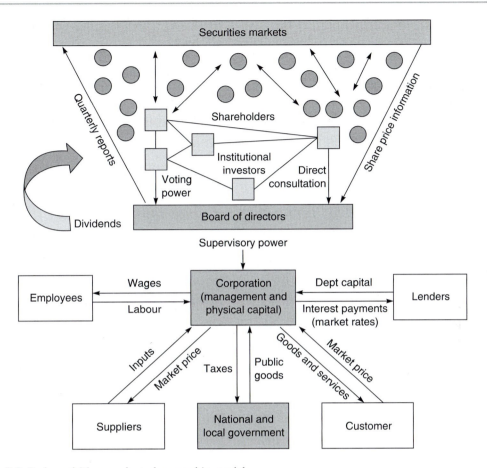

**Figure 3.2** Berle and Means adapted ownership model.

Source: Adapted from Blair, M. (1995), *Ownership and Control: Rethinking Corporate Governance for the 21st Century*, Washington DC, Brookings Institution.

making decisions. (Streeck 2001; Aglietta and Reberioux 2005: 54)

The US legal structure is dedicated to achieving market liquidity and shareholder value with highly developed securities market law to impose disclosure of information to the capital markets. The Securities and Exchange Commission (SEC) regulates the capital markets, supervising the value chain, including harmonising the accounting standards, auditing and financial analysis. In contrast corporate law is developed by the individual states in the US, with competition to attract company registrations, with Delaware dominating in this regulatory competition. Companies therefore have a degree of flexibility in their corporate

governance. The performance of fiduciary duties by directors is reinforced by the high risk of litigation. Yet there is some controversy regarding the nature of fiduciary duties, and it is argued these should be exercised in the interests of the shareholders and the company. This legal framework allows managers significant room to manoeuvre (Aglietta and Reberioux 2005: 56).

The German model of governance and law traditionally appeared the direct opposite of the US, with financial market law specific to each state, undeveloped capital markets and highly concentrated ownership. Financial transparency is lower, and the banks play a more direct intermediary role, acting simultaneously in the role of suppliers of credit, share owners, and proxy holders for

the voting rights of their customers, as well as members of the supervisory board. In contrast federal corporate law regulates the internal organisation of companies, with a dual structure, of board of directors (*Vorstand*) and a supervisory board (*Aufsichtsrat*). The codetermination system is guaranteed by both corporate and labour law at the federal level, with worker representatives joining shareholder representatives on the supervisory board. This whole system is designed to integrate compromise in German companies between the interests of shareholders, management, workers and creditors. This strong procedural integration internally, has the corollary of weak transparency and capital market liquidity externally (Aglietta and Reberioux 2005: 57).

In France capital markets are more developed, and regulated by the Commission des Operations de Bourse (COB) modelled on the SEC. As in Germany, corporate governance is regulated more by corporate law than financial markets law. There is the possibility of a dual structure board, though most companies have a single structure, the dualistic structure is adopted by some large companies. Employee involvement is less than in Germany, but exists through consultation in the works council, and since the councils have some rights of professional advice and legal redress, it does represent an element of co-supervision. As with the German system, there is in French law a holistic sense of the company as an autonomous entity with a corporate interest, as articulated in the Vienot I (1995) report on corporate governance commissioned by MEDEF (French Business Confederation) and the AFEP (French Association of Private Businesses) (Aglietta and Reberioux 2005: 59). The Vienot report states:

> In Anglo-Saxon countries, the emphasis is primarily placed on the objectives of fast maximization of share value, whereas, on the European continent in general and in France in particular, it is placed rather on the corporate interest of the company … The corporate interest can be defined as the greater interest of the body itself, in other words the company considered as an autonomous economic agent pursuing its own ends, distinct notably from those of its shareholders, employees, creditors (including the tax authorities), suppliers and customers, but which correspond to their common general interest, which is to ensure prosperity and continuity of the company.
>
> (1995: 8)

From this comparison a further characterisation of the two major competing systems of corporate governance based on their regulatory structures and the related distinctive conceptions of the firm is possible:

- The US approach has a resolutely favourable orientation to shareholders through strong regulation of capital markets. High disclosure requirements are maintained, along with intervention by the SEC. In contrast corporate law regarding direct regulation of intra-firm relations is weak. Formal integration of employees into decision-making does not exist, but informal cultural integration may occur. The distribution of power regarding the ultimate destiny of the firm is assumed to rest with the external shareholders, with a property rights conception of the firm prevailing, and fairly immediate and measurable shareholder value assumed to be the major driver.

- The continental European approach has less emphasis on capital markets, which have traditionally been less important in this system, and favours internal regulation of the firm. Corporate and labour law plays a much greater role orchestrating the deliberative structures between the main participants in the firm. The controlling interests of majority shareholders protect management from capital market fluctuations. A holistic, partnership based conception of the firm prevails, expressed in commitments to the corporate interest and worker involvement, with the major driver being the generation of sustained company value to be distributed among all participants and the wider community. (Aglietta and Reberioux 2005: 59)

The slightly unreal sense of the European approach to corporate governance, compared with the sharp ring of reality regarding the US approach to corporate governance, reflects the extraordinary ascendancy of the US model since

the 1990s with the industrial renaissance of the New Economy there. Yet as recently as the 1980s it was apparent that the earlier manufacturing based US economy could not compete with Japanese or German industry (Porter 1992). Structural weaknesses in the US approach to corporate governance caused this competitive failure, including the precedence given to finance capital with the high rate of interest extracted from industrial concerns, causing the erosion of strategic investment in organisational capability (Lazonick 1992: 480), the failure to adequately accept 'the collective nature of human endeavour' (Piore 2004: 142), and the essential basis of team production (Blair and Stout 1999; Blair 2004). Though a new institutional accommodation may have been constructed in the 1990s, whether this will have any longevity remains to be seen. Nonetheless, the US approach to corporate governance is becoming hegemonic.

## The peculiarities of the Anglo-American institutions

The emergence of the United States as the greatest industrial power early in the twentieth century, gave a particular significance and influence to Anglo-American institutions of corporate governance that has survived to the present day. In great measure this influence is due to the success in maintaining the largest and most liquid capital markets, which are integral to the Anglo-American system. Examining the political and legal roots of Anglo-American institutions is important for an understanding of the nature of contemporary corporate governance, and the ongoing insistent pressures for global convergence around this system. Ira Millstein (2001) describes the development of company law and corporate governance in the US as essentially based on self-regulation to achieve performance, punctuated by legislative intervention when things go wrong, as periodically they do. Hence the Wall Street crash and accompanying evidence of stock market abuses, led to the formation of the Securities and Exchange Commission. As US corporations began to perform less competitively in both the domestic and international marketplace, courts empowered more active independent directors.

A further political dimension to the development of US corporate governance is highlighted by Mark Roe in his influential work *Strong Managers, Weak Owners: The Political Roots of American Corporate Finance* (1994), which put forward the thesis that rather than being the result of self-selection, the increasing dispersal of ownership that Berle and Means had noted was the result of a legal framework that determinedly fragmented financial institutions. This legal framework was largely introduced by World War II, and discouraged or prevented institutional investors from amassing large blocks of shares (for example the Glass-Steagall Act (1932) for banks, and the Investment Company Act (1940) for mutual funds). He suggests successive political interventions to weaken financial intermediaries altered the structure of America's large public firms, making corporate managers more powerful: 'Populist fears, interest group manoeuvring and American political structure all had a cumulative effect that repeatedly led Congress and the states to fragment financial institutions, their portfolios, and their ability to network together. These political decisions gave rise to the distinctive form of the modern American corporation: scattered shareholders, with managers in control' (1994: x). This deep popular mistrust of concentrated financial power in the US deterred financial institutions from taking a close interest in the activities of corporate executives. In contrast in both Europe and Japan, the banks were allowed to build lasting relationships with corporations, which delayed for many decades the influence of equity markets, and encouraged industrialists to work in partnership with financial institutions.

La Porta *et al.* (1998, 1999) in response to Roe's *politics matters* thesis offered a *law matters* thesis arguing the level of the dispersion of ownership increases in direct proportion to the level of legal protection offered to minority shareholders. This protection is a result of the legal tradition in different countries. Common law countries such as the United States, UK and Australia provide stronger guarantees to minority shareholders than is the case in civil law countries such as France, Germany and Italy. In jurisdictions with weaker minority shareholder protection a concentrated structure of ownership is invariably found. La Porta *et al.* (1999) support their argument with

a wide array of evidence demonstrating that the Berle and Means model of separation of ownership and control is a phenomenon based in the Anglo-American world. Throughout the rest of the world the predominance of majority shareholdings and family companies suggest little separation of ownership and control has actually taken place.

Initially La Porta *et al.* accepted that all of the major industrial economies appeared to perform well despite different legal and ownership structures. Later they insisted that while most of the world had civil law and concentrated ownership, the common law system where judicial decision created a flexible response to new developments created better protection for shareholders, facilitating wider share ownership and the growth of equity markets (La Porta *et al.* 2000). In a further elaboration by La Porta *et al.* (2002) regarding corporate governance and valuation, they argued that while concentrated ownership provides close monitoring of management thereby eliminating the agency problem between owners and managers, it gives rise to a different agency problem of controlling shareholders taking advantage of minority shareholders in public corporations. Therefore La Porta *et al.* suggest a legal solution to increasing the depth of equity markets and the dispersal of shareholding in strengthening the law protecting investors to encourage greater participation in the market (Pinto 2005: 21).

A more pragmatic view is put by Easterbrook (1997) who suggests that different corporate structures are efficient, otherwise they would not survive, and that the law follows markets rather than determining them. Cheffins (2001) also insists the law is not the primary explanation, and emphasises the role of financial intermediaries who facilitate the public offerings of shares including for example in the UK the Stock Exchange, and the role of the City institutions which develop shared values and traditions of self-regulation. Coffee argues on similar lines:

> The growth of securities exchanges and the rise of dispersed ownership correlate most closely not with specific legal rules or protections, but with the appearance of a private sector that was largely free from direct governmental interference. More specifically, private institutions – most notably, stock exchange rules and bonding mechanisms by which investment bankers pledged their reputational capital – probably played a greater role than mandatory legal rules in the early rise of dispersed ownership. The common law, however, facilitated the emergence of these private institutions, while the civil law system tended to place them directly under the control of the state. Initially, the relative role accorded to self-regulation seems to have depended on the strength or weakness of the formal legal institutions in the particular country. Thus, active self-regulation was more visible in the US than in the UK, because judicial corruption and regulatory arbitrage were significant problems in the US, but not in the UK.
>
> (2001: 6)

In the later part of the twentieth century US corporate management were confronted however by two new challenges to their power that served to regulate their behaviour, in the rise of the takeover as an instrument of market control, and the increasing prominence of the institutional investors as dominant shareholders. The market for corporate control periodically has threatened incumbent corporate managers, however the growth of institutional shareholders has presented a quieter but more insistent pressure. As a result of the increasing wealth of American society and the growing popularity of pension funds, insurance and mutual funds, the institutional investors came to hold a greater share of US equities. The total equity holdings of institutional investors increased from 12.6 per cent of US equity markets in 1960, to 51 per cent in 1999 (OECD 2001), and has continued to grow. As institutional investors came to own the majority of shares in most large corporations, this qualified the Berle and Means model of the publicly held corporation with widely diffuse shareholders, and though the leaders of the institutional investors rarely exercised their potential power, certainly their influence exercised a degree of restraint on most corporate executives.

A century of legal and regulatory effort was invested in the US to achieve some resolution to what Swanson defines as 'The major governance problem … the intricate balance between maximising the efficiencies necessary to create wealth and ensuring that the controlling

parties are accountable to those with a stake in the enterprise' (1996: 417). The assumption that this equilibrium has been reached in the Anglo-American model of corporate governance in anything other than a partial and temporary way however, is a little optimistic. Furthermore, as Cheffins (2001) demonstrates with regard to the UK, as the only major industrial country to evolve along similar lines of ownership and control to the US, the resolution of this corporate governance equilibrium has scarcely been achieved there either. In this light, it is surprising that the Anglo-American model of corporate governance was so energetically canvassed worldwide as the route other countries should take towards resolving their corporate governance problems. Further examination is merited of the nature of the Anglo-American system to understand its manifest strengths and often concealed weaknesses.

## BANK, MAJORITY AND MARKET BASED FINANCE

Related closely to the development of law and regulation in corporate governance, is the issue of corporate finance. From where a company derives the finance it requires to develop and grow is one of the most fundamental questions any enterprise faces. The two principal ways of raising external finance are through bank finance or equity finance by selling shares on the stock market. Once this critical choice between alternative sources of finance is made there are profound implications for the governance structures resulting. Williamson argues, 'Debt and equity are treated not mainly as alternative financial instruments, but rather as alternative governance structures. Debt governance works mainly out of rules, while equity governance allows much greater discretion' (1998: 567).

The evolution of capital markets is divided by Rybczynski (1997) into three phases, bank oriented, market oriented and securitised. Though at each stage banks remain responsible for payments services and liquidity, over time there is adjustment in the allocation of saving, monitoring and disciplining of users of external finance, and in the management of risk. In the bank phase the

external funding of firms is obtained from banks in the form of loans, with banks monitoring the performance of borrowers. In this phase banks play a dominant role in the economy as financial intermediaries, and may in some markets hold equity stakes in firms. In the market oriented phase, banks face competition from other providers of financial products, with the growth of the institutional investors, and individual holdings of securities. Banks remain the major source of external funding for firms, but money and capital markets begin to develop. As other sources of external finance develop, monitoring begins to be shared with the other financial institutions. In the third securitisation phase the market provides most finance to firms, and also to the financial sector. Corporate bonds and commercial paper replace bank loans, and mortgages and consumer credit are securitised. Allocating savings and monitoring is undertaken by the financial markets through rating agencies, investment banks and institutional investors. New financial products are developed such as derivatives, that allow pricing and trading of risks, and new financial expertise emerges (Davis 2000: 3–4).

Historically the evolution of capital markets has proceeded at a different pace regionally, and the result is a varying emphasis on the importance of different kinds of finance and the related governance structures. Davis (1996, 2002) elaborates the distinctions arriving out of different financing into four paradigms of corporate governance:

- direct control via debt;
- market control via equity;
- market control via debt;
- direct control via equity.

### Direct control via debt

This governance system is associated with Germany and Japan, where a close relationship is maintained with a small number of creditors and equity holders, and monitoring is delegated to the bank as a trusted intermediary. Wide cross-shareholdings exist among companies, with banks themselves as significant shareholders, and in Germany having a substantial presence on supervisory boards as both equity holders and creditors.

Bank influence is further increased by being able to exert control over the voting rights of individual investors who have transferred their proxies. The influence of other shareholders, including other institutions is limited by voting restrictions, the strong countervailing influence of other corporate shareholders, and the lack of disclosure of detailed financial information, combined with the formal rights to board representation of other stakeholders including employees, suppliers and creditors.

## Market control via equity

This is the governance system ideally associated with the UK and US, in which greater dependence on equity finance by companies involves disclosure to the market of widely dispersed shareholders who may exercise influence by buying or selling shares on liquid equity markets that reward performing companies with higher share prices, and sanction poorly performing companies with lower share prices, that make them more vulnerable, including to the possibility of takeover. Takeover activity is the most dramatic way of resolving apparent conflicts between management orientations and shareholders' interests:

> Those firms which deviate most extensively from shareholders' objectives – and which consequently tend to have lower market values as shareholders dispose of their holdings – have a greater likelihood of being acquired. The threat of takeover, as much as its manifestation, acts as a constraint on managerial behaviour. Institutional shareholders, both directly and via non-executive directors can have an important role to play in this context both in complementing takeover pressures as a monitoring constraint on management behaviour, and in evaluating takeover proposals when they do arise.
>
> (Davis 1996: 83)

## Market control via debt

In the past takeovers were resorted to normally in very particular circumstances where either an incumbent management was clearly slipping, or where the synergies to be released from a takeover were apparently too great to resist. However in the 1980s this all changed with the arrival of junk bonds: bonds issued by companies considered to be higher credit risks, considered speculative rather than investment grade, with a higher chance of default than other bonds. Banks and institutions now joined in to finance highly leveraged takeovers through the issue of a vast amount of junk bonds. Debt was seen as a way of reasserting control on managers, since without internal resources, they needed to return to the market either for further debt or equity capital or for any new initiative (Jensen 1986). One disadvantage of loading companies with debt though, was that directors and shareholders in highly leveraged firms might have an incentive to engage in high risk projects, since under limited liability their creditors would bear most of the cost if the venture was unsuccessful. Disenchantment with highly leveraged takeovers set in with an increase in the bankruptcy rate, the diversion of management energies engaging in takeover and defence strategies, the panoply of defence mechanisms from takeover erected across the corporate sector, and the onset of recession at the end of the 1980s.

## Direct control via equity

Searching for a more positive way of monitoring and influencing management of corporations in the 1990s onwards, the investment institutions have launched a corporate governance movement to restore the traditional rights of shareholders to elect the board of directors, and influence the choice of strategic policies of management. Formal and informal engagement with management by major institutions has developed, and the sophistication of institutional investor corporate governance policies increased. Indexing strategies by leading institutional investors force funds to hold shares in companies that observe certain policies. Most institutions prefer to stay with the index, but even active investors who try to achieve greater influence in selective investment strategies, need to consider the significant cost in disposing of shareholdings, and are often driven to

further increase their control over companies due to the illiquidity of the market (Davis 1996: 84).

However there is a fifth paradigm for financing and governance of enterprises, which is more universal than the other approaches, and often co-exists with them, and that is *Managerial Control Via Retained Earnings*. In all governance systems most of the finance for expansion and innovation comes through the growth in the revenue of companies, and the retention of these earnings for further investment. This organic approach to capital investment is the essential well-spring of the corporate system. Of course this internal source of finance buttresses the position of the incumbent management, though it can be argued they are in the best position to judge both the need for new investment in the company, and the most appropriate means of raising finance. This approach until recently at least, has fared better in the German and Japanese systems. However, despite the repeated strenuous efforts to incorporate more energetic market disciplines, the use of retained earnings for investment has remained central to the Anglo-American model also, as Bill Lazonick insists:

> The financial basis of innovative strategies in the United States has always been, and remains, retained earnings. For strategic management of going concerns, retained earnings permit new investments in organization and technology to be financed without incurring legal obligations to pay returns. Retained earnings represent low-cost finance, and control over retained earnings is the quintessential mode of securing financial commitment. In addition, a stream of retained earnings can be used to pay the interest charges on investments that are externally financed. Depending on projected sales revenues, earnings retention, and bond rates, strategic management can choose a debt-equity ratio that leverages retained earnings without jeopardizing the financial ability of the firm to implement its investment strategy.
>
> (1992: 457)

Lazonick argues that contrary to economic folklore, common share issues have never been important to US industry to finance business expansion, and in contrast to the large volume of bond issues, new share issues have been responsible for only a small proportion of the capital raised in the US (1992: 457; Taggart 1986). New share issues essentially gained their prominence from owner-entrepreneurs taking their firms public. Beyond that, share issues have been significant more recently for acquisition and restructuring strategies. Finally much of the recent frenzied attention given to equity markets is the result of the arrival of stock options as the primary form of executive compensation in the US which over time switched managers' focus from the performance of their company in product markets, to their share performance in equity markets:

> The ability of managers to buy stocks at a discount transformed career employees into substantial owners. The exercise of stock options meant a stream of dividends if the managers held onto the stocks, or, in a rising market, capital gains if the managers (usually after a restricted period) sold the stocks. Ownership income began to dwarf compensation income for top managers ... With capital gains income over twenty times dividend income, and hence constituting the bulk of their total income, the lesson for top managers who were motivated by such matters ... was to prevent even short-run declines in the market value of their companies' stocks. Strategic managers of industrial corporations joined the money managers of institutional portfolios in focusing on the bottom line of their companies' quarterly reports.
>
> (Lazonick 1992: 462)

Despite the way equity markets have seized the public attention in recent decades, a final form of governance and finance remains the most popular in large parts of the world, that is *Direct Control Via Majority Group*.

## Majority group control

As extensive research by La Porta *et al.* (1999) and Claessens *et al.* (2000) demonstrates the most prevalent form of control over companies throughout the world, is not market control but

direct control by majority groups. Even in Japan and Germany where bank influence has been greatest, this was heavily supported by large cross-holdings of shares between enterprises. In other countries the majority shareholders are often family members, often with one figure in a dominant ownership and control position. The OECD comments

> It is commonly accepted that the structure of ownership in the US and the UK is widely dispersed while in other countries the situation is one of concentrated ownership. This picture is, however, somewhat exaggerated. While the median largest voting block in these two countries is 10 per cent or less and 30–60 per cent in other countries, there are also a number of companies with very concentrated voting power ... As in other countries these companies often reflect the dominance of a family holding. Much the same pattern emerges when considering the second and third largest voting blocks, with the UK rather more similar to Europe than to the US.
>
> (2004: 18)

Who the majority shareholders are also differs widely with financial institutions important in many countries with the exception of France. The nature of the major institutional influence is also different with pension funds very important in the US and the UK. The importance of banks in Japan needs to be qualified by the fact that insurance companies are the banks' own major shareholders. With regard to the non-financial sector, individuals are dominant in the US but in most other countries, except the UK, it is other companies that tend to have cross-shareholdings in each other. This reflects the prevalence of, and commitment to, company groups in many countries. The OECD continues:

> Groups of companies are often associated with particular control devices such as pyramids and cross shareholdings. One study examined 2890 companies in Europe finding that nearly 30 per cent of them were in the third or lower down layers but that a third also showed no deviation of cash flow from voting rights. The lowest deviation for the average cash to

voting rights ratio was in the UK while there were large deviations in Belgium, France and Germany, with a rather complex picture emerging for Italy. In Italy the governance system is characterised by voice rather than by exit of the important shareholders. Powerful families, financial holding companies and cross shareholdings are a common feature. Corporate networks, voting agreements and hierarchical groups, especially in Belgium, France and Italy, are a device for concentrating voting power without concentrating ownership and cash flow rights. They also shield the controlling group from hostile take-overs. However, they also open the system to abuse of minority shareholders.

> (2004: 19)

Bratton and McCahery (2002) contrast the relative merits of the market and majority ownership system, (which they characterise as blockholding systems, with majority or near-majority holdings of stock in the hands of one, two, or a small group of large investors). They refer to how widely dispersed shareholding prevents close monitoring of management, but go on to insist:

> Market systems have countervailing advantages. Their shareholders cheaply can reduce their risk through diversification. Relative to shareholders in blockholder systems, they receive high rates of return. The systems' deep trading markets facilitate greater shareholder liquidity. These capital markets also facilitate corporate finance, providing management with greater flexibility as to the type and sources of new capital than do markets in blockholder systems. More generally, they provide an environment relatively more conducive to management entrepreneurship, as reflected in increased investment in new technologies. Finally, although market system shareholders and their outside-director agents cannot access full information about firm operations, their very distance from operations yields a countervailing benefit. Distance makes them relatively immune to capture by the management interest and assures objective evaluation of the information they do receive. A practice of objective evaluation means relatively fewer barriers to

disinvestment and related features of downside restructuring.

(2002: 26)

Concentrated ownership offers a different set of advantages:

Blockholder systems, like market systems, leave management in charge of the business plan and operations. But large-block investments imply a closer level of shareholder monitoring. In addition, the coalescence of voting power in a small number of hands means earlier, cheaper intervention in the case of management failure. The systems' other primary benefit stems from the blockholders' ability to access information about operations. This lessened information asymmetry permits blockholders to invest more patiently. The longer shareholder time-horizon in turn frees management to invest for a long term and creates a more secure environment for firm-specific investments of human capital by the firm's managers.

(2002: 27)

Concentrated ownership has survived in most countries of the world as the most common form of ownership and control, and whatever its limitations, retains the greatest influence in the corporate governance systems of most countries. However in the two most powerful economies associated with this form of governance, Germany and Japan, questions have been raised concerning the central role assumed to be played by the banks. Roe (1994) examined the monitoring practice of banks in Germany, and though he found significant bank shareholdings and governance input, this did not involve an activist role in investment and divestment policies, and banks tend to act in a largely lender's role. Gorton and Schmid (1996) suggest the role of German bank monitoring has changed over time, and that earlier there were firm performance improvements depending on how much equity banks owned, though this changed by the 1980s. Baums (1998) argues though the banks held a significant place in the German system of corporate governance, with just three of the largest banks holding 37 positions of 231 positions reserved for stockholders

in the supervisory boards of the 24 non-financial companies which composed the DAX 30 in 1998, their real influence was limited by the personal interlocks between the publicly listed firms, and the codetermination regime. Baums insists real influence was in the hands of a small number of individuals who controlled more than half the positions available on the boards of DAX 30 companies.

Equally the relationships in Japan are more complex than simply bank lenders acting as idealised shareholder monitors. Aoki (1990) suggests that before the long economic crisis of Japan commencing in the early 1990s, the system involved interdependencies between vertically related nonfinancial firms, nonhierarchical management practices, and a highly articulated incentive structure that included the norm of life time employment in the major corporations. Japanese banks did play a key role in providing substantial funds to firms, allowing investment plans to proceed with diminished sensitivity to internal cash flow (Hoshi *et al.* 1991). If this allowed sustained growth during the long Japanese march to overwhelm overseas markets, continuing expansionary lending when opportunities and cash flow were drying up as the bubble was about to burst could not have helped the corporations they were supposed to be monitoring. When attention turns as in Germany, to the role of industrial cross-shareholdings in the Japanese *keiretsus*, the purpose of these was largely to stabilise long-term relational contracts among members of vertical production groups, rather than to exercise any monitoring function (Bratton and McCahery 2000).

Many commentators have argued there will a be a gradual unwinding of majority group control at least in the leading industrial countries as equity markets deepen, as institutions continue to grow and invest overseas, and as national regulation becomes less benign towards group formation and existence. There has been a rapid growth of the number of listed companies in France, Germany, and Spain, and a remarkable growth in market capitalisation across all European markets. A significant measure of the scale of this growth is stock market capitalisation as a percentage of Gross Domestic Product, which in the Netherlands is approaching US and UK levels.

In Germany the 50 per cent capital gains tax on the sale of shares, which locked financial institutions into their web of cross-shareholdings, was abolished in 2002, and created the possibility of reducing vast blocks of shares, and precipitating merger and acquisition activity and shareholder activism (Coffee 2002).

The rapid and sustained growth of market capitalisation in the stock markets of Europe at least, will unsettle the established groups and networks of the past. Davis and Steil argue: 'In corporate finance, major changes are in prospect as institutions impact on bank-based systems of corporate governance … European and Japanese financial systems are likely to shift to an Anglo-Saxon paradigm under pressure from institutionalization, although the processes will be slow' (2000: 6). Yet the institutional and cultural differences which persist, and the complementarities that make these different systems both coherent and viable, are a resilient manifestation of *path dependence* in the view of Bebchuk and Roe (2004). While insistent market pressures may cause changes to occur, enduring institutional complementarities will survive.

### The market for corporate control

The market for corporate control whereby a company perceived to be not performing well, or to have hidden assets which were not being utilized, could be put into play, is one of the most severe disciplinary mechanisms in the market based model of corporate governance. Though always present, this was a particularly brutal restraining influence on management in the US in the 1970s and 1980s whether it was the threat of a takeover bid, or cash or leveraged buyout. Such takeovers usually involved both the removal of the incumbent management and the radical restructuring of the company to release the revenue to meet the cost of the takeover. 'While merger and acquisition activity in the 1980s positively restructured some overextended conglomerates, it also had a downside. It was associated with reductions in plant and R&D expenditures, showed no net positive effects on productivity, and did not have clear efficiency advantages once its redistributional elements (from incumbent employees to shareholders) were factored into the analysis' (Jacoby 2002: 18).

Yet even in the 1980s takeover rates rarely exceeded 1.5 per cent (the number of bids as a percentage of the number of listed companies) and they declined steeply later. Moreover only 4 per cent of all US deals were hostile, suggesting the threat of hostile takeover was greater than the reality (Becht *et al.* 2002: 70). However, by the 1990s, with the help of the courts, corporate management had erected a series of defences against takeovers. In marked contrast takeovers were a comparatively rare event in Europe, and hostile takeovers unheard of, particularly in Germany.

Yet with the new found enthusiasm for equity markets in Europe in the 1990s, corporate takeovers became a more widespread and aggressive phenomenon throughout the continent. Occasionally the most publicised takeovers involved US or UK corporations such as General Motors acquiring half ownership of Saab in 1989, or Ford Motors' takeover of Volvo Motors in 1999. The largest hostile takeover threatened in German industrial history occurred in 2000 when the UK mobile phone group Vodafone bid $199 billion for Mannesmann which shocked the German public and led to a broad debate on the future of the German model of capitalism. German trade unions and the Mannesmann works councils strongly rejected Vodafone's bid, in order to defend the German culture of corporate governance which is based on strong employee involvement and co-determination. With the employees' viewpoint supported by almost all major political parties in Germany, Vodafone reacted to the criticism by saying that, after a takeover of Mannesmann, it would fully accept the German system of industrial relations and corporate governance (see Case Study 7).

Hostile takeovers were also experienced within European countries, in Italy with the bids of Olivetti for Telecom Italia; and Generali for INA; and in France with the bids of BNP for Paribas; and Elf Aquitaine for Total Fina. As European companies which had always been active acquiring companies outside Europe, began bidding for each other with greater enthusiasm, the number of takeovers increased significantly in the 1990s, but never reached the frequency experienced in the US and UK (Table 3.3). This provoked

|        | Australia | Canada | US | EU 15 | Total–UK | Ex–UK | Other |
|--------|-----------|--------|------|-------|----------|-------|-------|
| Number of announced uncontested takeovers[1] | | | | | | | |
| *1989* | 81  | 184 | 1,188 | 550 | 316 | 234 | 114   |
| *1990* | 69  | 193 | 834   | 597 | 290 | 307 | 188   |
| *1991* | 107 | 269 | 790   | 817 | 252 | 565 | 363   |
| *1992* | 46  | 194 | 746   | 824 | 181 |     |       |
| *1993* | 100 | 215 | 789   | 803 | 196 | 607 | 456   |
| *1994* | 124 | 224 | 1,015 | 816 | 221 | 595 | 614   |
| *1995* | 162 | 296 | 1,106 | 806 | 219 | 587 | 753   |
| *1996* | 142 | 277 | 1,115 | 676 | 195 | 481 | 745   |
| *1997* | 107 | 258 | 1,150 | 574 | 201 | 373 | 726   |
| *1998* | 103 | 231 | 1,203 | 653 | 234 | 419 | 893   |
| *1999* | 100 | 289 | 1,236 | 801 | 271 | 530 | 1,180 |
| Number of announced contested takeovers[2] | | | | | | | |
| *1989* | 3  | 6  | 45 | 36 | 32 | 4  | 10 |
| *1990* | 2  |    | 12 | 24 | 22 | 2  | 5  |
| *1991* | 8  | 1  | 7  | 34 | 31 | 3  | 2  |
| *1992* | 10 | 2  | 7  | 20 | 15 | 5  | 4  |
| *1993* | 10 | 1  | 11 | 15 | 11 | 4  | 5  |
| *1994* | 8  | 11 | 33 | 11 | 8  | 3  | 4  |
| *1995* | 18 | 19 | 59 | 22 | 14 | 6  | 7  |
| *1996* | 22 | 8  | 45 | 20 | 13 | 7  | 11 |
| *1997* | 12 | 17 | 27 | 23 | 11 | 12 | 5  |
| *1998* | 12 | 14 | 19 | 14 | 12 | 2  | 5  |
| *1999* | 15 | 6  | 19 | 42 | 21 | 21 | 6  |

**Table 3.3** Number of takeovers, by region.

Source: Becht, M., Bolton, P., and Röell, A., (2003), *Corporate Governance and Control*, in G. M. Constantinides, M. Harris and R. Stulz (eds), Handbook of Finance, 2003, Elsevier.
Notes
[1] Under the Thomson Financial Data (TFSD) definition a tender offer that was recommended by board of the target company to its shareholders.
[2] Under the TFSD definition a tender offer that was initially rejected by the board of the target company.

questions regarding managerial accountability and the nature of the firm (Deakin and Slinger 1997). A protracted debate in the European Community on the Takeover Bid Directive reflected differing conceptions of the firm, with the liberal conception of the firm belonging to the shareholders, opposed by the continental conception of the company as a community, with management obliged to act in the wider corporate interest (Aglietta and Reberioux 2005: 67).

In the end the text left considerable freedom for member states to make their own choice of rules regarding takeovers. In France a series of reforms in 2001 eased the path of takeovers, though not entirely as the law established an obligation to inform and consult with the works council of targeted firms. In Germany there was a strengthening of anti-takeover devices, as though accepting a takeover becomes obligatory when a shareholder exceeds a threshold of 30 per cent of voting rights, the law allowed managers to erect takeover defences as long as this occurred before any bid took place. The role of the supervisory board is increased during takeovers, and the works council is required to be informed by both sides (Aglietta and Reberioux 2005: 70). It appears that with regard to takeover regulation a specifically European solution is emerging.

In conclusion regarding the impact of different modes of financing, Aglietta and Reberioux (2001) conceive of three corporate governance regimes, which may coexist and compete with each other: internal control, majority group control, and market control (Table 3.4). In a later formulation (2005) they elaborate the three regimes as: *Internal control* involves control by banks and constraint by debt, with the dominant strategy being internal growth resulting in the entrenchment of technocratic managers. *Majority shareholding group control* involves an alliance between majority shareholders, managers, and/or institutional investors. While institutional investors rely on governance charters, majority shareholders can exert influence through the board of directors. For the two kinds of investor the dominant strategy is return on equity capital. *Control by the stock market* is the third regime, with a dominant strategy as the maximisation of market value through external growth, and to protect the company from takeover bids. The success of one of these forms of control over the others depends on the dominant financial logic:

> The performance of the firm is determined by the interdependencies between the strategy of the managerial team and the financial partners ... The firm has relations with three types of financial agents: the banks, which are assumed to represent all credit markets; the controlling group of shareholders; and the shareholders and potential inventors who are preoccupied by the dividend yield and the liquidity of their shares. The firm pursues its own objectives, which are those of its managers. The firm is not the agent of any principal. However it takes into account the constraints imposed by the financial players. Its objectives are those which enable the managers to perpetuate their power. The growth of the firm through the investment of its profit is the primary source of this power. Nonetheless, the threat of the market for corporate control obliges managers to concern themselves with their survival.
>
> (Aglietta and Reberioux 2005: 85)

## ALTERNATIVE CORPORATE GOVERNANCE SYSTEMS

Whatever the pressures towards convergence the alternative corporate governance systems continue to demonstrate profoundly different characteristics and orientations. The dispersed ownership, market based, Anglo-American

| Forms of control | Control by debt | Control by the securities market | Control by shares |
|---|---|---|---|
| Nature of control and basis of evaluation | Solvency prime rate + bank risk premium | Market for control (take-over bid; public offer of exchange) market price/private evaluation of the firm's potential | Financial evaluation of performance (EVA/MVA) |
| Style of governance and constraints on the company | Long-term commitment | Threat to oust the controlling group | Charters of governance |
| | Solvency constraint | Maximisation of share price | Maximisation of the financial return on equity |
| Types of capitalism | Corporative | Predator | Shareholder value |

Table 3.4  Corporate governance regimes.

Source: Aglietta Michael and Regis Breton (2001), 'Financial Systems, Corporate Control and Capital Accumulation', *Economy and Society*, 30, 4, 433–66. Table 2: Types of Corporate Governance, p. 444.

corporate governance system and the concentrated ownership, European and Asian relationship based corporate governance systems are described by a variety of names that reflect the emphasis of their different characteristics: including market systems and blockholder systems, rules based and relationship based systems, and market and bank based systems. The simplest characterisation is that between outsider and insider based systems.

Market based outsider systems are typified by dispersed ownership, a clear separation of ownership and control, lower debt/equity ratios, and sophisticated financial markets. In this system there is less incentive for outsiders to participate in the control of the corporation, except insofar as they do so through the equity markets, and the severest sanction is hostile takeover. The interests of outside stakeholders are not formally represented, and investors themselves often have less interest in the strategic goals of the enterprise than in the short term returns that are available in the market based system. In contrast insider systems are typified by highly concentrated ownership which is closely connected with the managerial control of the enterprise, and high debt/equity ratios, with a higher rate of bank credits due to the closer relationship with banks that are often represented on the board of major corporations along with other stakeholders including related firms and employees. In these insider systems hostile takeovers are rare and there is often a dense network of supportive relationships with related businesses that occasionally can develop into collusion.

An intense debate has continued since the 1990s concerning the relative merits of the different corporate governance systems, often with the assumption that the Anglo-American system with stronger security markets and higher levels of disclosure represents a more advanced and efficient mode of corporate finance and governance, and leading to the conclusion that inevitably there will be either an early – or more gradual – shift of the European and Asian systems of corporate governance towards the Anglo-American model (Hansmann and Kraakerman 2001; Branson 2001; McDonnell 2002; McCahery *et al.* 2002; Gordon and Roe 2004; Hamilton and Quinlan 2005). This argument for inevitable convergence tends

to underestimate the extent of the different orientations and objectives of the alternative systems, and fails to appreciate the significance of different cultures and conceptions of what a company is. In different regions of the world there are deeply embedded differences regarding business values and ways of doing things, and very different relationships with stakeholders.

Within the different systems there exist profoundly contrasting beliefs on the role of the market, that influence the way the corporation is considered: simply as a bundle of tradable assets in the most venal interpretation of the market based system; but as a productive institution to be passed on to future generations in the best interpretation of the insider governance system. Consequently different measures of performance are applied, with the market based system looking for short term returns, and the European and Japanese systems having much longer term horizons (Table 3.5).

As a result of the differences in corporate governance structure and objectives, the different systems demonstrate unique strengths and weaknesses: they are good at doing different things, and they all have weaknesses (Moerland 1995; Dore 2002). Anglo-American governance systems support a dynamic market orientation, with fluid capital which can quickly chase market opportunities wherever they occur. This agility, intelligence and speed equipped the United States to capitalise on the new economy of electronics, software, media, financial and professional services: an industrial resurgence that reasserted the US global economic ascendancy. The weakness of this system is the corollary of its strength: the inherent volatility, short termism and inadequate governance procedures that have often left US manufacturing industry stranded, and caused periodic stock market panics and occasional crashes that left the least well informed investors with serious losses.

Adopting a very different orientation, European enterprise as typified by the German governance system traditionally has committed to a long term industrial strategy supported by stable capital investment and robust governance procedures that build enduring relationships with key stakeholders (Cernat 2004; Lane 2003). This was the foundation of the German economic

| Feature | Anglo-Saxon | Germanic | Latin | Japanese |
|---|---|---|---|---|
| **Orientation** | Market oriented (an active external market for corporate control) | Market-oriented (relatively oligarchic, influenced by networks of shareholders, families and banks) | Network-oriented | Network-oriented |
| **Representative countries** | USA, UK, Canada, Australia, NZ | Germany, Netherlands, Switzerland, Sweden, Austria, Denmark, Norway, Finland | France, Italy, Spain, Belgium, Brazil, Argentina | Japan |
| **Prevailing concept of the firm** | Instrumental (as a means for creative shareholder value) | Institutional (autonomous economic units coming out of a coalition of shareholders, corporate managers, suppliers of goods and debts, and customers) | Institutional | Institutional |
| **The board system** | One-tier (governance with one level of directors, making no distinction but executives and non-executives | Two-tier (executive and supervisory board, the latter monitoring, appointing or dismissing managers; large shareholders on the board and high pressure from banks) | Optional (France) in general one-tier | Board of directors, offices of representative directors, of auditors, de facto one-tier |
| **Main stakeholders to exert influence on managerial decision-making** | Shareholders | Industrial banks (mainly in Germany; in general, oligarchic group inclusive of employees' representatives) | Financial holdings, the government, families, in general oligarchic groups | City banks, other financial institutions, employees in general oligarchic groups |
| **Importance of stock and bond markets** | High (requiring continued action and performance) | Moderate or high (legal and regulatory bias against non-bank finance) | Moderate or poor | High (legal and regulatory bias against non-bank finance) |

Table 3.5 Corporate governance alternative systems.

| Feature | Anglo-Saxon | Germanic | Latin | Japanese |
|---|---|---|---|---|
| **Is there a market for corporate control?** | Yes | No | No | No |
| **Ownership concentration** | Low | Moderate or high (very high in Germany) | High | Low or moderate |
| **Compensation based on performance** | High | Low | Moderate | Low |
| **Time horizon of economic relationships** | Short-termism (management and governance myopia) | Long termism | Long termism | Long termism |
| **Strengths** | Dynamic market orientation, fluid capital, internationalisation extensive | Long-term industrial strategy, very stable capital, robust governance procedures | | Very long-term industrial strategy, stable capital, major overseas investment |
| **Weaknesses** | Volatile, short-termism, inadequate | Internationalisation more difficult, lack of flexibility, inadequate investment for new industries | | Financial speculation, secretive governance procedures, weak accountability |

Table 3.5—Cont'd

Sources: Adapted from Keenan J. and Aggestam M. (2001), 'Corporate Governance and Intellectual Capital: Some Conceptualizations', *Empirical Research Based and Theory Building Papers*, 9, 4, Blackwell Publishers, *Taxonomy of Systems of Corporate Governance*, Table 1, p. 261. Clarke, T. and Bostock, R. (1994), 'International Corporate Governance: Convergence and Diversity', in, T. Clarke and E. Monkhouse, *Rethinking the Company*, London: Financial Times Pitman.

miracle which carried the country forward to becoming the leading exporter in the world of products renowned for their exceptional quality and reliability including luxury automobiles, precision instruments, chemicals, and electrical engineering. For some decades in the post-war era Germany appeared to have resolved extremely well the dual dilemmas of achieving economic prosperity and social stability. Again the weaknesses of the German system are the corollary of its strengths: the depth of relationships leading to a lack of flexibility, which make it difficult to pursue initiatives for new businesses and industries while accumulating costs in established companies, the resulting inability or unwillingness

to hire labour becoming associated with sustained unemployment.

In a very Southern European way the Latin variant of corporate governance as practised in France and Italy is highly network oriented, with dominant holdings by the state, families, or industrial groups. Protective ownership concentration provides for stability and long term horizons, with strong relationships with stakeholders. This governance system has allowed the Southern European countries to specialise in selected industries with notable success. For example in France state sponsored prestige industries such as aerospace, nuclear and high-tech train manufacture industries have flourished, along with an array of

leading international luxury goods companies. Italy remains the world leader in high quality fashion goods, particularly designer clothing, that have delighted the world (Goyer 2001). Yet in this system, weak governance accountability and frequent network and pyramid control diminishes the integrity of the equity market: the strength of the blockholder relationships precludes others from becoming involved, and casts a shadow over the probity of corporate dealings.

Finally the Asian corporate governance system is the most network based of all, with the firm as the institutional centre of long enduring and deep economic relationships of investors, employees, suppliers and customers (Claessens and Fan 2002). In the Japanese system traditionally there was a close dependence on bank finance and insider control. This insider approach has yielded the longest investment horizons of all, and was the key to the Japanese success in progressively dominating overseas markets in the US and Europe in advanced electronic goods that created and defined consumer markets, as well as in quality low cost automobiles and motorcycles, products that required persistent skill development and patient innovation. The Japanese economic miracle came to an abrupt and shattering end when paying the price for its own success, the hugely speculative bubble burst in the early 1990s, with the resulting decade-long disorientation revealing the weaknesses of Japanese secretive and unaccountable governance.

## CONTROL MECHANISMS IN CORPORATE GOVERNANCE

Efforts were made since the origins of the joint-stock company and associated investment and governance systems to redress the evident weaknesses that each system periodically exposed. Every system of corporate governance was punctuated, to a lesser or greater extent by periodic failures as well as notable successes. Problems of accountability, transparency, fairness and openness of governance and finance have persisted widely, though expressed in different ways in different governance systems. Successive attempts to enhance the independence and accountability of directors, to improve disclosure and to

make equity markets more transparent have yielded results, but new problems and issues have inevitably arisen as old abuses have been eliminated. For example the disaffection with the entrenched managerialism of poorly performing US corporations in the early 1980s led to a revival of the market for corporate control: the threat of takeover it was thought would discipline managers, and replace those managers who could not realise the true value of corporate assets (Walsh and Seward 1990; Goldstein 2000; Davis 1991). What began as a revitalising force ultimately resulted in the use of junk bonds in over-priced and reckless financing deals that disrupted corporations rather than stimulating them.

Periodic crisis has inevitably led to insistent calls for better regulation of corporate governance. The Cadbury Report in the UK in 1992 proved a watershed in the international movement to improve corporate governance. Called at the instigation of the London Stock Exchange as a result of a series of large bankruptcies of companies that had recently received favourable audit reports (including Maxwell, Polly Peck and the Bank of Credit and Commerce International), Cadbury set out a code of best practice that was subsequently emulated by countries worldwide as part of their stock exchange listing requirements (Aguilera and Cuervo-Cazurra 2004). Central to the code was the division of responsibilities at the head of the company, with independent non-executive directors responsible for the audit committee, and remuneration of senior executives, and the board reporting on the effectiveness of internal financial controls and verifying the business as a going concern. Companies were left with a choice whether to comply with the guidelines or to offer an explanation to the market as to the reason for their divergence.

These principles represented an important step forward in restoring a sense of the responsibility and accountability of boards and directors, however this was only effective and meaningful in the context of the efficacy of wider institutional disciplines, and the work of other reputational intermediaries in corporate governance (Table 3.6). Hence the independence and accountability of boards of directors requires the reinforcement of the duty of disclosure policed by effective regulators and well-functioning legal systems. In addition,

| Disclosure | ■ Securities laws on full disclosure of financial results and self-dealing transactions<br>■ Ownership disclosure rules<br>■ One-share, one-vote rule. In general, rules to prevent or restrict pyramid ownership structures<br>■ Strong publicly enforced civil and criminal sanctions against insiders for violating the disclosure and self-dealing rules<br>■ Civil liability risk for insiders<br>■ Honest, sophisticated and well-functioning courts<br>■ Honest, sophisticated securities agency and prosecutors for criminal cases both furnished with staff, skills and budget to accomplish their tasks efficiently |
|---|---|
| Board of directors | ■ Independent directors who can control self-dealing transactions<br>■ Procedural controls on self-dealing transactions with review by independent directors, non-interested shareholders, or both<br>■ Civil liability risk for independent directors who approve gross self-dealing transactions.<br>■ Independent directors on auditing and compensations committees |
| Market environment | ■ Market transparency rules (time, quantity and price of trades promptly disclosed to investors)<br>■ Investor property rights protection<br>■ Stock exchange with reliable listing standards and active surveillance of insider trading to fine or delist trespassers.<br>■ Enforced ban on market manipulation<br>■ A culture of disclosure ('concealing bad news is a recipe for trouble')<br>■ Active financial press and securities analysts' profession<br>■ Reliable judiciary system and widespread law enforcement |
| Reputational intermediaries     Accountants | ■ Good accounting and auditing rules<br>■ Accounting review of self-dealing transactions<br>■ Civil liability risk for accountants<br>■ An institution with competence and independence to write accounting rules |
|     Lawyers | ■ Sophisticated accounting profession<br>■ Securities lawyers to ensure issuers abide by the law and rules of disclosure<br>■ Civil discovery rules and class action procedure to protect minority rights<br>■ Liability risk<br>■ Lawyers' review of self-dealing transactions |

Table 3.6 Reputational intermediaries for sound corporate governance.

| Investment bankers | ▪ Sophisticated banking profession to investigate the issuers of securities |
| | ▪ Civil liability risk for investment bankers |
| Other reputational intermediaries | 1 Rating agencies that furnish not only credit-risk rating but also country-risk ratings worldwide |
| | 2 Venture capital funds that allow new enterprises to be financed and monitored, and also provide them with reputational capital |
| | 3 Public regulators, like central banks and securities exchange commissions |
| | 4 Self-regulatory organizations (SRO), either voluntary or mandatory, subject to regulatory oversight |
| | 5 Corporate monitoring firms (Latham 1999) |

Table 3.6—Cont'd

Source: Apreda Rodolfo (2003), 'The Semantics of Governance', University of CEMA, Working Paper 245, September, 20.

market transparency, well-run stock exchanges with effective restrictions on market manipulation and competent securities analysts and financial journalists are necessary. Finally the engaged and capable practice of a range of professional intermediaries is required including independent accountants and auditors, sophisticated lawyers and bankers, and active external monitoring agencies (Black 2000; Nolke 2003).

Despite the apparently increasing rigour of the extensive monitoring and disciplinary mechanisms of corporate governance, all of the methods available have limitations that have created the possibility for executives, who are determined to do so, to readily escape effective monitoring, at least for significant periods of time, until poor performance cannot be concealed any longer. Bebchuk and Fried (2003) reveal how successive efforts to incentivise senior executives by linking their pay to performance and aligning their interests to shareholders with stock options, can either be manipulated, or reward managers when equity markets are inflated rather than corporate performance improving. Similarly, transparency can be camouflaged and board committees unduly influenced. Finally, executives have built defences against the market for corporate control, and ensured they benefit whatever occurs (Table 3.7). The difficulties experienced in exercising effective governance with regard to managerial activity,

combined with the inevitable cycle of market growth and recession, and the tendency for ambitious strategies to come adrift when tested by a sudden collapse in the market, provokes recurring problems and periodic crises in corporate governance (MacAvoy and Millstein 2004; Roe 2005; Aglietta and Reberioux 2005).

## CRISES IN CORPORATE GOVERNANCE

Cycles of corporate governance in their normal form are associated with examples of corporate failure, and board and executive negligence revealed when long periods of expansion are replaced by recession. However longer – and more dramatic – cycles of systemic governance failure occur when burgeoning prosperity is followed by catastrophic collapse, most spectacularly in the Wall Street crash. That such events have not been consigned to history was revealed by the Asian financial crisis of 1997/1998, when the equity and currency markets collapsed, in what were up till this point portrayed as the high performance economies of South-east Asia. International agencies took this crisis as evidence of the inherent weakness of Asian modes of corporate governance, and as proof of the need to adopt rules based systems of governance and market disciplines (Clarke 2000).

| Device | Rationale | Limits |
|---|---|---|
| **Incentive pay** | | |
| Indexing wage on performance | Aligning managers' and rank-and-file workers' interests | Possible manipulation of performance by managers |
| Bonus linked to profit | Aligning managers' interests and firm strategy | |
| Stock options | Aligning CEO interest with shareholders' wealth | Still a major gap between CEO and shareholders' interests |
| Attribution of stock of the company | Aligning CEO interest with shareholders' wealth | Loosely correlated with CEO strategy and large benefits during financial bubble |
| **Transparency** | | |
| Public disclosure of CEO's remuneration | Trigger *outrage* from shareholders and institutional investors | *Camouflage* tactic by managers in spite of statements in favour of transparency |
| **Remuneration setting** | | |
| Creation of an independent remuneration committee | Prevent self-determination of remuneration by CEOs | The CEO may largely control the committee |
| Large number of independent members of the board | Prevent excessive remuneration by the detriment of shareholders | The income of members may depend on their generosity to the manager |
| Survey by consultant firms of CEO remuneration | Set an objective benchmark | The reference to average or median remuneration induces spill-over and excessive pay increases |
| **Market for corporate governance** | | |
| Firing of CEOs | Incentive to commitment | Exceptional configuration in the past |
| Threat of takeover | Puts a limit on CEO opportunism | Golden parachute for losers; CEO income may increase even if shareholders suffer value destruction |

Table 3.7 How efficient are the various methods of controlling managers?

Source: Bebchuk, Lucian Ayre and Fried, Jesse M. (2003), 'Executive Compensation as an Agency Problem', *Journal of Economic Perspectives*, 17, 3, 71–92.

However, just as the OECD, World Bank and IMF were increasingly confidently projecting the Anglo-American market based outsider system of governance as the preeminent model from which all other countries might learn, the Enron disaster occurred in 2001 closely followed by a series of other massive bankruptcies and scandals of leading corporations in the US including WorldCom, Tyco, Adelphia, Global Crossing and Arthur Anderson. The Sarbanes–Oxley Act was

rushed through Congress in an atmosphere of corporate crisis, in an effort to enforce financial discipline and impose tighter rules of accountability upon executives and directors (Gordon 2002; Coffee 2002).

The imposition of more stringent rules is unlikely to be effective if there are structural problems in US governance systems that remain unreformed. To illustrate, just one of the fundamental structural flaws Sarbanes–Oxley did not confront: the power and rewards of chief executives of US corporations have in recent decades escalated in ways that distort and frequently destabilise the governance system. Congress did not attempt to separate the roles of chair and chief executive, positions formally separated in most countries to ensure some balance of power and openness on the board. In contrast in the US, though the practice of CEOs filling boards with their friends is now less evident, in many corporations the CEO remains in a very dominant position in relationship to the board, and often only subject to challenge when things go badly wrong. The increasing adoption of a lead independent director on boards of US corporations is a step towards balancing the power of the CEO with the weight of non-executive board directors, but this is not the same as having an independent chair. Though more US companies are capitulating to the demands for an independent chair, other CEOs/presidents/chairs are maintaining a resolute opposition to any diminution or redistribution of their powers. (The combined role is 'part of the American way of life' one outraged US CEO insisted in a broadcast radio debate – 'it's part of the American CEO's way of life' some other directors later retorted).

Paradoxically it was the 1990s, when the greatest effort was made to align executives better with shareholders' interests with the issue of stock options, which witnessed the greatest accretion of executive power, reflected in the explosion of CEO compensation that occurred during this decade. It is particularly worrying that this pattern of extreme inequality is being conveyed as an acceptable component of the Anglo-American corporate governance system to other countries of the world, and is beginning to have some effect in this regard: in countries such as Germany and Japan where executive rewards have traditionally been modest relative to employee rewards, the first indications of a disruption of this equitable arrangement are being experienced.

The corrosive greed that became an integral part of the incentive system in US corporate governance yielded a more sinister fruit in the protracted spate of corporate frauds and bankruptcies of 2001/2002 leading to the collapse of the NASDAQ and NYSE. The apparently dynamic, competitive and performance oriented US economy of the 1990s over time degenerated as executives – faced with the necessity to demonstrate ever increasing returns – resorted to illegal means to do so (Boyer 2005; Aglietta and Reberioux 2005). Creative accounting and an often criminal collusion between executives, auditors and analysts fed a speculative bubble which finally burst, but not before many executives had cashed in their options, leaving their own employees destitute and superannuation funds depleted around the world.

Reacting to this betrayal, John C. Bogle, a long-standing CEO of a US mutual fund condemns what he describes as a 'pathological mutation' from traditional owner capitalism to new forms of managerial capitalism (2005). He rages against the

enormous transfer of wealth from public investors to the hands of business leaders, corporate insiders, and financial intermediaries during stock market booms and bust. Much of the responsibility for this subversion of capitalism lies in the diffusion of ownership of corporate America, and the resultant vacuum of ownership power ... Our traditional gatekeepers – corporate directors, auditors, the financial community, and regulators and legislators – failed to protect the owners against overreaching by management, reinforcing the principle that 'somebody's gotta keep an eye on these geniuses'.

Bogle refers to a study of the five highest-paid executives in each of 1,500 companies in the S&P 500, Mid-Cap 400, and Small Cap 600 during 1993–2003 which found that the amount paid totalled over $300 billion. During this same period, reported corporate earnings grew 1.9 per cent per year, while executive pay increased from 4.8 per cent to 10.3 per cent of company earnings.

Meanwhile, some 1,570 public companies restated earnings from 2000 to 2004, seven times the 218 companies that did so in 1990–1994. Many executives within these firms received bonuses based on the inflated results, but Bogle knew of none that returned part or all of their bonuses upon restatement (2005: 111).

The European and Asian forms of corporate governance also have from time to time experienced some acute difficulties. Though the Europeans have not witnessed anything quite as catastrophic as the US corporate collapses in 2001/2002, there have periodically been disasters, for example the Ahold scandal revealed European companies were not immune to inflated earnings (a weakness apparently contracted in the companies' US operations). The Parmalat debacle revealed a leading Italian listed company was used for many years as personal property by its chief executive, who apparently felt free to bestow unlimited cash and resources of the publicly owned company on his family members. There are continuing doubts concerning the close network relationships that typify much of European enterprise (see Case Studies 4 and 5).

Systemic weaknesses are more apparent still in Asian modes of governance, where the separation of ownership and control has not taken hold, and highly incestuous family relationships determine the direction of most companies:

> In all East Asian countries control is enhanced through pyramid structures. and cross-holdings, among firms. Voting rights consequently exceed formal cash flow rights, especially in Indonesia, Japan and Singapore. We find that more than two thirds of firms are controlled by a single shareholder. Separation of management from ownership control is rare, and the top management of about 60 per cent of firms that are not widely held is related to the family of controlling shareholder.
>
> (Claessens *et al.* 2000)

Research by Claessens *et al.* reveals countries in Asia with a higher concentration of ownership of companies among a few families or block-holders show the least progress in adopting institutional reforms. Hence insider controlled companies are frequently associated with a neglect of minority shareholder rights, as legal and judicial systems are not developed or active, and widespread corruption is often tolerated.

It is clear that corporate governance – always a work in progress – is presently at something of an impasse. The strenuous efforts by the OECD to enhance and extend corporate governance regulation will no doubt continue, as will the ongoing commitment to advance company law in many national jurisdictions. However, while the law and regulation might set careful parameters, in market based systems monitoring and enforcement to be viable requires the active vigilance of market institutions that in the recent past has often proved wanting. The rapid rise of the institutional investors however presents a new opportunity for the exercise of the shareholder mandate, the question is will this make corporations not only more accountable, but more responsible?

## THE INCREASING IMPORTANCE OF INSTITUTIONAL INVESTORS

The growing economic significance of institutional investors suggests they may be central to the future transformation of corporate governance. The institutional investors' simultaneous and contradictory desires for the immediate results of short term returns, sustained performance, and corporate social responsibility are creating corporate governance confusion. As the power of the institutions expands further they could either become an irresistible force for further economic instability induced by short-termism, or they could impress upon markets and companies' longer-term horizons, and the pursuit of sustainability. The implications of the increasing scale and activity of the institutional investors upon corporate governance have yet to be fully understood and appreciated including:

1 the complex relationships that exist across the institutional investment sector, in which corporate governance will play a greater role as the funds under the control of these institutions further increase;
2 the increasing sophistication of the corporate governance policies of the institutional investors;

3 the significance of the institutions' own governance as they seek to influence the entities in which they invest, and the criticality of the governance of the investment value chain, the complexities of which have often remained hidden;

4 the efficiency and effectiveness of existing methods of institutional investor participation in corporate governance, including voting procedures, the conduct of AGMs and other forms of corporate engagement with institutional shareholders;

5 the nature of investment institutions' trustees' roles, resources and expertise in carrying out their responsibilities;

6 how in carrying out their fiduciary duties institutional investor principals and agents exercise their discretion with regard to investment risk, performance, investment horizons and sustainability.

## Increasing scale and activity

As the financial scale and significance of the institutional investors, including the insurance companies, pension funds, mutual funds, and the fund managers, continues to increase, they are destined to play an ever-increasing role in economic life.

The concentration of wealth in the hands of the investment institutions has gradually accumulated over recent decades, but recently this accumulation has accelerated significantly. OECD figures indicate the total assets of the pension funds and life insurance companies in the United States reached $13.43 trillion by 2004, equivalent to 115 per cent of US GDP; in the UK the assets of pension funds and insurance companies totalled $2.47 trillion, amounting to 116 per cent of GDP; in the Netherlands pension fund and life insurance assets were $813 billion, equivalent to 140 per cent of GDP; and in Australia reached $582 billions by 2004, which was the equivalent of 91.3 per cent of GDP (Table 3.8). While it is the case that countries with different insurance, pension and social security provisions including Germany, Japan and France have invested less in private pensions and life insurance, there are indications of a sustained increase in the assets of the institutional investors across the industrial countries caused by demographic changes and institutional reforms (principally the increasing reluctance of the state to bear the social security costs of an ageing population).

A growing proportion of this investment is in equities, exceeding 50 per cent of the total of the institutional investors' portfolio in the US, UK and Australia by 1999 (OECD 2001), and for major

| OECD countries | Total assets for pension funds + life insurance investments (2003) | | Total assets for pension funds + life insurance investments (2004) | |
|---|---|---|---|---|
| | Millions of $ | As a % of GDP | Millions of $ | As a % of GDP |
| Australia | 393,765 | 74.7 | 582,886 | 91.3 |
| Canada | 618,724 | 72.2 | 662,448 | 77.3 |
| Denmark | 178,408 | 84.2 | 221,356 | 91.7 |
| France | 847,335 | 48.2 | 1,055,250 | 60 |
| Germany | 713,988 | 29.7 | 878,653 | 31.9 |
| Japan | 2,093,976 | 48.7 | 2,250,987 | 48.2 |
| Netherlands | 709,708 | 138.4 | 813,135 | 140.4 |
| Switzerland | 522,283 | 162.3 | 549,486 | 153.2 |
| United Kingdom | 2,121,652 | 118 | 2,475,540 | 116.2 |
| United States | 12,252,046 | 111.9 | 13,432,423 | 115 |
| **Total** | **20,451,885** | **88.83** | **22,922,164** | **92.52** |

Table 3.8 Pension funds and life insurance assets in selected OECD economies, 2003–2004.

Source: Abridged version from 'OECD Global Pension Markets in Focus', December 2005.

pension funds the proportion in domestic and overseas equities has been 65 per cent+ for some time (Figure 3.3). As a consequence, the institutional investors have become the major shareholders not only in the United States, United Kingdom and Australia, but in almost all other advanced industrial countries. Collectively assuming the role of majority shareholders has invested the institutions with considerable responsibilities for the effectiveness of corporate governance systems. Active shareholders are the key to market-based regulation. As Adrian Cadbury the originator of the most influential corporate governance code of best practice, and Ira Millstein the chair of the OECD Business Sector Advisory Group recently cautioned, 'Without the threat of active and engaged shareholders, the entire corporate system lacks its basic foundation' (2005: 17). This principle is recognised in law in most jurisdictions, as in the well-known Delaware opinion which states that, 'the shareholder franchise is the ideological underpinning upon which the legitimacy

of directorial power rests' (*Blasius Industries, Inc. v. Atlas Corp.*, 564 A.2d 651, 659 (Del. Ch. 1988).

The effectiveness of an enabling approach to regulation, Cadbury and Millstein go on to argue, depends on the degree to which shareholders, and especially institutional investors, are prepared to use their influence to support governance standards. 'Codes of good practice gave investors an agenda for their dialogues with boards and encouraged them to engage in such dialogues' (Cadbury and Millstein 2005: 11). This attribution of a driving role for institutional shareholders in the application of higher standards of corporate governance was first made in the Cadbury Report:

The widespread adoption of our recommendations will turn in large measure on the support which all shareholders give to them. The obligation on companies to state how far they comply with the Code provides institutional and individual shareholders with a ready-made

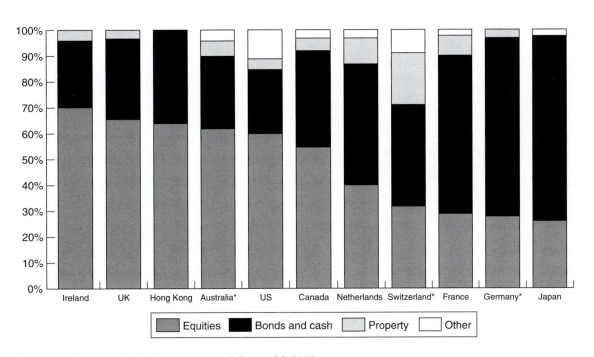

**Figure 3.3** Pension fund allocation around the world, 2003.

Source: Watson Wyatt (2004), *The Role of Equities in Pension Funds*, Technical and Policy Paper, Europe, November, Zurich: Watson Wyatt.

Notes

*Allocations as at 31 December, 2003. Switzerland. Other includes cash.

agenda for their representations to boards. It is up to them to put it to good use. The Committee is primarily looking to such market-based regulation to turn its proposals into action.

(1992: 52)

Yet it is often commented the shareholder franchise, at least as far as the institutional investors are able or willing to exercise it, is largely mythological (Bebchuk 2005). Andrew Clearfield responsible for international corporate governance at TIAA-CREF the world's largest pension fund with $324 billion in assets, puts the matter starkly in perspective:

As the consensus in favour of a more shareholder-friendly approach to corporate governance has gained ground over the past ten to fifteen years, one factor has remained curiously constant: the inertia of the bulk of shareholding institutions in the face of initiatives seemingly in their own interest. Institutional shareholders do not like to vote shares against incumbent managements. Often, they prefer not to vote shares at all … Having won back rights denied minority shareholders since the ascendancy of managerial capitalism, institutions which control more than half the world's

wealth seem as disinclined to exercise their prerogatives as the mythical small investor from the hinterland ever was.

(Clearfield 2005: 114–115)

## Patient capital?

Expectations that the financial institutions might exert a beneficial impact upon standards of corporate governance and corporate performance have in the past often proved unrealistic. Institutional investors are not a monolithic body. Different types of institutional investors have different investment strategies and time horizons (Figure 3.4). Corporate governance is less of a concern if a share holding is a very transitory price based transaction. While the life insurance and pension funds have long term horizons and often look to equity investments to offer durable and stable returns, the behaviour of other market participants is often focused on the shorter term, and more interested in immediate fluctuations in stock prices than in the implications of corporate governance for the future prospects of a company. Lazonick suggests that even when institutional investors are disposed to take a longer term view, they are subjected to the performance pressures

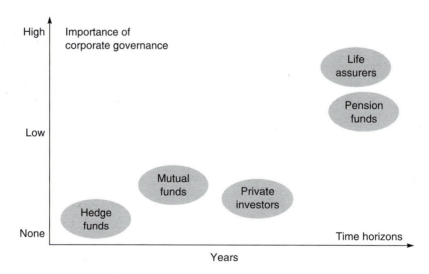

Figure 3.4 Institutional investor concern for corporate governance.

Source: Morley Fund Management (2003), Morley, London.

induced by institutions focusing on immediate returns:

> Pension fund managers can generally take a longer-term perspective on the returns to their portfolios than can the mutual-fund managers. Nevertheless even the pension funds (or insurance companies) are loath to pass up the gains that, in a speculative financial era, can be made by taking quick capital gains, and their managers may feel under personal pressure to match the performance of more speculative institutional investors. The more the institutional investors focus on the high returns to their financial portfolios needed to attract household savings and on the constant restructuring of their portfolios to maximize yields, the more their goals represent the antithesis of financial commitment. Driven by the need to compete for the public's savings by showing superior returns, portfolio managers who invest for the long term may find themselves looking for new jobs in the short term.
>
> (1992: 475)

As a result of the institutional investors increasing reliance on sustaining high rates of return to satisfy their beneficiaries, imperceptibly (and often not consciously) they have become implicated as one of the insistent forces pressuring corporate management towards unacceptable practices in order to inflate their earnings and dividends. That is, the institutions themselves are implicated in the causation of the volatile market conditions they often deplore:

> Although the rise of institutional investors over the past twenty years has fueled hopes that their large stakes give them an incentive to monitor, until now institutional investors have made only limited forays into corporate governance. Rather than acting like long-term investors, institutional investors – under pressure to show strong performance of their pension and mutual funds – tend slightly more often to have short-term horizons and 'bubble expectations' that produce distorted investor decision-making (and can have destabilizing effects when bubbles burst).
>
> (Jacoby 2002: 18)

## Hedge funds: the wolf in shareholder's clothing?

The hedge funds have the most transitory and sometimes quixotic interest in the companies and markets in which they invest. Hedge fund investment styles whether driven by opportunism, arbitrage, leverage, or risk, are aggressively focused on securing high returns for the fund, but normally are too arbitrary and fleeting to claim any real interest in anything but the immediate fortunes of the companies they deal in. At this point the rationality of *investing*, is totally overwhelmed by the urge of *gambling* (Niederhoffer 1999: 188–192). As William H. Donaldson, chair of the US Securities and Exchange Commission put it, 'Over time the key question has changed from "what is the best investment?" to "where are the best short-term profit opportunities?" These are two different questions that more often than not will yield different answers' (2005: 4).

If hedge funds had remained a marginal (and slightly suspect) investment category for rich investors this might not have presented too much of a problem, but there has been a phenomenal growth in hedge funds, and there is evidence they are becoming part of mainstream investment strategies. In the US hedge assets grew from $50 billion in 1993 to $592 billion in 2003, an increase of 1084 per cent. (In the same period mutual fund assets in the US increased by 289 per cent from $1.6 trillion to $6.4 trillion) (SEC 2003: 1). By early 2006 Reuters reported that globally 9,000 hedge funds had accumulated assets of $1.18 trillion.

Hedge funds are entities that hold a pool of securities and other assets that in the US do not register their securities offerings under the Securities Act, and are not registered as an investment company under the Investment Company Act. While investment goals vary among hedge funds many seek to achieve a positive, absolute return rather than measuring their performance against a securities index or other benchmark. Hedge funds employ a number of strategies investing in a wide variety of financial instruments. Often the aim is to achieve substantial leverage, sell securities short and employ hedging and arbitrage strategies. It could be argued (and once was by Alan Greenspan, then chair of the Federal Reserve) that

hedge funds by taking speculative, value driven trading positions, enhance liquidity and contribute to market efficiency. Further it could be said they offer a valuable portfolio diversification as hedge fund returns in many cases do not correlate with the broader debt and equity market. Hedge funds avoided registration under the Investment Company Act firstly by having fewer than 100 investors, and by selling their interests only to highly sophisticated investors (SEC 2003: vii–ix).

Hedge funds invest in equities and use leverage and short selling to 'hedge' the portfolio's exposure to movements of the equity markets. However, from their origin hedge funds have skirted controversy, and provoked concerns of inducing systemic risks in financial markets. Early rushes into hedge funds in the 1960s and 1970s were cut short by high losses and bankruptcies. High performance in the late 1980s and early 1990s was tarnished by the claim that hedge fund speculation was responsible for the UK pound having to drop out of the European Currency System in 1992. Similarly, hedge funds were accused of compounding the Asian financial crisis in 1997/1998. In the most critical hedge fund disaster, Long Term Capital Management (LTCM) with two Nobel prize winners in economics on its board, developed a complex model to take advantage of fixed income arbitrage deals, and in 1998 had assets of $4.72 billion and had borrowed over $124.5 billion, and had off-balance sheet derivative positions amounting to $1.25 trillion. In September 1998 when the Russian government defaulted on their bonds, investors bought US treasury bonds, and sold Japanese and European bonds, and left LTCM – which had bet catastrophically the wrong way – with total losses amounting to $4.6 billion. Fear of a chain reaction of debt liquidation that might undermine financial institutions world wide, the New York Federal Reserve bank organised a bail-out by the banks to avoid a wider collapse. William J. McDonough, President of the Federal Reserve Bank of New York, before the Committee on Banking and Financial Services, US House of Representatives on 1 October 1998 justified the rescue in terms of the systemic risk:

Two factors influenced our involvement. First, in the rush of Long-Term Capital's counterparties to close-out their positions, other market participants – investors who had no dealings with Long-Term Capital – would have been affected as well. Second, as losses spread to other market participants and Long-Term Capital's counterparties, this would lead to tremendous uncertainty about how far prices would move. Under these circumstances, there was a likelihood that a number of credit and interest rate markets would experience extreme price moves and possibly cease to function for a period of one or more days and maybe longer. This would have caused a vicious cycle: a loss of investor confidence, leading to a rush out of private credits, leading to a further widening of credit spreads, leading to further liquidations of positions, and so on. Most importantly, this would have led to further increases in the cost of capital to American businesses.

His successor as President and Chief Executive Officer of the Federal Reserve Bank of New York, Timothy F. Geithner, just a few years later offered a more benign view of the increasing role of hedge funds:

Hedge funds play a valuable arbitrage role in reducing or eliminating mispricing of financial information. They are an important source of liquidity, both in periods of calm and stress. They add depth and breadth to our capital markets. By taking risks that would otherwise have remained on the balance sheets of other financial institutions, they provide an important source of risk transfer and diversification. They don't perform these functions out of a sense of noble purpose, of course, but they are a critical part of what makes the US financial markets work relatively well in absorbing shocks and in allocating savings to their highest return. These benefits are less conspicuous than the trauma that has been associated with hedge funds in periods of financial turmoil, but they are substantial.

(Geithner 2004)

Whilst hedge funds may have increased liquidity, they have undoubtedly greatly increased volatility in the process. Continuous trading by

hedge funds has largely accounted for the dramatic increase in the intensity of share trading. A Credit Suisse First Boston Report (2005) cited studies indicating that hedge funds account for between 40–50 per cent of trading activity in the New York Stock Exchange, London Stock Exchange, and account for over 70 per cent of the activity in the convertibles market. More often recently hedge funds have gone beyond share trading to aggressively intervene in the governance of corporations in pursuit of immediate returns:

> As the funds have grown and diversified, they have gone beyond simply creating volatility in stock prices with short-selling activities based on minor fluctuations in quarterly returns. The funds no longer remain passive investors. Rather, they are taking an active stance in the performance of their stocks. If the funds do not see adequate results, they demand changes in strategy, management compensation, director mix, and will even bid for the companies themselves. Further, with billions of dollars on hand, a fund may conduct a buy-out without seeking funding in the open market. The fund manager's justification for the fund's extreme actions is the same as those expressed by both corporate raiders of the 1980s and institutional investors alike. Specifically, the fund managers claim that they are acting to 'help' shareholders reap value. However, hedge funds are not the same breed of investment pool seen in the past … Lack of outside control has given hedge funds free rein to operate, which they have done, by utilizing the nuances associated with corporate voting structures in order to completely entrench their control over corporations.
>
> (Kulpa and Long 2006: 3)

Recently, hedge funds have been at the centre of much merger and takeover activity. In April 2006 Daniel Vasella the head of Novartis, Europe's second largest pharmaceutical group, called for regulators to look into the role of hedge funds in speculation over his company's takeover plans. A slew of rumours of takeover deals was destabilising major European companies not only Novartis and Astra-Zeneca, but Vodafone, BT,

and others. Hedge funds make money from takeovers by arbitraging funds on the difference between a target company's share price after a takeover announcement and the closing price at completion of the deal. 'We've now gone beyond greed and have moved into hubris in the market. It's a lot like 1986/87 in the US', said one anonymous UK based multi-billion dollar hedge fund manager' (*Financial Times*, 18 April 2006).

The US Securities and Exchange Commission (2003) report on the *Implications of the Growth of Hedge Funds* expressed the following concerns:

- *The lack of SEC regulatory oversight of hedge fund*: The SEC instituted 38 enforcement actions involving hedge fund fraud and significant losses to investors in 1999–2003. However, with no regulatory oversight there was an inability to detect fraud at early stages, and intervention occurred only after significant losses had occurred.
- *The lack of meaningful information about hedge funds and hedge fund advisers*: Despite the considerable growth of the hedge fund industry the SEC did not have information about how many hedge funds operated in the US, their assets or who controlled them.
- *The valuation of hedge fund portfolio securities*: The lack of independent valuation of a hedge fund's portfolio of securities when hedge funds have powerful incentives to achieve superior performance as a means to retain investors and raise additional capital.
- *The retailisation of hedge funds*: The original exclusion hedge funds from securities regulation was because they were intended only for sophisticated investors, but with the growth in wealth in the 1990s, more people qualified to invest who had minimal investment experience, and with the proliferation of publicity on hedge funds it was clear a general solicitation to invest was taking place.
- *Conflicts of interest*: Investment advisers must act solely in the best interests of the clients consistent with fiduciary obligations, however hedge fund advisers have substantial conflicts of interest as investors in the fund themselves. Recognising that some of these conflicts are inevitable they must be disclosed to the clients.

Given this litany of regulatory concerns it is more than slightly surprising that institutional investors have proved among the most enthusiastic investors in these vehicles as the SEC comments:

> Perhaps the greatest change in terms of indirect exposure of individual investments in hedge funds has been the frequency with which pension plans, universities, endowments, foundations and other charitable organizations are investing in hedge funds. Pension plans were among the earliest hedge fund investors. The pace of these investments, however has increased over the past few years. The SEC is concerned that recent infusions of funds from public and private pension plans, universities, endowments, foundations and other charitable organizations into hedge funds may raise public policy concerns that heretofore have not been examined. These concerns do not relate to the ability or propriety of pension plan sponsors or trustees making investment decisions to place plan assets into hedge funds. Indeed, many trustees may believe that hedge fund investments are critical parts of a prudent investment strategy. Instead our immediate concern stems from the increasing presence of these investors in hedge funds over which neither the Commission nor any other regulatory authority exercises meaningful oversight.
>
> (2003: 82)

Though inflows of investment into hedge funds remained strong ($47 billion in 2005), some of their appeal is lost when they under-perform rather than outperform the rest of the market as they did in the fourth quarter of 2005, and again in the second quarter of 2006. However, facing lower returns, some hedge funds might be pushed into pursuing even riskier strategies in search of higher returns. At this stage the question is whether hedge funds are searching for market volatility to diversify their return strategies, or attempting to create volatility to achieve this. In this context, in January 2006 the Securities and Exchange Commission required hedge funds with assets over $25 million to register as financial advisers under the Investment Advisers Act (OECD 2006). The SEC

registration order to hedge funds was overturned on appeal by the federal court in August 2006; however, by this time the majority of hedge funds had registered with the SEC, and most determined to remain registered as part of their courtship of institutional investors.

## Private equity

As with hedge funds, private equity firms are similarly attracted by the lack of regulation, substantial profit opportunities, and ready availability of low-interest finance in the market for corporate control. Private equity has been around for a long time, but globally has enjoyed phenomenal growth from $100 billion in 1994 to $900 billion in 2005. Private equity firms raise significant funds from investors, then seek businesses to acquire, usually involving taking on considerable debt. The business is then revamped and floated on the stock exchange or sold to another company. Traditionally, private equity has involved: *venture capital*, providing essential seed funding to innovative young businesses; *management buy-outs* (MBOs) joining with existing management to takeover part of a business; and *expansion capital*, offering funds for established businesses that need to expand. In one sense private equity therefore plays a valuable role in providing investment funds for growth and development of corporations (*Australian Financial Review*, 16 September 2006).

However, there is another face to private equity which is less acceptable. As with hedge funds, private equity often operates through stealth in search of information asymmetries. If this simply involved discovering and turning around sleepy companies with management who had accumulated excessive capital and who ran 'lazy' balance sheets, few might object. However, 'the risk is where predatory companies do no more than strip down and excessively leverage stable companies with a view to refloating them to a less discerning public. Debt-fuelled takeovers help lift the share-market in the short term, but they will generate longer-run problems if corporations' strong balance sheets are left in tatters' (*Australian Financial Review*, 16 September 2006).

The resemblance of this predatory approach to the leveraged buy-outs (LBOs) fuelled by junk

bonds in the 1980s is confirmed by the presence among the contemporary leading private equity firms of major players from that era including Kohlberg Kravis Roberts & Co. (KKR), celebrated in *Barbarians at the Gate* for the $31.4 billion leveraged buy-out of RJR Nabisco, which left a trail of enriched investment bankers and lawyers, and many dissatisfied investors including pension funds. This huge deal was only finally eclipsed by the buy-out of the US private hospital operator HCA Inc. in July 2006 for $33 billion with KKR involvement. The conditions which have allowed private equity to flourish in a new era include the caution of mainstream companies following the NASDAQ crash, the regulatory impact of Sarbanes–Oxley, and the flood of liquidity and negative real interest rates in recent years. However, though many current private equity deals are aimed at a fast turnaround and resale of companies, paradoxically one of the strengths of private equity is the capacity to work to longer time horizons of three to five years if necessary, without needing to show the quarterly returns of listed companies. It is one of the tragedies of the governance of the investment value chain that institutional investors and listed corporations are now geared to much shorter investment horizons than many private equity firms.

## Breaking the short-term cycle

An inclination towards short-termism has long been associated with market economies afflicting both investors and corporations: limiting the investment in tangible and intangible assets to concentrate on immediate performance while undermining the longer-term value adding capability of the firm (Hayes and Abernathy 1980; Porter 1992). Causes of short-termism include the pressures induced on corporations by the excessive expectations of capital markets; the narrow financial focus of performance indicators; the short-term incentive systems applied to fund managers and corporate executives; and the resulting individual orientations and organisational cultures that develop in this context (Marginson and McAulay 2005). There are many indications that accompanying the increasing turnover of share trading is the increasing pressure

towards short-termism. William H. Donaldson the Chairman of the SEC insisted:

> Analysts have become obsessed with the question of whether a company meets its quarterly EPS numbers, and not with whether a company is built to last. And because of the considerable clout of the sell-side analyst, this shift from long-term thinking to short-term results has echoed through to company managements and to professional investors. The focus on short-term results has had a counter-productive influence on companies, on investors and on analysts themselves. For companies, the short-term outlook has given rise to the disturbing syndrome of trying to force earnings into an artificial model of uninterrupted quarter-to-quarter growth. One study found that from 1999–2004, nearly half of the companies in the Dow Jones Industrial Average always met consensus earnings estimated, or beat them by a penny. 'Making the numbers' often results in unsound corporate strategies, which pay no regard to the cost of postponed investment. Such a goal is often achieved only by bending accounting standards.
>
> (2005: 5)

A recent indication of how damaging the cumulative impact of short-termism can be was revealed in a survey of 400 financial executives, 80 per cent of whom admitted that in order to meet short term earnings targets they would decrease discretionary spending in areas such as research and development, advertising, maintenance, and hiring staff. More than half the executives said they would delay new projects, even if it meant ultimate sacrifices in value creation (Graham, Harvey and Rajgopal 2005). As the report of a group of US investors, fund managers and executives brought together by the CFA Institute Centre for Financial Market Integrity commented:

> These results demonstrate that short-termism is a larger issue than companies simply using *accounting* actions to meet quarterly earnings expectations. These are *real* actions – asset sales, cuts in research and development, and forgone strategic investments – that

corporate managers use to hit 'the quarterly earnings number'. Although the creation of long-term company value is widely accepted as management's primary responsibility, this research suggests that managing predominantly for short-term earnings expectations often impairs a manager's ability to deliver such value to shareowners.

(2006: 3)

To break the vicious short-term cycle the CFA recommended:

1 *Earnings guidance*: Ending the practice of providing quarterly earnings guidance and support higher-quality, long term, fundamental guidance principles, that will allow more skilled analysts to differentiate themselves.
2 *Incentives and compensation*: Align corporate executive compensation with long term goals and strategies, align asset managers incentives with long term performance and improve disclosure of asset managers performance metrics.
3 *Leadership*: Endorse corporate leadership in communicating long term strategic objectives and related performance benchmarks rather than quarterly earnings guidance, and promote an institutional investor focus on long term value.
4 *Communication and transparency*: Encourage the use of corporate long term investment statements to shareholders written in plain language rather than accounting and legal language, explaining the company's operating model, and encourage institutional investors to make long term investment statements to their beneficiaries.
5 *Education*: Encourage widespread corporate participation in dialogue with asset managers and other financial market leaders to better understand how their companies are valued in the marketplace, and educate investors and trustees in their long term fiduciary duties to their investors (2006: 2).

Another group of UK institutional investors have suggested an enhanced analytics initiative to make extra-financial factors likely to have a long term effect on the business results more prominent, including corporate governance, executive remuneration, occupational health and safety, human capital practices and the environmental and social impact of corporate activity. This is seen as a lever of change, increasing the quality of relevant research pertaining to these issues, with benefits for both investors and corporate managers (O'Loughlin and Thamotheram 2006).

## A NEW ERA FOR INSTITUTIONAL INVESTORS?

The massive developments in the scale of the institutional investors, together with increases in their level of corporate governance activity, suggests the possibility of the beginnings of a new era in the relationships between investment institutions and the corporates in which they invest. The rapid and sustained growth of the financial institutions since the 1990s, due in part to changing demographics (which may be perceived to a degree as a *democratisation of the financial institutions* as they come to represent a larger share of the wealth of a greater percentage of the population) has profound implications. The OECD comments:

The emergence of institutional investors as the dominant holders of financial assets and as increasingly important participants in capital markets is one of the distinguishing features of the present financial landscape – and one that is likely to become more prominent in the years ahead. Institutional investors exercise a dominant influence on developments in primary and secondary securities markets, in the money market and in the foreign exchange market. They dominate a substantial part of securities trading in both cash and derivative markets. They also influence the development of fund management and risk management opportunities ... Despite the preponderance of fixed-income assets in institutional portfolios, investments in equities kept more or less the recorded level in recent years. As from 1997 share holdings have been the most important asset class reaching $13.6 trillion in 2001, followed by bonds which stood at $12.9 trillion.

(2003: 9–10)

The current value of assets managed by the investment industry worldwide is estimated at $42 trillion, pension fund assets in the US and UK alone amounting to $7.4 trillion (UNEP 2005a). In Australia, Rainmaker Research projects an increase of superannuation industry assets from $650 billion to more than $2.3 trillion by 2014, with growth increasing to 13.5 per cent per year, up from 10 per cent per year over the last ten years. (The introduction of super choice from 1 July 2005 may further exacerbate competitive pressures, lead to new investment strategies, and compound the potential governance problems involved (*Australian Financial Review*, 12 April 2005).) The investments of the institutions are spread between bonds, shares and other assets, but the increasing share ownership of the institutions, means they now own the majority of the shares in virtually all of the largest listed corporations worldwide, including companies listed on the S&P 500; FTSE 500; Euronext 100 and all of the other major stock exchanges. Corporate governance standards and reforms will develop in future as a matter of greater institutional investor concern as more of the public will have more of their wealth invested in companies they will insist should behave responsibly. Yet the governance mechanisms by which beneficiary concerns are communicated to trustees of funds, and the way in which fund managers interpret their fiduciary duties, or if they even recognise these duties, are by no means clear.

## Corporate governance and corporate performance

Widespread doubts remain in the institutional investment industry regarding any contribution improved corporate governance might make to corporate performance. There are two principal measures of performance: one measured by the corporation's profitability and the other by its market valuation. Only under market efficiency are these equivalent and its absence will have implications for the metric used when measuring the relationship between corporate governance and corporate performance. (Though widely accepted in both financial economics and legal scholarship the *efficient capital markets hypothesis* has

subsequently been subject to extensive revision due to the expanding body of work on the heterogeneous expectations of investors; how arbitrage may move some kind of information into price and more slowly and less completely than earlier believed; and the behavioural finance literature on what happens to market prices when market participants do not behave as if they possessed rational expectations (Stout 2003).)

It is apparent that the relationship between corporate governance and performance is not by any means straightforward, as the Association of British Insurers (ABI) commented to the UK Modern Company Law Review: 'It has been suggested that the beneficial impact of corporate governance codes is as much a means of guarding against wealth subtraction as the promotion of wealth creation. Whichever perspective is adopted it is difficult to quantify the beneficial impact of corporate governance codes though we consider it to be significant' (DTI 2000). Even as an essential component of risk management, corporate governance has not convinced everyone in the investment community, though 'The evidence continues to mount that, if nothing else, weak corporate governance structures may be a good predictor of investment risk' (Clearfield 2005: 115).

With regard to a more positive impact of corporate governance upon corporate performance, the evidence from a large number of research studies stretching back to the 1950s remains mixed (Zahra and Pearce 1989; Stiles and Taylor 2002). Researchers have struggled with the multiple variables involved, and on occasion have been disappointed, looking for an early 'governance effect' in share price behaviour following changes in company boards, or takeover defences (Clearfield 2005: 120). The OECD states: 'Establishing an empirical relation between corporate governance and performance is exceedingly difficult since there is considerable leeway in specifying measures of performance and indicators of corporate governance are very restricted.' Then the OECD favourably cites longitudinal studies recently completed in the US that have demonstrated high governance risk correlates with lower performance, and more robust governance is associated with more sustained performance (Gompers *et al.* 2003; Cremers and Nair 2004). (However only in the US could robust

governance be defined as the non-existence of takeover defences that strengthen management and other stakeholders vis-à-vis shareholders as in the Gompers *et al.* study.) Research in Europe and beyond has discovered a more significant outperformance by companies with higher standards of governance in large samples of companies (Drobetz *et al.* 2004; Bauer and Guenster 2003; Gill 2001).

## The reluctance of the institutions to exercise governance oversight

There are many reasons why even those in the investment community convinced of the value of corporate governance are reluctant to exercise governance oversight. Traditionally the Wall Street rule was to walk away from any company where there were doubts regarding the management, rather than engage in the effort to change the company, though the spread of indexation throughout the investment industry has diminished this possibility. With investments virtually across the whole market, and with an overriding interest in maintaining stability in the market, there exists a deep-seated preference among institutional investors for quiet diplomacy with

companies thought to be neglecting important aspects of governance (Figure 3.5). In many contexts the regulatory position of assuming a bolder monitoring role is often uncertain amid serious concerns regarding insider activity. In the UK, as in other jurisdictions, government and regulators often put out mixed signals: on the one hand calling for greater disclosure and dialogue between corporations and investors as helpful in maintaining a sound corporate governance system and effective financial markets, and at the same time regulators insist companies cannot disclose price sensitive information until it is released to the market as a whole. The question is when does dialogue around softer forms of information become in itself price sensitive, which can only be resolved by the professional judgement of the participants (Al-Hawamdeh and Snaith 2005).

With regard to the wider investment community, the division of labour among consultants, advisers, and fund managers competing almost purely on quantifiable performance criteria, means governance does not really feature. Any effective efforts to improve corporate governance necessarily benefit all shareholders, and the efficient markets hypothesis implies there is no excess return from governance activism. Furthermore Clearfield identifies some more subtle psychological and

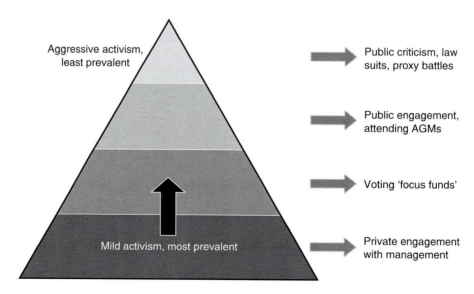

**Figure 3.5** Monitoring activities by institutional investors.

Source: ACGA (2005), *Degrees and Types of Activism in Asia: 2005*, Singapore: ACGA.

structural issues that confine institutional investor engagement: 'Fund managers tend to identify more with the managers they are supposed to monitor than with the clients it is their duty to protect. They are apt to be disinterested in shareholder initiatives to improve corporate governance, viewing this as an uneconomic attempt to restrain the "motor" of their investment' (2005: 117). And yet, like it or not, fund managers are at a critical interface between institutional investors and the corporates they are invested in, the investment and ownership decisions fund managers make have an important corporate governance dimension whether they recognise this or not (Figure 3.6).

Bebchuk adds that shareholder intervention is opposed as it is argued it would lead to disruption of corporate management; enable shareholders with special interests to undermine share value; allow bad choices in the removal of directors; further enforce short term perspectives on corporations attempting to meet shareholder demands; deter directors from serving on boards of publicly listed corporations; and ultimately, even if increasing shareholder power were to make directors more attentive to shareholder interests, it could well make them less attentive to other essential stakeholder interests. All this paints shareholders in a rather bad light. However, there is little evidence that insulating boards of directors from shareholder engagement makes them any more responsive to other stakeholder interests; and given the almost universal tendency of institutional shareholders to defer to boards, and to challenge boards only in the most exceptional of circumstances, it is unlikely that this pattern of extremely responsible, and some might suggest over-cautious, behaviour in protecting their investments could be replaced overnight by irresponsible activism (Bebchuk 2005: 29).

There is a structural divide in investment organisations between corporate governance advisers with a legal or regulatory background, and portfolio managers and analysts with a highly quantitative orientation towards performance assessment: 'The numerate are seldom at ease entrusting their fortunes to the literate' (Clearfield 2005: 118). Charkham and Simpson examine the implications of this division of labour pervasive in the investment institutions:

Those who analyse the company's performance will look at the numbers rather than the words, because they appear to facilitate comparisons with past performance, with other firms in the sector, and with the market as a whole. There is a relentless pressure to replace judgement with formulae, so as to be able to

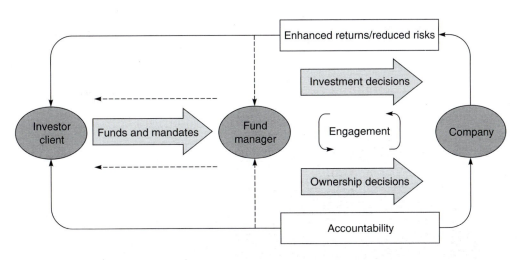

Figure 3.6 Investment fund managers' role in corporate governance.

Source: Mays, S. (2003), *Corporate Sustainability: An Investor Perspective*, Mays Report, Department of Environment and Heritage, Commonwealth of Australia, 19.

replace the skilled by the semi-skilled. This rests in part on the fallacy that numbers are more precise and accurate than words. As anyone who has compiled a set of accounts knows, almost every number is a judgement.

(1999: 207)

This division is expressed most clearly in time horizons. The investment industry is geared to short periods of time with performance milestones consisting of quarters, and renewal of contracts on a yearly basis. In contrast, corporate governance campaigns may take years for the benefits to manifest themselves (Clearfield 2005: 119). Corporations can be caught between managing their earnings to achieve better quarters and option results, while appeasing governance campaigners that they are thinking strategically of the longer term (Cadbury and Millstein 2005: 19).

## How institutions get involved in corporate governance

Though historically the institutional investors have been reluctant to exercise their potential influence, there are indications in the US, UK and to a more limited extent in Australia, that the institutions are now playing a more active role in pressing for higher standards of corporate governance, and more sustained corporate performance. Institutions continue to prefer quiet diplomacy to public voting, but are a little more prepared today to break cover. As a survey of shareholder activism at large US corporations between 2000 and 2003 conducted by Monks *et al.* (2004) demonstrates, shareholder proposals have extended from executive remuneration, poison pill and other board defence mechanisms, through board elections, director nomination, board independence and leadership, auditor independence, and stock options (Figure 3.7).

AMP Capital one of the larger institutional shareholders in Australia recently stated:

We aim to take corporate governance seriously. We believe that it is our responsibility to make the best investment decisions we can on behalf of our clients, but also to ensure that the companies we invest in are managed in the shareholder's best interests. For many years it has been AMP Capital's policy to vote at every meeting where it has the voting authority to do so … It is believed that by adopting high standards in relation to corporate governance and social responsibility (environment, employment and community relationships) companies can avoid potential damage to earnings or reputation and therefore enhance and protect the long term wealth-creation of their shareholders.

(2006: 1)

In 2005 AMP voted on 1,824 resolutions at 381 company meetings. The voting record is illustrated in Figure 3.8, with most company resolutions not supported relating to non-salary compensation and director election. This pattern of paying particular attention to remuneration of directors and executives is repeated in the US and UK, as in Australia. The explanation for this focus on executive reward is not simply outrage at rapidly escalating remuneration unrelated to company performance, or worry regarding the sustained transfer of wealth from shareholders to management. Cadbury and Millstein suggest a more profound reason for this concern with compensation processes and levels is that, 'Excessive executive compensation is generally the most visible example of management self-interest prevailing over the fulfillment of fiduciary duties'.

It is a matter of some concern that the renewed efforts of the institutional investors to exercise their responsibilities in voting, has to a degree been undermined by the inefficiency of the voting process. In the UK the Myners (2004) review of impediments to voting concluded that 'the system for voting shares is not as efficient as it should be, with problems that are largely the product of a process that is still quite manually intensive, where the chain of accountability is complex, where there is a lack of transparency and where there is a large number of participants each of whom may give a different priority to voting'. A year later Myners (2005) reported a significant improvement in the automation of the process, making it more transparent, and allowing an audit trail that instructions were received and votes recorded correctly. Similar problems in Australia remain to be addressed, and AMP refers to simple data entry errors occurring, registry records being

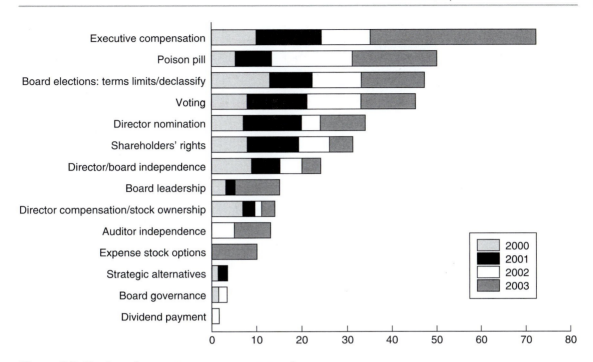

**Figure 3.7** Number of corporate governance proposals.

Source: Monks, Robert, Miller, Anthony and Cook, Jacqueline (2004), Shareholder Activism on Environmental Issues: A Study of Proposals at Large US Corporations (2000–2003), *Natural Resources Forum*, 317–330.
Note: Number per year in each subcategory ($N = 732$).

out of date, other operational errors by the share registry, and errors by companies in compiling the number of shares for their disclosure to the ASX (2006: 9).

The Myners solution to these problems is for the introduction of electronic voting with issuers, institutional investors and intermediaries transmitting and receiving votes by this means. By the end of 2004, 88 per cent or issuers in the FTSE 100 had facilitated the use of electronic voting, and 41 per cent in the FTSE 250. Regardless of the availability of electronic voting, not all shares are voted, and in 2004 61 per cent of FTSE 100 shares were voted (Myners 2005: 3–4).

The most important issue that shareholders are asked to vote on is the election of the directors of the company. Bebchuk highlights the significance of this event:

The importance of shareholders' power to replace directors as a mechanism for ensuring

director accountability is reinforced by the fact that other potential mechanisms are weak or non-existing. To begin with, according to established principles of corporate law, courts abstain from substantive review of the merits of director decisions and from imposing liability for decisions that could have been shown to be wrong had such a review been undertaken. In adopting this approach, courts have been moved not only by the significant difficulty of second-guessing directors' decisions but also by the existence of shareholder power to replace directors whose performance they find unsatisfactory. Thus, for example, in the recent decision in the Disney case, Chancellor Chandler stated that 'redress for [directors'] failures must come … through the action of shareholders … and not from this Court'.

(The Walt Disney Company Derivative Litigation, Consolidated C.A. No. 15452, Opinion decided August 9, 2005)

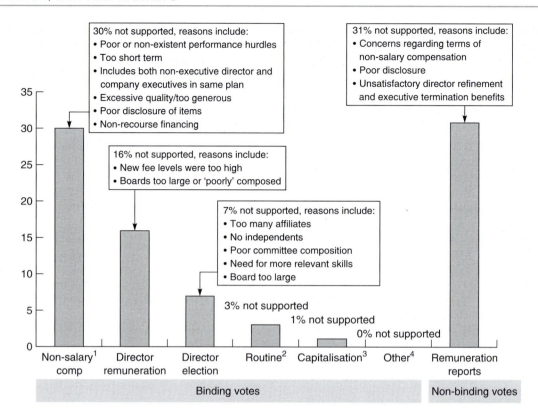

**Figure 3.8** Resolutions not supported by AMP Capital Investors, July–December 2005.

Source: AMP Capital Investors (formerly AMP Henderson Global Investors) (2006), *AMP Capital Investors' Corporate Governance Mid-Year Update*, August.

Notes

[1] Relates to employees' stock and option plans, various long term incentive plans, retirement plans etc.

[2] Accepting financial statements, general amendments to constitution, appointing auditors, etc.

[3] Approval or ratification for DRP share issues placements, etc.

[4] Shareholders' resolutions (self nominated directors), re-organisations and mergers, anti-takeover provisions.

In the United States what can be best described as an unusual voting system has been adopted in the majority of states including Delaware where most Fortune 500 companies are registered. This *plurality* voting system for directors allows voters to either vote 'yes' or withhold their vote. Votes withheld carry no weight, and it is not possible to register a 'no' vote. The charade becomes compounded since the proxy process of nominating a candidate for the board is expensive and difficult and the majority of elections are uncontested. The leading institutional investors including CalPERS,

TIAA-CREF, and AFL-CIO are now contesting this bizarre electoral process, and pressing for a majority voting system as in the rest of the world (Cadbury and Millstein 2005: 24).

## The governance of investment institutions

If the institutional investors are to play a more active role in corporate governance it is important they put their own house in order first. The institutions themselves have not enjoyed a

blameless existence through the historical cycles of governance. Bogle (2005) gives a contemporary account of some of the worst lapses in the sector:

- *Conflicts of interest in investment banking*: In April 2002 Eliot Spitzer, the New York Attorney General brought an enforcement action regarding serious conflicts of interest in US investment banking. Large investment banks had called on their research analysts to make buy recommendations to customers, not on the basis of unbiased evaluation, but to enhance the firm's support of initial public offerings they underwrote, and to attract new underwriting clients. The attorney general found 'fraudulent research reports … exaggerated or unwarranted claims … receiving payments for research … and inappropriate spinning of initial public offerings (essentially awarding shares to win potential underwriting clients). The action was settled with the investment banking firms agreeing to pay $1.4 billion, including penalties of $488 million, disgorgement of $388 million of profits, and payment of $512 million into a fund to sponsor independent research and investor education. The settlement also required structural reforms to sever the links between investment banking and research, and to restore the integrity of investment research (Bogle 2005: 77).

- *Mutual funds market – timing scandal*: Mutual funds with assets aggregating to more than $1.2 trillion dollars (a quarter of the total assets managed in the mutual fund industry in the US), were exposed when Elliot Spitzer brought civil actions against four mutual fund management companies, charging they had conspired with and aided preferred investors, including hedge funds (that described this strategy as 'mutual fund market timing') to undertake illegal acts. The investors involved bought and sold fund shares at closing prices based on late-breaking events that took place after the market has closed, and traded international funds in the US at values set in foreign markets before the trades took place (Spitzer made the comparison to allowing favoured investors to bet on a horse race after the horse had crossed the finishing line). The managers received high

interest rates on the loans they made to the traders, and required large investments in other funds on which the managers earned high fees. The market timing scandals were estimated to have cost long-term fund investors up to $3 billion in dilution of their returns (matched by the gains made be the short term speculators) (Bogle 2005: 143).

The US investment industry is not alone in the high fees and shady dealings which Bogle vigorously exposes: the UK investment industry has experienced its share of disasters too. The UK life and pensions industry manages $765 billion worth of funds, controlling 42 per cent of all personal sector holdings. Deregulation in the retail industry led to a long bout of misselling to vulnerable clients. As the UK Consumers Association (CA) put it,

> The retail industry (with a few exceptions) has never been interested in the lower-medium income consumers. It sold rip-off products which meant that it took consumers on average around 10 years to break-even – even when stock markets were booming. Millions lost billions of pounds on personal pensions and mortgage endowments due to exorbitant charges – especially the poor. The CA estimates the total cost of detriment attributable to the life insurance sector over the past two decades is in the region of 30 billion pounds – this includes pension misselling scandals and other market failures such as unreasonably high cost financial products.
>
> (CA 2004: 3).

Though billions of pounds in compensation was clawed back from the publicly embarrassed industry, this was often too late to help the victims of misselling, and was paid out of 'orphan assets' (assets held in the companies where policy holders could no longer be traced), 90 per cent of which rightly belonged to the wider policy holders rather than the companies themselves (CA 2001).

As the international investment institutions have developed massively in recent decades, a recurrent pattern of misselling, high costs, and astronomical (and often hidden) fees has

periodically been exposed in the industry. Bogle, the chief executive of *Vanguard* mutual fund in the United States for more than two decades sadly reflects on where the industry went wrong:

> In my Princeton senior thesis, I envisioned substantial future growth for the mutual fund industry, fostered by a 'reduction in sales charges and management fees'. Alas, that happy scenario was not to be. Indeed, after approximately moving lower as the industry grew over the next decade, fund expense ratios (expenses as a percentage of fund assets) began a relentless upward rise ... Although equity fund assets grew 1,600 fold during this period from $2.5 billion to $4 trillion, expenses rose at an even faster 2,400 fold rate, from $15 million in 1950 to $37.1 billion in 2004. Fund managers not only failed to deliver to their investors the huge economies of scale that were available, they arrogated those economies largely to themselves.
>
> (2005: 155)

The nadir of this reckless disregard for customers' interests was reached in Australia with the collapse of HIH, the largest bankruptcy in the country's history. An indulgent management was revealed in the subsequent Royal Commission of Inquiry to have lacked basic actuarial risk management skills or moral judgement, as they bled the company into extinction, in the process – as the largest general insurer – throwing thousands of other businesses into jeopardy which could not operate without insurance, and damaging the national economy as a result (HIH Royal Commission 2003).

However, these illustrations of particular weaknesses exposed in the institutional investor sector, are of less significance than the systemic impact of the investment institutions. Any sense that as they grow in scale and influence they may prove a powerful force for more responsible governance has to be tempered by the historical record of the institutions. Though the institutions have taken pride in their integrity and responsibility, often they have tended to follow the market rather than lead it. For example as the junk bond wave destabilised the market for corporate control in the US in the 1980s, it was the willingness of institutional investors to hold masses of low-grade, high-yield securities that made possible the new issues of junk bonds to finance bigger and bigger takeover deals. 'As US industry faced its greatest competitive challenges in the 1970s and 1980s, industrial enterprises required more, not less, financial commitment. Yet, as the institutional investors succeeded in their search for higher yields, less financial commitment is what they got' (Lazonik 1992: 470, 476). Similarly in the 1990s the institutional investors joined in the general euphoria that resulted in the massive inflation of the market capitalisation of technology stocks, that inevitably caused the NASDAQ spike, and their beneficiaries suffered the consequences in the equally inevitable market collapse that resulted. Lazonick questions the legitimacy of the claim that returning control to shareholders will present a better prospect for business development, 'Organisational commitment requires financial commitment. And the history of successful industrial development suggests that, in the provision of financial commitment for continuous innovation by going concerns, putting corporate governance in the hands of "owners" is more of a problem than solution' (1992: 485).

The institutional investors will need to ensure their investment and governance policies can stand up to more critical and open scrutiny in the future than was the case in the past. If the investment institutions are going to play a more active and influential role in mandating corporate governance they will need to ensure their own governance policies reflect best practices and are entirely transparent. Firstly, they owe this as a fiduciary duty to their ultimate beneficiaries. Secondly, by ensuring their own affairs are fully in order, they are better positioned to insist upon better governance and board performance in the companies they invest in (Cadbury and Millstein 2005: 20). Institutional investors will be held to account in the same exacting way as listed corporations are regarding the independence and competence of their directors, the appointment and election processes observed, how conflicts of interest are dealt with and how they exercise their fiduciary duty.

Increasing levels of transparency inevitably will be called for as the institutional investors become more prominent and influential.

Institutional governance will be actively bench-marked against the expressed policies of corporate governance ratings and advisory agencies such as Institutional Shareholder Services (ISS), and Governance Metrics International (GMI), and the International Corporate Governance Network (ICGN). International and national agencies are increasingly going to turn their attention from the present focus on corporate governance, to examining the internal governance of the investment institutions themselves, and for example assessing the extent to which they meet the OECD guidelines proposed for pension fund governance (2005b) and for insurers' governance (2005c).

The stability and security of the investments made by the institutional investors will increasingly prove a matter of the greatest importance, in terms both of the efficiency of firms and also the efficiency of allocating capital to companies, and the role of corporate governance in making a positive contribution to each. For some years the focus of governance has been upon the major corporations. In the future this interest will extend to the governance of the investment institutions, and how this impacts upon corporate governance. As two of the most influential authorities on international corporate governance have commented, 'Whilst some attention has been focused on institutional internal governance, we do not think the issue has yet gained the attention it is due, given the institutional charge of protecting other people's money. We know, however, of no systematic review of the internal governance of the institutional investor community. One is needed' (Cadbury and Millstein 2005: 20). Among the theoretical issues such research on the governance of the institutional investor community will need to examine are included:

▪ the complexity resulting from institutional investors becoming the financial intermediaries between individuals and corporates, the complex governance and regulatory relationships involved, and the additional agency costs (Schnieder 2000);
▪ the implications of the emergence of fiduciary capitalism, and how agents (fiduciaries) can effectively monitor other agents (boards of directors) (Hawley and Williams 1997; Woidtke 2002);

▪ the social implications of maximising shareholder value when the institutional investors enjoy majority ownership (Hawley and Williams 2000);
▪ the link between corporate governance and corporate performance and risk (Romano 2000);
▪ the impact of strategic investor alliances to curtail corporate managerial opportunism and manipulation (Noe 2002);
▪ the competing pressures from institutions for immediate results (shareholder value) and for sustained performance and corporate social responsibility (Clarke and dela Rama 2003; UNEP 2005b; Sullivan and Mackenzie 2006).

More needs to be known about how well the institutional investors are progressing with their own governance; the governance of the investment value chain; and the corporate governance of the entities they invest in, and issues of concern which may need further regulatory intervention. Better insights and assurance are required by the beneficiaries of the institutional investors, and particularly to superannuation fund members regarding the fiduciary responsibility and diligence attached to the stewardship of their investments.

Comprehending the governance of the investment institutions however will require looking across the whole of the investment value chain, examining the responsibilities, relationships, roles and understandings that together compose the governance of the investment community, the asymmetry in market power and information among various stakeholders, and the complex of regulatory relationships involved. 'Given the twin separations between beneficiary and institutional investor and between institutional investor and asset manager, important principal-agent issues might arise. Self-interested behaviour of agents (such as asset managers) may not always be in line with those bearing the risks (such as the corporate sponsors and ultimate beneficiaries). These agency problems give rise in turn to some of the distinctive effects of institutional investors on capital markets' (Davis and Steil 2001) Figure 3.9 demonstrates the elaborate network of participants and regulators in the institutional investor value chain in Australia, which is typical of the dense, and often hidden, pattern of relationships

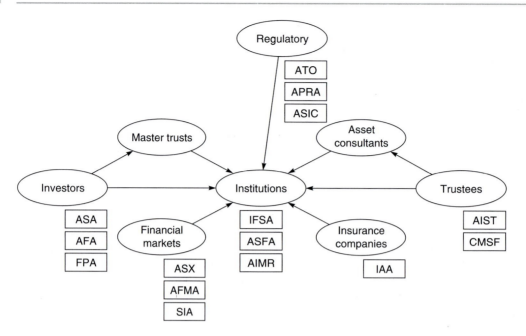

**Figure 3.9** The complex governance and regulatory relationships of the institutional investors.

Source: UTS Centre for Corporate Governance (2002).

and regulation at the heart of the financial industry that is becoming the increasingly influential driver of the international economy. Achieving a better understanding of the governance of this complex network of investment relationships is the next great frontier of the advancing corporate governance movement.

## CONCLUSIONS

This survey of the institutional elements of corporate governance highlights the distinctive origins and development of different corporate governance systems. The critical influence of finance, law and markets in sustaining alternative corporate governance values, structures and practices

was emphasised. The enduring distinctiveness and viability of market and relationship based systems of governance was considered. How the panoply of corporate governance controls have failed to prevent recurrent corporate governance crises was examined. Finally the impact of the new emerging force in corporate governance represented by the increasing vastness of the institutional investors was discussed. A series of dilemmas was posed as to whether institutional investors will ever be able to exercise effective governance oversight, and if they do, if this will result in further pressures towards short-termism in corporate performance, or whether the institutions will encourage higher standards of corporate governance and longer term horizons.

# 4
# Anglo-American Corporate Governance

## INTRODUCTION

This chapter sets out the essential elements of the Anglo-American approach to corporate governance. The cycle of crisis and reform that has proved most pronounced in the Anglo-American market based system is considered with regard to the reform path of the United States, United Kingdom and Australia and New Zealand. The impact of the new doctrine of shareholder value upon the workings of the governance system is investigated, and the direction of the increasingly financially driven markets of these countries considered. The excitement of the new economy that transformed the corporate landscape is discussed, and the experience of the long boom of the 1990s. The resulting Enron failure which precipitated a series of similar corporate collapses, and the dramatic fall of the NASDAQ is put into context. The regulatory aftermath of the Sarbanes–Oxley Act, and renewed efforts at reform in the UK and Australia are reviewed. This chapter aims to present some of the strengths and weaknesses of the Anglo-American approach to corporate governance in the context of the business development and crises that have occurred.

## MARKET BASED SYSTEMS OF CORPORATE GOVERNANCE

The *outsider* systems of corporate governance of the United States and the United Kingdom are among the longest established and have influenced much of the rest of the world. This is because of the strength of the US and UK capital markets, and the vast growth of their investment institutions that have become increasingly active

internationally. The Anglo-American outsider system has been adopted in many other countries including Australia and New Zealand, and is at the heart of agency theory, and associated corporate governance principles and company law elaborated over the last century, that has proved deeply influential in defining the activity and purpose of corporations internationally. The central characteristics of the market-based outsider model of corporate governance are:

- diffuse equity ownership with institutions having very large shareholdings;
- shareholder interests are considered the primary focus of company law;
- there is an emphasis on effective minority shareholder protection in securities law and regulation;
- there is a stringent requirement for continuous disclosure to inform the market.

In economies that have adopted this model of corporate governance, shares are widely distributed among individuals and institutions (Nestor and Thompson 2000: 5). In these countries a growing amount of the national wealth is held by institutions including insurance companies, pensions funds and mutual funds. The considerable growth in the financial assets of institutional investors since the 1990s, particularly the Anglo-American investment institutions, has important implications for the ownership and control of industry internationally, and for corporate governance. For some time institutional investors have been the dominant owners of equity in the UK, and they achieved this position more recently in the US. The institutional investors are charged with the responsibility to secure the maximum

return on their investments for their beneficiaries, and in accordance with their mandates. Typically, in the past the institutional investors demonstrated little interest in influencing the companies they invested in, employing strategies of portfolio diversification and indexation. However, more recently there is evidence of institutional investors becoming more actively engaged.

Outsider systems of corporate governance are characterised as *disclosure based*, as the dispersed investors require reliable and adequate information flows in order to make informed investment decisions. Regulation is intended to ensure all investors remain fully informed, and to prevent privileged groups of shareholders exclusively accessing and sharing information. The role of the banks is less central in the outsider model of corporate governance, normally bank finance is short term, and usually banks are encouraged to stay at arm's length in their dealings with corporations. Equity finance has been more important

as a means of developing companies (Nestor and Thompson 2000: 7). Equity shares have become the most significant assets in the portfolios of US and UK institutional investors (Table 4.1). While there has been a considerable growth in the equity markets of Germany and France most institutional investment in these countries remains in bonds and loans. In the Japanese economy the proportion of institutional investment held in shares declined at the end of the troubled 1990s, though the recent recovery of Japanese companies and financial institutions has restored confidence in the share market.

Under the Anglo-American system shareholders formally have the right to use their voting power to select the board and decide on the key issues facing the company, but in practice fragmented investors rarely exercise this control when faced with an informed and determined management. Investors' capacity to discipline management is greater in their freedom to buy or sell the

| | 2000 | 2001 | 2002 | 2003 | 2004 | 2000–4 (% change) |
|---|---|---|---|---|---|---|
| **Total** | **$17,627.0** | **$15,310.6** | **$11,871.0** | **$15,497.0** | **$17,204.4** | **−2.4** |
| Household sector | 7,806.2 | 6,604.2 | 5,047.8 | 6,375.8 | 6,521.6 | −16.5 |
| State and local governments | 97.1 | 100.7 | 80.3 | 84.5 | 89.1 | 8.2 |
| Rest of the world[2] | 1,643.2 | 1,572.7 | 1,260.8 | 1,669.0 | 1,906.1 | 16.0 |
| Commercial banking | 11.9 | 8.9 | 3.5 | 15.1 | 19.6 | 66.4 |
| Savings institutions | 24.2 | 27.9 | 29.1 | 30.4 | 28.2 | 16.5 |
| Bank personal trusts and estates | 356.8 | 200.7 | 181.1 | 213.1 | 223.4 | −37.4 |
| Life insurance companies | 891.9 | 811.3 | 708.9 | 919.3 | 1,091.5 | 22.4 |
| Other insurance companies | 194.3 | 173.9 | 152.3 | 182.7 | 209.0 | 7.6 |
| Private pension funds | 1,915.0 | 1,562.1 | 1,096.7 | 1,491.9 | 1,690.0 | −11.7 |
| State and local govt retirement funds | 1,223.1 | 1,084.0 | 869.8 | 1,084.4 | 1,204.7 | −1.5 |
| Federal government retirement funds | 55.6 | 49.1 | 45.9 | 79.9 | 99.3 | 75.4 |
| Mutual funds | 3,227.3 | 2,836.1 | 2,188.0 | 3,051.6 | 3,697.2 | 14.6 |
| Closed-end funds | 36.6 | 31.1 | 33.7 | 52.3 | 81.4 | 122.4 |
| Exchange-traded funds | 65.6 | 83.0 | 98.2 | 146.3 | 217.7 | 231.9 |
| Brokers and dealers | 77.2 | 85.1 | 74.9 | 100.5 | 125.3 | 62.3 |

Table 4.1 US institutional ownership equities, 1990 and 2004 ($ billions, market value at end of year).[1]

Notes
[1] Excludes mutual fund shires.
[2] Holdings of US issues by foreign residents.
Sources: WFE (2005), *The Financial Services Roundtable FS Fact Book 2006*, Board of Governors of the Federal Reserve System.

shares of the company, influencing the stock price and market perception of the company. When a company is thought to be badly managed, shareholders can respond by selling shares and thereby depressing the share price to the point where the company becomes a ready target for hostile takeover. Though takeovers do occur from time to time, the market for corporate control model assumes full disclosure of information, strict adherence to trading rules, and a liquid stock market (Nestor and Thompson 2000: 8). Moreover many institutional investors have become so large that they need to be in the whole market in order to spread their risk, and it is more difficult for them to abandon, rather than to attempt to help remedy, a company they have invested in which is experiencing governance problems or other difficulties.

In the United States the board of directors is entrusted with the important responsibility to monitor the company on behalf of shareholders. However, in the US boards of directors are often dominated by the company management. Attempts have been made to achieve greater accountability by introducing a majority of non-executive directors, but according to Lorsch and MacIver (1989), outside directors have limited time, knowledge and expertise in the companies that they are responsible for in principle. Non-executives often lacked any group cohesion of their own, but felt a need to fit into the values of the companies they join the board of. The OECD (1995: 22) comments: 'It is generally conceded in English-speaking countries boards have great difficulty in fulfilling the oversight function in a meaningful way, because they have traditionally worked on a collegial basis under the dominance of senior management. Until recently one tier boards have, more often than not, tended to ratify strategic decisions of management'. There are many ironic paradoxes in the Anglo-American approach to corporate governance, which corporate regulation over two centuries has never fully resolved.

A century of legal and regulatory effort has been invested in the US to achieve some resolution to what Swanson (1996: 417) defines as 'The major governance problem ... the intricate balance between maximising the efficiencies necessary to create wealth and ensuring that the

controlling parties are accountable to those with a stake in the enterprise'. However, the assumption that this equilibrium has been reached in the Anglo-American model of corporate governance in anything other than a partial and temporary way is a little optimistic. Furthermore, as Cheffins demonstrates with regard to the UK, as the only major industrial country to evolve along similar lines of ownership and control to the US, the resolution of this corporate governance equilibrium has scarcely been achieved there either. In this light, it is surprising that the Anglo-American model of corporate governance has been so energetically canvassed worldwide as the route other countries should take towards resolving their corporate governance problems. Further examination is merited of the nature of the Anglo-American system to understand its manifest strengths and often concealed weaknesses.

## US CORPORATION REGULATION

The regulation of corporate governance in the United States has occurred when a crisis has caused potential breakdown in the financial and industrial system, resulting in a raft of legislative interventions in the banking and securities industries (Figure 4.1). The 1929 great crash was a defining moment in US history, not only did the collapse cause widespread financial catastrophe, it undermined public belief in the integrity of financial and equity markets, and ushered in the long depression that scarred the optimism and endeavour of the American people. Following the Wall Street crash there was a banking panic that led to the closing of the banks for an extended period just after Roosevelt took office in 1933. The *Glass-Steagall Act* (1933) and the *Banking Act* (1933) divided investment banking from commercial banking. Commercial banks were prohibited from collaboration with full-service brokerage firms or participating in investment banking activities. This was intended to protect bank depositors from the additional risks associated with security transactions. (The Act was dismantled in 1999 by the Gramm-Leach-Billey Act and consequently the distinction between commercial banks and brokerage firms has blurred: many banks own brokerage firms and provide investment services.)

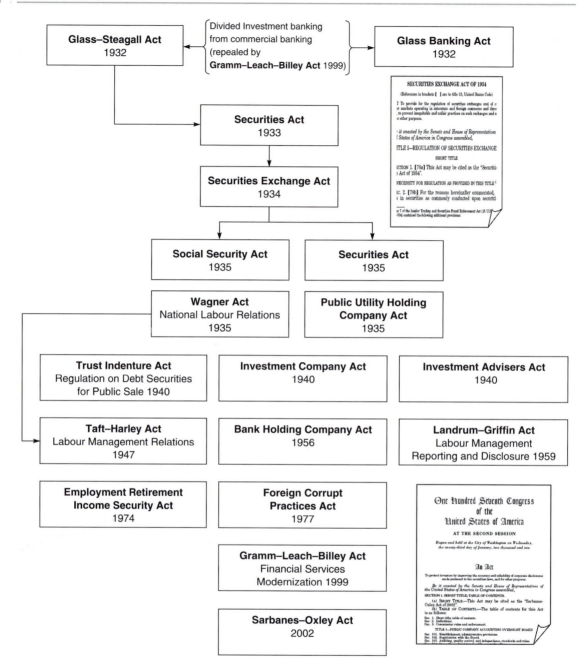

**Figure 4.1** US reform of corporate governance regulation, 1932–2002.

Source: Clarke, T. (2006).

The framework of securities legislation in the US consists of a series of related but separate statutes that are administered by the Securities and Exchange Commission. The *Securities Act* (1933) was concerned with distributions of securities.

It specifies the information companies must provide when issuing securities in the public markets. It requires prospectuses with a significant amount of affirmative disclosure including financial and other significant information to be provided for

investors before public sale. The Act prohibits deceit, misrepresentations and other fraud in the sale of securities.

The *Securities Exchange Act* (1934) created the Securities and Exchange Commission (SEC), empowered with broad authority over all aspects of the securities industry including the power to register, regulate and oversee brokerage firms, transfer agents, and clearing agencies, as well as securities self-regulatory organisations such as the NYSE and NASDAQ. This was concerned with publicly traded stocks after they were issued, and has been amended on numerous occasions. The main regulations concern the following:

- Publicly traded firms are required to file accounting returns periodically. Directors, officers and holders of 10 per cent or more of the shares are also required to provide information on a regular basis.
- Solicitation of proxies is controlled.
- Regulation of tender offers was added in 1968.
- Oversight of the stock exchanges and over the counter markets. Self-regulation is encouraged through self-regulatory organisations such as the New York Stock Exchange, the National Association of Securities Dealers, registered clearing agencies and the Municipal Securities Rulemaking Board.
- Prevention of market manipulation.
- Prevention of insider trading.
- Control of credit to purchase securities by the Federal Reserve System.
- Regulation of clearance and settlement processes.
- Regulation of markets in municipal securities.

The third statute was the *Public Utility Holding Company Act* (1935) which was concerned with the regulation of electric and gas holding companies. The *Trust Indenture Act* (1939) supplemented the *Securities Act* (1933) for situations where debt is being issued, and applies to debt securities such as bonds, debentures and notes that are offered for public sale. It required the filing of an indenture with the SEC which provides information on the obligations of the trustee in the event of default.

Customers of investment companies were perceived to be especially susceptible to unscrupulous behaviour by the managers of these companies because of the liquid nature of their assets. The *Investment Company Act* (1940), which was subsequently amended both in 1970 and 1980, was designed to prevent some of these abuses. The Act regulates the organisation of companies, including mutual funds, that engage primarily in investing, reinvesting, and trading in publicly offered securities. The Act is designed to minimise conflicts of interest that arise in these complex operations. It requires companies to disclose their financial condition and investment policies to investors when stock is initially sold and, on a regular basis. The focus of this Act is on disclosure to the investing public of information about the fund and its investment objectives, as well as on investment company structure and operations. Regulatory provisions were designed to ensure:

- honest management;
- participation in management by security holders;
- adequate and feasible capital structures;
- effective financial disclosure;
- prevention of selling abuses;
- desirable incentives for managers through restrictions on forms of compensation.

The *Investment Advisers Act* 1940 required all investment advisers to register with the SEC, including firms or sole practitioners involved in advising others about securities investment. Finally, the *Securities Investor Protection Act* (1970) is designed to protect investors in the event of a broker going bankrupt. All brokers and dealers registered with the SEC are required to be a member of the Securities Investor Protection Corporation which provides protection up to pre-specified limits in the event of bankruptcy (Allen and Herring 2001: 20–22).

## Delaware

Within the framework of securities law established at the federal level, US company law is the responsibility of the individual states. While this may be intended to allow a degree of local autonomy and responsiveness, as businesses may decide in which state they can be incorporated, the prospect

of regulatory competition is real. The state of Delaware has undoubtedly won this competition and plays a vital role as the national company law maker in the United States. Though Delaware has achieved such a dominant position of market power in the regulation of corporations, there is little chance that US company law will become part of federal jurisdiction in the near future. Delaware has accumulated the greatest expertise in the determination of company law, which is an important part of its attraction. But all states, and particularly Delaware, are subject to insistent pressures from corporate management for example in the development of anti-takeover legislation, and the danger of regulatory capture is very real. As McCahery and Vermeulen argue:

> The US legal system traditionally views company law in general as a local matter reserved to the states' governments. Consequently, the corporation statutes of some states may differ appreciably from those of most other states on many critical matters. Once US business owners decide to incorporate, they must select an attractive state of incorporation. Under traditional conflict-of-law rules, courts will respect this choice even if the corporation in question has no other contact with the chosen state. The corporate laws of the incorporating state govern the basic rights and duties of a corporation and its participants. At the end of the nineteenth century, New Jersey and Delaware, concerned about incorporation decisions, adopted modernised general incorporation statutes. Eventually, Delaware's statute made it the leading incorporation state in the United States since the 1920s, presently serving as the state of incorporation for nearly half of the corporations listed on the New York Stock Exchange and more than half of all Fortune 500 firms. In addition, Delaware is also the leading destination for firms that opt to reincorporate … Delaware's specialised chancery court, arguably preserve Delaware's leading position over time. Delaware's corporate law plays a key role in the evolution of companies in the United States, because Delaware law provides an alternative set of rules that serve firms and their legal advisers across the country. Consequently, many commentators have

dealt with the vexed question of whether the choice of Delaware's corporate law eventually leads to value maximisation. In other words, is regulatory competition better described as a 'race to the bottom' or as a 'race to the top'?
> (McCahery and Vermeulen 2005: 789–780)

At a higher level there is though a more complex interplay between state and federal politics and law making, and the exercise of the interests of corporations, investors and their lobbyists in the United States. Though the states do contribute most of the detail in corporate law, and competition between the states may determine this, the relationship of the states with Washington is a critical determinant, as federal authorities can displace the states if a legal issue is important enough. The SEC and Congress will intervene if issues seriously impact on the economy or public opinion, and this confines and conditions state lawmaking. Mark Roe presents an institutional analysis of the federal-Delaware relationship that reveals the constant political and legal bargaining that takes place in the exercise of public choice, and the likelihood of drastic federal intervention when things get out of hand at the state level:

> Corporate law issues can always go federal or attract federal attention. The SEC is always on stand-by, and Congress takes up issues that deeply affect the economy or the opinion polls. These possibilities confine the range of state lawmaking and, on occasion, condition it. The structure privileges state-level deals between managers and investors in Delaware. Although managers historically have had the upper hand in Delaware, they don't fully dominate there. Delaware doesn't let them dominate fully, not just because of, or perhaps even in spite of, state competition. It doesn't let them dominate or they themselves choose to be moderate because if it did, the game could move to Washington, where new players could induce new results. Hence, local interest groups compromise and local decision makers are even handed, even if local politics doesn't demand compromise or even handedness. Sometimes, despite local compromise, the issue is so big generating headlines in the media and fears for the economy that it attracts federal attention.

Different coalitions can, and do, emerge at the federal level. Sometimes the managers or the investors find new coalition partners at the federal level and thereby break the Delaware deal. Delaware limits the range of the first decision-making stage by keeping out corporate outsiders and public policymakers. Sometimes managers and investors can make their deal there and then unite at the federal level to fight off other forces. Sometimes probably more often than not their interests are sufficiently similar that they both want the states and not the federal authorities to make corporate law. But sometimes Delaware loses control of the agenda. It loses control when the public is sufficiently motivated that Congress acts because the economy is weak or because scandals dominate the media. Congress ousted Delaware most recently with Sarbanes–Oxley after the Enron and WorldCom scandals hit the headlines.

(2005: 45)

## Corporate failure and the reform of corporate governance

Though the US system may have partly evolved out of the pragmatic development of case law at the state level in response to changing circumstances, this is a sub-text compared to the major legislative interventions that have resulted at times of crisis. As Millstein (2001: 10) notes: 'This minimally intrusive system also leaves room for abuse. The US system has had to make many adjustments to counter mistakes generated by too much discretion. Our regulatory system has evolved over time, in reaction to the failure of corporations to live up to public expectations, and in reaction to outright abuse. At various points in our corporate history, fraud, larceny and mismanagement have not been all that unusual – and ultimately they have led to law and regulation'. Expanding confidence in the American economy 1920s with rising output, sustained growth, and an increase in personal wealth led to the speculative euphoria of 1928 and 1929 centred on New York that led to the Wall Street crash. The market collapse revealed market manipulation, insider trading, general mismanagement and

a reckless trampling of shareholder rights, with the loss of 86 per cent of market capitalisation between 1929 and 1933 (Soros 1998: 145).

The long depression that followed provoked deep misgivings about the nature of the economic system unleashed upon an apparently defenceless public.

> Congress enacted the Securities Act 1933 and the Securities and Exchange Act 1934 to address these problems, primarily through the regulation of corporate financial disclosure to improve transparency. These laws and the rules that followed also imposed liability on officers and directors for fraud and abuse, and established the SEC to enforce these measures, and among other things, to regulate solicitation of shareholder proxies by public corporations. Congress opted for honest and fair disclosure as the primary tool for securities regulation, obviating the need for more detailed substantive regulation.

(Millstein 2001: 11)

As Figure 4.2 demonstrates there is a pattern discernible in corporate governance regulation not only in the United States but around the world that during periods of recession, market failure and corporate collapse, legislation is introduced to deal with evident weaknesses in corporate governance. However, during times of expansion and economic confidence, corporate governance concerns are often neglected as both corporates and investors concentrate on the business of accumulating wealth.

In the long post-war expansion of the US economy, concerns regarding corporate governance were subordinated to enjoyment of the new found opportunity and prosperity. As long as the economy was doing well, and US corporations were successfully growing, the fact that managers had become the dominant players in a new form of 'managerial capitalism' was not of great consequence. Times were good, and executives were able to assume iconic status, in a system that appeared self-regulating as well as self-perpetuating, which delivered corporate engines of wealth creation that were the envy of the world such as IBM, Sears, GE, Exxon, US Steel, Alcoa, Procter & Gamble and GM

**Figure 4.2** US corporate governance legislation and the Standard and Poor index, 1990–2002.

Source: Clarke, T. (2006).

(Millstein 2001: 14). For a time at least it seemed that US executives were immune from either internal monitoring (their handpicked boards advised, they did not monitor), and from product market competition (corporations had grown large enough with sufficient resources to ignore product market messages until they got really serious, and there was little takeover activity). Slowly this complacency began to unravel, as the economic buoyancy on which it was based began to slip away. In the 1970s there was a series of corporate failures that provoked concerns regarding not only the ability of managers, but the capacity of boards of directors to monitor their actions. For example the SEC launched an investigation into management failure at Penn Central in the early 1970s. The SEC criticised the board of the nation's largest railway corporation for the lack of outside directors with the financial skills to recognise the financial problems of the company. The SEC approved a new rule of the NYSE that required all listed companies to establish audit committees composed entirely of independent directors in 1977 (Millstein 2001: 14–15).

The rise in regulatory concern was linked to a fall in economic performance. The 1970s was a period in which US corporations appeared to

be intent on 'expansion and conglomeration for their own sake', as symbols of the aggrandisement of their executives, rather than in terms of superior returns. As they became larger and more top heavy US corporations failed to take sufficient notice of the growing competitive threat of foreign imports. Two important developments occurred early in the 1980s which catalysed the corporate system in the United States: firstly the growth in the assets of institutional investors, and secondly the application of junk bonds which opened up the market for corporate control to new bidders and new targets. Gilson (2006) identifies three central characteristics of hostile takeovers that proved the catalyst for corporate governance transformation:

■ *new profit opportunities* created by changes in product markets, failure of conglomeration, and the growth of excess capacity/free cash flow;

■ *new financial mechanisms* created by the development of junk bonds to fund hostile takeovers;

■ *new investors* created by the growth of the investment institutions, consequent changes in the distribution of shareholdings, and the increasing focus on share price and performance by the institutions.

Three corresponding changes occurred in management's position in corporate governance:

- *increased business risk* from the aggressive focus of competitors, and the enhanced leverage of potential acquirers;
- *increased employment risk* from more efficient monitoring by directors and investors;
- *increased incentive compensation* as the major portion of CEO pay became linked to performance.

By the 1980s it appeared as if the US corporate system had turned in upon itself, with 'a growing fascination with Leveraged Buy-Outs (LBOs), and Management Buy-Outs (MBOs), junk bonds and a casino-like atmosphere, where corporations became tradeable commodities rather than essential engines of wealth' (Millstein 2001: 15). Managers came to believe themselves compelled to focus on short term stock market performance at the expense of strengthening their businesses in the longer term. A paradox of this period is that it represented a reassertion of the power of financial markets over corporate executives. The growth in financial engineering paralleled the decline of many of the leading US corporations of the mid-twentieth century. In comparison, in the 1980s Japanese and German industry seemed destined for ascendancy, as they relentless pursued export success in key manufactured goods sectors including luxury cars and consumer electronics.

Hostile takeovers are often regarded as the most brutal but effective way to bring financial market pressure to bear on poorly performing management. In the US and UK at least, takeovers are thought to discipline and replace inefficient managers, and the ever-present threat of takeover pressures managers to remember to service the interests of shareholders (though not in Europe where hostile takeovers are rare). In the 1980s an explosion of debt-financed takeovers backed by investment banks threatened even large well-established companies. Hostile takeovers were justified as necessary restructuring according to free cash flow theory (servicing takeover debt is supposed to spur the reallocation of resources to their most efficient uses, ensuring the paying out of surplus cash flow over time rather than maintaining

the existing excessive retention levels). However, this became a speculation in firms themselves as financial rather than productive assets, as low debt firms were seen as takeover targets to be filled with debt (Kaufmann and Englander 1993). For a time in the 1980s junk bond debt leveraged buy-outs seemed like a tsunami likely to engulf established companies:

'Until 1977 virtually all new issues of publicly traded bonds in the United States carried a Standard and Poor's investment grade rating of BBB or better. Although some low-grade bonds were traded in secondary markets, they were "fallen angels", bonds originally issued with an investment grade rating but subsequently downgraded to below investment grade. During 1977, Drexel Burnham Lambert began making substantial initial public offerings of low-grade bonds. From 1977 through 1989, the market for low-grade bonds grew from $1.1 billion to a total outstanding stock of $205 billion, about one quarter of all marketable corporate debt in the United States' (Allen and Herring 2001: 30; Blume *et al.* 1991).

Leading the charge of leveraged buy-outs (LBOs) was the firm of Kohlberg Kravis Roberts & Co. (KKR) which specialised in identifying, purchasing and restructuring underperforming or undercapitalised firms. If this began as a revitalising force in American industry, as others entered the LBO market, most notably Michael Milken's Drexel Burnham Lambert with high yield (junk) bonds, what transpired was a frenzy of overpriced buy-outs and reckless financing. Incumbent management felt forced to make divestitures, assume debt and recapitalise their companies to make them unattractive to corporate raiders (Kaufmann and Englander 1993). The Business Roundtable of US industrial leaders complained this was a diversion from long term strategic management to short term financial management.

In the US as the likelihood of takeover became more imminent with the invalidation of state anti-takeover laws in 1982, and the availability of increasingly sophisticated financial instruments to leverage takeovers became more prevalent, with the possibility of major corporations being broken up, incumbent corporate management took defensive action. From 1983 shareholders were asked to approve *shark repellents*, corporate charter amendments intended to erect barriers to takeover,

and *poison pills* entitling shareholders to purchase shares at a deeply discounted rate should a takeover occur without board approval. These measures made those intent on acquisition negotiate with the board, rather than simply the shareholders. As Gerald Davis (1991) indicates the rate of adoption of poison pills increased from 5 per cent of *Fortune* 500 companies in 1986 to 60 per cent by 1989, limiting the constraint of capital markets on managerial control of corporations. If the reform of corporate governance was to continue other means beyond the market for corporate control would be required.

The aggressive and often unethical practices of the junk bond investment banks caught up with Drexel Burnham Lambert, the most profitable investment bank on Wall Street in the mid-1980s, as it pleaded guilty to six felony charges in 1989 and agreed to pay $650 million in fines to the government. Drexel conducted 50 per cent of the trading in junk bonds, and when Michael Miliken the chief architect of the low-grade bond market was indicted on racketeering and securities fraud, Congress ruled that the thrift institutions which at that time had a substantial holding should liquidate their portfolios of low-grade bonds. Lack of confidence prompted a sharp decline in the liquidity of low-grade bonds, and the ratings agencies dropped their rating on Drexel's issues, meaning institutional investors could no longer buy them, leaving Drexel to file for bankruptcy (Allen and Herring 2001). Though the junk bond market collapsed in 1989, hostile takeovers resumed in the 1990s provoking waves of corporate restructuring and a new corporate ideology of *shareholder value*, as only those companies that continually released value to shareholders were regarded as safe.

## Further efforts at reform

As belief in the market for corporate control as the instrument to monitor and discipline corporate management evaporated, attention turned once again to the dysfunctional boards of US corporations to see if they could be reinvigorated with sufficient authority to exercise their responsibilities. In order to enhance the oversight functions of boards and limit the powers of chief executives, committees for critical tasks were established from

the 1980s in large US corporations. These tasks included the remuneration of executive directors, nomination of new board members, and auditing. Most CEOs of large companies in the US could no longer decide their own pay, select their own board, and audit their own financial performance. But in many companies CEOs continued to wield considerable power in the board room, partly because they also retained the role of chair. In an effort to progress the reform process further Lipton and Lorsch (1991) made a series of proposals that appear very modest now but at the time seemed quite radical:

- a board maximum of ten directors, with two independent directors for every inside director;
- an outside director to be nominated as the 'lead' director where the CEO is also the chair;
- boards to meet several times a year with the major shareholders;
- the independent directors to describe remedial action in the annual report if the company under-performs for three out of five years.

Another perhaps more potent check on management was the more active role played by institutional shareholders. Leading the charge of shareholders on corporate governance practices in the United States is the Council of Institutional Shareholders whose members have over $1.5 trillion dollars invested. Several of the large pension funds, most notably CalPERS, the Californian public pension fund have proved particularly influential. However, the pension funds of New York City, the State of Connecticut, State of Minnesota, and TIAA-CREF (the Teachers Insurance and Annuity Association College Retirement Equities Fund of New York with in excess of $259 billion of assets under management) are also all beginning to make their mark. These are among the largest wealth management companies in the world, and as their growth has accelerated since the 1980s with the changing demographics of the industrial world, they are becoming larger financial entities than the corporates they are investing in. The sheer scale of the financial assets of the institutional investors, and the massive increases in the assets of insurance companies, pension funds and investment companies between them, together with the fact that the

greatest increase in the financial assets of the institutional investors between 1990 and 1999 was in shares and bond holdings, suggests they will develop as a major force in corporate governance in the United States in the future, in a way they have not proved in the past.

## UNITED KINGDOM

The UK with the US developed the Anglo-Saxon model of corporate governance to the fullest degree, and has been active in the export of the model to many countries for nearly two centuries, commencing when the UK was the workshop of the world in the nineteenth century, but continuing during the more pressing times for the UK economy in the period after World War II. The UK has the largest and most influential investment institutions relative to the size of its economy, and companies more dependent upon the equity market than any of the large industrial economies (Table 4.2). Both UK financial institutions and equity markets are among the most internationalised in the world, with investors from the rest of the world holding a significant amount of total equity. As in the US the corporate governance

debate was originally sparked by the weak performance of domestic companies, the lack of accountability of executive management, and the fact that management compensation appeared unrelated to performance (OECD 1995: 28).

Compared to the US, the decline in the industrial fortunes of the UK occurred decades earlier, and public distress at the performance of UK companies and management and resulting unemployment was much greater. By the 1970s much of UK manufacturing industry was in sharp decline, and a vast wave of restructuring, takeovers and closures seemed to offer considerable pain with very little gain except for the investment banks, lawyers, accounting firms and management consultants who brokered the deals. The sustained lack of competitiveness of large parts of UK industry relative to German manufacturers in higher value added goods, and to Japanese manufacturers in mass produced goods was for many years a national scandal. Meanwhile the City of London was far more interested in investing capital overseas where returns were higher, and the investors in the London Stock Exchange seemed far more interested in squeezing dividends out of hard pressed companies than in industrial regeneration, product development or employment.

| Investor type | GBP billions | % of total equity owned |
|---|---|---|
| Rest of the world | 483.2 | 32.6 |
| Insurance companies | 254.2 | 17.1 |
| Pension funds | 232.6 | 15.7 |
| Individuals | 208.4 | 14 |
| Unit trusts | 27.5 | 1.8 |
| Investments trusts | 48.5 | 3.2 |
| Other financial institutions | 158.9 | 10.7 |
| Charities | 16.2 | 1.09 |
| Private non-financial companies | 9.6 | 0.6 |
| Public sector | 1.4 | 0.09 |
| Banks | 39.7 | 2.7 |
| Total | 1480.2 | |

Table 4.2 Share ownership in the UK (total equity owned as per 31 December 2004.)[1]

Source: UK National Statistics/Share Ownership 2004.
Note
[1]Unidentified holders have been allocated proportionally across all beneficial sectors.

Extensive privatisation and the forced march to a service economy seemed to offer less hope for the recovery of the economy than government and market proponents enthused. As in the United States, the 1980s deregulation of financial markets in the UK released a huge growth in the activity of international financial institutions centred in the City of London, though the benefit of this for the rest of the UK economy remained in some doubt.

In 1991 there occurred a sequence of failures of companies including Maxwell Communications Corporation (MMC), Bank of Credit and Commerce International (BCCI) and Polly Peck, all of which had recently received clear auditors' reports. More general concerns included: the standards of the audit and accountancy professions (Cadbury 1992); the lack of accountability, disclosure and transparency of boards to shareholders (Monks and Minow 1991); concerns over the adequacy of board structures and processes (Lorsch and MacIver 1989); the quality of directorial competencies; the apparent lack of corporate social responsibility; the destabilising impact of the growth of merger and acquisition activities (Pound 1992); the short term basis of corporate performance (Gregg *et al.* 1993); the spate of business fraud; and the evident weakness of corporate self-regulation. These problems were exacerbated by the development of more complex corporate structures and as a result modern company law was unable to keep pace with modern corporate reality (Hopt 1984). Corporate governance reform was released to bring some order into a very disorganised set of practices and regulations (Figure 4.3).

## Cadbury reforms

These concerns galvanised the London Stock Exchange, accountancy profession and Financial Reporting Council into establishing a committee on the Financial Aspects of Corporate Governance. The committee was chaired by Sir Adrian Cadbury, and formulated the Cadbury Code of Best Practice, which subsequently has inspired similar corporate governance codes in many countries of the world. They recommended that listed companies should incorporate a formal *statement* into their report and accounts outlining

whether or not they complied with each of the code's provisions. In respect of areas of non-compliance the company had to provide an explanation of why they had not complied. The report recommended that the compliance statements made by the companies be reviewed by auditors prior to release of the annual report.

This *comply or explain* provision was a brilliant innovation in corporate governance which was adopted internationally in other codes, as having set out a series of principles of good practice, companies were given the opportunity if they felt it necessary to explain why their practice in a specific aspect of governance was different. Once disclosed to investors and the wider public, they could then decide whether this was a convincing enough reason for the company to differ. Thus there was the possibility for intelligent engagement by companies in applying the code, and the flexibility to be different if a convincing argument could be made, which allowed necessary room for some differences at least in the governance of companies (and perhaps for the development of new good practices). In fact most large companies quickly complied with almost all of provisions of the code, though occasionally the investment community did accept *comply or explain* exceptions.

The central recommendations of Cadbury (1992) were:

- There should be a clearly accepted division of responsibility at the head of the company, ensuring a balance of power and authority.
- Boards should include non-executive directors of sufficient calibre and number to carry significant weight in the board's decisions.
- Boards should have a formal schedule of matters specifically reserved to it for decision to ensure that the direction and control of the company is firmly in its hands.
- Non-executive directors should bring an independent judgment to bear on issues of strategy, performance and resources, including key appointments and standards of conduct.
- The majority of non-executive directors should be independent of management and free from any business or other relationship.
- Non-executive directors should be selected through a formal process and both this process

Figure 4.3 UK reform of corporate governance regulation, 1992–2005.

Source: Adapted from Taylor, B. (2004).

and their appointment should be a matter for the board as a whole.

- Executive remuneration should be subject to the recommendations of a remuneration committee made up entirely or mainly of non-executive directors.
- An audit committee comprising of at least three non-executives should be established.
- The directors should report on the effectiveness of the system of internal financial control, showing the business as a going concern.
- The audit committee should meet the auditors at least once a year, without the executive directors, to ensure that there are no unresolved areas of concern.

Following publication of the code the London Stock Exchange introduced a requirement into the listing rules requesting all companies include a statement of compliance, or non-compliance and explanation, in their annual report and accounts. Institutional investors and investment banks urged those listed companies for which they provided sponsorship and advice to adopt the provisions. These principles now have become firmly established in corporate governance not only in the UK but across the world, though at the time of publication adherence to this good practice, even in large corporations, was at best partial in many countries.

Some sceptics might argue you cannot legislate against malfeasance, but the Cadbury Committee made a more balanced conclusion: 'No system of corporate governance can be totally proof against fraud and incompetence. The test is how far such aberrations can be discouraged and how quickly they can be brought to light. The risks can be reduced by making the participants in the governance process as effectively accountable as possible. The key safeguards are properly constituted boards, separation of the function of chair and of chief executive, audit committees, vigilant shareholders and financial reporting and auditing systems which provide timely disclosure. Although the great majority of companies are both competently and well run and audited under the present system of corporate governance, it is widely accepted that standards within the corporate sector have to be raised. The way forward is through clear definitions of responsibility and

an acceptance by all involved that the highest standards of efficiency and integrity are expected of them. Expectations of corporate behaviour are continually rising and a corresponding response is looked for from the shareholders, directors and auditors. The machinery is in place. What is needed is the will to improve its effectiveness' (1992: 53).

The Code of Best Practice approach of Cadbury was not only taken up by subsequent UK reports. As the following Hampel Report stated Cadbury 'struck a chord in many overseas countries; it has provided a yardstick against which standards of corporate governance in other markets are being measured' (1998: 1.5). Bockli (1998: 198) a leading Swiss company lawyer has suggested, 'it is hard to imagine today any discussion of corporate governance could bypass the Cadbury Report and the corresponding Code of Best Practice'. The Cadbury Code was characterised by Vinten (1998: 18–19) as 'the world leader' in corporate governance reform. Moreover, the Cadbury initiative propelled the UK through a series of further corporate governance reforms in a relatively positive approach to the improvement of corporate governance, even if the original volition was provided by unprecedented corporate failures and the loss of investor confidence in the quality of financial reporting (Figure 4.4).

## Further UK reform

Further UK reforms of corporate governance followed the Cadbury code, gradually developing a comprehensive approach to better standards of corporate governance in all its aspects (Manifest 2004).

## Greenbury Report (1995)

The Greenbury Report proposed new guidelines for director remuneration. During the 1990s the issue of directors' remuneration was becoming a primary concern for investors and the public at large. In particular, the levels of remuneration of directors in privatised industries were rising rapidly and remuneration packages were failing to

**Figure 4.4** UK corporate governance regulation and FTSE 100 index, 1992–2002.

Source: Clarke, T. (2006).

provide the necessary incentives for executives to perform. Greenbury outlined:

- the *role of a remuneration committee* in setting the remuneration packages for the CEO and other directors;
- the *required level of disclosure* needed by shareholders regarding details of directors' remuneration and whether there is the need to obtain shareholder approval;
- specific guidelines for determining a *remuneration policy* for directors; and
- *service contracts* and provisions binding the company to pay compensation to a director, particularly in the event of dismissal for unsatisfactory performance.

Greenbury recommended a *maximum notice period of 12 months* for executives rather than three years as suggested by Cadbury, which reduced the cost of removing underperforming executives. However Greenbury did not enjoy the acceptance of Cadbury, as it was thought it did not address the issue of linking executive pay with performance sufficiently.

## Hampel Report (1998)

The Hampel Report focused on disclosure and best practice, and represented something of a

corporate reaction to the enthusiasm Cadbury had generated for reform. The report emphasised *principles* of good governance rather than explicit *rules* in order to reduce the regulatory burden on companies and avoid 'box-ticking' so as to be flexible enough to be applicable to all companies. Sharply narrowing the focus, Hampel viewed governance from a strict principal–agent perspective regarding corporate governance as an opportunity to enhance long term shareholder value, which was asserted as the primary objective of the company. This was a new emphasis from the Cadbury Code which had primarily focused on preventing the abuse of the discretionary authority entrusted to management. The report favoured greater shareholder involvement in company affairs, and for example the report recommended that unrelated proposals should not be bundled under one resolution for shareholders, and that institutional shareholders should adopt a considered policy on voting. However in another conservative step, Hampel did not believe that directors' remuneration should be a matter for shareholder approval in general meeting.

## Combined Code (1998)

The Combined Code (FRC 1998) outlined a mandatory disclosure framework and was revised in 2003 following the publication of the

Higgs Report. Section 1 of the code is comprehensive covering topics including the composition and operations of the board, directors' remuneration, relationships with shareholders, the supply of information, accountability and audit. As with Cadbury the code is powerful enough to effect specific recommendations and flexible enough to be applicable to most companies.

Section 2 of the code covers shareholder voting, dialogue with companies and the evaluation of governance disclosures. As institutional investors invest on behalf of the shareholders they represent, they have a responsibility to hold the companies in which they invest to account. The code recognises that the responsibility for maintaining good dialogue and mutual understanding belongs to both companies and institutional investors. Finally when evaluating the quality of governance disclosure by companies, institutional investors are to give due weight to all relevant factors, a provision that has been more closely defined by the institutions themselves. Subsequently the Turnbull Report (1999) offered further advice on compliance with mandatory disclosure.

## Myners Report (2001)

The Myners Report was commissioned 'to consider whether there were factors distorting the investment decision-making of institutions'. The report highlights a number of problems with the current system:

- There are unrealistic demands made of pension fund trustees as they are being expected to make crucial investment decisions without either the resources or the expertise required.
- Consequently there is too heavy a burden placed on investment consultants who advise the trustees to ensure the decisions made are correct.
- The critical job of asset allocation in the selection of which markets as opposed to which individual stocks to invest in is under-resourced.
- There is a lack of clarity about objectives at a number of levels: for instance, the objectives of fund managers, when taken together appear

to bear little relation to the ultimate objective of the pension fund.

The review concludes the present structures used by the various types of institutional investors to make investment decisions lack both efficiency and flexibility, which often means that beneficiaries' money is not being invested in ways which will maximise their interests. Myners outlined some basic principles of an effective approach to investment decision-making, which if adopted by pension funds and other institutional investors would likely result in a more efficient system (Manifest 2004).

## AUSTRALIA AND NEW ZEALAND

Australia and New Zealand's approach to corporate governance follows the Anglo-Saxon model. They are shareholder economies in which private enterprise is about maximising returns for investors. 'Those who own equity dominate because the law has traditionally equated the interests of the company with those of shareholders. Australian corporate law traditionally falls for the most part within these parameters' (Ford 2001: para. 8.130). Australia has a well-established stock market, and a greater number of listed companies per million people than either the US or the UK. However, according to Cheffins (2001) Australia has some distinctive features in its development of an *outsider* model of corporate governance that distinguishes it from the US and UK. Whereas the majority of large companies in these countries are quoted on the stock exchange, in Australia only a minority of the top 500 companies have shares traded on the stock exchange. Furthermore, ownership structure is more concentrated in Australia than in the US or UK, with only 11 out of the 20 largest publicly quoted companies in 1999 classified as 'widely-held' (that is they did not have a shareholder who owned 10 per cent or more of the equity). A similar pattern exists with smaller companies, and in 1996 approximately 45 per cent of the companies that made up Australia's ASX All Ordinaries Index had a shareholder other than an institutional investor that owned 20 per cent or more of the shares (Stapledon 1998), and therefore could not

be claimed to be 'widely-held'. Since neither large companies nor small companies could be claimed to be generally 'widely-held' it could be concluded the separation of ownership and control has taken hold to only a limited degree in Australia.

This view is put forward more strongly by Dignam and Galanis (2004) who through an examination of share ownership patterns, institutional investor activism, private rent extraction, the market for corporate control and blocks to information flow, insist the corporate governance system of Australia's listed market in fact has many of the characteristics associated with insider systems:

- significant blockholders engaged in private rent extraction;
- institutional investor powerlessness;
- a strong relationship between management and blockholders, which results in a weak market for corporate control;
- a historic weakness in public and private securities regulation, which allows the creation and perpetuation of crucial blocks to information flow (2004: 26).

Australia has some of the frontier tradition of the United States; however, the vibrancy of this continued much later into the twentieth century, and the effort to regulate this coordinated at the federal level has occurred only in recent decades. A raw form of wild capitalism originating in the resources industries squared up against a strong-willed workerism, and together drove the economic development of the country. Episodes of corporate scandal were recurrent in Australia's business history, culminating in the excesses of the 1980s boom with colourful rogues exposed as crooks, as Sykes comments on the staggering scale of this corporate meltdown:

> The corporate booms and busts of the 1980s were the greatest ever seen in Australian history. The boom saw a bunch of corporate cowboys financed to dizzy heights by greedy and reckless bankers. Large sectors of Australian industry changed hands. Ownership of the major brewing and media companies changed completely ... Alan Bond built an enormous empire on debt and creative accounting. The ensuing bust saw awesome

destruction. The collapses included Australia's largest industrial group (Adelaide Steamship); the ninth largest enterprise in the nation, measured by revenue (Bond Corporation); nearly half the brewing industry (Bond Brewing); all three major commercial television networks (Bond Media, Qintex, Channel Ten); Australia's largest car renter (Budget); the second largest newspaper group (Fairfax); Victoria's largest building society (Pyramid); and Australia's largest textile group (Linter). Severe problems were faced by Australia's largest company, as measured by revenue (Elders), its largest media group (News) and the other half of the brewing industry (Fosters) ... The devastation was equally great among the financiers. Total write-offs and provisions by banks and financiers amounted to $28 billion. Australia's three largest merchant banks (Tricontinental, Partnership Pacific and Elders Finance) had to be rescued by their parents. Two of Australia's four state banks (State Bank of Victoria and State Bank of South Australia suffered devastating losses and were investigated by Royal Commissions. One of those (The SBV) was taken over by the Commonwealth Bank. The other two state banks, the Rural & Industries Bank of Western Australia and the State Bank of New South Wales, were deeply scarred. The four major trading banks (Westpac, National, Commonwealth and ANZ) had to write billions of dollars off their loan books, the suffering being particularly heavy in Westpac and ANZ. The losses of foreign banks operating in Australia were even higher proportionately, some of the worst being those of Hongkong Bank Australia, Standard Chartered, Security Pacific and Bank of New Zealand.

> (1996: 1)

All the evidence suggests Australian business has maintained an unusually high degree of blockholder control, much closer to the level experienced in insider governance systems. Even as late as 2003 Governance Metrics International conducted a wide-ranging corporate governance review of the largest 50 listed companies in Australia and was concerned by the large number of related party transactions, described as 'astounding by US or UK standards'.

More worryingly still, only 21 of the companies surveyed had a policy of board scrutiny of related party transactions (2003). Lamba and Stapledon discovered not only a large number of block-holders in Australian companies, but that private blockholders had an incentive to remain:

> There is a positive and highly statistically signif-icant relationship between the level of related party transactions and whether the blockholder is a widely held corporate entity or a fam-ily entity … Interestingly, there is no rela-tionship between the level of related party transactions and the likelihood of the block-holder being a government entity, that is, either the Commonwealth of Australia, a State of Australia, or an overseas government. Thus, higher levels of private benefits are directly related to the likelihood that the controlling blockholder will either be a corporate entity or a family entity, but not a government entity … In particular, where private benefits are com-paratively high, the company is more likely to have a blockholder with a controlling stake.
>
> (2001: n.5)

Institutional investors in Australia did not until recently enjoy much success at restraining these evident excesses, Henry Bosch suggests, 'Before the crash of 1987, the term 'corporate gover-nance' was rarely used in Australia and few people gave much thought to the concepts now covered by it. Shareholders were essentially passive … Institutional shareholders paid almost no atten-tion to the way that companies were governed, and if they were dissatisfied with one of their investments, they took the 'Wall Street Walk' and sold their shares' (2002: 270–273). Nor was the Australian takeover market particularly active in redressing corporate governance failure:

> The Australian listed market is therefore char-acterised by a small amount of hostile takeover activity, a concomitantly large number of friendly transactions and a very successful record of management in fighting off hostile bids. These characteristics suggest not only a strong relationship between management and blockholders, but also that a market discipline mechanism present in the UK and the US is

absent from the Australian listed market. Block-holders exercise control over the key decision as to the sale of the company.

> (Dignam and Galanis 2004: 20)

Presiding over this winner-take-all frontier corpo-rate culture was a weak, divided and ineffective regulatory structure with no single regulator, and a *Corporations Law*, consisting of the *Corpora-tions Act* (1989) and the Corporations Acts of the individual states. Regulators at the state level all had different priorities and different but inade-quate powers and resources, with each applying different corporate laws. Paul Barry maintains, 'Australia also had itself to blame for what cer-tain businessmen had been allowed to get away with, because its system of corporate regulation in the 1980s was pathetically inadequate' (1990: 289). Any attempt to introduce national regula-tion failed due to political resistance, and the reluctance of the states to give up a source of rev-enue. It was only the excesses of the 1990s that allowed agreement on the federal government tak-ing responsibility for company law and regulation. This was not overdue as Sykes indicates:

> … At the end, investors were left excoriat-ing corporate cowboys such as Alan Bond, Christopher Skase and Laurie Connell. While these and other men deserved blame, it should have been spread more widely. Australia, after all, is no stranger to corporate cowboys. The country has had them in almost every decade of its existence.
>
> (1996: 1)

The commitment to reform of corporate gov-ernance in Australia produced a national secu-rities regulator the Australian Securities and Investment Commission (ASIC), and a single corporate statute the *Corporations Act* 2001 (Figure 4.5). ASIC is empowered to regulate investments and securities, enforce the business and listing rules of financial markets including the Australian Stock Exchange, and to police the *Corporations Act*. However, corporate reg-ulation remains a complex constitutional com-promise, as while securities regulation is by ASIC, enforcement is the responsibility of the Commonwealth Director of Public Prosecutions

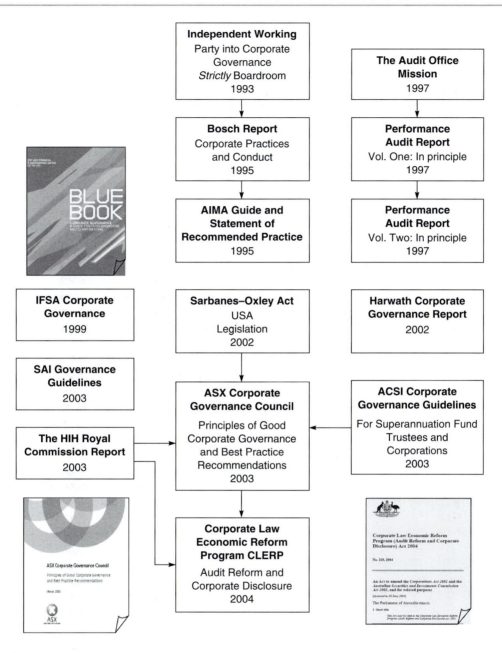

**Figure 4.5** Australian reform of corporate governance regulation, 1992–2004.

Source: Clarke, T. (2006).

and Commonwealth Attorney General. The banking industry is regulated by ASIC, but the Reserve Bank of Australia, and the Commonwealth Department of Treasury also have regulatory responsibility. The Australian Prudential Regulatory Authority also regulates the banking and financial services industry including pension funds. The state based stock exchanges merged into the Australian Stock Exchange in 1987 which demutualised in 1998. ASIC therefore is best described not as the single regulatory authority, but as the *lead regulator.* There is some evidence that this continuing division of regulator powers has diminished the power of regulation, limited the

pressure on company disclosure relative to other countries, and left the under-resourced regulator, in the past at least, with a hands-off approach to much routine infringement of company law (Dignam and Galanis 2004: 26). A very gradual reform process took place, and Australia only arrived at a definitive ASX corporate governance code in 2003 (Figure 4.6).

## New Zealand

As sympathetically considered by Joseph Healey in his book *Corporate Governance and Wealth Creation in New Zealand* (2003) the equity market in New Zealand has remained weak since the 1990s compared to the growth of the Australian market:

The market capitalization of the NZSE 40 at the end of 1994 was $42.4 billion, and by the end of 2001 was $42.8 billion. In other words there was little or no change. By contrast, the Australian market had grown from A$282 billion in 1994 to A$733 billion by

the end of 2001. In 1986 the NZSE 40 was also $42.4 billion and the Australian figure A$137 billion. The average market capitalisation of NZSE 40 companies at the end of 2001 was $320 million, up $10 million on the corresponding figure in 1994. In Australia the average market capitalization during the period had grown from A$250 million to A$550 million.

(Healey 2003: 30)

Financial markets in the advanced countries have experienced a series of far-reaching interrelated changes since the 1980s:

- progressive deregulation of financial markets;
- globalisation of financial markets;
- financial product innovation;
- increasing prominence of institutional investors in the market.

The new competitive environment in capital markets may have facilitated new sources of investment and more efficient management of risk. But more mobile capital has meant for New Zealand

Figure 4.6 Corporate governance and regulation in Australia.

Source: Clarke, T. (2006).

investment that is more short term, more arm's length and diffuse. Large-scale companies are most likely to benefit from these developments and New Zealand has few of these, and smaller companies face problems in a financial system that is globally integrated (Healey 2003: 207).

At 43 per cent of GDP the New Zealand equity market is one of the smallest markets relative to GDP compared to other countries. In contrast, the miracle economy of Ireland was 30 per cent of the New Zealand market in 1990 and is now 300 per cent of the New Zealand market. Healey (2003: 214–215) diagnoses the following problems with New Zealand's public equity market:

- the small size of firms;
- a dividend philosophy which treats equity as if it was a fixed income security and not a residual risk. If dividends do not go down during a recession they may be taking priority over investment, with under-investment in the potential of future growth;
- the New Zealand stock market does not enjoy a strong reputation, with the perception that there are not the reporting, compliance and governance standards of other advanced industrial markets.

In 2001 the New Zealand government approved stringent rules on shareholder protection. Under the new Takeover Code an investor buying more than 20 per cent of a company normally will have to make a bid for at least 50 per cent and offer the same price to all equity owners. A study by the ANZ bank in 2000 of corporate governance practices in 500 companies found the cost of weak governance estimated at 7 per cent of GDP. The ANZ study recommended that pension fund managers be mandated to report on the governance standards of the companies they invest in, and their own policies to improve such standards (OECD 2001a: 6).

## SHAREHOLDER VALUE ORIENTATION

During the 1990s the Anglo-Saxon shareholder value based approach to corporate governance became reinvigorated in the US, UK, Australia, New Zealand and other countries that adopted this model. This model also began to have a strong influence in European and Asian economies that formerly sustained more stakeholder or collective conceptions of corporate governance. In the context of global competition, international investment patterns, and the aggressive growth of international mergers and acquisitions, assuming the primary objective of releasing shareholder value often seemed the only sure way not only for international business success, but for corporate survival itself.

The shareholder value view upholds a property conception of the company. In its most extreme form, as developed by the Chicago School of law and economics, the company is treated as a nexus of contracts through which the various parties arrange to transact with each other. This theory claims the assets of the company are the property of the shareholders, and managers and boards of directors are viewed as the agents of the shareholders with all of the difficulties of enforcement associated with agency relationships. Though the shareholder value orientation is assumed to be an eternal belief, firmly rooted in law, with strong historical foundations, none of this is anything more than a recent ideological convenience. Shareholder value in its current manifestation was a construct of financial economists in the 1980s, and meant to deal with the *lack* of shareholder value orientation widely apparent in US industry at the time.

Historically, American corporations have demonstrated a broad conception of the orientation towards a wide constituency of stakeholders necessary in order to build the enterprise. Over time and with the increasing market power of large corporations, managements' sense of accountability might have become overwhelmed by complacency and self-interest. However, to attempt to replace self-interested managers, with managers keenly focused entirely upon delivering value to shareholders, is to replace one form of self-interest with another. Any broadening of the social obligations of the company was dangerous according to the shareholder value school of thought, 'Few trends could so thoroughly undermine the foundations of our free society as the acceptance by corporate officials of a social responsibility other than to make as much money

for their stockholders as possible' (Friedman 1962: 113). The difficulty is whether in trying to represent the interests of all stakeholders, company directors simply slip the leash of the one truly effective restraint that regulates their behaviour – their relationship with shareholders. These views were expressed with vigour by liberal economists, and enjoyed the support of leading business leaders and senior politicians. More practically, such views reflected how US and UK companies were driven in the period of the 1980s and 1990s, with an emphasis upon sustaining share price and dividend payments at all costs, and freely using merger and takeover activity to discipline managers who failed in their responsibility to enhance shareholder value. It was the economic instability and insecurity created by this approach that was criticised in the report by Porter (1992).

Monks and Minnow (2001: 40) have attempted a recent restating of the essential principles of the shareholder theory of the firm, which is more tolerant of the interests of other constituents, but insists they are best served by acknowledging the supremacy of the ultimate owner:

> It seems to make most sense to envision a hypothetical long-term shareholder, like the beneficial owner of most institutional investor securities, as the ultimate party at interest. That allows all other interests to be factored in without losing sight of the goal of long term wealth maximisation. But without a clear and directly enforceable fiduciary obligation to shareholders, the contract that justifies the corporate structure is irreparably shattered. It is difficult enough to determine the success of a company's strategy based on only one goal – shareholder value. It is impossible when we add in other goals … The only way to evaluate the success of a company's performance is to consult those who have the most direct and wide-reaching interest in the results of that performance – the shareholders. The problem is one of effective accountability (agency costs). Only owners have the motive to inform themselves and to enforce standards that arguably are a proxy for the public interest.

It could be questioned whether a singular focus upon shareholder interests really is the key to sustainable corporate performance and effective accountability. In an era of increasing participation of consumers, environmental, employees and other economic groups, to assume that shareholders alone are capable of effective monitoring is untenable. An irony is that shareholders, particularly the scattered army of individual shareholders, have not been particularly well looked after or informed in the recent past, even by companies espousing shareholder value views. Who then does the shareholder value ideology benefit?

Deakin (2005) examines how the market for corporate control in the 1980s used the takeover mechanism as the catalyst to ensure managers of large corporations acted in the interests of shareholders. Many of the measures developed during this era have now been internalised in companies, for example the near-universal adoption by listed companies of the accounting metrics of earnings per share, economic value added, and returns on capital employed which in various ways benchmark corporate performance by reference to shareholder returns. However, the enthusiasm of top executives for these measures corresponds closely with them receiving an increasing amount of their reward in stock options:

> Share option schemes, from a small beginning in the mid-1980s, are now a near universal feature of executive pay in large US and UK corporations. Share options represented a revolution in the way senior managers were paid and incentivised. In the immediate post-war period, professional managers often did not own shares (let alone have options to purchase shares) in the companies they ran; indeed, separation from the concerns of shareholders was often viewed in a positive light. With the advent of share options, as managers saw their own wealth increasingly tied up with that of the company's share price, managerial attitudes also began to change. Fewer of the leaders of large corporations were engineering or technical experts in their field; instead accounting, legal and financial skills were now the most highly valued. The goal of the senior managerial class with the goal of share price maximisation has thereby become even more complete.
>
> (Deakin 2005: 14)

Financially driven managers fitted well into an increasingly financially driven market environment of the 1990s with equity values, targets of current and future earnings, and an intensified interest in share price against the background of the longest bull market and economic upswing in history. This *financialisation* of business activity in the Anglo-American regime denoted a profound change in orientation involving a concentration on financial results, with a shift of focus from production markets to capital markets, with the danger of the concentrated forces of the capital market far more mobile and threatening, than the old forces of the product market of dispersed consumers. This shift in focus had great implications for the competitiveness of much of US and UK manufacturing industry in the 1980s, and was to provide an unstable platform for future business development (Froud *et al.* 2000). An excessive focus on immediate market returns, often serves to simply increase the extent and cynicism of market manipulation (Redmond 2005: 854).

At times in the 1970s and 1980s it appeared that the market-based shareholder value orientation was damaging the US and UK economies as the relentless pursuit of short term returns was associated with downsizing, loss of market share, and sometimes the abandoning of whole industries to overseas competitors with longer investment horizons. Towards the end of this period Michael Porter (1992) wrote a report for the US Council on Competitiveness on *Capital Disadvantage: America's Failing Capital Investment System*, in which he contrasted the *fluid* capital investment system of the US, with the *dedicated* capital investment system of Germany and Japan. While the US system focused purely on financial goals and measures and short term performance, the German and Japanese systems were characterised by long term investment in industrial strategies to boost productivity and capability. However as the industrial fortunes of the respective countries appeared to reverse in the 1990s, these lessons were forgotten, and shareholder value ideology was mightily reinforced as the unquestioned doctrine of the western corporate world.

With the renaissance of the *new economy* in the United States the Anglo-American corporate governance system once again became generally regarded as the most robust. It was related to the largest economy, with the largest concentration of leading corporations, the deepest and most fluid capital markets, a dispersed shareholding base, and well-established laws and regulatory institutions, and in the 1990s was increasingly regarded as the winning formula. One of the 'strengths of the US system lies in its encouragement of self-regulation by corporate entities, supported by law around basic principles, but not mandated point by point. The US system enables people who know the corporation most intimately to effect its operation, so that the corporation can be positioned to achieve the highest level of efficiency and competitiveness it is capable of within its economic environment' (Millstein 2001: 10).

## The new economy

Just at the time it looked as if the American economy was about to enter a long period of gradual decline, much as Britain experienced a century earlier, suddenly the US staged a remarkable recovery. Reasserting its place at the forefront of the information technology revolution, the US economy in the 1990s achieved higher productivity and sustained growth without a rise in the rate of inflation. As competitors in Europe and Japan faltered, the US was portrayed as a *new economy* with attributes that not only defied economics but confounded history, an economy that:

- grows without apparent threat of recession;
- continues to expand without increasing inflation;
- constantly restructures itself for greater efficiency and productivity;
- replenishes and revitalises itself through new technology and capital investment;
- functions without excessive debt, either public or private;
- maintains a balanced budget;
- increasingly becomes globalised and export driven (Weinstein 1997).

There was much evidence that apparently supported this optimism: US competitiveness and

productivity led the advanced economies; there was a faster expansion in industrial output than any advanced country; and GDP per capita second only to Singapore. The US appeared to have endorsed its leadership of technological advance and diffusion (OECD 2001d). This reinvention of the US economy created a sense of triumphalism, that the US system of fluid capital markets and flexible labour markets was the most dynamic in the world. Silicon Valley became the envy of every country, with its clusters of energetically innovative high technology companies producing the new software and technology the rest of the world apparently possessed an insatiable appetite for.

Despite warnings from the economist Paul Krugman and others that this sudden burst of productivity could be cyclical rather than permanent, the euphoria in the economy grew as hundreds of billions of dollars were invested in the apparently endless rise of the NYSE and booming NASDAQ, the world's largest electronic stock market. With apparently unlimited demand for new investment opportunities, telecommunications, computer hardware and software companies and other high technology firms experienced an unprecedented rise in their market capitalisation.

The economic significance of the increasing use and potential applications of internet technology was at the core of this industrial and investment revolution. A new knowledge and information based networked economy was becoming established, with the potential to capitalise on Metcalfe's law that as the scale of a network expands linearly, its use expands geometrically. This set the scene for the arrival of a horde of dot.com companies in the late 1990s which claimed in the prospectuses for their Initial Public Offerings (IPOs) that the heavy internet traffic visiting their websites could readily be translated into burgeoning sources of revenue. Belief was suspended in the scramble to make serious money overnight in the dot.com revolution. It was this mentality that Alan Greenspan, chair of the Federal Reserve Bank of the United States, famously dismissed as *irrational exuberance* (Shiller 2000). The scene was set for the biggest collapse in the NASDAQ and NYSE since the Wall Street crash of 1929.

## The Enron shock

Many large US corporations in the 1990s became caught up in this get-rich-quick approach to business. Most notable among them was Enron which transformed itself from a small gas pipeline company into the largest energy trader in the world. Effectively it abandoned interest in producing or transporting energy, but simply made itself the key trader in electronic energy markets. Enron then attempted to transfer this *asset light* model into the telecommunications business creating new markets for bandwidth. Enron's business model appeared to be based on brilliant innovation, but it was the dramatic and sustained profit growth that really captivated investors. Achieving this explained Enron's intense focus on its credit rating, cash flow and debt burden. The company's *asset light* strategy amounted to disposing of assets to engage in financial engineering, and ultimately led to actions taken by Enron to move billions of dollars in assets off its balance sheet to separate but affiliated companies.

> To accomplish its objectives, Enron had been relying increasingly on complicated transactions with convoluted financing and accounting structures, including transactions with multiple special purpose entities, hedges, derivatives, swaps, forward contracts, prepaid contracts, and other forms of structured finance. While there is no empirical data on the extent to which US public companies use these devices, it appears that few companies outside of investment banks use them as extensively as Enron. At Enron, they became dominant; at its peak, the company apparently had between $15 and $20 billion involved in hundreds of structured finance transactions.
>
> (Senate 2002: 8)

When the company encountered business problems, in the effort to convince the market that rising revenues and profits would continue indefinitely at Enron, it created off-balance sheet entities to hide tens of billions of liabilities and boost reported earnings. For a while this deception worked, but when Enron had to restate its earlier reported earnings, the end came very quickly (Figure 4.7).

**Figure 4.7** Enron's rise and fall.

Source: Clarke, T. (2006).

The euphoria the new economy was built upon was suddenly punctured in 2001/2002 by the spectacular sequence of US corporate crises involving Enron, WorldCom, Tyco International, Adelphia Communications, Global Crossing, Quest Communications, Computer Associates, and Arthur Andersen and others. The collapse of Enron, the largest bankruptcy in US history, led to thousands of employees losing their life savings tied up in the energy company's stock. Federal indictments charged Enron executives with devising complex financial schemes to defraud Enron and its shareholders through transactions with off-the-books partnerships that made the company look far more profitable than it was (see Case Study 1).

WorldCom's rise and fall on the back of the telecoms and Internet boom of the late 1990s was even more precipitous than that of Enron (Figure 4.8). WorldCom ironically named one of *Fortune* magazine's most admired global companies in 2002, wrongly listed over $3 billion of its 2001 expenses, and $797 million of its first quarter 2002 expenses as capital expenses, which were not reflected in the company's earnings results. WorldCom agreed to restate all of its earnings results for 2001, as well as those for the first quarter of 2002. Meanwhile the vast compensation

packages Bernie Ebers and the other WorldCom executives came to light, together with hundreds of millions of dollars of illicit loans to the executives. The SEC in June 2002 charged WorldCom with massive accounting fraud (see Case Study 2). In January 2002 Global Crossing filed for Chapter 11 bankruptcy protection, listing assets of 22.4 billion and debts totalling 12.4 billion dollars, the fourth largest bankruptcy in US history. The company was accused of employing misleading transactions and accounting methods that gave the appearance that the company was generating hundreds of millions of dollars in sales and cash revenues that did not actually exist.

At Adelphia Communications the former CEO John Rigas, two of his sons, and two other former executives were charged with conspiracy, securities fraud and wire fraud and with looting the company of hundreds of millions of dollars. At Tyco tens of millions of dollars in fraudulent bonuses were uncovered, and $13.5 million dollars in unauthorised loans to key Tyco managers (see Case Study 3). This represented an unprecedented display of accounting fraud, regulatory failure, executive excess, and avoidable bankruptcy, with resulting widespread disastrous losses incurred by employees, pension funds,

**Figure 4.8** The rise and fall of WorldCom.

Source: Clarke, T. (2006).

and other investors. What was alarming was that each element of the corporate governance system in these cases appeared to have failed, as the *Australian Financial Review* commented, 'The collapse of Enron has disclosed that every component of the infrastructure of US capitalism was dysfunctional. Companies' accounts were misleading, their auditors conniving, their lawyers conspiring, the ratings agencies asleep, and the regulators inadequate. "Faith in corporate America hasn't been so strained since the early 1900s", claims *BusinessWeek* magazine' (*US Crisis of Confidence, AFR*, 4/5 May 2002: 24).

Enacted on July 30, 2002 with an alacrity induced by general outrage, the Sarbanes–Oxley Act significantly changes the corporate governance and reporting requirements applicable to any company, including any non-US company, that is required to file reports with the SEC because it has listed securities on the NYSE or a NASDAQ market, or made a registered offering of securities in the United States. Meanwhile the NYSE and NASDAQ issued new listing standards intended to harmonise with the Sarbanes–Oxley Act.

## Wider implications of Enron and the Sarbanes–Oxley Act

In the emerging mosaic of new laws, regulations and listing rules that have emerged as a result of the Enron experience, promising to impose new corporate governance standards on the boards of companies, it will be the Sarbanes–Oxley Act which will have the most enduring implications not just for US companies, but for overseas companies whose securities are traded in the United States. Specific provisions of Sarbanes–Oxley and the recommendations of NYSE, implemented immediately include:

- Annual reports must be accompanied by CEO and CFO certifications that the report fully complies with reporting requirements and fairly presents in all material respects companies financial results (s. 906).
- CEO and CFO must certify statements concerning the company's internal accounting controls and disclosure controls and procedures.
- Personal loans to directors and officers are prohibited.

■ If a company restates its accounts due to material non-compliance of the company, as a result of misconduct, its CEO and CFO must reimburse the company for any bonus or equity, or incentive based compensation paid, and for any profits from sales of the company's securities realised during the 12 month period after the first publication of the accounts.

■ The act provides protection for employees who assist in investigations or proceedings that involve violations of US federal securities laws and fraud statutes.

The Act also empowers the SEC to adopt rules to require the NYSE and NASDAQ to prohibit the listing of a company's securities unless the company has an audit committee comprised entirely of independent directors, that meets certain requirements to its responsibilities and operation. The Act creates an oversight board to register and inspect auditors set auditing standards. The Act requires the SEC to adopt rules for reporting companies to include in their annual reports a management report on internal controls and to require independent auditors to attest to these management reports. Finally, the SEC must adopt new rules to require disclosure of material off-balance sheet transactions and a code of ethics for finance officers.

The new listing standards published by NYSE and NASDAQ in the light of the new legislation, embody in significant respects, what were best practices internationally:

■ populating boards with a majority of independent directors;

■ tightening standards of independence;

■ further restricting audit committee composition and adopting new responsibilities for audit committees;

■ instituting wholly independent compensation and nominating/governance committees and adopting specific responsibilities for these committees;

■ convening regular meetings restricted to the non-management directors;

■ performing regular board and committee evaluations;

■ publishing company-specific governance guidelines and codes of conduct and ethics.

There is some evidence Sarbanes–Oxley is having an impact on company policies and practices regarding corporate governance. For example a PwC survey of large US multinationals found 84 per cent companies changed their auditing control and compliances procedures in the light of Sarbanes–Oxley. Companies are now reporting more fully their critical accounting policies in annual reports. A survey by Shearman and Sterling of the recent annual reports found 95 out of 100 Fortune 100 companies thought that accounting policies affecting contingent liabilities, goodwill, pension benefits, and income taxes, are among the most critical (House Committee on Financial Services (HCFS) 2003: 6).

In board reform particularly, the separation of the roles of chair/CEO, the US has been slower to act (and interestingly this tough issue was not tackled in Sarbanes–Oxley). But in keeping with the trend to accountability and establishing effective checks and balances, the Business Roundtable an association of CEOs of 150 leading corporations reported that 55 per cent of Roundtable companies had an independent chair, independent lead director or presiding outside director (HCFS 2003: 10). Another criticism of Sarbanes–Oxley and similar legislative efforts in other countries is that corporate governance will become focused on compliance to the detriment of essential entrepreneurship and risk taking. Survey evidence suggests that boards are managing to rise to the challenge of pursuing accountability and risk-taking at the same time (HCFS 2003: 11).

The Investor Responsibility Research Centre reviewed SEC filings for 1,250 companies in the S & P 500, MidCap and SmallCap Indexes and found the number of audit committee meetings in 2003 increased on average by 39 per cent over 2002. Another survey by the American Corporate Counsel Association (ACCA) and national Association of Corporate Directors (NACD) suggests the majority of directors and corporate counsel think the recent scandals will not restrict risk-taking or entrepreneurial ventures by senior management. A further survey by PwC of CEOs of the 400 fastest growing US companies found that only 15 per cent are publicly listed and therefore immediately subject to Sarbanes–Oxley (HCFS 2003: 11). A final clue to the new context for corporate governance in the US for which

Sarbanes–Oxley has set the mood, are the decisions of the Delaware Supreme Court, the most experienced state judiciary in corporate law in the country, in the state where the highest number of large corporations are registered. In a sobering series of opinions in cases from mid-2002 to mid-2003 involving the performance by directors of their fiduciary duties, in every one of the cases, the court held for the shareholders and against the directors (HCFS 2003: 13).

However some critics have questioned whether Sarbanes–Oxley can in itself resolve some of the fundamental problems of the highly incentivised US market based system of corporate governance. Gordon (2002: 1234–1235) contends the Enron experience challenges some core beliefs and practices that have underpinned the academic analysis of corporate law and governance, including mergers and acquisitions, since the 1980s: 'These amount to an interlocking set of institutions that constitute "shareholder capitalism" American-style, 2001, that we have been aggressively promoting throughout the world. We have come to rely on a particular set of assumptions about the connection between stock market prices and the underlying economic realities; the reliability of independent auditors, financial standards, and copious disclosure in protecting the integrity of financial reporting; the efficacy of corporate governance in monitoring financial performance; the utility of stock options in aligning managerial and shareholder interests, and the value of employee ownership as both an incentive device as well as a retirement planning tool'.

## New York Stock Exchange: Grasso's fall

The sad fate of Dick Grasso the former chair and CEO of the New York Stock Exchange is a salutary lesson for anyone involved in corporate governance. On 25 May 2004 Eliot Spitzer the New York State Attorney General launched a lawsuit against Grasso, charging him with deception, conflict of interest and the receipt of excessive pay.

Grasso resigned from the NYSE in September 2003 after his vast pay package became public (Figure 4.9). He insisted his compensation was justified; however, shock waves went through the exchange when it was revealed he would be

**Figure 4.9** NYSE's annual profit vs. CEO Dick Grasso's annual compensation ($ millions).

Source: Webb Dan K. (2003), *Report to the New York Stock Exchange an Investigation Relating to the Compensation of Richard A. Grasso*, New York: Winston & Strawn, LLP.

receiving a lump sum payment of $139.5 million. The Securities and Exchange Commission chair immediately fired a letter to the NYSE Board demanding an explanation for this large sum. The Exchange launched its own inquiry and on 28 January 2005 the State Supreme Court Justice Charles E. Ramos declared the Webb Report should be made public. The document details board meetings and other events leading to the award of Grasso's pay package. It maintains he received unreasonable levels of compensation and benefits, and blames the NYSE board members for failing to monitor properly Grasso's activities. The report slams the ex-CEO for having enjoyed direct control over the people and processes used in settling his pay, and suggests there are grounds for demanding Grasso return over $50 million.

This all needs to be put in the context that Grasso as head of the NYSE was responsible in 2002 for the new corporate governance listing rules following Sarbanes–Oxley, that attempted to eliminate the excesses revealed in the Enron and WorldCom sagas. The fact that Grasso was essentially in a regulatory role, is a telling indication that reform has not run as deeply into the psyche of America's business people and regulators as might have been hoped. Grasso was one of the most important and influential regulators of corporate behaviour in the United States, and

yet appears to have ignored fundamental corporate governance procedures himself, while he was publicly calling for them to be respected by others. The NYSE is the largest and most powerful stock exchange in the world, and is expected to demonstrate leadership not largesse.

Dick Grasso joined the NYSE in 1968 as a listings clerk. He became chair and chief executive in 1995. He is accused of running the stock exchange like an old time political boss, as if he owned it. He controlled the composition of the board and the agenda. He fought to maintain the traditions of the stock exchange, and though he invested in new technology, he feared the advance of the NASDAQ. He rode the wave of the longest stock market boom in history, and was acclaimed for his bravery and determination in opening the market only six days after the September 11 terrorist bombings on the NYSE's doorstep. However, like many over-powerful figures surrounded by people he has appointed, Grasso lost the plot a few years ago as the 2001/2002 market crash wiped trillions off the value of stock, and the profits of the exchange collapsed. Grasso had allowed his pay to inflate massively during the recent good years, and instead of making any downward adjustment proceeded to eat into the faltering profits of the exchange with his inflated compensation claims (see chart). In 2002 the NYSE earned $28 million, barely a quarter of its 1998 profit, while Grasso earned $12 million, double his 1998 compensation.

## Big on marketing light on regulation

Under his reign the NYSE presented a glossy and successful image to the world, but the tragedy is that while marketing and communication budgets were regularly increased, the regulatory departments of the exchange were denied resources. When the exchange's arbitration chief requested further funding to deal with the rising number of arbitration cases, he was told there were more pressing issues. In early 2003 Grasso campaigned for the nomination of Citigroup chair and then CEO Sandy Weill as a representative of the public on the board of the exchange. This was just after Citigroup had agreed to pay $400 million to settle a case in which regulators accused the firm of misleading investors through stock research. Several members of the NYSE nominating committee questioned this recommendation and offered alternative candidates, but Grasso held firm. Uproar ensued and when New York Attorney General contacted Grasso he insisted it was the nomination committees' decision. Spitzer threatened to publicly denounce the nomination and Weill withdrew his name from consideration.

Things came to a head when Grasso pushed for permission to withdraw $135.5 million in accumulated retirement pay and other benefits: some members of the board objected to this move until 2007 when Grasso was due to retire. The item was passed at a board meeting in August 2003 when the most vociferous opponent was on vacation.

When details of Grasso's compensation package began to leak out the public backlash was overwhelming. This was seen as a clear case of the regulator breaking the rules. By way of comparison in 2001 when Grasso's total compensation was $30,550,000, his boss the SEC chair William Donaldson earned $142,500, and Alan Greenspan the chair of the Federal Reserve Bank (and the most powerful regulator in the world) earned $171,900! In October 2006 in New York Grasso was ordered by the State Supreme Court to repay $100 million, and the legal action threatened to continue for some years.

## Advancing inequality in the United States

The hundreds of millions of dollars in compensation routinely claimed each year by the leading US business and financial leaders has to be put into the perspective that although the United States is the most prosperous country on earth, it is typified by mounting, severe and very visible inequality. While CEO salaries inflated through the roof, in recent years average earnings in America actually went down. Looking at the distribution of stock market holdings, the richest 1 per cent of the population own 36.9 per cent of these assets, and the richest 10 per cent own 79 per cent, in contrast 80 per cent of the population own only 9.4 per cent of these assets (Figure 4.10). Looking at the boom time of the

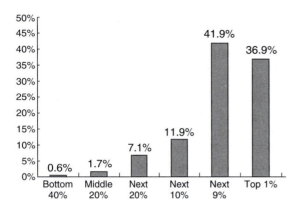

**Figure 4.10** Distribution of stock market holdings, by wealth class, 2004.

Source: Economic Policy Institute, *The State of Working America 2006–2007*, www.epi.org

1990s this advancing prosperity in the US hardly touched most of the population, and the meagre gains they made have been lost since 2001 (Figure 4.11). Some would defend this extreme level of inequality as the price of incentives and performance, but given the awful impact on the quality of most people's lives, it hardly makes the Anglo-American model as attractive as it is often portrayed by the rich and famous who have benefited from it.

## CORPORATE GOVERNANCE REFORM AROUND THE WORLD

### Corporate failure in other countries: the One-Tel and HIH collapse

The United States was not alone in feeling a sense of acute unease regarding standards of corporate governance. In Australia during the same period two corporate collapses occurred at One-Tel and HIH which were in context, if not in scale, almost as spectacular as those that had occurred across the Pacific. The A$5 billion HIH Insurance failure in 2001 was the largest bankruptcy in the country

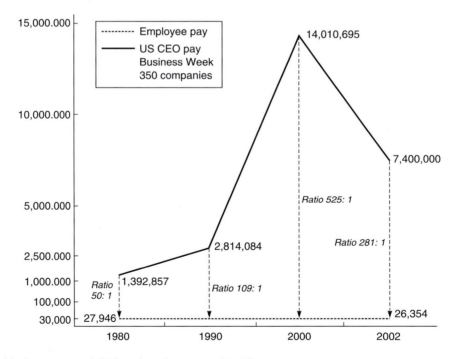

**Figure 4.11** Comparison of CEO and worker pay in the US, 1990–2002.

Source: Adapted from Ertuk, I., Froud, J., Johal, S., and Williams, K. (2005), Pay for Corporate Performance or Pay as Social Division? Rethinking the Problem of Top Management Pay in Giant Corporations, *Competition and Change*, 9(1): 49–74.

ever. As a consequence, for a period much of the insurance industry in Australia was jeopardised, and many people found it difficult or impossible to obtain public liability insurance or professional indemnity insurance, and their livelihoods were threatened. A royal commission into the affair was called, and the CEO and a parade of executives and directors were called to give evidence over a 12 month period of what was probably the most intensive cross-examination ever experienced by Australian executives. What transpired was a catalogue of accounting, actuarial and auditing failure, unrestrained executive greed, the complete failure of the board to monitor or even know what was occurring, excessive CEO powers, poor business decisions, and a consistent failure to exercise the responsibilities of a public company. The Commissioner Justice Neville Owen made the following observations about the causes of the failure:

> Corporate regulation in Australia in the late 1990s and into the present decade was replete with mechanisms designed to detect danger signals and promote the financial health and longevity of commercial entities. The law imposes duties and responsibilities on corporate officers and others such as auditors to ensure that problems that may adversely affect the solvency of a commercial entity are detected at an early stage. When problems of this nature are detected, corporate officers have a responsibility to take action. In the case of a company such as HIH, the corporate officers must inform the regulators and the public of the company's true financial position. The law also confers on regulators significant powers to act on the information that is provided and to obtain other information to protect the public interest. Despite these mechanisms, the corporate officers, auditors and regulators of HIH failed to see, remedy or report what should have been obvious. And some of those who were in or close to management of the group ignored or, worse, concealed the true state of the group's steadily deteriorating financial position. The governance of a public company should be about stewardship. Those in control have a duty to act in the best interests of the company. They must use the company's resources productively. They must understand that those resources are not personal property. The last years of HIH were marked by poor leadership and inept management. Indeed, an attitude of apparent indifference to, or deliberate disregard of, the company's underlying problems pervades the affairs of the group. Those responsible for the stewardship of HIH ignored the warning signs at their own, the group's and the public's peril. The culture of apparent indifference or deliberate disregard on the part of those responsible for the well-being of the company set in train a series of events that culminated in a calamity of monumental proportions.
>
> (HIH Royal Commission, 2003: vol. 1, 10)

The royal commission report led to the federal government referring 56 possible breaches of the law to relevant agencies. Justice Neville Owen also made 61 policy recommendations that have spurred a regulatory reform agenda with the goal of a more stable and robust financial system. In his report Justice Owen said he believed the most important failing of HIH directors was the abandonment of their ethical responsibilities to the company and shareholders. He suggested the rediscovery of fiduciary duty will be the most effective way of restoring trust in corporate governance (see Case Study 9).

At One-Tel two young entrepreneurs had secured nearly a billion dollars in investments from the Murdoch and Packer business empires in their telecoms start-up. The appearance of startling success was secured by selling telephone services at such low prices that the subscriber list grew with breathtaking speed, encouraging further investments in the company. But a fatal flaw in the business model of the company was that the telecom services were being offered to subscribers at lower than the price the company was paying for them itself. The business could only survive as long as it could raise new capital investment more rapidly than it was burning money. Mounting losses were ignored, until inevitably bankruptcy ensured, with both Murdoch and Packer losing hundreds of millions of dollars, together with an army of small investors. The CEO Jodie Rich often commented about the One-Tel Board, 'I don't know what it's there for'. Tragically, apparently

neither did some of the board directors who were representing the interests of major business corporations, and who did not seem to notice as the One-Tel venture slipped from ecstatic hype to unavoidable bankruptcy.

## US company earnings misstatements

Meanwhile the earnings misstatements scandal that commenced with Enron in 2001, rather than subsidising, continued to grow as implementation of Sarbanes–Oxley unearthed proliferating reporting problems in US corporations, that seemed to be growing each year, and did little to reassure investor confidence. General explanations for this alarmingly high rate of earnings restatements include the pressure for faster disclosure in the US in quarterly earnings guidance; the increasing complexity of accounting as business transaction themselves become more technically complex; or these problems could be coming to light simply because of increased transparency of business and accounting (ICAEW 2005: 18). There are also some more specific explanations for this very high rate of earnings restatements:

1 *Implementation of section 404 of the Sarbanes–Oxley Act 2002*: Sarbanes–Oxley requires companies and their auditors to review all internal financial controls, and this more intense scrutiny is revealing problems never noticed before. This could prove a transitional problem, or prove a continuing issue.
2 *Greater sensitivity to the definition of 'material' differences in earnings*: In the past companies avoided the embarrassment of restating earnings by convincing auditors that subsequently discovered accounting errors were not large enough to be 'material', and in theory a key accounting figure out by as much as 5 per cent could be dismissed as 'not material'.
3 *Newfound assertiveness among auditing firms*: Prior to Sarbanes–Oxley auditing firms that relied on large consulting contracts from their clients were reluctant about challenging those clients on accounting issues.
4 *Updating former estimates when the real numbers become available*: Part of the commonplace fudging of corporate accounting is missed estimates of matters such as bad debt reserves, restructuring charges, and contingencies. Having to announce earnings adjustments later is more likely to encourage managers to estimate better up front.
5 *Advancing the moment of revenue recognition*: Most revenue misrecognition may be due to technical difficulties interpreting different accounting standards or defining when contract performance has occurred. However at some point optimistic accounting degenerates into deliberately advancing the moment of revenue recognition in a speculative way to fraudulently enhance earnings which is what got Enron into trouble.

However it is difficult to escape the conclusion that whatever the other explanations might be, a great deal of the earnings restatements currently taking place are due to a breakdown in internal controls, which is a matter of some concern:

These restatements aren't just about revising subjective judgments or complying with esoteric, complex accounting pronouncements. In hundreds of instances, they stem from basic misapplications of simple rules or critical breakdowns in corporate controls and competencies. The good news is that, thanks to renewed urgency by auditors and their regulators, investors at least are getting better accounting (hopefully) on the next go-around. For that, they also can thank the renewed public-policy focus on the need to maintain strong internal controls. Simply put, internal controls are the systems, checks and balances that companies must keep in place to ensure that their financial accounts are recorded and presented accurately. Careful scrutiny of these controls, through independent testing and reporting by outside auditors, is what Section 404 of Sarbanes–Oxley mandated. By and large, this testing is what uncovered the weaknesses at the heart of the current rash of financial misstatements. Without this testing, we feel certain that investors still would be relying today on false financial statements at many of the thousands of companies that have restated their accounts over the past few years.

(Glass, Lewis and Co. 2006: 1)

## Sarbanes–Oxley costs of implementation

However, many business executives were concerned about the cost of implementing Sarbanes–Oxley, the time involved, and the unrelenting paperwork that was a distraction from more productive activities. Chair Donaldson conceded there were problems: 'We understand that the process of implementing the requirements of Section 404, as well as the related SEC and PCAOB rules, has consumed considerable time, energy, resources and has generated intense debate. Our staff and the Commission and I have all heard stories ... of substantial and unanticipated expenses, including internal overhead, audit fees and software expenses, companies pulling staff from other strategic projects to help with internal control reporting, management and auditors talking past one another, and duplicative testing procedures with little or no reliance on prior work (SEC 2005: 6).

According to one estimate the cost of audit fees for US corporations increased from $342,000 in 2001 to $1,342,000 in 2005 for S&P Small-Cap companies, from $650,000 to $2,240,000 for S & P Mid-Cap in the same period, and from $3,200,000 to $8,400,000 for S&P 500 companies as a result of the additional work involved in implementing Sarbane–Oxley (Foley and Lardner 2006a: 6). Clearly there has proved a great deal of work for companies in Section 302 of Sarbanes–Oxley involving both CEO and CFO signing off on quarterly and annual financial reports, including financial disclosure, and confirming that they have made appropriate disclosures to the auditors regarding internal controls. This together with Section 404, which requires the company management to assess and publicly report on the effectiveness of the company's internal controls, and the Public Company Accounting Oversight Board's (PCAOB) Audit Standard Number 2 which requires auditors to attest to management's assessment of internal controls, and to provide a separate opinion on the effectiveness of internal controls have stretched many companies' management. However, there have been some benefits from this prolonged and testing application of more rigorous internal controls. One survey of 274 finance managers by Financial Executives International (FEI) recorded

the following benefits:

■ 55 per cent agreed that compliance with Section 404 resulted in more investor confidence in financial reports;
■ 44 per cent agreed that financial reports were more reliable;
■ 38 per cent agreed that financial reports were more accurate; and
■ 32 per cent agreed that compliance with Section 404 helped to prevent or detect fraud.

However, when asked if the benefits of compliance exceeded the costs only 14 per cent on average agreed, while 85 per cent said the costs have exceeded the benefits. Interestingly, although some managers referred to the attractions of taking their public company private to avoid the burden of Sarbanes–Oxley, in another survey of private organisations 86 per cent of the managers surveyed said that Sarbanes–Oxley and other corporate governance reform requirements have impacted on their organisation (Foley and Lardner 2006b). A lot of the problems with Section 404 have come from uninspired and over-zealous implementation, often guided by expensive consultants, as William J. McDonough, chair of the Public Company Oversight Board, stated:

Instead of using judgment to tailor audit programs to the nature and size of an audit client, some auditors are applying a checklist approach to all audit clients, regardless of their complexity. There is no one-size-fits-all approach to assessing company's internal controls. Auditors should apply AS-2 in a manner that is proportional to the quality of management's monitoring of controls, as well as the complexity of the company. Untailored checklists to me are an early sign of poor quality judgments, which can lead to poor quality auditing. On the other hand, I have no doubt that some of the complaints being lodged about the assessment process being too rigorous and too extensive are being lodged in response to good auditors making hard decisions, auditors that are putting pressure on exactly the points of poor quality financial reporting that need to be squeezed.

Whatever actions we take, we must not undermine the work of auditors who are using their best professional judgment to drive exactly the kind of improvements in quality financial reporting that the Act intended.

(SEC 2005: 9)

The PCAOB released a policy statement that auditors should integrate their audits of internal controls with their audits of client's financial controls, tailor their audit plans to risks facing individual clients, and use a top-down approach that begins with company-level controls, to identify further testing of only those accounts and processes that are relevant to internal control over financial reporting (PCAOB 2005: 2). In contrast the approach to risk management that begins with a bottom-up, tick the box auditor perspective can lead to more unnecessary work as well as missing the major risks a company may face. Such misinterpretation of the intentions of the reform process not only damages the possibility of the reform having any effect, it greatly undermines the respect for regulatory intervention.

## Rules-based and principles-based approaches

Largely influenced by the US legislation, over the following years almost every country in the developed and developing world tightened up their corporate governance regulations considerably. It was clear that the monitoring and enforcement of corporate governance would be a great deal more active in the future than it may have been in the past. However, instead of the 'rules-based' approach of Sarbanes–Oxley the regulators in many countries including the UK, Canada, Australia and Hong Kong opted for a 'principles-based' approach to the reform of corporate governance. The advantage of 'playing by the rules' is that this requires all members of a community to exhibit minimum standards of practice. However, in order to gain acceptance by a majority of members, the standards enforced by rules have to be essentially the minimum acceptable practices. The worry about rules is that as soon as they are enforced, imaginative ways are invented to get around the rules without breaking them. It is true though that the tough rules based approach in the United States has considerably improved the standard of corporate reporting, and significantly reduced concerns about suspected collusion between auditors, bankers, and corporate officers as occurred in the Enron case. In contrast principles-based approaches set no hard and fast rules, and standards of practice can be encouraged to improve over time. Principles work to influence a broad set of practices meeting the expectations of the stakeholder community at large. The implications are that you have to maintain confidence in your actions, and over time this should leverage companies towards higher standards, as minimal compliance will not impress the wider business and stakeholder community.

## The myth of Anglo-American corporate governance

At this point it is worth emphasising that the US is firmly in the rules-based camp, and the UK has been a leader of the principles based approach, not just in accounting but in corporate governance generally. In this regard the Institute of Chartered Accountants of England and Wales (ICAEW) have decried the 'myth of Anglo-American corporate governance' and highlighted the significant and ongoing differences between the two systems: 'There is a perception of an Anglo-American corporate governance model because both the US and the UK have widely dispersed share ownership and focus on shareholder value. Each country has a common law legal system, long established and efficient stock exhanges and companies with a single, unitary board structure. However, while there are strong similarities between the US and the UK the fundamental balance of responsibility, accountability and power accorded to market participants is different. Hence the assertion that Anglo-American corporate governance is, in fact, a myth' (ICAEW 2005: 5). Bush (2005) presents a detailed account of the many differences in the approach towards reporting and shareholder rights of the two countries divided by a common language (Table 4.3).

The enhanced engagement of UK institutional investors is beginning to yield results in the UK

| Attribute | UK | US–SEC |
|---|---|---|
| Basis of laws affecting the core framework of financial reporting | UK company law: civil law, generally law of contract/property | Federal regulation – with tort-based remedies stemming from breaches (not contract/property law) |
| Purpose of audit | Agency conflict; Protection of the company itself 'stewardship' | Agency conflict; Conveying of false information to the market influencing the pricing of shares; 'General purpose' |
| History of company law | Companies Acts have evolved by following accepted existing best practice | 1933/34 Securities Acts; Big bang federal legislation to address governance *deficiencies* and the lack of financial reporting requirements in state law – but *without impinging on state law in matters of governance* |
| Applicability of laws affecting audits of companies | All companies irrespective of status of listing | Only SEC listed entities |
| Primary purpose of audited accounts | Accountability | Pricing of shares |
| Pre-emptive protection of property available to members | Yes. Body of members is sovereign. Civil freedom to act prospectively or reactively in binding way | No. Delaware Courts tend to judge *retrospectively*, e.g. Hollinger. Boards are sovereign, and self-appointed. *Voting on director reappointment non-binding* |
| Model intended to address failing companies ahead of potential crisis | Yes | Not so long as inefficiencies in the micro-economy of the company are 'priced' |
| Who is overseeing who? | Auditors act for shareholders | Auditors act for boards |
| Auditor 'independence' in law | Independent of whole board | Only independent of executive board and management |
| What is the intended path of accountability? | Shareholders to judge whole board, and the self-discipline of frank public disclosure | Independent directors to assess management's presentation free of 'scienter', in order to fulfil regulatory requirements |
| Legal basis underpinning accounting standards | Principles – 'economics' | Rules – 'letter of law' |
| Development of accounting/auditing practice, as led by the law | 'Rounded'. Income and balance sheets. Returns seen in terms of capital efficiency, not mere 'pricing' | Focused heavily on earnings. Record in practice of being weak on off-balance sheet risk |
| Form of opinion | True and fair view | Fairly presents |
| True and fair override | Yes | No |
| Status of audit report | Evidence from a trusted objective expert | Certification |
| Auditor liability | Contractual | Mainly tort |
| Do *investors* have any responsibility to read/use accounts | Yes | No |

**Table 4.3** Key differences between UK and US reporting frameworks and shareholder rights.

| Attribute | UK | US–SEC |
|---|---|---|
| External points of reference where difficulty | Actual members (sections 390, 392 and 394) | With dematerialised markets, only lawyers and SEC |
| Expression by an auditor of uncertainty in 'audit' reports | Allowed | Disallowed (counter to certification objectives) |
| 'Bias' other than fraud to be tested as part of audit | Yes SAS 470, now included in ISA UK and Ireland ISA 520 | No, and *not* in ISAs |
| Additional work for new issues handled under a specialised non-audit assignment | Yes. Reporting Accountant role. Different to statutory auditing | No, unless IPO |
| Role of audit committees | Execution of responsibility of *whole* unitary board in presenting financial statements – for shareholders. And for *internal purposes* | Oversight of management with insider access to accounting systems. 1.5 tier boards |
| Oversight of audit committee by shareholders | Normal director accountability of each member of audit committee | Limited binding rights of shareholders in Delaware to alter composition of audit committees |
| Right to call EGMs | Yes | Not Delaware |
| Binding re-election of individual directors | Yes | Delaware votes non-binding |
| Compliant with OECD principles (2004) | Yes | Not Delaware |
| Pre-emption rights for new issues | Yes | Not Delaware |
| Rights to audited financial information | Companies Act | Not Delaware |
| Protection of parties afforded by core reporting/ governance regime | Holders of shares. A large majority of UK equity is not traded in any one year | Buyers and sellers in capital markets. Not holders who did not trade |

Table 4.3—Cont'd

Source: Bush, Tim (2005), *Divided by Common Language: Where Economics Meets the Law – US vs Non-US Reporting Models*, London: Institute of Chartered Accountants of England and Wales (ICAEW).

market in a way not yet seen in the United States, unsettling the long history of institutional investor passivity:

> Boards of directors are supposed to hold managers accountable and to report to shareholders about managerial conduct. The relationship between directors and managers has historically been strong, either due to its cosiness or to its contractual nature, and it has recently improved thanks to pressure from regulatory groups and market forces. The relationship between board and shareholders

has been largely ignored. Montgomery and Kaufman (2003) suggest that there are two serious flaws in the shareholder–board relationship that are likely to threaten the entire equilibrium of the corporate governance system: 1) poor exchange of information between boards and shareholders and 2) shareholders' failure to influence boards. Consequently, directors are supposed to represent constituencies who are unclear about their preferences and who have few mechanisms to demand director accountability ... Historically, shareholders have been almost universally passive

towards the board for various reasons ... In the UK ownership concentration is higher, and institutional investors are key owners, unlike their American counterparts. British institutional investors (generally speaking) have been more interested in influencing managerial change and making boards of directors accountable.

(Aguilera 2005: 45–46; Black and Coffee 1994)

## FURTHER CORPORATE GOVERNANCE REFORM IN THE UK

The Enron fallout and the insistent influence of the strident Sarbanes–Oxley Act propelled the further reform of corporate governance internationally. In the UK the sedate progress of corporate governance reform quickened slightly.

### Higgs Report (2003)

The report examined the role, independence and recruitment of non-executive directors. Higgs viewed the non-executive director's role as:

- making contributions to corporate strategy;
- monitoring the performance of executive management;
- satisfying themselves regarding the effectiveness of internal control;
- setting the remuneration of executive directors; and
- being involved in the nomination, removal and succession planning of senior management.

The Combined Code recommended that boards should comprise at least one-third non-executive directors, a majority of whom should be independent. However, the Code did not detail how to assess independence. Therefore Higgs outlined a series of tests of independence such as length of service (maximum 10 years), associations to executive management, financial interest or significant shareholding. In particular, cross-directorships were identified as compromising independence, the simplest case being where two directors act as executive directors and non-executive directors alternatively at two companies. The report recommended a number of changes to the Combined Code and a revision of the Code in July 2003 incorporated most of the Higgs recommendations.

### Tyson Report (2003)

Following a recommendation in Chapter 10 of the Higgs Review concerning board composition, Professor Laura Tyson, Dean of the London Business School, was asked to lead a group to look at how companies might draw on broader pools of talent with varied and complementary skills, experience and perspectives to enhance board effectiveness.

Factors such as a company's size, the make up of its customer and employee base, the extent of its participation in global markets, its future strategies, and its current board membership are important determinants of its non-executive director requirements. Diversity in the backgrounds, skills and experiences of non-executive directors enhances board effectiveness by bringing a wider range of perspectives and knowledge to bear on issues of company performance, strategy and risk. Board diversity can also send a positive and motivating signal to customers, shareholders, and employees and can contribute to a better understanding by the company's leadership of the diverse constituencies that affect its success. Broader, more rigorous and transparent search processes for non-executive directors would not only enhance board talent and effectiveness but would also foster greater diversity in the background, experience, age, gender, ethnicity and nationality of non-executive directors' (2003: 2).

Tyson recommended the monitoring of best practice on achieving rigorous and transparent processes for non-executive director appointments processes, and progress on building diverse boardrooms, with case studies of best practice at individual companies. Research was needed on the impact of board diversity on board performance.

## Revised Combined Code (2003)

The Financial Reporting Council (FRC) agreed the final text of a new Combined Code that came into effect at the end of 2003. The main features of this new code are:

- new definitions of the role of the board, the chair and the non-executive directors;
- more open and rigorous procedures for the appointment of directors and from a wider pool of candidates;
- formal evaluations of the performance of boards, committees and individual directors, enhanced induction and more professional development of non-executive directors;
- at least half the board in larger listed companies to be independent non-executive directors;
- the separation of the roles of the chair and the chief executive to be reinforced;
- a chief executive should not go on to become chair of the same company;
- closer relationships between the chair, the senior independent director, non-executive directors and major shareholders;
- a strengthened role for the audit committee in monitoring the integrity of the company's financial reporting, reinforcing the independence of the external auditor and reviewing the management of financial and other risks.

## Myners (2004)

Paul Myners published *Review of the Impediments to Voting UK Shares*, in January 2004 for the Shareholder Voting Working Group, a network of investment industry and corporate bodies, was produced in response to the need to address concerns, 'that the system for voting the shares of UK issuers is not as effective and efficient as it should be'. Specifically, as stated in the report, problems have arisen from the fact that the, 'process … is still quite manually intensive … the chain of accountability is complex … there is a lack of transparency and … there is a large number of different participants, each of whom may give a different priority to voting'. While he states that if the existing paper-based system, which has a number

of structural weaknesses, were to be, 'overhauled and upgraded', it would lead to improvements being seen, his overriding conclusion is that, 'electronic voting remains the key to a more efficient voting system, and all parties – issuers, institutional investors and the intermediaries – need to make conscious efforts to introduce electronic voting capabilities in 2004'. Further to this, he recommends that, 'issuers in at least the FTSE 350, investment managers, custodians and proxy voting agencies should all have introduced the necessary system changes so that electronic voting capabilities are universally available (and) that beneficial owners … make direct and specific enquiries of their agents and others to establish the extent to which they have, or will have, introduced electronic voting capabilities to be used this year'.

## Modern Company Law Review (1998–2001)

In March 1998 the UK Department of Trade and Industry launched a long-term fundamental review of core company law. This review was led by an independent steering group whose aim was to develop a simple, modern, efficient and cost-effective framework for carrying out business activity in Britain for the twenty-first century. The CLR presented its final report to the Secretary of State on 26 July 2001. The government published an initial, partial response in a white paper of July 2002, and then published a full statement of its proposals in the white paper of 17 March 2005. This document included draft clauses and explanatory material on many elements of the bill. Additional draft clauses and explanatory material have subsequently been published.

The roots of this reform go back to the RSA *Tomorrow's Company* Inquiry (1992–1995) that researched the sources of sustainable business success, and suggested this was to be found in companies adopting *inclusive* relationships with all of its stakeholders. This was followed by the three year inquiry, Modern Company Law Review, which for the first time addressed the fundamentals of the reform of company law, which in the UK was particularly antiquated (Company Law Review Steering Group 2000).

The review examined directors' and auditors' duties and liability; investigated shareholder rights;

explored new means of corporate reporting and disclosure, including an operating and financial review statement by companies that set out their wider operations and impact beyond simply financial terms; and considered the particular issues of smaller companies' reporting and accountability. Despite this consistent effort at reform, government and institutional investors continue to search for more robust means to both regulate corporate governance and ensure that companies are directed towards sustained generation of wealth.

As a result of the work of the Company Law Reform Group the Department of Trade and Industry recommended that boards foster *inclusive* relationships with employees, customers, suppliers and the community. There was a keen debate that continued for some years on whether or not a more stakeholder focused model should be adopted. (The stakeholder model recognises a wider range of interests impacting upon the performance of corporations. The company is assumed to be responsible to a range of stakeholders including shareholders, employees, creditors and communities in which they operate.) The report finally recommended that a shareholder oriented, but inclusively framed, duty of loyalty was most likely to lead to optimal conditions for companies to contribute to the overall health and competitiveness of the economy. The report recommended measures aiming to:

- create monitoring obligations for non-executive directors;
- increase the proportion of non-executive directors on boards;
- change the appointment methods for non-executive directors in order to minimise the role which executive directors play in appointing non-executive directors;
- tighten the definition of director independence;
- strengthen the independence of the company chairperson. (OECD 2001a: 7; Company Law Review Steering Group 2000)

Meanwhile a new legal requirement in the UK compelled pension funds to explain any commitment to social issues in their investment principles. Corporations were coming under increasing pressure not only for financial performance, but also to demonstrate social and environmental performance. Hermes, one of the largest UK pension funds, led a group of investor institutions in 2001 to call upon companies to disclose the effect of social, environmental and ethical matters on their performance. In another instance of pressure for higher standards of governance by investment institutions, the National Association of Pension Funds (NAPF) published guidelines that go beyond the London Stock Exchange Combined Code. The guidelines recommend:

- the separation of the position of chair of the board and CEO;
- a ten part test to determine the independence of board members;
- avoiding the re-pricing of executive share options in situations of under-performance;
- an annual shareholder vote on the report of each company's remuneration committee.

Since the pension and life insurance industry in the UK manage the savings of millions of people, with assets of over 1,500 billion pounds representing over half the total equity market, it is likely their views will have increasing influence with corporations.

## FURTHER CORPORATE GOVERNANCE REFORM IN AUSTRALIA: CLERP 9

The Australian government has engaged in a series of proposals forming the Corporate Law Economic Reform Programme (CLERP), and the ninth paper in this series was published in 2002. One objective of these reforms has been the continuous improvement of standards of disclosure and corporate governance in the Australian market.

The Australian government tried to appear unruffled by the Enron events, insisting that the more robust and long-standing disclosure requirements in the Australian market made any further unanticipated corporate failures unlikely. However, HIH and One-Tel were salutary enough, and a further round of the Australia Corporate Law Economic Reform Programme (CLERP 9) 2002 quickly published a new series of requirements for

companies registered in Australia:

■ To ensure the independence of the auditor:

- there needed to be the periodic rotation of audit partners
- non-audit services offered by the audit company were to be disclosed
- audit committees were to become mandatory in the Top 500 ASX listed companies
- auditors must attend the AGM of the company
- auditor should be able to limit liability.

■ To ensure continuous disclosure:

- the penalties for companies involved in market manipulation were increased to a maximum of $1 million
- ASIC was to impose penalties via infringement notice
- Penalties were to extend beyond the company to any person involved
- ASX's tougher approach to disclosure to avoid false markets was endorsed.

■ To improve the conduct of shareholders' meetings:

- there should be plain English notifications
- rules on the bundling of resolutions.

■ Annual reports were to include:

- disclosure of directors' other directorships.

■ Whistleblowing:

- employees were encouraged to report to ASIC suspected breaches of law.

## ASX corporate governance principles

In 2003 the ASX Corporate Governance Council, which comprehensively represented bodies along the investor/corporate supply chain, published an influential report *Corporate Governance in Australia*. The report argued that corporate governance was important to Australia because:

Demonstrably good corporate governance practices are increasingly important in determining the cost of capital in a global market. Australian companies must be equipped to compete globally and to maintain and promote investor confidence both in Australia and overseas. In an examination of our corporate governance practices, Australia starts from a position of strength. However it is important that we continue to review those practices to ensure they continue to reflect local and international developments and position Australia at the forefront of best practice.

(ASX 2003: 4)

The report established a new set of best practice recommendations and encouraged companies to re-examine their corporate governance practices to determine whether and to what extent the company might benefit from a change in their approach. This was not a 'one-size-fits-all' policy: 'It states aspirations for best practice for optimizing corporate performance and accountability in the interests of shareholders and the broader economy. If a company considers that a recommendation is inappropriate to its particular circumstances, it has the flexibility not to adopt it – a flexibility tempered by the requirement to explain why' (ASX 2003: 5). Under Listing Rule 4.10 of the ASX listed companies are required to provide a statement in their annual report disclosing the extent to which they have followed the ASX best practice recommendations in the reporting period. Under the 'if not, why not' approach, where companies have not followed all the recommendations they must identify the recommendations that have not been followed and give the reasons for not following them. This way the investment community is informed and can judge whether explanations offered are convincing. The essential corporate governance principles determined by the ASX Council are that a company should:

■ Lay solid foundations for management and oversight:

- recognise and publish the respective roles and responsibilities of board and management.

- Structure the board to add value:

  - have a board of an effective composition, size and commitment to adequately discharge its responsibilities and duties.

- Promote ethical and responsible decision-making:

  - actively promote ethical and responsible decision-making.

- Safeguard integrity in financial reporting:

  - have a structure to independently verify and safeguard the integrity of the company's financial reporting.

- Make timely and balanced disclosure:

  - promote timely and balanced disclosure of all material matters concerning the company.

- Respect the rights of shareholders:

  - respect the rights of shareholders and facilitate the effective exercise of those rights.

- Recognise and manage risk:

  - establish a sound system of risk oversight and management and internal control.

- Encourage enhanced performance:

  - fairly review and actively encourage enhanced board and management effectiveness.

- Remunerate fairly and responsibly:

  - ensure that the level and composition of remuneration is sufficient and reasonable

and that its relationships to corporate and individual performance is defined.

- Recognise the legitimate interests of stakeholders:

  - recognise the legal and other obligations to all legitimate stakeholders.

## CONCLUSIONS

The saga of corporate governance crisis and reform does not convey the inherent superiority of this system above all others that the proponents of the Anglo-American approach proclaim. The undoubted success of the Anglo-American economies in the twentieth century which distinguished them as among the most prosperous in the world, was nonetheless punctuated by periodic corporate governance failure, sometimes almost of a catastrophic nature. The capacity of the system for reform and regeneration is very real, but also the apparently inherent instability and volatility in this increasingly market based system. Whether current reforms will reduce the frequency of market and corporate failure remains to be seen. How well the Anglo-American system can respond to the increasingly critical demand for corporate social responsibility is another pressing question at this stage, to which the analysis returns in Chapters 7 and 8. It is interesting at this stage to examine the relative merits of the European and Asia Pacific modes of corporate governance.

# 5
# European Corporate Governance

## INTRODUCTION

This chapter explores the fascinating diversity of corporate governance forms in Europe, and the distinctive features of this relationship based approach. The importance of bank finance and business networks are examined, which traditionally provide sources of finance and resources that in the Anglo-American system is the role of equity markets. The different political and legal structures of Europe have produced a rich array of corporate governance codes which are outlined. The deeper transformations of the industrial and governance systems of Germany, France and Italy are examined. Notable failures in European corporate governance are discussed as the backdrop to the sustained movement for corporate governance reform. The efforts of the European Commission to achieve a modernising of company law and enhancing of governance is considered. Whether this amounts to a harmonisation or convergence of corporate governance in Europe is a controversial question, made sharper by the impact of the Anglo-American ideology of shareholder value which is seen as an increasing threat by many. The increasingly international role of Europe is mentioned, and the prospects of a more active shareownership. Finally the struggles of the transitional economies of Eastern Europe are considered. What is apparent is the profound sense of flux and change in Europe, matched by a determination to hold on to essential values.

## EUROPEAN RELATIONSHIP BASED APPROACHES

European countries exhibit a rich diversity in corporate governance practices, structures and participants that reflect differences in history, culture, financial traditions, ownership patterns and legal systems. Nevertheless a common understanding is emerging regarding the importance of corporate governance for developing modern corporations and growing economies. The major difference between the corporate governance systems of the US and UK, and that of European countries is that the Europeans emphasise cooperative relationships and reaching consensus, whereas the Anglo-Saxon tradition emphasises competition and market processes (Nestor and Thompson 2000). With the move towards equity financing and broader share ownership in Europe in the 1990s, it seemed at times as if the shareholder value market based system was inexorably advancing, but important elements of the European tradition have proved resilient and enduring.

The European *insider* model relies on the representation of interests on the board of directors. More diverse groups of stakeholders are actively recognised including workers, customers, banks, other companies with close ties, local communities and national government. Stable investment and cross-shareholdings mean the discipline of management by the securities market is not strong, and similarly the market for corporate control is weak with hostile takeovers rarely occurring. That is, long-term large shareholders give the company a degree of protection from both the stock market and the threat of takeover. This is the continental European system with a supervisory board for oversight of management, where banks play an active role, inter-corporate shareholdings are widespread, and often companies have close ties to political elites.

In most European countries (and indeed in most countries in the world) ownership and

control are held by cohesive groups of insiders who have long-term stable relationships with the company (La Porta *et al.* 1999). Groups of insiders tend to know each other well and have some connection with the company in addition to their investment, for example through family interests, allied industrial concerns, banks and holding companies. Insider groups monitor management that often acts under their control. The agency problem of the outsider system is much less of an issue in this context (Nestor and Thompson 2000: 9).

## BANK FINANCE AND BUSINESS NETWORKS

Countries with insider systems tend not to have developed the institutionalisation of wealth of the English speaking countries, and there are no pension funds, mutual funds and insurance companies of comparable scale and significance. In place of this corporate finance is highly dependent upon banks with companies having high debt/equity ratios. Banks often have complex and long standing relationships with corporations, rather than the arm's length relations of equity markets. Consequently displacing the emphasis upon public disclosure of market based systems, the insider system is based more on deeper but more selective exchange of information among insiders. For example, though there has been a substantial diminution of the holdings of the banks and of other non-financial companies holdings in German companies in recent years,

these ownership relationships remain much more substantial than in Anglo-American economies (Table 5.1). Though there has been a significant growth in the holdings of the financial sector of German equities, the holdings of German pension funds remains small relative to other countries (Figure 5.1).

Insiders exercise control of a company either by majority ownership of voting shares, or by owning significant minority holdings and employing a combination of devices to increase their control over the company. Included among the devices to redistribute control from the majority to the minority are:

- arranging pyramid corporate structures;
- shareholder agreements;
- discriminatory voting rights; and
- procedures intended to reduce the participation or influence of other minority investors.

Pyramid structures enable people to dominate a company with only a small share of the total equity of the company. Multiple share classes can enable the insider group to have increased voting power (Nestor and Thompson 2000: 10).

Shareholder agreements are means by which groups of shareholders who individually hold small amounts of equity, act in concert to constitute a working majority, or at least form the largest block of shareholders. Such agreements can give the participants preferential rights to acquire shares, and can cover issues such as how the chair will be selected. In the past many

| Owners | 1993 | 1994 | 1995 | 1996 | 1997 | 1998 | 1999 | 2000 | 2001 | 2002 | 2003 |
|---|---|---|---|---|---|---|---|---|---|---|---|
| Banks | 12.8 | 12.1 | 12.9 | 13.4 | 13.0 | 12.0 | 13.0 | 11.5 | 11.5 | 10.9 | 9.0 |
| Insurance | 6.6 | 6.1 | 6.3 | 6.3 | 7.7 | 7.2 | 7.8 | 8.2 | 9.3 | 13.3 | 13.2 |
| Other financial | 6.0 | 6.3 | 6.2 | 7.1 | 8.9 | 10.1 | 12.7 | 14.4 | 13.3 | 14.3 | 13.5 |
| Households | 19.9 | 19.4 | 18.8 | 18.4 | 18.1 | 17.5 | 16.9 | 16.5 | 14.4 | 13.0 | 13.9 |
| Non-financial companies | 42.8 | 45.2 | 45.8 | 44.0 | 40.0 | 40.1 | 34.9 | 36.2 | 36.8 | 32.9 | 32.5 |
| Government | 2.0 | 2.0 | 1.8 | 1.8 | 2.0 | 1.3 | 0.7 | 0.6 | 0.6 | 0.8 | 0.9 |
| Foreign | 10.0 | 9.0 | 8.2 | 9.1 | 10.1 | 11.8 | 14.0 | 12.5 | 14.1 | 14.8 | 17.1 |

Table 5.1 Distribution of share ownership in German publicly traded companies.

Source: Vitols, S. (2005), 'Changes in Germany's Bank-Based Financial System: Implications for Corporate Governance', *Corporate Governance: An International Review*, 13, 3.

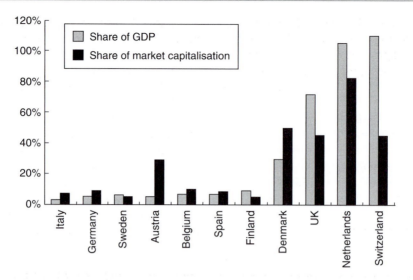

**Figure 5.1** Weight of pension funds in the economy and financial markets, 2001.

Source: Eurosif (2006), Active Share Ownership in Europe, *European Handbook*, 27, http://www.eurosif.org/publications/active_share_owenership_handbook.

companies operating with shareholder agreements have treated the AGM as merely a formal exercise that is tightly controlled by management. Restrictions are placed upon voting, with limited possibility of participating in decision-making (Nestor and Thompson 2000: 10).

In this context the validity of applying exclusively Anglo-American inspired corporate governance reform programmes to Europe could be questioned. The agency cost reasoning of the outsider system aims to secure the accountability of corporate executives through enhancing the power of non-executive directors who it is often assumed will represent shareholder interests. In contrast in many countries of Europe majority shareholders are often in a dominant position with strong financial incentives to monitor management closely. Agency costs do not have the same resonance in insider systems where the danger is that majority shareholders, who may be board members will collude closely with management. In this system the priority for reform needs to be protection of minority shareholders and other stakeholders liable to be neglected by the majority shareholders and management acting in concert.

Thus the report on corporate governance by the Belgian financial regulator and the Brussels Stock Market issued in 1998 instead of stressing the importance of accountability, called for managerial independence from the dominant shareholders. Similarly the Italian corporate governance code issues in 1999 insisted that directors of a publicly quoted company should always act autonomously, even when a controlling shareholder has already assessed the operational choices (Cheffins 2000: 17). Whether change may occur, and how quickly in the insider system is a question as yet unresolved.

In Italy and in various insider control oriented countries, companies are becoming increasingly eager to tap equity markets to finance expansion and acquisitive activity. A move towards the stock market is therefore taking place. If this trend towards public ownership becomes sufficiently strong, controlling shareholders could fade away as part of a shift towards the outsider/arm's length pattern of ownership and control which exists in the UK and in the US. At least in the short term however, this sort of radical change seems unlikely. A more plausible scenario is that public ownership will become increasingly prevalent but controlling shareholders will continue to play

a dominant role. For some time yet, then, ensuring that minority shareholders are adequately protected should remain a higher priority than enhancing managerial accountability.

(Cheffins 2000: 18)

## REGIONAL VARIATIONS

The continuing defining feature of European corporate governance is its institutional diversity. However, if two broad regional variations are identified, the Latin forms of corporate governance existing in Southern Europe, and the Germanic systems predominating in Northern Europe, the fact is that in recent years both variations have come under increasing pressure to assume elements of the Anglo-American market based approach to corporate governance.

An analysis of corporate governance in Italy reveals one of the least reconstructed systems among the advanced industrial countries. Italian corporate governance is characterised by a poor capital market, and almost non-existent market for corporate control, with banks that have a stake in corporate financing but play a minor part in governance. This leaves the field open for major active investors or blockholders, to monitor senior management, with minority shareholders likely to be ignored. Andrea Melis suggests, unlike the US system summarised by Roe as 'strong managers, weak owners', that in Italy the reality is almost the reverse with 'weak managers, strong blockholders, and unprotected minority shareholders'. In some senses it is remarkable that branches of Italian industry have succeeded in spite of, rather than because of, its corporate governance. Yet the bankruptcy of Parmalat in 2003 has exposed a similar disregard for accounting conventions as witnessed in the US, and focused attention on the manifest weaknesses in the Italian system of corporate governance.

In France the corporate governance system was dominated by cross-shareholdings – what Morin calls a 'financial networked economy', which inspired by the US shareholder value model is now transforming towards a 'financial market economy'. These changes have been hastened by the influence of the large Anglo-Saxon institutional investors in the ownership structure of the largest French firms, without any equivalent French institutional investors able to mobilise long term investment funds. The switch from defined benefit pensions schemes where the employer bears the risk, and pensions fund trustees can follow long term and prudent investment policies, to defined contribution pensions schemes where the employee bears the risk, have changed pension fund investment strategies towards higher risk strategies with more explicit attempts to target equities and portfolios that will outperform the market. In turn this more aggressive investment strategy places corporate management under growing pressure to deliver value.

## DIFFERENT POLITICAL, LEGAL AND REGULATORY STRUCTURES

For some decades the European Union has moved towards common internationally recognised standards with the introduction of the common European currency, free flow of capital, goods, services and people across borders of the countries of the European Union. Some developments in corporate governance have suggested further integration of economies including the privatisation of state owned companies that often begin to operate internationally and have an international shareholder base; the growth and diffusion of shareholding both within and between countries; the increased merger and takeover activity among large European corporations to create global players, and the increasing activity of Europe's larger stock exchanges (Weil, Gotshal and Manges 2002: 1).

However a series of important distinctions remain among the European countries, which also distinguish the European approach from other models of corporate governance policy and practice (Weil, Gotshal and Manges 2002: 3–5):

■ *Company law*: Many countries of Europe have a distinctive tradition of company law influenced by prescriptive Roman law, in France regulations on incorporation were inspired by the Napoleonic code, in Germany regulation insisted upon a board of supervision separate from the company's board of directors to represent and protect shareholder's interests.

Company law is embedded in different and often unique political, cultural and social traditions.

- *Employee representation*: Employee representation is embedded in law in Austria, Denmark, Germany, Luxembourg and Sweden. Employees of companies of a certain size have the right to elect some members of the supervisory board. In Finland and France company articles may provide this right. In other European countries it is the shareholders who elect the members of the supervisory board.

- *Stakeholder issues*: Different European countries articulate the purpose of corporate governance in different ways, some put the emphasis upon a broader range of stakeholder interests, others emphasise strongly the ownership rights of shareholders. The majority of corporate governance codes in Europe expressly recognise the interconnection and mutual dependency of corporate success, shareholder returns, employee security and well-being, and the interests of wider stakeholders.

- *Shareholder rights and participation mechanics*: Laws and regulations relating to the equitable treatment of shareholders, including minority rights in takeovers, and other transactions vary significantly among countries. Limits on shareholder participation rights pose barriers to cross-border investment. The codes on these issues call for equitable treatment for all shareholders, for disproportional shareholder voting rights to be avoided or at least disclosed, and for the removal of barriers to shareholder participation in general meeting.

- *Board structure, role and responsibilities*: Two-tier board structures are a legal requirement for large companies in many countries in Europe, but similarities in practices between unitary and two-tier boards are significant. Both types recognise a supervisory function and a management function, although the distinction between them is more formally recognised in the two-tier board. The unitary board or the supervisory board are responsible for appointing management, ensuring financial reporting and control systems are functioning appropriately, and ensuring the corporation complies with the law. Each board system has different strengths. The one-tier system may allow closer relationships and better flow of information between directors and executives; however, the two-tier system allows a clearer separation between the supervisory body and the executives being supervised.

- *Supervisory body independence and leadership*: The purpose of the supervisory board is to ensure accountability and provide strategic guidance, leaving management with the capacity to make operational decisions. Codes concerning unitary board structures urge companies to appoint independent outside directors who are distinct from the management team, and often call for the chair and CEO roles to be separate. Codes that relate to two-tier boards emphasise the importance of independence between the supervisory and management bodies.

- *Board committees*: Many supervisory board duties can be delegated to board committees, particularly where the interests of management and the interests of the company may be in conflict. Similarly under the unitary board structure an increasing amount of work is delegated to board committees, often with a membership largely of independent directors.

- *Disclosure*: Variations in disclosure requirements and resulting differences in information provided to investors is a potential impediment to a single European equity market. Nevertheless the amount of disclosure is increasing, and there is more agreement about the type of information that needs to be disclosed. In part, this is due to the promotion of international accounting standards. Consolidation of stock exchanges across Europe may further encourage common standards of disclosure. There is a growing awareness across Europe of the importance of disclosure for shareholders, and particularly relating to disclosure of executive remuneration. There is growing interest in the significance of both mandatory and voluntary social and environmental reporting.

If the main driver of the Anglo-American countries towards the urgent adoption of corporate governance reform were the recent series of financial scandals and related failures of listed companies, in Europe, with its staid and rather stable (if often inequitable) governance practices, the main

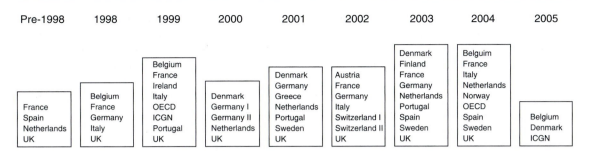

| Pre-1998 | 1998 | 1999 | 2000 | 2001 | 2002 | 2003 | 2004 | 2005 |
|---|---|---|---|---|---|---|---|---|
| | | | | | | Denmark<br>Finland<br>France<br>Germany<br>Netherlands<br>Portugal<br>Spain<br>Sweden<br>UK | Belguim<br>France<br>Italy<br>Netherlands<br>Norway<br>OECD<br>Spain<br>Sweden<br>UK | |
| | | Belgium<br>France<br>Ireland<br>Italy<br>OECD<br>ICGN<br>Portugal<br>UK | | Denmark<br>Germany<br>Greece<br>Netherlands<br>Portugal<br>Sweden<br>UK | Austria<br>France<br>Germany<br>Italy<br>Switzerland I<br>Switzerland II<br>UK | | | |
| France<br>Spain<br>Netherlands<br>UK | Belgium<br>France<br>Germany<br>Italy<br>UK | | Denmark<br>Germany I<br>Germany II<br>Netherlands<br>UK | | | | | Belgium<br>Denmark<br>ICGN |

**Figure 5.2** Recent flurry of new corporate governance codes in Europe.

Source: Eurosif (2006), Active Share Ownership in Europe, *European Handbook*, 19, http://www.eurosif.org/publications/active_share_ownership_handbook.

attraction was increased *access* to investment capital in a more competitive international economy. The flurry of new corporate governance codes in Europe was in large part determined by the intention not to be left behind in accessing new sources of investment (Figure 5.2).

European interest in corporate governance improvement – and associated company law reform – and in the development of codes has grown throughout the past decade, gaining considerable momentum in the late 1990s. This interest has paralleled heightened competition brought about by enhanced communication and transportation technologies, and the reduction of regulatory barriers in the European Union and internationally. It has also paralleled growth in the importance of equity markets and a trend toward broader-based shareholding in many EU Member States. Increasing interest in corporate governance improvement and attempts to articulate generally accepted norms and best practices is the result of numerous factors. Chief among them is the recognition that a firm's ability to attract investment capital, which is now internationally mobile, is related to the quality of its corporate governance.

(Weil, Gotshal and Manges 2002: 8)

## THE DEVELOPMENT OF EUROPEAN CORPORATE GOVERNANCE CODES

In the development of European corporate governance codes the inspiration of the original Cadbury code was very evident. The ideas put forward in Cadbury were discussed widely in France, and the resulting Vienot Report first issued in 1995 by a working group established by the French employers' associations was referred to as 'the Gallic equivalent of Britain's Cadbury report' (Cheffins 2000; Wymeersch 1996; Jack 1995). When the Peters Committee in 1997 issued a Code of Best Practice for the Amsterdam Stock Exchange, this was characterised as 'the Dutch answer to the Cadbury Report' (van der Velden and Hepkema 1998). The Association of Belgian Companies released corporate governance recommendations in 1998 based on the Cadbury Code and the Brussels Stock Exchange established a set of benchmark guidelines for good corporate governance. Similarly Spain in 1998 developed a set of corporate governance guidelines supported by its National Stock Market Commission with listed companies obliged to comply or explain (Segura 1998; Rogerson 1999). In 1999 Italy established a committee composed of corporate, regulatory and stock market representatives to approve a code of corporate governance, and invited the Stock Exchange to require listed companies to disclose whether they were complying with the code guidelines (Cheffins 2000: 281).

To what extent this commitment towards corporate governance reform reflected a realisation that the practices of the past were no longer tenable in an increasing transparent business world, where investment capital moved more freely and would not tolerate the neglect of shareholders' interests is an open question. At the beginning probably there was a sense of simply matching

the regulation of close economic neighbours by developing similar codes, however over time it is likely that the engagement in the codes became more real, if only because of increasing pressure from regulators and shareholders:

> The corporate governance codes ... emanate from nations with diverse cultures, finance traditions, ownership structures and legal origins. Given their distinct origins, the codes are remarkable in their similarities, especially in terms of the attitudes they express about the key roles and responsibilities of the supervisory body and the recommendations they make concerning its composition and practices. It is important to note that *the codes tend to express notions of 'best practice' – but translations of best practice ideals into actual practice may take time to achieve.* If the ideals expressed in the codes reflect a dramatic difference from common practice, and the potential benefits of reform efforts are not well communicated and understood, codes may meet with resistance. Investor interest in the codes and investor support for the practices the codes recommend appear to wear away resistance over time.
> (Weil, Gotshal and Manges 2002: 3)

Though the European Commission has made recurrent efforts to coordinate the route to corporate governance reform, it is clear that member countries have enjoyed the experience of navigating their own path (Figure 5.3). Though agreeing in principle to the objective of harmonisation of standards for corporate control, each member state has regarded the specificities of its own system as beyond the understanding of Brussels law makers. 'Corporate governance is an interesting example of the dialectic in the European integration process between integration and disintegration, between the need for more centralisation in certain areas (such as monetary policy), and the insistencies by Member States on respect for national traditions and cultures (the *subsidiarity test*)' (Lannoo 1999: 270). In the meantime though the European Commission has provided some leadership and encouragement, all of the member countries have devised their own codes of corporate governance as outlined below.

## European Commission

### Modernising Company Law and Enhancing Corporate Governance (2003)

This directive is aimed at a modern, dynamic, interconnected industrialised society. A flexible company law, and corporate governance framework will enhance the real economy. The report outlines why the European regulatory framework for company law and corporate governance needs to be modernised. The main objectives are to strengthen shareholder rights and foster the efficiency and competitiveness of business.

## France

### Vienot Reports (1995, 1999)

The first Vienot Report reviewed the principal issues concerning membership, powers and operation of the boards of French listed companies. The second Vienot Report was largely concerned with the separation of powers of the offices of chair and chief executive officer, and the disclosure of executive remuneration. The reports encourage voluntary adoption of best practice standards *(voluntary)*.

### Recomandations Sur Le Gouvernment D'Enterprise (1998, 2001, 2004)

This report looks at the governance of the enterprise. It covers issues such as general meetings, disclosure, transparency and remuneration. This report was originally published in 1998, updated in 2001 and 2004.

## Italy

### Draghi Reform (1998)

The 1998 Draghi Reform required company boards to improve their monitoring and compliance; observe 'principles of correct administration'; review internal controls, administrative and accounting systems; appointment of at least three

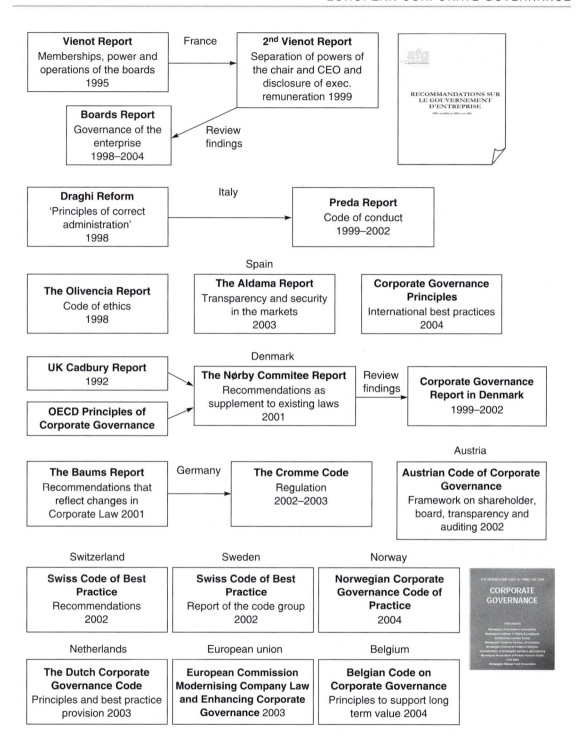

**Figure 5.3** Multiple corporate governance reform processes in Europe.

Source: UTS Centre For Corporate Governance (2006).

auditors and ensure that at least one statutory auditor is elected by minority shareholders.

## Preda Code (1999, 2002)

The Preda Code established a code of conduct for listed companies. The code is a means of fostering the proper control of business risks and dealing adequately with the conflicts that arise between directors and minority and majority shareholders. It creates mandatory disclosure framework in connection with listings rules to encourage improved practice and encourage voluntary adoption of best practice *(disclosure – comply or explain)*.

## Spain

### Olivencia Report (1998) Aldama Report (2003)

The Olivencia Report established a code of ethics for the boards of directors of listed companies. The Aldama Report looked at fostering transparency, disclosure, directors' responsibilities, and security in the market and in listed companies *(voluntary – comply or explain)*.

### Corporate Governance Principles (2004)

The purpose of this report is to provide Spanish company boards and directors with a set of principles which relate to international best practices for good corporate governance.

## Denmark

### Norby Report (2001)

The Norby Committee was influenced by the UK Cadbury Report and the OECD Principles of Corporate Governance. The report is divided into seven parts and the recommendations should be seen as a supplement to existing laws. Copenhagen Stock Exchange recommends that listed companies disclose on a comply or explain basis *(voluntary)*.

### Corporate Governance Report (2003)

The 2003 Corporate Governance Report was prepared by the Copenhagen Stock Exchange Committee on Corporate Governance. This report incorporates the findings of the Norby Committee on corporate governance and annual reports of companies.

## Germany

### Baums Report (2001)

The Baums Report was published in response to the globalisation of financial markets that placed German corporate law under pressure to adapt to ever changing requirements. The report made nearly 150 proposals or changes to existing German law and looked at how the system be developed so it is attractive for foreign and domestic investors.

### Cromme Code (2002–2003)

The Cromme Code presents essential statutory regulations for the management and supervision of German listed companies and contains internationally and nationally recognised standards for good and responsible governance. It aims at making the system transparent and understandable *(disclosure – comply or explain)*.

## Switzerland

### Best Practice for Corporate Governance (2002)

Published by the peak business body the report is intended for public limited companies. Certain provisions are addressed to institutional investors and intermediaries. The purpose is to set out guidelines and recommendations but not force Swiss companies into a regulatory straitjacket.

## Sweden

### Code of Corporate Governance (2004)

The purpose of this report is to establish a Swedish code of corporate governance. The aim is to help improve corporate governance in Swedish companies. Another aim is to enhance understanding and confidence in Swedish corporate governance on the part of foreign investors.

## Norway

### Code of Practice (2004)

The purpose of the code is for listed companies to practise corporate governance more comprehensively than is required by legislation. It is also intended to strengthen confidence in listed companies among shareholders, the capital market and other interested parties.

## Netherlands

### Peters Report (1997)

The report encourages voluntary adoption of best practice standards and voluntary disclosure *(voluntary disclosure encouraged).*

### Principles of Good Corporate Governance (2003)

The code is based on the principle accepted in the Netherlands that a company is a long-term form of collaboration between the various parties involved. The code contains the principles and concrete provisions which the persons involved in a company and stakeholders should observe in relation to one another.

## Belgium

### Recommendations of the Federation of Belgian Companies (1998)

This report encourages voluntary adoption of best practice standards, and voluntary disclosure.

### Code of Corporate Governance (2004)

The code was an initiative of the Banking, Finance and Insurance Commission; Euronext Brussels and the Federation of Belgian Enterprises. The code contains nine principles and its main objective is to support long term value creation.

## Code convergence?

Though the codes all have distinctive approaches and values, there are some defining principles almost all of them share (Table 5.2). As corporate governance codes have proliferated across European countries, there has been an inevitable tendency on the part of the European Commission to 'attempt to achieve a greater degree of coordination between them, for the sake of bureaucratic tidiness' (Cadbury 2002: 229). An early report recommended guidelines for convergence in the following terms:

> Considering the specificity of national corporate governance systems and the sensitivity to centralizing legislation, the Working Party proposes a set of Guidelines for the operation and control of a corporation in the European Union. These Guidelines should function as a minimum framework for corporate governance standards in the EU. It is suggested that all listed corporations should comply with these Guidelines; other companies, especially those in which there is a high degree of public interest, should attempt to meet the requirements to the extent possible.
>
> (CEPS 1995: ii)

The response to this proposal of Adrian Cadbury, who was responsible for the first code, to this call for uniformity was firm:

> The ... proposal has not been implemented and I believe it to be wrongly directed, as well as otiose. National codes have had an important part to play in raising governance standards. They can take account of the considerable differences between countries within the EU in terms of patterns of ownership, corporate structures, and legal and regulatory

| | Comply or explain with principles or codes | Defining audit functions and limits on auditors | Improving transparency | Defining and controlling conflicts of interest | Improving or easing voting. Greater role for AGM | Role for independent directors |
|---|---|---|---|---|---|---|
| Belgium | | + | | + | + | + |
| USA | | + | + | + | | + |
| Spain | + | + | + | + | | |
| Germany | + | + | + | + | | |
| Austria | | + | | | | |
| Ireland | | + | | | | |
| Finland | | | | | | |
| Portugal | | | | + | | |
| Netherlands | | + | + | | + | |
| Greece | | + | + | + | | + |
| Czech Republic | | + | + | + | + | |
| Australia | | | + | | | |
| Turkey | | + | | | + | |
| Poland | + | + | + | + | | |
| Switzerland | + | + | + | + | | + |
| UK | | | + | | | |
| Italy | + | | + | + | + | + |
| Hungary | | | | | | |
| Sweden | | | | | + | |
| Mexico | + | | + | | + | |
| Korea | | | + | + | + | + |
| France | | | + | | + | |
| Canada | | + | | | + | |
| Japan | | + | + | | + | + |
| Denmark | | | | | | |
| Slovak Republic | | | | | | |
| New Zealand | | | + | | | |
| Norway | | | | | | |
| Luxembourg | | | | | | |
| Iceland | | | | | | |

**Table 5.2** Summary of recent changes to company law and regulation. (+ Indicates a recent legal or regulatory change.)

Source: *Corporate Governance: A Survey of OECD Countries*, © OECD 2004. Country submissions to OECD and OECD company law and corporate governance database.

frameworks. The risk of attempting to amalgamate them into a European Code would be that they would lose their cutting edge in the interest of uniformity and, as a result, would add nothing of value … Convergence on governance principles makes sense, because it goes to the heart of the matter. There is no virtue in trying to harmonise governance structures, because the structural design of boards is not ultimately decisive. Structure is important; its precise form is less so. The effectiveness of governance systems depends primarily on the clarity with which responsibilities are assigned within them and the quality of the people who undertake those responsibilities. As Demb and Neubauer's researches have shown, the ways in which boards in practice are involved in matters of governance vary considerably,

even within the same national setting. What matters is that the principles of sound governance should be observed, within whatever structures boards and the shareholders choose to adopt.

(2002: 230)

## THE TRANSFORMATION OF CORPORATE GOVERNANCE SYSTEMS

### Germany

The German business sector is typified by a relatively strong concentration of ownership of individual enterprises; the importance of small and medium-sized unincorporated companies; a close correspondence between owners and managers; and a limited role played by the stock market. 'The German corporate governance regime is not only bank based, but also has weak rights for minority shareholders, a lower rate of return for shareholders and a weakly developed market for corporate control. Moreover, it coincides with a system of co-determination and centralised wage bargaining which gives labour a prominent role in the firm's decisions on restructuring and pursuing product market strategies' (Beyer and Hassel 2002: 310).

The central characteristics of the corporate governance of German enterprises is the insider nature in which all interested stakeholders – managers, employees, creditors, suppliers and customers are able to monitor corporate performance.

Large firms defined as AGs and GmbHs with more than 500 employees, are by law required to have a dual board structure. The two-tier board structure reflects a functional difference, laid down in law, between the strategic role of the supervisory board (*Aufsichtsraat*) and the day-to-day running of business taken care of by the management board (*Vorstaand*). Overlaps in membership between the two boards are not allowed within the same firm and symmetric cross-overlaps between two firms are also prohibited.

(OECD 1995b: 86)

In the 1990s German companies were engaged in internationalising their operations and became more dependent on global capital markets. The increasing internationalisation of regulatory standards within the framework of integrated capital markets placed pressure upon leading German corporations to formally at least declare a new commitment to shareholder value (while often retaining traditional adherence to stakeholder values and practices). A number of German companies including Daimler-Benz adapted their accounting and governance practices in order to list on the New York Stock Exchange.

A series of legislative and regulatory initiatives were progressed to drive the reform of corporate governance. A tax reform was approved in 2000 abolishing the 50 per cent capital gains tax on corporate sales of shares in other companies, paving the way for German corporations and financial institutions to begin unwinding the vast blocks of cross-shareholdings. These stable blocks of shares held in networks, had protected German companies from any likelihood of hostile takeover. In the new market environment without such large blockholdings of shares, it is likely there will be an increase in mergers and takeovers, and shareholder activism. It is assumed this will make German industry more competitive by eliminating protections against takeovers.

Finally development took place of a new code on corporate governance and a review of company law was undertaken with a view to improve disclosure, independence of audit, the operation of supervisory boards, and shareholder protection. Together these initiatives are intended as a response to increasing national and international shareholder activism. However, in the wake of Enron and the international fall in technology stocks, the fledgeling *Neuer Markt* that listed high-tech companies in Germany collapsed in 2002, dampening enthusiasm for the stock market there. Meanwhile German institutional investors and shareholders tempted to invest in the US market by the promise of higher returns also lost money.

The German system of control has been called a passive form in the sense that unfavorable developments are prevented. As a form of corporate governance, this may allow a necessary longer-run orientation of firms and may therefore have its advantages. One of the

shortcomings of the German system is, however, that it is geared to the incumbent firms and not to the uncertain terrain of the new firms. It is amazing that Germany has managed to solve its structural adjustment mainly in the existing firms, and not by new firms. Indeed, there are only a very few examples that new firms have gained eminence in the German economy. The German approach to corporate governance may be good in marginal improvements, but it is deficient in leapfrogging to new approaches and new products. Incremental technological improvements along established lines, mainly in the export-oriented automobile, machine building, chemical industry, and electro-technical industry are therefore typical for the German industry. In contrast, there was a more remarkable restructuring in the corporate sector of the United States, where the equity markets have forced management to restructure (Holmstrom 1999; Mayer 1998). In Germany, as on the continent, management has greater freedom not to restructure. The block holder model is not good in Schumpeterian innovations, i.e. in major technological breakthroughs.

(Siebert 2004: 41)

In an illustration of how adaptation of corporate governance institutions may attempt to support innovation, Vitols (2001) examines the development of the *Neuer Markt* and the initial public offering (IPO) explosion in Germany. The bank-based financial system of Germany was regarded as providing stable, long term finance to industry, however in the 1990s it came under criticism for failing to support high tech companies. 'Interestingly enough, the same elements that were previously seen as strengths are now partially seen as weaknesses: the German banks' preference for making loans to established, capital-intensive companies, according to this view, starves new technology-based firms of needed high-risk venture capital'. In response to this perceived weakness the Frankfurt Stock Exchange established the *Neuer Markt* in 1997, modelled on the NASDAQ, to serve the needs of both investors and young companies launching high risk technologies. The rapid growth of the *Neuer Markt* and sudden substantial increase in IPOs in Germany, led to

speculation that Germany could close the gap with the US in high tech industries. However, this new market was concerned with the diffusion rather than development of radical innovations, and displayed some continuities with the pre-existing insider model of small-firm governance. Yet though the *Neuer Markt* promised higher standards of accountability, it was plagued with scandals, and though at its peak companies listed on the index had a market value of 234 billion euros, this collapsed to 12 billion euros, before the closure of the market at the end of 2003.

The combination of the further integration and internationalisation of the financial markets of Germany, together with concerns regarding the *governing coalition* of banks, blockholders and employees in German industry, and long standing issues with the disclosure and transparency of German financial reporting, increased the demand for changes in corporate governance. A series of accounting scandals propelled legal reforms in Germany including the law for strengthening of control and transparency (KonTraG) in 1998, extending the role of the supervisory board, the law on transparency and disclosure (TransPuG) in 2002 sanctioning a corporate governance code, and the accounting enforcement act (BilKoG) in 2004 establishing additional outside supervision of company accounts. These reforms towards transparency and investor protection enhanced the position of outside investors, who as small investors did not have significant influence in the traditional German system of corporate governance (Goncharov *et al.* 2006: 422).

## Supervisory boards

The commitment to codetermination in Germany has survived largely unscathed through the company law reforms that have so far taken place, despite the fact that Anglo-American commentators are now so far removed from the basic tenets of social democracy that they seem to believe the supervisory board must come from another planet. To company directors and executives from the United States and Britain it is now fundamentally inconceivable that employees could be members of the board (even a supervisory board). This hardening attitude is an illustration

that the market based system has compounded social inequality as well as material inequality measurably in recent decades. However social democracy still survives in north European countries, if not entirely intact, certainly in some fundamentals. The German industrial project, which proved highly successful for most of the second half of the twentieth century was to invest in high quality production with a highly skilled workforce. Companies substantially invested in their employees and offered security of employment, and workers reciprocated with commitment and ingenuity. This was the social and economic basis that enabled the supervisory board to function in Germany and other countries.

North European managers used to working with supervisory boards traditionally have accepted them as a useful part of the governance apparatus of the company. Having to negotiate with and seek the final approval of the supervisory board for major investments, restructuring activity, product and market development, together with other major decisions, was a skill German managers developed and led to more consensual relationships and committed strategies. The structure

and operation of one supervisory board in a medium-sized chemical company is illustrated in Figures 5.4, 5.5 and 5.6. There is a dual system with a separation of duties between the board of management (BoM), and the supervisory board (SB), with the BoM responsible for operational control, and the SB exercising oversight including approval of business plans, defined transactions, and annual financial statements (Figure 5.4). On the supervisory board there is equal representation of shareholder representatives and employee representatives, though the chair of the SB is drawn from the shareholder representatives and has a casting vote (Figure 5.5). The work of the supervisory board is supported by a range of committees including audit, personnel, strategy and technology, each of which has assigned duties (Figure 5.6). In reality the dual supervisory board and board of management structure of governance is not as totally different from the developing practice of the unitary board in the Anglo-American system. The importance of independent non-executive directors has become firmly established in the unitary board, and increasingly they form a majority of the

**Figure 5.4** The dual system (1): segregation of duties.

Source: Heins-Bunde, Joachim (2006), *SGL Carbon*, Discussion Paper, Henley Management College, UK, 4 October.

**Figure 5.5** The dual system (2): equal representation of employee and shareholder representatives.

Source: Heins-Bunde, Joachim (2006), *SGL Carbon*, Discussion Paper, Henley Management College, UK, 4 October.

**Figure 5.6** Activities of supervisory board.

Source: Heins-Bunde, Joachim (2006), *SGL Carbon*, Discussion Paper, Henley Management College, UK, 4 October.

board, and take responsibility for the committees, it could be argued this is in effective a supervisory board that operates as part of the full board in a unitary structure. The only substantial difference is the direct representation of shareholders and of employees in the European supervisory board.

## France

France and Italy are the European countries with the smallest ownership of company shares by financial institutions. The majority of shares traditionally have been owned by non-financial enterprises, which reflects an elaborate structure of cross and circular ownership. That is, companies own each other's shares in a circular relationship. No external party can readily gain entry to the network, or seize control of any entity in the network, and all of the member companies support each other against outsiders. 'Cross participation among companies is an important element of French corporate governance. It shields managers from the short-term pressures of the market by making a change in corporate control more difficult – a feature that may be conducive to long-term, relation-specific investments, but one that also weakens pressures to maximize performance' (OECD 1997: 111).

Another distinguishing feature of France is the concentration of ownership, which is higher than in any other G7 (Group of Seven) industrialised country with the exception of Italy. In France half the firms are controlled by one single investor owning the absolute majority of capital. On boards the role of non-executive directors is muted, as business tends to be dominated by the President Directeur General (PDG) who combines the functions of the chair and chief executive. The independence of the PDG is reinforced by the legal notion that enterprises should pursue the *interet social de l'enterprise*. This law is interpreted in two ways: that management has to act in the interests of shareholders, but also that management has to act in the interest of the enterprise, for example to ensure its survival (OECD 1997: 113).

However, France is responding to the pressure for greater transparency and accountability

by foreign investors who by 2001 held 50 per cent of the equity in large public companies. The business federation MEDEF has accepted the disclosure of the remuneration of top executives, and the government proposed to separate the powers of the President Directeur General. Yet though France has among the most open capital markets in the world, the number of non-French directors appointed to French companies is extremely low. While there are signs of a general improvement in corporate governance among some of France's leading corporations, the dramatic losses of Vivendi in CEO inspired overseas adventures (that took a French water company to Hollywood and back), indicated the country is not immune to corporate governance failures.

Corporate governance has an essential role to play in the performance of companies, not just in securing accountability, and this includes promoting innovation and the institutions that support new industries. Goyer (2001) citing Michael Porter's *The Competitive Advantage of Nations* (1990) and Hall and Soskice's *Varieties of Capitalism* (2001) insists 'corporate governance is a key element shaping the innovation process in advanced industrial nations'. He charts the system of corporate governance in France that supported the strategy of innovation firstly led by the state under *dirigisme*, and subsequently by the large French firms since the mid-1980s. As the innovative capacity of French firms in industries such as aircraft, electrical products, life sciences, and railway equipment developed, the system of corporate governance adapted from supporting the central role of the state, to providing autonomy for senior managers as they restructured and pursued acquisitions internationally including in the United States:

> The system of corporate governance did change over time while the innovative capabilities of French firms remained specialized in the same areas ... From the early 1950s to the mid-1980s, the system of corporate governance served to support the central and guiding role of the state as well as to preserve the bilateral character of the policy-making process in France. From the mid-1980s to the early 1990s, the system of corporate governance

provided autonomy for top managers as they redrew work relations inside the firm and proceeded to acquire American firms. The current period is characterized by the institutional complementarity between the innovative capabilities of French firms and the institutional features of corporate governance.

(2001: 154)

## Italy

The Italian corporate governance system has a history of problems with a pyramidal structure in place in most companies. The Italian corporate governance system is characterised by 'a high degree of direct ownership concentration, both for listed and unlisted companies' (Bianco and Casavola 1999: 1058). 'Weak managers, strong blockholders and unprotected minority shareholders' summarise the Italian corporate reality (Melis 2000: 347; 2004; Becht 1997). The strong blockholders are usually families or coalitions associated with such families. The blockholders have a strong influence over management due to their large ownership of the corporation, and also through cross-shareholdings with other groups and companies. In the great majority of companies the control structure is characterised by the dominance of the main shareholder (Biancha *et al.* 1997).

Corporate governance in Italy is built around family capitalism, the involvement of banks and financial institutions (although usually not directly through large ownerships), considerable state presence (although this is changing) and the widespread use of pyramidal groups. The pyramidal group structure in particular, allows the entrepreneur at the top of the pyramid to control a large set of assets (Bianco and Casavola, 1999). As Melis pointed out (2000: 348), 'The structure of these groups is usually quite complex. Despite the rules of ownership disclosure, their exact control structure is difficult to trace, especially at an international level'. While Anglo-American corporate governance exhibits justified concerns about the abuse of power by senior executives of the company, the Italian system is concerned with 'the abuse of power from the blockholder' (Becht 1997; Melis 2004: 354).

## Provera and the reform of corporate governance at Telecom Italia

An insight into the intricate mysteries of Italian corporate governance can be gained by examining the case of Telecom Italia. There exists in Telecom Italia a relatively pyramidal structure with the presence of a substantial single blockholder. Marco Tronchetti Provera is chair and/or CEO of each of the companies that form a pyramid at the base of which is a substantial shareholding in the Telecom Italia ownership structure. He is a strong blockholder of the Telecom Italia company. Provera's many other financial interests will serve to enhance his influence over other Telecom Italia stakeholders, such as the company's own managers and other minority shareholders. Telecom Italia is making significant efforts to ensure their corporate governance standards match international best practice. This is evident in the board's adoption of a 'Code of Self-Discipline', the majority of the board is composed of independent directors, and the three board committees (internal control, remuneration and strategy) have a majority of independent directors. In addition there is a board of statutory auditors composed of five independent members with two of the independent directors being representatives of minority shareholders, and the implementation of specific anti-corruption practices to form part of the company's internal control system.

However, all of these apparently robust efforts to achieve more rigorous, and independent corporate governance mechanisms are potentially vitiated by the fact that of the 10 independent members of the 19 member board of directors, 6 independent directors are drawn from the slate presented by Olimpia (and 4 from a slate drawn up by minority shareholders). With the 3 executive directors of the board and a further 6 non-executive directors, the Telecom Italia board has the appearance of independence but this may not be the reality. While the transparency and accountability capabilities within Telecom Italia through the board and internal controls have improved, Provera's influence may in practice undermine this. As the main blockholder within Telecom Italia, Provera would have, if not the final say, a strong influence in any corporate governance decisions within the company. Central to this control is the SPV Olimpia.

## Olimpia

The main corporate governance questions on special purpose vehicles (SPVs) are:

▪ Why have they been established?
▪ Who established them?

With regard to the setting up of Olimpia as a special purpose vehicle (SPV) within Telecom Italia, questions need to be asked to its purpose, duration, magnitude and the decision makers behind its establishment. While SPVs are generally set up as short term financial solutions (in most cases to offset financial difficulties), they do call into question a company's accountability, transparency and financial strength. Overt reliance on SPVs contributed to the collapse of Enron and Parmalat. Financial markets took a serious view with the revelation of the magnitude of these vehicles and their importance to the financial health of these two companies. If Olimpia is shown to be an SPV as a temporary measure and a definite end-life, its establishment made known and having the approval of its statutory auditors and shareholders, and a financial weight not exceeding more than 17.03 per cent of Telecom Italia's ownership, then there is degree of danger for Telecom Italia to have Olimpia as such an influential SPV, though this may be monitored and limited. The corporate governance reforms within Telecom Italia are a step in the right direction. The reforms are promoting transparency and accountability in the company. The changes within Telecom Italia are not merely cosmetic nor need they be superficial in their effect. However, these reforms must also be seen in the context of the residual governance structure of having an influential blockholder in place, and the powerful presence of Olimpia S.p.A with the oversight of Marco Tronchetti Provera. This suggests the commitment of Telecom Italia to international corporate governance standards is being honoured in form rather than substance.

## CORPORATE GOVERNANCE FAILURE IN EUROPE

Though there is much evidence of widespread weaknesses in corporate governance in Europe, in recent times Europe has not experienced the frequency and scale of corporate failures witnessed in the United States. However, there have been sufficient accounting and corruption scandals to convince regulators that the accountability and transparency of the system was badly in need of reform. There have been two spectacular crashes in Europe which are reminders of how things could go wrong. The first at Ahold in 2002 was at the time described as 'Europe's Enron', the second at Parmalat in 2003 brought more than a note of ridicule to the standards of European corporate governance.

Parmalat was a dairy products company that had rapidly grown into a global concern, but demonstrated more ingenuity in illicit financial engineering than in dairy. For well over a decade, from about 1990 to 2003, Parmalat continued to borrow huge amounts of money from global banks and justified those loans by inflating its revenues through fictitious sales to retailers. By 1995, the company was losing more than $300 million annually in Latin America alone, so Parmalat decided to move some of its debt off the company's consolidated financial statements. It did so through three shell companies based in the Caribbean. These firms pretended to sell Parmalat products, and Parmalat would send them fake invoices and charge costs and fees to make the 'sales' look legitimate. Then Parmalat would write out a credit note for the amount the subsidiaries supposedly owed it, and take that to banks to raise money. To make the debt disappear, Parmalat management developed a network of 260 international offshore speculative entities. These companies were used to conceal losses, through a mirror-game which made them appear as assets or liquidity, while the company started to issue bonds in order to collect money. The security for such bonds was provided by the alleged liquidity represented by the offshore schemes. When the Bank of America on 17 December 2003 denied the authenticity of the existence of 3.9 billion euros, the Parmalat house of cards collapsed, it filed for administration, and all of its senior executives were arrested (Figure 5.7). All of this was made possible because the governance system of Parmalat was a fraudulent pyramid which left the company totally under the control of its founder Calisto Tanzi (see Case Study 5).

**Figure 5.7** Parmalat share price collapse.

Source: Compiled from Milan Stock Exchange, Yahoo Finance, various media news sources.

Ahold went from being a global food retailer and distributor that had grown to become the world's third largest grocer powerhouse to become Europe's Enron, when it made public an Enron-style financial accounting fraud by announcing 'accounting irregularities' at its US Food service (USF unit) on 24 February 2003. The irregularities were that it had overstated earnings by at least $500 million in 2001 and 2002, prompting its Amsterdam and New York-listed shares to lose more than 60 per cent of their value, credit ratings downgraded to junk, forcing Ahold to rely on an expensive emergency credit facility to pay its bills and facing a €12 billion debt. The crisis was deep and prolonged for customers, investors and employees alike (Figure 5.8).

According to the SEC fillings, Ahold was found responsible of three counts of fraud: the inflation of promotional allowances at US Food service (Ahold wholly owned subsidiary), the improper consolidation of joint ventures through side letters (control letters), and accounting errors and

irregularities that resulted in the overstated; net income, net operating income and net sales for the years 2000, 2001 and the first three quarters of 2002. As the investigation was completed in July the same year – 470 accounting irregularities and 278 internal control weaknesses were uncovered. The CEO at the time, Cees van der Hoeven and CFO Michiel Meurs immediately resigned, quickly followed by other senior managers and directors. Leaving the company as Lehman Brothers analyst Christopher Gower observed shortly after the scandal: 'with no management, no clarity on accounts, no clarity on financing, future strategy or disposals' (see Case Study 4).

## THE REFORM OF EUROPEAN CORPORATE GOVERNANCE INSTITUTIONS AND PRACTICES

The European Commission is committed to the continuous improvement of corporate governance

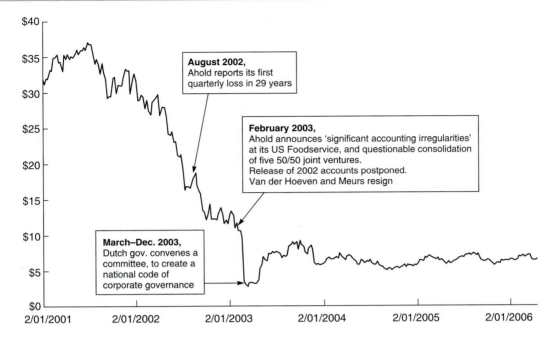

**August 2002,**
Ahold reports its first
quarterly loss in 29 years

**February 2003,**
Ahold announces 'significant accounting irregularities'
at its US Foodservice, and questionable consolidation
of five 50/50 joint ventures.
Release of 2002 accounts postponed.
Van der Hoeven and Meurs resign

**March–Dec. 2003,**
Dutch gov. convenes a
committee, to create a
national code of
corporate governance

**Figure 5.8** Ahold share price collapse.

Source: Compiled from Yahoo Finance (2006), various media news sources.

in the region and in a statement on this to the European Parliament insisted:

'Good company law, good corporate governance practices throughout the EU will enhance the real economy:

■ An effective approach will foster the global efficiency and competitiveness of business in the EU. Well managed companies, with strong corporate governance records and sensitive social and environmental performance, outperform their competitors. Europe needs more of them to generate employment and higher term sustainable growth.

■ An effective approach will help to strengthen shareholders' rights and third parties' protection. In particular, it will contribute to rebuilding European investor confidence in the wake of a wave of recent governance scandals. The livelihood of millions of Europeans, their pensions, their investments are tied up in the proper, responsible performance and governance of listed companies in which they invest' (Commission of the European Communities 2003: 3).

In 2002 a report was presented by the Winter Committee on 'A Modern Regulatory Framework for Company Law in Europe'. The policy objectives of this were:

■ effective protection of shareholders and third parties to achieve a high degree of confidence in business relationships;
■ distinguishing between categories of companies with a more stringent framework for listed companies;
■ measures aimed at combating fraud and abuse.

With over 40 codes relating to corporate governance adopted since the 1990s, the Winter report did not suggest another code, but recommended the European Union to focus its efforts on the reduction of legal and regulatory barriers to cross-border voting (participation barriers), as well as the reduction of barriers to shareholders' ability to evaluate the governance of companies (information barriers). This formed part of a five year plan to improve disclosure, governance mechanisms, and shareholder democracy (one shareholder/one vote).

## FEE Report on European Corporate Governance

The Federation des Experts Compatables Europeens (FEE) published a report on the financial and auditing aspects of corporate governance (2003). FEE is the representative body for the accountancy professions in Europe, with representation from 41 bodies from 29 countries. The FEE report was a response to the recent corporate governance debates in the United States and Europe, and to the European Commission's Communication on Company Law and Corporate Governance, and the preceding influential Winter Report on this subject. In establishing the context the report admits 'to the role of accounting errors or fraud in the demise of a number of important companies. Many of the recent corporate failures could be attributed to a lack of integrity on the part of management where individuals were involved in aggressive accounting, earnings management or fraudulent financial reporting to manipulate share price, borrowings and bonus plans'.

The report goes on to insist, 'Confidence in financial planning, and in audit, is a key factor in ensuring confidence in capital markets' (2003: 7). The purpose of the report is to contribute to the effort to restore confidence in capital markets by enhancing corporate governance by providing financial information of the highest quality.

FEE supports the conclusion of the Winter Report and the European Commission that there is no need for a separate corporate governance code. To ensure adequate coordination however, some principles and common benchmarks are required for national codes (soft law). The FEE paper concentrates on the intersection and mutual dependency between financial reporting, corporate governance, and audit. The intersecting areas include:

- internal control;
- financial reporting including financial statements and accounting policies;
- oversight by non-executive directors including activities of the audit committee;
- reporting by external auditors to shareholders and management;
- internal audit;
- shareholders' meeting.

The work of the FEE was complicated by the fact that they needed to deal with companies with unitary boards as well as companies with two tier boards (supervisory and management board). Included among the universal key messages of the FEE analysis are:

- the importance of an appropriate balance of power at board level, so that no individual or group has unfettered control of the company;
- the importance of the independence of audit committees, and of independent non-executive directors;
- requirements for comprehensive disclosure on corporate governance, with progress not only on identifying the core issues to be reported, but in establishing the conceptual underpinnings;
- a wider brief for audit committees beyond examining core issues of financial reporting, to reviewing wider aspects of internal control;
- use of extended ('long form') reports to boards by external auditors in combination with oral presentation and in-depth exchange of views;
- establishing a policy on the provision of non-audit services from auditors, keeping under review the auditor's role and independence.

The Sarbanes–Oxley Act focuses on internal control in relation to external financial reporting and the controls over information filed with the SEC. Both the FEE and Winter reports go beyond this to emphasise the wider aspects of internal control and related processes of risk management. Essentially the belief is that effective internal control systems should be designed to encompass all major areas of risk and vulnerability in a company's operation including corporate governance issues.

## MODERNISING COMPANY LAW AND ENHANCING CORPORATE GOVERNANCE

In 2003 the European Commission adopted an *Action Plan for Modernising Company Law and*

*Enhancing Corporate Governance in the European Union,* the main objectives of which were:

- to foster efficiency and competitiveness of business;
- to strengthen shareholder rights and their party protection.

In pursuit of this the Commission adopted recommendations on company directors, established the European Corporate Governance Forum, the Advisory Group on Corporate Governance and Company Law, revised the accounting directives, simplified the company law directive, and the directive on cross-border mergers.

> Harmonisation of the rules relating to company law and corporate governance, as well as to accounting and auditing, is essential for creating a Single Market for Financial Services and products. In the fields of company law and corporate governance, objectives include: providing equivalent protection for shareholders and other parties concerned with companies; ensuring freedom of establishment for companies throughout the EU; fostering efficiency and competitiveness of business; promoting cross-border cooperation between companies in different Member States; and stimulating discussions between Member States on the modernisation of company law and corporate governance.
>
> (European Commission 2005b)

In 2005 a series of further issues were submitted for consultation including the following.

## Shareholder democracy

A variety of exceptions to the 'one share, one vote' principle existed in Europe, including multiple voting rights, voting right ceilings, priority (or preference) shares, depositary receipts, or non-voting shares. These exceptions enable shareholders to control companies without holding a corresponding proportion of the share capital or bearing a corresponding financial risk. While the principle of proportionality between risk-bearing capital and control was the rule in some member

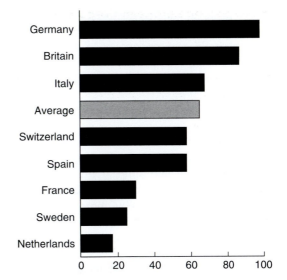

**Figure 5.9** What shareholders' democracy? Companies applying 'one share/one vote' principle.

Source: Association of British Insurers: Deminor Rating (2005).
Note: Companies in the FTS Eurofirst 300 Index.

states it was the exception (Figure 5.9). This had implications for the formation of groups and pyramids that could dominate companies with minority holdings.

## Corporate restructuring and mobility

This proposal would enable the transfer of the registered office of a company in the European Union without first having to wind up the company in the home member state, and subsequently reincorporating in the host member state. The 10th Company Law Directive on cross-border mergers was adopted and was due to be transposed into national legislation by the end of 2007.

## Legal forms of enterprises

On 8 October 2004 the Societas Europaea (SE) was created with the entry into force of the Statute of the European Company, this makes it possible for European companies to merge across borders, and to operate across the European Union with

reduced costs and unified management. The issue was whether companies needed more flexibility to establish SE and operate on a Europe wide basis.

## Simplification and modification of European company law

This proposal concerned a range of initiatives to codify, consolidate and simplify European company law to make legislation less burdensome, easier to apply, and thereby more effective in achieving its goals.

## CONVERGENCE OR HARMONISATION?

The question of whether countries will converge towards a common corporate governance system, or sustain the present diversity of institutions is one of the key issues facing the continent. Lower economic growth and higher unemployment in Europe compared to the Anglo-American countries since the mid-1990s, undermined some of the confidence in Europe's social model (though by 2005 Germany had returned to its former position as the world's largest exporter). Despite the pressures towards adopting Anglo-Saxon modes of corporate governance, the divergences in both the policy and practice of corporate governance in Europe have thus far resisted any move towards European standards. With greater market integration, the developing influence of institutional investors, and privatisation it is likely the market will play a greater role. However, debates on company law harmonisation in the European Union have been held up by countries not wishing to see elements of their own systems of corporate governance disappear in the harmonisation process. One explanation for this impasse is the *institutional complementarity thesis* which justifies the continuing diversity of systems, rejecting the 'one-best-way' strategy adopted by the 'convergence thesis'. Instead a plurality of models is assumed, each corresponding to local circumstances, supported by a cluster of social norms and regulation, enabling balanced economic development. As Reberioux argues what is often presented as the practical economic inevitability of convergence,

is in essence a profoundly ideological and political argument:

> Two competing theories behind forms of corporate governance can thus be discerned. In the first case, the US model – the predominance of widely held corporations controlled by their owners – is presented as optimal. If one adds a general law that institutions are evolving toward efficiency, then one obtains the convergence thesis: the European system is bound to change in the direction of the Anglo-Saxon one; it is only a matter of time. From a neo-institutionalist perspective, this process of convergence is seen as the result of rational micro-behaviour by individuals when crafting their governance structure (Williamson 1995) ... Without delving further into a complex debate, it is worth noting that the micro-efficiency of shareholder value has not yet been proved, and probably never will be. The fundamental reason is that shareholder sovereignty is not an efficient arrangement, but rather a power relationship, that is a particular (societal) way to design a corporation ... The *institutional complementarity thesis* provides a contrasting perspective on the continuing diversity of capitalist systems (Amable 2000). The core of this theoretical approach is a rejection of the 'one best way' strategy adopted by the convergence thesis in analysing institutions. Rather, a plurality of models is assumed, each corresponding to local circumstances. The focus should not be upon a particular (isolated) institution, but on the cluster of social norms that underpin national regulation. This societal approach emphasises the systemic links between institutions that enable balanced economic development.
>
> (2000: 117–118)

The diversity of corporate models is valuable and is rooted in societal characteristics that together shape the competitiveness of the different models. Though shareholder value may be gaining ground due to the influence of Anglo-Saxon institutional investors, a stakeholder approach is closer to the reality of European social democracies, and the outcome of the confrontation between the two competing philosophies is highly uncertain.

It is unlikely that imported Anglo-Saxon capital related features of corporate governance will work well with continental labour-related aspects of corporate governance as represented in supervisory boards. It is likely any such European compromise would be more unstable than existing systems (Reberioux 2000; Cernat 2004).

A more pessimistic view is offered by Christel Lane who reviews the evidence on the German case and concludes that a new Anglo-American logic of corporate governance is diffusing beyond the major corporations of the DAX 30, and that this is not simply attributable to external constraints, but to powerful actors within the German economy including large banks and insurance companies. This is significant firstly because Germany has been the paradigm for the model of coordinated capitalism as distinct from competitive or liberal market capitalism. If the cohesive German system is in the process of fundamental change, then other continental European business systems are likely to be vulnerable. Secondly, Lane argues it is wrong to assume the adoption of the Anglo-American model is simply about changes in capital markets and corporate financing:

> Because forms of corporate governance structure most other relationships within firms and even in society as a whole, they are inherently connected with a distribution of power and material welfare. They therefore decisively shape the logic of the whole political economy. Hence there is strong concern, particularly but not only on the part of labour, with the consequences of change for the distribution of surplus and control to various stakeholders in the firm, as well as the future viability of the production paradigm of diversified quality production.

## THE IMPACT OF SHAREHOLDER VALUE

The sharpest point of the advance of Anglo-Saxon modes of corporate governance is the principle of shareholder value as the central objective of corporations. Ultimately the direction of the development of corporate governance in Europe will be determined by the extent to which shareholder value orientations and their accompanying managerial practices take hold. Jurgens, Naumann and Rupp (2000) suggest the most visible manifestation of change in the direction of a shareholder value economy in Germany are the internal changes by management introducing shareholder value oriented management control and incentive systems. They claim that these changes have primarily affected a handful of large companies such as DaimlerChrysler and Siemens, though these flagship companies have linkages that flow through to the rest of the economy. One reason companies such as DaimlerChrysler and Siemens should have changed direction is their falling market capitalisation relative to other European corporations. Other recent changes include the role of the banks, the loosening of traditional cross-holdings and inter-locking directorate structures, and the growing influence of institutional investors with value orientations. However, they contrast German society where private pension schemes are just developing, with Anglo-Saxon countries where the interests and behaviour of private households drives shareholder value orientation.

Beyer and Hassel examine the interdependence between economic institutions captured in the idea of *institutional complementarities* and the impact upon this of internationalisation, with reference to the changing distribution of net value added in large German firms. The lower return to shareholders traditionally prevailing in Germany is possible with a weak market for corporate control since managers cannot be pressured by the threat of hostile takeovers, and lower returns for shareholders implies higher rates of retained earnings which enables a more consensus oriented approach to restructuring in line with a higher skill level and employee involvement in the firm. This contrasts considerably with the distribution arrangements in Anglo-American corporations:

> In Anglo-American countries, corporate owners have a fundamental problem of expropriating the return on their investment. Since the relationship between owners and management is market-driven and does not depend on owners trusting in the fair treatment by management or wider strategic business goals, investors have to strive for a high share of return. Their principal problem is to extract a high enough return from the company so

that management is not inclined to overinvest in order to improve its own position (Jensen 1986; La Porta *et al.* 2000). At the same time, investors in Anglo-American countries also have the means to extract a higher return from a company, not only because their legal position is stronger but also because the market for corporate control forces companies to anticipate and meet shareholders' expectations. Dividends are used as a signalling device for shareholders to indicate a high return on investment. Since corporate ownership serves to secure either bank credits or to stabilise inter-firm relations in the majority of German companies, rates of return on investment often play a secondary role. Corporate aims are frequently not stated in terms of return on investments, but in the maximisation of growth or sales. Moreover, minority investors do not have the means to enforce higher returns other than to disinvest, because their position is relatively weaker. As an actor, minority shareholders hardly play a role in company policies. As a consequence, we should find higher returns for investors in Anglo-American countries compared to German firms.

(Beyer and Hassel 2002: 315)

Successive changes in corporate governance practices in Germany since the mid-1990s have begun to have an impact pushing towards a more market based system however including:

▪ an increase in the legal protection for minority shareholders;
▪ the evolution of more offensive takeover practices and regulation;
▪ a changing approach by major blockholders – banks and companies – towards cross-shareholding, reducing their monitoring role.

While public policy has facilitated these changes it is corporations that have driven them, taking active steps towards disengaging in cross-shareholdings and interlocking directorships, towards more transparency and shareholder value, and towards a more active market for corporate control.

In their survey of large German firms Beyer and Hassel find a small but significant change in the distribution of net value added towards shareholders in the payment of dividends, resulting from the increasing orientation of firms towards international financial markets and the increasing importance of the market for corporate control, though this did not as yet appear to have affected the relationship between management and employees, though this might happen in time (Figure 5.10; Table 5.3). The direction of the changes of the German system will be negotiated for some time to come; however undoubtedly there will be changes from the closed financial networks of the past towards a more internationalised system, with consequent developments towards international accounting standards, auditing, and board supervision.

Further differences in approaches to corporate governance across Europe can be highlighted by examining the governance of the largest firms in different industry sectors. There has been a common EU-wide movement towards financial market integration, product market deregulation, and privatisation suggesting the convergence of business practices, ownership patterns and regulatory frameworks. However Goldstein's (2000) study of the evolution of corporate governance and regulation in the privatised telecommunications companies in the four largest EU economies reveals that relative to their British counterparts, companies in continental Europe still show a higher degree of ownership concentration and stability, and employ less frequently governance practices such as executive incentive remuneration packages, and specialised board committees. Corporate governance remains heavily influenced by durable national institutions, and distinctive political traditions regarding the role of the corporation in society, 'just' levels of executive remuneration, the concept of public service, and the legitimacy of state involvement in corporate restructuring.

The car industry has for long been identified as an indicator of major industrial trends and in recent years has been singled out by the capital markets as a value destroyer in terms of shareholder value, with the resulting low market capitalisation exposing them to the threat of hostile takeover. In this context the flagship European car companies including Fiat, PSA, Peugeot-Citroen, Renault and Volkswagen have all made shareholder value a greater priority.

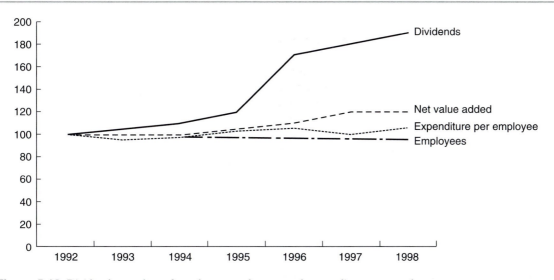

**Figure 5.10** Dividends, number of employees and personnel expenditure per employee.

Source: Beyer, J. and Hassel, A. (2001), The Effects of Convergence: Internationalization and the Changing Distribution of Net Value Added in Large German Firms, *Economy and Society*, 31(3): 309–332.

|          | Labour | Creditors | Government | Dividends | Retained earnings |
|----------|--------|-----------|------------|-----------|-------------------|
| 1992–4   | 85.3   | 5.4       | 5.2        | 2.0       | 2.2               |
| 1996–8   | 78.4   | 4.3       | 6.8        | 2.8       | 7.8               |
| %        | −8.1   | −20.4     | +30.8      | +40.0     | +254.5            |

**Table 5.3** The distribution of net value added in large German firms, 1992–1994 and 1996–1998 (as % of net value added).

Source: Beyer J. and Hassel Anke (2001: 320).
Note: Table 5.3 shows the distribution of net value added in 1992–4 compared to the period 1996–8 as an average for fifty-nine large German companies. The change over time largely supports the assumption of a changing distribution of net value added due to a convergence to Anglo-American practices: the shares of net value added are paid out as dividends and as taxes as to the Government have increased, while the share for labour has decreased. It is, however, unclear why the share of retained earnings has also increased significantly, which was not to be expected.

All of these companies are protected by strong family ownership or state ownership. However, while Fiat has introduced shareholder value and accompanying governance practices rapidly, at the other extreme Volkswagen has adopted a more measured approach attempting to balance the interests of labour and capital. Yet none of the companies required the support of the stock market to raise capital for its operational activities, including major project investments. This is true also for the financing of large acquisitions. Nor have most of the companies used stock options as a major incentive for management. The most important reason for the companies to be concerned about the stock market and their share price, is the lingering threat of hostile takeover. To resist this threat they have engaged in a dual strategy of attempting to enhance their stock market valuation and of erecting barriers against hostile takeovers. Ironically there is evidence that the gross profit margins of these European producers are in inverse proportion to their adoption of

shareholder value policies. It appears that the corporate governance systems in the advanced industrial countries of Europe are still in a state of flux, and that ownership concentration, institutional structures, shareholder value and management control continue to be negotiated. However, at the margins of Europe in the transitional economies, corporate governance change has proved a great deal more problematic.

## REASSESSING THE INTERNATIONAL ROLE OF EUROPE

### Isolationism/protectionism will not work

The European Commission claims 'Resorting to protectionism and trying to shield jobs and industries from international competition is not a viable option' arguing,

> The European economy is inextricably linked to the world economy. Happily, upon close inspection many of the allegedly negative implications of rising international trade and investment for jobs, wages and living standards are belied by the evidence. However, widespread public concerns should not be dismissed too easily. In order to realise the potential gains from globalisation, production structures will have to shift considerably towards further specialisation and diversification into new areas of relative comparative advantage, and this process is likely to be associated with considerable frictions.
>
> Throwing sand into the wheels of deeper international economic integration, as contemplated by some, in order to reduce adjustment costs is not a viable option. Clearly, it is difficult for policy-makers to withstand protectionist tendencies in the face of concentrated, localised short-term adjustment needs, when the gains from economic integration are dispersed and only materialise in the medium to long term.
>
> But living in a fortress will not benefit us; it will only reduce economic efficiency, income and employment opportunities in the long run. And it will weaken our bargaining stance against trade barriers in other countries,

thereby undermining job creation at home in those sectors that would benefit from economic integration. Moreover, past experience of defensive policies which try to shield established firms or industries from new sources of competition and/or which have tried to protect people within specific jobs has largely been negative.

(2005: 13)

Though economic growth has been slower in Europe since the 1990s, there are a number of indications of the growing economic significance of the European Union, which now represents by far the largest market in the world, including the growth in overseas investment from Europe and the increasing significance of European stock exchanges.

### EU dominates global FDI

One reflection of the growing integration of the pan-European economy into the world economy is that it is now the largest investor of direct investment in other countries (including other European countries):

> The EU-15 is by far the largest investor 'abroad' (the data is not adjusted for intra-EU FDI), accounting for half of the world's outward FDI stock. In 1980 it was 39 per cent compared to 43 per cent for North America. North America's share has since fallen to 29 per cent. Developing countries' share of outward FDI stocks has been relatively stable over the past 25 years at low levels and in 2003 accounted for 10 per cent. Most of this FDI originates in the Asia/Pacific region. Africa accounts for less than half a per cent of the global outward FDI stock. Inward foreign investment is distributed a bit more evenly, with developing countries accounting for 28 per cent in 2003. Of this, the Asia/Pacific region (64 per cent) and Latin America and the Caribbean (28 per cent) have the largest shares. However, developing countries have not been able to benefit proportionally from the increase in FDI over the past quarter of a century – in 1980 their share stood at 44 per cent of global FDI stocks.

Again, the EU is, at 40 per cent in 2003, the largest recipient of FDI ahead of North America (22 per cent). Central and Eastern Europe, despite the progression since the early 1990s, still accounts for only 3 per cent of the global inward FDI stock.

(European Commission 2005: 24)

## Euronext

The pan-European stock exchange Euronext with subsidiaries in Belgium, France, the Netherlands, Portugal and the United Kingdom, quickly became a force in Europe and beyond. Euronext was formed in September 2000 in a merger of the stock exchanges of Amsterdam, Brussels and Paris, in order to take advantage of the harmonisation of the European Union financial markets. In 2002 the group merged with the Portuguese stock exchange BVLP and the London based futures and options exchange LIFFE. Euronext.liffe is the subsidiary of Euronext responsible for all options and futures contracts trading, formed by the merger of the derivatives activities of the various constituents of Euronext with LIFFE. In the relatively short time of its existence, Euronext came to rival the well-established London Stock Exchange, and with the revived German Bourse represented a strong European challenge to London. (This was accentuated when it appeared either Euronext or the German Bourse might acquire the London Stock Exchange. However, the welcoming of overtures from the New York Stock Exchange to merge with Euronext might have appeared flattering to the Euronext executives, but was less warmly received by many Europeans as a US takeover of a promising new European initiative) (see Chapter 7).

As the demographics of Europe changes, and governments withdraw from some of their pension responsibilities, the financial institutions managing insurance and superannuation will grow considerably. What impact they have on European corporate governance remains to be seen, as so far it has been the overseas investments of US and UK institutions that have had the most influence:

The driving role is sometimes taken by foreign institutional shareholders, as their weight in those countries' economies is growing. In fact, research indicates that foreign investors have already been key lobbyists for shareholder-friendly legislation on some markets such as France. Indeed, the primary actors prompting change in many corporate governance systems are institutional investors and often foreign institutional investors. To be sure, the presence of foreign shareholders is not always well accepted. Their demands tend to clash with historically established balances of power between investors, companies and their stakeholders. They are often perceived as 'breaking' existing social models. But as their role in fuelling economies is also increasingly acknowledged, so are their rights as stakeholders of those economies ... Globalisation is driving the evolution of company-investor relationships. Investors have more holdings abroad, and companies rely more on shareholders, particularly foreign institutionals, to finance their growth. In economic terms more countries are starting to veer towards the *outsider model*, even though cultures might not change as fast. As a result, corporate governance is currently undergoing profound modifications.

(Eurosif 2006: 17–27; TIAA-CREF 2001)

The level of activity of active ownership varies significantly among European countries (Table 5.4).

## CORPORATE GOVERNANCE IN TRANSITIONAL ECONOMIES

If Western Europe experienced prolonged contention concerning the consequences of reform of its corporate governance systems, the experience of Eastern Europe in its transition from command to market economies was far more difficult. The often painful transition of the Eastern European economies towards market systems reveals there is no ready formula to replace centrally planned economies with efficient market economies (Neumann and Egan 1999; McCarthy and Puffer 2002). Questions of corporate governance have been at the heart of the effort at privatising major corporations, and the failure to find satisfactory answers to these fundamental questions has often left economies weak and companies disoriented. The vacuum created by

| State of local activism | Countries |
|---|---|
| Established market culture for institutional investors and many fund managers | Ireland, UK |
| Driven by a limited number of (but nonetheless powerful) activist players | Denmark, Netherlands, Sweden, Switzerland (pension funds or institutional investors) <br> Austria, France, Germany, Italy (research organisations or fund managers) <br> Greece (Institutional investors) |
| Driven by strong small shareholder associations | Denmark, France, Germany, Netherlands |
| Rather non-existent | Other countries |

**Table 5.4** Penetration of active share ownership in some European countries.

Sources: Deutsche Bank Corporate Governance Research, TUAC, Eurosif, *Active Share Ownership in Europe: 2006 European Handbook*, p. 26.

the lack of effective corporate governance mechanisms allowed managers of state enterprises to exercise insider control and strip corporate assets during the process of privatisation. The Czech Republic was once regarded as a model for post-communist transition, yet Neumann and Egan explain how inadequate restructuring of major companies in the privatisation process, and insufficient efforts at legal and regulatory oversight have left a trail of bank failures and stock market scams. The country is now introducing reforms in the areas of capital market supervision, banking supervision, minority shareholder rights, and stock market regulation. In a bid to reduce market failure and provide economic stability, it is adopting elements of both the German and Anglo-Saxon models.

Looking further across the East European transition economies Joseph Stiglitz (1999) surveyed the wreckage of the economies subjected to market shock therapy. Tragically many of these economies have gone backwards rather than forwards after ten years or more of transition to market economies and poverty has become rampant. 'The quandary of the failure of so many experiments is particularly vexing when economic theory was so clear in its predictions: distorted prices, central planning, and attenuated incentives arising from the absence of clear property rights meant that resources were not efficiently allocated. Reducing those distortions, decentralising

decision-making, and privatising – even if not done perfectly – should have moved countries closer to their production possibilities curve. Output should have soared – instead it plummeted' (1999: 31–32). With corporations hopelessly in arrears with creditors, and effectively bankrupt banks, Stiglitz can only offer the solution of a government takeover of large proportions of existing assets, with a subsequent process of reprivatisation paying greater attention to problems of corporate governance than the first disastrous effort.

## Russia

In their account of corporate governance in Russia, McCarthy and Puffer argue that having experienced the most flagrant abuses of shareholder rights, and management enriching themselves, as in the excesses at Gazprom, the upheaval of 'wild capitalism' is now over and Russia is destined to apply more exacting governance standards. Yet Radygin and Malginov (2004: 33) chart the hard road to transforming the governance and performance of privatised corporations:

In Russia, the achievement of a considerable enhancement of economic agents' economic efficiency upon their privatization is far from

being evident. There are several reasons for this: the specifics of the Russian privatization process in early '90s (a giant role played by managers, prevalence of insiders in the primary post-privatization ownership structure, due to respective privileges) has led to many privatized companies' failure to get a new efficient owner. The consequent capital redistribution took a lot of time, which encouraged the continuous degradation of enterprises' production capacity and decreased their weakness in terms of adjustment to new conditions. Furthermore, the 1997–98 financial crisis has proved genuine concerns about the ability of the Russian commercial banks (along with a number of other categories of outsiders), lacking both financial capacity and managerial skills, to efficiently exercise corporate control and strategic ownership of shares. In many cases, such shareholders have proved to be incapable to ensure an efficient restructuring of acquired enterprises of the real economy sector and to bear the costs related to the control over them.

The state sponsored enthusiasm for a market alternative to the vast public sector in Russia, delivered through an insider model of majority shareholder domination, has created a potent cocktail of constant intermingling of the governance of the state, financial institutions and industrial magnates, which is unstable and fractious:

> The intense conflicts of interests between various bureaucratic structures within the government system, large financial structures, top management and their lobbying of their interests camouflaged under structural and legal restructuring made direct sales based upon negotiations and auctions (that were the main

privatization methods in Western countries) ineffective … As a result of the ownership redistribution and struggle for corporate control the prevailing feature of the Russian corporate sector now is concentrated property of insiders, including large external shareholders, who participate directly in management or who strictly control employed managers. Minority shareholders in most cases are kept away from the decision-making process. The investment policy is aimed at the use of own funds. The main property and corporate control redistribution are going on outside organized markets. The greater part of joint-stock companies formally belong to public companies, but are really operating as private enterprises.

> (Radygin and Malginov 2004: 34–35)

## CONCLUSIONS

The transformation of corporate governance in Europe is a fascinating but clearly unfinished portrait. The canvas encompasses immense diversity in the institutional arrangements and practices of corporate governance. Though these might be dismissed as archaic and in need of drastic reform from an Anglo-American point of view, the peculiarities of the different corporate governance systems do serve a purpose as far as their adherents are concerned. The distinctiveness of Europe has produced some of the most valued corporations in the world, together with an exceptional quality of life in many communities. Though Europe has embarked on a process of change in corporate governance and company law in recent years to integrate better into international financial and product markets, there are important signs that the commitment to social democracy will survive this experience.

# 6
# Asia Pacific Corporate Governance

## INTRODUCTION

This chapter explores the diverse approaches to corporate governance practised in the Asia Pacific countries. The special qualities of the relationship based approach to corporate governance are considered, and the pervasiveness of family owned businesses, embedded in business networks. The traditionally informal and often weak corporate governance mechanisms of this region are examined, where boards lack authority, and financial institutions fail to monitor. Despite the evident weaknesses in corporate governance this region has maintained the fastest economic growth, until the East Asian systemic financial crisis hit in 1997, and the lessons of the crisis for corporate governance reform are studied. The distinctive corporate governance systems of the giant economies of Japan, China and India are examined, and the extensive transformations that are taking place in each of those countries. Finally, the extensive development of corporate governance codes of practice throughout the Asia Pacific is considered, and the continuing efforts towards more durable reforms.

## ASIA PACIFIC RELATIONSHIP-BASED APPROACHES

The countries of the Asia Pacific also have a rich cultural diversity with different political and legal structures, and social traditions. Not only does this make for significant national differences in corporate governance policy and practice, but many countries in Asia are still engaged in a process of institutional development. Most countries of the region have corporate governance systems that are essentially based around close relationships, usually involving family control, and ongoing close relationships with creditors, suppliers, and major customers. In some systems this is reinforced by close relations with regulators and state officials.

This *relationship-based* form of conducting business contrasts with the *rules-based* systems that predominate in western industrial countries where there is a combination of internal and external controls exerted on companies. In western countries internally company directors are responsible for exercising a duty of care and diligence, which includes ensuring financial controls are effective. This financial discipline is reinforced by annual audit of the company accounts. Externally the company operates within a framework of company law that is enforced by regulatory authorities. Finally there is the enveloping discipline of the capital market, the effect of which is to exercise a commercial discipline upon companies. In broad terms this institutional structure existed in many East Asian economies by the 1990s, though unfortunately the structures did not work properly.

In Korea, Malaysia and Thailand for example, in the recent past the market and regulatory structures were undeveloped and therefore unable to ensure effective market discipline. In a less developed legal and institutional environment, the information asymmetries – between those on the inside who know what is happening and others left in ignorance – are more severe. Since it is difficult to enforce contracts, contract costs are higher. It is difficult to enforce contracts because courts are weaker, regulators less active and influential, and the economy is undergoing more rapid change than in advanced industrial countries. In addition, developing countries tend not to have the administrative agencies capable of enforcing accounting

standards, financial disclosure, and stock market listing rules (Prowse 1998).

A related problem is that Asian economies have a considerable concentration of ownership of companies. Most companies in Asia either have a majority shareholder, or a tightly knit group of minority shareholders who act in concert to control the company. Often the company is part of an extensive corporate network, which in turn has majority shareholders. The most common company form in East Asia is the diversified conglomerate, which is controlled and managed by a single extended family. Companies with widely dispersed ownership are rare in Asia. In this context it is difficult to protect the rights of minority shareholders. Though there are usually laws and penalties against insider trading and related party transactions, as well as on the conduct of substantial transactions and takeovers, it is open to question how often and how rigorously these are enforced (Prowse 1998).

## FAMILY CONTROLLED COMPANIES AND BUSINESS NETWORKS

A widespread business concern is that the most rapid economic growth in the world is occurring in Asia on weak institutional foundations. 'The most prominent features of the Asian business landscape include the predominance of family-run firms, the informal nature of stakeholder relations and the legal and economic diversity of the region' (OECD 2003: 10). The OECD reports that approximately two-thirds of listed companies in Asia are family run, and almost all private companies. These firms have demonstrated a flexibility and dynamism that has resulted in strong economic growth and substantial increases in living standards for several decades.

A particular feature of the Asian corporate landscape, however, is a tendency for such individuals (and their families) to establish large interlocking networks of subsidiaries and sister companies that include partially-owned, publicly-listed companies. On the one hand, the use of such subsidiaries and sister companies permits investors not only to place their money with the management team of their

choice, but to direct this money to the markets and industries in which particular subsidiaries specialise and which investors believe hold the greatest potential for profits. On the other hand, such pyramidal structures can lead to severely inequitable treatment of shareholders. By conducting operations through a complex network of subsidiaries, controlling shareholders acquire control of operations and/or cash flows disproportionate to their equity stake in individual companies. The extent of this disproportionate control is frequently opaque to outsiders and undisclosed by insiders. A particular challenge for corporate-governance reform in Asia is, therefore, to encourage the dynamism and growth of family businesses while channelling their energies and operations into structures that are more transparent and, consequently, more clearly equitable for non-family investors.
(OECD 2003: 10)

As Figure 6.1 indicates, in most economies in East Asia, families are in a position to exercise ownership and control over many listed entities. 'In all East Asian countries control is enhanced through pyramid structures and cross-holdings, among firms. Voting rights consequently exceed formal cash flow rights, especially in Indonesia, Japan and Singapore. We find that more than two thirds of firms are controlled by a single shareholder. Separation of management from ownership control is rare, and the top management of about 60 per cent of firms that are not widely held is related to the family of controlling shareholder' (Claessens *et al.* 2000). This dominance of companies by families casts doubt on the relevance of the theory of the separation of ownership and control, and of the principal/agent model that informs much of western thinking regarding corporate governance. However, memories of the Asian financial crisis, which was also a crisis in corporate governance, are too recent to make people sanguine about the future. As the OECD indicates there is in Asia a tendency to establish interlocking networks of subsidiaries and sister companies that include partially owned listed companies. This allows investors to support the management team of their choice, and invest in industries in which particular subsidiary companies specialise.

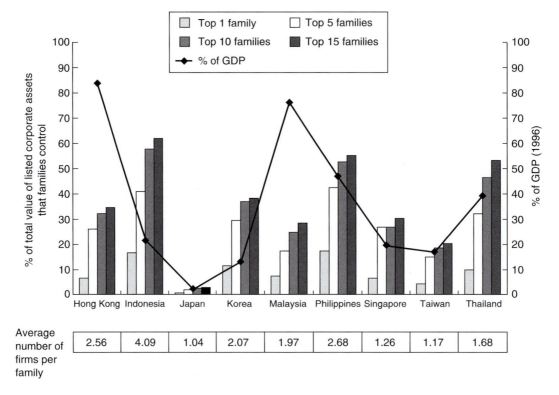

| Average number of firms per family | 2.56 | 4.09 | 1.04 | 2.07 | 1.97 | 2.68 | 1.26 | 1.17 | 1.68 |

**Figure 6.1** Concentration of family control of corporate assets in East Asia.

Source: Adapted from Claessens, S., Djankov, S., and Lang, L. (2000), The Separation of Ownership and Control in East Asian Corporations, *Journal of Financial Economics*, 58: 108.

The second prominent feature of Asian business is the strength of informal stakeholder relationships, as even in the largest enterprises other principal investors will often be family members or friends: 'The informal nature of Asian stakeholder company interaction can produce real and lasting benefits for stakeholders that equal or exceed those offered through more formalistic approaches based on "rights". At the same time, trends towards more globalised markets and greater minority shareholder activism are leading to evolutionary changes in business relationships, as well as to debate about recasting informal interests as formal rights enjoying formal mechanisms for redress' (OECD 2003: 11).

Culturally the Asian family business is patriarchal (and occasionally matriarchal), and traditionally tends to have close relations also with long-standing employees, suppliers, distributors and others. This patriarchy involves a unitary and often authoritarian structure of authority, but within that considerable depth exists in reciprocal relationships, long before lifetime employment was instituted by large Japanese corporations with all its attendant benefits beyond pay, the Chinese family firm traditionally offered security and support to loyal employees.

## WEAK GOVERNANCE MECHANISMS AND INSTITUTIONS

For some decades countries of the Asia Pacific have established all of the necessary mechanisms and institutions of corporate governance, however they were frequently nominal, almost ceremonial, with little active operation or meaning. Neither internal mechanisms nor external monitoring institutions made much difference in a culture of business as usual. Claessens and Fan in

a review of corporate governance issues in Asia emphasise the lack of protection of minority rights insisting that most studies do not suggest that firms in Asia are badly run, but,

> the returns went disproportionately to insiders, accompanied with extensive expansion into unrelated businesses, high leverage and risky financial structures. The usage of group structures created internal markets for scarce resources. However, the internal markets were prone to misallocate capital due to the agency problem. Conventional governance mechanisms were weak to mitigate the agency problem, as insiders typically dominated boards of directors and hostile takeovers were extremely rare. Neither did external financial markets provide much discipline, partly as there were conflicts of interest, but mostly as there existed rents through financial and political connections, which combined with the moral hazard of a large public safety net for the financial system.

## Boards

The boards of directors of companies in Asia often serve a nominal and sometimes a perfunctory role. There is often no clear role for non-executive directors, and little knowledge of the formal obligations and functions of company officers. Boards are effectively dominated by majority shareholders. A result is that disclosure and transparency are often minimal, making it more difficult for regulatory authorities to take action, even if they wished to. Furthermore, institutional investors and fund managers are under-developed, which reduces the extent of external monitoring by powerful institutions. The OECD claims that boards in developing countries are frequently dysfunctional:

> While board competencies, structures and practices vary across countries, the board everywhere plays a central role in the governance of the company. A strong board participates effectively in company strategy and provides proper incentives for management, maximising value for all shareholders while protecting the legitimate interests of all stakeholders. In contrast boards in developing and emerging market economies all too often fall into one of two categories. One is the *rubber stamp* board that plays little role in governance. In this case the company is run by a controlling shareholder who deals directly with management. Board meeting and decisions are formalities. The other is the *family* board. Here, the controlling shareholder, important executives – often relatives of the controlling shareholders – and long trusted advisors do make strategic business decisions. This kind of board can be quite effective at furthering the interest of the family that controls the company. Unfortunately, this interest may conflict with that of other investors, as well as the long term interests of the company. Controlling shareholders are frequently in a position to choose all members of the board. These board members in turn may feel obliged to act in the interests of that controlling shareholder. They may even go as far as to see themselves as the *delegate* of the controlling shareholder: someone who votes as directed. In turn minority shareholders and in some cases stakeholders have demanded to have their own delegates on the board. However … regardless of how they are chosen, board members should be capable of exercising informed and independent judgement, acting as a representative of all shareholders.
>
> (2003: 164–165)

## Finance

Banks and other financial institutions have a role in making sure that companies follow corporate governance principles and exercise prudent financial controls in advanced industrial countries. Government intervention in banks in East Asia, including rescuing depositors when banks have failed, provides an incentive to relax risk controls on the part of companies. Commercial operations appear to carry less risk when governments are ready to intervene in this way. In this context businesses can be inclined towards over-investment, inducing investment cycles of boom and bust in the markets.

Yet corporate finance is dominated by banks operating in this way in East Asia. For example in Malaysia, which has one of the more significant securities markets in the region, banks still provided over 85 per cent of funds to the corporate sector in 1997, compared to 15 per cent raised in the capital markets. Debt has a less disciplining effect when insolvent businesses can rely on the government to rescue them. Corporate debt increased considerably in the 1990s in East Asia, with the inducement of rapidly rising asset prices, and the encouraging belief that governments were operating a too-big-to-fail policy that led companies to invest as much as they could borrow in fixed assets (Clarke 2002). Yet with all of these institutional weaknesses the export led economic growth of East Asia was truly astonishing.

## ECONOMIC GROWTH AND CORPORATE GOVERNANCE

'From 1965 to 1990 the twenty-three economies of East Asia grew faster than all other regions of the world. Most of this achievement is attributable to seemingly miraculous growth in just eight economies' (World Bank 1993: 1). The World Bank research report, *The East Asian Miracle*, characterised the high performing Asian economies (HPAEs) led by Japan, into the four tiger economies of Hong Kong, Republic of Korea, Singapore and Taiwan, joined later by the newly industrialising economies (NIEs) of Indonesia, Malaysia and Thailand. What caused East Asia's success? The World Bank (1993: 5) offered the following explanation:

In large measure the HPAEs achieved high growth by getting the basics right. Private domestic investment and rapidly growing human capital were the principal engines of growth. High levels of domestic financial savings sustained the HPAE's high investment levels. Agriculture, while declining in relative importance, experienced a rapid growth and productivity improvements. Population growth rates declined more rapidly in the HPAEs than in other parts of the developing world. And some of these economies also got a head start

because they had a better educated labour force and a more effective system of public administration. In this case there is little that is 'miraculous' about the HPAEs' superior record of growth; it is largely due to superior accumulation of physical and human capital.

Whatever weaknesses remain unresolved in corporate governance, the Asia Pacific has for a second time become the epicentre of world economic growth, and once again has become the favoured region of the IMF and World Bank:

For several decades, growth has been very strong in the region as a whole – even spectacular in the newly industrialized economies (NIEs) and, more recently, China. Between 1981 and 2001, the number of people living in extreme poverty declined dramatically in East Asia (by over 400 million in China alone). At the same time, given the presence of both early and late developers, Asia continues to display wide disparities in per capita income, ranging from over $33,000 in Singapore to $2,000 in Bangladesh. Average income levels in developing Asia as a whole are still well below those in other regions. Asia's remarkable growth performance reflects strong total factor productivity (TFP) growth, as well as rapid accumulation of both physical and human capital. In turn, these accomplishments were driven by a more favorable institutional and policy environment than observed in other developing economies, including in particular greater trade openness, macroeconomic stability, financial development, and in many cases educational attainment. Looking ahead, further improvements in policies and institutional quality would help to sustain high sectoral productivity growth rates and facilitate the continued shift of resources from agriculture to industry and services, hence supporting sustained rapid growth, convergence toward advanced-economy income levels, and the elimination of poverty across the region.

(IMF 2006: 1)

What is most impressive about the economic lift-off of the Asia Pacific, is that the historical sequence of development, commencing with

Japan, has translated so readily firstly to the East Asian countries, and now to the giant economies of China and India. Asia's real income per capita has increased sevenfold between 1950 and 2005, closing the gap with the advanced industrial countries. There remain 700 million people living in extreme poverty in Asia mainly in rural areas, but across Asia there are increasing indications of economic prosperity, as the IMF argues:

> Within Asia, there have been significant, well known differences across countries in the timing of their initial 'takeoff' into sustained growth and, more broadly, the start of their 'integration' into the world economy. Later developers, including China, appear to have started their takeoff at lower income levels than Japan or the NIEs. At the same time, the overall pace of growth in later developers does not appear significantly different from that experienced by Japan and the NIEs at similar stages of the integration process. A similar story emerges when looking at broader development indicators. Asia's share of world trade more than doubled during 1970–2005, whereas Latin America's decreased. Within Asia, all regions have captured a rising share of world trade, but the rapid expansion in China's trade over the past decade stands out, even though it started from a very low base. Asia has also enjoyed an especially rapid increase over the last half century in levels of educational attainment.
>
> (IMF 2006: 2)

Apparently the weak institutional foundations of the Asian economies have not halted the impetus for rapid economic growth; however, the question is how stable and sustained this growth can be without a firmer base? This question was posed most dramatically at the end of the first economic miracle period with the East Asian Financial crisis of 1997.

## EAST ASIAN FINANCIAL CRISIS

The unique combination of high investment and sustained high growth rates of the Tiger economies of East Asia was seen as an inspiration to the other developing economies when

abruptly the Asian financial crisis broke. Erupting in June 1997 in Thailand, it quickly swept through the Philippines, Indonesia, Malaysia, Singapore and South Korea, impacting upon Taiwan and Hong Kong. Meanwhile, Japan was experiencing a deepening crisis in its financial institutions. The financial systems of East Asia began to collapse at the moment the Thai government announced a 'managed float' of the baht. This confirmed the warning signals of the bankruptcy of Hanbo Steel in Korea at the start of the year, and the failure of Finance One, the largest finance company in Thailand in May 1997.

The strenuous efforts of governments and repeated interventions of the International Monetary Fund did not prevent the spread of currency depreciation, collapsing stock markets, crashing asset prices, and contagious corporate failures and financial insolvencies. This process of enveloping panic intensified as domestic credit dried up and foreign investors disappeared. The total loss of stock market capitalisation in dollar terms ranged from 42 per cent (Hong Kong) to 88 per cent (Indonesia) in the period 30 June 1997 to 3 July 1998 (Clarke 2002) (Table 6.1). This was no ordinary financial crisis, the scale of the disaster for the countries concerned was similar to the great Wall Street crash in which there was an 86 per cent loss in market capitalisation between 1929 and 1933 (Soros 1998: 145). While share prices in East Asia plummeted to the floor, the stock markets of the west rebounded (Figure 6.2).

The crisis exposed underlying vulnerabilities both in governance structures and values. An international confidence crisis was fuelled by a growing realisation of the structural weaknesses of economies often governed by crony capitalism, opaque accounting and auditing systems, and too close relations between business and the state. Unprecedented growth over three decades brought over-confidence with savings not always applied to productive investments, currency appreciations, mismanaged firms and misaligned strategies. 'Speculative bubbles involve the mass delusion that asset prices will rise relentlessly' (Lingle 1997: 88). In many senses the Tiger economies were victims of their success, with burgeoning prosperity encouraging excessive borrowing and the wasteful use of resources,

|  | Currencies (%) | Stock index (%) | Market fall |
| --- | --- | --- | --- |
| Indonesia | −83.2 | −35.0 | −$96bn (−88%) |
| Thailand | −40.2 | −48.0 | −$40bn (−66%) |
| Malaysia | −39.4 | −56.0 | −$217bn (76%) |
| Philippines | −36.1 | −33.8 | −$43bn (−58%) |
| South Korea | −34.1 | −58.7 | −$111bn (−71%) |
| Singapore | −16.5 | −43.5 | −$91bn (−53%) |
| Hong Kong | Nil | −43.2 | −$223bn (−42%) |

**Table 6.1** Dimensions of the East Asian crisis 1997–1998.[1]

Sources: Bank of International Settlements; IMF; World Bank; Asia Week 17 July 1998; Jones Lang Wootton; Dataquest.
Note: [1](Fall in currency exchange rate for $ between 30 June 1997 and 3 July 1998. Percentage decline in stock market index between 30 June 1997 and 3 July 1998. Fall in stock market capitalisation in $ billions, between 30 June 1997 and 3 July 1998)

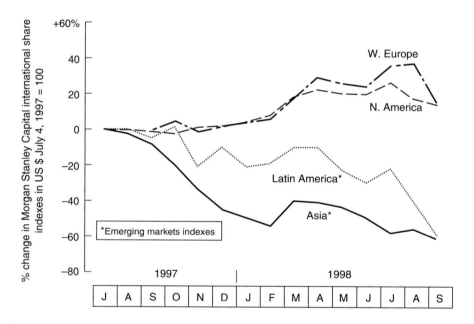

**Figure 6.2** Change in share indexes of East Asia region, 1997–1998.

Source: Adapted from Bloomberg IHT.
Note: *Emerging markets indexes.

inadequate supervision of the financial sector and lack of transparency in business. Complacency during the time of seemingly endless economic growth was replaced by inability to act decisively at a time of crisis.

How could all this have happened in economies that were formerly celebrated for their robustness and efficiency? Surveying the institutional structures of Korea, Malaysia and Thailand, Prowse (1998) concludes:

Market and regulatory institutions that play an important role in ensuring market disciplines are relatively undeveloped in the East Asian

economies. In a less evolved regulatory, legal and institutional environment, information asymmetries are more severe, contracting costs are higher because standard practices have not developed, enforcement of contracts is more severe, contracting costs are higher because standard practices have not developed, enforcement of contracts is more problematic because of weak courts, market participants and regulators are less experienced, and the economy itself is likely to be undergoing more rapid change than in developed countries. In addition to having a weak judicial system, developing countries are unlikely to have administrative agencies that can handle issues that benefit from detailed rule making and non-legal administrative enforcement such as accounting standards, financial disclosures and stock market listing rules.

The scale of Asia's equity markets was still tiny compared to the west, and could readily be marginalised (Figure 6.3). The total vulnerability

of the East Asian economies to international financial markets was cruelly exposed during the financial crisis as the IMF recommended austerity measures.

## THE BEGINNING OF REFORM

An export-led recovery took several years to manage; however the question remains whether the return to economic growth is on firmer institutional foundations and is sustainable? It is likely that only a fundamental programme of the reform of corporate governance institutions and practices in East Asia is likely to produce results. All of the countries concerned are committed to reform of corporate governance, but as the countries focus once again on economic growth and business development, the worry is that corporate governance may once again be considered of marginal importance. A range of external agencies have an interest in sustaining the reform process including the IMF, World Bank, and Asian Development

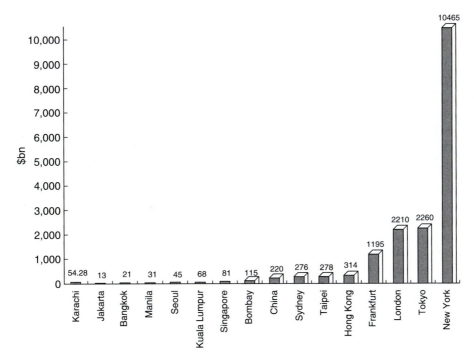

**Figure 6.3** Market capitalisation of stock exchanges in Asia Pacific, 1998.

Source: Stock Exchanges Respective Annual Reports (1998).

Act, and they have all engaged in major initiatives to facilitate and support the reform process. Moreover, international investors will not be sympathetic to economies that are not consistently raising their standards of corporate governance.

The reform process is taking different paths in different countries, but the main principles and objectives can be outlined as:

- ensuring clear and effective financial control structures within firms;
- developing external monitoring and control with improvements in the legal framework, regulatory agencies, and the disclosure environment;
- advancing training and development programmes to encourage understanding of corporate governance procedures and issues.

It is likely that significant reform of the Companies Acts in the countries of East Asia will be required to clarify internal control structures. The commitment to adopting codes of best practice in corporate governance is necessary. A more prescriptive regulatory approach is required given the widespread failure of systems of voluntary standards in East Asia, with more powerful securities commissions ensuring compliance. Included as important elements of corporate governance codes would be provision for:

- decision-making structures and roles within firms to ensure effective governance and financial controls, including representation by non-executive directors;
- clearer definition of duties and responsibilities, with clear procedures for exercising these duties;
- more rigorous monitoring and reporting requirements to ensure the transparency of management's actions and the company's performance.

What this entails is the development of a disclosure-based corporate governance and regulatory regime. Firms should be required to disclose all material information at the time of first listing, and update this on a periodic basis. In developed capital markets, firms depend on market prices and the exercise of due diligence to ensure disclosure of all material information. With the less well developed capital markets of East Asia, investors will need regulators to adopt a more active role in defining and enforcing appropriate accounting, financial reporting and disclosure standards. Codes of best practice can be best enforced from the entry points to stock market listing, together with stringent enforcement with government contracts ensuring contractors demonstrate best governance practice.

Additional procedures to encourage good practice include the legal requirement to abstain from voting on connected party transactions; and the practice of ensuring prior shareholder approval in substantial matters involving interested party transactions. Enhanced legal controls against insider trading and reinforcing takeover codes is necessary. Improving the performance of accounting, auditing, financial reporting and disclosure standards, enforcing due diligence and fiduciary obligations of both company officers and financial intermediaries will offer minority shareholders some protection against systematic abuse by majority shareholders. Equally more timely and continuous disclosure will contribute to more accurate assessment of credit and market risk.

Developing the knowledge and capacity of shareholders, company officials and other stakeholders in their rights and responsibilities will form part of the institution building that will help corporate governance standards. A more active role for shareholders will encourage self-enforcement, and the pursuit of those in violation of the law.

In conclusion, corporate governance development in East Asia requires action on three related fronts:

- activating the mechanisms in firms for more accountable and transparent operations;
- ensuring more effective control and regulation of firms by external agencies;
- extending education and training to develop understanding of sound corporate governance practices.

These reforms will allow investors to make more intelligent and critical judgements on which companies to entrust with their money.

## Japan

Presently Japan is recovering from a prolonged period of disorientation. After being the miracle economy of the 1970s and 1980s with the highest growth rate, it must have been hard to come to terms with more than a decade of repeated economic recessions following the end of the bubble economy in 1990. Major Japanese corporations continued to do exceptionally well in export markets, particularly Toyota, but the financial institutions remained weak and unreformed for some time (reform in Japan was once described as at best *glacial*). Also Japan has experienced a number of what are referred to as *the recent unfortunate incidents* including the New York Daiwa Bank, Sumitomo Corporations copper losses, Nomura Securities, Mitsubishi Oil, and the collapse of Yamaichi Securities under a mountain of off-balance sheet liabilities (it transpired that one of the main architects of this operation was one of the company's auditors!). However, as in the rest of the industrial world, the emphasis is now upon a new commitment to reform and revitalisation of corporate governance.

The formal legal features of the Japanese corporate governance system resemble those in most other advanced industrial countries. Corporate law in Japan was modelled on the German system, with the establishment of limited liability companies since 1899. As in most OECD countries, the majority of enterprises are organised as public-limited companies, though in Japan a significant number of medium-sized firms are private-limited corporations. In 1995 there were 2,263 public-limited companies listed on the Japanese stock exchange (which requires a share equity of 1 billion yen or more). In terms of the number of listed companies and the size of market capitalisation, Japan lies in the middle of the US/UK heavily equity based markets, and European countries with smaller equity markets (OECD 1996: 147).

Johnstone (1995) suggests there are four underlying institutional factors critical to understanding the Japanese corporate system:

■ a financial system based on bank rather than equity financing, with *keiretsu* of industrial groups and banks;

■ government policies which consistently protected industries deemed vital to economic development, and encouraged the development of oligopoly;
■ barriers to the entry of foreign companies by legal obstacles and traditional business norms;
■ the peculiarities of the Japanese labour market with a distinctive brand of labour/management cooperation in the form of lifetime employment and investment in human capital.

Together these factors allowed Japanese management to pursue long-term strategies based on winning market share rather than short term profit maximising, with an emphasis on product quality and manufacturing techniques. Long-term growth strategies were possible according to Johnstone because Japanese managers were freed by the institutional structures in which their corporations operated from threats from shareholders, trade unions, domestic speculators, competitors and foreign capital.

The functioning of all of the major institutions and mechanisms of corporate governance including shareholders, banks and boards of directors, is rather different in Japan. Beginning with the board of directors, in the west the board is largely appointed from outside the company and serves to monitor management. In Japan the board plays a more strategic and decision-making role and is drawn from the ranks of management who are employed by the company. Putting it simply: in the west the board members are outsiders representing the shareholders, in Japan the board members are insiders leading management (Yasui 1999: 4). This reflected the lifetime employment pattern traditionally offered by large Japanese corporations, as managers looked forward to board membership as a reward for loyalty to the company. This structure is inherently hierarchical, and makes it difficult for the board to supervise the president or officers of the company. This hierarchy is extended into the board with vertical reporting lines between the president, and senior and junior members of the board.

Another problem of this approach is that over time there is a tendency for the size of boards to grow as more managers need to be rewarded. In 1998 the average board size was around 20, with some boards reaching as many as 40 members.

As a result, most companies formed a board committee of the president and some senior board members who made all of the essential management decisions which are ratified later by the main board as a formality. Thus the role of Japanese boards is superficial both in terms of supervising the executive management and in terms of responsibility for the company.

In reality, however in Japan the respective roles of directors and managers have not necessarily been clearly defined. Further, the distinction between the governance role of the board of directors on the one hand and the management role of managers on the other, is further complicated by the existence of a separate board of auditors whose role is to audit the activities of the management. This body has meant that in practice the Japanese board of directors has not necessarily been equipped with sufficient governance authority or capability, while the board of auditors has been little more than a cosmetic shell.

To provide some counterbalance, the Japanese Commercial Code requires statutory auditors to be appointed by the shareholders, who are responsible for the supervision of the directors. Statutory auditors have the authority to demand management reports, examine operational and financial information, attend board meetings, and demand the suspension of a director if they believe the director is contravening the law. Statutory auditors cannot be directors or employees of the company, but they are often former employees or from business partners and the main banks, and therefore are not likely to be fully independent. Japanese directors despite being legally responsible to shareholders, have few incentives to emphasise shareholder value. There are few share option schemes, and remuneration is largely according to position in the management hierarchy. Moreover, the consensus orientation of Japanese organisations hardly allows for representation of external interests. Japanese directors identify more with their fellow managers and employees rather than shareholders (Yasui 1999: 6).

The ownership structure of Japanese companies is also different than in western countries. The banks and other business corporations have traditionally been larger shareholders than in the Anglo-American markets, though both have now reduced their share ownership substantially (Table 6.2). This is part of the cross-shareholding pattern of Japanese corporations originating in the early 1950s aimed at raising capital while preventing hostile takeovers. When stock prices in Japan soared in the 1970s and early 1980s the shareholdings created hidden profits for companies, strengthening their financial base, though this was undone when the Japanese financial bubble burst in the early 1990s. The significant change that has occurred in recent years

| Shareholder distribution in Japan (%) | 1950 | 1970 | 1980 | 1990 | 2000 | 2003 | 2004 | 2005 |
|---|---|---|---|---|---|---|---|---|
| Government and local government | 3.1 | 0.6 | 0.4 | 0.3 | 0.4 | 0.3 | 0.2 | 0.1 |
| Banks, trusts companies | 12.6 | 13.7 | 17.5 | 20.9 | 19.2 | 17.4 | 11 | 11.6 |
| Pension trusts | – | 0.0 | 0.4 | 0.9 | 5.5 | 4.5 | 2.0 | 2.0 |
| Investment trusts | – | 2.1 | 1.9 | 3.7 | 2.8 | 3.7 | 2.3 | 4.2 |
| Life and casualty insurance | – | 13.7 | 16.1 | 15.8 | 10.9 | 8.0 | 4.2 | 3.0 |
| Other financial institutions | 11.9 | 3.4 | 3.8 | 3.3 | 1.4 | 2.1 | 1.3 | 2.0 |
| Other business corporations | 11.0 | 23.9 | 26.2 | 30.1 | 21.8 | 25.1 | 17.4 | 19.8 |
| Foreign shareholders | – | 4.9 | 5.8 | 4.7 | 18.8 | 21.8 | 16.5 | 22.2 |
| Individual shareholders | 61.3 | 37.7 | 27.9 | 20.4 | 19.4 | 20.5 | 45.6 | 36.8 |
| Total | 100 | 100 | 100 | 100 | 100 | 100 | 100 | 100 |

Table 6.2 The distribution of share ownership in Japan, by type of shareholder.

Source: Takaya Seki (2005). Tokyo Stock Exchange (2006), http://www.tse.or.jp/english/data/research/english2005.pdf.

is the considerable growth in the holdings of foreign investors in Japanese companies, up from 4.7 per cent in 1990 to 22.2 per cent in 2005. This has implications for the governance of Japanese corporations and the orientations of Japanese managers.

This concentrated pattern of shareholding has created considerable stability. The top ten shareholders of companies listed on the Tokyo Stock Exchange have held on average 44 per cent of the outstanding stock of a company (Yasui 1999: 8). The concentrated ownership structure gives key shareholders considerable influence over management, but these shareholders are usually affiliated companies in the same corporate group or *keiretsu*. Traditionally, they have put more emphasis on expanding their business with the company rather than seeking short-term returns.

The position of the main banks is central to the Japanese corporate governance structure and functioning. As the major creditor and a major shareholder the main bank was positioned to carry out effective monitoring in three forms:

■ *Ex ante*: Monitoring of the investment decisions of the company, examining loan applications.
■ *Interim*: Monitoring performance of the ongoing business and projects carried out by the company, examining cash flows at the company's accounts.
■ *Ex post*: Evaluating the financial performance of the company, and when a company experiences difficulty, intervening to take corrective measures (Aoki and Okuno 1996).

The main banks are well positioned to restructure companies when necessary, and in return they received long term benefits through fees, deposits, and interest rates on loans from companies and they had very economical costs of information gathering. The Japanese government encouraged this main bank system in its policies, and in turn was the regulator of the main banks. However, a drawback of this main bank system is that it allows increasing borrowing by companies without sufficient risk assessment. As banks competed to lend volumes of money with regulated interest rates, companies began making investments in projects with lower expected returns which contributed to the Japanese economic bubble.

Deregulation of the Japanese banks occurred in the 1980s, which strengthened the bargaining power of firms and weakened the main banks. With the bursting of the bubble economy in the early 1990s, the banks had accumulated problem assets, which eroded their capital base. This prevented the main banks in some recent bankruptcy cases from saving the companies, or bearing a large burden of the liquidation costs. Banks have needed to dispose of their shares, weakening the relationship with client companies (Yasui 1999: 13). Successively there has been a weakening of cross-shareholding in Japan, as economic performance has worsened and the negative effects of owning shares in other companies become apparent with low dividends and collapsing share prices. This problem was particularly severe for the banks and insurance companies who have had to write off huge problem assets, and who can no longer afford the costs of holding problematic share portfolios (Yasui 1999: 13).

As Japanese institutional investors have reduced their share portfolios, the influence of overseas investors has become greater. Overseas investors are looking for an economic return and have begun to be active in pressing for greater accountability to shareholders from Japanese corporations. In turn, Japanese institutions have begun to be more active in attempting to raise standards of corporate governance. Japanese corporate managers are beginning to listen to these demands, and look for investments with better returns. Incentive schemes and stock options are being introduced. There is a new emphasis on transparency and disclosure. Efforts are being made to simplify the dense Japanese business structures with holding company forms and consolidated accounts.

Boards of directors have been restructured: for example the Sony Corporation reduced its board from 38 members to 10, introducing 3 independent directors. As the role of directors was strengthened, so was the independence and role of statutory auditors increased. However, in many Japanese companies there has been less enthusiasm about appointing independent directors, or establishing remuneration and appointment committees, continuing to place more reliance on the statutory auditors.

## Japanese model of transition

In 2000 the Japanese government began a two year programme to modernise company law, examining boards, independent directors and auditors. Japanese corporations are coming under pressure from shareholders to end the secrecy regarding executive compensation, and at the 2000 AGM Sumitomo Bank became the first financial institution in Japan to reveal the compensation package of their executives. As a result of the government making it easier for investors to sue, there has been an increase in the number of lawsuits brought against executives.

Though Japanese companies may be moving in the direction of the Anglo-Saxon model, this movement is one of degree. The distinctive interrelated elements of the Japanese economic and social system, together with legal, regulatory, financial market and employment system will continue to have a powerful effect (Yasui 1999: 20). However, supporters of the Japanese system such as Dore (2000) and others contend that the welfare capitalism of Japan has delivered much more for the Japanese people than stock market capitalism ever will. Some have argued that cross-shareholding and the associated *keiretsu* system is relatively resilient, and that these might be associated with alternative governance mechanisms. This is a trust-based form of governance where there is relational contracting, in which is generated a diffuse sense of obligation to individual trading partners (Learmont 2002). Jacoby examines further the unique stakeholder culture of the Japanese enterprise:

> A recent study identifies six main features of Japanese-style corporate governance: stable shareholders, an emphasis on steady payment of dividends, heavy reliance on banks for debt financing, internal labor markets for managers, managerial pay cuts to protect employee jobs, and a stakeholder ethos that includes employees as a key bloc. Currently, 82 percent of Japanese firms have four or more of these characteristics; only 5 percent have but one or two of these characteristics Although not a social democracy, Japan's approach to corporate governance has strong similarities to the stakeholder system of continental Europe.

> In Japan there is concentrated ownership by banks and other companies; a preference for voice over exit; and expectations (albeit not regulations) that a company should be responsible to employees and suppliers as well as shareholders. What's important to note is that these practices are not legally required yet are regularly complied with. Perhaps a key factor here is not social democracy so much as the 'all in one boat' mentality that prevailed in postwar Japan and Europe as ethnically homogeneous societies with a discredited business class and restive labor movements sought to rebuild their economies along new and more cooperative lines. Moreover, in Japan the Occupation created a postwar legal muddle, which led to various private rules regarding shareholder rights, takeovers, and banks; this is consistent with a line of legal scholarship that views norms as low-cost substitutes for public rules.

> (Jacoby 2001: 9)

As the return to economic growth of Japan has proceeded in recent years, the commitment to economic and structural reform has gathered pace, for example in the takeover defence guidelines which established principles of eliminating excessive defensive measures, protecting shareholders' interests, disclosing to shareholders any defensive measures and seeking shareholder agreement, and ensuring the reasonableness of defensive measures by submitting them to scrutiny and limiting their duration. According to the Japanese trade organisation, JETRO (1995), these changes have led to a surge in merger and acquisition activity in Japan, and could prepare the way for cross-border merger and takeover activity. What this amounts to is a significant change in the Japanese model. For example the influence of cross-holdings by other Japanese firms is firmly balanced now by the holdings of overseas shareholders. Instead of orienting towards the main bank Japanese managers are increasingly facing out towards their shareholders (Figure 6.4).

Certainly JETRO is fully committed to the transformation:

> Individual Japanese firms are also introducing other measures to achieve efficiencies and to

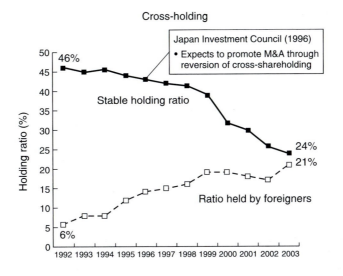

Cross-holding

Japan Investment Council (1996)
• Expects to promote M&A through reversion of cross-shareholding

Stable holding ratio

Ratio held by foreigners

Surveillance

**Japanese companies in the 80s**

Used to create stable relationships with shareholders by cross-shareholding, and so have management under main Bank's surveillance. Therefore it was possible for management to innovate

**Japanese companies today**

Now stockholders provide surveillance, and so companies improve management on their own in order to enhance long-term corporate and shareholder value

High ratio held by foreign investors in selected Japanese firms

| | | | |
|---|---|---|---|
| Hoya Corp | 56% | Canon Inc | 52% |
| Fuji Photo Firm | 49% | ROHM Co. LTD. | 49% |
| Kata Corp | 47% | Takeda | 41% |

**Figure 6.4** The Japanese model transformation.

Source: Adapted from Japanese External Trade Organization JETRO (2005), *Focus: Japan Enters New Phase in its Recovery*, Japanese Ministry of Economy, Trade and Industry.

control costs. Sanyo, for example, a major electronics firm, recently announced plans to initiate a comprehensive restructuring, involving a 15 per cent workforce reduction. Sanyo's new CEO, Tomoyo Nonaka, the first woman ever to head a leading Japanese electronics group, noted in a Financial Times article titled 'Sanyo wields axe to achieve turnaround' that 'there will be no taboos' in the restructuring program. For its part, Sony appointed a foreigner,

Howard Stringer, as Chief Executive, in an effort to restore the firm's role as an innovative global powerhouse. Restructurings and consolidations are a hard reality of business, even where so-called 'new economy companies' are concerned. For instance, in the game software sector, Sega has merged with Sammy, Bandai with Namco, and Takara with Tomy. A third area where there are positive developments are actions taken by Japanese managers to focus on shareholder value. This is manifest in the rising number of dividend payout increases and share buybacks announced in recent years. Japanese companies are also according more importance to communicating with outside investors, sometimes hiring investor relations firms to connect with shareholders. Many analysts believe Japan's changing corporate environment, coupled with supportive policy moves, is opening up a range of new opportunities. U.K.-based Hermes, for example, has partnered with Nissay Asset Management of Japan (Namco) to create one of many new funds seeking to foster change on under-performing companies. Wataru Tanaka, the president of Namco, told the Financial Times 'the time is right to introduce a new investment philosophy based on encouraging shareholder friendly management'

(JETRO 1995)

Japan has already reached the level of momentum needed to sustain its economic recovery efforts, for example, the movement to clean up Japan's financial system is eliminating overcapacity and debt. What will remain of the Japanese model is another question. Toriihara offers a graphical view of the stages of transition of Japanese corporate governance starting with the high growth period of the 1960s with the ascendancy of Japanese-style management involving mutual dependence among companies, lifetime employment, coordinated industry groups and ambiguous accounting. Then there was the 1980s bubble induced by changes in the capital market, globalisation and corporate scandal, resulting in the lost decade of the 1990s. Now Japan faces an indeterminate world of further corporate governance reforms and shareholder value (Figure 6.5). The question is can Japan continue

with its unrivalled manufacturing expertise and commitment to innovation and research and development in this new corporate governance institutional structure (Hosono, Tomiyama, and Miyagawa 2004)?

Ahmadjian and Okumura (2006) refer to the corporate governance *vacuum* in Japan that had to be filled by the end of the 1990s:

The main bank system no longer functioned, as large firms procured capital elsewhere and the banking system was too focused on survival to do much monitoring. While cross-shareholdings remained, changing accounting regulations meant that firms and financial institutions have to consider the market value of these shares and treat them as financial investments. Foreign portfolio investors, strongly committed to Anglo-American governance practices, dominated Japanese equity markets. The government also had retreated from the business of industrial policy and reduced, if not eliminated *amakudari* board appointments of retired government officials. The business environment had changed from a clear course of catch-up with the industrialised Western nations to one requiring risky, uncertain decisions about investments in new technologies and markets. A new corporate governance system was necessary to respond to this new structure of ownership and business environment.

(2006: 137)

What will this new corporate governance system be? Ahmadjian and Okumura suggest a two tier system with the Japanese companies with a high proportion of foreign ownership following an Anglo-American path, leaving most domestic oriented firms keeping to the old system. Perhaps before this happens the special capabilities of the Japanese system may reassert themselves in the international economy.

## China

China is rapidly developing into the largest industrial economy in the world. The country has sustained the strongest and most consistent

**Figure 6.5** Transitions of Japanese corporate governance, 1960s–2000.

Source: Toriihara, M. (2004), *Corporate Governance in Japan*, Policy Dialogue on Corporate Governance in China, 26 February, Paris: OECD.

economic performance of the region since the 1980s with an annual average economic growth rate in excess of 8 per cent. While the economies of East Asia went into reverse during the 1997–1998 financial crisis and then suffered a further reversal in the tech-wreck of 2000–2001, China's economy continued to grow strongly and helped to stabilise the region. China's exports reached $325 billion in 2002, more than double the 1996 level of $150 billion. This export performance now rivals that of Japan and the ASEAN 5 countries (Indonesia, Malaysia, Philippines, Singapore, and Thailand). Entry of China into the World Trade Organisation is likely to increase the export momentum of China. Finally China since the 1990s has received large amounts of foreign direct investment (FDI) and in 2002 received a record $53 billion in direct investment from other countries, exceeding the amount received by the United States, and becoming the world's largest recipient of FDI (EAU 2003).

This momentous economic progress in the most populous country on earth has been achieved in spite of pervasively weak corporate governance foundations. Though there has been a commitment to economic reform stretching back to the early 1980s, at times the progress of reform has stumbled. China has avoided the harmful social and economic dislocation experienced throughout Eastern Europe in the sudden lurch towards market systems. However, there is a widespread recognition in China that it is unlikely sustained economic growth can continue without the development of more robust institutions of corporate governance.

There are five types of enterprise predominating in China:

■ state-owned enterprises (SOEs);
■ town and village enterprises (TVEs);
■ joint-ventures (JVs);
■ foreign owned enterprises;

- Chinese listed public companies (Clarke and Duh 1998).

The state owned enterprise model dominated from the 1950s through to the 1980s in a negotiated system of central planning. An SOE law of 1988 called on the SOEs to separate themselves from government, and exercise their responsibilities as businesses. From 1992 Deng Xioaping supported the call for the introduction of a market economy, and China began the slow process of corporatisation of SOEs by which they could eventually transform into state owned corporations or public listed corporations. In contrast the town and village enterprise (TVE) sector of the economy has often represented a bubbling entrepreneurship in tens of thousands of small and medium sized companies, a few of which have grown to the size of large conglomerates, despite the fact they are supposed to be community based enterprises, and have uncertain ownership and governance structures.

In all of these enterprise forms the relationship that binds people together is guanxi – the sense of durable reciprocity. Boisot and Child (1996: 624) suggest the western preoccupation with the relevance of property rights to economic performance has failed to recognise that property rights,

> can be a complex mixture that does not constitute a simple binary set of possibilities – 'state' vs 'private'. In China a bundle of property rights is exercised by different bodies and de facto property rights tend to emerge from continuing processes of negotiation between central, regional, community and private interests ... The Chinese system of network capitalism works through the implicit and fluid dynamic of relationships. On the one hand this is a process that consumes much time and energy. On the other hand, it is suited to handling complexity and uncertainty.

Joint-ventures with Chinese partner companies were the traditional means by which overseas companies entered China. Though they brought the benefit of foreign technical expertise combined with local market knowledge, again the governance structures of joint-ventures often exhibited a degree of tension and uncertainty, as both parties discovered opportunities or disadvantages in the arrangement. More recently the Chinese government has considerably eased its insistence of the formation of joint-ventures if overseas companies wish to enter China. Negotiations with wholly foreign-owned enterprises could lead to similar benefits flowing to the Chinese economy as in joint-ventures, including technology transfer, skill development, and retained earnings.

## China's reforms

Around 1,200 large companies in China have diversified their ownership through public listing. Accompanying this process a legal framework of company law, contract law, accounting and securities laws has also been established. The financial system has become more independent of political influence, and regulators' capacity strengthened. A corporate governance code has been introduced for listed and non-listed companies by the China Securities Regulatory Commission and the State Economic Trade Commission. Notwithstanding this commitment towards reform, there remains considerable scope for advancing the rigour of corporate governance policy and practice in China (Tenev, Zhang and Brefort 2002).

In the SOE sector poor performance remains widespread due to weak incentives for managers to maximise value. Furthermore, government agencies engaging in protectionist practices shield firms from market competition. When government is considering state owned companies to become listed companies, it is often those with strong local government links that are selected, often leaving controlling shareholders able to exploit companies through related party transactions. Banks lack the capacity and incentives to monitor companies' behaviour, and bankruptcy of SOEs is largely an administrative process, with state owned banks suffering the same weaknesses as the SOE enterprises.

Corporatisation and ownership diversification has introduced new institutional forms of control, without dismantling the old informal representation structures, and for example the role of chair

of the board of directors and party secretary will often be combined. Key decisions are often made informally, with boards assuming decorative functions. Power effectively is exercised by controlling shareholders and government agencies. The quality of audits is often compromised in this context, as accounts often bear little relation to the commercial transactions that have actually taken place.

Chinese listed company shares are classified as A shares, B shares, and H shares. A shares are issued by domestic companies and are available to domestic investors only and traded in the RMB currency. B shares are issued by domestic companies registered on the mainland, but traded in hard currency by foreign investors, including overseas Chinese and institutions in Hong Kong and Taiwan. Individual domestic investors have been allowed to trade B shares since 2001. H shares are issued and listed by domestic companies in Hong Kong. Shares of listed companies are classified further into state shares, legal person shares, and tradable shares, with each type accounting for around one-third of all shares.

State shares are held by central and local governments, represented by state asset management or investment companies. State shares can also be held by the parent of the listed company, typically a state owned enterprise. These state shares are not tradable, yet they normally form the largest shareholding in the enterprise. The state therefore remains the controlling shareholder in listed enterprises, revealing the limitations of China's effort to diversify ownership, and the lingering power of the party and state as the country moves gradually towards a market based system.

A survey of corporate governance by the World Bank in China recommended the following policies for reform (Tenev, Zhang and Brefort 2002):

- alleviating the negative impact of dominant state ownership on market discipline and on the regulatory capacity of the state;
- building an institutional investor base to facilitate shareholder activism;
- strengthening the role of banks, enhancing creditor's rights in the case of default, with options for banks to engage in reorganisation and restructuring of client companies.

The weaknesses in the financial institutions of China remain worrying. A People's Bank of China report suggests that of the 62,656 enterprises that completed transfers of ownership by the end of 2000, 51.2 per cent had failed to repay their bank debts. Non-performing loans are estimated at between 25 per cent and 40 per cent of the total. Poor economic performance of SOEs imposes a burden on the banking system and government finances (Tenev, Zhang and Brefort 2002). However one reason the SOEs continue to make losses is the extensive social obligations they maintain for government.

Commitments were given during the World Trade Organisation negotiations to increase the pressure to move from a relationship-based to a rules-based system of corporate governance. Abandoning the bond of traditional and political relationships, and replacing these with the impersonal rules of governance and institutions will not be easily achieved. Yet only greater transparency in business and government activities will encourage further international investment into China to facilitate its economic progress.

## India

India is the second giant Asian country to join the ranks of the miracle economies (even if the economic miracle in India is heavily concentrated in a few states and a handful of internationally successful companies). If China has become the manufacturing centre of the world, India has embarked on becoming the business and information technology service centre of the world, and is enjoying some success in this quest. If the economic growth rate of India does not quite match that of China, it is substantial and sustained enough to offer many business opportunities for the thriving entrepreneurs of the country. However, it was not always thus: India until two decades ago was a centralised, heavily regulated economy which was virtually stagnant, and riddled with corrupt corporate governance practices. As Chakrabarti recalls the state financial institutions smothered enterprise at birth:

In the absence of a developed stock market, the three all-India development finance

institutions (DFIs) – the Industrial Finance Corporation of India, the Industrial Development Bank of India and the Industrial Credit and Investment Corporation of India – together with the state financial corporations became the main providers of long-term credit to companies. Along with the government owned mutual fund, the Unit Trust of India, they also held large blocks of shares in the companies they lent to and invariably had representations in their boards. In this respect, the corporate governance system resembled the bank-based German model where these institutions could have played a big role in keeping their clients on the right track. Unfortunately, they were themselves evaluated on the quantity rather than quality of their lending and thus had little incentive for either proper credit appraisal or effective follow-up and monitoring. Their nominee directors routinely served as rubber-stamps of the management of the day. With their support, promoters of businesses in India could actually enjoy managerial control with very little equity investment of their own. Borrowers therefore routinely recouped their investment in a short period and then had little incentive to either repay the loans or run the business. Frequently they bled the company with impunity, siphoning off funds with the DFI nominee directors mute spectators in their boards.

(2005: 25)

The saga sadly did not end there as even after bankruptcy companies remained under protection almost indefinitely:

This sordid but increasingly familiar process usually continued till the company's net worth was completely eroded. This stage would come after the company has defaulted on its loan obligations for a while, but this would be the stage where India's bankruptcy reorganization system driven by the 1985 Sick Industrial Companies Act (SICA) would consider it 'sick' and refer it to the Board for Industrial and Financial Reconstruction (BIFR). As soon as a company is registered with the BIFR it wins immediate protection from the creditors' claims for at least four years. Between 1987 and 1992 BIFR took well over two years on an average

to reach a decision, after which period the delay has roughly doubled. Very few companies have emerged successfully from the BIFR and even for those that needed to be liquidated, the legal process takes over 10 years on average, by which time the assets of the company are practically worthless. Protection of creditors' rights has therefore existed only on paper in India. Given this situation, it is hardly surprising that banks, flush with depositors' funds routinely decide to lend only to blue chip companies and park their funds in government securities.

(Chakrabarti 2005: 26)

India has a notoriously poor system of corporate insolvency: according to Goswami (2001) 32 per cent of company liquidations took more than 20 years and 59 per cent took more than 10 years. The inadequacy of the system allows management to act irresponsibly and undertake excessively risky investments without the fear of insolvency and ultimate liquidation when creditors pursue their rights. It is also detrimental to the countries' financial sector, with a high cost of capital and a significant proportion of non-performing loans due to capital misallocations to non-optimal uses (Kimber *et al.* 2005: 188).

Fortunately, prolonged process of economic and governance reform is under way in India and has yielded some results. The interest in corporate governance coincided with the realisation that to raise capital at competitive rates there was a need to demonstrate greater disclosure, transparency and shareholder returns. The Confederation of Indian Industry released a voluntary code in 1998 titled *Desirable Corporate Governance: A Code*. The document set out detailed disclosure guides that were subsequently adopted by many of the largest listed companies. A further development occurred with the publication of an additional and mandatory code in 2000 by the principal regulator, the Securities and Exchange Board of India (SEBI) (Kimber *et al.* 2005: 185). The heavily amended Indian *Corporations Act 1956* is now under review. The Confederation of Indian Industry has called for the new legislation to achieve 'a balanced approach that recognized an international trend, i.e. flexibility and greater self-regulation by companies, subject to better disclosure, more efficient enforcement of law,

and prompt and deterrent punishment to those who violate the law' (CII 2004).

Earlier takeover regulation was reformed in India as part of the programme of economic reforms undertaken in the mid- to late 1990s. The reform facilitated corporate restructuring through merger and takeover activity since 1997 and has become an important vehicle for corporate growth (Kar 2001).

> India's *Companies Act* requires that company valuations in mergers or acquisitions are subject to court approval; in addition the SEBI has issued a separate 'Regulation for Takeovers' to protect investors. While the financial market in India is certainly freeing up, these changes are also influenced by central government concerns relating to economic stability and employment. For example, employee groups in India are resisting these developments as concern grows about the potential for job losses as financial markets are deregulated and state-owned enterprises are privatised to become more competitive. Arguably, the 2004 elections in India were strongly influenced by concerns that less advantaged sectors were losing out in the face of deregulation and privatization.
>
> (Kimber *et al.* 2005: 191)

However the reform process has accompanied a major growth in market capitalisation of Indian companies. The market capitalisation of the Bombay Stock Exchange (Mumbai), the oldest stock exchange in Asia, has risen dramatically to $730 billion in October 2006, and is now one of the five largest stock exchanges in the world in terms of transaction volume. Between 1991 and 2006 a total of $39 billion in foreign investment has been attracted to India, with the anticipation of hundreds of millions more arriving over the next five years.

## THE DEVELOPMENT OF ASIA PACIFIC CORPORATE GOVERNANCE CODES

The countries of the Asia Pacific have been as enthusiastic about developing codes of corporate governance as have regulators in Europe and the Anglo-American world (Figure 6.6). However, there is even more doubt about the substance and quality of enforcement. Promulgating a code of corporate governance is an important step, but effective implementation of higher standards of governance beyond a few leading companies is far harder.

## Thailand

### Thai Code of Best Practice for Directors (1999)

Published by the Stock Exchange of Thailand, this is not a legal requirement but it should be used as guidelines for all board members concerning their behaviour while holding such appointments. Management under these guidelines should help to ensure a high standard of best practice on behalf of the company and its shareholders.

## Malaysia

### Malaysian Code of Corporate Governance (2000)

This code is principally an initiative of the private sector. The need for a code was inspired in part by a desire of the private sector to initiate and lead a review and to establish reforms of standards of corporate governance at a micro level. Self-regulation is preferable over statutory regulation and this is reflected in the standards developed in this report.

## Indonesia

### Indonesia Code of Corporate Governance (2001)

The code is intended to allow for more constructive and flexible methods of raising standards of corporate governance in Indonesian companies, as opposed to adopting the more prescriptive approach of imposing mandatory regulations having the force of the law.

Thailand

**Code of Best Practice
for Directors**

Guidelines on Behaviour
for Board Members
1999

Malaysia

**Malaysian Code of
Corporate Governance**

Self-regulation over
statutory regulation
2000

Indonesia

**Indonesia Code of
Corporate Governance**

Code to raise the standards
of corporate governance
2001

China

**Chinese Code of
Corporate Governance**

An enforceable framework
for all listed companies
2002

India

**Kumar Mangalam Birla
Committee Report**

Recommendations that
distinguishes responsibilities
and obligations of the board
2002

Philippines

**SEC Corporate
Governance**

Reforms to raise investor
confidence
2002

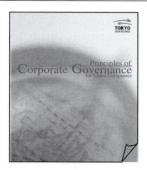

Hong Kong

**Hong Kong
Corporate Governance**

2004

Japan

**Japanese
Corporate Governance**

Principles of Corporate
Governance
2004

Singapore

**Singaporean Code of
Corporate Governance**

Requirements under the
Singaporean Exchange
Listing Rules
2005

**Figure 6.6** Asia Pacific reform of corporate governance regulation.

Source: UTS Centre for Corporate Governance (2006).

## China

### Chinese Code of Corporate Governance (2002)

Published by the China Securities Regulatory Commission, the code is applicable to listed companies. The code promotes the standardisations and operations of listed companies and to bring forward the healthy development of the securities market in China.

## India

### Kumar Mangalam Birla Committee Report (2002)

The committee's report contains a set of recommendations which distinguishes responsibilities and obligations of the boards and the management in instituting the system of good corporate governance and emphasises the rights of shareholders demanding corporate governance.

## Philippines

### SEC Code of Corporate Governance (2002)

Published by the Securities and Exchange Commission, the code aims to actively promote corporate governance reforms to raise investor confidence; to develop the capital market and help achieve high sustained growth for the corporate sector.

## Hong Kong

### Hong Kong Code of Corporate Governance (2004)

This report summarises responses to a proposed corporate governance code. Issued by the Hong Kong Stock Exchange, most respondents were supportive of the exchange's effort to enhance corporate governance in Hong Kong.

## Japan

### Japanese Corporate Governance: Principles of Corporate Governance (2004)

This report outlines five principles of corporate governance. They are: the rights of shareholders; equitable treatment of shareholders; relationships with stakeholders; disclosure and transparency; and responsibilities of board of directors, auditors or board of corporate auditors.

## Singapore

### Singaporean Code of Corporate Governance (2005)

This code replaces the code issued in 2001. Compliance with the code is not mandatory but listed companies are required under the Singaporean Exchange Listing Rules to disclose their corporate governance practices and give explanations for deviations from the code.

## CONTINUING REFORM

### Due diligence of directors

The OECD principles require that directors act with *due diligence and care*. This principle derives from a blend of law, regulation and appropriate directoral practice. Directors are effectively granted considerable latitude in deciding the business affairs of a company.

This latitude means that directors should not be held liable for the consequences of their exercise of business judgement – even for judgements that appear to have been clear mistakes – unless certain exceptions apply. These exceptions include fraud, conflicts of interest and failure to engage in the basic activities of the director's role (such as attending meetings, seeking to inform oneself and deliberating meaningfully before making important decisions). The rationale for this relatively 'hands-off' policy is that courts and agencies are ill-suited to second-guess the business

judgement of directors and that if these state bodies began to do so there would be no end to the litigation and administrative actions that would result.

(OECD 2003: 52)

Participants in the OECD Roundtable discussions in Asia have identified areas where directors are fundamentally failing in their task, reducing the board to a series of nominal and often rudimentary tasks. Among the problems that require attention in the Asian context are:

- poor director attendance;
- little preparation and participation;
- a lack of *healthy scepticism* on the part of directors.

Another issue in Asia is that board appointees frequently include people who lack the experience of capacity to inform themselves fully and take a responsible role in the board deliberations. In some cases relatively junior employees or inexperienced relatives of controlling shareholders find their way onto boards of directors as straw men meant to cover for *shadow directors*:

Such shadow directors do not occupy board seats themselves but are the real decision makers. In other cases, a simple dearth of suitable candidates leads to the appointment of the clearly unqualified. At least two OECD-member countries in the Asia/Pacific area, Australia and Korea, have developed attribution rules to impose liability upon shadow directors. Among non-OECD-member countries in Asia, Malaysia has also instituted such rules, while the Hong Kong China Companies Ordinance applies to any officer of the company and any person in accordance with whose directions or instructions the directors of the company are accustomed to act. Other Asian jurisdictions should follow suit.

(OECD 2003: 53)

The OECD records how efforts are being made to widen the perspective of what constitutes *due diligence and care*. It argues codes of conduct can further promote director performance, and the number of Asian countries that have developed

codes through private sector organisations, stock exchanges or regulatory bodies is increasing. Some of these codes adopt a phased approach, toughening the expected standards over time, or placing higher demands upon directors of larger companies. As noted in the World Bank (2002) survey and more recently in the discussions of the Asian Roundtable on Corporate Governance, there is often a wide discrepancy between principles and practice in developing countries, where the institutional fabric is still being constructed and made operational. In this context it is not safe to assume anything with regard to corporate governance, and the governance details of companies must be confirmed with regulators and other informed professions.

In Tokyo in June 2003 the OECD *White Paper on Corporate Governance in Asia* was released. This was compiled from a series of meetings of the Asian Roundtable on Corporate Governance between 1999 and 2003 of policy-makers, regulators and business leaders.

It is part of the effort to stimulate Asian business leaders and controlling shareholders to re-think their relationships with their companies and minority shareholders. All Asian countries have substantially revamped their corporate governance laws and regulations, the task now is to ensure the implementation and enforcement of this new framework. The commitment given is that Asian Roundtable Countries will work towards full convergence with international standards and practices for accounting, audit and non-financial disclosure. Where for the time being, full convergence is not possible, divergences from international standards and practices, and the reasons for these divergences) will be disclosed by companies.

(OECD 2003)

The independence and diligence of boards of directors was called into question in the OECD roundtables because of the persistent problems of neglect of minority shareholders. A series of recommendations of the roundtable includes boards of directors improving their participation in strategic planning, monitoring of internal control systems. It also recommended that any transactions involving managers, controlling shareholders

and other insiders should be subject to independent review. This includes delineation of a core set of related-party transactions that should be prohibited outright. These measures are to be reinforced by strengthening the legal and regulatory framework ensuring that non-controlling shareholders are protected from exploitation by insiders and controlling shareholders. This involves increasing the capacity of regulators to monitor companies for compliance with these requirements with substantial penalties for wrongdoing, clarifying and strengthening the fiduciary duty of directors in the interests of the company, and prohibiting indemnification of directors for breaches of fiduciary duty. Finally, to restore confidence in both debt and equity markets a similar reform of the corporate governance of the banks is recommended. The OECD concludes, 'The effort that has gone into compiling this detailed report demonstrates the degree of commitment to reform in Asian markets, the continued growth and success of the region depends on effective and widespread implementation of these principles' (2003).

Research by Claessens (2004) *et al.* reveals countries in Asia with a higher concentration of ownership of companies among a few families or blockholders show the least progress in adopting institutional reforms, judicial efficiency, rule of law, and absence of corruption (Figure 6.7). Hence, insider controlled companies are frequently associated with a neglect of minority shareholder rights, as legal and judicial systems are not developed or active, and widespread corruption is often tolerated. Berglof and Claessens consider further the potential mechanisms for enforcement of corporate governance in Asia. Systemic weaknesses are more apparent still in Asian modes of governance, where the separation of ownership and control has not taken hold. They consider how enforcement can be achieved by private ordering, private law enforcement, public enforcement and state control. Different mechanisms can be applied utilising these different forms of enforcement, and often these can be reinforcing. Berglof and Claessens detail the relative importance of different corporate governance mechanisms in developing and transition countries and what scope there is for policy intervention. For example, the market for corporate control is likely to be ineffective when ownership is highly concentrated, and the most effective policy intervention therefore is to remove managerial

**Figure 6.7** Countries with higher concentration of wealth show less progress in institutional reforms.

Source: Claessens, Stijn (2004), Corporate Governance and Development, *Focus*, 1: 1–44.

defences, secure disclosure of ownership and control, and strengthen the banking system as forms of discipline. Shareholder activism can be important in large firms with dispersed shareholders, but if this is to happen minority protection needs to be strengthened, together with enhancing the governance of institutional investors themselves (Table 6.3).

| Corporate governance mechanism | Relative importance in developing and transition countries | Scope of policy intervention |
| --- | --- | --- |
| **Large blockholders** | Likely to be the most important governance mechanism | Strengthen rules protecting minority investors without removing incentives to hold controlling blocks |
| **Market for corporate control** | Unlikely to be important when ownership is strongly concentrated, can still take place through debt contracts but requires bankruptcy system | Remove some managerial defences, disclosure of ownership and control, develop banking system |
| **Proxy fights** | Unlikely to be effective when ownership is strongly concentrated | Technology improvements for communicating with and among shareholders, disclosure of ownership and control |
| **Board activity** | Unlikely to be influential when controlling owner can hire and fire and has private benefits | Introduce elements of independence of directors, training of directors, disclosure of voting, cumulative voting possibly |
| **Executive compensation** | Less important when controlling owner can hire and fire and has private benefits | Disclosure of compensation schemes, conflicts of interest rules |
| **Bank monitoring** | Important, but depends on health of banking system and the regulatory environment | Strengthen banking regulation and institutions, encourage accumulation of information on credit histories; develop supporting credit bureaus and other information intermediaries |
| **Shareholder activism** | Potentially important, particularly in large films with dispersed shareholders | Encourage interaction among shareholders, strengthen minority protection. Enhance governance of institutional investors |
| **Employee monitoring** | Potentially very important, particularly in smaller companies with high skilled human capital where threat of leaving is high | Disclosure of information to employees, possibly require board representation; assure flexible labour markets |
| **Litigation** | Depends critically on quality of general enforcement environment but can sometimes work | Facilitate communication among shareholders; encourage class action suits with safeguards against excessive litigation |
| **Media and social control** | Potentially important, but depends on competition among and independence of media | Encourage competition in and diverse control media; active public campaigns can empower public |

Table 6.3 The corporate governance mechanisms in developing and transition countries.

| Corporate governance mechanism | Relative importance in developing and transition countries | Scope of policy intervention |
|---|---|---|
| **Reputation and self enforcement** | Important when general enforcement is weak, but stronger when environment is stronger | Depend on growth opportunities and scope for rent seeking. Encourage competition in factor markets |
| **Bilateral private enforcement mechanisms** | Important, as they can be more specific, but do not benefit outsiders and can have downsides | Requiring functioning civil commercial courts |
| **Arbitration, auditors other multilateral mechanisms** | Potentially important, often the origin of public law; but the enforcement problem often remains, audits sometimes abused, watch conflicts of interest | Facilitate the information of private third party mechanisms (sometimes avoid forming public alternatives) deal with conflict of interest, ensure competition |
| **Competition** | Determines scope for potential mistreatment of factors of production including financing | Open up all factor markets to competition including from abroad |

Table 6.3—Cont'd

Source: Berglof, E. and Claessens, S. (2004), 'Corporate Government and Enforcement' World Bank Policy Research Working Paper 3409, September.

However, Jamie Allen the Secretary General of the Asian Corporate Governance Association (ACGA) believes that Asia's regulatory performance is not impressive: 'The authorities are reasonable enough at tackling smaller problems such as mis-selling of financial products', but he said 'big deals and insider trading issues are not well dealt with. Regulators are better at writing the rules than enforcing them' (*Ethical Corporation* May 2006). The ACGA with CLSA Asia Pacific Markets each year completes an index of the relative performance in corporate governance of 10 Asian countries, surveying over 400 companies, with 30 to 50 companies included in each of the 10 countries. The questions asked to determine relative corporate governance performance cover five fields:

1 *Corporate governance rules and regulations*: (19 questions) New focus on audit committees, pre-emption rights, shareholder meetings and rule implementation.
2 *Enforcement (public and private)*: (18 questions) New focus on insider trading, disclosure of enforcement action by regulator, exercise of voting rights by investors.
3 *Political and regulatory environment*: (10 questions) More focus on actual autonomy of regulator, availability of information on laws and regulations, range of legal remedies.
4 *IGAAP (accounting and auditing)*: (13 questions) Focus on practices as well as rules; information on standards.
5 *CG culture*: (18 questions) New focus on large-caps (vs the rest), mid caps, split between chairman and CEO, internal controls, voluntary voting by poll.

The results obtained from 2000 to 2004 are included in Table 6.4. There is a significant difference in performance between those countries that have a long established concern for corporate governance, and the countries that have discovered it more recently. Over time there has been an improvement in the performance of some of the countries, but not all. This is partly explained by the application of more rigorous methodology, that there are

| Rank | Country | 2000 | 2001 | 2002 | 2003 | 2004 |
|------|---------|------|------|------|------|------|
| 1 | Singapore | 7.5 | 7.4 | 7.4 | 7.7 | 7.5 |
| 2 | Hong Kong | 7.1 | 6.8 | 7.2 | 7.3 | 6.7 |
| 3 | India | 5.6 | 5.4 | 5.9 | 6.6 | 6.2 |
| 4 | Malaysia | 3.2 | 3.7 | 4.7 | 5.5 | 5.8 |
| 5 | Korea | 5.2 | 3.8 | 4.7 | 5.5 | 5.8 |
| 6 | Taiwan | 5.7 | 5.3 | 5.8 | 5.8 | 5.5 |
| 7 | Thailand | 2.8 | 3.7 | 3.8 | 4.6 | 5.3 |
| 8 | Philippines | 2.9 | 3.3 | 3.6 | 3.7 | 5.0 |
| 9 | China | 3.6 | 3.4 | 3.9 | 4.3 | 4.8 |
| 10 | Indonesia | 2.9 | 3.2 | 2.9 | 3.2 | 4.0 |

Table 6.4 Corporate governance in selected countries of Asia Pacific, 2000–2005.

Source: Adapted from CLSA Asia Pacific Markets and ACGA (2005).

| Exchange | (USD millions) | | |
|----------|----------|----------|----------|
| | End 2005 | End 2004 | % Change 2005/2004 |
| *Asia - Pacific* | | | |
| Australian SE | 804,014.8 | 776,402.8 | 3.6% |
| Bombay SE | 553,073.7 | 386,321.1 | 43.2% |
| Bursa Malaysia | 180,517.5 | 181,623.8 | −0.6% |
| Colombo SE | 5,720.0 | 3,657.0 | 56.4% |
| Hong Kong Exchanges | 1,054,999.3 | 861,462.9 | 22.5% |
| Jakarta SE | 81,428.1 | 73,250.6 | 11.2% |
| Korea Exchange | 718,010.7 | 389,473.4 | 84.4% |
| National Stock Exchange India | 515,972.5 | 363,276.0 | 42.0% |
| New Zealand Exchange | 40,592.5 | 43,731.3 | −7.2% |
| Osaka SE | 2,969,814.6 | 2,287,047.8 | 29.9% |
| Philippine SE | 39,817.8 | 28,602.0 | 39.2% |
| Shanghai SE | 286,190.3 | 314,315.7 | −8.9% |
| Shenzhen SE | 115,661.9 | 133,404.6 | −13.3% |
| Singapore Exchange | 257,340.6 | 217,617.8 | 18.3% |
| Taiwan SE Corp. | 476,018.0 | 441,435.8 | 7.8% |
| Thailand SE | 123,885.0 | 115,390.4 | 7.4% |
| Tokyo SE | 4,572,901.0 | 3,557,674.4 | 28.5% |
| *Total region*[1] | *9,310,171.3* | *7,524,363.6* | *23.7%* |

Note:
[1] Asia Pacific Total region excludes Osaka and NSE India to avoid double counting with Tokyo SE and Bombay respectively.
Data combine the main and SMEs market capitalizations. They include common and preferred shares, and exclude investment funds, rights, warrants, convertibles, foreign companies.

Table 6.5 Market capitalisation of selected Asia Pacific countries, 2005.

Source: WFE (2005), *Annual Report*, Paris: World Federation of Exchanges.

weaknesses in the details of laws and regulations that may have appeared convincing initially, there are gaps between national accounting policies and practices, and finally some major corporate governance practices are not gaining traction among listed companies. Though the economies of Asia are once again expanding rapidly, and the stock exchanges are getting stronger, doubts remain about the vigour and the integrity of the institutions that are supporting and regulating this vast generation of wealth (Table 6.5).

## CONCLUSIONS

The Asia Pacific countries are presently among the most dynamic in the world, and economic growth appears certain to accelerate further. But the near-collapse of the economic systems of East Asia in 1997 is a salutary lesson of the importance of building solid institutional and governance foundations to support increasing economic activity if it is to be reliable and sustainable. All of the Asian countries have embarked on reform of corporate governance, though the considerable divide between policy and practice could undermine the integrity of the reform. One of the great weaknesses of the reform movement is the often unthinking application of Anglo-American policies and interests to the corporate governance problems of the Asia Pacific, as the price for accessing western capital markets. Eliminating corruption and extending principles of accountability and transparency may be necessary, but this does not necessarily mean assuming that shareholder value is the only purpose of business. The Asia Pacific region will build stronger institutions if it reflects wider and more deeply rooted social values than this.

SIX

# 7

# The Globalisation of Corporate Governance

## INTRODUCTION

This chapter asks whether a universal corporate governance system is either necessary or desirable. The increasingly recognised premium for good governance is considered in the context of a globalising economy. The implications of the deregulation of finance and the globalisation of capital markets is examined, with a focus on the growth of equity markets and the dominant position of the New York Stock Exchange. The movement towards the globalisation of regulation that is accompanying the globalisation of markets is presented. The considerable impact of the OECD principles of corporate governance is studied with the international development of corporate governance standards. The convergence thesis is debated, examining different theoretical arguments for and against the inevitability of convergence of corporate governance systems. Finally, the future direction of corporate governance trends is questioned, with the likelihood of greater complexity rather than uniformity emerging from current developments.

## A UNIVERSAL CORPORATE GOVERNANCE SYSTEM?

Having reviewed three resolutely different approaches to corporate governance in the Anglo-American, European and Asia Pacific models, the question arises: is one system more robust than the others and will this system prevail and become universal? The answer to this question appeared straightforward in the 1990s. The US economy was ascendant, and the American market based approach appeared the most dynamic and successful. Functional convergence towards the market based system seemed to be occurring, inexorably driven by forces such as:

- increasingly massive international financial flows which offered deep, liquid capital markets to countries and companies that could meet certain minimum international corporate governance standards;
- growing influence of the great regional stock exchanges, including the NYSE and NASDAQ, London Stock Exchange, and Euronext – where the largest corporations in the world were listed regardless of their home country;
- developing activity of ever-expanding Anglo-American based institutional investors, advancing policies to balance their portfolios with increasing international investments if risk could be mitigated;
- expanding revenues and market capitalisation of multinational enterprises, (often Anglo-American corporations, invariably listed on the New York Stock Exchange even if European based), combined with a sustained wave of international mergers and acquisitions from which increasingly global companies were emerging.
- accelerating convergence towards international accounting standards; and a worldwide governance movement towards more independent auditing standards, and rigorous corporate governance practices.

Together these forces have provoked one of the liveliest debates of the last decade or so concerning the globalisation and convergence of corporate governance (Hansmann and Kraakerman 2001; Branson 2001; McDonnell 2002;

McCahery *et al.* 2002; Hamilton and Quinlan 2005). How high the stakes are in this debate is revealed by Gordon and Roe:

> Globalization affects the corporate governance reform agenda in two ways. First, it heightens anxiety over whether particular corporate governance systems confer competitive economic advantage. As trade barriers erode, the locally protected product marketplace disappears. A country's firms' performance is more easily measured against global standards. Poor performance shows up more quickly when a competitor takes away market share, or innovates quickly. National decision makers must consider whether to protect locally favored corporate governance regimes if they regard the local regime as weakening local firms in product markets or capital markets. Concern about comparative economic performance induces concern about corporate governance. Globalization's second effect comes from capital markets' pressure on corporate governance. First, firms have new reasons to turn to public capital markets. High tech firms following the US model want the ready availability of an initial public offering for the venture capitalist to exit and for the firm to raise funds. Firms expanding into global markets often prefer to use stock, rather than cash, as acquisition currency. If they want American investors to buy and hold that stock, they are pressed to adopt corporate governance measures that those investors feel comfortable with. Despite a continuing bias in favor of home-country investing, the internationalization of capital markets has led to more cross-border investing. New stockholders enter, and they aren't always part of any local corporate governance consensus. They prefer a corporate governance regime they understand and often believe that reform will increase the value of their stock. Similarly, even local investors may make demands that upset a prior local consensus. The internationalization of capital markets means that investment flows may move against firms perceived to have suboptimal governance and thus to the disadvantage of the countries in which those firms are based.
>
> (2004: 2)

## THE PREMIUM FOR CORPORATE GOVERNANCE

In this vein a series of surveys of international investor opinion conducted by McKinsey (including a survey of South America undertaken in cooperation with the World Bank) inquiring what premium investors were prepared to pay for the shares of well governed companies proved highly influential. Three surveys conducted in 1999–2000 covering Asia, Europe and the United States, and South America discovered that:

> Three-quarters of the investors say that board practices are at least as important as investment performance when they evaluate companies for investment ... Over 80 per cent of the investors say that they would pay more for the shares of a well-governed company than for those of a poorly governed one with a comparable financial performance. (A well governed company was defined as one that has a majority of outside directors with no management ties on its board, undertakes formal evaluation of directors, and is responsive to requests from investors for information on governance issues). Directors should also hold significant shareholdings in the company, and a large part of their pay should come in the form of stock options ... In fact, the size of the premium the institutional investors say they are willing to pay for good board governance reflects the extent to which they believe that there is room for improvement in the quality of financial reporting in a particular country. Financial reporting in Asia or Latin America, for instance, is both limited and, often, of distinctly poor quality. As a result, investors all over the world believed that their investments in Asia and Latin America are better protected by well-governed companies that respect shareholders' rights.
>
> (Coombes and Watson 2000: 74–76)

The weight of popular opinion in the investment industry appeared to be supporting this association of governance criteria with investment decisions, as in a further survey of investors in the US and Europe conducted by Russell Reynolds, which found that approximately half of European

investors, and over sixty per cent of US investors had decided not to invest in a company, or reduced their investment, because of what they regarded as poor governance practices (2000). (Though it is slightly ironic that the McKinsey survey of the need for companies to reform their governance includes the insistence that directors should hold significant shares in the company and receive a large part of their pay in stock options, when both parts of this received wisdom more recently were rejected by many corporate governance guidelines around the world, which prefer to see directors adopting a more objective stance and not having their own fortunes inextricably linked with the companies they are directors of, but retaining the freedom to resign on principle should this prove necessary.) Nonetheless, the McKinsey survey confidently concludes with a resounding call for companies internationally to attend to their governance if they are to succeed:

> Companies and policy makers should take heed. If companies could capture but a small part of the governance premium that is apparently available, they would create much greater shareholder value. Moreover, companies that fail to reform governance will find themselves at a competitive disadvantage when they try to obtain capital to finance growth. High governance standards will prove essential to attracting and retaining investors in globalised capital markets; failure to reform will probably hinder companies with global ambitions.
>
> (Coombes and Watson 2000: 747)

In the inevitable contest implied by such calls between the insider, relationship based, stakeholder oriented corporate governance system and the outsider, market based, shareholder value oriented system, it is often implied that the optimal model is the dispersed ownership with shareholder foci for achieving competitiveness and enhancing any economy in a globalised world. The OECD, World Bank, IMF, Asian Development Bank and other international agencies, while they have recognised the existence of different governance systems and suggested they would not wish to adopt a one-size-fits-all approach, have nonetheless consistently associated the *rules-based*

outsider mode of corporate governance with greater efficiency and capacity to attract investment capital, and relegated the relationship based insider mode to second best, often with the implication that these systems may be irreparably flawed. The drive towards functional convergence was supported by the development of international codes and standards of corporate governance.

The vast weight of scholarship, led by the financial economists, has reinforced these ideas to the point where they appeared unassailable at the height of the new economy boom in the US in the 1990s (which coincided with a long recession for both the leading exponents of the relationships based system, Japan and Germany), supporting the view that an inevitable convergence towards the superior Anglo-American model of corporate governance was occurring. This all appeared an integral part of the irresistible rise of globalisation that was advancing through the regions of the world in the late 1990s and early 2000s, with apparently unstoppable force. Economies, cultures and peoples increasingly were becoming integrated into global markets, media networks, and foreign ideologies in a way never before experienced. It seemed as if distinctive and valued regional patterns of corporative governance would be absorbed just as completely as other cultural institutions in the integrative and homogenising processes of globalisation. The increasing power of global capital markets, stock exchanges, institutional investors, and international regulation would overwhelm cultural and institutional differences in the approach to corporate governance.

Yet just as there are many countries that continue to value greatly the distinctions of their culture and institutions, they would not wish to lose to any globalised world, people also believe there are unique attributes to the different corporate governance systems they have developed over time, and are not convinced these should be sacrificed to some unquestioning acceptance that a universal system will inevitably be better. The field of comparative corporate governance has continued to develop however, and a different and more complex picture of governance systems is now emerging. The objectives of corporate governance are more closely questioned; the qualities of the variety and relationships of different

institutional structures are becoming more apparent; the capability and performance of the different systems more closely examined; and different potential outcomes of any convergence of governance systems realised. While capital markets have acquired an apparently irresistible force in the world economy, it still appears that institutional complementarities at the national and regional level represent immovable objects.

## WHAT GLOBALISATION MEANS

The controversy regarding what is involved in globalisation is worth examining more closely. The experience of globalisation represents a profound reconfiguration of the world economy compared to earlier periods of internationalisation. 'An international economy *links* distinct national markets; a global economy *fuses* national markets into a coherent whole' (Kobrin 2002: 7). As the growth of foreign direct investment exceeded the growth in world trade, the centrality of corporations' internationalisation strategies to the evolving pattern of the industrial and investment processes of globalisation became increasingly apparent. With regard to resolving the resulting tensions the OECD maintained:

> Globalization of industry refers to an evolving pattern of cross-border activities of firms involving international investment, trade and collaboration for purposes of product development, production and sourcing, and marketing. These international activities enable firms to enter new markets, exploit their technological and organizational advantages, and reduce business costs and risks. Underlying the international expansion of firms, and in part driven by it, are technological advances, the liberalization of markets and increased mobility of production factors. These complex patterns of cross border activities increasingly characterize the international economic system and distinguish it from the earlier predominance of arms-length trade in finished goods. National economies are becoming more closely integrated as firms spread their operations and assets across countries. This brings greater economic efficiencies and welfare, as well as

more intense competition, greater need for adjustment and more demands on national and international policy. The current challenge for many countries – in a situation of low economic growth and high unemployment – is to ensure effective adjustment while minimising related international frictions, so that the potential welfare and efficiency gains from globalization are attained.

> (OECD 1996: 9)

However a more critical view of the impact of globalisation is becoming widespread in large parts of the developing world (as well as in the older industrial parts of the developed world). It is the perception that behind the appearance of a universal global interconnectedness and opportunity, what is occurring is the aggressive advance of a US inspired hegemony, with the pre-eminence of international markets, the abandonment in many circumstances of social welfare, and the intensification of poverty and inequality that causes such widespread disquiet with the globalisation phenomenon.

> Because of globalization many people in the world now live longer than before and their standard of living is far better ... Globalization has reduced the sense of isolation felt in much of the developing world and has given many people in the developing countries access to knowledge well beyond the reach of even the wealthiest in any country a century ago ... Those who vilify globalization often overlook its benefits. But the proponents of globalization have been, if anything, even more unbalanced. To them, globalization (which is typically associated with accepting triumphant capitalism, American style) *is* progress; developing countries must accept it, if they are to grow and fight poverty effectively. But to many in the developing world, globalization has not brought the promised economic benefits.

> (Stiglitz 2002: 4–5)

In essence is globalisation simply the ascendancy of US inspired liberal consensus on deregulation, privatisation, structural adjustment programmes and limited government? (Held and McGrew 2002: 4) In its present form is the globalisation

process sustainable, or will the economic and social imbalances it generates create greater international instability?

The World Commission on the Social Dimension of Globalisation established in conjunction with the ILO considered this issue:

> The current process of globalization is generating unbalanced outcomes, both between and within countries. Wealth is being created, but too many countries and people are not sharing in its benefits. They also have little or no voice in shaping the process ... Many of them live in the limbo of the informal economy without formal rights and in a swathe of poor countries that subsist precariously on the margins of the global economy. Even in economically successful countries some workers and communities have been adversely affected by globalization. Meanwhile the revolution in global communications heightens awareness of these disparities.
>
> (ILO 2004: x)

To appreciate the scale of the problem, it is useful to examine the economic impact of globalisation. Table 7.1 demonstrates the vast, if uneven, growth in world GDP, exports, foreign direct investment and portfolio investment since the 1980s. Though the people of the rest of the world have sustained an intense effort to achieve economic growth, the high income advanced industrial countries have *increased* significantly their percentage share of world GDP from 73.6 per cent in 1985 to 80.5 per cent in 2002. This was maintained by dominating 72.9 per cent of exports of goods and services, 76.6 per cent of inflows of foreign direct investment, and a total of 88.9 per cent of inflows of portfolio investment. Economic ascendancy of the advanced industrial countries was achieved despite the output growth rate of the developing countries in aggregate exceeding the growth rate of the developed countries in recent years: the problem for the developing world is that this growth is from such an exceedingly low base that in absolute terms these countries on the whole continue to fall further behind (UNCTAD 2005: 3).

The pervasive characteristics of globalisation contributing to this unequal transformation of the world economy include the liberalisation of international trade; expansion of foreign direct investment; emergence of massive cross-border financial flows; increased competition in global markets; policy decisions to reduce national barriers to international economic transactions; impact of new technology, especially in the sphere of information and communications; the acceleration of global environmental degradation; and the social impact of globalisation in compounding inequality. The industrial countries strong economic base and abundance of capital and skill have allowed them to gain the most substantial benefits from globalisation, with the increasing market power of MNEs, the global growth of financial markets allowing higher returns in emerging markets, technological leadership, and strengthening of international rules on intellectual property rights. Only a minority of developing countries have benefited, including the East Asian countries. China and India represent the greatest development achievements of the contemporary world, but have not followed orthodox liberalisation strategies in order to develop their economies (World Commission 2004: 37).

A problem of political governance which pervades this new era Held contends, is that contemporary processes of globalisation and regionalisation are creating overlapping networks of power which cut across territorial boundaries, and strain a world order designed according to the Westphalian principle of the exclusive national sovereign rule over a bounded territory. As a result, effective power is shared and negotiated between diverse forces and agencies both public and private, at local, national, regional and international levels (2003: 161). 'The infrastructure of global governance has evolved into a complex and multi-layered system which has no single centre of authority' (McGrew 2000: 142). The multi-lateral system for developing and implementing international policies lacks policy coherence, transparency and accountability. These are problems for nation states to work through together if the tensions and conflicts unleashed by globalisation are to be relieved, though any efforts in this direction will occur in a context where international financial markets and multinational corporations are exerting immensely greater influence than ever before.

| | Billion of $ | | Increase of 2002 compared to 1985 | % share of world level | |
|---|---|---|---|---|---|
| | 1985 | 2002 | | 1985 | 2002 |
| **Gross domestic product (GDP)** | | | | | |
| China and India | 558.5 | 1922.4 | 3.4 fold increase | 4.4 | 6 |
| Low income countries excl. India | 579.3 | 634.7 | 1.1 fold increase | 4.5 | 2 |
| Middle income countries excl. China | 2234.1 | 3702.9 | 1.7 fold increase | 17.5 | 11.5 |
| High income countries | 9393 | 25867 | 2.8 fold increase | 73.6 | 80.5 |
| **World** | **12765.2** | **32127** | **2.5 fold increase** | **100** | **100** |
| **Exports of goods and services** | | | | | |
| China and India | 79.1 | 685.1 | 8.7 fold increase | 3.4 | 8.7 |
| Low income countries excl. India | 82.5 | 215.2 | 2.6 fold increase | 3.6 | 2.7 |
| Middle income countries excl. China | 433.9 | 1227.2 | 2.8 fold increase | 18.7 | 15.6 |
| High income countries | 1718 | 5732.6 | 3.3 fold increase | 74.3 | 72.9 |
| **World** | **2314** | **7860.2** | **3.4 fold increase** | **100** | **100** |
| **Inflows of foreign direct investment** | | | | | |
| China and India | 1.7 | 62 | 37.4 fold increase | 2.9 | 9.8 |
| Low income countries excl. India | 1.9 | 7.1 | 3.7 fold increase | 3.3 | 1.1 |
| Middle income countries excl. China | 9.7 | 79.1 | 8.1 fold increase | 16.8 | 12.5 |
| High income countries | 44.7 | 484.3 | 10.8 fold increase | 77.1 | 76.6 |
| **World** | **58** | **632.6** | **10.9 fold increase** | **100** | **100** |
| **Inflows of total portfolio investment** | | | | | |
| China and India | 2.3 | 49.8 | 22 fold increase | 1.7 | 6.9 |
| Low income countries excl. India | 0.05 | 0.07 | 1.3 fold increase | 0.038 | 0 |
| Middle income countries excl. China | 9.1 | 30 | 3.3 fold increase | 6.7 | 4.2 |
| High income countries | 123.8 | 639.9 | 5.2 fold increase | 91.6 | 88.9 |
| **World** | **135.2** | **719.8** | **5.3 fold increase** | **100** | **100** |

Table 7.1 Evolution of income, exports and capital flows, 1985–2002.

Source: Gunter, B., and Hoeven, R. (2004), 'The Social Dimension of Globalisation: A Review of the Literature', Working Paper 24, Policy Integration Department, World Commission on the Social Dimension of Globalisation, International Labour Office, Geneva: ILO, June, p. 3.

## Deregulation of finance

In particular, the deregulation, internationalisation and innovation of the world monetary system is having the most dramatic impact of all (Turner 1991). The international financial system ostensibly is there to lubricate the processes of trade, foreign direct investment and international production. Yet the cumulative impact of the integration of the forces of international finance has periodically destabilised large parts of the world:

Financial liberalization created the policy environment for expanded capital mobility. But the increase in capital flows was greatly boosted by the revolution in ICT. This made possible the improved and speedier knowledge of foreign markets, the development of 'round the world and round the clock' financial transactions, and

the emergence of new financial instruments, especially derivatives. Since the late 1980s there has been a global trend towards financial liberalization … The governance structure of the global financial system has also been transformed. As private financial flows have come to dwarf official flows, the role and influence of private actors such as banks, hedge funds, equity funds and rating agencies has increased substantially. As a result, these private financial agencies now exert tremendous power over the economic policies of developing countries, especially the emerging market economies. Rating agencies determine whether countries can have access to sovereign borrowing and, if so, the cost of this. The assessments of stock analysts have a profound influence on the flow of funds into stock markets, while the decisions of hedge fund managers often impact on national currencies.

(World Commission 2004: 27–34)

The other great force in the globalisation saga is the escalating scale, universal operations, and increasing revenues of the multinational enterprises. The brand images of the leading multinationals have been impressed on the public consciousness of the world with apparently limitless advertising and marketing budgets. The advancing market capitalisation of the increasing number of multinationals has contrasted with the halting economic growth of the majority of nation states. The autonomy and power of multinational enterprises relative to national states has often been subject to some exaggeration; however, there is much evidence to justify the increasing economic significance of multinational enterprises, and as Calder and Culverwell (2005: 16) argue, the increasing involvement of these corporations in the economies of developing countries is one of the main concerns in recent globalisation debates. The sales of the largest 100 multinationals increased from $3.2 trillion to $4.8 trillion between 1990 and 2000 (UNCTAD 2002: 90). Foreign employment by multinational enterprises grew from 24 million people in 1990 to 54 million people in 2001 (UNCTAD 2002: xv). During this period private sector corporations commenced construction and operation of approximately 2,500 infrastructure projects in developing

countries with a total investment of $750 billion (World Bank 2002: 1). 'Weak public sector governance in some developing countries has meant that transnational corporations (TNCs) are often operating in areas with far weaker environmental and social standards than those in their "home" countries, where human rights are being abused and/or where corruption is endemic. These conditions have been seen to create the risk that the activities of TNCs in these countries will lead to negative environmental and/or social impacts and to human rights abuses' (Calder and Culverwell 2005: 16).

A number of initiatives from the UN, World Bank and OECD have attempted to address these issues, including the OECD *Guidelines for Multinational Enterprises* offering detailed guidance on good business conduct regarding human rights, accountability, disclosure, employment, environmental protection, bribery and taxation. Though these guidelines are a comprehensive statement on internationally agreed principles, they fail to provide sufficient detail on key issues such as the provision of a living wage, human rights and tax compliance; the guidelines do not directly apply to small and medium sized enterprises; and their applicability to global supply chains is contested (Calder and Culverwell 2005: 46).

## GLOBALISATION OF CAPITAL MARKETS

A major driver of the globalisation phenomenon has proved the massive development of finance markets, and their increasing influence upon every other aspect of the economy:

Financial globalisation, i.e. the integration of more and more countries into the international financial system and the expansion of international markets for money, capital and foreign exchange, took off in the 1970s. From the 1980s on, the increase in cross-border holdings of assets outpaced the increase in international trade, and financial integration accelerated once more in the 1990s. In EMU, monetary integration boosted the integration of financial markets, which had begun under the single market programme, even further.

The internationalisation of finance was driven by technical advances, above all the decrease in the cost of communication and information processing as well as policy changes, in particular the spreading liberalisation of cross-border financial flows … Plainly, trade integration (which is beneficial in itself) and financial integration reinforce each other in various ways. The past decade has also seen widespread improvements in macroeconomic and structural policies that may to some extent be linked to a disciplining effect of financial integration. Moreover, there is evidence that financial linkages have strengthened the transmission of cyclical impulses and shocks among industrial countries. Financial globalisation is also likely to have helped financing the build-up of significant global current account imbalances. Finally, a great deal of the public and academic discussion has focused on the series of financial crises in the 1990s, which has highlighted the potential effects of capital account liberalisation on the volatility of growth and consumption.

(European Commission 2005: 19)

The complex explanation for this massive *financialisation* of the world economy is pieced together by Ronald Dore thus:

- the advance of neo-liberal policies involving smaller government, a belief in free enterprise, and competitive markets as the basis of allocation;
- cutbacks in state welfare, insurance and pensions, combined with tax incentives to direct personal savings to equity markets, accompanied by financial deregulation, new financial products, futures and derivatives;
- the huge growth of private insurance and pensions, with a shift of savings from fixed-interest deposits to investment funds;
- the supply of funds to equity markets greatly exceeds what is required for new issues, and corporations shift from bank to direct market finance, becoming more involved in financial markets;
- the growth of company treasuries, and share buybacks to raise share price and facilitate share-swap acquisitions become central

corporate strategies, increasing the influence of finance managers;
- asset price inflation becomes rampant in swollen stock markets exhibiting greater volatility;
- speculation becomes an integral part of financial management for individuals, institutions and corporations;
- pressures build to increase the profit share of national income at the expense of the labour share;
- financial services take up an ever larger share of advertising, economic activity and highly skilled human resources;
- banks respond to the decline in loan business with a shift to earning fees for financial and investment services and own account trading;
- shareholder value is preached as the sole legitimate objective and aspiration of corporations and executives;
- the reinforcement of the international financial services industry, which is US dominated, extending the belief in the success and power of the American economy and ideology;
- insistent and demanding calls for 'level playing fields' from the World Trade Organisation and Bank of International Settlements (BIS), with pressures for the further liberalisation of financial markets, and greater international competition forcing international financial institutions, and other corporations to work within the same parameters (Dore 2000: 4–6).

What is resulting from this insistent impulse of the increasingly dominant financial institutions are economies (and corporations) increasingly dependent upon financial markets: 'Global integration and economic performance has been fostered by a new dynamic in financial markets, which both mirrors and amplifies the effects of foreign direct investment and trade driven integration. The economic performance of countries across the world is increasingly supported by – and dependent on – international capital flows, which have built on a process of progressive liberalisation and advances in technology since the 1980s' (European Commission 2005: 8).

## THE GROWTH OF EQUITY MARKETS

A vital dimension of the increasing financialisation of the world economy is the growth of capital markets, and especially the vast growth of equity markets, where volatility has been experienced at its furthest extremities. The American zone equity markets (entirely dominated by the NYSE and NASDAQ) were propelled from a total of $4,000 billion in 1990 to $22,653 billion in 2006 (Figure 7.1). This onward progress was violently punctuated by the market collapse of 2001/2002, with a fall from $16,450 billion in 2000 to $11,931 in 2002. The European zone markets grew from just over $2,000 billion in 1990 to $15,434 in 2006, experiencing a similar shock with the fall from $9,588 billion in 2000 to $6,465 billion in 2002. Finally, market capitalisation in the Asia Pacific zone grew more steadily from just under $4,000 billion in 1990 to $11,838 billion dollars in 2006, with a fall from $4,918 billion in 2000 to $3,968 in 2001 before recovery occurred (World Federation 2007: 50).

The extent that equity markets are far more enthusiastically embraced in the Anglo-American world is revealed by the value of share trading between 1990 and 2004. In the Americas share trading reached a peak of $34,070 billion in 2000, collapsing to $17,899 billion in 2003, before recovering to $35,909 billion in 2006 (Figure 7.2). In the European zone trading reached a peak of $17,430 in 2000, collapsed to $9,884 billion in 2002, and recovered to $21,512 billion in 2006; while in the Asia Pacific trading has grown steadily but comparatively slowly from $4,991 billion in 2000 to $12,100 billion in 2006, with a relatively slight fall in 2002 to $4,119 billion (World Federation 2007: 56).

Because they have adopted regional time zones which fit their trading patterns over the 24 hours of each day opening with the Asia Pacific markets, followed by the European, and closing with the US markets, the World Federation of Exchanges has to an extent concealed the enormous concentration of equity markets by including South America with the United States, Africa and the

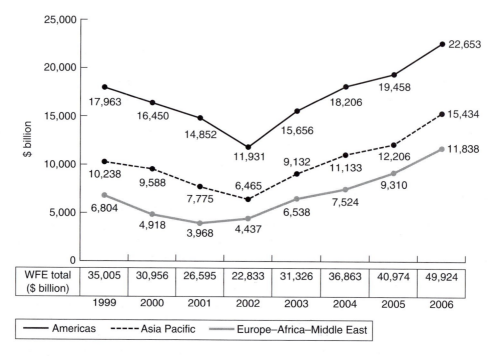

**Figure 7.1** Recent evolution of domestic equity market capitalisation.

Source: World Federation of Exchanges (WFE) (2005), *Annual Report and Statistics 2007*, p. 29.

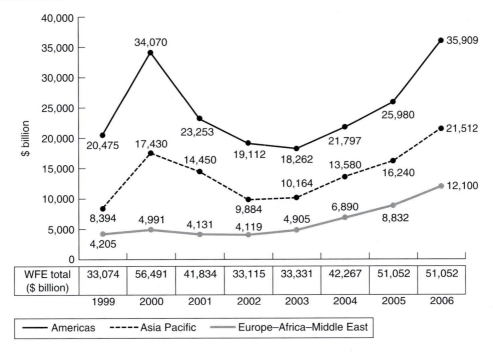

| WFE total ($ billion) | 33,074 | 56,491 | 41,834 | 33,115 | 33,331 | 42,267 | 51,052 | 51,052 |
|---|---|---|---|---|---|---|---|---|
| | 1999 | 2000 | 2001 | 2002 | 2003 | 2004 | 2005 | 2006 |

——— Americas    - - - - Asia Pacific    ——— Europe–Africa–Middle East

**Figure 7.2** Evolution of share trading, by region.

Source: World Federation of Exchanges (WFE) (2005), *Annual Report and Statistics 2007*, p. 31.

Middle East with Europe, and South Asia with South-east Asia, Japan and Australia. A more accurate picture of the paucity of equity markets in the developing world is gained from Table 7.1 where for example in 2002 inflows of total portfolio investment into low income countries amounted to 0.009 per cent of the world total, and into middle income countries (excluding China) portfolio investment amounted to 4.2 per cent of the world total, while the high income countries claimed almost 90 per cent of the total inflows of portfolio investment.

The supremacy of the New York Stock Exchange is very apparent, with a market capitalisation almost as large as the other members of the ten largest exchanges put together (Table 7.2). When the market capitalisation of the major Anglo-American stock markets of the NYSE, NASDAQ, London, Toronto, Australian and American Stock Exchanges is combined the total is $21,141 billion, while the other 44 stock exchanges which are members of the World Federation of Exchanges together have a combined market capitalisation of $15,425 billion.

This concentration of equity market activity is even more apparent in share trading (Table 7.3), with the NYSE, NASDAQ and London having a combined total of share trading of $25,554 billion while the stock exchanges of the rest of the world have a total of $14,810 billion (World Federation 2004: 50–56). What this demonstrates is the overwhelming predominance of Anglo-American institutions and activity in world equity markets, and how to a great extent these markets reflect largely Anglo-American interests, as the rest of the world depends more on other sources of corporate finance. This absolute pre-eminence of equity markets is a recent phenomenon. Historically, the primary way most businesses throughout the world (including in the Anglo-American region) have financed the growth of their companies is internally through retained earnings. In most parts of the world until recently this was a far more dependable source of finance rather then relying on equity markets. Equity finance has proved useful at the time of public listing when entrepreneurs and venture capitalists cash in their original investment, as a means of acquiring

| Exchange | End 2006 ($ bn) | End 2005 ($ bn) | % change in $ | % change local currency |
|---|---|---|---|---|
| 1 New York Stock Exchange | 15,421 | 13,310.6 | 15.9 | 15.9 |
| 2 Tokyo SE | 4,614 | 4,572.9 | 0.9 | 1.9 |
| 3 NASDAQ | 3,865 | 3,604.0 | 7.2 | 7.2 |
| 4 London SE | 3,794 | 3,058.2 | 24.1 | 8.8 |
| 5 Euronext | 3,708 | 2,706.8 | 37.0 | 22.5 |
| 6 TSX Group | 1,715 | 1,482.2 | 62.6 | 63.1 |
| 7 Deutsche Börse | 1,701 | 1,221.1 | 14.7 | 14.3 |
| 8 Hong Kong Exchanges | 1,638 | 1,055.0 | 34.1 | 20.0 |
| 9 BME Spanish Exchanges | 1,323 | 959.9 | 37.8 | 23.3 |
| 10 Swiss Exchange | 1,212 | 935.4 | 29.6 | 20.0 |

Table 7.2 Largest stock exchanges in market capitalisation, year-end 2006.

Source: World Federation of Exchanges, Annual Report, (2007: 29).

| Exchange | 2006 $ bn | 2005 $ bn | % change in $ | % change local currency |
|---|---|---|---|---|
| 1 New York Stock Exchange | 21,789 | 14,125 | 54.3 | 54.3 |
| 2 NASDAQ Stock Market | 11,807 | 10,087 | 17.1 | 17.1 |
| 3 London Stock Exchange | 7,583 | 5,674 | 33.7 | 30.5 |
| 4 Tokyo Stock Exchange | 5,825 | 4,427 | 31.6 | 36.4 |
| 5 Euronext | 3,805 | 2,901 | 31.2 | 28.2 |
| 6 Deutsche Borse | 2,742 | 1,912 | 43.4 | 40.0 |
| 7 BME Spanish Exchanges | 1,941 | 1,568 | 23.8 | 21.0 |
| 8 Borsa Italiana | 1,596 | 1,300 | 22.7 | 19.8 |
| 9 SWX Swiss Exchange | 1,396 | 975 | 43.0 | 43.2 |
| 10 Korea Exchange | 1,340 | 1,204 | 11.2 | 3.5 |

Table 7.3 Largest exchanges in share trading value, 2005–2006.

Source: World Federation of Exchanges, Annual Report (2007: 31).

other companies, or providing rewards for executives through stock options. Equity finance is used much less frequently during restructuring or to finance new product or project development (Lazonick 1992: 457). In Europe and the Asia Pacific region however, this finance was in the past provided by majority shareholders, banks, or other related companies (to the minor extent it was needed by companies committed to organic growth rather than through acquisition, and where executives traditionally were content with more modest personal material rewards than their American counterparts).

## New York Stock Exchange

The burgeoning significance of the equity markets is a comparatively recent phenomenon, even in the United States. The New York Stock Exchange was a very different beast in the middle decades of the twentieth century with a total of 3 million shares traded daily in 1960 compared to 1,582 million shares in 2005. During this time the average turnover of shares increased from 12 per cent to 102 per cent, transforming the periodic trading of shares into a daily event. Alongside this has been a sustained and increasingly vast

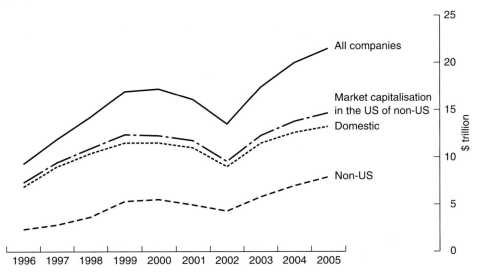

**Figure 7.3** Market capitalisation of NYSE listed companies, 1996–2005.

Source: Adapted from the World Federation of Exchanges (2006).

growth in total market capitalisation of NYSE listed domestic companies from $600 billion in 1970 to $13.3 trillion in 2005 (Figure 7.3).

The attraction of these vast pools of available capital proved irresistible to many large non-US companies from different parts of the world, which began to list on the NYSE in increasing numbers, growing from just 24 non-US companies listed in 1960 to 458 in 2004. These are among the largest and most successful of the companies of Europe, Japan and other countries. At first only one or two adventurous overseas companies succeeded in listing on the NYSE, but over time it became a badge of global corporate ambitions to be dual-listed in the home country, and in New York. In some cases this is the prelude to moving stock exchange listing completely to the NYSE, as in the case of News Corporation which after more than fifty years of having its base in Adelaide moved its listing from Australia to the United States in 2004. Greater access to the US investment institutions is a particularly strong factor, though most institutions do have policies to invest an increasing proportion of their assets overseas, there is invariably a limit to this, and listing on the NYSE is a means to higher investment rating, more ready availability of US institutional investment, and increased share price.

Why domestic stock exchanges were less promising is illustrated in Table 7.4: though the Tokyo and London stock exchanges have considerable resources and influence, they cannot compare with the might of the NYSE. Other stock exchanges around the world have remained small, until the recent growth in Euronext, the Deutsche Bourse and other European exchanges. As corporations became more international in their operations, and more distant from the banks, shareholder base and institutions that formerly helped to fund the development of their operations, the prospect of listing on the NYSE was increasingly difficult to dismiss (though some corporations that regarded themselves as national champions succeeded in doing so).

As overseas corporations have gravitated towards the United States, US investors have assumed a growing interest in holding non-US equities. Figure 7.4 illustrates how US investors have placed up to 2 trillion dollars in non-US equities, around 10 per cent of the total of all equity holdings. Originally the vast bulk of this investment was in the leading corporations of Europe and Japan, but now US investors are prepared to venture further afield if the returns, governance and risk conditions are appropriate. These new and emphatic investment criteria

|      | All WFE members | NYSE | NYSE (% of all) | NASDAQ | Tokyo | London | Deutsche Börse | Euronext |
|------|-----------------|------|-----------------|--------|-------|--------|----------------|----------|
| 2005 | 40.90 | 13.30 | 33 | 3.60 | 4.60 | 3.10 | 1.20 | 2.70 |
| 2004 | 37.10 | 12.60 | 34 | 3.50 | 3.60 | 2.80 | 1.20 | 2.40 |
| 2003 | 31.30 | 11.40 | 36 | 2.80 | 3.00 | 2.40 | 1.00 | 2.10 |
| 2002 | 23.10 | 9.00 | 39 | 2.20 | 2.10 | 1.80 | 0.70 | 1.60 |
| 2001 | 26.80 | 11.00 | 41 | 2.90 | 2.30 | 2.10 | 1.10 | 1.80 |
| 2000 | 30.90 | 11.50 | 37 | 3.60 | 3.20 | 2.60 | 1.30 | 2.30 |
| 1999 | 35.60 | 11.40 | 32 | 5.80 | 4.00 | 2.80 | 1.40 | 2.40 |
| 1998 | 26.30 | 10.30 | 39 | 2.50 | 2.40 | 2.30 | 1.10 | 1.80 |
| 1997 | 22.30 | 8.90 | 40 | 1.70 | 2.10 | 2.10 | 0.80 | 1.30 |
| 1996 | 20.10 | 6.80 | 34 | 1.50 | 3.00 | 1.70 | 0.70 | 1.10 |
| 1995 | 17.50 | 5.70 | 33 | 1.20 | 3.50 | 1.30 | 0.60 | 0.90 |
| 1990 | 9.60 | 2.70 | 28 | 0.30 | 2.80 | 0.90 | 0.40 | 0.50 |
| 1980 | 2.90 | 1.20 | 41 |      | 0.40 | 0.20 | 0.07 | 0.09 |

Table 7.4 Global comparison of market capitalisation of domestic listed companies 1980–2005 ($ trillions). Source: WFE (2006), *Annual Report*, Paris: World Federation of Exchanges.

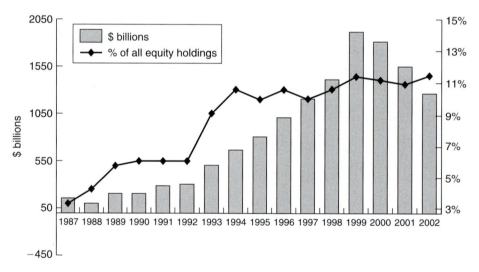

Figure 7.4 Investor holdings of non-US equities.
Source: Adapted from Federal Reserve Board of Flow of Funds.

have caused considerable disquiet in foreign corporations used to more patient and forgiving capital investment. The insistence on achieving higher rates of return on investment, on adopting more international governance standards, and on adhering to more disciplined risk management impressed upon European and Japanese corporations by deep-pocketed and assertive US institutional investors has proved something of a challenge.

The NYSE and NASDAQ are not simply much larger markets than the rest of the world; they are traded much more actively. As the turnover (the trading value as a proportion of market capitalisation) of the US markets increased from 12 per cent per year in 1960 to 46 per cent in

1990 and on to 102 per cent in 2005, the incentives, behaviour and values of market participants changed also. What were once widely considered substantial investments for the long term in industries thought to have a future, is often now reduced to elaborate formulae to extract the maximum value in the shortest possible time, before moving quickly on to the next money making opportunity almost regardless of the fate of the companies left behind (witness the catastrophic fall of General Motors' share price and market capitalisation in 2005 when it was realised the company had some difficult liabilities and market competition to confront). The commitment of the US markets to *trading in shares* rather than *investing in companies* has been apparent for some time (Table 7.5), and reached a dizzy – sanity defying – peak of speculation of $19.8 trillion annual trading on the NASDAQ in 2000 during the extraordinary and short-lived boom in new technology stocks.

The euphoria of the US equity markets did reach across the Atlantic with a flurry of new listings, which formed part of a sustained growth in the market capitalisation of European stock exchanges as a percentage of GDP (Figure 7.5). This substantial development of the equity markets of France, the Netherlands, Germany, Spain, and Belgium and other countries began to influence the corporate landscape of Europe,

and was further propelled by the formation of Euronext. Along with the growth in market capitalisation in European exchanges occurred a gradual increase also in trading value. It appears that contemporary equity markets inevitably will be associated with high levels of trading activity.

The important role of equity markets in fostering further international financial integration is recognised by the European Commission:

Globally, portfolio investment is the largest asset category held cross-border; global portfolios (equity and debt securities) amounted to 19 trillion US dollars at the end of 2003 (IMF CPIS, preliminary data). Turnover in international financial centres is very substantial. At the London Stock Exchange, 7.6bn euro worth of foreign equity was traded on a daily basis in May 2005. That represents 45 per cent of the total London trading volume. The part of turnover of foreign equity in the New York and Frankfurt stock exchanges stands at 8 per cent and 7 per cent, respectively. Currently, 235 EU firms are listed in US stock exchanges and 140 US firms in London, Frankfurt or at Euronext. Moreover, an agreement on equivalence of accounting standards has been reached, in April 2005, between the US Securities and Exchange Commission and the European Commission.

| Year | All WFE members | NYSE | NYSE (% of all) | NASDAQ | Tokyo | London | Deutsche Börse | Euronext |
|------|-----------------|------|-----------------|--------|-------|--------|----------------|----------|
| 2004 | 41.80 | 11.40 | 0 | 8.50 | 3.20 | 5.10 | 1.50 | 2.50 |
| 2003 | 33.60 | 9.70 | 29 | 7.10 | 2.00 | 3.60 | 1.30 | 1.90 |
| 2002 | 33.80 | 10.30 | 30 | 7.50 | 1.60 | 4.10 | 1.20 | 2.00 |
| 2001 | 40.30 | 10.50 | 26 | 11.00 | 1.70 | 4.60 | 1.50 | 3.20 |
| 2000 | 51.80 | 11.10 | 21 | 19.80 | 2.30 | 4.60 | 2.10 | 1.80 |
| 1999 | 34.30 | 8.90 | 26 | 10.50 | 1.70 | 3.40 | 1.60 | 1.30 |
| 1998 | 24.50 | 7.30 | 30 | 5.50 | 0.80 | 2.90 | 1.50 | 1.10 |
| 1997 | 20.10 | 5.80 | 29 | 4.50 | 0.90 | 2.00 | 1.10 | 0.70 |
| 1996 | 14.30 | 4.10 | 29 | 3.30 | 0.90 | 1.40 | 0.80 | 0.50 |
| 1995 | 10.90 | 3.10 | 28 | 2.40 | 0.90 | 1.20 | 0.60 | 0.40 |
| 1990 | 5.90 | 1.30 | 22 | 4.50 | 1.30 | 0.50 | 0.50 | 0.20 |
| 1980 | 0.90 | 0.40 | 44 | 0.07 | 0.20 | 0.04 | 0.02 | 0.02 |

Table 7.5 Global comparison of annualised trading ($ trillions).

Source: WFE (2005), *Annual Report*, Paris: World Federation of Exchanges.

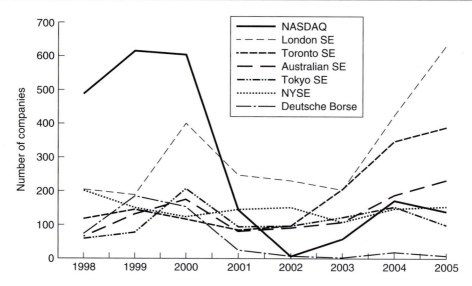

Figure 7.5 New listings in major markets, 1998–2005.

Source: WFE respective annual reports.

As equity markets come to play a more powerful role in corporate life in Europe, Japan and other parts of the world, a set of assumptions and practices are also disseminated which may confront long standing values and ideals in the economies and societies concerned. Specifically, the ascendancy of shareholder value as the single legitimate objective of corporations and their executives, usually accompanies increasing dependence upon equity markets. Dore cites a Goldman Sachs study of manufacturing value added in the United States, Germany and Europe in general, which concluded that: 'The share of gross value added going to wages and salaries has declined on trend in the US since the early 1980s. In fact, for the US, this appears to be an extension of a trend that has been in place since the early 1970s ... We believe that the pressures of competition for the returns on capital available in the emerging economies have forced US industry to produce higher returns on equity capital and that their response to this has been to reserve an increasingly large share of output for the owners of capital' (Young 1997).

This insistent pressure to drive increases in capital's returns at the expense of labour inherent in Anglo-American conceptions of the nature of equity finance is roundly condemned by Dore as the negation of essential values previously considered central to economic good in both Europe and Japan:

Multiple voices are urging Japanese managers to go in the same direction. The transformation on the agenda might may be variously described – from employee sovereignty to shareholder sovereignty: from the employee-favouring firm to the shareholder-favouring firm; from pseudo-capitalism to genuine capitalism. They all mean the same thing: the transformation of firms run primarily for the benefits of their employees into firms run primarily, even exclusively, for the benefit of their shareholders ... It means an economy centred on the stock market as the measure of corporate success and on the stock market index as a measure of national well-being, as opposed to an economy which has other, better, more pluralistic criteria of human welfare for measuring progress towards the good society.

(2000: 9–10)

## GLOBALISATION OF REGULATION

The OECD is the international agency charged with promoting policies for economic growth and

development among the advanced industrial market economies that form its membership, and also assumes responsibility for encouraging non-member countries in a similar market-oriented direction. The OECD has been at the forefront of policy analysis and promotion of the expansion of world trade, foreign direct investment, global capital markets and the globalisation of economies. The OECD has led the way in forging an international acceptance of international corporate governance principles, and has been supported in this work by the World Bank, Asian Development Bank, the UN and other international agencies who have promoted a series of regional forums of government, regulators, corporate executives and professionals to develop and disseminate best practice. These forums are also committed to institutional building and company director development. The work of the OECD on corporate governance was a natural extension of its interest in the productivity of corporations and economies and the efficiency and expansion of international markets. An early influential report *Corporate Governance: Improving Competitiveness and Access to Capital in Global Markets* (1998) was developed by the Business Sector Advisory Group, a distinguished group of international business representatives chaired by Ira Millstein on the New York law firm Weil, Gotshal and Manges. The report put forward an eloquent argument for pluralism and adaptability in corporate governance policy and practice:

> Because worldwide the corporation is the essential engine driving the private sector economically, and because corporate governance can be critical to competitive performance in all of a corporation's markets (goods, services, capital and human resources), the quality of corporate governance can affect the dynamism of the private sector and ultimately the credibility of market economies in providing economic growth and promoting citizen welfare ... The task of adapting, refining and adjusting corporate governance is a necessary and ongoing process. To be competitive, both corporations and investors must be allowed to innovate relentlessly and to adapt their governance practices to new economic circumstances; corporate governance should be

viewed as 'work in progress'. For this reason, the Advisory Group rejects a 'one-size-fits-all' approach to corporate governance practice and focuses this Report on a set of general policy perspectives and guiding norms in a context of pluralism and adaptability. To enable flexibility, experimentation and continuous improvement the design of corporate governance relationships and practices should be left to market forces: corporate governance should remain, basically, decisions by individual actors in the private sector. While the need to protect investor rights is undisputed, the Advisory Group believes the market-driven solutions emerging from competition among alternative practices are generally superior to those mandated by regulating authorities. This market-based perspective does not exclude a role for government. Policy makers and regulatory bodies have a distinct and important responsibility for shaping a regulatory framework, compatible with their respective societal values, that allows market forces to work and permits investors and companies to design their governance arrangements in accordance with respective needs.

(1998: 15)

Whether the OECD was able to live up to these ideals of pluralism and adaptability in the development of subsequent policy recommendations on corporate governance, and whether market forces were as tolerant and understanding of flexibility and differences in approaches to corporate governance are questions worth exploring. The advisory group establish three conditions as essential to governance flexibility and adaptability:

- permissive regulation, which allows for a range of ownership and contracting structures at the company level;
- availability of alternative options for corporate governance arrangements; and
- positive public attitudes towards diversity and innovation in the area of corporate governance (1998: 34).

If these conditions are satisfied then different regions, countries and corporations would in principle be able to select the type of governance

arrangements appropriate to its needs, in an informed market for governance arrangements. The advisory group suggest this flexibility might cover ownership structure, legal status, board structure, ownership transactions, and contracts with resource providers. As long as full disclosure takes place, and the existing rights are recognised with respect to all corporate governance adjustments then diversity is acceptable:

'For an economy to maintain a competitive business sector, it is necessary to foster a positive perception of flexibility in corporate governance arrangements by highlighting the pivotal role flexibility plays in supporting entrepreneurship, growth and competitiveness across all sectors of society' (OECD 1998: 37). Yet the market focused OECD principles of corporate governance which resulted did not appear to embrace diversity this warmly, and often, at least in the way the principles were interpreted, suggesting a more uniform view of what constitutes appropriate corporate governance, giving rise to some concerns about the globalisation of corporate governance regulation: 'It is difficult to imagine how corporate governance practices which are completely alien … can be accommodated'. The winner of the corporate governance model competition is likely to be the system which imposes the least cost on the corporation and supports the sole purpose of profit maximising. In other words an Anglo-American model.

(Dignam and Galanis 1999: 399)

## OECD Principles of Corporate Governance (1999)

The OECD principles have become the most influential internationally and define corporate governance as involving 'a set of relationships between a company's management, its board, its shareholders and other stakeholders … [it] also provides the structure through which the objectives of the company are set, and the means of attaining those objectives and monitoring performance are determined'. The experience of the Asian crisis, that revealed a systemic failure in corporate governance, was a spur to the publication

by the OECD of its *Principles of Corporate Governance* in 1999:

In the aftermath of the Asian financial crisis in 1997, the OECD Council Meeting at Ministerial level called upon the OECD to develop, in conjunction with national governments, other relevant international organisations and the private sector, a set of corporate governance standards and guidelines. The *OECD Principles of Corporate Governance* were agreed in 1999 and are intended to assist member and non-member governments in their efforts to evaluate and improve the legal, institutional and regulatory framework for corporate governance in their countries, and to provide guidance and suggestions for stock exchanges, investors, corporations and other parties that have a role in the process of developing good corporate governance.

(2004a: 7)

This framework of principles was endorsed by the World Bank, International Monetary Fund, and Asian Development Bank. If the UK 1992 Cadbury Report provided the inspiration for many other countries around the world to establish a corporate governance code, the OECD principles provided the stimulus to revise and apply more rigorously the principles of corporate governance that were becoming part of the international business and regulatory culture. The principles were the most influential global corporate governance guidelines and were designed to be acceptable within any framework of corporate governance found within any OECD member nation. However, the OECD argued the principles are not designed to be a panacea for all corporate ills and need to be seen as a fundamental starting point from which to build. The reasons why many countries were focusing on reforming corporate governance were highlighted by the OECD (1999: 2):

Corporate governance is only part of the larger economic context in which firms operate, which includes, for example, macro-economic policies, and the degree of competition in product and factor markets. The corporate governance framework also depends on the legal, regulatory and institutional

environment … While a multiplicity of factors affect the governance and decision-making processes of firms, and are important to their long term success, the Principles focus on governance problems that result from the separation of ownership and control … The degree to which corporations observe basic principles of good corporate governance is an increasingly important factor for investment decisions. Of particular relevance is the relation between corporate governance practices and the increasingly international character of investment. International flows of capital enable companies to access financing from a much larger pool of investors. If countries are to reap the full benefits of the global capital market, and if they are to attract long term 'patient' capital, corporate governance arrangements must be credible and well-understood across borders. Even if corporations do not rely primarily on foreign sources of capital, adherence to good corporate governance practices will help improve the confidence of domestic investors, may reduce the cost of capital, and ultimately induce more stable sources of financing.

Having indicated the advantages of moving from a relationship based to a rules based model of corporate governance, the OECD indicated the common elements that corporate governance framework should possess, and highlighted five broad areas of corporate governance which are essential to any sound model of governance. The five principles are directed at the rights of shareholders, the equitable treatment of shareholders, the role of stakeholders in corporate governance, disclosure and transparency, and the responsibilities of the board.

This framework of corporate governance principles was intended to have universal appeal, but there was some sub-text that they were essentially derived from the fundamentals of the market-based system, and were particularly aimed at the exponents of the insider systems with relationship based approaches, especially in the developing economies where corporate governance failure was assumed to be more likely. (In the event the next cycle of spectacular corporate governance failure occurred a lot closer to home than

anticipated.) However, the portrayal of the four essential ethical and practical elements underlying the OECD principles are more universal in their appeal:

- *Fairness*: Equitable treatment, protection against misappropriation of assets.
- *Transparency*: Timely and accurate disclosure on all material matters – finances, performance, ownership.
- *Accountability*: Effective monitoring of management by the board, and accountability of board to the company and shareholders.
- *Responsibility*: To abide by national laws and regulations, act ethically towards stakeholders.

There was considerable evidence that the OECD principles were having a significant impact, at least in terms of national regulators' acceptance and business leaders' approval across the industrial world, and in many developing economies. However, in terms of practical implementation of the principles, there was a different story. In a survey by the World Bank (2002) of fifteen corporate governance country assessments across five continents the following were the key findings:

- None of the countries assessed complied with the OECD principles in all respects, yet all countries were engaged in corporate governance reforms to bring their legal and regulatory frameworks into compliance with the OECD principles.
- Generally, there was a discrepancy between the letter of the law and actual practices. The enforcement of shareholder rights and equitable treatment of shareholders needs strengthening. Business transactions have traditionally taken place on the basis of relationships and trust. Corporate governance reform is a way to extend this trust to all market participants via enforcement of shareholder rights.
- The OECD principles assume that countries have an efficient legal and regulatory framework in place and that securities regulators have the means and capabilities to enforce the rules and regulations of their capital markets, but this is often not the case. Typically courts are under-financed, unmotivated, unclear as to how the law applies, unfamiliar with the

economic issues, or even corrupt. Securities regulators have little direct power to enforce penalties.

■ A 'menu of choice' approach to corporate governance standards provides a means for issuers and investors to choose the markets and companies that are most appropriate to their specific risk profile.

The OECD ambitious approach underestimated the difficulties of attempting to implement general guidelines across countries at different stages of economic and legal development. The legal and ethical basis of the OECD principles is based on Western legal and ethical concepts, and focuses on the governance issues arising out of the separation of ownership and control. As Iu and Batten (2001) illustrate this approach presents serious issues in developing regions such as Asia, where the separation of ownership and control substantially has not yet occurred.

> Economic liberalisation has provided the illusion of a world in which past barriers have been removed and also a world in which nations are becoming more similar. The conduct of commerce between nations on homogenous terms and conditions does not translate into homogenous cultural constructs. National identities remain. Cultural differences also remain. Thus the 'starting point' becomes the major impediment to implementing the selected international standards ... Given cultural differences between jurisdictions, concepts may not be interpreted with the same effect as originally intended. The danger, therefore, is that the fundamental characteristics, values and intentions of the original law are lost in the transfer, if interpreted without reference to the underlying context.
>
> (Iu and Batten 2001: 51–52)

Indeed the OECD was alerted to this at the Asian Corporate Governance Roundtable that 'indiscriminate mixing and matching concepts from different legal traditions, also risks producing legislation that is ineffective, ignored or distortion producing. Asia is littered with past mistakes of this kind' (Jordan 1999: 5). The OECD placed too much reliance on the introduction of a set of regulatory principles, when the accompanying cultural and behavioural changes present a much greater challenge (if they are accepted as worthy of achievement at all by people who have played little role in their construction). As the Confederation of Indian Industry (1998: 5) put it, 'effectiveness of corporate governance systems cannot merely be legislated by law ... The best results would be achieved when companies begin to treat the code not as a mere structure, but as a way of life'.

## OECD Principles (2004)

The uneven application of the Principles, and the slow process of moving from official sanction to actual implementation in many parts of the world, may have alerted the OECD to the fact that further efforts might be required if it was to achieve the universal acceptance of the guidelines it desired. However, the unforeseen and unprecedented series of corporate failures beginning with Enron and WorldCom in the United States, which for a time at least seemed highly contagious, and the dramatic intervention of the US Congress with the rapid passage of the Sarbanes–Oxley Act, caused the OECD to engage in a sudden re-evaluation of its strategy:

> Policy concerns with corporate governance issues has been driven in recent years primarily by a series of corporate scandals and failures in a number of countries. Although bankruptcies are to some extent a cyclical phenomenon, and especially so following an asset price bubble, systemic weaknesses have also been evident. This was particularly true with respect to financial disclosure and audit integrity but at a deeper level such weaknesses do raise questions about whether boards have been able to exercise independent judgement with respect to the oversight of management. The importance of preventing such weaknesses is already a key element of the Principles which were widely accepted in member countries. This raises the question as to why weaknesses were not foreseen and how implementation might have been better organized.
>
> (OECD 2004a: 4)

In a rare moment of critical reflection, the OECD dropped its normal diplomatic reserve and confronted the extensive catalogue of corporate failure due to governance disasters since the 1980s, and put this into the context of the reasons for wider business failure (Box 7.1). Though the recent events clearly had caused the OECD to examine governance failures more critically, it tended to respond to the crisis by urging more strongly the recommendations it had already developed, rather than engaging in any deeper questioning of the fundamental instability of the market based system it was essentially wedded to. While calling for greater efforts from national governments and others in meeting the challenge of evident weaknesses in corporate governance, the solution offered appears to be the more robust implementation of the OECD principles, combined with a greater adjustment to international capital market requirements:

> Since the Principles were agreed, activity in this area by member countries has surged. National principles, codes and review committees have proliferated and in some cases significant policy initiatives are either coming into place or are under consideration. A number of countries are also involved in reviewing their company law. The reasons for this activity are varied. In some cases the concern has been to 'tweak' the system and to preserve, for example, competitiveness in capital markets. In these cases countries have sometimes chosen to use codes and principles put forward on a non-governmental basis. In other cases, corporate failures and scandals have called into question the veracity of published financial information and have placed governments under pressure to also take policy initiatives of a legal or regulatory kind. Yet the question remains whether these developments in member countries are sufficient to deal with both the immediate tensions and the longer term challenges, and whether the assumptions on which action is based are adequate … The integrity of corporations, financial institutions and markets is essential to maintain confidence and economic activity, and to protect the interests of stakeholders. To maintain market integrity, the Ministers agreed to implement best practices in corporate and financial governance which 'entails an appropriate mix of incentives, balanced between government regulations and self-regulation backed by effective enforcement'.
>
> (2004: 7)

---

### Box 7.1   OECD: the Governance Debacle

Large corporate failures have often stimulated debate about corporate governance, leading to regulatory action and other reforms. In the UK the collapse of the Maxwell publishing group at the end of the 1980s stimulated the Cadbury code of 1992, and cases through the 1990s such as Polly Peck, BCCI and recently Marconi stimulated a series of further enquiries and recommendations. Widespread distress among both banks and *chaebol* in Korea in 1997 was viewed as not only macroeconomic in origin but as also reflecting governance weaknesses. In Germany the cases of Holtzman, Berliner Bank, and more recently Babcok have served the same catalytic role as did the collapse of HIH (a large insurer), Ansett Airlines and One Tel in Australia. Crédit Lyonnaise and Vivendi have raised many governance issues in France; and in Switzerland the events at Swissair have had a similar effect. Large failures of both financial and non-financial institutions in Japan have also led to regulatory responses and to legal changes. Finally, the cases of Enron, World Com and Tyco have initiated major debate and legislation in the US. At other times, large collapses (or near collapses) in some countries have either led to no systematic follow-up or to only some minor regulatory changes.

In thinking about these incidences of corporate failure, several features stand out. First, some cases are clearly related to bad

business plans (even though *ex ante* they might have appeared visionary) and to poor managerial decisions. In some instances, government policy or informal pressure and regulatory forbearance have also been a contributing factor. Poor business plans and risk management have usually become apparent as macroeconomic conditions have tightened. However, in many of the cases cited above legitimate questions have arisen about the quality of the board (including the supervisory board in Germany) and whether it was in any position to exercise independent judgement. In addition, it has sometimes appeared that the board did not demand additional information from the management, but had actually almost become a part of it. Business failures might also be due to broader forces and not to corporate governance weaknesses. Thus from the macroeconomic viewpoint some companies will often need to go out of existence, the question being how efficiently the exit process works. In part this is determined by the efficiency of the bankruptcy system, but it is also related to timely decisions by the company which are related to its corporate governance arrangements. For example, in Germany and Japan massive overcapacity in the construction sector probably cannot be reduced without companies disappearing but in many cases the situation might have been handled in a more timely fashion.

Second, some collapses have involved fraud (in the everyday sense if not the legal one) or the active cover-up and dissimulation by management, or indeed both. Enron and Worldcom are recent examples of the two categories and there is now a huge literature about these two cases. Maxwell, BCCI and Polly Peck in the UK were similar. In many cases, the fraud or cover-up in question was already illegal under existing statutes, and questions have arisen about the quality of regulatory oversight (e.g. HIH in Australia, Enron in the US). The most recent cases, but also some before, have in addition also involved, by omission or commission, auditors and external lawyers of the firm. But although sanctions were imposed in a number of cases, the problem was not viewed as systemic.

Third, pension claims have emerged as a new feature of large collapses. The Maxwell case in the UK involved the abuse of pension funds by dominant directors. In Germany, Japan and in other countries where pension liabilities are covered more or less by internal corporate provisions, incompetence or fraud against the main firm will have the same effect of endangering pension assets. The more recent failures (Enron in particular) have brought out another aspect, which is the limited possibility at times for a pension scheme to diversify. The mechanism includes lock-up provisions which force employees to continue to hold the company's stock when prudence might indicate otherwise. OECD member countries have also experienced a number of banking and insurance failures during the last decade. Such cases have often led to reviews of the regulatory system and to reform measures. In some instances (e.g. the S&L collapse in the US) criminal charges have been brought and successfully prosecuted. But apart from tighter monitoring of the 'fit and proper person' test for directors and major owners, the issue of governance does not appear to have been pursued with the same vigour as in the cases of non-financial collapses. However, this situation might now be changing. In sum, although financial and non-financial corporate failures cannot all be attributed to corporate governance deficiencies, such weaknesses have certainly played a role and contributed at least to the scale of the distress which is of added importance now given the rising value of pension liabilities. Weak corporate governance has been an important factor, and also in the banking sector. In addition, the cases cited also pointed to the need to review enforcement and regulatory oversight.

Source: OECD (2004), *Survey of Governance Trends in OECD Countries*, Paris: OECD, 9–10.

The OECD criticises the limited response to its past recommendations, and refers to 'forces which are driving governments to reconsider governance arrangements, many of which were not long ago regarded as either excellent or at least as not presenting serious policy problems'. The OECD identifies three key forces (all market based) impacting on corporate governance:

- The 'strong stock market correction' exposed some systemic weaknesses with respect to audit and disclosure and threw into question assumptions about how boards were carrying out their duties. These weaknesses also contributed to financial market instability.
- Longer-run trends in both global and domestic financial markets were bringing corporate governance arrangements under pressure to adjust.
- A growing body of research confirming that corporate governance and financial market arrangements was exerting an important influence on growth prospects, a key policy concern.

(However this explanation refuses to acknowledge that it was the insistent pressure of financial markets upon companies to demonstrate sustained performance improvement, that prompted executives to manipulate earnings, which when exposed led to a long series of corporate collapses in the US. That is, the market instead of being the solution to the problem of corporate governance, was closer to being the cause of the problem.)

Extensive consultations took place with both OECD member and non-member countries prior to the 2004 revision of the corporate governance principles, including 25 meetings of 5 regional corporate governance roundtables through which the OECD promotes corporate governance reform in partnership with the World Bank. Reflecting the great heterogeneity in both OECD and non-OECD countries, the modified principles retain a non-binding, principles-based approach, which recognises the need to adapt implementation to varying legal, economic and cultural circumstances, and identifies six key areas of corporate governance:

- *Ensuring the basis of an effective corporate governance framework*: The corporate governance framework should promote transparent and efficient markets, be consistent with the rule of law and clearly articulate the division of responsibilities among different supervisory, regulatory and enforcement authorities.
- *The rights of shareholders and key ownership function*: The corporate governance framework should protect and facilitate the exercise of shareholders' rights.
- *The equitable treatment of shareholders*: The corporate governance framework should ensure the equitable treatment of all shareholders, including minority and foreign shareholders. All shareholders should have the opportunity to obtain effective redress for violation of their rights.
- *The role of stakeholders in corporate governance*: The corporate governance framework should recognise the rights of stakeholders established by law or through mutual agreements and encourage active co-operation between corporations and stakeholders in creating wealth, jobs, and the sustainability of financially sound enterprises.
- *Disclosure and transparency*: The corporate governance framework should ensure that timely and accurate disclosure is made on all material matters regarding the corporation, including the financial situation, performance, ownership, and governance of the company.
- *The responsibilities of the board*: The corporate governance framework should ensure the strategic guidance of the company, the effective monitoring of management by the board, and the board's accountability to the company and the shareholders.

The revisions strengthened the 1999 principles in response to four areas of concern:

- ensuring the basis for an effective corporate governance framework, including effective regulatory and enforcement mechanisms;
- improving possibilities for the exercise of informed ownership by shareholders;
- strengthening of board oversight of management; and
- increasing attention to conflicts of interest through enhanced disclosure and transparency.

SEVEN

The emphasis is now greater on ensuring the wider regulatory framework actually works, without which the governance principles will have little effect: the chair of the OECD steering group, Veronique Ingram of the Australian Treasury, maintained 'The revised Principles emphasise the importance of a regulatory framework in corporate governance that promotes efficient markets, facilitates effective enforcement and clearly defines the responsibilities between different supervisory, regulatory and enforcement authorities. They also emphasise the need to ensure transparent lines of management responsibility within companies so as to make boards and management truly accountable'.

The OECD continued to maintain a non-binding, principles based approach, recognising – at least formally – the need to adapt the recommendations to a wide range of cultural, legal and economic circumstances in the 30 member OECD countries and beyond. However, there is an attempt to provide more guidance on how the principles can be implemented and enforced by reference to evolving practice.

With regard to investors the aim is to lower the cost and increase the incentive to make informed use of ownership rights. Institutional investors are called on to disclose their corporate governance policies, how they decide on the use of their voting rights and how they manage conflicts of interest that may compromise their voting. It is suggested that restrictions on consultations between shareholders about their voting intentions should be eased to reduce the cost of informed ownership. The rights of shareholders have strengthened in the revised principles:

■ Shareholders should be able to remove board members and participate in the nomination and election processes.
■ Shareholders should also be able to make their views known about the executive and board remuneration policy of the company, and any equity component should be subject to their approval.

With regard to the board, its responsibilities have been more clearly specified to address corporate ethics, compliance with laws and standards, and oversight of internal control systems covering financial reporting, all of which the OECD suggests have at one time or another appeared weak:

■ The duties and responsibilities of the board have been clarified as *fiduciary* in nature, which is particularly important where company groups are concerned.
■ The principle covering board independence and objectivity has been extended to avoid conflicts of interest and to cover situations characterised by block and controlling shareholders.

An effective corporate governance framework should promote transparent and efficient markets the OECD argues, be consistent with the rule of law, and clearly articulate the division of responsibilities among different supervisory, regulatory and enforcement authorities. With regard to the exercise of ownership, there is widespread agreement that corporate governance weaknesses in many OECD countries can be attributed to an important extent to a lack of effective ownership participation which the OECD now seeks to encourage. Finally, with reference to dealing with conflicts, the OECD argues one of the most striking lessons of recent years is that conflicts of interest are widespread and can be quite pernicious.

For example, many countries have witnessed insider boards that have become part of management, rather than an active monitor of its performance. In other cases, boards appear to act simply as rubber stamps, responding to the wishes of a controlling shareholder. In a number of cases controlling shareholders have pursued their interests at the expense of minority shareholders. Complex financial institutions and complex corporate structures around the world have also thrown into stark relief the question of conflicts of interest, which have been most apparent in some brokerage research and funds management.

(Jesovar and Kirkpatrick 2005: 128)

Conflicts of interest, which can and often do lead to actions to the detriment of shareholders, investors and stakeholders, take many different

forms, so they are dealt with in several chapters of the principles. In general, the principles now advocate not only disclosure, but also statements by the parties involved as to how the conflict is being managed. The special conflicts between controlling shareholders and minority shareholders, which are particularly pronounced in a number of developing and emerging market economies, are also explicitly addressed. The provisions include the following:

- the principles covering disclosure have been strengthened, particularly with respect to conflicts of interest and related-party transactions;
- a new principle recognises the role of various providers of corporate information, such as rating agencies and analysts, whose advice should not be compromised by conflicts of interest;
- the duties of the auditor have been strengthened, and include accountability to shareholders and a duty to the company to exercise due professional care in the conduct of the audit. Greater attention is paid to ensuring auditor independence, including steps to manage and minimise potential conflicts of interest; and
- greater attention is paid to the protection of minority shareholder rights.

In conclusion the revised OECD principles highlight many pressing and unresolved problems of corporate governance, and offer much helpful policy guidance. However, an inherent weakness in the approach of the OECD is to attempt simultaneously, in the same policy document, to deal with the critical issues arising out of the post-Enron fallout in the Anglo-American region on the one hand, and to address the rather different set of fundamental governance issues facing the developing world on the other hand. The OECD corporate governance principles have had considerable influence on the advance of policy and practice in corporate governance in both the developed and the developing world; however, the impact may have been more beneficial if the different stages of economic and regulatory development across countries and regions might have been more explicitly recognised.

## International development of corporate governance standards

The OECD was joined in its efforts to raise the standard of corporate governance by the World Bank, Asian Development Bank, UN and other international agencies, in a collective drive to equip companies throughout the world with the governance structures and processes that might assist their growth and success, but also increase their chance of attracting capital investment from increasingly well-informed markets (Figure 7.6). This extensive series of international reports did offer the chance to make a more focused address to the specific governance problems of the different regions of the world. Among the influential publications of policy guidelines were the following.

1 Commonwealth Association for Corporate Governance (1999), *Principles for Corporate Governance in the Commonwealth*: The report contains guidelines intended to facilitate best business practice and behaviour, whether to the private-sector or state-owned enterprises. These guidelines are neither mandatory nor prescriptive and have been designed as evolutionary in concept. The guidelines are a 'continuum', remaining flexible and responsive to further developments of corporate governance in the global economy.

2 European Bank for Reconstruction and Development (1999), *Corporate Governance: Foundation for Capital Flows*: This special issue of the EBRD journal 'Law in Transition' focuses on corporate governance and its role in managing capital flows, with specific reference to the damaged economies of Eastern Europe. As an international financial institution the EBRD needed to satisfy itself that organisations in receipt of bank financing are properly organised and their treatment of shareholders is transparent and complies with the legislation.

3 World Bank (2000), *Corporate Governance: A Framework for Implementation*: This report develops a framework for corporate governance reform based largely on the operational experience of the World Bank Group and practitioners in the field. This framework is used to identify

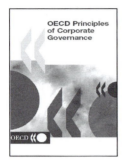

| OECD Principles of Corporate Governance 1999–2004 | 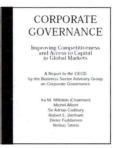 |

| OECD Business Sector Advisory Group 1998 |

| Commonwealth Association for Corporate Governance 1999 | European Bank for Reconstruction and Development 1999 |

| APEC & Pacific Economic Co-operation Council 2001 | 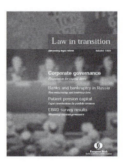 |

| United Nations Economic Commission for Africa 2002 |

| Asian Development Bank Principles for Business Enterprises 2003 | European Commission of Corporate Governance 2003 |

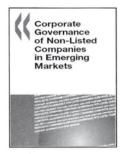

| OECD Guidelines on Corporate Governance of state-owned Enterprises 2005 |  |

| Corporate Governance of Non-listed companies in Emerging markets 2006 |

**Figure 7.6** Development of international principles of corporate governance guidelines.

the major elements and processes of reform required in emerging market economies and the contribution the World Bank Group, together with its partners, can make to the objective of promoting enterprise and accountability.

4 APEC & Pacific Economic Co-operation Council (2001), *Guidelines for Good Corporate Governance Practice*: This report was written in the wake of the 1997 East Asian Crisis. The crisis underscored the critical importance of

structural reforms in the governance of the business enterprise. The guidelines provide a non-binding and voluntary framework for the implementation of global best practices, consistent with core OECD principles. The focus of these guidelines is on the role of the board of directors in ensuring sound corporate governance practices.

5 United Nations Economic Commission for Africa (2002), *Guidelines for Enhancing Good Economic and Corporate Governance in Africa*: These guidelines are intended to provide a framework of policies, processes, instruments, codes, standards, indicators, best practices and enforcement mechanisms that can be adopted and/or adapted by African countries to demonstrate their commitment to good economic and corporate governance practices.

6 Asian Development Bank (2003), *Corporate Governance Principles for Business Enterprises*: This report contains principles aimed at businesses. The objectives of the principles are to assist: (a) enterprises' design and implement their own corporate governance guidelines by benchmarking their practices against these principles, (b) domestic and institutional investors, fund managers as well as the ADB, in their quest for excellence in corporate governance in investee enterprises, and (c) governments in designing corporate governance regulations.

7 European Commission (2003), *Modernising Company Law and Enhancing Corporate Governance*: This directive is aimed at a modern, dynamic, interconnected industrialised society. A flexible company law, and corporate governance framework will enhance the real economy. The report outlines why the European regulatory framework for company law and corporate governance needs to be modernised. The main objectives are to strengthen shareholder rights and foster the efficiency and competitiveness of business.

8 OECD (2005), *Guidelines on Corporate Governance of State-Owned Enterprises*: These extend the guidelines on corporate governance to the state-owned sector, focusing on the 'complex undertaking' of finding a balance between the state's responsibility for actively exercising its ownership functions, such as the nomination and election of the board, while at the same time refraining from imposing undue political interference in the management of the company. Also focuses on how a level playing field can be ensured for private-sector companies which are competing with state-owned enterprises.

9 OECD (2006), *Corporate Governance of Non-Listed Companies in Emerging Markets*: This publication provides policy-makers, board members managers, equity providers, creditors and other stakeholders an overview of the issues to be addressed in establishing good corporate governance of non-listed companies. While the corporate governance debate has mostly focused on listed companies with dispersed shareholdings, issues such as financial transparency, the role of access to outside capital and conflict resolution are just as important for non-listed and family controlled companies which play a major role in many economies.

On the whole, all of these reports stay close to the OECD line of the importance of reforming corporate governance to be able to attract global capital at lower rates and create better companies as a result. The World Bank (2000) report though broke new ground in indicating why accountability and integrity in corporate governance has an important role to play in assisting the economic development of poor countries where domestic investors needed to be protected.

'While the recent economic and financial crises in East Asia and elsewhere had a multitude of underlying causes, weak corporate governance has consistently been seen as a major contributor that needs to be addressed to revive investor confidence and decrease the impact and likelihood of future shocks. Good corporate governance is not only about its increasing importance to international investors but also its protection of domestic investors. Unlike international investors who have sophisticated instruments to diversify their overall portfolio risk, domestic investors are often captive to local markets and risk losing their life's savings when transparency is lacking and governance systems are defective. In an environment that does not protect minority shareholders' rights, these investors cannot risk investing in corporations directly, thus limiting their ability and potential to participate in or contribute to their

economy's development. As a group, however, they represent a large pool of stable, long-term resources critical to the development process'. (World Bank 2000).

Official reports by international agencies were supplemented by many other corporate governance reports by private international organisations, which reflected some particular viewpoint, or attempted to bring together trends and developments in particular regions or industries and suggest the directions for further development. Among the more influential of these reports and guidelines on corporate governance by international organisations were the following:

1 Asian Corporate Governance Association (2000), *Building Stronger Boards and Companies in Asia*: This report provides a snapshot of corporate governance policies and practices around Asia. The report finds that Asian corporate governance does not entirely follow either the Anglo-American model or German model. Local business practices are the main determinants of Asian corporate behaviour.

2 New York Stock Exchange (2003), *Corporate Governance Rules*: These rules apply to companies listed on NYSE. These rules highlight the importance of independent directors. Listed companies must have a majority of independent directors, and a majority of them must sit on nominating, audit and remuneration committees. Because many of the largest global companies are listed on the NYSE, regardless of where their company registration is, and their headquarters are based, inevitably the NYSE rules have an international, not simply national, influence.

3 Business Roundtable (2005), *Principles of Corporate Governance*: This report by an influential group of US business leaders contains 'principles that should help guide the ongoing advancement of corporate governance practices and advance the ability of public corporations to compete, create jobs and generate economic growth'.

4 International Corporate Governance Network (2005), *Statement on Global Corporate Governance Principles*: The purpose of ICGN is to provide a network for the exchange of views and information about corporate governance issues internationally for investment institutions, and for the development of corporate governance guidelines. This statement reflects and endorses the revision of the OECD Principles in 2004, and suggests practical guidance on implementation from an investor's perspective.

5 Institutional Shareholder Services (2006), *International Corporate Governance Policy Update*: The ISS produces policy updates for US and international markets for institutional investors, as an indication of the way they will vote in AGMs, and recommend others to vote. The 2006 updates include ISS positions on boards in Europe and South Africa, anti-takeover devices in Japan, and audit committees in South Korea.

Such a wide panoply of advocacy carries more than the suggestion of a universal consensus regarding the necessary advance of international corporate governance standards. However, dissident voices do exist. The critique of the precedence given to market forces in the international corporate governance movement is widespread in Europe (Rhodes and Apeldoorn 1998; Rebevioux 2000; Lane 2003; Cernat 2004). There is also an extensive literature suggesting the present emphasis on corporate governance reform along international standards in the developing world may represent a misplaced order of priorities (Clarke and dela Rama 2006). Soederberg offers the most strenuous objections insisting the standardisation of corporate governance codes and practices is part of a new disciplinary landscape in the developing world imposed by powerful international agencies:

The disciplinary force of shareholder activism is strengthened institutionally by the G7 nexus, specifically the OECD, Standard and Poors, the World Bank and ADB ... One step toward this goal is the act of universalising standards, such as corporate governance, which in effect serves to recreate the existing power structures of the neo-liberal market-centric system ... While it is too early to decipher the effects of the efforts to build a new international financial architecture, through, for example, the standardisation of corporate governance, it is not too soon to dispel the common-sense assumption that these strategies are based on universal

values ... Corporate governance in its present form and content, represents specific material interests.

(2003: 23–24)

In a more measured analysis, Stiglitz (2003), formerly the chief economist of the World Bank, emphasises the importance of addressing the multi-dimensional nature of the problems of developing economies including introducing integrated policies for finance, governance, technology, research and education, rather than focusing on one element, if progress is to be made, whilst avoiding the capital market liberalisation that can lead to instability in these vulnerable economies (and which is often associated with the need to attract international investment). Grindle (2004) considering the general governance demands made of developing countries calls for a 'more nuanced understanding of the evolutions of institutions and government capabilities; being explicit about trade-offs and priorities in a world in which all good things cannot be pursued at once; learning about what's working instead of focusing solely on governance gaps; and grounding action in the contextual realities of each country' (2004: 525).

However, rather than develop a more nuanced understanding of the different strengths and weaknesses of the various systems of corporate governance, and how the progress of reform could be carefully timed to match wider institutional and economic developments, and asking the questions about which systems work best in which contexts for what purposes, there has instead been a rush to recognise an emerging convergence in international corporate governance, with the implication the most sensible thing to do is simply to adapt as quickly as possible entirely to this self-evident consensus.

## CONVERGENCE OF CORPORATE GOVERNANCE

Underlying the energy and apparent variety of the corporate governance guidelines and policy documents appearing in such profusion since the 1990s is an implicit but confident sense that an optimal corporate governance model is indeed emerging: 'An optimal model with dispersed ownership and shareholder foci ... The OECD and World Bank promote corporate governance reform ... Influenced by financial economists and are generally promoting market capitalism with a *law matters* approach, although for political reasons, they do not advocate too strongly market capitalism and allow for other corporate governance systems (i.e. concentrated ownership)' (Pinto 2005: 26–27).

Other authorities are less diplomatic in announcing the superiority of the Anglo-American approach that other systems must inevitably converge towards. Two eminent US law school professors, Hansmann and Kraakman, in an article prophetically entitled *The End of History for Corporate Law* lead the charge of the convergence determinists:

Despite very real differences in the corporate systems, the deeper tendency is towards convergence, as it has been since the nineteenth century. The core legal features of the corporate form were already well established in advanced jurisdictions one hundred years ago, at the turn of the twentieth century. Although there remained considerable room for variation in governance practices and in the fine structure of corporate law throughout the twentieth century, the pressures for further convergence are now rapidly growing. Chief among these pressures is the recent dominance of a shareholder-centred ideology of corporate law among the business, government and legal entities in key commercial jurisdictions. There is no longer any serious competitor to the view that corporate law should principally strive to increase long-term shareholder value. This emergent consensus has already profoundly affected corporate governance practices throughout the world. It is only a matter of time before its influence is felt in the reform of corporate law as well.

(2001: 1)

The irony of this profoundly ideological claim (the most recent in a long historical lineage of similar appeals), is that it attempts to enforce the consensus it claims exists, by crowding out any

possibility of alternatives. This is not an isolated example, but the dominant approach of much legal and financial discussion in the United States, whereas McDonnell insists the prevailing view is: 'The American system works better and that the other countries are in the process of converging to the American system. Though there is some dissent from this position, the main debate has been over why countries outside the United States have persisted for so long in their benighted systems and what form their convergence to the American way will take. The scholarly discussion has converged too quickly on the convergence answer' (2002: 2).

It is worth asking by what standards or criteria a system of corporate governance may be defined as 'optimal'? Most economic analyses simply substitute 'efficient' for optimal, but McDonnell offers three relevant values:

1 efficiency;
2 equity;
3 participation.

In considering efficiency there is the question of: how well the governance system solves agency problems; how well the system facilitates large scale coordination problems; how well the systems encourage long term innovation; and how they impose different levels of risk on the participants. Distributional equity is another important value, but again is difficult to measure. For many, distributional equity suggests an increased equality of income and wealth, but others find this less compelling. In some instances, equity may conflict with efficiency: it could be argued the US system is more efficient, but inevitably results in greater inequality. Finally, there is the value of participation, both in terms of any contribution this may make to the success of the enterprise, and as an end in itself in enhancing the ability and self-esteem of people. Corporate governance systems affect the level of participation in decision-making very directly, whether encouraging or disallowing active participation in enterprise decision-making (McDonnell 2002: 4).

Arguably each of these values is of great importance, and the precise balance between them is part of the choice of what kind of corporate governance system is adopted. Yet there

appears increasingly less opportunity to exercise this choice:

> The universe of theoretical possibilities is much richer than a dominant strand of the literature suggests, and we are currently far short of the sort of empirical evidence that might help us sort out these possibilities. Most commentators have focused on efficiency to the exclusion of other values. Moreover, even if convergence occurs, there is a possibility that we will not converge on the best system. Even if we converge to the current best system, convergence still may not be desirable
>
> (McDonnell 2002: 2)

## History and politics

In the past, these critical political choices on which system of governance provides the most value in terms of efficiency, equity and participation have been made and defended. Mark Roe's (1994, 2003) path dependence thesis rests on how political forces in America, anxious about the influence of concentrated financial or industrial monopolies, resisted any effort at concentration of ownership or ownership through financial institutions, resulting in dispersed ownership. In contrast, European social democracy has tended to favour other stakeholder interests, particularly labour, as a system that promotes welfare among all citizens and attempts to prevent wide disparities. In turn this can be viewed as a reaction to the historical rise of fascism and communism (Pinto 2005: 22). Fligstein and Freeland (1995) adopt a similar historical view that the form of governance is a result of wider political and institutional developments:

1 the timing of entry into industrialisation and the institutionalisation of that process;
2 the role of states in regulating property rights and the rules of competition between firms; and
3 the social organisation of national elites (1995: 21).

In this way characteristic institutions of the US economy can be traced back to distinctive political and regulatory intervention, resulting for example in weak banks, diversified companies,

and the dominance of the diversified (M-form) corporations. In contrast in Europe and Japan the regulatory environment encouraged a very different approach:

> Regulatory policy in the United States had the unintended consequence of pushing U.S. companies in the direction of unrelated diversification, whereas in Germany and Japan it continued on a pre-war trajectory of discouraging mergers in favour of cartels and of promoting corporate growth through internal expansion rather than acquisitions. In other words, modern regulatory policy in the U.S. produced corporations who relied on markets to acquire ideas and talent, whereas in Germany and Japan it produced corporations whose primary emphasis was on production and on the internal generation of ideas through development of human capital and organizational learning. The implications for corporate governance are straightforward: corporations favour shareholders in the U.S. so as to obtain capital for diversification and acquisitions; they favour managers and employees in Germany and Japan so as to create internal organizational competencies.
>
> (Jacoby 2001: 8)

A very different reading of these events is offered by Rajan and Zingales (2003), who argue that widely dispersed shareholders is related to the development of liquid securities markets and the openness to outside investments, while it was not social democracy but protectionism that kept European and Japanese markets closed from competition with concentrated ownership. As financial economists they favour the globalisation route to open market based competition, which they see as the way to unsettling local elites, achieving dispersed ownership, raising capital, and improving corporate governance.

## Law and regulation

Following a different line of analysis the substantial empirical evidence of La Porta *et al.* (1998, 1999, 2000, 2002) concerning countries with dispersed and concentrated ownership, which demonstrates differences in the legal protection of shareholders, was very influential. In many countries without adequate laws guaranteeing dispersed shareholder rights, the only alternative appeared to maintain control through concentrated ownership. This led to the conclusion the law determined the ownership structure and system of corporate finance and governance. Jurisdictions where the law was more protective encouraged the emergence of more dispersed ownership (Pinto 2005: 19).

Coffee (2001) extends La Porta *et al.*'s acceptance that in the common law system there was greater flexibility of response to new developments offering better protection to shareholders, to the argument that the critical role of the decentralised character of common law institutions was to facilitate the rise of both private and semi-private self-regulatory bodies in the US and UK. In contrast in civil law systems the state maintained a restrictive monopoly over law-making institutions (for example in the early intrusion of the French government into the affairs of the Paris Bourse involving the Ministry of Finance approving all new listings). Coffee concludes that it was market institutions that demanded legal protection rather than the other way around:

> The cause and effect sequence posited by the La Porta *et al.* thesis may in effect read history backwards. They argue that strong markets require strong mandatory rules as a precondition. Although there is little evidence that strong legal rules encouraged the development of either the New York or London Stock Exchanges (and there is at least some evidence that strong legal rules hindered the growth of the Paris Bourse), the reverse does seem to be true: strong markets do create a demand for stronger legal rules. Both in the U.S. and the U.K., as liquid securities markets developed and dispersed ownership became prevalent, a new political constituency developed that desired legal rules capable of filling in the inevitable enforcement gaps that self-regulation left. Both the federal securities laws passed in the 1930's in the U.S. and the Company Act amendments adopted in the late 1940's in the U.K. were a response to this demand (and both were passed by essentially

'social democratic' administrations seeking to protect public securities markets). Eventually, as markets have matured across Europe, similar forces have led to the similar creation of European parallels to the SEC. In each case, law appears to be responding to changes in the market, not consciously leading it.

(Coffee 2001: 6)

## Culture: deep causation

In the search for explanations, some have attempted a philosophical approach including Fukuyama who conceives of business organisations as the product of trust, and the different governance systems as built of different forms of trust relations (1996).

Regarding the social foundations and development of ownership structures and the law, other writers have examined the correlations between law and culture. Licht (2001) examines the relevance of national culture to corporate governance and securities regulation, and explores the relationship between different cultural types and the law: 'A nation's culture can be perceived as the mother of all path dependencies. Figuratively, it means that a nation's culture might be more persistent than other factors believed to induce path dependence. Substantively, a nation's unique set of cultural values might indeed affect – in a chain of causality – the development of that nation's laws in general and its corporate governance system in particular' (2001: 149).

In working towards a cross-cultural theory of corporate governance systems, Licht (2001) demonstrate that corporate governance laws exhibit systematic cultural characteristics.

A comparison between a taxonomy of corporate governance regimes according to legal families ('the legal approach') and a classification of countries according to their shared cultural values demonstrates that the legal approach provides only a partial, if not misleading, depiction of the universe of corporate governance regimes. Dividing shareholder protection regimes according to groups of culturally similar nations is informative. The evidence corroborates the uniqueness of common law

origin regimes in better protecting minority shareholders. However, statutes in the English Speaking cultural region offer levels of protection to creditors similar to the laws in the Western European or Latin American regions. Our findings cast doubt on the alleged supremacy of common law regimes in protecting creditors and, therefore, investors in general. Finally, we find that analyses of corporate governance laws in Far Eastern countries, a distinct cultural region, would benefit from combining an approach that draws on cultural value dimensions and one that draws on legal families.

(Licht 2001: 32)

Licht *et al.* conclude that corporations are embedded within larger socio-cultural settings in which they are incorporated and operate. Cultural values are influential in determining the types of legal regimes perceived and accepted as legitimate in any country, and serve as a guide to legislators. Hence cultural values may impede legal reforms that conflict with them, and the naivety underlying quick-fix suggestions for corporate law reform (2001: 33–34).

Culture also influences what are perceived as the maximands of corporate governance – for example in the debate over stockholders' versus stakeholders' interests as the ultimate objective of the corporation: 'The corporate governance problem therefore is not one of maximising over a single factor (the maximand). Rather, it calls for optimising over several factors simultaneously' (Licht 2003: 5). Berglof and von Thadden (1999) suggest the economic approach to corporate governance should be generalised to a model of multilateral interactions among a number of different stakeholders. They argue that though protection of shareholder interests may be important, it may not be sufficient for sustainable development, particularly in transitional economies. Licht concludes: 'Every theory of corporate governance is at heart a theory of power. In this view, the corporation is a nexus of power relationships more than a nexus of contracts. The corporate setting is rife with agency relationships in which certain parties have the ability (power) unilaterally to affect the interests of other parties notwithstanding pre-existing contractual arrangements. In the present

context, corporate fiduciaries are entrusted with the power to weigh and prefer the interests of certain constituencies to the interests of others (beyond their own self-interest). Given the current limitations of economic theory, progress in the analysis of the maximands of corporate governance may be achieved by drawing on additional sources of knowledge' (Licht 2003: 6).

## Institutional complementarities

A further development of the path dependence thesis, is the emphasis on the interdependence of economic and social institutions: 'Corporate governance consists not simply of *elements* but of *systems* … Transplanting some of the formal elements without regard for the institutional complements may lead to serious problems later, and these problems may impede, or reverse, convergence' (Gordon and Roe 2004: 6). Optimal corporate governance mechanisms are contextual and may vary by industries and activities. Identifying what constitutes good corporate governance practice is complex, and cannot be templated into a single form. One needs to identify the strengths and weaknesses in the system but also the underlying conditions which the system is dependent upon (Pinto 2005: 31; Maher and Andersson 2000). The institutions that compose the system of corporate governance and complement each other consist not just of the law, finance and ownership structure.

Complementarities may extend to such things as labour relations and managerial incentive systems. In Germany and Japan the corporation's long term relations with banks, customers, and suppliers, facilitates long term commitments to employees. The commitment to permanency promotes extensive firm-specific training, which contributes to flexible specialisation in the production of high quality goods. In contrast in the United States employer training investments are lower than in Japan and Germany, employees are more mobile, and there is less firm-specific skill development. Similarly, in the US fluid managerial labour markets make it easier for ousted managers to find new jobs after a hostile takeover. In contrast in Japan management talent is carefully evaluated over a long period of time through career employment and managerial promotion systems. Jacoby contends 'It is difficult to disentangle the exogenous initial conditions that established a path from the *ex post* adaptations … What's most likely to be the case is that capital markets, labour markets, legal regulations, and corporate norms co-evolved from a set of initial conditions' (2001: 17). He continues with a warning to those who might wish to randomly transplant particular institutional practices into other countries:

Given institutional complementarities and path dependence, it's difficult for one country to borrow a particular practice and expect it to perform similarly when transplanted to a different context. Two examples: First, despite numerous calls for the Japanese to do more in the way of venture capital, the fact is that Japan lacks the fluid labor markets, legal expertise, and equity-related compensation schemes that are the underpinnings of the U.S. venture-capital approach. The Japanese nevertheless do have high rates of innovation, but they achieve it via corporate spin-offs and big-company funding rather than venture capital. Second, were the Japanese or Germans to adopt a U.S.-style corporate governance approach that relies on takeovers to mitigate agency problems, it would prove highly disruptive of managerial incentive and selection systems presently in place. Hostile takeovers also would be disruptive of relations with suppliers and key customers, a substantial portion of which exist on a long term basis. In Germany and, especially, in Japan, there is less vertical integration of industrial companies than in the United States or the United Kingdom. Rather than rely primarily on arms-length contracts to protect suppliers and purchasers from opportunism, there is heavy use of relational contracting based on personal ties, trust, and reputation. Personal ties are supported by lifetime employment; the business relations are buttressed by cross-share holding. In short, imitation across path-dependent systems is inhibited by the cost of having to change a host of complementary practices that make an institution effective in a particular national system.

(Jacoby 2001: 18)

Another way of understanding this, Jacoby suggests, is through the concept of multiple equilibria, which leads to the conclusion there is no best way of designing institutions to support stability and growth in advanced industrial countries:

> Multiple equilibria can arise and persist due to path dependence, institutional complementarities, bounded rationality, and comparative advantage. Sometimes multiple equilibria involve functionally similar but operationally distinctive institutions, such as the use of big firms as incubators in Japan versus the U.S. approach of incubation via start-ups and venture capital. Other times different institutions create qualitatively different outcomes. That is, a set of institutions, including those of corporate governance, may be better at facilitating certain kinds of business strategies and not others. Companies – and the countries in which they are embedded – can then secure international markets by specializing in those advantageous business strategies because foreign competitors will have difficulty imitating them. For example, the emphasis on specific human capital in Germany and Japan is supportive of production based technological learning, incremental innovation, and high quality production, all areas in which those economies have specialized. By contrast, the U.S. emphasis on resource mobility and on high short-term rewards directs resources to big-bang technological breakthroughs. In short, there are substantial gains to be reaped from sustaining institutional diversity and competing internationally on that basis.
>
> (Jacoby 2001: 25)

The discussion of corporate governance is often framed in static efficiency terms, Jacoby contends, as if it was possible to measure the comparative performance of national governance institutions in a static framework. This is inadequate for understanding the dynamic properties of governance systems, especially concerning innovation and long term growth. 'When there are multiple equilibria and bounded rationality regarding what constitutes an institutional optimum, we are operating in the world of the second best. In that world, there is no reason to believe that

revamping a governance system will necessarily move an economy closer to an economic optimum. The economic case for the superiority of Anglo-American governance – and of the Anglo-American version of "free markets" as we know them, as opposed to a theoretical ideal – is actually rather weak' (Jacoby 2001: 27).

## Rushing towards convergence

For Hansmann and Kraakman convergence of corporate governance systems towards the shareholder-oriented model is not only desirable and inevitable, it has already happened. They boldly confirm:

> The triumph of the shareholder-oriented model of the corporation over its principal competitors is now assured, even if it was problematic as recently as twenty-five years ago. Logic alone did not establish the superiority of this standard model or of the prescriptive rules that it implies, which establish a strong corporate management with duties to serve the interests of shareholders alone, as well as strong minority shareholder protections. Rather, the standard model earned its position as the dominant model of the large corporation the hard way, by out-competing during the post-World War II period the three alternative models of corporate governance: the managerialist model, the labour-oriented model, and the state-oriented model.
>
> (2001: 16)

For Hansmann and Kraakman alternative systems are not viable competitively, only the lack of product market competition has kept them alive, and as global competitive pressures increase any continuing viability of alternative models will be eliminated, encouraging the ideological and political consensus in favour of the shareholder model.

Hansmann and Kraakman dismiss the three rivals they set up for the victorious shareholder model. The managerialist model is associated with the US in the 1950s and 1960s, when it was thought professional managers could serve as disinterested technocratic fiduciaries who would

guide the business corporation in the interests of the general public. According to Hansmann and Kraakman this model of social benevolence collapsed into self-serving managerialism, with significant resource misallocation, imperilling the competitiveness of the model and accounting for its replacement by the shareholder driven model in the US (Gordon and Roe 2004).

The labour-oriented model exemplified by German co-determination, but manifest in many other countries, possesses governance structures amplifying the representation of labour, which Hansmann and Kraakman claim are inefficient because of the heterogeneity of interests among employees themselves, and between employees and shareholders. Firms with this inherent competition of interests would inevitably lose out in product market competition. Finally the state-oriented model associated with France or Germany entails a large state role in corporate affairs through ownership or state bureaucratic engagement with firm managers, allowing elite guidance of private enterprise in the public interest. Hansmann and Kraakman argue this corporatist model has been discredited because of the poor performance of socialist economies (Gordon and Roe 2004).

At the height of the NASDAQ boom when Hansmann and Kraakman wrote their visionary article it might have appeared that the shareholder model in its US manifestation was certainly globally hegemonic in all of its manifestations. However the post-Enron world is less easily convinced of the inevitable and universal superiority of the US model of governance, and Hansmann and Kraakman may have written off the prospects of Japan and Europe a little too presumptuously. To take some examples: firstly as Toyota has consolidated its grasp of the global car market with technological supremacy (leaders in fuel-cell and hybrid engineering), and by 2005 Toyota at $134 billion had a larger market capitalisation than General Motors ($16 billion), Ford ($19 billion) and DaimlerChrysler ($45 billion) combined. Meanwhile GM and Ford were engaged in large scale restructuring and downsizing (GM announcing 113,000 redundancies in March 2006 the largest number ever by any corporation), and it was feared both companies were not far from facing

Chapter 11 bankruptcy due to their legacy costs in pensions and health care from another more profitable and less responsible era.

Secondly, the Toulouse based Airbus founded as a state sponsored consortium of aerospace companies drawn from several European countries leading with a strong customer focus and innovative designs, went from being a newcomer in the global civilian aerospace market in the 1970s to becoming the leader by 2005. With a string of technological 'firsts' including the first twin aisle twin engine commercial jet, the first 'fly-by-wire' commercial aircraft, and A380 first double-decker aircraft with 550 passengers, Airbus has captured the imagination of the industry. In contrast the long established former world leader Boeing, though it was responsible for many of the early innovations in civilian aircraft, and consolidated its position of dominance with a string of acquisitions of other aerospace manufacturers in the last ten years, has struggled to sustain its technological edge.

Finally, after some time in the doldrums the industrial powerhouse of Germany is regaining its ascendancy, becoming the world's leading exporter in 2005 with $970.7 billion, followed by the United States with $904.3 billion, China with $762 billion and Japan with $595.8 billion. This industrial renaissance was led by the *Mittelstand*, the small and medium sized family companies that composed the majority of German industry, with a focus on exports leading to strong growth. Eberhard Veit, chief executive of Festo, a leader in automation technology, explained the decision to invest for the long term in this bionic products business, meant growth of 5 to 10 per annum. 'We have growth every year, which is better than having peaks and troughs, because it motivates workers. We have brought 100 new products to the Hanover Messe (the largest industrial trade fare in the world), and that certainly would not be done at a listed group' (*Financial Times*, 25 April 2006). None of these graphic illustrations offers much support for Hansmann and Kraakman's messianic vision of the innate advantages of the shareholder value approach in international competition, the best that could be salvaged from their over-confident thesis, is that the different corporate governance systems may be better at doing different things.

As Douglas Branson concludes regarding the globalisation and convergence debate, 'seldom will one see scholarship and advocacy that is as culturally and economically insensitive, and condescending, as is the global convergence advocacy scholarship that the elites in United States academy have been throwing over the transom. Those elites have oversold an idea that has little grounding in true global reality' (2004: 276). Bebchuk and Roe's (2004) view still holds that neither shareholder primacy nor dispersed ownership will easily converge. Path dependence has evolved established structures not easily transformed, and complementary institutions make it more difficult to do so. 'Thus keeping existing systems may in fact be an efficient result. This lack of convergence allows for diversity and suggests that globalisation will not easily change the models' (Pinto 2005: 29).

## DIVERSITY IN CORPORATE GOVERNANCE

A more realistic global perspective than the convergence thesis is that there will continue to be considerable diversity both in the forms of corporate governance around the world. Different traditions, values and objectives will undoubtedly continue to produce different outcomes in governance, which will relate closely to the choices and preferences people exercise in engaging in business activity. If there is convergence of corporate governance, it could be to a variety of different forms, and it is likely there will be divergence away from the shareholder oriented Anglo-American model, as there will be convergence towards it.

A surprising claim of Thomsen (2003) is that as US and UK board structures adopt more actively a committee structure with subcommittees of independent outsiders for the key committees of remuneration, auditing and nomination, which the SEC and NYSE insist upon in the US, and which is a central part of the Combined Code in the UK, there are elements of a two tier system of control, which is also implicit in the full separation of the CEO and chair's role. Certainly boards of directors in the US and UK in recent years have felt a more immediate responsibility to recognise

a wider range of relevant constituencies as stakeholder perspectives have once again become a more prominent part of corporate life. In US firms the spread of equity based compensation, recognition of the growing importance of intellectual capital, and the adoption of high performance work practices, have all reemphasised the importance of human capital in a context where previously labour was marginalised in the interests of a single minded shareholder ethos (Jacoby 2001: 26). It is ironic that as European and Japanese listed corporations are being forced to recognise the importance of shareholder value, Anglo-American corporations are being sharply reminded of their social responsibilities (Figure 7.7).

Thomsen illustrates the transition from a shareholder to a stakeholder view with the symbolic change in rhetoric of the Coca-Cola company from an earlier mission statement: 'At the Coca-Cola Company our publicly stated mission is to create value over time for the owners of our business. In fact, in our society, that is the mission of any business: to create value for its owners'. To a more recent statement by its President, 'Fundamentally, the Coca-Cola company, is built on a deep and abiding relationship of trust between it and all its constituents: bottlers … customers … consumers … shareowners. … employees … suppliers … and the very communities of which successful companies are an integral part. That trust must be nurtured and maintained on a daily basis' (2001: 313). The widespread adoption among leading Anglo-American corporations of triple bottom line reporting, publishing social and environmental reports alongside their financial reports, and actively demonstrating their corporate social responsibility in other more practical ways, suggests this is more than simply a rhetorical change. The formal adoption of *enlightened* shareholder value in the UK Companies Act indicates a significant move forwards from the more naked pursuit of shareholder value.

Further unlikely, but nonetheless real, evidence that the United States system could in some important ways converging towards the European model is unearthed by Thomsen (2003). Firstly an unanticipated consequence of the increasing use of executive stock options in the US has caused a degree of reintegration of ownership and control. Holderness *et al.* (1999) compared

**Figure 7.7** Corporate governance objectives.

Source: Clarke, T. (2006).

a comprehensive cross-section of 1,500 publicly traded US firms in 1935 with a modern benchmark of more than 4,200 exchange listed firms for 1995. They discovered that the percentage of common stock held by a firm's officers and directors as a group rose from 13 per cent in 1935 to 21 per cent in 1995 (1999: 52–53). This is partly attributable to the entry into the market of new firms with high ownership concentration (for example in high tech start ups), and the exit of old economy firms with dispersed ownership due to merger and acquisitions. Dennis and Sarin (1999) find average CEO ownership of 7.2 per cent for a random sample of listed firms. Mehran (1995) examined the ownership of outside blockholders in the US, which he classified as individuals or entities owning at least 5 per cent of total stock (as this triggers a mandatory SEC filing). He discovered that 56 per cent of randomly selected manufacturing firms had outside blockholders (23 per cent were individuals, 23 per cent other corporations, and 54 per cent institutions).

This pattern of insider ownership and extensive blockholding in the US does not demarcate the American system as sharply from the European as is often suggested. And the trend may be in this direction as apparently the stock market in Anglo-American systems responds positively to higher ownership by financial institutions, and one reason for this may be the perception of better monitoring) (Thomsen 2003). The increasing

importance of institutional investors in the US, and in every other market, means that ownership relations are once again becoming more concentrated (even if the ultimate beneficiaries are highly diffuse). This institutional ownership has begun to create forms of relational investing, which could over time lead to more exercise of voice and less of exit by US shareholders (Jacoby 2001: 26). Finally the return of blockholding in the US may be enabled by US banking deregulation and the abolition of the Glass Steagal Act and Bank Holding Company Act, which over the longer term could enable US banks to play a more active role in investment banking and corporate governance as in the European system. As US banks grow larger they would be able to take positions in individual firms without incurring excessive risk (Thomsen 2003). Much attention has been focused upon the pressures driving large listed German corporations to focus more directly on the creation of shareholder value, and upon the insistent pressures for Japanese corporations to demonstrate more transparency and disclosure. Less attention has been paid to the developing pressures upon Anglo-American corporations to exercise greater accountability towards institutional investors and more responsibility in relation to their stakeholder communities (Figure 7.8).

With multiple institutions exerting interdependent effects on firm level outcomes (Aguilera and

**Figure 7.8** Multiple convergence of governance institutions and relationships.

Source: Clarke, T. (2006).

Jackson 2003: 448), and with different values informing the objectives for the enterprise in different cultures (Hofstede 2004), the scenario for convergence and diversity of corporate governance models is more complex and unpredictable than many commentators have suggested. A pioneer of corporate governance possessed a more compelling grasp of the possibilities that convergence and divergence may occur *simultaneously:* that is, an insistent increase in diversity within an overall trend towards convergence:

> Looking ahead towards the next decade it is possible to foresee a duality in the developing scenarios. On the one hand, we might expect further diversity – new patterns of ownership, new forms of group structure, new types of strategic alliance, leading to yet more alternative approaches to corporate governance. More flexible and adaptive organisational arrangements, entities created for specific projects, business ventures and task forces are likely to compound the diversity. Sharper differentiation of the various corporate governance types and the different bases for governance power will be necessary to increase the effectiveness of governance and enable the regulatory processes to respond to reality ... But on the other hand, we might expect a convergence of governance

processes as large corporations operating globally, their shares traded through global financial markets, are faced with increasing regulatory convergence in company law, disclosure requirements and international accounting standards, insider trading and securities trading rules, and the exchange of information between the major regulatory bodies around the world.

> (Tricker 1994b: 520)

In this analysis the strength of diversity rather than uniformity becomes apparent; 'There is then value in maintaining international diversity in corporate governance systems, so that we do not foreclose future alternatives and evolutionary possibilities. The argument resembles the argument for biodiversity in species' (McDonnell 2002: 18). The importance of diversity for the exercise of choice and creativity is paramount, and reveals the dangers involved in national and international policymaking vigorously advocating a one-size-fits-all prescription for corporate governance (McDonnell 2002: 19). Indeed this essential dynamism of corporate governance was fully recognised in the OECD business advisory group's report:

> Entrepreneurs, investors and corporations need the flexibility to craft governance arrangements

that are responsive to unique business contexts so that corporations can respond to incessant changes in technologies, competition, optimal firm organization and vertical networking patterns. A market for governance arrangements should be permitted so that these arrangements that can attract investors and other resource contributors – and support competitive corporations – flourish. To obtain governance diversity, economic regulations, stock exchange rules and corporate law should support a range of ownership and governance forms. Over time, availability of 'off the shelf' solutions will offer benefits of market familiarity and learning, judicial enforceability and predictability.

(OECD 1998a: 34)

## FUTURE TRENDS

Contemplating the future of corporate governance systems is a hazardous business. Each of the systems is facing pressures to change. The long term stakeholder orientation of the German and Japanese governance systems is under insistent pressure to deliver shareholder value, particularly from overseas investment institutions. However, the market oriented short termism of the Anglo-American approach is itself being challenged by international, national and community agencies to recognise wider social and environmental responsibilities. The German and Japanese systems are faced with demands for increased transparency and disclosure from both regulators and investors, while Anglo-American corporations are faced with repeated calls for greater accountability from institutional investors and other stakeholder communities.

Bratton and McCahery (1999: 30) recognised four possible outcomes from the present pressures to converge, and the resilient institutional resistance encountered:

1  a *unitary system* as there is strong convergence towards a global system which assembles the best elements of both major governance systems and combines them together (the least likely alternative);

2  a *universal market based system* as anticipated by the Chicago School of financial economists, representing the triumph of the rules based outsider system;

3  an *improved variety of governance systems* in which there is weak convergence, but some learning from each other between the different national systems;

4  a set of *viable distinctive governance systems*, based on distinctive institutional complementarity each having a unique identity and capability.

Contrary to all of the predictions of an early and complete convergence of corporate governance systems, the final two alternatives are the closest to the present state of play, and are likely to be for some time to come, as this differentiated system has a proven robustness and usefulness (Figure 7.9).

### Complexity of corporate governance forms

It is likely the campaign to raise standards of corporate governance will continue for some time in all jurisdictions of the world. There will be a strenuous effort to secure commitment to the essential basis of trust identified by the OECD as fairness, transparency, accountability and responsibility. However, this will occur in countries with different cultures, legal systems, and economic priorities. To assume that all countries will adapt to the same corporate governance structures is unrealistic. It is likely that fundamental features of the European and Asian approaches to corporate governance will be maintained, even where the apparatus of market-based corporate governance is formally adopted. Often these differences will be perceived as part of the cultural integrity and economic dynamism of the economy in question. At the same time countries will adopt the important universal principles such as international accounting standards, but within a culturally diverse set of corporate structures. This is part of the evolving and dynamic complexity of corporate life, in which both convergence and divergence can occur simultaneously.

SEVEN

**Figure 7.9** Corporate governance convergence: alternative directions.

Source: Adapted from Bratton and McCahery (1999). Comparative Corporate Governance and the Theory of the Firm: The Case against Global Cross Reference, *Columbia Journal of Transnational Law*, 38: 213–297.

## CONCLUSIONS

As pressures to conform to international standards and expectations increase, the resilience of historical and cultural differences will continue. The business case for diversity is, if anything, even more compelling. There will be a continual need to innovate around new technologies, processes and markets. This will stimulate new organisational and corporate forms, the shape and objectives of which will be hard to predetermine. However, an enduring lesson of the recent experience of corporate governance failure, is that it is in the interests of firms, investors, and economies wherever they are based in the world, and whatever system they adopt, to commit to strive for the highest standards of governance.

# 8
# Corporate Social Responsibility

## INTRODUCTION

This chapter considers the overwhelming movement presently driving towards corporate social responsibility. Bridging the great divide between corporate governance and corporate social and environmental responsibility is the next great challenge for business. Corporate social responsibility has many interpretations, but essentially is based on a realisation that the wasteful and exploitative practices of industry in the past can no longer be afforded by people or the planet. It is just not sustainability that is currently at issue – it is survival. The publication of the Stern review on *The Economics of Climate Change* (2006) has helped to propel the business world into an urgent recognition of the dramatic consequences of unrestrained industrial activity, and how little time there is to attempt to put things right (Figure 8.1). Business corporations will respond, or will be made to respond by shareholders, stakeholders and government, to the demand that they act with greater responsibility in their use of resources and impact on the community and environment. The legitimacy of corporate social responsibility is examined in this chapter from a governance perspective firstly in terms of enlightened shareholder value, and the duty to promote the success of the company, and secondly in terms of responsible investment, and the potential of socially responsible investment strategies. An examination of the increasing sophistication of corporate reporting of social and environmental matters is made. The conclusion is that only a fundamental redesign of corporate forms, objectives and value measures can fully meet the realities of responsibility.

## THE SIGNIFICANCE AND IMPACT OF CORPORATE SOCIAL RESPONSIBILITY

The narrow focus of corporate governance exclusively upon the internal control of the firm and simply complying with regulation is no longer tenable. In the past this has allowed corporations to act in extremely irresponsible ways by externalising social and environmental costs. In the name of normal business activity, corporations were too often given a licence to destroy people's lives and damage the environment. 'Just as evolution has made the shark a perfect eating machine, the device of limited liability has allowed the corporation to perfect its function ... The function perfected by limited liability is that of permitting corporations to externalise the costs of stock price maximisation, that is to push those costs onto others. The corporation is the perfect externalizing machine' (Mitchell 2001). Corporate objectives described as 'wealth generating' too frequently have resulted in the loss of well-being to communities and the ecology. But increasingly in the future the *licence to operate* will not be given so readily to corporations and other entities. A licence to operate will depend on maintaining the highest standards of integrity and practice in corporate behaviour. Corporate governance essentially will involve a sustained and responsible monitoring of not just the financial health of the company, but the social and environmental impact of the company.

A substantial increase in the range, significance and impact of corporate social and environmental initiatives in recent years suggests the growing materiality of sustainability. Once regarded as

**Figure 8.1** The economics of climate change.

Source: Stern Review (2006), *The Economics of Climate Change*, Stern Review, 8, Figure 1.4: The link between greenhouses gases and climate change.

a concern of a few philanthropic individuals and companies, corporate social and environmental responsibility appears to be becoming established in many corporations as a critical element of strategic direction, and one of the main drivers of business development, as well as an essential component of risk management. Corporate social and environmental responsibility (CSR) seems to be rapidly moving from the margins to the mainstream of corporate activity, with greater recognition of a direct and inescapable relationship between corporate governance, corporate responsibility, and sustainable development.

The burgeoning importance of this newly revived movement is demonstrated by the current frequency and scale of activity at every level (Calder and Culverwell 2005: 43). Among international organisations the United Nations is coordinating a public-private partnership between UNEP and 170 banks, insurers and asset managers worldwide including Deutsche Bank, Dresdner Kleinwort Wasserstein, Goldman Sachs, HSBC and UBS to explore the financial materiality of environmental, social and governance (ESG) issues to securities valuation (UNEP 2004a). Early in 2005 the UN convened a group of 20 of the world's largest institutional investors to negotiate a set of Principles for Responsible Investment, which will be published in a *Working Capital Report* in early 2006 as a guide to the investment community on how to incorporate environmental, social and governance issues into their investment decision-making and ownership processes.

This builds on the work of the UN Global Compact with more than 1,500 corporate signatories, which is working with the world's leading stock exchanges and the World Federation of Exchanges to advance the principles of corporate responsibility in capital markets and with public corporations (UN 2000).

In 2005 institutional investors representing 21 trillion dollars in assets came together for the third Carbon Disclosure Project meeting, collectively requesting the world's largest corporations to disclose information on greenhouse gas emissions and their approach to the management of carbon risks (UNEP FI 2005a). Finally, 36 of the world's largest banks, representing more than 80 per cent of the global project finance market, have adopted the Equator Principles, a set of voluntary principles outlining environmental, social and human rights disciplines associated with project finance above $50 million (Freshfields Bruckhaus Deringer 2005a). The principles originally were developed by the International Finance Corporation (IFC), the private sector investment arm of the World Bank. The OECD also is active in the promotion of corporate social responsibility in its guidelines for the operations of multinational corporations; and the European Union is actively encouraging corporate social responsibility as the business contribution to sustainable development (OECD 2000; European Commission 2003, 2004). At the national level a growing number of governments in Europe, and across the globe, have identified strongly with the call for corporate social and environmental responsibility, even with the evident difficulties in applying the Kyoto Protocol and creating an effective international climate policy regime.

At the corporate level the World Business Council for Sustainable Development, and World Economic Forum Global Corporate Citizenship Initiative has projected corporate responsibility in the minds of the international business elite (WBCSD 2002, 2004; WEF 2005). Other business organisations active in promoting CSR include the Business Leaders' Initiative on Human Rights, the Conference Board, Business in the Community, and Business for Social Responsibility. A large number of leading corporations have signed up for the Global Reporting Initiative and more

than 2,000 international corporations now publish reports on their CSR performance (many accessible on www.csrwire.com) (GRI 2002). Reinforcing the new found willingness on the part of corporate executives to disclose their commitments to CSR are the new indices including the Dow Jones Sustainability Index and FTSE4Good. Finally, there are a proliferating number of consultancies, NGOs and campaign groups offering guidance and actively monitoring CSR activities along the entire length of the global value chain (World Bank 2003).

Questions are often addressed to the sincerity of corporate social and environmental initiatives; the legality of company directors engaging in these concerns; equally, the legality of the trustees of investment institutions attending to these interests; and the verifiability of CSR activities and outcomes. The aim of this chapter is to clarify the continuing and emerging legal and commercial basis for corporations to pursue corporate social and environmental responsibility; the ongoing legal and material support for institutional trustees to prioritise socially and environmentally responsible investments; to examine developments in verification on corporate reporting of CSR performance; and to consider some illustrations of current best practice.

## THE INTEGRITY OF CORPORATE SOCIAL RESPONSIBILITY

Despite the recent burst of enthusiasm for corporate social and environmental responsibility in some quarters of the business community, the concept and practice still provokes a degree of understandable scepticism (partly due to CSR's record of lapsing into amoral apologetics for unacceptable corporate behaviour) (Najam 2000; Christian Aid 2004; Corporate Responsibility Coalition 2005; OECD Watch 2005). David Vogel in a review conducted for the Brookings Institute, *The Market for Virtue: The Potential and Limits of Corporate Social Responsibility* (2005), contends there are many reasons why companies may choose to behave more responsibly in the absence of legal requirements to do so, including strategic, defensive, altruistic or public spirited

motivations. However despite pressure from con-sumers for responsibly made products, the influ-ence of socially responsible investors, and the insistent call for companies to be accountable to a broader community of stakeholders there are important limits to the market for virtue:

> CSR is best understood as a niche rather than a generic strategy: it makes sense for some firms in some areas under some circumstances. Many of the proponents of corporate social responsibility mistakenly assume that because some companies are behaving more responsi-bly in some areas, some firms can be expected to behave more responsibly in more areas. This assumption is misinformed. There *is* a place in the market economy for responsible firms. But there is also a large place for their less respon-sible competitors … Precisely because CSR is voluntary and market-driven, companies will engage in CSR only to the extent that it makes business sense for them to do. Civil regulation has proven capable of forcing *some* companies to internalize *some* of the negative externalities associated with *some* of their economic activi-ties. But CSR can reduce only some market failures.

> (2005: 3–4)

Vogal concludes that CSR has a multidimen-sional nature, and that companies, like individuals, do not always exhibit consistent moral or social behaviour, and may behave better in some coun-tries than others depending on the social and environmental policies existing there. Since the origins of capitalism there have always been more or less responsible firms, and though it may be heartening that executives in many highly visible firms may be becoming more responsive (if only as a result of external stakeholder pressures) the reality is that the amounts wasted on the losses due to financial fraud, and the very substantial – and some would argue unwarranted – increases in executive compensation in corporations in the recent period far exceed any resources companies have devoted to CSR.

In a similar vein Deborah Doane who is Chair of the Corporate Responsibility Coalition in the UK, is sceptical regarding optimism about the power of market mechanisms to deliver social and environmental change, referring to the key myths informing the CSR movement as:

- The market can deliver both short term finan-cial returns and long term social benefits.
- The ethical consumer will drive change.
- There will be a competitive 'race to the top' over ethics amongst businesses.
- In the global economy countries will compete to have the best ethical practices.

In support of her argument that these are largely mythological trends, she highlights the insistence of stock markets upon short term results, and the failure of companies to invest in long term benefits; the considerable gap between green con-sciousness expressed by consumers and their consumer behaviour; the inconsistency between companies' alignment to CSR schemes and their successful efforts to bring about the sustained fall in corporate taxation in the United States and other jurisdictions in recent decades; and finally the evidence emerging in developing countries of governments competing to *reduce* their insistence on the observance of social and environmen-tal standards to attract international investment (Doane 2005).

It may well be the case that further legisla-tive and regulatory intervention will be required to ensure all corporations fully respond to the grow-ing public demand that they recognise their wider social and environmental responsibilities. However, it is useful to examine how far CSR objectives can be achieved within existing law and regulation. If there is substantial evidence of leading corpo-rations demonstrating it is possible to voluntarily commit to social and environmental performance and to achieve commercial success – perhaps because of, rather than in spite of, ethical com-mitments – then it will be more straightforward to press for the legislative changes necessary to deal with corporations that refuse to acknowledge their wider responsibilities, as well as finding appropri-ate legislative support for companies that wish to develop further their CSR commitments.

In the meantime, the practical fact is that corporations and governments currently are struggling with an 'almost bewildering array of international CSR initiatives' (Calder and Culverwell 2005: 7; McKague and Cragg 2005).

Reviewing the efforts to develop CSR following the World Summit on Sustainable Development, a survey by the Royal Institute for International Affairs of stakeholders from governments, businesses and civil society groups identified a range of significant weaknesses in current approaches to promoting CSR which governments should seek to address:

- an over-proliferation of CSR initiatives at the international level and lack of clarity about how these initiatives relate to each other in a coherent way;
- an excessive focus on getting businesses to make commitments to CSR and not enough focus on enabling them to implement them effectively;
- an absence of credible monitoring and verification processes of CSR initiatives;
- a lack of effective mechanisms of redress for communities affected by companies that flout national or international norms on sustainable development or human rights;
- a lack of engagement with developing country governments and their sustainable development priorities (e.g. economic development and poverty reduction);
- a failure to bridge the governance gap created by weak public sector governance of the private sector in many developing countries;
- the limited impact on national and international sustainable development goals;
- a lack of government involvement and/or investment in international CSR initiatives, which is contributing significantly to their underperformance (Calder and Culverwell 2005: 7).

## DEFINING SOCIAL AND ENVIRONMENTAL SUSTAINABILITY

The rapidly developing interest in sustainability and corporate social and environmental responsibility has resulted in a plethora of definitions and interpretations of the two concepts from international agencies, consultancies and practitioners (Calder and Culverwell 2005; McKague and Cragg 2005). A first difficulty is that the most commonly employed acronym, CSR,

refers to corporate social responsibility, though in most interpretations is meant to include environmental responsibility also. The use of the simpler term corporate responsibility and acronym CR is not in widespread use, though it would more readily embrace all corporate responsibilities. The UN's recent adoption of the environmental, social and governance (ESG) acronym may become influential, since it explicitly links governance to social and environmental responsibility.

More confusingly still, in some definitions CSR is subsumed under sustainability, while in others sustainability is included within CSR. One source of this confusion is that often different levels of analysis are being addressed. At the highest level the sustainability of the planet is at issue, and at lower levels the sustainability of economies and societies, industries and organisations. Corporate sustainability is a critical issue because of the economic scale and significance of these entities and their growing impact on the economy, society and environment. 'Corporations have magnified capacities relative to individuals, in their financial resources, scale of operations, organisational capacity and capacity for social and individual harm' (Redmond 2005: 1). Once the primary (in some cases sole) concern was to produce goods and services that might generate the profits to achieve the financial sustainability of the corporation (everything else was written off as externalities). 'Defining limited liability is simple. It means that no matter how much environmental damage a corporation causes, no matter how much debt if defaults on, no matter how many Malibus explode or tires burst or workers or consumers die of asbestosis, no matter how many people it puts out of work without their pension benefits or other protections; in short, no matter how much pain it causes, the corporation is responsible for paying damages (if at all) only in the amount of assets it has' (Mitchell 2001).

Increasingly today the social and environmental impact of the corporation will be assessed in deciding whether it is viable or not, by governments, regulators, or other stakeholders, even if the corporations' management are reluctant to make this assessment. The *licence to operate* can no longer be readily assumed for any corporation, and in an increasing number of contexts needs to be earned with verifiable evidence of

the social and environmental responsibility of the corporation.

Definitions of CSR and sustainability range from the basic to the most demanding, from a specific reference to a number of necessary activities to demonstrate responsibility, to a general call for a comprehensive, integrated and committed pursuit of social and environmental sustainability. The following representative range of definitions of CSR is in ascending order from the least to the most demanding:

- The integration of stakeholders' social, environmental and other concerns into a company's business operations (EIU 2005: 2).
- The commitment of businesses to contribute to sustainable economic development by working with their employees, their families, the local community and society at large to improve their lives in ways which are good for business and for development (World Business Council for Sustainable Development 2002).
- Corporate social responsibility is at heart a process of managing the costs and benefits of business activity to both internal (for example, workers, shareholders, investors) and external (institutions of public governance, community members, civil society groups, other enterprises) stakeholders. Setting the boundaries for how those costs and benefits are managed is partly a question of business policy and strategy and partly a question of public governance (World Bank 2002: 1).
- A concept whereby companies integrate social and environmental concerns in their business operations and in their interaction with their stakeholders on a voluntary basis (European Commission 2001).
- A company's commitment to operating in an economically, socially, and environmentally sustainable manner, while recognising the interests of its stakeholders, including investors, customers, employees, business partners, local communities, the environment, and society at large (Certified General Accountants Association of Canada 2005: 20).
- CSR is essentially about how the company makes its profits, not only what it does with them afterwards. CSR is about how the company manages first, its core business

operations – in the board room, in the workplace, in the marketplace, and along the supply chain; second, its community investment and philanthropic activities; and third, its engagement in public policy dialogue and institution building (Kennedy School of Government Corporate Responsibility Initiative 2004: 33).
- A business approach embodying open and transparent business practices, ethical behaviour, respect for stakeholders and a commitment to add economic, social and environmental value (SustainAbility 2005).
- Sustainability performance refers to an organisation's total performance, which might include its policies, decisions, and actions that create social, environmental and/or economic (including financial) outcomes (AccountAbility 2005: 10).

Sustainability as a whole (planet, environment, species) is an altogether more ambitious project with more expansive definitions than CSR. Corporations have a vital role to play in this also, beginning with a modest recognition of their necessary subordination to the interests of maintaining a balanced ecosystem. Sustainability is defined as:

- Meeting the needs of the present generation without compromising the ability of future generations to meet their needs (Bruntland Commission 1987).
- Sustainable development, sustainable growth, and sustainable use have been used interchangeably, as if their meanings were the same. They are not. Sustainable growth is a contradiction in terms: nothing physical can grow indefinitely. Sustainable use, is only applicable to renewable resources. Sustainable development is used in this strategy to mean: improving the quality of human life whilst living within the carrying capacity of the ecosystems (IUCN, UNEP, WWF 1991).

Putting the entire field into perspective, according to the *Global Reporting Initiative (GRI) 2002 Sustainability Reporting Guidelines*:

- *Environmental impact* means an organisation's impact on living and non-living natural systems, including ecosystems, land, air and water.

Examples include energy use and greenhouse gas emissions.

- *Social impact* means an organisation's impact on the social system within which it operates. This includes labour practices, human rights and other social issues.
- *Economic impact* means an organisation's impact both direct and indirect on the economic resources of its stakeholders and on economic systems at the local, national and global levels.

## TOMORROW'S MARKETS

The economies of the world are on an unsustainable development path. Trends identified in *Tomorrow's Markets: Global Trends and Their Implications for Business* (2002) a joint publication of the World Resources Institute (WRI), United Nations Environment Programme (UNEP), and the World Business Council for Sustainable Development (WBCSD) illustrate the diversity, severity and complexity of the challenges society and business face to survive and discover new sources of value:

### People

- *Population*: Expanding population in developing regions will create large markets dominated by the young with questionable access to the developed world's standard of living (2.4 billion of today's total population of 6.2 billion people are children and teenagers). More than 80 per cent of the world's population live in developing countries and 85 per cent will live in developing countries by 2025.
- *Wealth*: Global wealth is rising but the income gap grows wider threatening civil society. The world is 78 per cent poor, 11 per cent middle income and 11 per cent rich.
- *Nutrition*: Millions of people are malnourished amidst an abundance of food, thousands die of hunger every day. In 1998, 791 million of the 826 million undernourished people lived in the developing world.
- *Health*: Life expectancy rises, yet preventable disease continues to limit development, and

epidemics threaten the viability of entire geographic regions.

- *Education*: Primary education is widespread, but opportunities for learning elude many: 113 million children are not in school, 97 per cent of them in developing countries, and 60 per cent of them female. One in every five adults – a total of 880 million adults – is functionally illiterate. This is a dramatic improvement over 1970 when one in three was illiterate.

### Innovation

- *Consumption*: Rising consumption creates environmental risks as well as business opportunities for innovation. Consumers in high-income countries spent $15.4 trillion of the $19.3 trillion (80 per cent) of total private consumption in 1998. Purchases by consumers in low-income countries represented less than 4 per cent of all private consumption.
- *Energy*: Escalating demand for energy propels economic development but threatens the earth's climate and ecosystem. The 1990s were the warmest decade since the 1880s, and 1998 the warmest year ever. World energy production rose 42 per cent between 1980 and 2000 and will grow 150–230 per cent by 2050.
- *Emissions*: Pollution increases threaten society and the integrity of ecosystems. Between 50–90 per cent of the mass of industrialised country environment outflows goes directly into the atmosphere.
- *Efficiency*: Throughput still grows even as energy efficiency and improves, adding to society's environmental footprint. But recycling is accounting for an increasing share of production, for example paper recycling into paper and fibre products has risen since the 1970s to about 40 per cent of total paper production worldwide.

### Natural capital

- *Ecosystems*: The productive capacity of the planet is in decline, threatening biodiversity, clean air provision and natural global temperature balancing. Nearly 26,000 plant species,

more than 1,100 mammals and 1,200 birds, 700 freshwater fish, and hundreds of reptiles and amphibians are threatened with extinction.

- *Agriculture*: Food production is the basis of many economies but threatens the ecosystem upon which it depends, threatening fish stocks and productive agricultural output. About 30 per cent of the potential area of temperate, sub-tropical, and tropical forests and about 40 per cent of temperate grasslands have been converted to agriculture.
- *Water*: Freshwater is growing scarce amidst competing human needs, millions exist daily without fresh water. Over the past century, world water withdrawals increased almost twice as fast as population growth.

## Connection

- *Urbanisation*: Urban growth concentrates business opportunities and societal challenges while undermining the social fabric for many. By 2050, 50 per cent of all people will live in urban areas as 60 million people become new urban dwellers yearly, the equivalent of adding the population of Paris, Cairo or Beijing every other month to the urban population.
- *Mobility*: People are more mobile, accelerating the flow of goods and knowledge and raising the demand for energy and infrastructure. Transport of people and goods is responsible for about one-fifth of worldwide energy consumption.
- *Communications*: Access to information and communication technologies enables economic opportunity, although many remain information poor. Over 50 per cent of the world's population has never used a telephone, only 7 per cent have access to a personal computer and only 4 per cent have access to the internet.
- *Labour*: As economies are becoming service-based, women are a becoming a growing part of the formal labour force. In developed countries the working population will shrink from approximately 750 million to 690 million between 2000 and 2025, whereas in the developing world the working population will

increase 43 per cent from 3 billion to 4 billion people.

## Roles and responsibilities

- *Democracy*: Democracy spreads, creating improved conditions for market-based economies. The number of democratic states in the world has grown from 22 democratic states out of 154 total countries in 1950, to 119 democratic states out of 192 total countries in 2000. The number of countries that have ratified the 6 major human rights conventions has grown from 10 per cent to 50 per cent of all countries between 1990 and 2001.
- *Accountability*: Civil society is demanding greater accountability and transparency from government and business as lack of trust threatens the effective operation of market-based economies. Currently 2,091 NGOs hold consultative status at the United Nations, compared to 928 in 1991 and just 41 in 1948.
- *Privatisation*: Private sector development is increasingly financing economic development. Foreign direct investment in developing countries has risen from about $24 billion in 1990 to $178 billion in 2000 as official development aid declined from about $55 billion to $39 billion (WRI; UNEP; WBCSD 2002).

As Sustainable Asset Management Group (SAM) (2003: 5) argue:

Understanding the implications of these trends on business is central to sustainability investing as, despite lower interest rates, increased risk-premia have effectively erased the benefits of low costs of capital for business. The implications of environmental degradation and weakened eco-system have been starkly demonstrated by the spiralling costs of environmental catastrophes. Financial losses due to natural disasters have doubled each decade since the 1950s, and UNEP estimates that natural disasters caused by climate change could cost $150 billion a year by 2012. Socio-cultural disruptions have also had severe financial implications recently: insurers had to cover $40 billion in losses after the September 11[th] disaster.

This leads SAM (2003: 2) to conceiving of a hypothesis of enlightened self-interest: 'Should extreme climactic events such as flooding occur, the civility of society is disrupted and hence the healthy functioning of the economy undermined. This impacts the possibility of a vigorous population of enterprises thriving which, in turn, compromises the possibility of successful investment. Sustainability investing therefore selects companies that contribute to the vibrancy of the socio-economic system and a sustainable planet'.

In the past companies did not recognise or acknowledge the environmental and social effects of their operations, such as the impacts releases to water have on river systems, or the effects of particular emissions upon human health. The United States Environmental Protection Agency (1995: 1) has developed a useful dichotomy – private versus social costs. The term environmental cost has at least two major dimensions: it can refer solely to costs that directly impact a company's bottom line (termed *private costs*) or it can also encompass the costs to individuals, society, and the environment for which a company is not directly accountable (termed *societal costs* by the EPA but typically referred to as externalities). 'Externalities generated by an organisation, although possibly ignored from an accounting perspective, are often recognised as costs by other entities'. (ICAA 2003: 19). Consideration of the range of environmental costs an entity might be encouraged to consider widens the scope of accounting systems, though makes measurement more difficult (Table 8.1).

| Tier | Description |
|------|-------------|
| 1 | **Conventional costs** <br> Includes the costs of direct raw materials, utilities, labour, supplies, capital equipment and related depreciation |
| 2 | **Hidden costs** <br> Includes the up front environmental costs, such as search costs relating to environmentally conscious suppliers, initial design costs of environmentally preferable products, regulatory costs which are often obscured in overhead costs, future decommissioning or remediation costs |
| 3 | **Contingent** <br> Defined in probabilistic terms and includes fines for breaching environmental requirements, clean up costs, lawsuits relating to unsound products |
| 4 | **Relationship and image costs** <br> These costs are difficult to determine and would seldom be separately identified within an accounting system. However they could be expected to have some influence on the value of some intangible assets, such as goodwill, brand-names and so forth. The sum of the costs in tiers 1 to 4 can be referred to as *private costs* and they can directly impact on an organisation's reported profit |
| 5 | **Societal costs** <br> These costs are often referred to as externalities and represent costs that an organisation imposes upon others as a result of their operations but which are typically ignored by the organisation. They could include environmental damage caused by the organisation for which they are not held accountable or adverse health effects caused by organisation-generated emissions for which the organisation is not held responsible. It is difficult and sometimes controversial to put a cost on these effects and with the exception of a few organisations worldwide, most entities ignore these costs when calculating profits. However, physical measures can be developed, and related KPIs can be used to assess performance |

Table 8.1 The range of environmental costs.

Source: Van Berkel, R. (2003), *Managing for Sustainable Development*, CPA Congress 2003, pp. 1–18, Table 4, p. 9.

Together the trends indicated provide the context in which business must operate in future suggest the following imperatives which all corporations will face:

- maintaining a licence to operate via transparency and accountability;
- serving society;
- generating more value with less impact;
- preserving the resource base;
- doing business in a networked world.

In summary the challenge is to find means of enduring value creation without social or environmental harm.

## FROM THE MARGINS TO THE MAINSTREAM?

However challenging the prospects, there are growing indications of large corporations taking their social and environmental responsibilities more seriously, and of these issues becoming more critical in the business agenda. KPMG since 1993 have conducted an international survey of corporate responsibility every three years which has revealed the developing prevalence of this commitment (Table 8.2). Surveying the largest 100 companies in a sample of advanced industrial OECD countries (with the addition of the Global 250 companies from 1999), KPMG (2005) find a steadily rising trend in companies issuing separate corporate responsibility annual reports. From 13 per cent of national 100 companies reporting on corporate responsibility matters in 1993, by 2005 this had risen to 33 per cent (up to 41 per cent if including information in annual reports). A more substantial increase in the Global 250 reporting occurred with 35 per cent reporting in 1999 and 52 per cent in 2005 (64 per cent including information in annual reports). Publication of corporate responsibility reports as part of the annual financial reports of companies often implies the issue is regarded as of greater salience, and companies often progress

| Survey year | 1993 | 1996 | 1999 | 2002 | 2005 |
|---|---|---|---|---|---|
| Research set (s) | Top 100 in 10 countries | Top 100 in 13 countries | Top 100 in 11 countries and global 250 | Top 100 in 19 countries and global 250 | Top 100 in 16[1] countries and global 250 |
| Total number of companies included | 810 | 1,300 | 1,100+ | 1,900+ | 1,600+ |
| Response rate | 85% | 69% | 98% | 96% | 98% |
| N100: % of companies with CR reports | 13% | 17% | 24% | 23% (28% for 11 countries in 1999) | 33% (41% including CR information in annual reports) |
| G250: % of companies with CR reports | – | – | 35% | 45% | 52% (64% including CR information in annual reports) |

Table 8.2 KPMG CSR surveys, 1993–2005.

Source: KPMG CSR Surveys (1993–2005), *KPMG International Surveys of Corporate Responsibility Reporting 2005*, KPMG International.

Notes
[1] Refers to 15 of the OECD countries (Australia, Belgium, Canada, Denmark, Finland, France, Germany, Italy, Japan, Netherlands, Norway, South Africa, Spain, Sweden, UK, US) and also South Africa.

from separate to integrated CSR and financial reports.

More importantly, the substance of company reports is changing, from purely environmental reporting up until 1999, to sustainability reporting (social, environmental and economic), which has become the mainstream approach of the G250 companies, and is becoming so among the national 100 companies. The two leading countries in terms of separate corporate responsibility reporting are Japan (80 per cent of top 100 companies) and the UK (71 per cent of top 100 companies) in 2005. The industrial sectors with the highest environmental impact tend to lead in reporting (in one sense self-evidently important, in another sense deeply curious). At the Global 250 level over 80 per cent of companies report in electronics and computers; utilities; automotive; and oil and gas sectors. The most remarkable increase in the Global 250 was in the finance sector, with a doubling of the rate of CSR reporting from 24 per cent in 2002 to 57 per cent in 2005. At the national level over 50 per cent of top 100 companies are reporting in utilities; mining; chemicals and synthetics; oil and gas; and forestry and paper sectors.

Finally the KPMG survey reveals a balanced range of business drivers for CSR reporting (Table 8.3), beginning with economic considerations (74 per cent of companies); ethical considerations (54 per cent); innovation and learning (53 per cent); employee motivation (47 per cent); risk management (47 per cent) and access to capital (39 per cent). The survey suggests there were solid business reasons for acting and reporting on CSR: 'The economic reasons were either directly linked to increased shareholder value or market share or indirectly linked through increased business opportunities, innovation, reputation, and reduced risk. Thirty-nine per cent of the companies reported improved shareholder value, and one in five (21 per cent) reported increased market share as an important reason for sustainability' (KPMG 2005: 18).

In a further international survey of 136 corporate executives and 65 executives of institutional investors on the importance of corporate responsibility (CR) the Economist Intelligence Unit (EIU) discovered a similar growth in interest:

A total of 88 per cent of executives said that CR is a 'central' or 'important' consideration in decision-making. This compares with 54 per cent of executives who said it was a 'central' or 'important' consideration five years ago. The biggest percentage change between now and five years ago was among European executives. A total of 46 per cent said CR was 'central' or 'important' five years ago compared with 84 per cent at the present time. In Asia, the proportion rose from 49 per cent to 82 per cent and in North America from 66 per cent to 88 per cent. The survey of professional investors reveals a sharper trend. Eighty-one per cent of those surveyed said CR was currently a 'central' or 'important' consideration in their investment decisions, compared with 34 per cent who said it was 'central' or 'important' five years ago. In fact, 14 per cent of them said CR was not a consideration at all five years ago. Now, not a single investor said it was not a consideration.

(EIU 2005: 5)

| Driver | % |
| --- | --- |
| Economic considerations | 74 |
| Ethical considerations | 53 |
| Innovation and learning | 53 |
| Employee motivation | 47 |
| Risk management or risk reduction | 47 |
| Access to capital or increased shareholder value | 39 |
| Reputation or brand | 27 |
| Market position (market share improvement) | 21 |
| Strengthened supplier relations | 13 |
| Cost saving | 9 |
| Improved relationships with governmental authorities | 9 |
| Other | 11 |

Table 8.3 Drivers for corporate social responsibility.

Source: KPMG CSR Surveys (1993–2005), *KPMG International Surveys of Corporate Responsibility Reporting 2005*, KPMG International.

As with the gap noticed earlier between consumer consciousness and behaviour, it is likely there will be a mighty gulf between the expressed concerns of executives for corporate responsibility and their

actual behaviour in different circumstances in the exigencies of difficult situations; however, simply expressing concerns is an advance over stony faced refusals to even acknowledge responsibilities that may have occurred in the past. 'Corporate responsibility is really about ensuring that the company can grow on a sustainable basis, while ensuring fairness to all stakeholders', says N. R. Murthy, the chairman of an Indian IT firm, Infosys' (EIU 2005: 2). Though some of the expressed concern may be part of the discourse of political correctness, there do appear to be grounds for a significant shifting of opinion among executives, as the EIU comments:

Until recently, board members often regarded corporate responsibility as a piece of rhetoric intended to placate environmentalists and human rights campaigners. But now, companies are beginning to regard corporate responsibility as a normal facet of business and are thinking about ways to develop internal structures and processes that will emphasize

it more heavily. In the not-too-distant future, companies that are not focusing on corporate responsibility may come to be seen as outliers. As companies focus on non-financial performance, an important yardstick of corporate responsibility, the measurement of intangibles, such as customer satisfaction and employee morale, are likely to become less vague and more credible.

(EIU 2005: 3)

One of the surprising results of the EIU survey was that after more than a decade of the exhortation of the primacy in all circumstances of shareholder value, the executives surveyed still possessed a balanced appreciation of the relative importance of key stakeholders to the company, identifying customers, employees and shareholders in that order (Figure 8.2). The EIU compiled some of the contextual highlights for these changes in executive views in the emerging evidence that corporate social and environmental responsibility is moving substantially

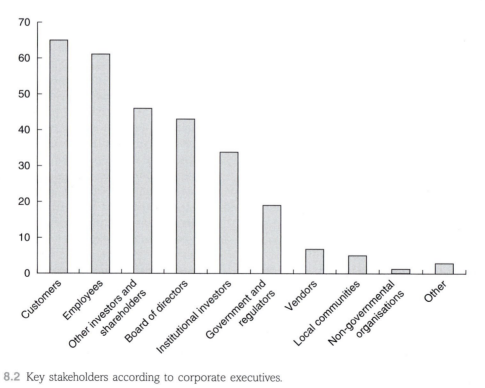

**Figure 8.2** Key stakeholders according to corporate executives.

Source: Adapted EIU (2001).

from the margins to the mainstream of economic activity:

- The New York-based GovernanceMetrics International (GMI), which covers corporate governance and CR, now produces in-depth rating reports on 2000 companies around the world and has a growing client base including TIAA-CREF, State Street Bank and ABP, the largest pension fund in Europe.
- More than 10,000 individuals and 3,000 listed companies have helped to develop the standards of the Global Reporting Initiative (GRI), an organisation based in Amsterdam, trying to create a single global measure for CR performance. Among its corporate clients implementing GRI standards are Bayer, Canon, Deutsche Bank, General Motors, Heineken and Shell.
- A group of five major European institutional investors, including the second-largest pension fund in the UK and the largest pension fund in the Netherlands, jointly stated in October 2004 that they would allocate 5 per cent of their budgets for the purchase of non-financial research analysis of such topics as corporate governance, labour management and environmental practices.
- One in every nine investment dollars under professional management in the US is now invested in socially responsible funds. This amounts to $2 trillion out of a total of $19 trillion in investible funds, according to the 2003 report on socially responsible investing (SRI) produced by the Social Investment Forum, the national trade body for the SRI industry.

(EIU 2005: 4–5)

At the confluence of these multiple emerging initiatives and trends towards greater corporate social and environmental responsibility there is emerging a dynamic stakeholder model for driving enlightened shareholder value (Figure 8.3). At many leading corporations the pieces of what is admittedly a very large and demanding puzzle are beginning to come together. The wider commitments to building engaged and inclusive relationships with employees, economic partners, the community and the environment becomes

a means of achieving enlightened shareholder value through access to a lower cost of capital, enhanced reputation, minimised risks and new business opportunities.

## THE LEGITIMACY OF CSR FROM A GOVERNANCE PERSPECTIVE

### Corporations enlightened shareholder value? The duty to promote the success of the company

The impact of the adoption of corporate commitments to wider forms of social and environmental engagement and reporting will be determined essentially by initiatives of leading companies and, in turn, this will be influenced by the insistent pressures companies encounter from the market, investors and stakeholders, and the perceived commercial benefit of assuming a broader accountability. However, the role of the law and of accounting standards in establishing a framework of accountability and management discipline is a significant factor. Historical analysis of the perception of company directors' duties, including legal interpretations, reveals much greater sympathy for corporations adopting a wider view of their responsibilities than the recently imposed tenets of shareholder value would suggest.

This balance of pursuing market opportunities while maintaining accountability has proved a defining challenge for business enterprise since the arrival of the joint-stock company in the early years of industrialism. The accountability and responsibility of business enterprise was constantly subject to question, and historically failed this test often in the view of the public. Maurice Clark deplored how business 'inherited an economics of irresponsibility' from the laissez-faire beliefs and practices of early industrialism (1916). He argued business transactions do not occur in isolation, but have wider social and economic consequences that need to be considered, impacting directly on employment, health and the environment. He insisted legal regulation may be required to ensure protection from abuses, but that this could never replace a general sense of responsibility in business that goes beyond the letter of the law, preventing competitive forces leading to a

**Figure 8.3** CSR stakeholder model driving enlightened shareholder value.

Source: Mays, S. (2003), *Corporate Sustainability: An Investor Perspective.* Mays Report, Department of Environment and Heritage Commonwealth of Australia, 11, 16.

race to the bottom. Hence the periodic outbreak of destructive competition needed to be restrained in Clark's view by 'an economics of responsibility, developed and embodied in our working business ethics (1916)'.

The debate concerning the true extent of the accountability and responsibility of business enterprise has continued to the present day, punctuated by occasional public outrage at business transgressions, and calls for greater recognition of the social obligations of business. At the height of the economic depression in the United States in 1932 Dodd made a dramatic plea in the pages of the *Harvard Law Review*: 'There is in fact a growing feeling not only that business has responsibilities to the community but that our corporate managers who control business should voluntarily and without waiting for legal compulsion manage it in such a way as to fulfill these responsibilities'. This resonated with Berle and Means' insistence that large corporations 'serve not alone the owners or the control, but all society'. Though Berle subsequently commenced a prolonged debate with Dodd on the subject of 'For Whom Are Corporate Managers Trustees', Berle (1955) later conceded to Dodd's argument that management powers were held in trust for the entire community (Wedderburn 1985: 6).

Such forthright views did not remain at the level of academic speculation, but often were translated into legal, policy and business interpretations and practice. For example in *Teck Corp Ltd v. Millar*, the Supreme Court of British Columbia, while retaining the identification of company interests with those of shareholders, nonetheless was prepared to grant directors a licence under their fiduciary duties to take into account wider stakeholder interests:

'The classical theory is that the directors' duty is to the company. The company's shareholders are the company ... and therefore no interests outside those of the shareholders can legitimately be considered by the directors. But even accepting that, what comes within the definition of the interests of the shareholders? By what standards are the shareholders' interests to be measured? A classical theory that once was unchallengeable must yield to the facts of modern life. In fact, of course, it has. If today the directors of a company were to consider the interests of its employees no one would argue that in doing so they were not acting bona fide in the interests of the company itself. Similarly, if the directors were to consider the consequences to the community of any policy that the company intended to pursue, and were deflected in their commitment to that policy as a result, it could not be said that they had not considered bona fide the interests of the shareholders' (*Teck Corp Ltd v. Millar* 1973: 313–14).

Wedderburn (1985: 12) documents an equivalent deep-seated and practical commitment of corporate responsibility to a wide constituency in the post-war beliefs of leaders of the British business community. A lively debate continues worldwide concerning the scope of directors' duties. In Australia the Corporations Act Section 181 obliges directors and other corporate officers to exercise their powers and discharge their duties:

- in good faith and in the best interests of the corporation;
- for a proper purpose.

Under common law directors are obliged to act in the interests of 'the company as a whole'. Traditionally this phrase has been interpreted to mean the financial well-being of the shareholders as a general body. (Though directors are obliged to consider the financial interests of creditors when the firm is insolvent or near-insolvent.) A recent generation of financial economists helped to translate this broad shareholder *primacy principle* into a narrow pursuit of shareholder value. There is a wider interpretation of shareholder value which suggests that only when all of the other constituent relationships of the corporation – with customers, employees, suppliers, distributors and the wider community – are fully recognised and developed that long term shareholder value can be released. However, the restrictive definition of shareholder value has often been associated with short-termism and a neglect of wider corporate responsibilities in the interests of immediate profit maximisation. Concerns have arisen that directors who do wish to take account of other stakeholder interests may be exposed.

Traditionally, commercial law in many European countries has supported a sense of the wider social and environmental obligations of companies, which continues despite a recent enthusiasm

for the principle of shareholder value as some large European companies for the first time seek the support of international investors. The UK has stood apart from Europe as an influential exponent of the Anglo-American market based approach to corporate governance. However, in an effort to jettison the company law rhetoric formed in the nineteenth century, and to make the law more accessible, a Company Law Review (CLR) steering group was established. The ensuing consultative document *Modern Company Law for a Competitive Economy: Developing the Framework* (2000) proposed for the first time that there should be a statutory statement of directors' duties (presently the core components of those duties is found in case law), and made a significant step in the direction of endorsing fuller corporate social and environmental reporting:

> Current accounting and reporting fails to provide adequate transparency of qualitative and forward looking information which is of vital importance in assessing performance and potential for shareholders, investors, creditors and others. This is particularly so in the modern environment of technical change, and with the growing importance of 'soft', or intangible assets, brands, know-how and business relationships. The full annual report must be effective in covering these, both as a stewardship report and as a medium of communication to wider markets and the public … we believe the time has come to require larger companies to provide an operating and financial review, which will cover the qualitative, or 'soft', or intangible, and forward looking information which the modern market and modern business decision-making requires, converting the practice of the best run companies into a requirement for all.
>
> (CLR 2000: 180–1)

These issues were extensively considered in the UK for several years in the deliberations of the Modern Company Law Review. Two approaches were considered:

- a pluralist approach under which directors' duties would be reformulated to permit directors to further the interests of other

stakeholders even if they were to the detriment of shareholders;
- an enlightened shareholder value approach allowing directors greater flexibility to take into account longer term considerations and interests of various stakeholders in advancing shareholder value.

In considering these approaches, the essential questions of what is the corporation, and what interests it should represent are exposed to light, as Davies eloquently argues:

> The crucial question is what the statutory statement says about the interests which the directors should promote when exercising their discretionary powers. The common law mantra that the duties of directors are owed to the company has long obscured the answer to this question. Although that is a statement of the utmost importance when it comes to the enforcement of duties and their associated remedies, it tells one nothing about the answer to our question, whose interests should the directors promote? This is because the company, as an artificial person, can have no interests separate from the interests of those who are associated with it, whether as shareholders, creditors, employers, suppliers, customers or in some other way. So, the crucial question is, when we refer to the company, to the interests of which of those sets of natural persons are we referring?
>
> (2005: 4)

As a member of the Corporate Law Review Steering Group, Davies goes on to defend the enlightened shareholder value view suggesting the pluralist approach produces a formula which is unenforceable, and paradoxically gives management more freedom of action than they previously enjoyed. An Australian legal expert, Redmond endorses this critique of widening the scope of directors' duties too greatly:

> The pluralist or multifiduciary model rests on a social, not a property, view of the corporation. It identifies the corporate purpose with maximising total constituency utility. This is an indeterminate outcome measure which

poses particular difficulties in translation into a legally enforceable duty. The indeterminacy of the criteria for decision and performance measurement also points to a probable loss of accountability for directors since it offers broad scope to justify most decisions. It is difficult to resist the conclusion of the UK review that either it confers a broad unpoliceable policy discretion on managers themselves or just gives a broad jurisdiction to the courts. The model needs either practical rehabilitation or a superior performance metric. It is not clear where either might be found.

(Redmond 2005: 27)

In the resulting UK Company Law Reform Bill (2005) the enlightened shareholder value view has prevailed in clause 156, which defines the essential directoral duty as:

### Duty to promote the success of the company

(1) A director of a company must act in the way he considers, in good faith, would be most likely to promote the success of the company for the benefit of its members as a whole.

(2) Where or to the extent that the purposes of the company consist of or include purposes other than the benefit of its members, his duty is to act in the way he considers, in good faith, would be most likely to achieve those purposes.

(3) In fulfilling the duty imposed by this section a director must (so far as reasonably practicable) have regard to:

(a) the likely consequences of any decision in the long term,
(b) the interests of the company's employees,
(c) the need to foster the company's business relationships with suppliers, customers and others,
(d) the impact of the company's operations on the community and the environment,
(e) the desirability of the company maintaining a reputation for high standards of business conduct, and
(f) the need to act fairly as between members of the company.

(4) The duty imposed by this section has effect subject to any enactment or rule of law requiring directors, in certain circumstances, to consider or act in the interests of creditors of the company.

This clause replaces the *discretion* of directors to have regard for stakeholder interests with a *duty* for directors to do this:

> As far as directors' duties are concerned, this is the heart of the enlightened shareholder value approach. The aim is to make it clear that although shareholder interests are predominant (promotion of the success of the company for the benefit of its members), the promotion of shareholder interests does not require riding roughshod over the interests of other groups upon whose activities the business of the company is dependent for its success. In fact, the promotion of the interests of the shareholders will normally require the interests of other groups of people to be fostered. The interests of non shareholder groups thus need to be considered by the directors, but, of course, in this shareholder-centred approach, only to the extent that the protection of those other interests promotes the interests of the shareholders. The statutory formulation can be said to express the insight that the shareholders are not likely to do well out of a company whose workforce is constantly on strike, whose customers don't like its products and whose suppliers would rather deal with its competitors.

(Davies 2005: 5)

In this way the Company Law Reform Bill treads a fine legal line between a sense of 'enlightened shareholder value' which is becoming best practice in many leading companies, and more radical claims for company law to adopt a more 'pluralist' sense of the ultimate objectives of the enterprise and the interests to be served. The reform manages this balancing act by suggesting that the pluralist objectives of maximising company performance to the benefit of all stakeholders can best be served by professional directors pursuing commercial

opportunities within a framework of standards and accountability:

> The overall objective should be pluralist in the sense that companies should be run in a way which maximises overall competitiveness and wealth and welfare for all. But the means which company law deploys for achieving this objective must be to take account of the realities and dynamics which operate in practice in the running of commercial enterprise. It should not be done at the expense of turning company directors from business decision-makers into moral, political or economic arbiters, but by harnessing focused, comprehensive, competitive decision-making within robust, objective professional standards and flexible, but pertinent accountability.
>
> (CLR 2000: 14)

The reform supports the ultimate power of shareholders to appoint or dismiss directors for whatever reasons they choose, and to intervene in management to the extent the constitution permits, and confesses: 'There is clearly an inconsistency between leaving these powers of shareholders intact and enabling or requiring directors to have regard to wider interests ... the effect will be to make smaller transactions within the powers of directors subject to the broad pluralist approach, but larger ones which are for shareholders subject only to the minimal constraints which apply to them' (CLR 2000: 26).

It is likely that the modern company law proposals, will over time facilitate the wider and more conscious adoption by UK companies of social and environmental commitments, and the willingness to report fully on them. In time it is possible that such social and environmental commitments will become part of a widespread company and management best practice, in the way that the commitment to quality in the production of goods and services has become universal.

Moreover, just as the UK in the publication of the Cadbury code of corporate governance ultimately influenced a considerable number of other countries to adopt a similar code, it is possible that other countries, particularly that share a common law tradition with the UK, will begin to review their company law with similar objectives

in mind. Twin inquiries taking place into corporate responsibility in Australia are now traversing this terrain. The Corporations and Markets Advisory Committee (CAMAC) commenced in March 2005 to consider whether directors' duties under the Corporations Act 2001 should include corporate responsibilities or obligations to take into account certain classes of stakeholders. The committee published an excellent discussion paper on *Corporate Social Responsibility* (available free at www.camac.gov.au).

The second inquiry, the Parliamentary Joint Committee on Corporates and Financial Services (PJC) began in June 2005 with a call for submissions on corporate social responsibility, and received over 120 extensive submissions from companies, consultancies, academics and other interested parties (available at http://www.aph.gov.au/Senate/committee/corporations_ctte/corporate_responsibility/index.htm). Together these inquiries will raise awareness of the issues involved in corporate responsibility considerably in Australia and it is likely that some significant modification of directors' duties will result at least in practice.

The possibility that this will be accompanied by an extension of the requirements for company reporting to include social and environmental matters receded, with the UK Chancellor's dramatic abandonment of the obligatory operating and financial review for listed companies in November 2006. However this was in the context of the European Union's Accounts Modernisation Directive (2003/51/EC) which also requires companies include environmental and social reports with their annual accounts necessary for an understanding of the companies' performance. There is here an irresistible new agenda for corporate responsibility.

One reason the agenda of corporate responsibility is increasingly irresistible is that while legal liability of corporations is deepening, what has been described as an emerging and hardening *moral liability* is exerting increasing influence (Figure 8.4). In this respect the legislative process lags behind what society thinks, values and respects. Moral liability occurs when corporations violate stakeholder expectations of ethical behaviour in ways that put business value at risk. There is an increasing convergence between these two forms of liability, as corporations come

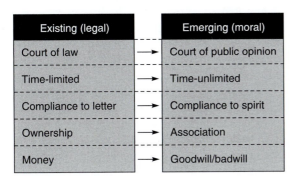

Figure 8.4 Legal and moral liability are converging.

Source: SustainAbility (2004), *The Changing Landscape of Liability: A Director's Guide to Trends in Corporate Environmental, Social and Economic Liability*, London: SustainAbility Ltd.

under scrutiny both by the law and – often more immediately and pointedly – by public opinion (SustainAbility 2004: 5). A graphic illustration of this was the James Hardie building company which having moved its corporate headquarters from Australia to the Netherlands, and the majority of its business activity to the United States, believed it had escaped responsibility for the legal liabilities of its remaining Australian subsidiaries to the thousands of asbestos victims now dependent on a seriously underfunded and almost bankrupt medical foundation Hardie had left behind to meet their claims. Massive public disapproval in Australia and internationally, and a commission of inquiry combined with the threat of legislative intervention, dragged James Hardie back to face the consequences of its irresponsible actions over many decades in the Australian market (Jackson 2004) (see Case Study 8).

## THE LEGITIMACY OF CSR FROM A GOVERNANCE PERSPECTIVE

### Investment institutions' effective portfolio management: the duty to address ESG issues?

Similar forces that are impressing corporations towards taking a greater regard of CSR issues are guiding investment institutions towards addressing environmental, social and governance issues more directly in their investment policies and practices. In the UNEP Finance Initiative on *The Materiality of Social, Environmental and Corporate Governance Issues to Equity Pricing* (2004) the interest of a growing number of institutional investors in approaches to asset management that explicitly include environmental, social and governance (ESG) criteria and metrics, either for ethical reasons or as relevant to investment performance was considered. Critical intermediaries are the brokerage firms that often have paid less consideration to ESG issues, often because they are driven by short term performance. A group of eleven international brokerage firms' analysts were commissioned to examine a range of industry sectors regarding the relevance of ESG to investment performance, and to submit detailed reports. Briefly their conclusions were:

- Environmental, social and governance criteria affect shareholder value both in the short and long term, and in some cases the effects could be profound. Research to determine the financial materiality of these criteria should use longer time spans than is currently employed for financial analysis.
- Governments could reduce barriers to environmental, social and corporate governance analysis by mandating and standardising the inclusion of these criteria in national and international corporate disclosure frameworks.
- Innovative techniques are being developed to perform financial analyses of environmental, social and corporate governance criteria in response to growing investor demand, including ranking surveys, portfolio analysis of best and worst performers, and scenario analysis to evaluate potential impact of upcoming regulation on sectors.

EIGHT

The survey discovered that brokerage houses in Europe are increasingly willing and able to respond to demand for ESG research. In contrast brokerage houses in the United States referred to perceived difficulty in analysis due to barriers associated with inadequate disclosure of these criteria.

A further fascinating research project of the UNEP Finance Initiative considered *A Legal Framework for the Integration of Environmental, Social and Governance Issues into Institutional Investment* (2005). The current value of assets managed by the investment industry worldwide is estimated at $42 trillion, pension fund assets in the US and UK alone amounting to $7.4 trillion. However the weighty responsibility of deciding where these assets are invested lies not with the owners, but with a small number of principals and agents. 'By influencing the way investments are made, the legal factors that inform the decisions made by this relatively small group have a profound effect on the behaviour of the entities in which these assets are invested and ultimately on the environments and societies with which these investment vehicles interact' (UNEP FI 2005: 6).

Despite the increasing evidence that ESG issues do have a material impact on the financial performance of securities and increasing awareness of the importance of assessing ESG related risks, the effort to achieve a greater regard for ESG issues in investment decision-making is often resisted on the basis that institutional principals and their agents are legally prevented from taking account of these issues. Just as it is assumed corporate directors can only be committed to shareholder value, it is often assumed that investment trustees can only be directed towards profit maximisation. However, the survey conducted by the international law firm Freshfields Bruckhaus Deringer confirms categorically that in each of the jurisdictions examined (France, Germany, Italy, Japan, Spain, UK, US, Australia and Canada) investment decision-makers retained some degree of discretion as to how they might invest the funds they control.

In the common law jurisdictions (US, UK, Australia and Canada) the rules are articulated in statute and in court decisions. In the other jurisdictions as civil law applies, rules are articulated as codes or in statutes. Though in none

of the jurisdictions do rules prescribe how principals should integrate ESG considerations into their decisions, in most cases it is left to principals to determine their investment approach within their legal obligations.

Fiduciary duties are the key discretionary limits of investment decision-makers in common law countries, the most important duties being the duty to act prudently and the duty to act in accordance with the purpose for which investment powers were granted (the duty of loyalty) (Figure 8.5).

In the US the modern prudent investor rule, which incorporates both a duty of care and a duty of loyalty, emphasises modern portfolio theory and provides that:

- investments are assessed not in isolation but in the context of their contribution to a total investment portfolio;
- there is no duty to 'maximise' the return of individual investments, but instead a duty to implement an overall investment strategy that is rational and appropriate to the fund;
- the investment portfolio must be diversified, unless it is prudent not to do so; and
- the prudence of an investment should be assessed at the time the investment was made and not in hindsight.

The effect of the modern prudent investor rule is that institutional decision-makers are given latitude to follow a wide range of diversified investment strategies: provided their choice of investments is rational and economically defensible, they are free to construct a balanced portfolio (UNEP FI 2005: 8). Other jurisdictions stipulate the duty to act conscientiously in the interests of beneficiaries, to seek profitability, recognise the portfolio approach to modern investment, and in some jurisdictions limits on the types of assets which may be selected for particular funds.

Two things which are critical in all jurisdictions are following the correct process, and pursuing proper objectives in terms of acting only in the interests of the beneficiaries. As with other investment criteria, different considerations will be given different weight, according to how conditions are defined and analysed. In some circumstances it may be decided that ESG considerations have

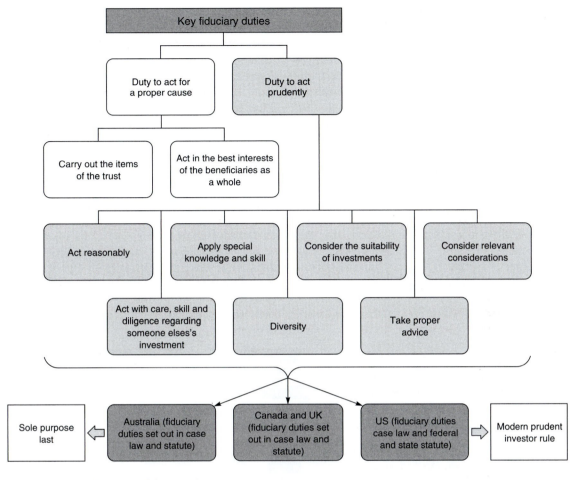

**Figure 8.5** Fund trustees' fiduciary duties.

Source: Freshfields Bruckhaus Deringer (2005), *A Legal Framework for the Integration of Environmental, Social and Governance Issues into Institutional Investment*, Geneva: UNEPFI, 15.

little material impact on financial performance relevant to a particular investment. However, this does not justify failure to identify such considerations and to assess the weight. It is becoming increasingly difficult to argue that ESG considerations are difficult to quantify, since goodwill and intangibles are now readily quantified. A majority of the jurisdictions surveyed have already legislated to require investment decision-makers, particularly of pension funds, to disclose the extent to which they take ESG considerations into account.

There is increasingly credible evidence that ESG considerations have a vital role to play in the proper analysis of investment value, and cannot be ignored as they would result in investments being given inappropriate value, for example:

Climate change is an obvious example of an environmental consideration that is recognised as affecting value. Following the recent release of a report by Mercer Investment Consulting noting the financial impact that climate change has already had on companies' costs, revenues, assets and liabilities, the UK Carbon Trust expressed the view that 'Pension fund trustees have a duty to address the financial risk posed by climate change when making investment decisions'.

(UNEP FI 2005: 11)

E
I
G
H
T

Investment institutions are not only becoming more alert regarding the ESG issues in their investment portfolio they are also beginning to take a proactive stance in terms of engaging in the environmental, social and governance performance of the corporations they invest in (Figure 8.6). Both in the US and UK the traditional passivity of the investment institutions is being cast aside in favour of more active involvement. Certainly they continue to prefer quiet influence to open confrontation, but in an increasing number of instances the institutional investors have demonstrated a willingness to use their power to insist on higher standards of governance, and there are some indications this may occur more frequently in future on wider ESG issues.

## SOCIALLY RESPONSIBLE INVESTMENT AND CORPORATE SOCIAL RESPONSIBILITY

In recent years, interest in socially responsible investing has grown around the world. The European Commission helped launch the European Sustainable and Responsible Investment Forum (Eurosif) in 2001. Eurosif unites existing forums in the UK, France, Italy, the Netherlands, Germany, Luxembourg, and Switzerland, and aims to encourage shareholder action on Corporate Social Responsibility (CSR) policies and publish reports on socially responsible investment issues to influence public policy.

Socially responsible investment (SRI) according to the UK Social Investment Forum (2001)

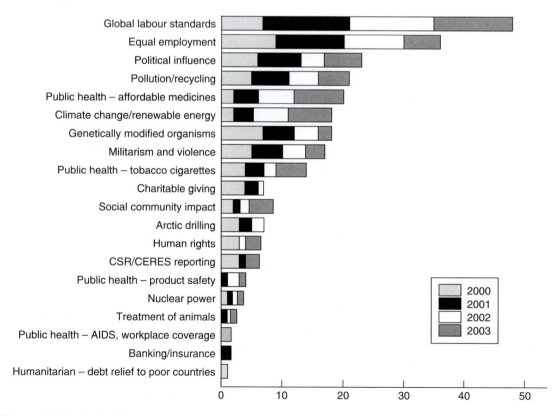

Figure 8.6 Institutional investor voting, 2000–2003.

Source: Monks, R., Miller, A. and Cook, J. (2004), Shareholder Activism on Enviromental Issues: A Study of Proposals at Large US Corporations (2000–2003), *Natural Resources Forum*, 28: 317–330.

'combines investors' financial objectives with their commitment to social concerns such as social justice, economic development, peace or a healthy environment'. In an influential green paper entitled *Promoting a European Framework for Corporate Social Responsibility* (2001: 4), the European Commission states simply 'Corporate social responsibility is essentially a concept whereby companies decide voluntarily to contribute to a better society and a cleaner environment'.

In France AFG-ASFFI the association of professional fund managers has requested that corporate boards consider the concept of sustainable development, social responsibility and the environment. French corporate law was amended to require listed companies to disclose in their annual reports how they take the social and environmental consequences of their activities into account in May 2001.

Meanwhile in the UK the Modern Company Law Review (2000) introduced the concept of an extended Operating and Financial Review (OFR) to include environmental policies and performance, and policies and performance on community, social, ethical and reputational issues. In 2000 the UK government passed regulations requiring pension funds to disclose the extent to which social, environmental, and ethical issues are taken into account in their investment decisions.

Responding to the new legislation in 2001 the Association of British Insurers (ABI) announced that it expected companies to assess and disclose the risks and opportunities in social, environmental and ethical matters (Gregory and Pollack 2002). As a result of these changes Sparkes (2002) calculates the total assets involved in SRI in the UK leapt from £22.7bn in 1997 to £224.5bn in 2001.

The first ethical investment fund, Asahi Life Socially Responsible Investment, was formed in Japan in 2001. At the end of October 2001 the Nikko Fund designed by Nikko Asset Management and Nikko Securities to serve the new interest in corporate responsibility had raised assets of one billion US dollars. From small beginnings in investment funds managed by religious organisations, according to the Ethical Investment Association's (EIA 2002) figures, SRI in Australia has grown dramatically rising to A$12 billion in 2006, (Figure 8.7).

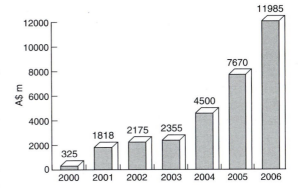

**Figure 8.7** Growth of SRI investment assets in Australia, 2000–2006.

Source: Ethical Investment Association (EIA) (2006), SRI Benchmarking Survey.

Finally in the US Socially Responsible Investing (SRI) is becoming firmly established. According to the biennial report of the Social Investment Forum, of the overall investment through professional managers amounting to $19.9 trillion in December 2000, over 11 per cent or $2.3 trillion dollars is invested in a socially responsible manner. The Social Investment Forum (SIF) breaks down these figures into $1.4 trillion employing screening only on social or environmental criteria; $601 billion in screening and shareholder advocacy funds; $305 billion in shareholder advocacy only funds; and $8 billion in community investment funds (Figure 8.8): www.socialfunds.com/news/article.cgi?sfArticleId=724.

As the stock markets of New York, London and much of Europe collapsed in 2002 and 2003 the SRI funds seemed to offer the safer haven of sustainable growth rather than the reckless gamble of massive booms followed by apparently inevitable appalling busts. Socially and environmentally responsible mutual funds in the United States continued their strong performance during the first quarter of 2003, according to data released by the Social Investment Forum. For the first three months of the year, 13 of the 18 (72 per cent) Forum-tracked screened mutual funds with $100 million or more in assets received top marks for performance from either or both rating agencies

E
I
G
H
T

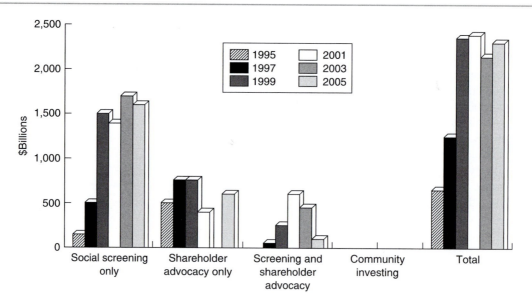

**Figure 8.8** Growth of SRI investments in the US, 1995–2005.

Source: SIF (2006), *2005 Report on Socially Responsible Investing Trends in United States: 10 Year Review*, Washington, DC: Social Investment Forum, Fig. 1.2, p. 2.

Morningstar and Lipper for the one- or three-year periods ended 31 March 2003. Socially responsible mutual funds continued to grow on a net basis during the first quarter of 2003 while the rest of the mutual fund industry contracted. According to Lipper, socially responsible mutual funds saw net inflows of $185.3 million during the first quarter of 2003. Over the same time, US diversified equity funds posted outflows of nearly $13.2 billion: www.socialinvest.org/areas/news/2003-Q1performance.htm.

Reflecting this trend towards SRI, and in all likelihood massively compounding it, is the advent of social and environmental reporting indices, such as the FTSE4Good Index and the Dow Jones Sustainability Index. The existence of these indices will attract more investors, fund managers and institutions to concentrate their minds on the potential benefits of socially and environmentally responsible investing. In turn this will lead more companies to both develop and to disclose their social and environmental policies and performance. At first appearing or not in the SRI indices may be a matter of corporate pride, but soon enough it will be a matter of access to an important and growing part of the investment market, and a part of the market prepared to invest for the longer term if the right corporate policies and practices are in place. If companies are not attracted to this prospect there is always the possibility of being compelled, for example in April 2001 the UK fund manager Morley, part of CGNU the UK's largest insurer, announced that it would not vote for FTSE 100 managements that did not disclose comprehensive reports on environmental issues. This assertiveness of investment institutions is set to grow, rather than diminish, and will require positive responses rather than clever evasion.

Corporate social responsibility is no longer the purview of just a handful of managers concerned with the social or environmental impact of their firm's operations and increasingly has become part of overall business strategy. Widespread economic and political concerns are at the heart of this movement, and a number of factors explain the growing interest in corporate social responsibility:

■ new concerns and expectations of citizens, consumers, public authorities, and investors in times of globalisation and industrial change;

- the increasing influence of social criteria on the investment decisions of individuals and institutions, as investors or consumers;
- growing concern about environmental degradation;
- the impact of new information and communication technologies on the transparency and circulation of information on business activity.

In the financial and corporate world, corporate social responsibility is increasingly accepted as a given with a positive impact on performance. An indication of this acceptance is the proliferation of voluntary codes of conduct. The majority of international businesses now would state that they take ethical issues into consideration in managing their risk; however, only a minority of them methodically and regularly evaluate their performance (Committee on Public Finance 2002).

It is useful to examine some of the investment strategies of the SRI funds, seek to demonstrate the principles and character of the developing different social and environmental investment indices, and investigate the potential impact upon corporate environmental and social reporting. There is mounting evidence that corporations, industries, markets, economies and ecologies are all in serious jeopardy in the foreseeable future, if social and environmental commitments are not fully engaged.

## SOCIALLY RESPONSIBLE INVESTMENT STRATEGIES

In exploring the development and implementation of SRI strategies, it is proposed to examine the two countries with the largest SRI institutional investment funds, the United States and the United Kingdom, and thirdly to look at Australia, where the potential for SRI remains considerable.

### United States

Socially responsible investment in the United States incorporates three strategies that work together to promote socially and environmentally responsible business practices, and encourage improvements in the quality of life throughout society as a result:

- *Screening*: The practice of including or excluding publicly traded securities from investment portfolios or mutual funds based on social and and/or environmental criteria. Generally, investors seek to own profitable companies that make a positive contribution to society. 'Buy lists' include enterprises with outstanding employer-employee relations, excellent environmental practices, products that are safe and useful, and operations that respect human rights around the world. Conversely, they avoid investing in companies whose products and business practices are harmful.
- *Shareholder advocacy*: The actions many socially aware investors take in their role as owners of corporate America. These efforts include entering discussions with companies on issues of concern as well as filing and voting proxy resolutions. Proxy resolutions on social issues are generally aimed at influencing corporate behaviour toward a more responsible level of corporate citizenship, steering management toward action that enhances the well-being of all the company's stakeholders, and improving social performance over time.
- *Community investing*: Financing that generates resources and opportunities for economically disadvantaged people in urban and rural communities in the US and abroad that are under-served by traditional financial institutions. Community investors make it possible for local organisations to create jobs, provide financial services to low-income individuals, and supply capital for small businesses, affordable housing, and community services such as childcare (Social Investment Forum 2001: 6).

With regard to the first SRI strategy of screening, in recent years tobacco is the most common screen employed by socially screened portfolio screens in the US (that is, companies involved in tobacco are screened out). The environment, human rights, employment/equality, gambling, alcohol and weapons are widely used screens by 50 per cent or more of screened portfolios

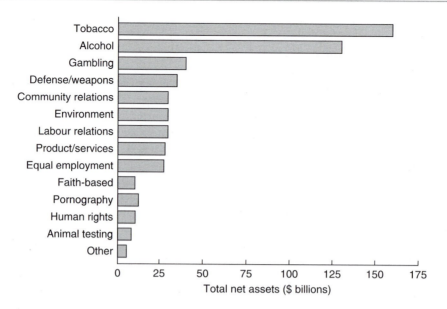

**Figure 8.9** Screens most commonly used in screened portfolios in the US, 2005.

Source: Social Investment Forum Foundation (2006), *2005 Report on Socially Responsible Investing trends in the United States: 10 Year Review*, Washington, DC: SIF, 8.

(Figure 8.9). Other common screens include labour relations, animal testing/rights, community investing and community relations. More specialised screens include executive compensation, birth control, and international labour standards. Over time screened portfolios have consistently broadened their screens employed, including negative screens (screening out companies for their poor environmental and social records), and positive screens (screening in companies that have excellent social and environmental records). In some cases new issues of social and environmental concern, such as international labour standards, emerge first through shareholder advocacy and as quantitative criteria are developed to apply them as portfolio screens.

The growth of screened portfolios is due to several factors. Socially responsible investment continues to perform financially well in relation to the market for both institutional and individual investors. Anti-tobacco sentiment goes beyond a social concern and has become a financial consideration. Investors are divesting from tobacco stocks due to concerns about public health, and admissions by the tobacco industry that it has marketed cigarettes to children and

withheld evidence about the health risks of smoking. Other factors contributing to a growth of socially screened investment options are the increased participation of retirement plans and employees increasingly moving assets into them. There is also a growth of screened religious funds. Investors are now presented with a growing range of products, SRI portfolios offer investors the ability to invest in a wide range of equities and bonds, as well as domestic, international and global options. All this has given increasing prominence to SRI with increasing media coverage, with greater familiarity among the public and investment professionals (Social Investment Forum 2001: 9–13).

The second SRI strategy of shareholder advocacy is the one that often hits the headlines and leads to set-piece confrontations between major corporates and influential members of the investment lobby. Of course though, 'shareholders have both a right and a responsibility to take an interest in the company's performance, policies, practices and impacts. The shareholder resolution process provides a formal communication channel between shareholders, management, and the board of directors, and with other shareholders, on

issues of corporate governance and social responsibility' (Social Investment Forum 2001: 14). There were 261 shareholder resolutions introduced in US companies in 2001 of which 156 were voted on receiving on average 8.5 per cent of the votes. This may not seem impressive, but the figures are deceptive for a number of reasons. Firstly, corporations are not used to any public display of dissent among their ranks, and are usually deeply concerned when issues that concern them become matters of open controversy. This leads to an increasing inclination on the part of many companies to engage in meaningful dialogue with shareholders or other stakeholders that have an issue to raise, before the issue becomes too controversial, and often this results in some form of settlement. If the matter does come before the AGM and the company wins the vote, this is often only because of the number of institutions that do not vote their proxies, and the management win by default. However where there is a genuine issue and there is a determination among a significant number of shareholders to see it resolved, often these prove pyrrhic management victories, as shareholder campaigns bring more institutions on board.

Analysts categorise shareholder resolutions into two categories: corporate governance and corporate social responsibility:

■ *Corporate governance resolutions* address issues such as confidential voting, board of director qualifications, compensation of directors and executives and board performance (Table 8.4).
■ *Social responsibility resolutions* most often address issues such as company policies and practices on the environment, health and safety, race and gender, tobacco, sweatshops, and other human rights issues (Table 8.5).

Illustrative of the issues addressed by shareholders' actions in 2003/2005 are compliance on labour standards, human rights, access to prescription drugs, restraint on genetically modified products, employment of people with disabilities, environmental damage and recycling (Table 8.5).

| Type of proposal | Proposed | | Withdrawn | | Voted on | | Average vote (%) | |
| --- | --- | --- | --- | --- | --- | --- | --- | --- |
| | 2003 | 2004 | 2003 | 2004 | 2003 | 2004 | 2003 | 2004 |
| Independent board chair | 42 | 59 | 9 | 8 | 30 | 36 | 26.10 | 28.30 |
| Limit consulting by auditors | 29 | 35 | 7 | 16 | 19 | 12 | 16.10 | 14.20 |
| Increase board independence | 8 | 14 | 1 | 0 | 5 | 13 | 27.50 | 26.10 |
| Majority vote to elect directors | — | 14 | — | 2 | — | 12 | — | 11.80 |
| Cumulative voting | 21 | 24 | 1 | 1 | 20 | 21 | 34.10 | 34.90 |
| Restrict executive compensation | 64 | 158 | 2 | 28 | 36 | 79 | 15.40 | 11.50 |
| Expense option value at time of grant | 115 | 50 | 27 | 11 | 69 | 34 | 47.40 | 53.30 |
| Vote on golden parachutes | 21 | 36 | 2 | 8 | 18 | 26 | 57.00 | 51.80 |
| Cap executive pay | — | 15 | — | 3 | — | 7 | — | 7.70 |
| Award performance-based stock options | 92 | 8 | 24 | 1 | 59 | 5 | 16.10 | 40.20 |
| Poison pill | 107 | 100 | 1 | 3 | 84 | 51 | 60.00 | 61.10 |
| Declassify board | 63 | 59 | 9 | 11 | 48 | 39 | 63.40 | 71.60 |
| Eliminate supermajority vote | 10 | 11 | 1 | 1 | 9 | 7 | 60.50 | 75.80 |
| Sell the company/maximise value | 4 | 13 | 0 | 1 | 2 | 4 | 3.20 | 25.10 |
| Other | 215 | 251 | 38 | 84 | 75 | 99 | — | — |
| **Total** | **791** | **847** | **122** | **178** | **474** | **445** | | |

**Table 8.4** US shareholder actions planned for 2003–2004, including key resolutions.

Source: SIF (2006), *2005 Report on Socially Responsible Investing Trends in the United States – 10 Year Review*, Washington, DC: Social Investment Forum, Figure 4.4 Key Corporate Governance Resolutions (2003–2004), p. 21.

| | Company | Resolution | Year | Management Opposed? | Vote (%) |
|---|---|---|---|---|---|
| 1 | **Coca-Cola Company** | **Review AIDS pandemic's impact on company** | 2004 | No | 97.9 |
| | Proponent: ASC Investment | | | | |
| 2 | **JC Penney Co., Inc.** | **Adopts sexual orientation and anti-bias policy** | 2003 | No | 93.3 |
| | Proponents: NYCERS, NYC Teachers, Trillium Asset Management | | | | |
| 3 | **Tyco International Ltd** | **Review and reduce toxic emissions** | 2004 | No | 92.2 |
| | Proponents: Christian Bros, Investment Service (CBIS) | | | | |
| 4 | **Cintas Corp** | **Review/report on vendor standards** | 2004 | No | 91.5 |
| | Proponent: NYCERS | | | | |
| 5 | **Fifth Third Bancorp** | **Adopt sexual orientation and anti-bias policy** | 2004 | No | 62.8 |
| | Proponent: NorthStar Asset Management | | | | |
| 6 | **Plum Creek Timber Co., Inc** | **Report on political donations and policy** | 2005 | No | 56.2 |
| | Proponent: Newground Social Investment | | | | |
| 7 | **Cooper Industries** | **Issue sustainability report** | 2003 | Yes | 44.3 |
| | Proponents: Benedictine Sisters, Domini Social Investments, St Joseph Health | | | | |
| 8 | **Dover** | **Adopt sexual orientation anti-bias policy** | 2003 | Yes | 42.8 |
| | Proponents: Walden Asset Management, Calvert | | | | |
| 9 | **Ryland Group Inc** | **Report using GRI guidelines** | 2004 | Yes | 42.2 |
| | Proponent: Calvert | | | | |
| 10 | **Gentex** | **Commit to/report on board diversity** | 2003 | Yes | 39.2 |
| | Proponent: Calvert | | | | |
| 11 | **Yum! Brands, Inc.** | **Issue sustainability report** | 2005 | Yes | 39.1 |
| | Proponents: CREA, Trillium, Christus Health, ELCA | | | | |
| 12 | **Yum! Brands, Inc.** | **Issue sustainability report** | 2003 | Yes | 39 |
| | Proponents: Trillium, Needmor Fund, CBIS, United Church Christ | | | | |
| 13 | **Emerson Electric Co** | **Adopt sexual orientation anti-bias policy** | 2005 | Yes | 38.9 |
| | Proponents: Domini, NorthStar, Pride Foundation | | | | |
| 14 | **AGCO Corp** | **Report using GRI guidelines** | 2004 | Yes | 38.3 |
| | Proponent: Calvert | | | | |
| 15 | **Apache Corp** | **Report on/reduce greenhouse gas emissions** | 2004 | Yes | 37.1 |
| | Proponent: Boston Common Asset Management | | | | |
| 16 | **Advance Auto Parts Inc.** | **Adopt sexual orientation anti-bias policy** | 2005 | Yes | 37.1 |
| | Proponent: NYC Pension Funds | | | | |
| 17 | **Yum! Brands, Inc.** | **Issue sustainability report** | 2004 | Yes | 32.9 |
| | Proponent: CREA | | | | |
| 18 | **CenterPoint Energy** | **Adopt sexual orientation anti-bias policy** | 2003 | Yes | 32.2 |
| | Proponents: NYCERS, NYC Teachers | | | | |

Table 8.5 US companies' highest votes on social policy resolution.

| | Company | Resolution | Year | Management Opposed? | Vote (%) |
|---|---|---|---|---|---|
| 19 | Gilead Sciences, Inc. | Review AIDS pandemic's impact on company | 2005 | Yes | 31.7 |
| | Proponents: Camilla Madden Trust, Catholic Healthcare West | | | | |
| 20 | Triquent Semiconductor | Report on involvement in ballistic missile defence | 2003 | Yes | 31.5 |
| | Proponent: Maryknoll Fathers and Bros. | | | | |
| 21 | Anadarko Petroleum Corp | Report on/reduce greenhouse gas emissions | 2004 | Yes | 31.4 |
| | Proponent: Trillium | | | | |
| 22 | Cooper Cameron Corp | Report using GRI guidelines | 2004 | Yes | 30.4 |
| | Proponent: Calvert | | | | |
| 23 | Delphi | Review/report on global standards | 2003 | Yes | 30.1 |
| | Proponents: Gen. Board of Pensions of United Methodist Church, Mercy Consolidated Asset Management, Benedictine Sisters | | | | |
| 24 | Home Depot Inc | Report on EEO | 2005 | Yes | 30 |
| | Proponents: Walden, NorthStar, Domini | | | | |
| 25 | Exxon Mobil Corp. | Adopt sexual orientation anti-bias policy | 2005 | Yes | 29.5 |
| | Proponents: NYCERS, Trillium, NorthStar, F&C Asset Management | | | | |

Table 8.5—Cont'd

Source: SIF (2006), *2005 Report on Socially Responsible Investing Trends in the United States – 10 Year Review*, Washington, DC: Social Investment Forum, Figure 4.5: 25 Highest Votes on Social Policy Resolution, p. 23.

These resolution are beginning to have more impact at large corporations' annual meetings, and will exert a greater effect as their voting strength continues to grow with much public support.

Leading the charge of the shareholders on corporate governance practices in the United States is the Council of Institutional Investors, whose members have over $1.5 trillion invested. Many of the institutions active on corporate governance are also active on CSR issues, including the pension funds of New York City, the State of Connecticut and State of Minnesota, State of California, and TIAA-CREF (the Teachers Insurance and Annuity Association College Retirement Equities Fund of New York with $259 billion of assets under management one of the largest wealth management companies in the world), seeing both governance and social issues having an impact on corporate performance (Social Investment Forum 2001: 14–19).

The final SRI strategy in the United States are assets invested locally by community development financial institutions, providing the financing which helps generate resources and opportunities for economically disadvantaged people in urban and rural communities. Community investors make it possible for local organisations to create jobs, provide financial services to low-income individuals, supply capital for small businesses, affordable housing and vital services like childcare. Though a much smaller part of the SRI world at $7.6 billion in 2001, this form of investing is growing rapidly (Social Investment Forum 2001: 20).

## United Kingdom

Demonstrating how SRI is rapidly becoming a global phenomenon, a dramatic catalyst occurred in the UK government's amendment of the

Pensions Act in July 2000 to require all occupational pension funds to declare whether and how they integrate social and environmental factors into their investment decisions. While pension funds are free to declare that they do not have any intention of doing so, this new legislation resulted in a new resolve by many pension funds to engage corporations in dialogue on social and environmental issues. A survey conducted by Environmental Resources Management (ERM) in 2000 revealed that 21 of the UK's largest 25 pension funds intended to implement socially responsible investment principles, representing nearly half of the $1.2 trillion in UK pension fund assets, which makes up about a third of all investment in the UK stock market.

The ERM survey asked pension funds how they anticipated investing against SRI criteria over the next two years. Nearly 90 per cent of the funds surveyed said they would include environmental, social and ethical impacts in their investments at some level, following the new law. 'If pension funds are going to seriously engage industry on issues such as human rights, child labour, and environmental pollution, they face a steep learning curve', said ERM director Tom Wollard. 'Not only are they going to have to decide what questions to ask companies, but also what they are going to do with the answers'. Around 70 per cent of the funds surveyed said they planned to implement active engagement of companies, rather than simply boycotting specific industry sectors such as tobacco and alcohol. While most funds were undecided about the level of social investment, two said they were committed to implementing social investing principles across 100 per cent of their funds, representing at least $180 billion in UK equities: www.ssocialfunds.com/news/print.cgi?sfArticleID=309.

The UK position in SRI was given a further boost when the Association of British Insurers (ABI) whose members accounted for a further 25 per cent of all London Stock Market investments launched new guidelines incorporating social responsibility. They called upon companies to establish formal systems to identify risks and opportunities arising from ethical and environmental issues, to disclose which of these issues are significant for business, and to describe the polices and management systems in place to address these risks: www.abi.org.uk. The ABI guidelines state: 'Public interest in corporate social responsibility has grown to the point where it seems helpful for institutional shareholders to set out basic disclosure principles, which will guide them in seeking to engage with companies in which they invest'.

However, a survey of pension funds published as *JustPensions* (Coles and Green 2002) two years after the introduction of the new legislation suggested that though the majority of pension funds had adopted SRI policies, they often did not have the capacity to implement or monitor these policies in practice. The survey consisted of 14 pension funds managing £170 billion about 20 per cent of the total value of the assets held by UK pension funds. The researchers' view of SRI best practice was essentially in terms of policies and people:

- *Policies*: A *Statement of Investment Principles* that states why social, environmental and ethical issues should be considered and why this is consistent with achieving satisfactory investment returns. The exercise of *voting rights* and *public disclosure of engagement activities* backs up the principles taken in the statement. The pension fund SRI principles are consistent with the values on social responsibility of the employer the pension fund is based on, where this is compatible with the interests of the scheme.
- *People*: Where investments are managed in-house someone is employed to monitor the social, environmental and ethical performance of investor companies. Where investment management is out-sourced, an assessment is made of the capability of the investment manager's people in monitoring this performance. Appropriate research is carried out into the social, environmental and ethical performance of companies invested in, both directly by reference to published information, and through the utilisation of research organisations. Formal training programmes are established for both trustees and investment managers on critical social, environmental and ethical issues.
- *Implementation*: The assessment of social, environmental and ethical issues is integrated into

the investment process and the risk management process. For all markets the assessment is viewed as being an essential part of good corporate governance and good management. Specific measurable goals are set, and good performance is rewarded. Pension funds collaborate in the consideration of particular issues, and within legal constraints, in the exercise of voting rights.

- *Transparency*: Information on how pension funds invest and assess social, environmental and ethical issues and good practice is shared with others through the pension funds website (Coles and Green 2002).

Examining how well pension funds lived up to this view of best practice the researchers found some examples of best practice in terms of statements of principles, including BP, Hermes, USS and West Midlands (the first three among the largest pension funds in the UK). The Universities Superannuation Scheme (USS) with £22 billion assets managed in 2001, had the most developed policy (Box 8.1).

But even funds with good SRI principles did not have a strong policy of backing this up with the use of voting rights and publicity. Furthermore, only a small number of pension funds had in-house specialists responsible for this remit, USS has a team of three Socially Responsible and Sustainable professionals. Hermes has added social responsibility to the remit of its specialist Corporate Governance team, and the Local Authority Pension Fund Forum has out-sourced this activity to the Pensions Investment Research Consultants (PIRC). Very few pension funds required their investment managers to use an SRI research organisation, and there was little formal training of pension fund trustees in SRI issues.

With regard to implementation some of the leading SRI pension funds do monitor and review the SRI activity of their fund managers, but these are the exceptions and in general there is little evidence this assessment taking place in most pension funds, and no evidence of it relating to rewards. A few pensions funds are actively collaborating around issues such as climate change, and some such as Strathclyde and West Midlands

---

### Box 8.1    Extract from Universities Superannuation Scheme

**UNIVERSITIES SUPERANNUATION SCHEME**

The Universities Superannuation Scheme (USS) is a global pension fund principally for academic and senior administrative staff in UK universities and other higher education and research institutions. As an institutional investor that takes seriously its fiduciary obligations to its beneficial and institutional members, USS aims to be an active and responsible long-term shareholder of companies and markets in which it invests. The Fund has a commitment to encourage responsible corporate behaviour which is based upon:

i)   the view that management of such issues is good for long term corporate performance and

ii)   a duty to protect and enhance the value of the fund's investments. This approach

is indeed widely recognised as one that greatly increases the likelihood of long-term value delivery and therefore to be in the long-term interests of pension fund beneficiaries.

As a fund that seeks to be a patient and long-term provider of capital, USS takes seriously its responsibilities to companies in which it invests and seeks to engage in constructive communication and dialogue as a basis upon which it is appropriate to discuss and question management behaviour.

USS therefore seeks to pay appropriate regard to relevant corporate governance, social, ethical and environmental considerations in the selection, retention and realisation of all fund investments. USS focuses its efforts on engagement, and thus seeks to use its influence as a major institutional investor to promote good practice by investee companies

and by markets to which the fund is particularly exposed. USS sees engagement as a necessary and important part of responsible ownership.

USS will engage with companies in which it invests on occasions when it thinks it is in members' long-term interests and will endeavour to identify problems at an early stage to minimize any loss of shareholder value. This approach may be adopted irrespective of whether the company is held in an active or passive fund or whether USS is underweight or not.

Instances when USS may intervene include when we have concerns about:

- The company's strategy
- The company's operational performance
- The company's acquisition/disposal strategy
- Independent directors failing to hold executive management to account
- Internal controls failing
- Inadequate succession planning
- An unjustifiable failure to comply with the Combined Code
- Inappropriate remuneration levels/incentive packages/severance packages
- The company's approach to corporate responsibility.

Source: Extract taken from pp.1–3 of USS (2004), 'Voting and Engagement Policy', London: USS, http://www.usshq.co.uk/policy statement

are publishing their investment policy on their websites and reports on engagement. The 2002 *JustPensions* survey demonstrates that a lot of the idealism and policy commitments offered by pension funds two years earlier in the UK in response to the change in legislation as revealed in the survey of the UK Social Investment Forum (Mathieu 2000) of the UK's largest 500 pension funds remains to be effectively implemented. However, even in the more hopeful earlier survey it was clear that different UK funds had different degrees of commitment to SRI (Figure 8.10).

## Australia

Australia has great potential for development in SRI, firstly, because unlike the United States and United Kingdom, the Australian superannuation scheme requires the majority of employees to make compulsory contributions to their pension funds, covering 81 per cent of all employees, that has resulted in superannuation funds managing A$454.7 billion in assets. Secondly, Australia has some of the finest natural assets in the world, though being the driest continent on earth, also has the most precarious ecology with drought and salinity constant threats, that might stimulate a heightened sense of environmental awareness. However, though SRI increased to A$12 billion

in 2002, this is a smaller proportion of investment than in the US or UK. Australian investors have been relatively slow to take up SRI, and the market is relatively immature. Environmental disclosure by corporates appears to be driven by regulatory needs rather than investors' and analysts' requirements. Presently legislation does not enforce disclosure on environmental, social or ethical considerations in investment decisions. There remains doubt whether SRI performance will be in the best interests of superannuation fund members, and some conservative views among trustees whether SRI investments might compromise their fiduciary responsibility. In the insurance sector also sustainability issues have not featured highly, and responses to the issue of environmental impairment are reactive (PwC 2001). How fragile is the grip of SRI in Australia despite the appearance of a dramatic increase in scale and significance is illustrated by the fact that the record of shareholder resolutions related to social responsibility in 2001 was limited to one resolution introduced at the Rio Tinto AGM, where 17.3 per cent of the votes cast represented A$2.6 billion in share value. In 2002 there was not a single shareholder resolution relating to social responsibility.

Yet improvement in understanding and acceptance of SRI is rapidly developing in Australia. A significant number of new SRI investment

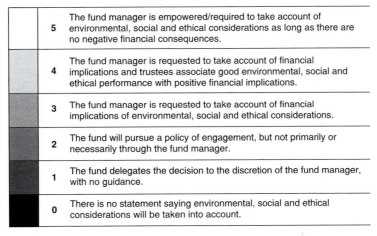

**Figure 8.10** Proportion of UK funds taking SRI concerns into account to differing degrees.

Source: Mathieu, Eugenie (2000), London: UKSIF.

products are being developed, and superannuation fund trustees are beginning to appreciate the significance of the SRI alternative. There is an increasing demand for the use of environmental screening as part of the investment process, and superannuation fund members are taking more interest in where their superannuation is invested. Banks are developing environmental risk assessment as part of their lending evaluation processes, and the insurance and re-insurance industry is developing a more comprehensive understanding of environmental risks. Biodiversity and salinity credits are being considered, as the government shows leadership on the issues of climate change, salinity and biodiversity (PwC 2001). However, Australia has some way to go in developing an optimum

social and environmental reporting and disclosure regime. The sudden realisation in 2007 in Australia that the country was experiencing the longest drought in 100 years was a salutary wake-up call.

## SOCIAL AND ENVIRONMENTAL INVESTMENT INDICES

The impact of the new Social and Environmental Investment indices will probably hasten all of the developments towards SRI so far observed by highlighting SRI issues, disseminating widely information about corporate social and environmental responsibility performance, and encouraging

greater reporting and disclosure by corporations of their CSR. This will help to create a wholly new investment climate in which any sense of SRI being marginal will be divested, as SRI investing moves into the mainstream. The rest of this chapter will review the salient features of the principal SRI Indices.

## Calvert

The Calvert Social Index is a broad-based benchmark for measuring the performance of large socially responsible US-based companies. The Calvin index is a product of Calvert which has been in the mutual fund business for 25 years, and manages $25 billion in assets in 27 screened and non-screened portfolios for 220,000 shareholders. It has become a leading provider of SRI mutual funds across equity, bond and money market portfolios. Calvert takes the 1,000 largest companies by market capitalisation in the US listed on the NYSE, and NASDAQ-AMEX. The social research department of Calvert then conducts an audit including product safety, environment, workplace issues, international operations and human rights, community relations and weapons contracting on each company.

The stocks that meet Calvert's social criteria make up the Calvert Social Index, and in September 2002 a total of 637 companies were in the index. Calvert reviews the index on a quarterly basis with companies reviewed for inclusion or exclusion on the basis of their social performance. Calvert states,

> We understand that few companies excel in all these areas and that a portfolio of 'perfect' companies meeting all our ideal standards does not exist. We conduct extensive research on all prospective investments, and our decisions to invest in a particular company are based on both quantitative and qualitative criteria. Calvert's social analysis is a dynamic process. We continually assess our screening analysis to ensure it reflects the evolution of traditional social issues, company best practices, public sentiment, and emerging social issues.
>
> www.calvert.com

## KLD BMSI

KLD Research and Analytics Inc provides social investment research, compliance and consulting services to investment institutions, and publishes a series of SRI indices and also SOCRATES a social research database on 650 US corporations. Among the indices KLD offers are:

- ■ **KLD BMSI**: The KLD Broad Market Social Index (BMS Index) consists of all companies in the Russell 3000 that pass KLD's screening criteria. The intent of the index is to give investors a benchmark of socially screened companies against which to compare investment results. Companies involved in alcohol, tobacco, firearms, gambling, nuclear power, and military contracting are excluded from considerations. All remaining companies are then evaluated for employee diversity, product, innovation, and community involvement among other criteria. All Russell 3000 companies passing these screens are included in the index that is reconstituted every June along with the Russell 3000.
- ■ **KLD DSI**: The Domino 400 Social Index (DSI) was launched in 1990 as the first benchmark for equity portfolios subject to multiple screens. The DSI has outperformed the S & P 500 on a total return and on a risk-adjusted basis since its inception.
- ■ **KLD NSI**: The NASDAQ Social Index is the first benchmark for socially and environmentally screened securities traded on the NASDAQ, reflecting the performance of approximately 180 of the largest US corporations in technology, financial, and telecommunications industries.
- ■ **KLD LCSI**: The Large Cap Social Index (LCSI) is a socially screened subset of the Russell 1000 Index. The LCSI represents approximately 92 per cent of available US market capitalisation: www.kld.com.

## FTSE4Good

FTSE have developed what is likely to become one of the most prominent and influential series of SRI indices, the FTSE4Good Global 100,

FTSE4Good US 100, FTSE4Good Europe 50 and FTSE4Good UK 50. In each case the index tracks the performance of the largest socially responsible companies in the relevant part of the world. The companies selected for inclusion in the FTSE4Good index are screened for their performance in three main areas:

- working towards environmental sustainability;
- developing positive relationships with stake-holders;
- upholding and supporting universal human rights.

Companies with operations in the sectors of tobacco production, weapons and nuclear power are currently excluded from the FTSE4Good series. An advisory board of 13 independent experts including members with a professional background in SRI, oversees the screening process and constituent selection.

The FTSE4Good distinguishes between companies that may have a greater impact in a specific area than others:

> In evaluating corporate performance in respect to human rights, stakeholder relationships and environmental sustainability, FTSE4Good is committed to the principle that the more substantial their impacts, the higher the standards that companies should measure up to. For example, in the current FTSE4Good criteria, companies that are expected to have high environmental impacts must meet more demanding criteria for index inclusion than those with low expected impacts. In addition, some industries are 'high impact' due to the nature of their supply chains. Here too, the Committee intends to try and develop suitable criteria for measuring companies' efforts.

Also the FTSE4Good plans to adopt significantly higher standards for human rights policies, systems and reporting as these become more common, particularly for those companies with the most significant investments in countries where human rights are most at risk. Because of the high profile of the FTSE4Good already there have been some controversies around the inclusion or exclusion of leading companies from the indices,

and it seems inevitable that these controversies will continue if the indices are doing their job: www.ftse.com/indices_marketdata/FTSE4Good/index_home.jsp.

## DJSI World

The other high profile SRI indices are the Dow Jones Sustainability Indexes (DJSI), established to track the performance of companies that lead the field in terms of corporate sustainability. All indices in the DJSI are assessed according to the same Corporate Sustainability Assessment and respective criteria. The DJSI consist of a global and European set of indices. The DJSI World first published in 1999 consist of a composite index and five narrower, specialised indices excluding companies that generate revenue from alcohol, tobacco, gambling, armaments and firearms or all of these industries. The European indices, the DJSI STOXX were first published in 2001, in combination with the European index provider STOXX Limited.

DJSI emphasise the commercial drivers of SRI:

> Increasingly, investors are diversifying their portfolios by investing in companies that set industry-wide best practices with regard to sustainability. Two factors drive this development. First, the concept of corporate sustainability is attractive to investors because it aims to increase long-term shareholder value. Since corporate sustainability performance can now be financially quantified, they now have an investable corporate sustainability concept. Second, sustainability leaders are increasingly expected to show superior performance and favourable risk/return profiles. A growing number of investors is convinced that sustainability is a catalyst for enlightened and disciplined management, and thus a crucial success factor.

www.sustainability-index.com

## ESI Global

The Ethibel Sustainability Index (ESI) set of indices was first published in 2002, developed by

Ethibel a leading European screening company in the field of SRI based in Brussels. Ethibel contracted Standard and Poor's to maintain and calculate the indexes. There are four regional indices: ESI Global, ESI Americas, ESI Europe and ESI Asia Pacific. The ESI applies the same criteria and gives equal weight to company scores on social, environmental and economic criteria, regardless of the type of company or the sector. It is recognised that different sectors and regions are facing different key CSR issues and that the concept of CSR is developing over time, and the methodology reflects these changes.

> The distinctive characteristics of Ethibel's methodology originate from the integration of the two strongest concepts of CSR: sustainable development and stakeholder involvement. Sustainable development focuses on the content of the research. All the aspects of the social responsibility of a company, including its social, environmental and economic-ethical policy, are taken into account: the people-planet-profit approach. A specific aspect of the Ethibel research process is the permanent dialogue with all the stakeholders, including the company, at every stage of the research and evaluation process.
>
> www.ethibel.org

### ECP Ethical Global Return

A further series of indices are published by the Italian company E.Capital Partners with a management team drawn from the finance department of SDA Bocconi University, the Ethical Global Return covering the 300 largest capitalisation companies incorporated worldwide which pass an Ethical Screening Methodology. The index invests in all developed stock markets, America, Europe, Asia Pacific, Australia. Ethical Euro Return includes the 150 largest capitalisation companies resident and incorporated in Europe which pass E.Capital's ethical screening. Ethical Global Gov. Bond, includes multi-currency government bonds that have passed the ethical screening test. Finally the Ethical Euro Corp. Bond includes euro-denominated

corporate bonds that have passed the ethical screening test. While many SRI funds in the United States exclude government bonds because of the exposure to investment in the Department of Defense, ECP's government bond indexes do not implement such exclusions. E. Capital Partners Analyst Oliviero Gobbi explained,

> We do not want to exclude all governments who support defense because we would have to exclude all government bonds. We prefer a positive approach that considers several points of view because we think it is possible to invest in government bonds in a socially responsible way. We analyze countries under several points of view: respect of human rights; compliance with international treaties; compliance with I.L.O. regulations; respect for the environment; and we exclude countries who have the death penalty ... We have excluded all the governments deeply involved in military activities from our benchmarks. We exclude, for example, the U.S.A., because of the death penalty.
>
> www.sri-adviser.com/article.mpl?
> sfArticleId=989;www.e-cpartners.com

## SRI IMPACT UPON CORPORATE ENVIRONMENTAL AND SOCIAL RESPONSIBILITY

This last comment by Oliviero Gobbi highlights how SRI might have had a remarkable impact in recent years, but there remains a very long way to go. It is deeply ironic that the United States, the country that has the largest SRI investment institutions and financial commitment, also has one of the worst human rights records in terms of imprisonment and the death penalty, is one of the world's worst polluters per head of population, and refused to sign the Kyoto agreement on global warming. The US is a market based economy and society, and it is not entirely contradictory that among the most influential opposition to these social and environmental transgressions should be applied through the market system.

How much pressure may be realistically applied through the influence of SRI and the

associated indices is still to be ascertained. And of course there will always be insistent pressures in the opposite direction, for example though the work of the World Health Organisation (which estimates that four million people die from smoking-related illnesses every year) and other agencies, 'suggest that tobacco is part of a group of sunset industries where ethical legitimacy has disappeared ... this is not a view shared by FTSE4Good. In January 2002 this index of ethical stocks was reported to be set to lift its ban on companies making tobacco, allowing them to join the listing by the end of the year. The index committee suggesting that it would admit tobacco companies if they were improving their records on issues such as public health, the environment and human rights' (Bendell and Shah 2002: 6).

A more optimistic prognosis would suggest that Socially Responsible Investment will add a huge impetus to the wide stakeholder alliance of customers, employees, managers, suppliers, communities and governments attempting to impress upon the process of value creation ethical, social and environmental concerns.

## CORPORATE REPORTING OF CSR

If the revival of interest in CSR is to continue to develop, and not descend into apologetics as previous efforts have done, and if the current wave of interest in ESG issues in the investment community is to bear fruit in more enduring returns, then what is absolutely critical is the accuracy and verifiability of corporate disclosure regarding CSR performance. In this regard the Global Reporting Initiative (GRI) Principles are an invaluable tool for working towards international confidence in the trustworthiness of corporate reporting. The overall aim of the GRI-based reporting is to:

- provide a balanced and reasonable representation of an organisation's sustainability performance;
- facilitate comparability;
- address issues of concern to stakeholders.

The GRI reporting principles are the underpinnings of corporate report content, and as such are as important as the content itself. The reporting principles are:

- **Transparency**: Full disclosure of the processes, procedures and assumptions in report preparation are essential to its credibility.
- **Inclusiveness**: The reporting organisation should engage its stakeholders in preparing and enhancing the quality of reports.
- **Auditability**: Reported information should be recorded, compiled, analysed and disclosed in a way that enables internal auditors or external assurance providers to attest to its reliability.
- **Completeness**: All material information should appear in the report.
- **Relevance**: Reporting organisations should use the degree of importance that report users assign to particular information in determining report content.
- **Sustainability context**: Reporting organisations should seek to place their performance in the broader context of ecological, social or other issues where such context adds significant meaning to the reported information.
- **Accuracy**: Reports should achieve a degree of exactness and low margin of error to enable users to make decisions with a high degree of confidence.
- **Neutrality**: Reports should avoid bias in selection and presentation of information and provide a balanced account of performance.
- **Comparability**: Reports should be framed so as to facilitate comparison to earlier reports as well as to reports of comparable organisations.
- **Clarity**: Information should be presented in a manner that is understandable by a maximum number of users while still maintaining a suitable level of detail (GRI 2002: 6).

The work of developing, implementing and verifying these reporting standards for corporate social and environmental responsibility will continue for many years to come, replicating the effort that is now being made in the quest to achieve better measurement and reporting of intangibles. However, the whole edifice of CSR and ESG analysis and valuation will rest on the adequacy and rigour of reporting standards.

## FUTURE DEVELOPMENTS: THE REDESIGN OF THE CORPORATION

It could be argued that the whole corporate social and environmental responsibility project, however worthy, is probably too little and too late. A more sympathetic view is that in its revived form CSR represents a new beginning in corporate reform that may be built on to create more substantial and enduring results. Certainly further efforts will be required to further ensure the accountability of corporations, on a universal and not simply voluntary basis. In extending accountability, directors of corporations should be licensed to have regard for the interests of other stakeholders, and to accept the costs of enterprise operations beyond what they are legally required to assume (Redmond 2005: 28). A group of business and community leaders in the US have projected a

vision of Corporation 2020 based on the imperative to redesign the corporation. The principles they advocate are that the purpose of the corporation is to harness private interests to serve the public interest, that fair returns to shareholders should not be at the expense of the legitimate interests of other stakeholders, that corporations should operate sustainably, and that corporations distribute wealth produced equitably among those who contribute to the creation of that wealth. Robert Hinkley offers a 28 word amendment to directors' duties which states that they are to act in the interests of the company 'but not at the expense of the environment, human rights, public health and safety, dignity of employees, or the welfare of communities in which the corporation operates' (Luis 2005).

It is possible to envisage a business world not characterised by the bipolar disorder of

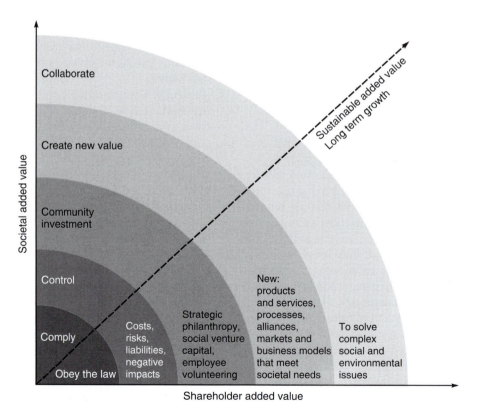

Figure 8.11 Corporate strategies to deliver value to society.

Source: Nelson Jane (2004), *The Public Role of the Private Enterprise; Risks, Opportunities and New Models of Engagement*, Working Paper, 1, for the Corporate Social Responsibility Initiative 2004–2006.

the ongoing shareholder/stakeholder debate. The effective integration of corporate social and environmental responsibilities could potentially release greater value for both shareholders and wider stakeholders (Figure 8.11): moving beyond compliance, to creating new value through new products and services that meet societal needs; collaborating to solve the complex and demanding social and environmental problems that threaten to grow beyond our control. Corporations capable of working in investors', stakeholders', and society's interests in a collaborative, creative and productive way would require a fundamental redesign of the concept of the corporation and the institution of the market. At this stage both prospects appear remote. However, we live in an industrial world where the problem of material production has essentially been solved. The primary remaining global dilemmas are that overproduction and massive surpluses still coexist with desperate poverty and need, and that the resource base for industry is rapidly depleting and damaging, potentially irreparably, the ecosystem. It is possible that confronting these dilemmas will force the rethinking of corporate objectives, structures, and activities that is necessary.

EIGHT

# CASE STUDIES

## Corporate Governance in Crisis

# CASE STUDIES IN CORPORATE GOVERNANCE

All of the enclosed case studies are of corporations experiencing a crisis of governance, with the exception of DaimlerChrysler which faced the challenge of merger of two different systems of corporate governance. It is much easier to find large amounts of accurate information concerning corporations that are in crisis, that have attracted the attention of the financial press, regulatory authorities and academics. Furthering this forensic analysis of companies struggling with often insoluble governance and strategic problems is illuminating, in at least learning of the warning signs to look out for, and the kinds of action that might have some effect when encountering a crisis.

It is a matter of some regret that the study of corporate governance does not focus more on the practice of corporate governance by corporations that are able to combine robust governance with strategic and sustainable success. Such companies do exist, and are far more numerous than the ones that fail. Fortunately, large corporations today provide a great deal of information regarding their governance on their web sites, and it is possible to investigate the characteristics of successful corporations by this means of comparing good practice. There is a list of significant corporate web sites in the Appendix to this volume, together with a wide range of academic, policy and regulatory authorities involved in corporate governance.

One reason corporate governance has become such an important subject for policy development and business education in recent years, is that it does provide a fascinating set of insights into how companies are actually run at the highest level. Delving deeper into what went wrong at times of crisis can be an exciting intellectual task, and help develop important forensic skills. What is slightly alarming is how history tends to repeat itself in a cyclical pattern. One Enron is perhaps enough, but it is possible to observe how practices that were employed in one infamous era are revived and used to wreak havoc again in another. For example the leveraged buy-out excesses in the takeovers of the 1980s appear to be revisiting in the aggressive acquisitiveness of private equity and the hedge funds in the mid- to late 2000s. This suggests that despite the important and vigorous efforts at reform and regulation, there will be more serious corporate governance crisis to examine and explain in future.

Included in this volume are ten cases. Three are drawn from the Anglo-American world, Enron, WorldCom and Tyco, and are stories of the consequences of executive ambition and greed out of control. Four of the cases come from European experience, Ahold and Parmalat, which demonstrated how corruption could affect the corporate governance systems of Europe just as badly as in the United States. The other two cases from Europe are the DaimlerChrysler merger demonstrating the huge difficulty faced in bringing two very different systems of governance into alignment; and the takeover of Mannesmann by Vodafone, revealing the clash of ideologies, interests and practices in the European and Anglo-American systems.

The final three cases are drawn from the Asia Pacific. Two of these cases are from Australia which is firmly part of the Anglo-American world of corporate governance, though it is located in the Asia Pacific region. The James Hardie case is a salutary lesson in how damaging an industry can be to the people it employs and who use its products, and how corporate governance is required to recognise and ameliorate these risks to limit the tragic consequences. HIH is another illustration of how corporate governance can go badly wrong, and how widely the damaging effects are felt. The final case is Nomura of Japan which shows how the lack of accountability and transparency in corporations in Asia can conceal more serious problems of fraud and corruption.

A matrix is provided listing the governance issues covered in each case (Table CI.1). Further reading and research will no doubt reveal other dimensions of these fascinating case studies which all have enduring lessons for those interested in seeing the development of higher standards of corporate governance policy and practice.

*Anglo-American Corporations*
Case 1 Enron
Case 2 WorldCom
Case 3 Tyco

*European Corporations*
Case 4 Ahold
Case 5 Parmalat
Case 6 DaimlerChrysler
Case 7 Vodafone–Mannesmann

*Asia Pacific Corporations*
Case 8 James Hardie
Case 9 HIH Insurance Group
Case 10 Nomura

| ISSUES | Case 1, Enron | Case 2, Worldcom | Case 3, Tyco | Case 4, Ahold | Case 5, Parmalat | Case 6, DaimlerChrysler | Case 7, Vodafone-Mannesman | Case 8, James Hardie | Case 9, HIH | Case 10, Nomura |
|---|---|---|---|---|---|---|---|---|---|---|
| Shareholders | X | X | X | X | X | X | X | X | X | X |
| Shareholders' value | X | X | X | | | X | X | X | X | X |
| Losses | | | X | X | | X | X | X | X | X |
| Bankruptcy | B | B | | | B | | | | B | |
| Fraud | X | X | X | X | X | | X | | X | X |
| Restructuring | X | X | | | X | X | | | | |
| Takeover | X | X | | | | X | X | | X | |
| Merger | X | X | | | | X | X | | X | |
| Acquisition | X | X | X | | X | X | X | | X | X |
| Origins | | | | | X | | | X | X | |
| Transformation | X | X | | | | X | X | | | X |
| Quality | | | | | | | | | | |
| Competitiveness | X | X | | | | X | X | | X | |
| Diversification | X | | | | | | | | | |
| Strategy | X | X | | | X | X | X | | X | X |
| Transparency | X | X | X | X | X | | | X | X | X |
| Succession | | | | | X | | | | X | |
| Interlocking directorships | | | | | X | | | X | | |
| Board performance | X | X | X | X | X | | | X | X | |
| Board representation | | | | | | X | | | | |
| Structure and principles | X | X | X | X | X | X | | | | |
| Financial aspects | X | X | X | X | X | | X | X | X | X |
| Chair CEO | X | X | X | X | X | | X | | X | |

Table Cl.1 Corporate governance matrix of cases and issues.

# Anglo-American Corporations

# Case Study 1
# Enron

## EXECUTIVE SUMMARY

Enron's transformation from a regular natural gas company into a financial trading, pseudo-investment bank was remarkable in the speed and breadth of this achievement. The company's ambitions were financed through manipulation of its accounts by setting up highly irregular special purpose entities, and utilising these to illegally conceal massive debts and other liabilities. This was all done with the complicity of its institutional advisers – auditors Andersen, and lawyers Vinson and Elkins – and the secondary complicity of its team of consultants and investment bankers. Enron's influence reached the upper echelons of the American political establishment, financing election campaigns and buying its way with favourable legislative clauses limiting regulation in the energy industry.

As a multinational company, Enron wielded extraordinary influence with third world governments in the management of developing countries' water and energy resources. The lives of millions of people throughout the world were badly affected by Enron, a company that most had never heard of. As with its 1980s counterpart, Drexel Burnham Lambert, Enron's collapse exposed the rampant abuses that occur during periods of expansion. Enron's dubious business practices are the yardstick by which all that is wrong in the American system of market capitalism will be measured. Concealed behind the rhetoric of global economic domination by the virtual corporation of the future projected by the Enron chair Ken Lay, CEO Jeffrey Skilling and CFO Andrew Fastow, were breathtaking personal greed and irresponsibility to consumers and the wider community. What for nearly a decade was regarded as the most advanced market and management practice of the most successful company in the US, was exposed as hubris built upon rampant graft and corruption.

## ENRON'S ORIGINS

The deregulation of what were once thought of as community goods to be delivered by state owned industries, such as electricity, water and telecommunications, emerged during the 1980s under the banner of Reaganism in the USA, and Thatcherism in the UK. Deregulation's supposed beneficiaries were consumers who would access lower prices from the increased competition brought by private sector participation in the deregulated industries. The move towards deregulations encouraged the establishment of new corporations, such as Enron founded in 1985, a natural gas pipeline company formed through the acquisition of Houston Natural Gas (HNG) by Inter-North of Omaha, Nebraska. The CEO of HNG was Kenneth Lay, and his contacts and vision led to his appointment as the chair and CEO of the new company.

Enron was a pioneer in the recently deregulated industry. Like WorldCom in the deregulated telecommunications industry, the creation of a market for the private sector in the natural gas area (previously operated entirely by highly regulated public utilities) created many opportunities for pioneers as market values were placed on the sector. Enron was not the only company lobbying for energy deregulation,

|  | Before deregulation | After deregulation | Impact |
|---|---|---|---|
| Generating power | Public utilities owned power stations and sold directly to customers | Power plants sold, new private owners compete to sell to utilities | Mixed impact and reaction. Critics attack removal of strategic planning and secure supply |
| Distributing power | Public monopolies tightly controlled to protect consumers | Private utilities compete to win consumer contracts on basis of price | Enron and others created new markets focusing on energy trading, energy becomes a commodity |
| Regulating the industry | Special federal and state commissions monitor prices charged to consumers and security of supply | Market competition theoretically to set prices between private suppliers, but some regulatory controls remain | Mixed political reaction. Some legislators oppose unhindered markets, consumers concerned, black outs begin |

Table C1.1 The impact of deregulation in the transformation of the US energy industry.

but deregulation helped Enron establish the trading markets that later became its core business. Energy corporations lobbied Washington intensively to deregulate the business and Washington began to lift controls on who could produce energy and how it was sold.

As new suppliers came into the market and competition increased, the price of energy became more volatile in a free market (Table C1.1). Enron saw the chance to make money out of market fluctuations, and decided to act as middle man offering to guarantee stable prices and taking a significant cut for this service. In 1989, Enron launched the Gas Bank, which allowed gas producers and buyers to trade and hedge gas supplies. During the early 1990s, Enron expanded into the energy sectors of other countries, such as power plants in England (Teeside) and India (Dabhol). While the UK operation was profitable, Dabhol proved a financial disaster leaving an unused, half-built plant as a testament to the rapacious attempt of Enron to extract exorbitant energy prices from the poor of India. This was typical of the Enron approach to making money in developing countries by seizing monopoly contracts and raising prices, that led to public riots in opposition in the Dominican Republic, Guatemala, Panama and Colombia. These overseas operations of

Enron were part of the US government's policy of encouraging private investment in oil and gas development in the third world, and facilitated by the World Bank.

Undeterred by the dramatic failure of its overseas adventures (which it attempted to conceal) Enron continued to expand the portfolio of industries in which it attempted to establish electronic trading markets including electricity, weather, coal, pulp, paper, plastics, metals, and broadband. As far as the executives of Enron were concerned, any industry could be transformed by the ready application of electronic trading markets.

**Trading futures: The new Enron model**

Kenneth Lay's vision was to expand the business by whatever means, and in response Jeffrey Skilling proposed trading futures in gas contracts between suppliers and consumers – effectively betting against future movements in the price of gas generated energy also known as the *asset light* strategy (trading energies and other commodities the way Wall Street trades capital). Having already primed the industry regulators, Skilling 'convinced the Enron Audit Committee to allow him to apply

mark-to-market accounting to those future markets. However, the problem was that for trading activities such as the long-dated gas and power deals, no liquid markets existed. In this context, mark-to-market accounting became mark-to-model accounting. Traders who were performing trades had considerable influence in how the deals were marked to model. With their bonuses depending upon the profitability of deals, there was an acute conflict of interest: there was nothing to restrain the traders from imagining the most remarkable returns from their future trades, ensuring them immediate huge bonuses' (Holton). This became the new Enron trading model, a microcosm of the deception the company based all of its financial projections upon.

Within a few years Enron became a massive player in the US energy market, controlling at its height a quarter of all gas business. Enron offered companies the chance to hedge against the risk of adverse price movements in gas and a range of other commodities, and shortly expanded its trading arm to include external factors such as weather risk. Over 90 per cent of Enron's income came from these trading activities.

## Enron's accounting fraud from JEDIs to SPEs

Enron formed a limited partnership with the California Public Employees' Retirement System (CalPERS) in 1993. This partnership was called the Joint Energy Development Investment Limited Partnership (JEDI), with the purpose of investing in natural gas projects. Participation of CalPERS meant that JEDI was an independent entity from Enron. Enron earned profits from the partnership, but none of JEDI's debt appeared on Enron's balance sheet. Later in 1997 Enron launched a new and larger limited partnership called JEDI II, to make Enron the sole investor in JEDI. But because JEDI would no longer be independent, and its debt would have to appear on Enron's balance sheet, CFO Andrew Fastow proposed forming another new venture, called Chewco Investments, to replace CalPERS as

an independent investor. With Chewco Enron would keep the debt off its balance sheet; however, this would only work if Chewco was seen to be independent from Enron. Rather than find a truly independent investor for Chewco, Fastow decided that one of his subordinates, Michael Kopper, could play the role of independent investor in Chewco.

Enron's portfolio of equity investments was increasing and Enron's 2000 annual report stated global revenues of $100bn, suggesting that income had risen by 40 per cent in three years. In reality real revenue was far lower as company managers found that mark-to-market losses were having an increasingly adverse effect on net income. In late 2000 Enron's shares hit an all time high of more than $90, but puncturing the euphoria was Enron's involvement in the energy crisis California was now suffering, blamed by many on the state's poor handling of deregulation, but by others on the aggressive and often rapacious pricing strategies of Enron and other private energy providers.

At about this time Andrew Fastow Enron's CFO designed a further scheme, Special Purpose Entities (SPE) transactions to buffer against future losses so it could keep its share price high, raise investment against its own assets and stock and maintain the impression of a highly successful company. (A special purpose entity (SPE) is a legal entity authorised to carry out specific activities as listed in its establishing legal document. The SPE provides its sponsor with financing and liquidity, while offering creditors protection against the sponsor's bankruptcy. A sponsor would typically create an SPE to carry out a specific function through some type of asset transfer. For example, an SPE might borrow cash from a third-party creditor. In exchange for that cash, the sponsor sells an asset to the SPE and then leases it back under an operating lease (sale-leaseback). Under certain circumstances, the debt used by the SPE to acquire the asset would be its own liability and would not appear on the sponsor's balance sheet (Holtzman *et al.* 2003).

Equally, investment money flowing into Enron from new partnerships ended up on the

books as profits, even though it was linked to specific ventures that were not yet up and running, subsequently amended numerous times, the deals clearly violated GAAP SPE requirements:

- there was no substantive capital investment;
- the equity level dropped below 3 per cent of assets;
- the SPE was controlled by Enron's CFO, who could not possibly have been an independent third party to the transactions.

The numerous amendments made to the agreement – before it was wound down – suggest that Enron shielded SPEs from the full losses that they had initially contracted to incur. Worst of all the SPEs could not provide an effective hedge against mark-to-market losses. By this time SPEs were hiding within other SPEs: it was a form of cannibalisation and self-destruction that ensured Enron collapsed like a house of cards (Table C1.2).

As Enron's need for off balance sheet debt grew so did reliance on the Special Purpose Entities, as Andrew Fastow's bullying of colleagues who questioned his methods increased, and treading the fine line between legal and illegal interpretations became a pastime. Fastow used many people to help him with the creation of the SPEs both Enron staff and external bankers, and most of them profited spectacularly from their association with financial manoeuvres that were evidently becoming increasingly desperate (Table C1.3).

However, the façade of reckless optimism and constantly fabricated good news could not last forever at Enron, and CEO Jeffrey Skilling probably realised the game was up when he resigned, giving personal reasons, on

| Generation | Vehicle or SPE name | Purpose |
|---|---|---|
| 1st | LJM2 | Fastow's main investment banking vehicle within Enron |
| 2nd | Raptors | Cross-guarantees that promised one entity to pay the obligations of a sister entity. Concealed cross-collaterisation debt of other SPEs and became dumping ground of choice for bad properties of other Enron divisions. |

Table C1.2  Example of an SPE descendancy: the descendants of LJM2.

Source: Adapted from Swartz and Watkins (2003).

| Employee | Contribution ($) | Profit ($) |
|---|---|---|
| Michael Kopper | 25,000 | 4.5m |
| Fastow Family Foundation | 25,000 | 4.5m |
| Kristina Mourdant | 5,800 | 1m |
| Ben Glisan | 5,800 | 1m |
| Others | 2,000 | 200,000 |
| Andrew Fastow | 1m (LJM1) | 23m (LJM1) |
|  | 3.9m (LJM2) | 22m (LJM2) |
|  |  | 13.9m (for salaries, consulting and management fees, partnership distribution) |

Table C1.3  How Enron employees in Fastow's division reached spectacular returns on investment into the SPEs.

Source: Adapted from Fox (2003); Swartz and Watkins (2003).

14 August 2001. He later denied he knew anything was wrong with the firm when he left, but in a damaging incident he had lost his temper in a conference call with analysts when asked why Enron could not produce a balance sheet. The longer the game went on, the more difficult it was for Enron to manufacture earnings from a business based on hypothetical values. After Skilling's resignation Enron's fate was sealed as it vainly sought to disentangle itself from the intricate accounting vehicles that disguised its indebtedness. By October 2001 Enron was forced to disclose a billion dollar write down related to the SPEs. Just six weeks after the first public sign of trouble, Enron which had $62 billion in assets, filed for bankruptcy. A series of other huge and well-regarded US companies soon followed in Enron's wake towards bankruptcy. In the words of Sherron Watkins an Enron Vice President, the company that once held the admiration of the business world, promised the future and envisioned itself to be the world's leading energy company, soon became a company whose 'past successes [were] nothing, but an elaborate accounting hoax' (Swartz and Watkins 2003: 362).

## THE DOT COM BUBBLE AND THE ENERGY CRISIS

Enron's dynamic ideas coupled with its stable old-economy energy background, appealed to investors and the share price soared. It traded heavily online by offering a free service that attracted a vast amount of sales. However, while Enron boasted about the value of products that it bought and sold – $880 billion in just two years – it didn't disclose whether these trading operations were actually making any profits. Enron's stock begun to fall in the wake of the dot.com deflation and energy price instability, which led to questioning of both the Enron virtual business model and the damage being caused to energy markets. Companies like Enron and Dynergy rushed into the energy trading, saw their share prices soar and then collapse on revelations of dubious deals and accounting fraud. As Figure C1.1 reveals, Enron maintained a similar stock price to the industry at around $20 to $26, then it began to separate from 1:1 relationship to a 3.5:1 in 2000 as the Enron stock soared to $90, yet within less than a year the stock was worthless.

**Figure C1.1** Timeline of Enron's collapse.

Source: Adapted from enron.com, Powers Report (2002)

As the US energy crises deepened, many people began to realise that Enron's business operations were not as sound as they seemed and the share price began a precipitous fall. Early in 2001 Enron's auditors, Andersen's, held a confidential meeting about concerns with the special partnerships and the full implications of moving money, stock and assets backwards and forwards in incredibly complicated deals; however the auditors stated that there were no legal issues to answer. As he was preparing to sell his own stock, Kenneth Lay dishonestly told employees and others that Enron stock was 'an incredible bargain' even after he had been warned of a potential scandal regarding the SPEs by an Enron executive.

On 16 October 2001 Enron announced it was taking a $544 million after tax charge against earnings related to trading transactions of LJM2, a partnership created by Fastow, and a reduction in shareholders' equity of $1.2 billion, and details began to emerge of the CFO Fastow's conflicts on interest, and thousands of offshore partnerships. Though on 1 November Enron secured a $1 billion line of credit from JP Morgan Chase and Citigroup, a few days later it made an announcement restating its financial statements for the period through 1997 to 2001 due to accounting errors relating to different Fastow partnerships LJM Cayman L.P. (LJM1) and a related party entity Chewco Investments. This restatement reduced Enron's reported earnings by $28 million in 1997 (of $105 million total), by $133 million in 1998 (of $703 million total), by $248 million in 1999 (of $893 million total), and by $99 million in 2000 (of $979 million total). The restatement reduced reported shareholders' equity by $258 million in 1997, by $391 million in 1998, by $710 million in 1999, and by $754 million in 2000. It increased reported debt by $710 million in 1997, by $561 million in 1998, by $685 million in 1999, and by $628 million in 2000. As the Powers Report (2002: 3) commissioned by the Board of Directors of Enron subsequently concluded 'These announcements destroyed market confidence and investor trust in Enron.'

A planned rescue takeover of Enron by Dynergy for $8 billion, was called off as it was discovered that company faced difficulties also, and on 2 December Enron filed for bankruptcy. During the death throes of the company, tens of thousands of employees' retirement savings that were tied to Enron stock were wiped out. As the stock was plummeting employees were unable to sell their stock for weeks due to what Enron described as a management change.

## THE COMPANY CULTURE

The Enron corporate culture clearly places profits first.

*(Fox 2003: 87)*

A stereotypical Enron employee was 'bright, young and fiscally ambitious'. Most employees at Enron were highly skilled: 40 per cent had degrees and 20 per cent possessed advanced degrees, with an advanced degree in econometrics highly regarded. To be employed at Enron was to be in 'a company of winners' (Swartz and Watkins 2003: 3). In this way Enron distinguished itself from its rivals in the natural gas sector. Enron was ambitious, innovative and made sure its employees were richly rewarded for joining a company based in the Texas heartland, far from the glamour of the West Coast and East Coast cities.

In Enron, its relatively flat structure allowed ideas to flourish. This emphasis on the intellectual assets of the company was enhanced when Skilling joined the company from consulting firm McKinsey & Co. Other long-time Enron partner organisations, such as Andersen and Vinson & Elkins would also provide a bank of potential employees for Enron. McKinsey had been long-time consultants to Enron and were behind the first major strategic change in Enron when Lay was looking for other ways to enhance the company's role in the newly deregulated businesses. As a McKinsey alumnus, Skilling brought to Enron the idea of 'flattening the management organisation so decisions could be made faster and knocking down walls so workers could communicate better' (Fox 2003: 34).

The other side of the coin for this highly innovative, relatively flat organisation was

the proliferation of highly competitive pro-grammes that weeded out the meek. This was encapsulated in the McKinsey-inspired Performance Review Committee (PRC) process, which instilled a 'competitive streak in every employee'. The PRC was unique in Enron's industry as Enron rivals 'felt it wouldn't inspire teamwork' (Fox 2003: 84). Not surprisingly paranoia set in, and sabotage would occur during the periods when the PRC was in action. Different business groups within Enron would 'compete against each other as though they were different companies' and while Skilling thought this would encourage competition, it 'solidified a compartmentalization of the company into contending fiefdoms' (Fox 2003: 85). As at Harvard Business School, the bottom 10 per cent of employees would be put on probation and some would be asked to leave the company: 'Employee X would lose faith that he was creating the future through association with Enron. And then he would stumble, and soon enough, he'd be branded a *loser*. Too lazy, too obstructive, or worse, just not smart enough' (Swartz and Waktins 2003: 5).

## THE KEY PLAYERS

### The public face of Enron: Kenneth Lay

Ken Lay was a political animal who relished the opportunity to show his power and influence as chair and CEO of Enron. In his early years he was an economist who had worked in the federal regulatory agency on energy and was comfortable within the corridors of the American political class. An astute man, he saw the opportunities of the private sector more financially rewarding than another job overseeing the regulation of utilities. During the 1970s and 1980s he worked his way up through various utilities, preaching deregulation, before joining HNG and becoming its CEO (Swartz and Watkins 2003). As CEO of Enron, he wanted to dominate the then heavily regulated market in a different way. He was an active proponent of markets free of government interference, lambasting Enron critics who were keen to keep the government

regulation on natural gas prices. He donated heavily to the Republican party and was on first name terms (as Kenny Boy) with the Bush political dynasty, corresponding regularly with George W. Bush.

Evidence showed that Enron was very well connected to the Bush administration, the Republican party, and to a lesser extent, the Democratic party (Figures C1.2 and C1.3).

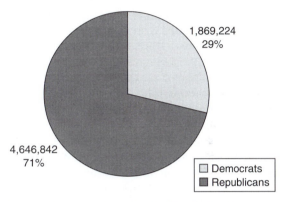

Total contributions during the elections 1989–2002
$6,516,066

**Figure C1.2** How Enron buys power: Enron's political contributions.

Source: Center for Responsive Politics/Federal Election Commission (2006).

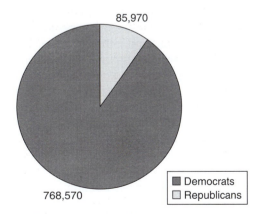

Total contributions $885,140

**Figure C1.3** How Enron buys power: Ken Lay's contributions.

Source: Center for Responsive Politics/Federal Election Commission (2006).

After the collapse of Enron, George W. Bush underplayed his friendship with Lay, when he suggested that he did not get to know Lay until after his election as President. In fact Lay donated three times more to Bush than to the Democrats, and records reveal that the Bush/Lay relationship went back many years to the time of Bush senior's presidency. It is also alleged that Enron executives had greater access to the formulation of Vice President Dick Cheney's energy policy than representatives of any other organisation, having met with Cheney or his aides 6 times over the course of 2001 alone. Since 1992, at least 21 agencies, representing the US government, multilateral development banks, and other national governments, helped leverage Enron's global reach by approving $7.2 billion in public financing toward 38 projects in 29 countries (Vallette and Wysham 2002).

The political links with the Republican party went deep with Lay, and indeed within Enron itself. In 1993, Enron hired former cabinet members of George Bush senior as Enron consultants: State Secretary James Baker and Commerce Secretary Robert Mosbacher. The biggest coup for Lay and Enron, was the acceptance of Wendy Gramm as an Enron board director. Gramm was the chair of the Commodity Futures Trading Commission (CFTC). She was also the wife of a Republican senator who was one of the party's main powerbrokers. In 1993, Gramm's committee exempted energy derivatives and other related swaps from government regulation. The boom to Enron's trading business was enormous – the company proceeded to make financial trades on all movements of the gas market. Gramm's role was invaluable in the institutionalisation of trading within the former pipeline company, and this act legitimised Enron's trading house status.

When George W. Bush became President, the years of political lobbying and donations paid off immediately for Lay and Enron. Lay had ambitions of returning to the political corridors of power but he was overlooked for the plum job of Energy Secretary. Perhaps as compensation, Lay and other Enron officials met with the Vice President, Dick Cheney, and other state officials, to formulate the country's energy policy. Cheney wanted Lay's input as 'Enron has a different take than most energy companies.' Where Gramm's role helped legitimise Enron's trading status, Cheney's recommendations encouraged the proliferation of Enron businesses: 'The US government should continue to support the development of efficient derivatives markets' which directly benefited Enron's Capital and Trade goals for 'a larger and unfettered energy derivatives market it was dominating' (Fox 2003: 225). Cheney also backed Enron in its strategy to enter the electricity market, recommending competition in the transmission of electricity: '[The government should] develop legislation to grant authority to obtain rights-of-way for electricity transmission lines' (Fox 2003: 226).

## The real force at Enron: Jeffrey Skilling

Though he only became Enron CEO towards the end, from his arrival at Enron from McKinsey and Co. in 1990, Jeffrey Skilling proved the driving force for change at Enron, and from his position as head of Enron Capital and Trade, he forged the aggressive trading culture that gave Enron its edge in an increasingly competitive energy business, which reached its nadir of profit seeking at any cost in the deregulated market of California. The Bush administration's support for Enron's commercial activities had devastating effects in the summer of 2000 for Californians. By 2000, wholesale electricity transmission was opened to nationwide competition. A national company would be able to trade electricity to a local (state) company. When a state needed power, it could theoretically buy the lowest electricity prices from a national provider. But competition also meant that when there was higher demand, prices would be at a premium, and electricity supply could be stemmed, so demand would increase, price would increase and profits would be astronomical. This is exactly what happened in California: the Californian energy crisis was a man-made catastrophe of rolling blackouts as Enron and other electricity traders limited supply, hiked up prices in the transmission

of wholesale energy (which was unregulated with no price controls) to the local electricity networks (which was regulated and had price controls). Power prices went from $59 to $234 megawatt per hour (MWh). The state shortage of electricity also flowed into other states. At one point Enron was buying at $250 MWh in California, and selling at $1,200 MWh to the state of Oregon (Fox 2003; Swartz and Watkins 2003).

The crisis forced the bankruptcy of local Californian electricity companies, and the temporary closure of schools, hospitals and businesses. The outrage from consumers was high, but the profits for Enron were enormous. The California crisis brought to Enron alone approximately $1.5 billion in the space of six months. The profit-taking during the Californian crisis was the peak of Enron's commercial activities, of putting profit before the public interest, (though both Skilling and Lay denied any responsibility for the California crisis, claiming it was all caused by the regulators. Skilling went as far as joking 'What is the difference between California and the *Titanic*? At least the *Titanic*'s lights were on as it sank!' – understandably this did not endear Enron to the California public who lobbied successfully for a reintroduction of regulation of the industry).

However, Enron was interested in acquiring the best company, prestige money could buy, and made hundreds of charitable donations in addition to many political donations. Enron had given large sums for the establishment of Rice University's James A. Baker Institute for Public Policy, and Kenneth Lay presented the annual Enron Prize for Distinguished Public Service to such luminaries as Mikhail Gorbachev and Alan Greenspan (Swartz and Watkins 2003). Greenspan, then chair of the Federal Reserve was offered a large cheque as well as trophy, both of which remained on the board table after he left.

Lay was the public face and the statesman of Enron and Houston, but left most of Enron's day-to-day operations to his chair and chief operating officer Richard Kinder. Kinder was the anointed successor to Lay but Lay never received the plum job offers he had expected – the Energy Secretary position or CEO of another conglomerate than Enron – and so Lay stayed on at Enron. Kinder decided to leave 'I want go somewhere where I can run my own show' (Fox 2003: 98). Kinder had 'effectively been running the company for quite a number of years, urging it forward but also imposing [fiscal] discipline' (Swartz and Watkins 2003: 98). Kinder could handle the dual role of Enron – the company's hard assets in pipelines and power plants, and the innovation of its trading arm.

However after Kinder left in 1996 the baton was passed to Jeffrey Skilling, though this did not occur before an almighty power struggle for the company's heart and soul, which ultimately determined the path the company took. Amidst all of this, Lay remained ignorant of the internal operations the company was engaging in. At private moments Skilling would ask his team, 'Do you think Ken understands what we do at all? Do you think he gets it?' Skilling would then answer his own questions: 'Nah … I don't think he gets it' (Swartz and Watkins 2003: 62).

### Enron International and Rebecca Mark

Enron International (EI) was the international development arm of the company and developed from its national power business in the USA. EI represented the heavy asset strategy of Enron. EI entered into major international projects in Europe, South America, the Middle East and Asia worth $19 billion to the company. It sought tangible (pipelines and plants) projects, alliances with governments, and its profit-making venture was traditional, in that project rate of investment return was more modest than the US trading group's (Swartz and Watkins 2003). EI was headed by Rebecca Mark – another Harvard Business School graduate in the company. Mark led Enron International into developing countries with her own brand of missionary zeal – instead of spreading the word of Christianity, Mark was spreading American capitalism to open the energy markets of the world (Fox 2003: 49).

Presumably Mark was immune to the hypocrisy of an American corporation preaching free market capitalism in developing

countries (who traditionally have government-owned utilities), yet receiving US government money in order to enter such markets. Enron International received the funding largesse of US government agencies to the tune of $400 million when it entered the Indian electricity market in Dabhol. However, Dabhol turned out to be a nightmare for Enron (and even more so for the Indian community). For foreign investment to work, and for the foreign investor to profit from its investment, short-term pain for the investor is inevitable. The different business and socio-cultural environment in India warranted a long-term commitment from EI in order for business relationships to be strengthened so that a modicum of trust could be achieved between EI and its local Indian partners.

Enron International was under pressure from its head office to produce spectacular investment results like its trading arm – and was impatient for immediate profits. EI increased its price requirement for its electricity from the local government, which was passed on to the Indian people. The reaction to this price hike was massive protests, hunger strikes and accusations of human rights violations. The first phase of the project was stalled as EI refused to continue the project without the government's honouring of the contract and EI filed a $300 million lawsuit against the Indian government. The US ambassador to India personally intervened saying the Indian stance on Dabhol would deter foreign investors to the country.

Though similarly motivated and encountering similar local discontent, EI's overseas investments in Colombia, Guatemala, the Dominican Republic, the UK and the Philippines had delivered more returns. By 1985 EI had generated EBITDA of $142 million; however, the trading arm of Enron headed by Skilling, Enron Capital and Trade (ECT), had generated EBITDA of $232.5 million. Skilling was determined Enron was going to pursue an *asset light* strategy. After EI was dissolved Rebecca Mark whose position within Enron was still secure, sought to find a role for herself within the new Enron under Skilling. However, Mark represented the old guard of Enron and as his nearest rival, Skilling was never

comfortable while she was still around. Kenneth Lay considered her his protégé as they shared similar strategic experiences, and the same charismatic personality that Skilling lacked. The succession struggle was proving a dilemma for Lay, 'Jeff is the number two officer in the company, but Rebecca is a very, very talented individual' (Swartz and Watkins 2003: 117).

Rebecca Mark sought to redeem herself by forming the water arm of Enron called Azurix. She entered the UK water business with the purchase of England's Wessex Water for $2.2 billion, and acquired another water business in Argentina. The vision was to ultimately compete with the two other heavy water resource companies at the time, Suez Lyonnais des Eaux and Vivendi. However, she was never secure in this new role as her rival Skilling and his team constantly undermined her confidence – both financial and personal. Skilling would complain to her in meetings: 'The organisation has no confidence in you'; 'Your deals don't make any sense' and 'You can't get your skirt high enough to get out of this one' (Swartz and Watkins 2003: 197). By 2000, a combination of bad luck, inexperienced trading strategy and covert financial traps – that Skilling had set – doomed Azurix. Mark resigned later that year, and the orphan child Azurix went through a rocky dismantling. In hindsight, Mark's resignation was the best outcome for her: she cashed in $80 million in share options, and escaped with her reputation before Enron's debacle two years later.

## Enron's Cassandra: Sherron Watkins

Sherron Watkins joined Enron in 1993 from Andersen. She was a stereotypical Enron employee, and had the drive and ambition which was essential in a company like Enron. Watkins survived many reorganisations in Enron, being privy to both the trading philosophy of Skilling and the asset strategy of Mark, as well as the internal company politics associated with both. By 2001, she had achieved a vice president position in the company and oversaw some SPEs, one being the JEDI portfolio and the other Whitewing. She worked directly under Fastow but was never

comfortable working with him as she would suffer what she called an 'ethical overhang' when dealing with the SPEs (Swartz and Watkins 2003: 262). Inside the company, Watkins overheard one colleague say in disbelief, 'I know it would be devastating to all of us, but I wish we would get caught. We're such a crooked company' (Fox 2003: 249). Outside the company Watkins received an inkling of how Enron was perceived when a former Enron business partner berated her over the way Enron treated them over a proposed acquisition that fell through, 'You just tell Ken Lay and Jeff Skilling they are the most unethical people I've ever met. I don't see how you can stay here and work at this company' (Swartz and Watkins 2003: 131).

In her involvement with Whitewing, she found out the transactions within the SPE were being recorded as cash flow instead of repayment of money borrowed. A higher cash flow helped Enron to ultimately meet its earnings that quarter. Watkins wondered whether all the other SPEs had the same accounting treatment as the ones she had just dealt with. As structured, 'the SPEs owed Enron hundreds of millions of dollars due to their hedges on Enron investment, but they had no ability to pay and LJM [Fastow's SPE-quasi investment fund] had no requirement to put more money into the Raptor [SPE descendant of LJM2]. It looked like pure manipulation of income statements because with Enron's stock supporting the Raptors, the true economic risk remained with Enron' (Fox 2003: 249). With JEDI (the natural gas investment arm of ECT), Watkins questioned the unrealised gains in the fair value assessment made by the core members of ECT over natural gas assets. When JEDI bought a company called C-GAS for $30 million she found Skilling's team was valuing the assets at $45 million 27 days after the close of the transaction. With her suspicions, she used her Andersen contacts to find out whether this had the approval of her former employer. When she found out that the external auditor approved this transaction, as it had approved the MMM method which the transaction used, she decided to leave Enron (Swartz and Watkins 2003).

## THE INTERMEDIARIES

### The role of the accountants: Andersen

One of the more poignant photos in the Enron saga was the picture of a group of Andersen employees, shredding reams of documents after it was known there would be a formal SEC investigation into Enron. Andersen's behaviour showed symptoms of auditor capture: they were not auditors any more but mere fronts for Enron. Andersen knew they were guilty, but they had to stem the appearance of how guilty they should appear. What made Enron endure during its lean years was through its use of SPEs. But Enron would not have been able to use these SPEs and therefore manipulate its accounts without the complicity of its auditor, Andersen.

Andersen helped Enron in structuring its SPEs, which not only helped increase Andersen's consulting fees (that were far more lucrative than auditing) but also strengthened the ties between them. Having Enron as its client ensured Andersen's prestige and so it made sure Enron was happy. Andersen did its best to find the 'legal and innovative way to transfer the risks and debt [of Enron]' (Fox 2003: 64). In hindsight any fee Andersen received for the approval of the SPEs, fell far short of the disaster caused by its loss of reputation, as its own collapse quickly followed that of Enron.

### The role of the lawyers: Vinson and Elkins

Often overlooked in the Enron saga, was the role the Enron lawyers Vinson & Elkins (V&E) played. V&E's complicity mirrored Andersen's, though they received less attention, and survived the Enron debacle. V&E were joined at the hip to Enron (Swartz and Watkins 2003: 204). They shared the same political ties (donating generously to George W. Bush), and were arrogant, edgy and aggressive like Enron. Similar to Andersen, V&E provided a lawyer's labour market for Enron. With the SPEs, V&E knew the process so well, despite it having such complicated arrangements, that they had

contracts ready to be signed, 48 hours after the formation of these vehicles. The Enron board relied more on the advice and approval of V&E, than on Andersen's. V&E were part and parcel of the SPE structures – they had approved most of them, especially the 'smaller' vehicles. When they investigated the conflicts of interest Fastow had in Enron, their conclusion was weak, 'the accounting treatment [for the] transactions are creative and aggressive, but no one has reason to believe that it is inappropriate from a technical standpoint ... the SPEs could be portrayed poorly if subject to a *Wall Street Journal* exposé or class action lawsuit ... [however] Ms. Watkins's concerns were thoroughly reviewed, analysed, and although found not to raise new or undisclosed information, were given serious consideration' (Swartz and Watkins 2003: 304). Vinson and Elkins was heavily criticised in the Powers Report: 'V&E did not bring a stronger, more objective and more critical voice to the disclosure process. The management board relied heavily on the perceived approval by V&E on the LJM structure and disclosure of transactions' (Swartz and Watkins 2003: 349).

### The role of the consultants: McKinsey & Co.

Unlike auditing, consulting is a lucrative business with less exposure to litigation. It is in the technical details, the implementation phase, with the possibility of false or misleading actions that the real possibilities of litigation arise – that is in the accounting/auditing process and the legal contracts. After all, consultants' advice can be taken or dismissed. In McKinsey's case, their advice to Enron to enter the electricity market was taken, while their warnings to Enron to avoid the broadband market were dismissed (Swartz and Watkins 2003). In the electricity market, McKinsey believed Enron could capture 5–8 per cent of the $290 billion electricity market, bringing an additional $300 million to the bottom line for Enron. In the broadband market, they warned Enron that broadband was rather different from gas pipelines. The internet was a

service-oriented business aimed at householders. It required call centres and service-friendly people. McKinsey believed Enron was neither interested nor good at service-orientation. Nevertheless, McKinsey's role in the downfall of Enron was pivotal. Within Enron, Skilling (a McKinsey alumnus) and the McKinsey mafia terrorised those whom they disliked or were critical of, and McKinsey effectively silenced the opposition to the *asset light* strategy Skilling pursued.

### The role of the banks

Enron's accounting machinations would not have been supported without the financial outlay provided by its banks. In this case Enron's banks have played roles as diverse as debtors, investors, guarantors and partners not only with the company but with the SPE structures. Enron had cajoled, and Fastow even enticed, the banks into entering such structures because the returns were so lucrative when they succeeded. When Enron was collapsing, its banks were still there, pumping money to prop up the company for they had invested so much in the company and would lose as much when Enron went bankrupt. JP Morgan Chase and Citigroup were fined over allegations that they had committed fraud with Enron by lending money for the company's wrongful conduct, and by duping and cheating investors. JP Morgan Chase paid $135 million while Citigroup paid $120 million. Citigroup also paid for its role in misleading Dynegy over the state of Enron's financial health. Lastly, Merrill Lynch settled $80 million over accusations it knowingly falsified accounts it had with Enron in the SPEs.

### THE FUNDAMENTAL PROBLEM WITH ENRON'S BUSINESS MODEL

Enron was celebrated by the strategy consultants McKinsey and Co., and by the leading management guru Gary Hamel in the first edition of his book *Leading the Revolution*, as inventing a new business model of the *asset*

*light* corporation that was going to transform the business world. Behind the management hype lay a much more prosaic reality which Enron finally confronted, and which was laid bare in the withering assessment of the US Senate (2002: 7) report on the Enron fiasco:

> One of Enron's key corporate achievements during the 1990s was creation of an online energy trading business that bought and sold contracts to deliver energy products like natural gas, oil or electricity. Enron treated these contracts as marketable commodities comparable to securities or commodity futures, but was able to develop and run the business outside of existing controls on investment companies and commodity brokers. The nature of the new business required Enron's access to significant lines of credit to ensure that the company had the funds at the end of each business day to settle the energy contracts traded on its online system. This new business also caused Enron to experience large earnings fluctuations from quarter to quarter. Those large fluctuations potentially affected the credit rating Enron received, and its credit rating affected Enron's ability to obtain low-cost financing and attract investment. In order to ensure an investment-grade credit rating, Enron began to emphasize increasing its cash flow, lowering its debt, and smoothing its earnings on its financial statements to meet the criteria set by credit rating agencies like Moody's and Standard & Poor's.

From this point Enron was increasingly obsessed with the financial engineering of its business rather than supplying energy or any other commodity, and the focus of Enron's management was almost entirely on manipulating its finances:

> Enron developed a number of new strategies to accomplish its financial statement objectives. They included developing energy contracts Enron called 'prepays' in which Enron was paid a large sum in advance to deliver natural gas or other energy products over a period of years; designing hedges to reduce the risk of long-term energy delivery contracts; and pooling energy contracts and securitizing them through bonds or other financial instruments sold to investors. Another high profile strategy, referred to as making the company *asset light,* was aimed at shedding, or increasing immediate returns on, the company's capital-intensive energy projects like power plants that had traditionally been associated with low returns and persistent debt on the company's books. The goal was either to sell these assets outright or to sell interests in them to investors, and record the income as earnings which top Enron officials called *monetizing* or *syndicating* the assets. A presentation made to the Finance Committee in October 2000, summarized this strategy as follows. It stated that Enron's 'energy and communications investments typically do not generate significant cashflow and earnings for 1–3 years'. It stated that Enron had 'limited cash flow to service additional debt' and 'limited earnings to cover dilution of additional equity'. It concluded that 'Enron must syndicate' or share its investment costs 'in order to grow'.

At this stage Enron took the fateful step that was to lead it into a virtual world of fraud and deceit on a scale never before witnessed in corporate life. Without the business partners to invest in Enron's risky ventures, Enron resorted to simply inventing them:

> One of the problems with Enron's new strategies, however, was finding counterparties willing to invest in Enron assets or share the significant risks associated with long-term energy production facilities and delivery contracts. The October 2000 presentation to the Finance Committee showed that one solution Enron had devised was to sell or syndicate its assets, not to independent third parties, but to 'unconsolidated affiliates' – businesses like Whitewing, LJM, JEDI, the Hawaii125-0 Trust and others that were not included in Enron's financial statements but were so closely associated with the company that Enron considered their

assets to be part of Enron's. Enron had a total of $60 billion in assets, of which about $27 billion, or nearly 50 per cent, were lodged with Enron's 'unconsolidated affiliates'.

(US Senate 2002: 8)

## CORPORATE GOVERNANCE FAILURE

Within Enron the responsibility for the collapse was attributed to Andrew Fastow and his finance division. Enron's organisation was unique – it allowed its CFO to run independent entities that were virtual hedges within Enron (Coffee 2002: 2). Fastow exploited this opportunity turning Enron into a vehicle to funnel money into his personal slush funds. Enron's spectacular collapse shook much of the US public's complacency and trust in its most prestigious business icons. The web of lies Enron spun over its finances imposed greater scrutiny of the integrity of the entire financial system as the venerable institutions of government, lawyers, accountants and banks appeared to have been seduced by the Enron multi-billion dollar charade. More worryingly, Enron's business interests appeared to reach the highest levels of government, with Lay being instrumental in the drafting of the country's energy policy.

The Powers Report (2002) noted Lay was the captain of the ship, but he did not give proper attention to the company he was leading, despite receiving more than $101 million when he sold his Enron shares before the problems unravelled. The Enron board which looked very dignified on paper, and included an accounting professor from Stanford and an English lord and former Thatcher cabinet minister, were equally impotent. The stewards had no clue to what was happening within the company, and trusted the outside advisers without question. When Watkins warned Lay of the danger the company was in, the board decided to have her employment contract investigated by lawyers. The Enron collapse undermined the belief that a board is able to represent the interests of shareholders, or other stakeholders. Enron's collapse seriously shook financial markets with the ensuing scandals of WorldCom, Tyco, Adelphia and many others, seeming to indicate 'systemic governance failure' (Coffee 2002: 4).

The passing of the Public Company Accounting Reform and Investor Protection Act, also known as the Sarbanes–Oxley Act 2002, was a direct result of Enron. Principally, this Act addresses the conflicts of interest in the auditing profession and established a public agency that regulates the profession, establishing auditing standards and imposing professional discipline. The Act did not address the corporate governance failures of other professional gatekeepers including lawyers, consultants and analysts. Nor did the Act address the herd behaviour of institutional fund managers, who demand short term results, and do not question how they might have been achieved.

On the long-term effects of Enron, Gordon (2002) proposes this 'matter will prove to be a very important event in the history of American shareholder capitalism' but the problem can never be solved because greed lies at the root of the problem, and that can only be restrained. Holmstrom and Kaplan (2003) argue that 'the legislative, regulatory and market responses to Enron will make the corporate governance system better though there is a danger of overreacting to extreme events', indeed they state the 'greatest risk now facing the US corporate governance system is the possibility of overregulation', dismissively suggesting 'the current problems arose in an exceptional period that is not likely to happen again soon' (Holmstrom and Kaplan 2003: 29). Overlooking the role Enron played in the exploitation of developing countries, consumers and employees, Holmstrom and Kaplan conclude that 'Enron was an experiment that failed [and] we should take advantage of its lesson by improving control structures and corporate governance so that other promising experiments can be undertaken' (2003: 29).

## THE ENRON TRIALS

The law proved less forgiving of the Enron misdemeanours than academic commentators.

As the investigation and trials of the senior executives from a series of other corporate failures including Adelphia, Tyco and Worldcom proceeded, the mood of US Congress, courts and general public became a lot tougher on dealing with the perpetrators of corporate crimes. Instead of the light sentences that white collar crime usually received, the sentences handed out to senior executives matched the spectacular nature of their frauds. Sensing this Andrew Fastow pleaded guilty to criminal charges in January 2004 and received a 10 year prison sentence. In contrast Kenneth Lay and Jeffrey Skilling resolutely maintained their innocence throughout, blaming anyone but themselves for the collapse of the company. In May 2006 Lay was convicted of six counts of conspiracy and fraud and faced 45 years in jail. Skilling was found guilty of 19 counts of conspiracy, fraud, insider trading and making false statements, carrying a combined sentence of 185 years. In July 2006 Kenneth Lay died at his home in Aspen, Colorado aged 64, before his sentence began. In October 2006 Jeffrey Skilling was sentenced to 24 years in jail, and ordered to pay $50 million into a restitution fund for Enron's victims.

On 15 June 2002, Andersen was convicted of obstruction of justice for shredding documents related to its audit of Enron. Since the US Securities and Exchange Commission does not allow convicted felons to audit public companies, the firm agreed to surrender its licences and its right to practise. In May 2005, the Supreme Court of the United States unanimously overturned Andersen's conviction due to flaws in the jury instructions. Despite this ruling it is highly unlikely Andersen will ever return as a viable accounting business. The firm lost nearly all of its clients when it was indicted, and there are over 100 civil suits pending against the firm related to its audits of Enron and other companies. From a high of 28,000 employees in the US and 85,000 worldwide, the firm is now down to around 200 based primarily in Chicago, dealing with the remaining lawsuits the firm faces.

The verdict on Enron's ultimate impact is still an open one. 'Half a decade after the spectacular collapse of the former $70 billion energy trader, it is unclear whether the crackdown on corporate governance that reached a crescendo in the wake of Enron's collapse has left an indelible impression on the ethical operation of corporate America … The burgeoning scandal over the timing of executive share options packages at an ever growing list of American companies shows the continuing propensity, and comfort, of some managers to push the envelope of acceptable corporate behaviour' (*Australian Financial Review*, 27 May 2006).

## Questions

1 Present an analysis of the multiple sources of corporate governance failure at Enron, and how these might be resolved in future.
2 What can be done to make corporate boards supervise companies better?
3 How can we make accounting more transparent and auditing more effective?
4 Is the extensive development of corporate regulation since Enron likely to prevent further large corporate failures?
5 Offer an analysis of the Enron saga in terms of the principle of shareholder primacy, or the significance of stakeholder engagement.

## REFERENCES

BBC (2006) *The Rise and Fall of Enron,* http://news.bbc.co.uk/1/hi/business/5018176.stm
*Business Week online,* Special Report Enron, http://www.businessweek.com
Coffee, J. (2002) *Understanding Enron: It's about the Gatekeepers Stupid*! Columbia Law School Center for Law and Economic Studies. Working Paper, 207, 30 July, http://papers.ssrn.com
Coffee, J. (2003) What Caused Enron? A Capsule Social and Economic History of the 1990s, *Columbia Law School Center for Law and Economic Studies*, Working Paper, 214, 20 January, http://papers.ssrn.com
Cruver, B. (2003) *Enron: Anatomy of Greed,* London: Arrow.
*Financial Times, The Enron Collapse,* http://specials.ft.com/enron/

*Fortune* (2001) *Why Enron Went Bust*, 9 December, http://www.fortune.com/fortune/investing/articles/0,15114,367052,00.html

Fox, L. (2003) *Enron: The Rise And Fall*, New Jersey: John Wiley.

Fuerman, R.D. (2002) *Accountable Accountants*, http://papers.ssrn.com

Gordon, J. (2002) What Enron Means for the Management and Control of the Modern Business Corporation: Some Initial Reflections, *University of Chicago Law Review*, 69(3): 1233–1250.

*Guardian, Enron*, http://www.guardian.co.uk/enron/

Holton G. (2002) *Enron Debacle: A Publication of Risk Glossary*, http://www.riskglossary.com/link/enron.htm

Holmstrom, B. and Kaplan, S.N. (2003) *The State Of US Corporate Governance: What's Right And What's Wrong?*, Chicago Graduate School of Business, Working Paper, 19 March.

Holtzman, M., Venuti, E. and Fonfeder, R. (2003) *Enron and the Raptors*, CPA Journal Online, New York Society of CPAs, http://www.nysscpa.org/cpajournal/2003/0403/features/f042403.htm

Mack, T. (1993) Hidden Risks, *Forbes*, 151(11): 54–56.

McLean, B. (2001) Is Enron Overpriced? *Fortune*, 5 March, http://www.fortune.com/fortune/investing/articles/0,15114,369278,00.html

McLean, B. and Elkind, P. (2003) *The Smartest Guys in the Room*, London: Viking.

*New York Times*, (2003) *Understanding Enron: a primer*, http://www.nytimes.com/2002/01/14/business/_ENRON-PRIMER.html

Powers, W. (2002) *Report of the Special Investigative Committee of the Board of Enron, Enron Corporation*, http://fl1.findlaw.com/news.sfindlaw.com/wp/docs/enron/specinv020102rpt1.pdf#search=%22Powers%20Report%20Enron%22

Public Broadcasting Services (PBS) (2002) *Investigating Enron*, http://www.pbs.org/newshour/bb/business/jan-june02/enron_2-26.html

Puscas D. (2002) *A Guide to the Enron Collapse*, http://wwwpolarisinstitute.org

Spacek, L. (1989) *The Growth of Arthur Andersen & Co. 1928–1973: An Oral History*, Academy of Accounting Historians Classic Series, New York: Garland Publishing.

Stevens, M. (1991) *The Big Six: The Selling Out of America's Top Accounting Firms*. Simon and Schuster: New York.

U.S. Senate (2002) *The Role of the Board of Directors in Enron's Collapse*, Committee on Governmental Affairs, United States Senate, 107 Congress, Report 107–70, 8 July.

Vallete, J. and D. Wysham (2002) *Enron's Pawn: How Public Institutions Bankrolled Enron's Globalization Game*, Sustainable Energy and Economy Network Report, Washington, DC: Institute for Policy Studies.

*Washington Post* (2003) *Enron Special*, http://www.washingtonpost.com/wp-dyn/business/specials/energy/enron/

Watkins, S. and Swartz, M. (2003) *Power Failure: The Inside Story of the Collapse of Enron*, New York: Doubleday.

Wilson, A. and Campbell, W. (2003) Enron Exposed: Why It Took so Long, *Business and Economic Review*, January–March.

# Case Study 2
# WorldCom

## INTRODUCTION

The report to the United States District Court in New York by Richard Breedon captured the essence of the WorldCom debacle in this way:

> The events at WorldCom, Inc. transformed one of the largest companies in America, possessing one of the two largest and most comprehensive communications networks in the world, into the scene of one of history's largest frauds. In WorldCom's saga approximately $200 billion in shareholder value was first created, and then destroyed. Tens of thousands of employees lost their jobs as the Company was forced into bankruptcy, and virtually all WorldCom employees lost the entire value of stock held in retirement accounts as well as the value of accumulated equity-based compensation. The accounting fraud and governance abuses at the old WorldCom were by any measure reprehensible, and can never be justified. At the same time, WorldCom was then, and is today, an enormous global company with more than 55,000 employees and over 20 million individual and corporate customers who freely choose its services as a competitor. After exhaustive multiple investigations, the fraudulent accounting activities seem to have involved fewer than 100 persons out of the entire employee base.
>
> (Breedon 2003: 12)

Following closely after Enron's failure, the WorldCom's $9 billion accounting scandal caused widespread chaos in the US telecom sector and the wider stock market in June 2002.

WorldCom grew in size and complexity in a relatively short period of time, but it was an even faster fall that shocked investors, analysts and the corporate world. WorldCom stock traded as high as $64.50 in mid-1999, but shares of WorldCom and other telecommunications companies slid when the dot.com bubble burst, and as the company crisis developed, shares plummeted as low as 20 cents. 'WorldCom repeatedly deceived investors, competitors, and regulators with false statements about its Internet traffic projections and financial performance' (Sidak 2003: 210). By late 2002 the company went into bankruptcy.

## WORLDCOM ORIGINS

In 1985, a group of motel owners decided to start a company in Jackson, Mississippi. called Long Distance Discount Service to take advantage of the liberalisation of the US telecommunications long distance call market. Former basketball coach Bernard Ebbers was the CEO of this company, and reputedly wrote the business plan on a napkin in a café. Four years later, LDDS merged with another company to become WorldCom. By late 1992, the company reported annual revenues of $948 million and by the end of 1995 $3.9 billion. During the 1990s, WorldCom grew to become the 25th largest company in America, the world's largest internet backbone provider and largest carrier of international voice traffic, and in its home market, the second largest provider of long distance services. The rapid growth of the company was mainly due to the huge expansion of the telecoms sector caused by

massive expansion of mobile telephony and of the internet. The elimination and relaxation of legal and regulatory barriers to markets, the advancement of new technologies and services including data transmission and internet services and consolidation of competitors' reduced costs and opened lines of business and increase revenue.

## Business

WorldCom was a major provider of communications services to the US government, corporations and consumers. The company's long-distance services included long-distance and local telephone call services, and prepaid calling (telephone) cards. The astronomical growth of the internet during the 1990s created demands for internet infrastructure, which WorldCom provided. At its height, the company controlled 37 per cent of the internet backbone market and at the time of its bankruptcy, WorldCom handled half of the traffic on the internet. WorldCom's internet services included providing the internet backbone services, hosting, virtual private networks, and wholesale internet service provider services. In Australia, WorldCom acquired UUNET, and with it, the internet service provider, Ozemail. Even in the throes of bankruptcy, WorldCom was awarded government contracts to provide communication services to the country's general services administration (GSA), and contracts to rebuild the communications infrastructure of Iraq.

## THE US TELECOMMUNICATIONS INDUSTRY IN THE 1990s

### Deregulation

In the 1980s the telecommunications industry in the USA was dominated by AT&T. Concerns about the monopoly the company had led to its divesture into 7 'Baby Bells', most notably Pacific Bell (PacBell) and Bell Atlantic. This coincided with calls for deregulation in the industry to bring new players in and lower telecommunication costs to consumers.

In 1996 when the Telecommunications Act was passed, there were 12 major Telco companies. By 2002, consolidation in the industry through mergers and acquisitions by players such as WorldCom saw the industry dwindle to 6 major Telco companies. Traditional voice and data traffic in the USA soon became concentrated into the hands of a few carriers. Hence, deregulation of the industry was something of a failure for the American public as twenty years after calls for increased competition the opposite occurred. Sidak notes deregulation in fact increased the costs and diminished the effectiveness of regulation (Sidak 2003: 211). Deregulation not only increased the transaction costs of the regulatory processes, but also saw the proliferation of imperfect information as the regulator (Federal Communications Commission or FCC) relied on the information given to it by the dominant carriers: 'This model did not take into account the fact competitors were sophisticated veterans of antitrust and regulatory battles' (Sidak 2003: 227).

Deregulation in telecommunications also saw deregulation in the accounting, banking and financial sectors. McChesney notes the flow-on effects of multiple deregulation created the telecommunications crisis of the late 1990s (McChesney 2002). It became a form of regulation on behalf of powerful interests with no one representing the public. WorldCom became one of the principal actors to take advantage of this regulatory-friendly environment.

### The bull market

The exponential rise of the internet and its commercial use in the 1990s saw massive over-investment by Telco players in long-distance networks that had little regulation, while under-investing in the heavily regulated local networks. The over-investment was fuelled by the bullish stock market of the 1990s. The Telco companies' paper profits exceed traditional industrial companies which allowed them to buy bigger players and encouraged the overvaluation of dot.com companies. billion-dollar market valuation of companies that had '.com' in their name became common and

stock options were the motivating currency for employees in the industry. Stock was also the fuel that kept WorldCom's acquisition engine running, and keeping its stock price high put extraordinary pressure on the company to meet the expectations of securities analysts.

This created a corporate environment in which reporting numbers to meet market expectations – no matter how these numbers were derived – became more important than accurate financial reporting (Thornburg 2004). WorldCom made false claims from false internet traffic reports that exaggerated revenue to its financial accounts. WorldCom's claim that internet traffic was doubling every one hundred days misled government officials and the business press (Sidak 2003: 228). John Sidgmore, and Bernie Ebbers would repeat this claim in 1998. The real figures showed annual growth of 70–150 per cent rather than 700–1,500 per cent as trumpeted by WorldCom. These claims intensified over-investment in the telecommunications sector and the expansion of long-distance and internet capacities. Yet this false reporting enhanced the value of the company's share price and its stance as a voice in telecom policies.

The attempt to reconcile its inflated claims with reality led to accounting transactions such as transferring line costs expenses to capital accounts in a way that was not consistent with generally accepted accounting principles. Manipulating a high stock price was part of the strategy to expand the companies' services, customer base and facilities rapidly through acquisition of existing telecommunications companies, acquiring desirable geographic or service markets (Table C2.1). 'The company achieved growth but by rather opportunistic and rapid acquisitions of other companies' (Thornburg 2004: 255). From 1985 to 2001 WorldCom acquired over 60 companies, and spent $66.5 billion from December 1996 to July 2001 on acquisitions. The MCI acquisition (three times larger than WorldCom) in 1998 for $37 billion was considered the largest takeover in history. However, WorldCom ran out of luck with its attempt to acquire Sprint in 1999 with $129 billion in a stock buy-out in stock and debt. The deal was vetoed by the Department of Justice and the European Union on concerns of it creating a monopoly. The new company would have been the largest communications company in the US and the merger would have put AT&T number two in the US for the first time in history.

Besides sustaining the stock price to fund these acquisitions, another problem WorldCom faced was the integration of acquired assets, operations and related customer services. In 1999, the *New York Times* warned that Ebbers would have to slow down buying corporations and 'learn to run what he has built' (Gimein 1999).

Significant questions were raised regarding the extent to which WorldCom effectively

| Date | Target company | Price ($ billions) | Business |
|---|---|---|---|
| December 1996 | MFS, UUNet | 12.5 | Internet access options, applications, and value added services |
| January 1998 | Brooks Fiber | 2.4 | Facilities-based CLEC |
|  | CompuServe | 1.3 | Internet service provider |
|  | ANS Communications | 0.5 | Internet service provider |
| August 1998 | Embratel | 2.3 | Brazilian long-distance provider |
| September 1998 | MCI | 40 | Long-distance service |
| October 1999 | SkyTel | 1.7 | Paging service |
| July 2001 | Digex | 5.8 | Web/application hosting service |
| Total | 7 companies | 66.5 | |

Table C2.1 WorldCom acquisitions, December 1996 to July 2001.

integrated acquired businesses and operations and the extent to which the Company integrated or expanded its systems and internal controls to accommodate new and changing businesses, cultures and reporting structures, as there was little attempt to integrate them. (Sidak 2003: 225). When MCI was taken over, the two companies remained distinct from each other. Operations were unintegrated, and subsidiaries were used simply to bolster the parent company's financial position. WorldCom was a patchwork of acquisitions (Sidak 2003: 225; see also Appendix C2.2) that allowed the company to report its financial statements any way it wanted to due to the complexity of its corporate structure.

## WORLDCOM FRAUDULENT REPORTING 2001–2002

Serious and sustained fraudulent reporting brought WorldCom's demise. Prior to the restatement of earnings made in June 2002, WorldCom was already under scrutiny: reports emerged in 2001 of commission, subscription, and contract fraud, all ultimately blamed on the company's missing internal controls or system deficiencies. Commission fraud was sales representative misrepresentation and transfer of accounts to enhance the commission payments of some of WorldCom's sales employees. Subscription fraud was the action of setting up accounts with stolen identities resulting in customers being billed for a phone service somebody else was using and also employees were accused of approving lines of credits for non-legitimate customers. Finally, contract fraud involved business customers finding out their calls were being charged at a higher rate than their contract rate. By 2002 WorldCom had obstructed refunds owing to customers of the order of $1.8 billion to $3.5 billion in billing credits by issuing policy obstacles that made refunds hard to obtain (*Voice Report* 2002; CoFS 2002: 133). WorldCom had the reputation of having twice as many customer complaints as the other telecom companies (Boyd Saum 2002).

However, what finally brought the company into bankruptcy was its fraudulent earnings reporting when WorldCom exaggerated its earnings by $3 billion in 2001 and reported lower costs. This was largely due to the capitalisation of operating expenses by its CFO that began in January 2001 and allocated $3.2 billion expenses to its MCI subsidiary to cover up the parent company's ongoing troubles. While it reported profits of $10 billion in its final year, another set of company books showed the company made a loss of $1 billion resulting in the company collecting $300 million in overpayments from the tax office (Internal Revenue Service, IRS).

The accounting restatement of $3.8 billion stated that the company improperly reported earnings in 2000, 2001 and the first quarter of 2002. Subsequently another restatement of $9 billion was made at the end of 2002 of company accounting errors, false reporting of expenses, fraudulent line costs, company perks and loans made to executives. The majority of the accounting restatement was related to

1 phone line costs: line costs are fees charged by other phone companies for connecting WorldCom's long distance customers to their local networks; WorldCom capitalised these costs on the balance sheet rather than expensing them;
2 inflating revenues with bogus accounting revenues from 'corporate unallocated revenue accounts'.

### The dot.com bubble and the stock collapse

The bursting of the hype-inflated dot.com bubble quickly undermined confidence in the whole telecoms industry that had intended providing the infrastructure for e-business. The entire US telecom industry was beset by excess capacity and slack demand (Boyd). Telecommunication companies shed more than half a trillion dollars in market value in less than two years. The massive profitability of the telecommunications sector was replaced with huge losses amounting to around $150 billion in 2002 in the leading firms (Figure C2.1). As the OECD (2004a: 313)

WorldCom key acqusitions and events vs. the closing stock price

**Figure C2.1** WorldCom's rise and fall.

diplomatically put it, 'In recent years, firms in the telecommunications services sector have experienced some of the largest losses in corporate history' (Figure C2.2). WorldCom, the most extravagant of the telecommunications companies, filed for bankruptcy; but Vodafone and Deutsche Telecom both lost over $23 billion; France Telecom over $20 billion; AT & T $13 billion; and NTT over $6 billion. Substantial losses were also encountered in communications equipment companies and in electronics and components. Together, these losses punctured the NASDAQ bubble and sent the New York Stock Exchange into a tailspin, losing 46 per cent of market capitalisation or $7,000 billion.

Commissioner Abernathy stated, 'WorldCom appeared to have resorted to financial deception to mask poor performance. This fraud compounded the [telecommunications/economy] downturn by shaking investors' confidence in the truthfulness of financial statements' (FCC evidence in Sidak 2003: 231). Domestic equity funds had $25 billion invested in telecoms shares while investors in the S&P 500 index funds indirectly owned telecom companies that have since gone bust including Global Crossing, Qwest, WorldCom and the other

10 telecom high fliers (Feldman and Caplin 2002). WorldCom common stock fell from a high on June 30, 1999 of $96.766 per share to a low of $46 per share by 30 June 2000. For the course of the next year it fluctuated between $24 and $12 per share and then the share price fell precipitously in 2002, prompting it be delisted from the NASDAQ stock market as of 30 July 2002 (Thornburg 2004: 23) (Figure C2.2).

## SEC investigation

In the wake of numerous SEC investigations into the accounting practices of telecommunications and other companies WorldCom disclosed on 11 March 2002 that it had received a confidential request from the SEC for voluntary production of documents and information. By 26 June 2002 the SEC commenced a civil injunctive action against WorldCom alleging violations of the antifraud and other provisions of the federal securities laws. The SEC complaint sought an injunction, monetary penalties, and prohibitions on destroying documents and making extraordinary payments to WorldCom affiliates. On 28 June 2002

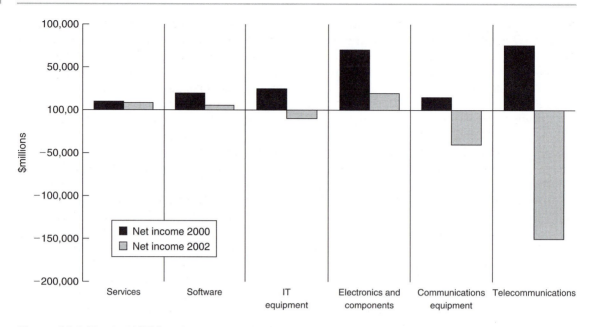

Figure C2.2 Top 250 ICT firms' net income, by sector.

Source: OECD, compiled from annual reports, SEC filings and market financials.

the district court ordered that WorldCom and its affiliates preserve all items relating to the company's financial reporting obligations, public disclosures required by the federal securities laws and accounting matters. The district court appointed a corporate monitor with oversight responsibility regarding all compensation paid by WorldCom (Thornburg 2004: 23).

## THE CORPORATE GOVERNANCE CULTURE

### Conflicts of interest

The emphasis on stock options during the internet boom as *the* performance incentive made management's main goal to meet analysts' expectations of earnings and stock price (Stern 2002b). This produced disproportionate pay increases for chief executives, for top executives and their boards of directors, that decoupled shareholders' interests in profit maximisation from management's interest in

personal wealth maximisation (Table C2.2). By 1999 the nine-member board was made up of insiders that supported Bernard Ebbers – invited executives from WorldCom's acquired companies (Haddad 2002). The board, especially the CEO, thrived on the rise of the company share price (ticker symbol: WCOM). Indeed WorldCom executives were 'more

| Person | Shares sold | Value/ proceeds |
|---|---|---|
| John Sidgmore (CEO) | 2,601,430 | $87,364,381 |
| Scott Sullivan (CFO) | 1,388,816 | $44,183,360 |
| Francesco Galesi | 3,517,004 | $29,176,146 |
| Bert Roberts (Chair) | 422,526 | $22,766,074 |
| Carl Aycock | 859,791 | $4,490,900 |
| Max Bobbitt | 34,343 | $1,821,875 |

Table C2.2 Shares sold by board members, 1996–2002.

Source: Adapted from CoFS (2002: 298).

responsible for inflating the internet bubble than anyone' (Odlyzko 2003: 228), as a higher share price meant higher personal net worth. The internecine relationships between top executives and their boards of directors which facilitated this largesse became relevant during the last ten years, and this was nowhere better illustrated than in WorldCom (Stern 2002a, 2002b; Stern and Krim 2002). The same generosity was not extended to employees: for example, the board approved a $10 million loan to the CEO while laying off 6,000 employees at the same time.

The WorldCom board was weak on corporate governance, frowned on internal audit, and was totally dominated by its CEO. The board unquestioningly backed Ebbers through the stupendous expansion – to the brink of the company's collapse. Strategic planning at WorldCom was done by Ebbers, and to a lesser extent by Sullivan. This planning was largely informal, lightly documented and to some extent consisted of oral discussions among a small number of executives (Thornburg in Stern 2002b). The board was at the mercy of Ebbers who would not let his senior management sell their shares without his permission.

## THE KEY PLAYERS

### The non-accountable CEO: Bernie Ebbers

Ebbers was obsessed with the company share price reaching $100, telling managers they had to figure out ways to keep on pushing it up. 'The value of my stock is worth a lot more to me than my job and my salary … I have to fire myself for the sake of my stock' (Ebbers in Mehta 2001: 88). At the time of bankruptcy Ebbers owed the company more than $400 million in personal loans, having loan repayment terms and sweetheart loan interest rates of about 2 per cent (Sidak 2003: 244). In part, this $400 million loan was to pay off Ebbers' other personal loans. WorldCom's directors were worried that Ebbers would dump his large holdings of company stock, either to finance his purchases or meet margin calls.

If he did, and the stock price plummeted, shareholders and the directors stood to lose. Over a seven year period Ebbers obtained over $800 million in personal loans from conglomerate financial institutions that had close ties to the company. Ebbers was one of the biggest borrowers from the Bank of America's private banking division since Bank of America acted as the lead bank on the $2.5 billion finance of WorldCom's acquisition of WilTel in 1995. During the 1990s, Ebbers' total debt exceeded $1 billion for yachts, farms, a marina, ranches and personal gifts (see Tables C2.3 and C2.4).

Ebbers' debt to WorldCom was closely related to the falling price of his WorldCom shares (Figure C2.3). As the share price collapsed, Ebbers' liquidity and capacity to service his vast loans to fund his reckless extravagance evaporated. By April 2002 when it became clear he couldn't repay back the company loan, the WorldCom board requested his resignation with a retirement package of $1 million per annum for life with $750,000 per annum for his wife after his death. This was on top of his compensation package that was worth $25 million from 1999 to 2001. The company also seized some of Ebbers' assets, the shipyard and the Canadian ranch to pay off company debts owed by Ebbers.

### The creative accountant: Scott Sullivan

*The company's balance sheet is strong, cash flow broke even during the 4th quarter, SG&A is being cut wherever possible and debt maturities are relatively light during the next 2 years. Growth would be revised to mid-single digit growth.*
        (Sullivan in 6 February 2002 Audit Committee minutes in CoFS appendix, 2002)

Scott Sullivan was the Chief Financial Officer at WorldCom and was one of Ebbers' most loyal lieutenants. At age 37 in 1998 CFO magazine named Sullivan as one of America's best CFOs and he was earning $19.3 million. He was widely respected in the company as the best in his profession. When it became clear the dot.com crash was more widespread than first thought, WorldCom, like

| Institution | Loan |
| --- | --- |
| Citigroup | $10m (1994) to buy 2 million shares of WorldCom |
| | $42.2m (refinance for Canadian cattle ranch) |
| | $499m (Timberland in Mississippi, Alabama and Tennessee) |
| | Total: $552m (88m repaid, still owed $464m) |
| Bank of America | $13.8m (March 1998) for Louisianan soybean and rice farm |
| | $800k (for Mississippi Columbus lumber timberyard) |
| | For a 46-foot yacht (1988), 60-foot yacht, 92-foot yacht, 121-foot yacht and for a 132-foot yacht, *Aquasition* (1996) |
| | $14m for *Intermarine Savannah* |
| | Total: $253m (repaid) |
| Toronto Dominion Bank | $65m (for Canadian cattle ranch) June 1998. |
| UBS PaineWebber | $51m, margin call on September 2000. Repaid |
| Morgan Keegan | $11.6m Repaid |
| Bank of North Georgia | $10.8m (April 2002 – repaid after sale of two yachts). Repaid |
| Morgan Guaranty | $10.8m (paid by Bank of North Georgia loan). Repaid |
| WorldCom | $415m loan to pay off margin calls (owed) |

Table C2.3 Ebbers' personal loans.

| Description | Value |
| --- | --- |
| Intermarine Savannah, yacht-building business | $50m |
| Douglas Lake Ranch, Canada 500,000-acre ranch with 20,000 cattle | $65m |
| Joshua Timberland LLC | $700m with a $460m mortgage |
| Build a house | $27m |
| WorldCom shares, to secure the margin loan from Citigroup (1994) | $10m |
| Gift to family member | $2m |
| Loan to friends | $1m |
| Fund own business | $22.8m |

Table C2.4 What Ebbers bought with WorldCom company loans.

other companies in the telecoms sector was severely affected. No definite motive has been offered as to why Sullivan started capitalising operating expenses in January 2001. For the next five quarters until the internal auditor Cynthia Cooper and her team discovered what was happening, Sullivan would make fraudulent entries in WorldCom's general ledger, directing the company comptroller David Myers to reduce the reported line costs and increase reported earnings to meet analysts' expectations and bolster the share price (O'Harrow and Stern 2002). Sullivan told Ebbers about this change in accounting practice (Stern and Krim 2002). The capitalisation of WorldCom's operating expenses enabled the company to claim in its books that the costs would be spread out over several years instead of immediately (Table C2.5).

When the accounting fraud was brought to light, Sullivan was asked to resign by the board, but his failure to do so led to an ignominious termination without a severance

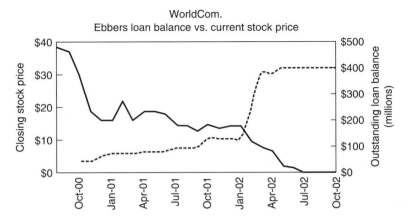

**Figure C2.3** Ebbers' loan balance vs. current stock price.

Source: Thornburg (2004).

By booking certain costs as a capital expense, WorldCom was able to boost its bottom line. A look at how the company conducted such accounting in 2001:

| WorldCom's accounting | Expense | | GAAP |
|---|---|---|---|
| 1 Accounts $3.1B in line costs, including telecom access and transport charges, as capital expenditure | Capital expense | Operating expense | 1 The $3.1b line cost expense is booked as an operating expense |
| 2 Plans to amortise $3.1b over a period of time, possibly as much as 10 years | Amortisation | Cost of business | 2 The entire $3.1b would have been counted as a cost of business for that quarter |
| 3 Reports net income of $1.38b for 2001 | Higher net income | Lower net income | 3 Net income for 2001 would have been a loss, amount to be determined |

**Table C2.5** Creative accounting.

Source: CoFS (2002: 285).

package on 24 June 2002. He had sold WCOM shares worth $44 million between 1996 and 2002 and had a $15 million family compound. In August 2002, Sullivan was indicted on charges of securities fraud, faced with seven charges of improperly manipulating the company's books and accused of fraudulently securing $4.25 billion for the company by making false statements to several banks.

### The pliant financial controller: David Myers

*If we disclose this, we close our doors, we can't operate. We have to keep hiding these losses or our business fails.*

*(Myers 2002)*

David Myers was the financial controller of WorldCom. Under instruction by senior management he ensured entries were made

to reduce WorldCom's reported costs thus increasing the company's earnings. These entries transferred costs from expense accounts to capital expenditures. Myers later admitted there was no justification for such action, and these adjustments did not meet GAAP. With the director of general accounting, Myers was arraigned on securities fraud and conspiracy. Myers was charged with three counts of conspiracy, securities fraud and making false statements to the SEC (O'Harrow and Stern 2002). He pleaded guilty to charges of manipulating and covering up the accounting of the company to inflate profits.

### The well-rewarded chair of the compensation committee: Stiles Kellett

Stiles Kellett was head of the company's compensation committee which approved the $408 million company loan and retirement package made to Ebbers. He had a close relationship with Ebbers and this was reciprocated. Kellett was permitted to rent the corporate jet for $1 per month. He paid a $400 per hour usage fee which was substantially below the market rate while the fuel used and crew was reimbursed. The one year lease expired the same month WorldCom restated its accounts. The lease deal was never disclosed by the company in its proxy statements and few people were aware that such an arrangement existed.

When this lease deal was made public, Kellett resigned in disgrace.

### The short-lived successor: John Sidgmore

John Sidgmore became the short-lived CEO of WorldCom after Ebbers' resignation. Sidgmore joined the WorldCom board after his company, MCI, was taken over. He sold over $87 million worth of shares primarily after the MCI's acquisition. Sidgmore appeared before the House Committee on the company's accounting scandal. Unlike Sullivan and Ebbers he answered the committee's questions. While Sidgmore's lack of responsibility for the company and conflict of interest was not as severe as the others in this section, Sidgmore entered into high price contracts with investment banks and consultants. These contracts were made without board approval and Sidgmore paid investment bankers such as Goldman Sachs and Lazard Freres millions of dollars in fees. Tainted with the old regime Sidgmore soon made way for the new CEO.

### THE INTERMEDIARIES

WorldCom's management could not have not have carried out this huge accounting fraud without a close and forgiving relationship with its bankers and auditors (Table C2.6).

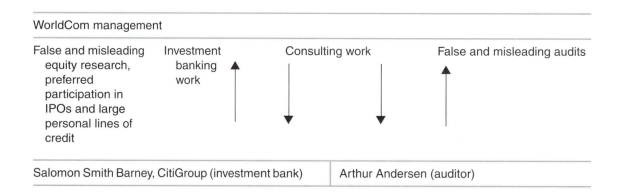

| WorldCom management | | | |
| --- | --- | --- | --- |
| False and misleading equity research, preferred participation in IPOs and large personal lines of credit | Investment banking work | Consulting work | False and misleading audits |
| Salomon Smith Barney, CitiGroup (investment bank) | | Arthur Andersen (auditor) | |

Table C2.6  Possible WorldCom conspiracies.

Source: Adapted from Sidak (2003: 247).

## The role of the investment bank: Salomon Smith Barney

Part of the Citigroup of companies, Salomon Smith Barney (SSB) was one of WorldCom's principal investment bankers. The relationship between WorldCom and Salomon Smith Barney was questionable on several levels: it was found that Salomon Smith Barney's Atlanta Brokers Group, staffed by a number of young and inexperienced account executives, allegedly gave unsuitable financial advice, under WorldCom management instructions to many WorldCom employees in connection with their 401 (k) retirement plan resulting in many WorldCom employees investing a large portion of their retirement nest eggs in WorldCom stock that left them vulnerable when the share price collapsed. At the peak of the dot.com hype SSB was at the centre of the telecom boom with deals in excess of $223 billion. SSB underwrote $22 billion of WorldCom deals over a period of five years (Royce in CoFS 2002: 61). Out of the $1.8 billion in telecom fees from 1997 to 2000 SSB received, more than $32.5 million were in fees from WorldCom. At the centre of the SSB-WorldCom relationship was the bullish telecom analyst Jack Grubman who had an inappropriately close relationship with WorldCom executives and and was accused of issuing misleading statements relating to the value of WorldCom stock.

## The role of the stock analyst: Jack Grubman

*What used to be a conflict [of interest] is now a synergy.*

(Thomas in Feldman and Caplin 2002)

Jack Grubman was a Salomon Smith Barney analyst who was considered a telecommunications industry expert. Once the most highly paid investment analysts on Wall St, earning $20 million a year, Grubman was the ultimate power broker in the telecom industry: every time he put a 'buy' on a company, its shares would jump high, enriching his investors (some of whom happened to be company directors).

He once boasted he sculpted the telecommunications industry.

Grubman's perceived strength in the industry was due in part to the personal relationships he had cultivated with the principals of the companies he analysed. He had a personal relationship with Ebbers, even attending his second wedding in 1999: 'I consider Mr. Ebbers someone I like, someone I liked to be around when I was around' (CoFS 2002: 82). Indeed this close relationship could be explained by the hundreds of millions of dollars his firm was also receiving in underwriting fees (CoFS 2002: 2). Though called an independent analyst, Grubman attended board meetings of WorldCom and even served on the WorldCom board as the official proxy solicitor on the company's bid to buy MCI. As he put it, this was 'synergy', not conflict of interest. Grubman repeatedly recommended share after share that his company was dealing with, most unabashedly with Global Crossing. Grubman never made a 'sell' recommendation on any company: 'We didn't have a sell. We had neutrals on companies that either went bankrupt, or [we] just suspended coverage' (Grubman in CoFS 2002: 70). (In fact few analysts at the time in Wall Street ever dared put a 'sell' on major companies.) When the internet sector crashed and reverberated into the telecoms sector, Grubman became an outcast.

Even before the leakage of the $9 billion accounting irregularity of WorldCom, serious doubts were being cast over Grubman's analytical skills as wave after wave of telecom companies he had recommended went bust (see Table C2.7). In February 2002, Grubman was sued by two former SSB brokers. In April 2002, *Money Magazine* pounced, wondering whether he was the worst analyst ever (Feldman and Caplin, 2002), as several of the companies filed for bankruptcy, and Grubman made little attempt to change his recommendations When Ebbers resigned from WCOM, this was a potent signal to the market that all was not well within the company. However, Grubman's recommendations did not put 'sell' on the company; he merely changed his 'buy' to 'neutral'. The following month WCOM was downgraded by Grubman

| Company | Fate |
|---|---|
| Metromedia Fiber Network | Recommended in 1997, share price went up by 500 per cent within 10 months. Did not go bust but needed financial restructuring |
| Qwest | Recommended in 1998, share doubled in 11 months. In 2003, the company is under investigation for financial problems after revealing it lost $3b over the past 3 years |
| Global Crossing | Salomon Smith Barney helped the company in its $397m IPO. Recommended in September 1998, share rose 375 per cent. In 2002, the company filed for bankruptcy, the 4th largest ever with $55b paper wealth evaporating |
| McLeod USA | Recommended. Filed for bankruptcy |
| Winstar Communications | Recommended. Filed for bankruptcy |
| XO Communications | Recommended, Grubman had good working relationship with management. Filed for bankruptcy |
| Broadwing | Recommended. Down 83 per cent |
| Allegiance Telecom | Down 90.7 per cent July 2002 |
| WorldCom | Emerged from bankruptcy as MCI |

Table C2.7  Grubman's recommendations.

Source: White, K. (2002), 'Profile: Bill Lytton, Counsel Tyco International', *Lawyers Weekly*, 29 November.

to 'suspend' status, the day after WorldCom announced its restatement. The collapse of sections of the telecom sector saw investigations by the National Association of Securities Dealers (NASD) into Grubman's close ties with many of the telecom companies he followed.

### The role of the auditor: Andersen

WorldCom's company auditor was Arthur Andersen, the same auditor as Enron. When Enron collapsed and Andersen's rubber stamp and conflict of interest roles were roundly condemned, WorldCom's internal auditor Cynthia Cooper sensed something was amiss at WorldCom. As with Enron, Arthur Andersen may have been inclined to support WorldCom's management in misleading audits since they were receiving substantial consulting work (Sidak 2003: 248). From 1999 to 2001 internal Andersen reports wrote that WorldCom's accounting was at 'maximum risk' (Stern 2002b) with significant risks related to 'overly aggressive revenue or earning targets'. Despite these warnings Andersen auditors did not take steps to seek accounting changes. In 2001 Arthur Andersen's entire service fees for WorldCom were $16.8 million and only 26 per cent of these fees were related to audit services. Tax consulting services comprised the bulk of the fees, while the rest of the charges were made of consulting services (Figure C2.4). On 6 February 2002 a meeting was held with the company's audit committee with Andersen presenting an audit of WorldCom for the financial year. Andersen gave WorldCom a clean bill of health, stating that WorldCom's key transaction processing areas were operating effectively, and Andersen did not have any disagreements with WorldCom management.

Andersen stated they were not aware of any irregularities or illegal acts committed by the company or by its employees, and that there were no significant difficulties encountered during the audit. There were no major issues discussed with management prior to Andersen being appointed as auditors. Andersen stated there were no

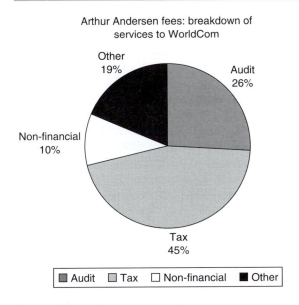

Arthur Andersen fees: breakdown of services to WorldCom

- Other 19%
- Audit 26%
- Non-financial 10%
- Tax 45%

Audit ☐ Tax ☐ Non-financial ■ Other

**Figure C2.4** Arthur Andersen fees.

material weaknesses in internal controls of the company, and they were comfortable with the company's classification of its CEO loan of December 2001. Andersen was not aware of any issues related to Andersen's independence that occurred during the company's fiscal year. WorldCom had no significant or unusual transactions Andersen claimed, nor did it have material transactions in controversial or emerging areas for which there was a lack of authoritative accounting guidance or consensus.

Melvin Dick was global managing director for Andersen and became the lead auditor in 2001 for WorldCom. His team spent 15,000 hours auditing the company (CoFS 2002: 92). On 4 February 2002 Dick stated the 'balance sheets and income statements are fairly presented in accordance with GAAP in the US' (Appendix of CoFS 2002). Dick was satisfied with the company's health, agreeing with the 'reasonableness of management's current judgments' and for the most part assessed WorldCom operations as being 'effective'. On the 15 May 2002 with the company shares in free-fall Arthur Andersen was replaced by KPMG as WorldCom's auditor.

## Role of the regulator

The FCC was established to promote 'a rapid, efficient, nation-wide and worldwide radio communication service with adequate facilities at reasonable charges'. The agency is empowered to regulate wire and radio communications and its duty is to guard the welfare of consumers and preserve competition among producers of telecommunications services (Sidak 2003: 253–254). *Regulatory capture* involves a regulatory agency being influenced by the companies or organisations it seeks to regulate. In the FCC's case a symptom of its capture was its reliance on self-reported industry data or asymmetry of information between itself and the companies it was supposed to regulate. Accounting data and related information filed by carriers was used by policy-makers to determine access charges, evaluate federal–state jurisdictional separations, set rates for unbundled network elements and calculate universal service support (Sidak 2003: 236). The FCC in fact relied on 'potentially misleading and harmful financial, accounting and market information produced by corporate sources subject to clear biases and market pressures' (Sidak 2003: 229).

An example of misleading data was the overstatement made by WorldCom in the growth in internet traffic volumes (Sidak 2003: 230) that led to overinvestment in this area with supply soon exceeding consumer demand. WorldCom flourished under the FCCs regulatory oversight: the FCC 'was oblivious to the largest accounting fraud in history, committed by a principal beneficiary of the market-opening deregulation efforts' (Sidak 2003: 259–260).

## THE WORLDCOM EMPLOYEES: THE WHISTLEBLOWERS

Many employees of WorldCom were not aware of the financial irregularities taking place, but a small group who did become aware questioned the validity of management's reasoning and demonstrated a determination to expose the truth.

## Cynthia Cooper: vice president internal audit

Cynthia Cooper exploded the bubble as she knew 'There are some things, terribly, terribly wrong at WorldCom' (Lacayo and Ripley 2002) and she realised 'There is a corporate governance revolution across the country. Internal audit departments are going to be taken more seriously'. She had joined the company a decade earlier, earning $15 an hour in customer service. She became the vice president of the internal audit division of WorldCom in 1998. WorldCom was an exciting, anti-jargon and entrepreneurial place to be: 'We were moving and shaking and acquiring companies' (Ripley 2002). Then in March 2002 an executive in the wireless division, Troy Normand, told her $400 million was taken out of his division's reserve account to boost the parent company's income. Cooper went to the auditors Andersen but was told it was not a problem. When she brought the subject up to Scott Sullivan, Cooper was told to 'back off and that everything was fine'. To Cooper, 'when someone is hostile, my instinct is to find out why'. With doubts over Andersen's efficacy after its role in Enron, Cooper and her internal audit team decided to retrace the footsteps of its external auditors, going behind the back of management directives by working late at night and keeping their project a secret. Cooper's 'fear of losing my job was very secondary to the obligation I felt', and she went against the very people she had admired who were 'typically racehorses, not workhorses … and very charismatic' (*Time*, 22 December 2002).

By May, Cooper and her team discovered the company's public reports had categorised billions of dollars of operating costs as capital expenditures. There was a sudden realisation then that WorldCom's problems were not due to the general downturn in the telecom sector but due to its internal accounting fraud. 'There was an adrenaline rush yet there was a great sadness' (*Time*, 22 December 2002). When management became aware of the internal audit's investigations, Ebbers ordered Cooper's division to have its funding (including employees' compensation expenses) halved with the intention of slowing down and discouraging further investigation (although this was later reduced to a 10 per cent cut by Sullivan).

The extent of the accounting fraud was so enormous that Cooper brought her concerns to the company's audit committee which was chaired by board member Max Bobbitt who had a year earlier tried to oust Ebbers from his CEO role. By mid-May, Bobbitt and the audit committee hired KPMG and recalled Dick to explain Andersen's failure to come across this billion-dollar hole. On 11 June Sullivan called Cooper to ask what the internal audit team was up to, and to possibly delay the investigation, but she refused. The next day Cooper confronted Myers in the hope there was some rationale behind the accounting manipulation, but Myers admitted it could not be justified. Sullivan was asked to offer an explanation but could not convince the board. The audit committee requested the resignations of Sullivan and Myers. On the same day, both KPMG and Andersen agreed Sullivan's accounting was improper and encouraged the company to make a financial restatement. After the debacle Cooper with the other whistleblowers at Enron (Sherron Watkins) and the FBI (Coleen Rowley) was designated as one of *Time*'s persons of the year in 2002. Her division became 'probably the most secure in the company and the company has carried out many of her recommendations' (Ripley 2002). Yet some of her colleagues despised what she did, telling her that Sullivan should have been given more time to find a way out of the accounting hole and that the company could have borrowed its way to avoid bankruptcy had her division kept quiet. However, Cooper insisted and the Breedon report confirmed, 'The vast majority of WorldCom is made up of capable, honest employees trying to do the right thing. Only a handful of people were involved in any wrongdoing' (*Time*, 22 December 2002).

## Troy Normand: wireless division accountant

Troy Normand was a mid-level employee from the company's wireless division who waved

a red flag to Cooper when he noticed some aggressive accounting occurring in his division (Johnson and Stern 2002). In 2000 when Normand first raised concerns about the accounting of line costs Sullivan told Normand there were 'business reasons' that justified the accounting. The following year Normand with two other colleagues, raised concerns about the state of the books with Myers whom they did not know was in cahoots with Sullivan about the accounting. Normand threatened to resign over the fudging of the prepaid capacity of the line costs but finally backed down as 'he was concerned for his job and the family he had to support' (Dreazen and Solomon 2002). Normand did not communicate his concerns to either external or internal audit until he notified Cooper in March 2002.

### Steven Brabbs: director, international finance and control

Steven Brabbs was former director of WorldCom's international finance and control division based in London. In 2000 Brabbs' unit was asked to restate their units' financial reports to make the unit look more profitable. When he probed this directive further Brabbs found out this order came from Sullivan. He was asked to record $33.6 million in operating expenses, which were expenses related to the capitalisation of line costs. Brabbs questioned this, but Myers shortly wrote to him saying he was not pleased this matter had been raised with Andersen without Myers' knowledge (Stern 2002d). Brabbs was agitated by this directive as it was illogical and was reluctant to change his unit's books, and as pressure was exerted, he refused to make the entry into his ledgers and on 10 July 2000, created a separate 'management company' to attribute the disputed $33.6 million expenses. This 'management company' was not a legal entity but rather emphasised his concerns, and he included a note saying the adjustment was instructed by Scott Sullivan. Andersen who was first informed by Brabbs of this adjustment went to WorldCom management and was told that

this was being corrected with the item booked as an expense in the next quarter. This was never done, and Brabbs' action went unexposed for the next two years until WorldCom went bankrupt.

### CORPORATE GOVERNANCE: THE DECLINE IN ETHICS IN THE 1990s

The US government reacted swiftly to WorldCom's downfall which had undermined confidence in America's market system (CoFS 2002: 4). Two weeks after WorldCom restated its accounts, WorldCom officers Ebbers (ex-CEO), Sullivan (CFO), Sidgmore (CEO) and Bert Roberts (Chairman), Dick of Andersen, and Grubman of SSB were subpoenaed to appear before the US House of Representatives financial committee. Ebbers and Sullivan refused to testify to what happened at WorldCom but the rest did. The committee explored the 'decline of ethics in American culture during the 1990s' (CoFS 2002: 1). WorldCom's executives were accused of deliberately attempting to hide billion dollar expenses, to prop up the share price and keep their paper wealth, at the expense of the pension funds of the house representatives' constituents. Sidgmore and Roberts apologised on behalf of WorldCom even though they made $87 million and $22 million respectively with the sale of their WorldCom stock.

### Shareholders

The biggest shareholders of WorldCom were the state pension funds in America. The Californian public employees' retirement fund lost $580 million as a result of WorldCom's bankruptcy, and the small state of Iowa pension funds lost a total of $30 million. CalPERS sued the company to regain some of the moneys lost. The company was fined $500 million meaning shareholders received 17 cents a share, a far cry from its $60 per share peak (Figure C2.5).

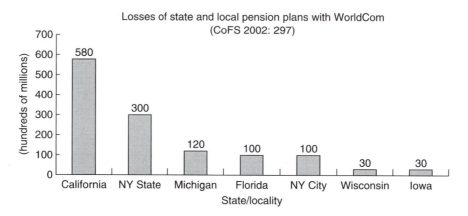

Figure C2.5  Pension fund losses due to WorldCom collapse.

## Government

*Your company is really vital to our country. It is vital to an incredible industry. It is vital to the competitiveness of American communication companies worldwide.*

(CoFS 2002)

WorldCom earned $1.7 billion or 8 per cent of revenue from American state and federal government contracts. It was in the governments' interest that WorldCom emerged from bankruptcy as they depended on WorldCom's services. In November 2002 WorldCom received government contracts post-restatement: one to provide telecom services for veterans' hospitals, another a contract extension with the general services administration (GSA) to provide long-distance telephone service for 77 federal agencies worth $331 million per annum. The following month WorldCom was awarded a $360 million contract to provide global communication services to the US State Department, and after its brand name change MCI received a contract to build a small mobile phone network in Baghdad (Stern 2002). Its interim 2002 CEO Sidgmore did not exaggerate WorldCom's importance to the US economy and industry when he said WorldCom was 'a key component of our nation's economic and communications infrastructure. Both commercial and national security interest, relies upon WorldCom's operations

continuing without disruption' (Krim and Stern 2002).

## Business rivals

Industry rivals like AT&T, Sprint and Verizon were glad to see the fall of WorldCom whom they 'blamed as the principal culprit in the telecom bubble – one that posted curiously high profits that they could never quite seem to match' (Eisenberg 2002). WorldCom had distorted the competition in the industry (Sidak 2003: 260). The fraudulent reporting by WorldCom during the 1990s on the financial performance internet infrastructure saw an overinvestment in the industry as WorldCom's distortion influenced policy-makers, and influenced competitors to raise their own costs by inducing inefficient investment in capacity and inefficient expenditure on customer acquisitions (Sidak 2003: 239).

## Market

WorldCom set a trading volume record for a single stock in a given day with over one billion shares trading hands. The financial community, still recovering from the billions lost after the dot.com bubble burst blamed WorldCom's financial improprieties for severe market declines in the telecommunications industry

(Sidak 2003: 231). WorldCom's accounting fraud destroyed at least $7.8 billion of shareholder wealth in other American telecommunication companies (Sidak 2003: 235).

## Employees

One of the first acts of the post-Ebbers era was a 'cost saving effort' of Sidgmore (CoFS 2002) that saw 17,000 employees sacked. The employees received some severance, but received no life insurance, no healthcare and no annual pension. A further 5,000 employees were laid off later in 2002 and 33 per cent of jobs were slashed in the internal computer and data-networking support division which had 6,000 employees worldwide. Overall WorldCom/MCI was left with 60,000 employees worldwide.

## GOVERNANCE REFORMS: RESTORING TRUST

When it finally arrived the regulators' intervention at WorldCom was robust:

> The SEC's enforcement proceeding in WorldCom has itself been highly innovative. The Commission filed charges of fraud against WorldCom almost immediately, after the Company announced the first discovery of the accounting problems, without waiting for a lengthy investigation to be completed. The SEC also sought the imposition of a corporate monitor immediately, which was a highly innovative remedy designed to create effective oversight of potential inappropriate activity immediately. The SEC also eventually sought and obtained far reaching affirmative relief as a part of its settlements with the Company. This relief included the requirement for this governance overhaul, and also the largest financial penalty of its type in history.
>
> (Breedon 2003: 13)

The preliminary settlement with the SEC involved a unique approach to enforcing a substantial commitment to corporate governance reform:

> In November of 2002, WorldCom and the SEC entered into a preliminary settlement of the SEC's action. The Company consented to the entry of a permanent injunction (the 'Permanent Injunction') by the Court against future violations of the federal securities laws. The Permanent Injunction also imposed several novel and far-reaching forms of affirmative relief. This relief included requiring
>
> (i) a company-wide program of training in accounting, financial disclosure and ethics,
> (ii) a comprehensive review of the Company's system of internal controls, and
> (iii) a review of the Company's corporate governance 'systems, policies, plans and practices' to recommend changes for the future.

The Permanent Injunction provides that: '[t]he Corporate Monitor, taking note of the report of the Special Investigative Committee and such other input as the Corporate Monitor shall deem appropriate, shall perform a review of the adequacy and effectiveness of WorldCom's corporate governance systems, policies, plans, and practices. This review will include but is not limited to inquiries into

> (1) whether WorldCom is complying with recognized standards of 'best practices' with respect to corporate governance;
> (2) whether WorldCom has sufficient policies and safeguards in place
>
> (a) to ensure that WorldCom's Board of Directors and all committees of WorldCom's Board of Directors (including without limitation the Audit Committee and the Compensation Committee) have appropriate powers, structure, composition, and resources, and
> (b) to prevent self-dealing by management;

(3) whether WorldCom has an adequate and appropriate code of ethics and business conduct, and related compliance mechanisms; and
(4) whether WorldCom has appropriate safeguards in place to prevent further violation of the federal securities laws.

(Breedon 2003: 14)

## Criminal charges

In September 2002, Myers was charged with three counts of conspiracy, securities fraud and making false statements to the SEC (O'Harrow Jr and Stern 2002). He pleaded guilty to charges of manipulating and covering up of the accounting of the company to inflate profits. In August 2002 Sullivan was indicted on charges of securities fraud, and faced with seven charges of improperly manipulating the company's books and was accused of fraudulently securing $4.25 billion for the company by making false statements to several banks. On 15 March 2005 Bernard Ebbers was found guilty of all charges and convicted of fraud, conspiracy and filing false documents with regulators – all related to the $11 billion accounting scandal at the telecommunications company he founded. He was sentenced to 25 years in prison.

Other former WorldCom officials facing criminal penalties in relation to the company's financial misstatements included former CFO Scott Sullivan who entered a guilty plea on 2 March 2004 to one count each of securities fraud, conspiracy to commit securities fraud, and filing false statements, and received a five year sentence in return for testifying against Ebbers. Former controller David Myers pleaded guilty to securities fraud, conspiracy to commit securities fraud, and filing false statements. Former accounting director Buford Yates pleaded guilty to conspiracy and fraud charges on 7 October 2002, and former accounting managers Betty Vinson and Troy Normand both pleading guilty to conspiracy and securities fraud on 10 October 2002.

## Other settlements

In March 2005, 16 of the 17 WorldCom former underwriters reached settlements after class actions from investors, with Citigroup (the parent company of Salomon Smith Barney) settling for $2.65 billion in May 2004. On 7 January 2005 the lead plaintiff of the New York State Common Retirement Fund announced a historic $54 million settlement with the majority of the former WorldCom directors. Of the $54 million, $36 million was funded by the defendants' insurers and $18 million was funded by the directors themselves. The $18 million represented over 20 per cent of the aggregate net worth of these individuals. This type of recovery from the personal holdings of corporate officials is extremely rare.

## Emergence from Chapter 11

WorldCom with $36 billion in debt re-emerged as MCI. Its reorganisation plan for the largest corporate bankruptcy in history involved $107 billion in assets. The board of WorldCom has been swept clean of board members during the Ebbers era. Not long after his House testimony, Sidgmore stepped down for Michael Capellas, the former Hewlett-Packard president. Unlike his predecessors, Capellas has the triumvirate role of chair, CEO and president. His $20 million contract over three years includes an 'unusual incentive provision that ties his future bonuses to the ethical standards of the scandal-plagued firm' (Stern 2002a). His bonus is linked to the accuracy of WorlCom's financial statements and to its own code of ethics. In 2004 the company emerged from Chapter 11 bankruptcy with a new name MCI, and about $5.7 billion in debt and $6 billion in cash. About half of the cash was intended to pay various claims and settlements. Previous bondholders ended up being paid 35.7 cents on the dollar in bonds and stock in the new MCI company. The previous stockholders' shares were valueless. Under the bankruptcy reorganisation agreement, the company paid $750 million to the SEC in cash and stock in the new MCI, which was intended to be paid to

wronged investors. In February 2005 Verizon Communications agreed to acquire MCI for $7.6 billion, with the deal closing on 6 January 2006. MCI was incorporated into Verizon, as Verizon Business.

## Questions

1 Outline the major corporate governance failings of WorldCom. What mechanisms might have corrected these before bankruptcy was inevitable?

2 Consider the benefits and costs of rapid strategic growth through acquisitions.

3 Are business ethics capable of withstanding the temptations of apparently unlimited executive reward through stock options?

4 Discuss the major responsibilities of external auditors in evaluating company financial statements as in the case of WorldCom, and to whom do the auditors owe this professional responsibility?

5 Was the telecoms crash in 2002 simply an inevitable result of rapid technological and market changes?

| Date | Event |
| --- | --- |
| 1985 | Former motel owner, Bernard Ebbers becomes CEO of Long Distance Discount Service, a service created by a group of motel owners |
| 1989 | LDDS merges with Advantage to become WorldCom |
| 1994 | Scott Sullivan named CFO of WorldCom |
| 1998 | WorldCom acquires MCI for $37B |
| 1999 | July: WorldCom share reaches high of $67.90 |
| 2000 | DoJ blocks WorldCom proposed acquisition of Sprint at $129b. Ebbers sells off 3m shares for $84m to pay off investment debts |
| September | Bank of America calls back Ebbers margin loan |
| 25 September | Ebbers asks Kellett, head of compensation committee for $50m loan. Kellett declines. Ebbers decide to sell shares in the company. Compensation committee alarmed as Ebbers' shares would flood the market and see price decline |
| 13 October | WorldCom shares slide by $11b. Ebbers asks for another $25m loan to meet other banks' margin calls |
| 14 October | Ebbers meet with Kenneth Lewis, Bank of America president, to ask for time and more loans. Lewis declines on both counts. Ebbers is lent $25m by WCOM board to prevent him from selling his shares |
| November | Kellett sell 67 per cent of WorldCom shares worth $53m |
| 2001 | |
| January | Sullivan start capitalising operating expenses |
| April | WorldCom director Max Bobbit plots to oust Ebbers from CEO position. Boardroom manoeuvre fails |
| | Bobbitt and Kellett urge Ebbers to find buyers for his properties. Ebbers has trouble letting go, refusing offers for his timberland, shipyard and ranch |
| 2002 | |
| 8 February | Ebbers takes out $366m company loan to cover share holdings |
| 6 March | Meeting of the audit committee of the company where Cooper outlined her concerns. In reply Ebbers proposed to cut 50 per cent of the internal audit's funds to discourage Cooper's division's investigation, this was later reduced to 10 per cent by Sullivan |
| 11 March | WorldCom states the company has complied with GAAP |

Appendix C2.1 Events in WorldCom history

| Date | Event |
| --- | --- |
| April | Ebbers borrows from Bank of North Georgia to pay off loan from Morgan Guaranty, part of J.P. Morgan. WorldCom had repaid Bank of America loan on shipyard, and angered at seeing the sale of two yachts. Company seize shipyard soon afterward |
| 3 April | WorldCom cuts 3,700 jobs |
| 22 April | Grubman downgrades WCOM from buy to neutral |
| 29 April | Ebbers resigns as CEO of WorldCom following meeting of Board. Board approve his retirement package of $1m p.a. for life, with $750,000 p.a. for his wife after his death. |
| 7 May | Ebbers asks Kellett if company can make him one final loan of $10m to cover Citibank margin call. Refused |
| 9 May | WorldCom bond rating lowered to junk status |
| 13 May | WorldCom is removed from S&P index |
| 15 May | Andersen fired as company's external auditor. |
| 16 May | KPMG appointed to take over Andersen as external auditor. |
| 1 June | Dick resigns as Andersen's partner |
| 5 June | Cooper meet Malone to discuss accounting irregularities |
| 11 June | Sullivan calls Cooper and asks Cooper to delay the audit |
| 12 June | Cooper and others contacted Bobbitt, chair of Audit Committee about line cost transfers. |
| 13 June | Cooper meets Bobbit and KPMG's Malone about investigation |
| 17 June | Cooper and others interview Myers, briefing Malone, and calling on Bobbitt |
| 18 June | Malone interviews Myers |
| 19 June | Bobbitt contacts Areen, another member of audit committee. Bobbitt and Areen contact outside counsel of Simpson Thacher & Bartlett. Malone interviews Sullivan |
| 20 June | Bobbitt meets Sullivan and informs him of investigation into propriety of transferring line costs to capital accounts. Areen and Bobbitt meet outside counsel. Bobbitt notifies Sidgmore and general counsel of company |
| | Audit committee meeting comprising of Bobbitt, Areen and Galesi (audit committee) with Sullivan, Myers, Cooper, Smith, Malone and Kroll of KPMG, Sidgmore, Salsbury, Beaumont (COO) and Simpson Thacher and Bartlett |
| | Meeting discusses line costs transfer to capital accounts for 2001 and 2002. Malone noted absence of documentation supporting transfer. Sullivan states this was done due to economic conditions but planned writedown later in 2002. Malone disagreed that writedown could have been possible in later 2002 |
| 21 June | Sidgmore meets lawyers. Advised to make restatement and full investigation. Bobbitt contacts Andersen partners in charge of audits in 2001 |
| 24 June | Second audit committee. Andersen decides company's financial statements of 2001 could not be relied upon. |
| | Line transfer by quarter were: |
| | 1q 2001: $771m |
| | 2q 2001: $610m |
| | 3q 2001: $743m |
| | 4q 2001: $931m |
| | 1q 2002: $797m |
| | Sullivan and Myers told they would be fired if they did not resign |
| 25 June | WorldCom announce $3.8 billion restatement. At close, WorldCom share price of 83 cents. Myers resigns and Sullivan fired without severance. |
| 26 June | NASDAQ suspend WorldCom share trading. SEC file civil action against WorldCom |
| 29 June | WorldCom lays off 17,000 workers |
| July | Files for bankruptcy |
| 1 July | WorldCom resume trading. Close at 6 cents per share. Over 1b shares are traded |
| 5 July | WorldCom is delisted from the NASDAQ |

| Date | Event |
|------|-------|
| 7 August | WorldCom reveals further $3.3b in accounting errors |
| August | Sullivan charged with securities fraud |
| 26 September | Former WorldCom controller, Myers, pleads guilty to criminal fraud in connection with the company's accounting scandal and bankruptcy |
| October | Stiles Kellett of $1 per month corporate jet lease fame resigns in disgrace |
| 10 December | Judith Areen, board member, resigns from WorldCom |
| 17 December | John Sidgmore and Bert Roberts tender their resignation as CEO and Chairman respectively, with directors Carl Aycock, Max Bobbitt, Francesco Galesi and Gordon Macklin also resigning to make way for a new board |
| 19 December | WorldCom awarded government contract to provide global communication services to the US State Department, worth around $360m over 10 years |
| 2003 | |
| January | Congressional testimony into WorldCom |
| 13 March | WorldCom writes off goodwill of $45 billion of companies acquired during the 1990s; devalues property, equipment and intangible assets from $44.8 billion to $10 billion |
| 14 April | WorldCom changes its name to its long-distance subsidiary, MCI |
| 19 May | MCI settle accusations of fraud by paying the SEC $500m penalty. The largest ever penalty in US corporate history. Investors would be paid 33.1 cents |
| 13 June | Reports link to Ebbers' prior knowledge of fudging with accounts |

Appendix C2.1—Cont'd

| Actor | WorldCom role | Post-WorldCom role |
|-------|---------------|--------------------|
| Carl Aycock | Director, asked for a $600,000 loan | Resigned to make way for new board |
| Judy Areen | Director who approved retirement package of Ebbers | Resigned to make way for new board |
| Max Bobbitt | WorldCom director since 1982, tried to oust Ebbers in 2001. Chairman of Audit Committee | Resigned to make way for new board |
| Melvin Dick | Arthur Andersen auditor, Global Managing Director | Resigned from Andersen |
| Bernie Ebbers | Chief Executive Officer | Investigated by SEC and Justice department, Convicted, 25 years jail |
| Francesco Galesi | Director who approved retirement package for Ebbers | Resigned to make way for new board |
| Jack Grubman | Salomon Smith Barney investment analyst | Left Citigroup, sued by other analysts |
| Scott Sullivan | Chief Financial Officer | Indicted on charges of conspiracy to commit fraud, Testified against Ebbers, 5 years jail |
| Stiles Kellett | Head of compensation committee | Resigned due to scandal over corporate jet lease arrangement |
| Gordon Macklin | Director who voted for retirement package for Ebbers | Resigned to make way for new board |

Appendix C2.2  The fate of former WorldCom actors.

| Institution | WorldCom role | Post-WorldCom role |
|---|---|---|
| Citigroup | Investment bank of WorldCom, parent of Salomon Smith Barney | Paid $400m in restitution to SEC to resolve fraud accusations involving conflicts of interest among Wall St analysts. |
| New York State Employees' Pension Fund | Pension fund | Lost $300m, filed a class-action lawsuit against MCI |

Appendix C2.2—Cont'd

# REFERENCES

Ackerman, D. (2005) *Bernie Ebbers Guilty, Forbes Magazine*, 15 March, http://www.forbes.com/home/management/2005/03/15/cx_da_0315ebbersguilty.html

BBC News on WorldCom, http://news.bbc.co.uk/1/hi/in_depth/business/2002/scandals/default.stm#WorldCom

Boyd, D.P. (2003) Chicanery in the Corporate Culture: WorldCom or World Con?, *Corporate Governance*, 3(1): 83–85.

Boyd Saum, S. (2002) *Ode to WorldCom's failure Salon*, http://www.salon.com/tech/feature/2002/07/13/schadenfreude/print.html

Breeden R. C. (2003) Restoring trust, Report to the United States Federal Court for the Southern District of New York *On Corporate Goverance for the Future of MCI, Inc.* Full report at http://www.thecorporatelibrary.com/spotlight/scandals/Restoring_Trust_Final-WorldCom.pdf

Brickley, Kathleen F. (2003) From Enron to WorldCom and Beyond: Life and Crime after Sarbanes–Oxley, *Washington University Law Quarterly*, 81, http://papers.ssrn.com/sol3/papers.cfm?abstract_id=447100

Committee on Financial Services (CoFS) (2002) *Wrong Numbers: The Accounting Problems at WorldCom*, Hearing, US House of Representatives 177th Congress, 8 July, US GPO, Washington, DC.

Dreazen, Y.J. and D. Solomon (2002) WorldCom Alerts about Accounting Went Unheeded, *Wall Street Journal*, 13 July.

*Economist* (2002) Too Many Debts; Too Few Calls: The Telecoms Crisis, 20 July.

Eisenberg, D. (2002) WorldCom: Showing Signs of Life, *Time*, 22 December, http://www.time.com/time/personoftheyear/2002/poyWorldCom.html

Feldman, A. and J. Caplin (2002) Is Jack Grubman the Worst Analyst Ever?, *Money Magazine*, 25 April, http://money.cnn.com/2002/04/25/pf/investing/grubman

Harmantzis, Fotios (2004) Inside the Telecom Crash: Bankruptcies, Fallacies and Scandals – A Closer Look at the WorldCom Case, http://papers.ssrn.com/sol3/papers.cfm?abstract_id=575881

Gimein, M. (1999) *Bernie Ebbers: A nineteenth century-style tech tycoon? Salon*, 6 October, http://www.salon.com/tech/log/1999/10/06/ebbers/index.html

Goldstein, M. (2002) *The Moon and $30M for Jack Grubman, The Street*, 16 August, http://www.thestreet.com/markets/matthewgoldstein/10038108.html

Google Directory on WorldCom, http://directory.google.com/Top/Society/Issues/Business/Allegedly_Unethical_Firms/MCI_WorldCom/?il=1

*Guardian* (2003) *WorldCom Special*, http://www.guardian.co.uk/WorldCom

Haddad, C. and Foust, D. (2002) World.Com's Sony Legacy, *Business Week*, 3790: 38–40.

Jeter, L.W. (2003) *Disconnected: Deceit and Betrayal at WorldCom*, New York: Wiley.

Johnson, C. and C. Stern (2002) WorldCom Charges Could Be Filed Soon; CFO, Controller May Be First Targets, *Washington Post*, 1 August.

Khanna, Vikramaditya S. (2003) Should the Top Behaviour of Top Management Matter?, *Georgetown Law Journal*, 91, http://papers.ssrn.com/sol3/papers.cfm?abstract_id=339940

Krim, J. and C. Stern (2002) WorldCom: Nation Needs US: CEO Apologizes for Scandal, Says Company's Services Remain Secure, *Washington Post*, 3 July.

Labaton, S. (2003) MCI Agrees to Pay $500m in Fraud Case, *New York Times*, 20 May.

Lacayo, R. and A. Ripley (2002) Persons of the Year, *Time*, 22 December, http://www.time.com/time/magazine/printout/0,8816,40194,00.html

Malik, O. (2003) *Broadbandits*, New York: Wiley.

Masters, B.A. (2004) Ex-WorldCom CEO's Defense Wins Delay, 20 October, http://www.washingtonpost.com/wp-dyn/articles/A46453-2004Oct19.html

Masters, B.A. and C. Stern (2003) WorldCom Agrees to Pay $500, MCI News, http://global.mci.com/news/infodesk

McChesney, R. (2002) *Deregulation's Big Lie, Salon.Com*, 16 July, http://archive.salon.com/tech/feature/2002/07/16/telecom_crisis/index.html

MCI (2003) News, http://global.mci.com/news/infodesk

Mehta, S.N. (2001) Can Bernie Bounce Back?, *Fortune*, 143(2): 84–90.

Mieszkowski, K. (2002) *Deregulation's Big Lie, Salon*, http://archive.salon.com/tech/feature/2002/07/16/telecom_crisis/print.html

Nuzum, C. (2002) ACCOUNT-ABILITY: WorldCom may not turn eyes from EBITDA, *Dow Jones Newswires*, 27 June.

O'Farrell, J. (2002) Capitalism's Cheatin' Heart, *Guardian*, 20 July, http://www.guardian.co.uk/enron/story/0,11337,764203,00.html

O'Harrow Jr., R. and Stern, C. (2002) WorldCom Controller Pleads Guilty; Myers Admits to Falsifying Numbers, Says He Acted at His Superior's Behest, *Washington Post*, 27 September.

Pulliam, S., Solomon, D. and C. Mollenkamp (2002) Easy Money: Former WorldCom CEO Built an Empire on Mountain of Debt – Eager to Win His Business, Many Banks Competed to Lend Ebbers Big Sums – Soy Beans, Yachts and Timber, *Wall Street Journal*, 31 December.

Ripley, A. (2002) The Night Detective, *Time*, 22 December, http://www.time.com/time/personoftheyear/2002/poycooper.html

Rosenberg, S. (1997) The net becomes WorldCom's fiefdom, Salon, http://archive.salon.com/21st/rose/1997/10/09straight.html

Securities and Exchange Commission v. WorldCom, http://www.sec.gov/spotlight/WorldCom.htm

Sidak, J.G. (2003) The Failure of Good Intentions: The WorldCom Fraud and the Collapse of the American Telecommunications after Deregulation, *Yale Journal on Regulation*, 20(2): 209–243, http://papers.ssrn.com/sol 3/papers.cfm?abstract_id=335180

Stern, C. (2002a) 6 Resign from WorldCom Board: Ex-CEO Sidgmore among Departees, *Washington Post*, 18 December.

Stern, C. (2002b) Ebbers Dominated Board, Report Says: World.Com Chief Reportedly Forced through Big Compensation Package, *Washington Post*, 5 November.

Stern, C. and J. Krim (2002) Ebbers Knew of Strategy, House Told; WorldCom Lawyers Brief Investigators, *Washington Post*, 12 July.

Teather, D. (2002) Corporate America's Path to a Very Public Humbling, *Guardian*, 19 December, http://www.guardian.co.uk/WorldCom/story/0,12167,862623,00.html

Thornburg, D. (2004) First Interim Report, *Bankruptcy Court Examiner*, November: 73.

*Time* (2002) Persons of the Year: The Interview, 22 December, http://www.time.com/time/personoftheyear/2002/poyqa.html

Treanor, J. (2003) A Thought Message to Corporate America, *Guardian*, 27 August, http://business.guardian.co.uk/story/0,16781,1029825,00.html

Voice Report, Telecom Managers (2002) Frustrating Policies Obstruct Refunds: WorldCom Holds at Least $1.8B in Billing Credits, 20 May, 23(10).

*Washington Post* (2003) *WorldCom Special*, http://www.washingtonpost.com/wp-dyn/technology/specials/WorldCom

World Com entry on Wikipedia, http://en.wikipedia.org/wiki/WorldCom

# Case Study 3
# Tyco

## EXECUTIVE SUMMARY

The rise of American CEOs to cult status was a product of the decade long bull market of the 1990s, and Dennis Kozlowski CEO of Tyco during this period led the company to great heights living a life of unbelievable extravagance, only to be convicted of 22 counts of grand larceny and fraud against the company shareholders. Unlike other companies where fraud and other charges were made public in 2001 and 2002, such as Enron, WorldCom and HealthSouth, Tyco was never in a cash crisis. Tyco under the direction of its CEO was an aggressive acquirer of companies and in the space of three years made around 700 acquisitions worth $8 billion by 2002. In total Tyco reputedly spent $63 billion acquiring, 1,000 companies with the purposes of achieving control of multiple international product products, boosting cash flow, and pursuing tax avoidance schemes.

When rumours of accounting irregularities started to resurface concerning Tyco's acquisitions the SEC initiated an investigation in December 1999 till July 2000 but it was not able to find anything illegal, and simply recommended some changes in procedures. However, this was the beginning of a growing lack of confidence in the veracity of Tyco's accounting. When Kozlowski acquired CIT Group in which he held substantial stock creating a conflicts of interest, this had a major adverse effect on Tyco's stock putting it into freefall by July 2002.

## TYCO'S ORIGINS

Tyco is one of the largest industrial and electronics conglomerates in the US. It was founded in 1960 at the height of the cold war as a research laboratory to service the American government. In 1962 it began commercialising its research and started functioning as a business. In 1964 Tyco went public and as a precursor to its later strategy acquired 16 companies. Throughout the 1970s and 1980s Tyco grew through acquisition and developed market leadership across an extensive range of electronics, fire and safety products, and packaging. However, it was with the appointment of Dennis Kozlowski as CEO in 1992 that the company grew astronomically, propelling it from an obscure manufacturer into an industrial powerhouse. Between 1994 and 2002 Tyco spent $63 billion acquiring, 1,000 companies. At one time Tyco's market capitalisation was higher than General Motors', Ford's and Sears' combined. In 2001, Tyco was a $93 billion market capitalisation company, a year later it was a $36 billion company (Figure C3.1).

### Aggressive acquisitions

Tyco grew mainly through its aggressive acquisition business strategy. The strategy was the main reason behind the company's growth and valuation. Kozlowski wanted to transform Tyco into the next General Electric. The company

**Figure C3.1** Tyco's share price and share trading, 2001–2006.

Source: Adapted from Yahoo Finance (2006).

had inappropriate large restructuring reserves for its acquisitions, and in 1999 Tyco came under SEC scrutiny over its merger-related accounting practices. The companies that were targets for Tyco were made to take unusual charges before formally becoming part of the corporation. The acquired companies slowed their revenue growth and/or wrote off significant assets before the takeover (Maremont 1999). Pooling accounting rules where the target's accounting statements were merged with Tyco's prior to acquisition, created more cash flow for Tyco. While unusual this was not illegal and the SEC prematurely dropped their investigation into the company's accounting. Kozlowski's response to the SEC investigation was one of surprise, he believed the company 'disclosed everything in the past … and we will go to even greater lengths. We're obviously going to err on the side of over-disclosure … we have nothing to hide' (Maremont 1999).

## THE COMPANY CULTURE

When Kozlowski reigned over the company he was admired for having a largely decentralised company structure. He had a frugal head office, notorious for its lack of executive facilities. However, a frugal and isolated head office also made it difficult for most employees to communicate with company officers. For example, the head office lacked an effective corporate legal infrastructure. Tyco had 100 lawyers working worldwide but only one at the company's executive headquarters. The prestige conferred on the selected few at head office showed in the arrogant directives they would send out to Tyco's other offices. A memorandum to employees at one division directed them to find cost savings by 'financial engineering'. At another division employees were told to 'create stories' to justify an accounting change that would improve Tyco's earnings (Verschoor 2003: 18). Tyco's company culture 'discouraged

subordinates from questioning top executives and discouraged contact between directors and second-tier managers' (Lavelle 2002) while its 'once-heralded lean, mean management structure (with only a few trusted lieutenants based at the headquarters), looks more like a set up to keep out prying eyes' (Symonds 2002).

## THE KEY PLAYERS

### CEO

Kozlowski seemed to consider Tyco little more than an extension of himself: he was the corporate equivalent of Louis XIV's famous phrase: 'L'état, c'est moi' (Varchaver 2002). It could be argued, 'Tyco's problems are not Tyco's problems … they are Dennis Kozlowski's personal problems' (Rynecki 2002). Dennis Kozlowski joined Tyco in September 1975 as an *internal auditor*. Some two decades later, Kozlowski became CEO in July 1992. Kozlowski's management style was based on his own personal experience and handpicked managers that were 'smart, poor, and want to be rich' and he never appointed a president, combining the roles of president of the company, chair of the board, and chief executive officer. At Tyco the isolation of the head office allowed Kozlowski to take control of everything, including internal audits of the complex conglomerate corporate structures.

Kozlowski started misappropriating money and assets in 1995, and over the next seven years he treated Tyco like his personal bank (Table C3.1) to fund items from the most mundane, such as $6,000 shower curtains, to the most extravagant, including a $2 million birthday party for his wife in Sardinia, Italy. Ultimately this confusion of his own and the companies' assets led to outright embezzlement of company funds to buy and hold his own personal line of credit of expenditures and to purchase and speculate on New York real estate. In July 2001 Kozlowski paid an unauthorised $20 million fee to his close friend and then Tyco director Frank Walsh, in connection with the acquisition of the

CIT Group, a financial services company. By 2002 Kozlowski with his CFO Mark Swartz had misappropriated over $600 million of company funds, though it was only after the Manhattan District Attorney charged him with sales tax fraud that the board requested his resignation from the company. Kozlowski resigned on 3 June 2002 and 'will be remembered as one of the great corporate hoodwinkers' (Symonds 2002). Though his first trial was declared a mistrial in April 2004, his second trial led to his conviction, and he was sentenced to between 8 and 25 years in prison in September 2005. The judge also ordered Kozlowski and Swartz to pay $134 million back to Tyco, and Kozlowski was fined $70 million. He was ordered to start serving his sentence immediately, and was led from the courtroom in handcuffs.

### CFO

Mark Swartz was Tyco's CFO and was the closest lieutenant to Kozlowski. While he did not misappropriate funds on such a scale, he emulated his boss by entering unapproved credits in 1999 against $25 million of Kozlowski's own employee loans. In 1999 Swartz's response to the SEC investigation into Tyco's merger-related accounting practices was largely rhetorical: 'we're going to do what we need to do, even if it's to hit someone over the head so they see exactly what we have buried in there' (Maremont 1999). Both Swartz and Kozlowski had a such tight control over the company's internal information, it was of course difficult for anyone to find any incriminating documents. As with Kozlowski, Swartz was charged with misappropriation of company funds. He was sentenced to between 8 and 25 years in prison in September 2005. In addition, Swartz was fined $35 million. Since Kozlowski and Swartz received a sentence of more than three years, they are liable to spend part of this in one of New York's maximum security prisons which include Attica and Sing Sing, however, Kozlowski was placed in Mid-State Correctional Facility in Upstate New York (Table C3.2).

| Type of monetary gain | Amount in $ |
|---|---|
| Key employee loans | 18,840,461 (principal balance) |
| | 25,000,000 (adjustment) |
| TyCom business (Florida relocation loans) | 32,644,338 (own unauthorised bonus) |
| | 95,962,653 (benefits to senior executives without board approval) |
| Unauthorised ADT automotive bonus | 17,188,034 (and 184,000 shares) |
| | 36,584,338 (and 261,500 shares) |
| Unauthorised Flag Telecom bonus | 8,219,650 (for Kozlowski) |
| | 15,378,700 (for senior executives) |
| Unauthorised fee to director Frank Walsh | 20,000,00 |
| Compensation | 26,454,603 (1997) |
| | 70,329,8401 (1998) |
| | 21,074,097 (1999) |
| | 137,493,424 (2000) |
| | 32,511,801 (2001) |
| Charitable contributions paid by company that enriched CEO | 43,000,000 |
| Unauthorised property transactions | 3,000,000 (overpayment on sale of property) |
| | Other amounts to be determined on 4 other properties (in NY Park Avenue, Florida and Nantucket) |
| Questionable business expenses | 20,000,000 (artwork, antiques and furnishings) |
| | 700,000 (movie rights) |
| | 1,000,000 (birthday party in Sardinia, Italy) |
| | 110,000 (use of *Endeavour* yacht) |
| | 1,144,000 (jewellery, clothing, florist, club memberships, wines, private ventures) |
| | 150,000 (personal expenses) |

Table C3.1 Kozlowski's misappropriations.

## General counsel

The company's general counsel was the other member of the embezzling triumvirate of the company. Unusually it was Tyco's finance department in charge of filing the company SEC reports and not its legal division. Its legal division perhaps was otherwise engaged. The company's general counsel, Mark Belnick, was accused of falsifying records to cover up $14 million in improper loans. When the embezzlement was unravelled, Belnick assisted New York prosecutors into the investigation of the company, only to be fired by the board over accusations that he had 'failed to cooperate with internal company investigation into improper conduct by any of its personnel' (AFP 2002). Coincidentally, Belnick's lawyer was Reid Weingarten who was also counsel for the ex-CEO of WorldCom, Bernard Ebbers.

On 15 July 2004 in New York, general counsel Belnick, accused of taking a $17 million bonus as a reward for helping conceal corporate wrongdoing, was acquitted of all charges by a Manhattan jury. Belnick was the highest-ranking corporate official to be acquitted in a jury trial since the December 2001 collapse of Enron sparked a round of corporate prosecutions. His case demonstrated the challenge prosecutors face when trying to prove that white-collar defendants knew their activities were against the law, legal analysts said.

| Date | Event |
| --- | --- |
| 1960 | Tyco is founded as a research laboratory |
| 1992 | Dennis Kozlowski, employed by Tyco since 1976, is named CEO |
| 1997 | The company merges with Bermuda-based security systems provider ADT |
| 13 March 2001 | Tyco announces $9.2 billion cash and stock deal to purchase the CIT Group, a commercial finance company. Tyco director Frank Walsh helps arrange the deal |
| 5 December 2001 | Tyco shares close at a high of $59.76 on the New York Stock Exchange |
| 14 January 2002 | *Business Week* magazine lists Tyco CEO L. Dennis Kozlowski as one of the top 25 corporate managers of 2001 |
| 22 January 2002 | Kozlowski announces plans to split Tyco into four independent, publicly traded companies. The announcement starts a slide in the price of Tyco shares |
| 29 January 2002 | Tyco shares drop sharply, one day after the company filed a proxy report with the Securities and Exchange Commission disclosing that Walsh got a $10 million fee on the CIT Group deal, and that another $10 million went to a charity where he was a director |
| 30 January 2002 | *The New York Times* reports that Kozlowski and Tyco CFO Mark Swartz sold more than $100 million of their Tyco stock the previous fiscal year despite public statements that they rarely sold their stock. Kozlowski and Swartz say they will buy 1 million shares with their own money |
| 3 June 2002 | Kozlowski resigns unexpectedly as *The New York Times* reports he is the subject of a sales tax evasion investigation by Manhattan District Attorney Robert Morgenthau's office |
| 4 June 2002 | Kozlowski is charged with illegally avoiding more than $1 million in sales taxes on paintings, including works by Renoir and Monet |
| 12 September 2002 | Morgenthau announces a criminal indictment accusing Kozlowski and Swartz of enterprise corruption for allegedly stealing more than $170 million from Tyco and obtaining $430 million by fraud in the sale of company shares. Former Tyco corporate counsel Mark Belnick is charged separately with falsifying records to conceal more than $14 million in company loans. They plead innocent. They are also accused by the SEC of failing to disclose huge sweetheart loans and other money taken out of the company |
| 17 September 2002 | Tyco, in an SEC filing, details a pattern of improper and illegal activities by its former management, including nearly $100 million in unauthorised payments to Tyco employees |
| 17 December 2002 | Former Tyco board member Frank Walsh pleads guilty in an alleged scheme to hide the $20 million in fees for the CIT Group deal |
| 7 October 2003 | The first trial of Kozlowski and Swartz begins with opening statements in which prosecutors characterise them as crime bosses who looted Tyco. Defence lawyers call them honest executives who deserved and disclosed all corporate payments and perks |
| 28 October 2003 | The jury is shown a video of a birthday party Kozlowski threw for his wife at a resort in Sardinia. Tyco paid roughly half the $2 million cost of the event, which featured entertainers clad in togas and an appearance by singer Jimmy Buffett |
| 25 November 2003 | Prosecutors show the jury a video of the $6,000 shower curtain and other lavish furnishings that decorated Kozlowski's Tyco-owned apartment in Manhattan |

Table C3.2 Tyco trial timeline.

| Date | Event |
|---|---|
| 10 February 2004 | Swartz testifies he didn't do anything he believed was illegal during the 11 years he worked at the company. Kozlowski does not take the stand |
| 5 March 2004 | Judge throws out enterprise corruption charge against Kozlowski and Swartz, the most serious count |
| 2 April 2004 | A mistrial is declared after a juror says she received a letter pressuring her to convict Kozlowski and Swartz. Some observers said the juror, Ruth Jordan, had previously appeared to make an 'OK' sign to defence lawyers. She subsequently denied making any gesture towards the defense team |
| 15 July 2004 | In a separate trial, former Tyco corporate counsel Mark Belnick is acquitted of charges that he received millions in loans from the company and failed to disclose the payments |
| 26 January 2005 | The second trial of Kozlowski and Swartz begins with opening statements in which prosecutors switch tactics to focus on money the two allegedly stole from Tyco |
| 27 April 2005 | Kozlowski, who did not testify at his first trial, takes the stand and testifies that the millions of dollars in Tyco payments and perks he received had been properly authorised and disclosed |
| 17 June 2005 | Kozlowski and Swartz are convicted of looting Tyco of more than $600 million in corporate bonuses and loans. Both are convicted of grand larceny, falsifying business records and other charges |
| 19 September 2005 | Kozlowski and Swartz are sentenced to eight and one-third to 25 years in prison |

Table C3.2—Cont'd

The jury deliberated for five days over two weeks before finding Belnick not guilty of grand larceny, securities fraud and falsifying business records. Prosecutors alleged during the 11-week trial that Belnick accepted cash and stock from Tyco chief executive L. Dennis Kozlowski as hush money and that he knew the bonus had not been approved by the Tyco board of directors.

### The role of accountants

The auditors for Tyco were PriceWaterhouse Coopers. After the 1999 SEC Tyco investigation into the company's accounting practices, PWC issued a statement saying the company's practices conformed to generally accepted accounting principles. Three years later, PWC auditors were under scrutiny on how it failed to disclose a $33 million bonus paid to Kozlowski. As a result of inconsistencies in PWC books, in 2003 Tyco brought in forensic accountants to examine the books as it was clear Tyco's outside auditors were aware of many of the transactions committed by Kozlowski and Swartz.

### SYSTEMATIC GOVERNANCE FAILURE

The Tyco experience showed the central purpose of the company executives was to further their own interests, not those of the shareholders of the company (or employees or any other stakeholders). The Tyco board, auditors and the SEC apparently were blind to the embezzlement. Tyco was notorious for not disclosing information to its shareholders and Tyco's tight and furtive corporate culture 'openly encouraged managers to push the rules of accounting to mislead investors

about the company's results' (Verschoor 2003: 18). It was only after the severity of the company's problems were revealed that Tyco finally disclosed to shareholders that it had spent $8 billion acquiring more than 700 entities from 1999 to 2001.

## An ineffective board

The board of Tyco was firmly under the thumb of its chair and CEO, Dennis Kozlowski. On the issue of internal audits the board did not insist on hearing directly from the company's internal auditors. The board did not receive timely information, nor did it insist on receiving adequate information. This gross failure of communication saw 'seemingly every single public statement by the company's senior management … contradicted by subsequent statements' (Sonnenfeld 2002: 109). Within five months of Kozlowski's resignation the new CEO of Tyco, Edward D. Breen, replaced the executive team and entire board of the company: 'I didn't know who knew what, who should have known what, and who should have raised their hand, and I was never going to be able to figure that out fast. So I wasn't going to take any chances' (Warner 2003).

## SEC

The SEC's ineffectiveness was highlighted again in the Tyco case. While its 1999 investigation focused on the company's accounting, the agency missed the embezzlement of Kozlowski, simply because it did not look at the company's internal auditing procedure. As Symonds (2002) asserts 'there were warning signs on the company's murky accounting practice but how were they missed?'

## CORPORATE GOVERNANCE REFORM

After the 1999 SEC investigation, Kozlowski gave reassurances on its corporate governance practice, 'Tyco already has started drawing up a list of prominent academic accounting

experts who could consult on ways to improve its disclosure practices' (Maremont 1999). This failed to materialise, but Edward Breen, the new CEO of Tyco, put the promise into practice by bringing Wharton academic and corporate governance expert Michael Useem to help with the corporate governance of the company. As a result, three main corporate governance controls were instituted:

- the creation of an ombudsman's office and company ombudsman;
- the creation of the senior vice president of corporate governance;
- all executive perks downsized, and Breen prohibited all corporate loans to senior executives and slashed executive compensation.

According to Useem, 'Tyco really needs to go from worst to first. It really does have to transform itself (Useem in Lavelle 2002)'. Useem suggested a company ombudsman would mean 'bringing problems to the board is a "sacred obligation"'. To Breen, this office would allow employees who had previously feared management, to register concerns confidentially. The senior Vice President for corporate governance officer would report directly to the board, creating another voice for better governance.

In an article in the *Harvard Business Review* (2003) E.M. Pillmore, Tyco's first Vice President for corporate governance set out what steps were necessary to dramatically transform the corporate governance systems at Tyco:

- bringing in a new CEO, Ed Breen;
- hiring some 60 new senior executives;
- bringing in an entirely new board of directors with strong backgrounds in finance and operations;
- meticulously checking all the books;
- making clear with the board who has authority over which transactions;
- having three executives report to the board, offering a window on day-to-day affairs.

Tyco was determined to create a stronger boundary between finance and operations management, 'In the heat of the new

economy … it became unfashionable for finance to exercise checks and balances on operations', Philmore explains, which is why abuses went unchecked in many companies.

## TYCO'S PRESENT AND FUTURE

Tyco's existing businesses were always viable and not as affected as they could have been by the recklessness of Dennis Kozlowski. The new CEO, Edward Breen, believed Tyco's solid businesses were unharmed by the embezzlement. While Tyco's share price fell from its 2001 height of $65 to $10 in the days immediately after the scandal, Tyco's shares were never suspended nor were there any doubts about the company entering Chapter 11 bankruptcy. The company had a good chance of emerging relatively unscathed from the misconduct of a few, and over time its share price improved and it reached $65 billion market capitalisation by 2006.

Today the company is the world's largest manufacturer of electrical and electronic components; the world's largest designer, manufacturer and installer of undersea telecommunications systems; the world's largest manufacturer, installer and provider of fire protection systems and electronic security services; and the world's largest manufacturer of specialty valves. Tyco's business is currently grouped into five broad categories: fire and security, healthcare, electronics, plastics and adhesives, and engineered products and services. The company operates in more than a hundred countries and employs 200,000 people. In the first quarter of 2007 Tyco separated into three companies:

- Tyco Healthcare;
- Tyco Electronics;
- Tyco Fire and Security and Tyco Engineered Products and Services (TFS/TEPS).

Each company will operate separately, with their own board of directors, CEO, management staff and financial structure. A separation management team was created to make the restructuring as efficient as possible.

Edward D. Breen, the current Tyco CEO will stay on with TFS/TEPS as CEO. If the 1990s was a time of reckless acquisition for Tyco (and many other companies), the 2000s are a time for careful focus and corporate coherence and accountability.

## Questions

1 Assess the strengths and weaknesses of the cult of the CEO with respect to Tyco's Kozlowski.
2 Examine the systematic failures in corporate governance at Tyco, and propose the reforms necessary to institute more effective corporate governance.
3 If Dennis Kozlowski was a child of the 1990s, examine the state of business ethics that existed in the 1990s.
4 Is there anything that might have stopped Kozlowski before the Manhattan District Attorney in 2002?
5 Investigate the conduct of the court trials of the CEO, CFO and Legal Counsel of Tyco, and how they delivered the verdicts that were awarded.

## REFERENCES

AFL/CIO (2002) *Executive Paywatch – Job Security Double Standard: Tyco International*, http://www.aflcio.org/corporateamerica/paywatch/jobsecurity/case_tyco.cfm

AFP (2002) *Tyco Trades Angry Shots*, News Limited, http://finance.news.com.au/common/story_page/0%2C4057%2C4489541%255E14305%2C00.html

Brooker, K. (2002) David Tice: A Tyco Critic, *Fortune*, 21 February.

*Business Week* (2001) Top 25 Managers of the Year; Managers to Watch: Dennis Kozlowski, Tyco International, 8 January.

CBSNews.com (2002) *New Trouble for Ex-Tyco Execs*, 12 September, http://www.cbsnews.com/stories/2002/09/17/national/printable522288.html

Findlaw (2002) *Tyco International vs. L. Dennis Kozlowski*, 12 September, http://www.findlaw.com

Greenberg, H. (2002) Does Tyco Play Accounting Games? *Fortune*, 17 March.

Lavelle, L. (2002) *Rebuilding Trust in Tyco*, *Business Week*, 25 November, http://www.businessweek.com/magazine/content/02_47/b3809105.htm

Maremont, M. (1999) Tyco Shies from All-stock Deals: Shift Reflects Accounting Queries, *Wall Street Journal*, 3 November.

Pillmore, E.M. (2003) How We're Fixing Up Tyco, *Harvard Business Review*, 81(12): 96–103.

Rynecki, D. (2002) *Stocks or Bonds? Bill vs. Bill*, *Fortune*, 12 August, http://www.fortune.com/fortune/specials/2002/retirement/bill_miller.html

Sonnenfeld, J.A. (2002) What Makes Great Boards Great, *Harvard Business Review*, September, 106–113.

Symonds, W.C. (2002) Tyco: How Did They Miss a Scam So Big?, *Business Week*, 30 September.

Varchaver, N. (2002) CEO's under Fire: The Biz Kozlowski. Midas Had His Gold, Elvis had His Cadillacs, Dennis Kozlowski Had His, Um, Shower Curtain, *Fortune*, 6 December.

Verschoor, C.C. (2003) The Ethical Alternative to Selfish Management, *Strategic Finance*, April, 18–20.

Warner, M. (2003) Exorcism at Tyco, *Fortune*, 14 April.

# European Corporations

# Case Study 4
# Royal Ahold

## EXECUTIVE SUMMARY

Ahold was designated 'Europe's Enron' before Parmalat snatched this title away. Ahold went from being an international food retailer and distributor that grew to become the word's third largest grocer, to having to make public an Enron-style financial accounting fraud by announcing 'accounting irregularities' at its US Food service (USF division) on 24 February 2003. The company had overstated earnings by at least $500 million in 2001 and 2002, prompting its Amsterdam and New York-listed shares to lose more than 60 per cent of their value in one day, with credit ratings downgraded to junk, forcing Ahold to rely on an expensive emergency credit facility to pay its bills and facing a €12 billion debt. The crisis was deep and prolonged for customers, investors and employees alike.

Ahold was found responsible on three counts of fraud: the inflation of promotional allowances at US Food service (a wholly owned subsidiary), the improper consolidation of joint ventures through side letters (control letters), and accounting errors and irregularities that resulted in the overstated net income, net operating income and net sales for the years 2000, 2001 and the first three-quarters of 2002. At the end of the investigation in July 2003, an astonishing 470 accounting irregularities and 278 internal control weaknesses were uncovered.

CEO Cees van der Hoeven and CFO Michiel Meurs immediately resigned, followed by other senior managers and directors leaving Ahold as Lehman Brothers analyst Christopher Gower observed shortly after the scandal: 'with no management, no clarity on accounts, no clarity on financing, future strategy or disposals, it's a long road back' (Karaian 2005). Worse, it was left in a liquidity crisis, embroiled with tough negotiations with both Dutch and American prosecutors, a series of run-ins with shareholders, analysts and the Dutch public who were angered by the demise of such a national icon (Karaian 2005).

## AHOLD'S ORIGINS

In 1887 Albert Heijn started with a small grocery store in Zaandam, just north of Amsterdam. The Netherlands-based holding company Ahold was listed on the AEX, the Amsterdam Stock Exchange, in 1948 and opened its first self-service supermarket in Rotterdam in 1955. The operating company of Albert Heijn became the supermarket leader in the Netherlands and a household word for quality and value-for-money. Shortly after, the queen awarded the company the designation 'Royal'. The store format primarily used by the Group was the supermarket, along with operating or servicing hypermarkets, discount stores, specialty stores, cash and carry stores and convenience stores.

Ahold operates in two market sectors: food retail and food service in 27 countries throughout Europe, North America, South America and Asia. It employs 450,000 people in 9,000 stores who service 40 million customers every week. Ahold's approach to global operations was emphasised in local controls, as the company

refers to its global operating strategy as being 'multi-local, multi-format, multi-channel'. It does not use Ahold as a brand name rather it utilises 26 brands that are derived from the local market. The company also adjusts its retail outlet formats to suit the local conditions, utilising everything from small local style stores to huge hypermarkets and makes sure it maximises the know-how of local management, by relying on local managers to determine their own product assortment, pricing policies, and store formats. On a global basis, its supermarkets jointly procure, source, and deliver products, and work from standardised IT networks. Ahold identified acquisition candidates based upon the following six criteria:

- It must be either no. 1 or 2 in regional market share, or have the potential to become no. 1.
- It must have an excellent customer reputation, as reflected in focus groups.
- Management must be very qualified and willing to work for Ahold.
- The company must be profitable and have the potential to increase profits.
- It must offer potential synergies.
- Its marketing must emphasise food quality, nutrition and safety.

### The 1980s–1990s: the unstoppable expansion

Ahold began its acquisitions in 1976 when it acquired a Spanish supermarket and the Bi-Lo chain (a South Carolina based chain) in the American South before the last of the Heijn family retired as CEO from the company in 1989. Under this CEO's leadership Royal Ahold had initiated an international expansion programme. In Northern Europe Ahold has a joint venture as the regions' largest food retailer, with over 3,000 stores in Sweden, Norway, Denmark, Latvia, Lithuania and Estonia as well as conducting food service operations in Sweden. In Southern and Central Europe Ahold operates over 1,150 stores. Its largest operations in the region are in Spain where it operates over 600 stores and the company has

smaller interests in Portugal, Poland, the Czech Republic and Slovakia.

Ahold was not able to make any significant expansions into Britain, France and Germany as the existing retail operations have effectively blocked the company from having a significant retail presence in those markets. However, Ahold reinforced its expansion during the 1990s, when it decided to do it by means of acquisitions as the engine of growth. When Cees Van der Hoeven joined Ahold he set the company on a path of global growth from 1993 to 2002 in which the company spent €19 billion buying 50 companies in four continents and €12 billion was borrowed to fund the expansion programme. These acquisitions turned Royal Ahold into the world's third-largest food retailer, behind Wal-Mart and Carrefour, the French largest grocer. But it was not until 1999 that the company expanded to Europe, Asia, Latin America and the United States, which delivered almost two-thirds of its operating profits at the time. The wider expansion programme was not a success and in 2003 the company announced that it would begin to divest most of its operations in South America and Asian markets to focus on more mature and stable markets.

As for the US holdings, Ahold acquired five additional food retail chains which operated over 1,600 stores. By 1996 Ahold bought the American, giant Stop and Shop chain in 1996. However, when the US Federal Trade Commission blocked the acquisition of the Pathmark chain in 1999 it undermined Ahold's ability to continue to expand in the US, and Ahold subsequently turned to diversifying into the wholesale food service industry; Ahold then acquired US Foodservice for $2.6 billion and PYA/Monarch for $1.6 billion in 2000 (Fink 2001). It expanded into food service by purchasing and expanding the operations of US Foodservice (a company that produces ready made meals, prepared foods and ingredients for restaurants and hotels). US Foodservice was considered the second largest food distributor in the US and Ahold estimated that its products reached 95 per cent of the American population.

The 2000 results revealed a 56 per cent increase in Ahold's worldwide sales to $50

billion, with a rise in operating earnings by 61 per cent, to more than $2 billion, further encouraging Ahold's thirst for growth, prompting doubts in their capacity to integrate and manage all their acquisitions and raising concerns on the amount debt reaching 12 billion euros. By late 2002 Ahold became the largest food provider in the Netherlands and one of the largest in the United States. At this stage Ahold operated 5,606 stores, including 790 franchise stores and 450 associated stores, with the majority of the franchise stores and associated stores located in the Netherlands (Albert Heijn the number one food retailer in the Netherlands and Schuitema, a Dutch retailer and food distributor (73 per cent owned) and online food retailer Peapod and a 60 per cent stake in Scandinavian food seller ICA AB, employed approximately 280,000 people. It operated primarily in Europe and the United States with some operations in Latin America and Asia Pacific.

## THE MAKING OF THE FRAUD

### The earnings fraud at US Foodservice

The decision to diversify into food service (a non-core activity) is considered the strategic mistake that initiated Ahold's problems and their fraudulent bookkeeping. With the exception of its 1998 acquisition of Giant in the Washington DC area, Ahold's further mistake was to buy second-tier retailers in slow-growth markets, together with grocery retail margins of 2 per cent to 4 per cent. This prompted the US Foodservice executives to manipulate vendor payments known as promotional allowances as a way to increase revenues. (Promotional allowances are rebates that vendors pay to companies like USF for committing to purchase a given volume.) According to SEC filling documents at the Maryland-based wholesale distribution company; managers recorded fictitious promotional allowances that reflected in the operating income on USF's financial statements sufficient to cover any shortfall in budgeted earnings. The way the suppliers'

rebates operated was by the supplier negotiating with the retailers a discount for its goods, and if the supplier achieves certain sales volumes within a specified period, the supplier rebates either a percentage or fixed amount of the original cost to the retailer. Additionally, some larger retailers negotiate sales 'over-riders', which are in effect discounts based upon sales figures for the whole year.

Further, US Foodservice's executives also provided Ahold's independent auditors Deloitte with false information by persuading several suppliers to confirm overstated rebates in letters. In accounting terms these discounts are supposed be regarded as lowering the cost of goods sold. It is normal practice for the retailer only to account for the discounts once the required level of sales has occurred; therefore, it should be treated as reduction of cost of sales and not as revenue. At Ahold the overstated promotional allowances aggregated for the period of 2000 and 2002 that resulted in false inflated operating and net income of $880 million, $110 million in 2000, and $510 million in 2001.

In this case the use of supplier discounts entries in the company accounts were manipulated to increase profit figures and they achieved this in a variety of ways: including booking the discounts rebates as profit, falsely entering larger discounts than had been agreed with the suppliers, and incorporating the discounts into the accounts in the wrong time period or before the required sales had actually been achieved. Two major US food-manufacturing companies, Sara Lee and ConAgra, acknowledged that their employees had assisted US Foodservice employees in the fraud. The US Justice Department and the Securities and Exchange Commission made a public announcement stating that it suspected that US Foodservice had used its market dominance to force its suppliers to assist in artificially inflating its profit figures. On 4 September 2003 at the annual meeting of the company, Henny de Ruiter, chair of Ahold's supervisory board, announced that 'promotional allowances' had been at the heart of the fraud.

## The joint venture sales fraud and the operating income errors

The SEC stated that, Ahold fully consolidated several joint ventures in its financial statements despite owning no more than 50 per cent of the voting shares and despite shareholders' agreements that clearly provided for joint control by Ahold and its JV partners. It never had the management control necessary to allow full consolidation of the ventures' results. However, to justify full consolidation of certain JVs Ahold gave its independent auditors side letters to the JV agreements, signed by Ahold and its joint venture partners which stated that Ahold controlled the joint ventures (SEC Litigation release No. 18929, October 13, 2004). On an annual basis Meurs would send out letters to the CEOs of Ahold's joint venture partners, asking them to agree that all decisions would be 'made by consensus' in Ahold. Meurs signed these 'control letters' and sent them to Deloitte. However, soon after executing the letters Ahold and its JV partners executed side letters retracting the control agreement. Meurs signed all but one of the control and rescinding letters on behalf of Ahold and Van der Hoeven co-signed one of the rescinding letters without the auditors

being aware of its existence. In September 2003 the Dutch public prosecutor fined Ahold €8 million for this practice (SEC 2006). The full consolidation of joint ventures caused Ahold's revenues to be overstated by €27.6 billion and operating income by €222 million from 1999 to 2001. In 2003 Ahold announced an investigation into the fraud and uncovered further potentially illegal transactions in Argentina (Figure C4.1).

## GOVERNANCE STRUCTURE IN THE NETHERLANDS

### Management and supervisory boards

In the Netherlands corporations are regulated under the Civil Code. Large public corporations are required to have a dual board structure that consists of a management board and supervisory board. Each board has defined responsibilities, powers and duties.

The management board is the executive body of the corporation and may be made up of individuals and or corporations. The members of the board have collective powers and responsibilities. The board also shares responsibility for all decisions and acts of the

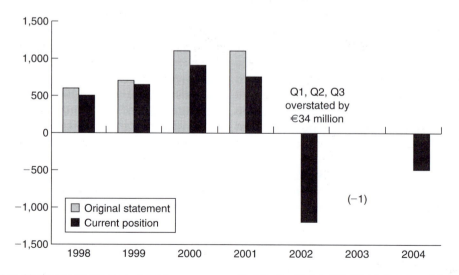

**Figure C4.1** Ahold overstatement of net income according to the Dutch GAAP (€ thousands).

Source: Ahold company reports.

board and for the acts of each individual board member. The management board is responsible for the management of the company and its representation to third parties. The board is also responsible for the company's business policies which must take into account the interests of the company, the shareholders, the employees and some social interests. The board oversees company operations, implements decisions made at shareholder meetings and prepares the annual accounts.

Members of the management board are nominated by and elected by shareholders. Members may be removed by a resolution from shareholders or from the supervisory board. The supervisory board is an advisory and supervision board. Its primary responsibility is to supervise the policy of the management board and the company's general course of business affairs. Members on the management board cannot be members of the supervisory board and there is a legal minimum of three members of this board. The supervisory board must inform shareholders and the works council of any impending board vacancies and board nominations. Shareholder meetings, the works council and the management board may propose candidates for the vacancies. Shareholder meetings and the works council may also object to particular nominations. The board itself can elect a new member; however this is normally done by shareholder votes. The powers given to the supervision board are dictated by the company's article of association. The board can only engage in executive functions: in exceptional circumstances it can give the management board specific operating instructions or policies. The board has the power and the duty to intervene to ensure the company operates within the law and its articles of association.

## MANAGEMENT AT AHOLD

### CEO

In 1993 Cees van der Hoeven, the former CFO, became Ahold's CEO. He promised 15 per cent annual earnings per share growth, and had ambitions to make Ahold one of the largest food providers in the world. At the time Ahold's sales were about 10 billion euros. Since arriving at Ahold, Cees van der Hoeven had led an expansion programme that had seen the company profits grow between 5 per cent and 10 per cent per annum. However, in 2002, signs began to appear of increasing disapproval of management by shareholders when, after declaring the company to be in line to achieve its 5–8 per cent profit growth forecast for the year, the third quartér results showed a profit decline of 15 per cent. The company had suffered its first quarterly loss in over twenty-five years of operations.

From 1993 to 2002 Ahold adopted a business model that established regional retail franchises that utilised centralised purchasing, distribution, merchandising and marketing and it created 'synergy groups' which shared information, distribution centres and marketing strategies. The company also adopted the strategic use of private label products where it believed it could compete profitably with existing brand manufacturers. The combination of Ahold's centralised business operations together with the private label products led to a significant increase in the level of competition from brand manufacturers. The impact of Ahold's considerable market share forced brand manufacturers to compete between themselves, improving the company's profitability. Also the use of private label products decreased the amount of available shelf space for brand products at Ahold stores. Favoured brand managers were given advantageous positions and priority in shelf allotment plans, something critical for sales success. Manufacturers had to reduce the number of products they sold and offer them at better prices to ensure they achieved the necessary shelf space. At the time of the crisis Cees Van der Hoeven resigned and in May 2003, was replaced by Anders Mobergs.

### CFO

Michiel Meurs became CFO in 1997, after a 16-year career with Dutch bank ABN Amro, he

was seen as a key player in Cees Van der Hoeven's expansion plan. At the time of the crisis he too, resigned along with many senior managers and directors.

## THE AFTERMATH

### Share price collapse

Once Ahold announced 'significant accounting irregularities' in February 2003, the market informed by the events at Enron and World-Com and not knowing what might come next, punished Ahold shares which lost 60 per cent of their value, Ahold's credit rating was cut to junk, and it was forced to rely on an expensive emergency credit facility to pay its bills (Figure C4.2). By October 2003 Ahold released the 2002 results and restated accounts back to 1998, erasing nearly €1 billion from profits. Ahold called 2003 a 'lost year' and 2004 its 'year of transition'. In 2004 the company recorded a net loss of €443 million on sales of €52 billion, compared with a net loss of €1 million on sales of €56 billion in 2003. The

2004 results were heavily impacted by exceptional charges, including a €495 million loss related to divestments, mainly in Latin America. (Those divestments however helped reduce net debt to €6.3 billion at the end of 2004 compared with €7.8 billion at the end of 2003.) (Karaian 2005)

### Charges

American regulators investigated the company for fraud, and three lawsuits were filed on behalf of shareholders. The Dutch securities watchdog also investigated possible insider trading based on a high volume of trades in the days prior to Ahold going public with its profit announcement. Dutch prosecutors demanded jail sentences of up to 20 months for former top managers for their role in one of Europe's largest financial scandals. Prosecutor, Hendrik Jan Biemond told the court, 'the trust in Dutch business in general and in Ahold in particular was very seriously damaged to an extent never heard of before … billions of euros were lost'. The prosecutor demanded a 20 month

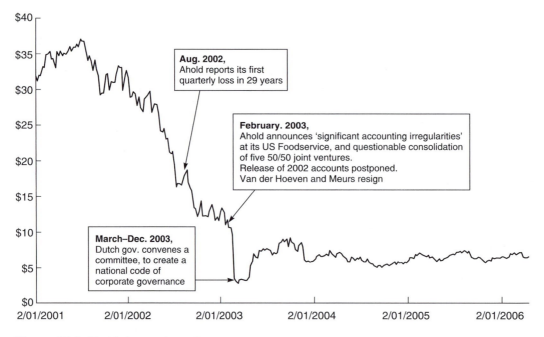

**Figure C4.2** Ahold share price collapse.

sentence, with six months suspended, for former chief executive Cees van der Hoeven, singled out for taking a leading role, and for ex-chief financial officer Michiel Meurs, described as an accomplice.

In July 2004 the SEC charged four US Foodservice executives with fraud, including former CFO Michael Resnick. Former purchasing executives Timothy Lee and William Carter settled charges paying fines of more than $300,000 (€232,000) between them. SEC deputy enforcement director Linda C. Thomsen said the 'defendants manipulated income; they accelerated income, and in some cases, they simply made it up. When questioned about it, they lied and induced others to lie' (Masters and Johnson 2004).

In September 2004 Dutch Public Prosecutor settled charges over joint-venture accounting with Ahold and its former top executives, fining the company €8 million. By October 2004 the SEC settled charges with Ahold and its former top executives with no fine. By January 2005 the SEC and US Justice Department pursued US Foodservice's suppliers, charging nine executives with fraudulently assisting the company to inflate profits.

## Heads rolling

In the aftermath of the investigation, CEO Cees Van der Hoeven and his CFO Michael Meurs resigned. James Miller the CEO of US Foodservice along with two other executives resigned. Ahold stated publicly that the company was not implicated in the fraud. Mark P. Kaiser the US Foodservice chief marketing officer and Tim Lee, a US Foodservice purchasing executive, were fired. The CEO of the Argentina retail chain Eduardo Oreu and his finance director José Sánchez also resigned. The chair of the supervisory board, Henny de Ruiter, led an interim management team until 4 September when at the General Meeting of Shareholders de Ruiter announced the appointment of Anders Moberg as the new president and chief executive along with Hannu Ryopponen the new chief financial officer. At the meeting, the chair disclosed

the findings of the forensic accounting investigation in which were uncovered 750 items that required some form of a response, the bulk of them being administrative and control procedures. The majority of the problems stemmed from the US Foodservice unit and its accounting for 'promotional allowances'. Subsequently on 17 September the supervisory board announced that they believed a new supervisory board should oversee the future of Ahold operations. To facilitate an orderly change a nomination committee was established to consider candidates for the positions on the new supervisory board. It also announced that at the October 2003 general meeting of shareholders the chair of the supervisory board, Henry de Ruiter, would resign. The position was taken by Karel Vuursteen, who was appointed to the board in May. The existing board remained until the annual general meeting in May 2004 when the new supervisory board would take over.

## Legislation

In the US, retailing and accounting guidelines were introduced in January 2003 to assist accountants in correctly accounting for supplier discounts in the formulation of accounts. However, the possibility exists of a legislative response to ensure compliance with the guidelines. France also introduced legislation in 1996 that requires French suppliers to show any refunds directly on their bills. The French legislation also makes 'over rider' agreements illegal.

## Convictions

On 22 May 2006 Cees van der Hoeven and former CFO Michiel Meurs were convicted of fraud but let off with a fine and no prison time: each was fined €225,000 ($290,000) and each received nine-month suspended sentences. 'What a disappointment', Peter de Vries, head of the Dutch shareholders' organisation VEB said in a written reaction, referring to the fines as a 'pittance' given that Van der Hoeven is

estimated to have €43 million ($55 million) in personal wealth. 'This judgment sends a signal to managers that no matter what they do, the risk of a heavy punishment is minimal', he said. 'In the United States, a conviction on the same facts would have led to a prison term of more than 10 years. Prosecutors, who had asked for 14-month prison terms, said they would appeal the ruling (Sterling 2006). A US class action lawsuit began in 2006.

## AHOLD'S FUTURE

New CEO Moberg and CFO Ryöppönen, who had worked together at Sweden's IKEA, announced in November 2003 the Road to Recovery plan, designed to raise at least €5 billion via rights issue and divestments by the end of 2005. In April 2004 Ahold's losses narrowed from €1.2 billion in 2002 to €1 million in the 2003 accounts, and by 2004 losses were reduced to €443 million on sales of €52 billion. Ahold began selling off some of its grocery chains in South America, and pulled out of Asia. In 2005 with a new board and executive management, Ahold signed €2.6 billion of divestment deals, beating its €2.5 billion target several months ahead of schedule. After reaching the depths in early 2003, Ahold's share price doubled, with analysts expecting an early return to profitability. The new CFO Ryöppönen explained the problem with the old reporting system at Ahold, and the strengths of the new system: 'The old structure was an "us and them" situation between CFOs of the units and the centre. Under ex-CFO Meurs each operating company ran finance on its own, with unit-level CEOs the sole point of contact for group CEO van der Hoeven. At headquarters, Meurs's group finance function concerned itself only with their role in helping the company meet the CEO's longstanding pledge of 15 per cent annual earnings per share growth, having little to no contact with finance staff out in the units'.

In 2004 Ryöppönen began a new matrix structure for finance based on the model he saw work at Ikea. An important aspect of this was splitting finance at Ahold into two functions – accounting/reporting and business controlling – and staff have dual reporting lines. The structure means that the accounting/reporting division has authority over rules and deadlines, with a solid-line reporting relationship with headquarters providing stronger oversight. Business controlling, on the other hand, focuses on 'what makes the business move'. It works on developing qualitative analysis and acts as strategic adviser to operational managers (Karaian 2005).

## Questions

1 What lessons can be learned from Ahold on the operations and accounting relationships between parent companies and their overseas subsidiaries?
2 Analyse the weaknesses of Ahold's approach to transparency and disclosure.
3 'The culture at Ahold was one where the economic pressure to reach growth targets overwhelmed legal and accounting principles'. Discuss.
4 What does the Ahold experience indicate regarding the relative weaknesses of corporate governance in the United States and in Europe?
5 Consider how global expansion compounds the corporate governance and financial risks of companies.

## REFERENCES

Ahold (2003) Address by Henny De Ruiter, Chair of the Ahold Supervisory Board, The Hague.

Ahold (2003) Ahold Apoints Moberg and Ryopponen to Corporate Executive Board, Zaandam.

Ahold (2003) Ahold Supervisory Board to Change Its Composition, Zaandam.

Ahold (2003) Serving Our Customers through a Strong Portfolio of Food Retail and Food Service Companies, Zaandam.

Arnold, S. (2002) Lessons Learned from the World's Best Retailers, *International Journal of Retail & Distribution Management*, 30(11): 562–570.

Chirinko, B., van Ees, H., Garretsen, H. and Sterken, E. (1999) Firm Performance, Financial Institutions and Corporate Governance in the Netherlands, University of Groningen.

de Jong, A., de Jong, D., Mertens, G. and Wasley, C. (2000) *The Role of Self-regulation in Corporate Governance: Evidence from the Netherlands*, Centre for Economic Research, Paper 2000–59, Tilburg University.

de Jong, A., Gispert, C., Kabir, R. and Renneboog, L. (2002) *International Corporate Governance and Firm Performance: An Empirical Analysis*, Centre for Economic Research, Tilburg University.

*Economist* (2002) Double Dutch, 365(8300): 59.

*Economist* (2003) Trouble in Store, 367(8324): 55.

*Economist* (2003) Europe's Enron, 366(8313): 55.

Fink, R. (2001) Royal Ambition, *CFO*, 17(4): 46.

*Food Engineering International* (2000) Ahold Branches into Foodservice, 25(2): 13.

Glynn, M. (2003) Royal Ahold Calls Accounting Problems at New York Grocery Chain 'Intentional', *The Buffalo News*, 2 June.

Grumbel, P. (2003) Get Ahold of the Problem, *Time Atlantic*, 161(10): 46.

Hillary, R. (1995) Dutch Retailer Ahold's US Masterplan Unfolds, *Brandweek*, 36(28): 5.

Hopkins, N. (2003) Ahold Finds More Black Holes in US, *The Times*, 27 May.

Johnson, C. and Masters, B. (2003) US Foodservice Suppliers Cited Rebate Problems, *Washington Post*, 19 March.

Karaian J. (2005) *Retail Therapy*, CFO Asia, June, http://www.cfoasia.com/archives/200506-03.htm

Karaian, J. (2005) *Retail Therapy*, CFO Europe, April, http://www.cfoeurope.com/displayStory.cfm/3821872

Kirkman A. (2001) *Another Look*, Forbes.com, 4 February.

Maassen, G. and van den Bosch, F. (1999) On the Supposed Independence of Two-Tier Boards: Formal Structure and Reality in the Netherlands, *Scholarly Research and Theory Papers*, 7(1): 31–37.

Masters, B. and Johnson, C. (2004) Ex-Officials of Colombia Firm Charged, *Washington Post*, 27 July.

Miller, K. (2003) The Enron of Europe?, *Newsweek*, 10 March, 41.

Peters, J. (1997) *Corporate Governance in the Netherlands: Forty Recommendations*, Committee on Corporate Governance.

Progressive Grocer (2003) Gauging the Ahold Fallout, 82(5): 6.

Selva, M. (2003) Wal-Mart, France's Carrefour Set Sights on Ahold Business, *Sunday Business*, 4 June.

SEC (2004) SEC Litigation release no. 18929, 13 October, http://www.sec.gov/litigation/litreleases/lr18929.htm

Securities and Exchange Commission (SEC) (2006) Fillings, Reason.

Sterling, T. (2006) Royal Ahold Ex-Execs Fined After Conviction, *Washington Post*.

*The Times* (2003) Ikea Veteran for Ahold, 5 March, http://www.washingtonpost.com/wpdyn/content/article/2006/05/22/AR2006052200269.html

*Times* (2003) Ahold Shares Surge, 28 February.

Tomlinson, R. (2002) The Biggest Grocer You've Never Heard Of, *Fortune*, 146(1): 42.

Valdmanis, T. (2003) Sara Lee Says Employees May Be Linked to Ahold Case, *USA Today*, 8 April.

Verbeke, L. (1997) Corporate Governance in the Netherlands, *Mondaq Business Briefing*, 27 May.

# Case Study 5
# Parmalat

## EXECUTIVE SUMMARY

Parmalat was termed 'Europe's Enron', a scandal that even overshadowed the disasters that beset the Dutch supermarket company Ahold, and the French media company Vivendi, when they expanded in North America. The principals of the company wove an elaborate web of financial deceit that eventually brought the whole company down with them. The story of a small, family-run delicatessen in Parma converted by Calisto Tanzy, into a global enterprise was hailed as one of Europe's biggest corporate success stories. Parmalat was considered a miracle in the Italian economy, was listed in the *Fortune* most admired companies, and by 2000 had operations in over thirty countries and reported revenues exceeding €6.6 billion. It is also the story of fundamental failure of corporate governance to exercise the most rudimentary audit and control over the financial dealings and reported position of the firm. Parmalat was a case of massive fraud where €16.8 billion went missing and the true level of its debt at the time was €14.3bn (£10bn), eight times more than the debt it admitted to. It was involved in a complex web of more than 200 subsidiaries, many in offshore tax havens including the Cayman Islands and the Antilles, with the purpose of hiding liabilities and moving money around subsidiaries to portray an image of solvency to regulators and investors, when the company was haemorrhaging funds.

## PARMALAT'S ORIGINS

Parmalat was established in 1961, by a then 22-year-old Calisto Tanzi who built upon an inherited family-run delicatessen. Parmalat is a combination of two words: 'Parma' (the Italian city where the company was established) and the Italian word for milk, 'latte'. Tanzi believed milk was an untapped market opportunity, and he established a small pasteurisation plant to industrialise the distribution of milk in the region in Collechio, a small town near Parma. Initially Parmalat competed with the government monopoly, the Milk Board, by using skimmed milk. In 1965 Parmalat began to sell milk with vitamin C, and marketed milk that came from herds free of tuberculosis. (Parmalat 2004). Opportunities to grow the company were helped with the innovation of the Swedish cardboard product Tetra Pak, which prolongs the life of milk and is more hygienic than bottles. This form of packaging also preserves the nutritional qualities of milk, and furthermore, it does not need to be refrigerated. Tetra Pak also allowed Parmalat to brand milk as Parmalat. As a sign of Parmalat's growing strength in the sector, the Milk Board's monopoly was dismantled in 1973.

### 1990s: Parmalat's international expansion

From the 1970s to the 1990s Parmalat became one of the most important food and beverage conglomerates in the world. Its milk came in

different forms (UHT, pasteurised, flavoured, sterilised and powdered); it had an extensive dairy range (cream, sauces, cheese, butter, yoghurt and other desserts); and it had entered the juice (nectars, iced teas, water) and staple foods sector (snacks, pastry, pizza, soups, and bread). Parmalat listed on the Milan Stock Exchange in 1990 eventually listing in over six stock exchanges around the world, once Parmalat was listed the company became a global player and extended to the Americas (North, Central and South), the rest of Europe, and Australasia, where it owns the Paul's brand of milk and related dairy goods. Parmalat competed against other multinational food groups, such as Nestlé, Danone and Unilever. In 1999 Bonlat subsidiary of Parmalat was set up in the Cayman Islands.

At the end of 2002 Parmalat Finanziaria S.p.A. was the listed holding of a multinational food group made up of more than 200 companies spread around 50 countries and operated 139 industrial plants, with more than 36,000 employees and a consolidated turnover of €7.6 billion (Ferrarini and Guidici 2005). Parmalat products were sold in 20 countries and around 45 per cent of the turnover was generated in Latin America. By then Parmalat group was seen as a lucrative client for investment banks, Chase Manhattan Bank in particular, and became very active on the capital market, issuing waves of bonds on the Euromarket.

## The Italian corporate governance environment

According to Bianco and Casavola (1999) in Italian companies there is a limited degree of separation between ownership and control, and control is achieved mainly by using pyramidal groups. Segato (2006) states that

Generally Italian Corporations both listed and unlisted are owned by a small number of shareholders. Parmalat's case was a clear example of this structure as it was a composite group of companies controlled by a strong majority shareholder, the Tanzi family

through the pyramidal device. In this type of organization a holding company controls directly or indirectly, the majority of voting rights of the companies that are part of the organization and the ultimate control over the entire organization is in the hands of either a single entrepreneur, a family or a coalition.

This type of ownership structure was very popular in Italy and more than 50 per cent of all Italian industrial companies belong to pyramidal groups. In Italy pyramidal groups, headed by families, coalitions, or the state have supplanted other forms of ownership. This ownership structure was recognised by the Italian regulator since the late 1940s, and was favoured by a neutral tax policy (i.e. dividends are taxed only once, no matter how many levels the control chain has) (Bianchi 1999). However, these shareholders are often linked by family ties or shareholders' agreements and are willing to wield their power over the corporation. Governance structures built around family capitalism are often linked by family relationships to other investors (Bianco 2004). In Parmalat the holding company of the organisation Coloniale S.p.A was under the control of the Tanzi family through several Luxemburg based companies. The family holdings were a pyramid on top of the pyramid of finance companies on top of the operations companies. Therefore, the Tanzi family was the ultimate shareholder of more than 50 per cent of Parmalat's equity (Figures C5.1 and C5.2).

The corporate monitoring structure of Italian listed companies required the presence of two gatekeepers: the board of statutory auditors and the external auditing firm. In this framework, Parmalat Finanziaria was composed of three members as the minimum legally required, but the original Parmalat board comprised largely executive directors and most of the non-executive directors were close to the Tanzi family. Only one or two members of the board could be described as independent and there was little in the way of control structures (i.e. audit and control committees). With the Tanzi family effectively having a controlling shareholding and a weak and compliant board

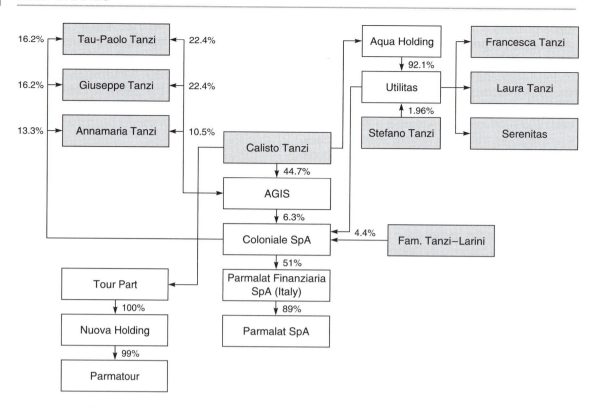

**Figure C5.1** The Tanzi pyramid holding I: the family holdings.
Source: Di Staso, K. (2004).

heavily under the influence of Calisto Tanzi himself (CEO and Chairman), there was no effective board oversight which consequently allowed the other corporate fraudulent activities to continue to be unchecked. The clear inefficiency of the board of statutory auditors was connected to its lack of information and its lack of independence from the controlling shareholders.

Italian corporate governance may be classified as a relationship-based corporate system which adopts the Latin approach (Melis 2004: 74). In this regard, Parmalat's structure was not unusual for an Italian corporation. As with the Fiat company and Agnelli family, Parmalat is strongly associated with the founder (usually led by a charismatic figurehead with a strong personality) and his family, the Tanzis. The Italian corporate governance system has a relatively weak capital market,

with the market for corporate control playing a limited role due to the concentrated control structure (Melis 2004: 74). The Italian system is little influenced by institutional investors (such as in the Anglo-American system), or by banks (such as in Germany and Japan). What made Parmalat rather different was that as a listed company it had a powerful group of institutional investors including a substantial foreign presence such as the Bank of America, Citigroup, Deutsche Bank, and a host of other Italian financial institutions.

Following in the wake of other corporate governance codes inspired by Cadbury in 1992, Italy launched two codes: the Draghi Reform (July 1998) and the Preda Code (July 2002). The former is statutory and regulates 'listed corporations on issues such as public bids, shareholders' agreements, minority shareholders' rights, and internal controls' while

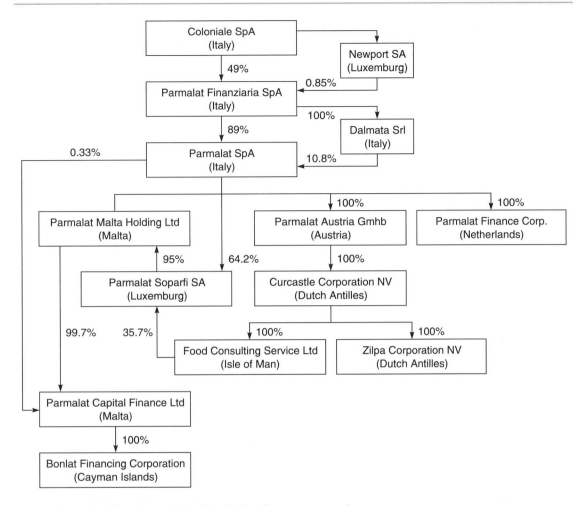

Figure C5.2 The Tanzi pyramid holding II: the finance companies.

Source: Adapted from Di Staso, K. (2004) and company reports.

the latter is voluntary and self-regulatory, covering the issues relating to the 'the board of directors, the board's composition and appointment, and the role of statutory auditors' (Melis 2004: 76–7). Nevertheless Melis argues, 'weak managers, strong blockholders and unprotected minority shareholders' summarise the Italian corporate reality (2000, 2004). The roles of chair and CEO are not usually separated. Non-executive directors 'often find [it] difficult to verify the information given by executive directors … [and accessing] information tends to be perceived [as being] against the implicit rules within the board' (Melis 2000: 352–353).

The board of directors was usually bereft of committees (such as audit, remuneration and nomination) that became present in the governance systems in other countries from the 1990s onwards.

In contrast to the Anglo-American system, strong blockholders are usually families, coalitions and other companies (who are usually associated with the said families and coalitions). Blockholders have a strong influence over management due to their large ownership of the corporation, but also through cross-shareholdings with other groups and companies. As Melis pointed out in 2000,

'The structure of these groups is usually quite complex. Despite the rules of ownership disclosure, their exact control structure is difficult to trace, especially at an international level'. Two Parmalat subsidiaries, Bonlat (established in 1999) and Epicurum, set-up in the Cayman Islands, did exactly that. Finally, while the Anglo-American corporate governance spheres exhibit justified concerns about the abuse of power by senior executives of the company, the Italian system is concerned with 'the abuse of power from the blockholder' (Melis 2004: 354).

## Parmalat's accounting fraud

In an early demonstration of financial wizardry in 1987 Parmalat spent €130 million on Odeon TV which it hoped to build into Italy's third major network, but the station collapsed after three years. To stave off bankruptcy, Tanzi engineered a so-called reverse merger, by which it sold itself to a dormant holding company already listed on the Milan stock exchange. The combined firm then raised about €150 million from outside investors. This enabled Parmalat to go public in 1990, and plug some of the gaps in its accounts. At the time, Parmalat had a market value of around €300 million.

In 1997 Parmalat began expanding outside the Italian market with a campaign of international acquisitions primarily in North and South America, all financed through debt. From 1990 to 2003, Parmalat continued to borrow huge amounts of money from international banks and justified those loans by inflating its revenues through fictitious sales to retailers. By 1995 the company was losing more than $300 million annually in Latin America alone, and at this point Parmalat decided to move some of its debt off the company's consolidated financial statements. It did so through three shell companies based in the Caribbean. These firms pretended to sell Parmalat products, and Parmalat would send them fake invoices and charge costs and fees to make the 'sales' look legitimate. Then Parmalat would write out a credit note for the amount the subsidiaries supposedly owed it, and take that to banks to raise money. To make the debt disappear, Parmalat management developed a network of 260 international offshore speculative entities. These companies were used to conceal losses, through a mirror-game which made them appear as assets or liquidity, while the company started to issue bonds in order to collect money. The lawyer of Parmalat Giafranco Zini helped to establish this colossal network of embezzlement, which included several groups of Luxemburg companies among them Olex Sa, Satalux and Third Millennium. Third Millennium was used to hold a part of the €500 million held by the mysterious Epicurum funds registered in the Cayman islands, from which credits disappeared without trace. Third Millennium was a personal financial stronghold of Fausto Tonna, the financial director of Parmalat. All of these companies could circulate cash, credits, debt and assets and when necessary make them disappear, and then reappear when needed (Figure C5.3).

The security for such bonds was provided by the alleged liquidity represented by the offshore schemes: Parmalat management invented assets to offset as much as $16.2 billion in liabilities, and falsified accounts over a 15-year period. By then Parmalat had invested $6.9 billion in interest swaps and high risk derivatives operations. Parmalat used derivatives and other complex financial transactions to disguise its financial situation through investment banks like Citicorp and Merrill Lynch. In one 1999 deal with Citibank which was done via a subsidiary of the bank called Buconero LLC, which literally means 'black hole' in Italian, the bank made a €117 million ($146 million) 'investment' in return for a chunk of the company's net profit. By setting up the transaction as an investment and not a loan (i.e. a perfectly legal manoeuvre), Parmalat made its borrowing costs appear smaller than they actually were. Thus the fake balance sheet figures allowed Parmalat to continue borrowing. Another part of the fraud was a system of double billing to Italian supermarkets and other retail customers: by billing twice for the same shipment of merchandise, Parmalat could create the impression

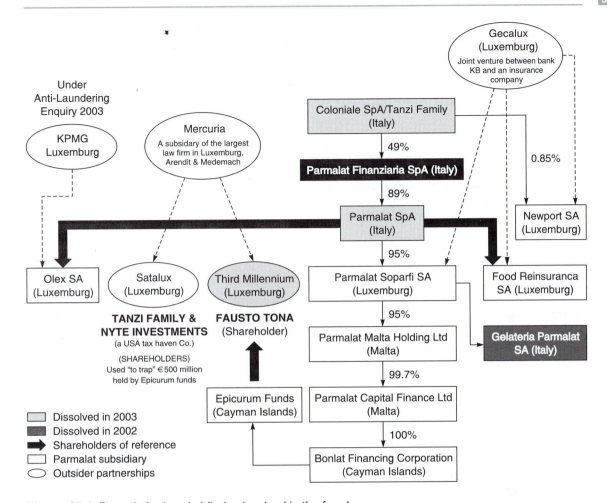

Figure C5.3 Parmalat's six subsidiaries involved in the fraud.

Source: Adapted from company reports.

that its accounts receivable were much larger than they really were. However when the debt became out of hand, Tanzi, the CFO Tonna and the two auditors came up with Parmalat's most audacious invention: a bogus milk producer in Singapore that supposedly supplied 300,000 tons of nonexistent milk powder to a Cuban importer via Bonlat (Time 2004).

## 2003: the crisis and the share price collapse

Essentially, the catalyst for the scrutiny and eventual insolvency of Parmalat was the company's failure to pay a total of €4 billion in routine payments to its creditors including farmers who had not been paid since August 2003. This was triggered when Parmalat was unable to retrieve the money to pay them from its Cayman Island account, the Epicurum Fund. In the past Parmalat had sought to issue bonds to pay its debts but by now it was unable to sell €500 million worth of bonds, and in September 2003 the company shelved plans to sell €300 million worth of bonds. This failure coupled with concerns over the non-payments, alarmed some of the holders and investors that included the Bank of America. In November the shares were hit after auditors started

questioning the accounting transactions with mutual fund Epicurum, another Cayman-based company linked to Parmalat. This forced Parmalat the following month to admit its failure to recover €496.5 million from Epicurum, needed to service debt. Parmalat notified the banks that €4 billion was temporarily housed in its Cayman Island subsidiaries, but the Bank of America questioned the veracity of this statement and produced a document showing that the transfer of €4 billion to the Cayman Island subsidiaries was, in fact, a forgery resulting in another revelation that the €4 billion hole in the accounts was in fact €8 billion. This announcement caused a crisis of confidence in the company and the spiral towards insolvency began (Figure C5.4).

By this time, the company's net debt had blown out to €14.3 billion, and the founder Calisto Tanzi became the focus of investigations and was accused of falsifying accounts, embezzlement and running the company into the ground. Tanzi admitted that he had diverted €500 million of the company's money into the family-run company Parmatour, and offered

to give up his family's 51 per cent stake in the company, including his two yachts in order to pay off the debt. But the response to this gesture was that it was perceived as being too little and too late: 'Shareholders, bondholders, lenders, employees and all the other stakeholders … have had enough of the nostalgia and pointless gestures, including this latest offering of probably worthless assets, private jets and personal yachts' (Arie 2004). On 15 December Tanzi resigned as chair and CEO and by 27 December 2003, an Italian bankruptcy court formally declared Parmalat insolvent. Days later under a government appointed administrator, Enrico Bondi, Parmalat sought bankruptcy protection from its creditors and Tanzi spent New Year's Eve 2003 in jail.

Parmalat Brazil was badly affected by the crisis: Brazil was one of the company's largest markets, and its brands are well known in the country. Unlike the Australian and American arms, the Brazilian operation set up in the 1970s, was a substantial operation, and is the second biggest buyer of Brazilian milk

Figure C5.4 Parmalat stock price collapse.

after Nestlé. However, during the 1990s there were deep suspicions about its activities (BBC 2004f) and this subsidiary was a key recipient of hundreds of millions of euros transferred by its Italian parent. The subsidiary was also in debt long before the scandal broke. It had debts of $1.8 billion, its president had resigned, and the company filed for bankruptcy protection. Parmalat's collapse had a negative effect on the dairy farmers and milk co-operatives who relied on big food corporations to buy their products. Most of these farmers and co-ops have not been paid since the scandal broke and the future for some of them is bleak. Parmalat Brazil employed 6,000 workers and production seriously fell. In early 2004 Parmalat's American arm was placed under bankruptcy protection. The assets of this subsidiary exceeded its debts and it was by no means in such dire straits as the rest of the company. However, this signalled the process of restructuring had started throughout Parmalat, and it was a move to save its profitable subsidiaries from creditors, as the US has a well-established bankruptcy protection procedure.

## THE COMPANY CULTURE

There were many signs that all was not well within the company: Parmalat had to meet Italian fund managers to explain its accounts, the company's bond issues were failures, and three CFOs resigned in the space of eight months. The downfall of Parmalat is attributed to the aggressive expansion and its disastrous family ventures. Once Tanzi had succeeded in the long-life milk market, he went on to buy up most of his competitors, then entered the Football market buying Parma Calcio (Parma's soccer club), the well-known Brazilian club Palmeiras, and a Chilean club named Audax Italiano, as one of Tanzi's main rivals in the dairy-product market Sergio Cragnotti was also involved in the football market. However, the family football clubs and the tourism enterprise Parmatour

turned out to be financial disasters, as was Odeon TV.

## THE KEY PLAYERS

### The founder: Calisto Tanzi and family

Tanzi faced trial for the pivotal role he played in Parmalat's collapse accused of building offshore companies in which non-existent assets were declared to offset real liabilities. Like Tyco these liabilities were accumulated when the company went on a global acquisition spending frenzy. Tanzi stated that while some of the faults were his, the €14 billion hole was his top managers' fault and 'the problems at Parmalat were due to bad management and company finances' (Arie 2004). Tanzi and his family interests' in the company, and the company's interests in the family businesses were extensive. Calisto's son Stefano was president of the football club owned by Parmalat and sat on the Parmalat board, while Calisto's daughter Francesca worked for the family's tourism business Parmatour, which received the €500 million diverted funds. Calisto's brother Giovanni, and Calisto's niece Paola Viconti also served as Parmalat board members (BBC 2004g). On 26 May 2004 Italian prosecutors indicted the entire board of Parmalat.

### The succession of CFOs

The signs that all was not well at Parmalat were backed up by the company's loss of three CFOs in one year: Fausto Tonna, Alberto Ferraris and Luciano del Soldato. Tonna helped create some of the financial vehicles to hide the losses of Parmalat, and Tanzi blamed him for being behind the company's financial ruin (BBC 2004a). He resigned on 28 March 2003 replaced by Ferraris, who only lasted 8 months in the job. Ferraris' replacement del Soldato, resigned within 4 weeks of taking up the job as CFO. The finances of Parmalat were unravelling and the CFO rotation was an indication of how fast Parmalat was sinking.

## THE INTERMEDIARIES

### The role of the banks

The banks of Parmalat, both local and foreign, played various roles as creditors, investors, bond issuers, and, depending on their close ties to the Tanzi family, as part of the Tanzi block. Parmalat's main local banks were Capitalia, Banco Intensa and San Paolo IMI. These three banks had some €1 billion of unpaid loans from Parmalat (Arie 2004). Bondi also asked these banks to pay €100 million to pay wages and suppliers of Parmalat in January 2004 to keep Parmalat afloat, this was in addition to the loan of €25 million the previous month to ensure Parmalat did not default on an outstanding bond. Other Italian banks exposed to Parmalat (BBC 2004c) included Banca Monte dei Paschi di Siena (€183 million), Unicredito (€150 million), Banca Nazionale del Lavoro (€110 million), Banco Popolare di Lodi (€100 million), Banca Popolari Unite (€100 million), Banco Popolare di Verona e Novara (€35 million), and Banca Lombarda (€35 million). One hapless banker and a personal friend of Tanzi, Franco Gorreri, stepped down as chair of the Monte Parma savings bank when he was arrested for his close connections to Parmalat. He had told investors that 'their money is safe' (BBC 2004d).

The Italian bank business practice of cultivating relationships may be profitable, but they are also costly. While foreign banks with investments in Italian companies do not play a proactive role, the Bank of America broke the mould when it blew the whistle on the initial missing €4 billion in Parmalat. Perhaps given the conspiracy of silence that descended around American financial institutions (especially Merrill Lynch, Salomon Smith Barney and Citigroup) closely associated with the collapses of Enron, WorldCom, Global Crossing and others, the Bank of America took the unusual initiative of going public with its information, thereby lifting the veil from the confidential relationship between bank and client. By doing so, not only did Bank of America's revelations trigger off the loss of confidence in Parmalat, it also ensured a wave of disquiet towards Bank of America's role in Parmalat. Some thought Bank of America might in fact be a villain in this saga, hiding the extent of its involvement with Parmalat.

The US SEC investigated the roles the Bank of America, JP Morgan, Merrill Lynch and the Spanish bank, Santander played in selling €8 billion worth of Parmalat bonds between 1997 and 2002, that were probably worthless (Arie 2004). In addition, the Bank of America faced accusations that it 'used privileged financial information to end up first in the queue of creditors'. Bondi suggested that the Bank of America knew in some way 'about the group's financial crisis' (BBC 2004i). It was also in a Bank of America account that the Cayman subsidiary of Parmalat was holding the now-missing billions. As a sign of how suspicious the Italian prosecutors were of Bank of America's role, three former executives of the Italian unit of Bank of America faced charges, while the Italian subsidiary was indicted (BBC 2004j). Foreign banks with significant interests in Parmalat, such as Citigroup, wrote off some €242 million in bad loans as the prospect disappeared of recovering any monies lent. Other foreign banks exposed to Parmalat (BBC 2004c) included ABN AMRO (€70 million), Barclays (45 million pounds) and UBS (€420 million of Parmalat bonds).

### The role of the brokerage houses

As the Parmalat scandal broke the company's share price (PRFI.MI) fell from a high of €3.09 to €0.11, before it was suspended. Some sixteen brokers rated Parmalat, and 18 December 2004 was the last date the shares were traded. The scandal publicly broke in late November, with the Bank of America information revealed in the first week of December. With a window of three weeks, the share price reflected the loss of investor confidence in the company. Parmalat shares nosedived, and at the very least, one might expect the financial analysts to reflect this market sentiment. Yet in a range of 1.00–5.00 where 1.00 is a strong buy and a 5.00 is a strong sell, the average brokerage house recommendation for Parmalat's last weeks was 2.75. In Parmalat's

final days of trading five brokers had a hold on Parmalat; three had a moderate buy, and one courageous broker even suggested a strong buy. Only four brokerage houses signalled a sell on Parmalat shares. Some of these brokerage houses were recommending a buy on Parmalat while simultaneously selling their holdings.

### The role of the auditors: Deloitte and Grant Thornton

From 1999 to 2003 the auditors Deloitte & Touche did not suggest any irregularity or any form of fraud. The auditors certified balance sheets, as local auditors who were honest or too curious were pushed away. During 1990–1999 Parmalat's auditor was the Italian branch of Grant Thornton International, one of the largest of the second-tier US accounting firms. In 1999 Parmalat was forced to change its auditor under Italian law, and it replaced Grant Thornton with the Italian branch of Deloitte Touche Tohmatsu. However, Grant Thornton continued to audit Parmalat's offshore entities (i.e. the web of financial companies that were closed down in the Dutch Antilles in 1999 and re-established in the Cayman Islands). In response, the US parent of Grant Thornton SpA, the long time auditor of Parmalat and its Cayman Island arms, washed its hands of any knowledge of the affairs of its Italian branch, effectively letting this branch of the partnership (now known as Italaudit SpA) face all the blame, and isolate the harmful effects it may have on the reputation of the US headquarters.

### The role of the lawyers

US authorities played an active role in bringing Parmalat to book. American investors were moderately affected by the Parmalat collapse and the US authorities, with their recent experience of delving into companies broken by executive excess acted with enthusiasm in helping Italian authorities pursue their lines of inquiry. For instance, in seizing the New York office documents of a Parmalat lawyer Gianpaolo Zini,

who was already in an Italian jail at this point (Arie 2004). Such is the global nature of crimes committed by multinational corporation, that international cooperation with white collar crime enforcement will be necessary.

### The role of the regulators

Regulatory obstruction occurred passively and actively by Parmalat staff and on orders of senior managers. Examples of this behaviour included denial of wrongdoing, concealment of various false statements by Parmalat, and failure to reveal documents to the regulators (i.e. Consob) or justice authorities and Parmalat was accused of deliberately deceiving the regulators. The company had a labyrinthine records system, which made it very difficult to be audited. The US Securities & Exchange Commission sued Parmalat for misleading investors in a 'brazen fraud'. A company computer and floppy disks turned over to investigators by a Parmalat employee, who disobeyed orders (from superiors) to destroy corporate documents, may help prosecutors uncover the web of deceit.

## CORPORATE GOVERNANCE

'While in the United States the main corporate Governance issue is defined as "strong managers, weak owners", the leading corporate governance issue in Italy is "weak managers strong blockholders and unprotected minority shareholders". It is clear that in the Parmalat case "the blockholder", the Tanzi family, used its power in the organisation to pursue personal interests to the detriment of the minority shareholders by funnelling most of the Parmalat companies' resources to the family's personal accounts' (Segato 2004). The Parmalat case exposed the many gaps and conflicts of interest in the corporate governance system of Italy: this scrutiny highlighted the failings of a system so reliant on ruling families running industrial enterprises with little or no monitoring at all from outsiders. However, the quick arrests

by Italian police of the main players involved in Parmalat somewhat stemmed the tide of investor dissatisfaction with Italian regulators and companies. Indeed the immediate arrests made were far quicker than WorldCom or Enron arrests. The total of twenty-nine arrests is far longer than the arrests made of executives at WorldCom, Enron, Global Crossing and Tyco combined.

However, the response of the financial market regulatory agency (CONSOB) and the Bank of Italy, to Parmalat's financial manoeuvres was disappointing. CONSOB did not start to investigate Parmalat until late 2003, when it became evident that market forces were discounting Parmalat stock in reaction to its business practices. The Bank of Italy was also criticised for not sharing with CONSOB important information on distressed and defaulted debt evident in the central bank records. The Italian government introduced statutes, long debated but hitherto unimplemented, on bankruptcy. The Italian central bank called for 'wide-ranging reforms to the way the Italian financial markets are regulated' and pointed out that the pre-existing climate of self-regulation was at an end: 'the crisis is not industrial but financial, the only solution is organic reform'. Italian reformers are also empowering a watchdog to supervise insurance companies and pension funds in addition to its scrutiny of the financial markets (BBC 2004b).

The ultimate effectiveness of such an Italian securities and companies regulatory institution, however, would depend upon its insulation from the kind of political meddling that undercuts many of Italy's regulatory bodies. But the Bank of Italy as the central bank, which is supposed to exercise control over the banking system, after deregulation, is itself controlled by the banks, that are its shareholders. These shareholding banks are Banca Commerciale (now Intesa–BCI), Credito Italiano (now Unicredito), IMI (now S. Paolo-IMI), and Banca Nazionale del Lavoro, among which were some of Parmalat's main creditors and bond-placers. Following the Parmalat scandal there was an unsuccessful battle to change this, by attempting to introduce local government representatives onto the boards of the Banking Foundations, which control Italian banks.

Milan bourse requires family-owned companies to appoint lead independent directors in the wake of Parmalat. The Milan bourse said listed companies will have to appoint 'a lead independent director' in order to protect investors in companies owned by families or controlled by an executive chair, as part of new rules for listed companies. The bourse has upgraded its corporate governance code for listed companies, the first time since 2002, and after Parmalat's collapse at the end of 2003. 'Parmalat showed up the weakness in controls at family-controlled companies', he said. Parmalat returned to the bourse after major financial restructuring.

## Implications for European corporate governance convergence

The Parmalat scandal has highlighted that national systems of corporate governance still count in Europe. After the initial shock when the scandal broke, the European markets saw Parmalat as an isolated case in Italy, not a European-wide affliction that would have a domino effect on other European corporations and countries 'the harmonisation of Europe's industrial and financial markets still has a long way to go. Local practices matter, never more so than when things go wrong' (*The Economist* 2004).The reaction to Parmalat of the European Commission was to put extra procedures in place with auditor rotation. The plan is to introduce tougher new auditing laws, ending the existing self-regulation, because: 'auditors are our major line of defence against crooks who want to cook the books' (BBC 2004h). The Parmalat scandal was a catalyst for long-awaited reforms in Italy; it has not been so for the rest of Europe.

## Financial implications

As much as $8 billion to $10 billion were missing from Parmalat company accounts and had

effectively disappeared. Consequently, there was a fear that the whole of the Italian financial system may be affected as foreign investors lost faith in the country. As well as losses to thousands of direct shareholders or investors, many dairy and factory workers in Italy and around the world could lose their pension and superannuation savings. Suppliers such as 5,000 dairy farms in Italy and Brazil's largest flour milling concern, Moinho Pacifico, depended on the company for the bulk of their business and had not seen any payments. The bankruptcy of Parmalat ran the risk of general corporate insolvency in Italy if there was a run on corporate bonds. The Italian government declared an emergency in its dairy sector and called for financial support from the EU.

The Italian government was aware of the systemic dimensions of the crisis, at least as concerns the Italian bond market. The main concern was of what would happen if the market demanded liquidation of money invested in corporate bonds. There was a recognition that the Italian regulator must quickly review current legislation protecting investors. There were 100,000 Italian owners of Parmalat bonds, mostly families and this was the third large insolvency hitting Italian investors in one year.

## The Parmalat trials

The chair and lead partner from the ex-Grant Thornton Italian branch and two partners from Deloitte individually faced indictments, while institutionally, these two firms are facing indictments over their role in Parmalat. Joining Bank of America, these three firms are the main focus of investigation by the Italian prosecutors in the Parmalat scandal. In June 2005 eleven people were convicted under plea bargaining arrangements that allowed them to avoid jail. The heaviest sentence of two and a half years was handed down to the former CFO Fausto Tonna, accused of weaving the web of offshore subsidiaries to disguise the true cash flow of the company. As Tonna had spent several months remanded in detention, it was likely he would pass the remainder of his sentence in community service. The lawyer Zini who received

a two year sentence, and others convicted and sentenced to two years, were covered by an Italian law that waives jail terms for first time offenders sentenced to less than two years. This included two former financial officers, internal auditors, and a brother and son of Calisto Tanzi.

Tanzi himself attempted to plea bargain, but was ordered to stand trial alongside 15 other people, including former executives of Parmalat, and of the Italian arm of Bank of America, and the auditing firm of Deloitte Touche and Grant Thornton. Curiously, Tanzi's line of defence was to blame the banks for his penchant for spending money on himself and his family: 'Parmalat … had a relation with its banks that was one of addiction', Tanzi said in a 16-page statement read out in court, reconstructing the events that led to Parmalat's 2003 collapse. 'The lenders themselves, the investment banks, were the ones who chased us, promising the group all the money it needed, even though the accounts were not entirely transparent and despite the fact we were constantly asking for debt while stating we had consistent liquidity. Already at the end of 1995 the group fell into a state of serious financial imbalance. It was unable to generate enough profits to service its debt with its own resources, having to repay debts with new credit lines', said Tanzi, 67, looking drawn as he spoke in the 40-minute address. 'This situation was presented to me by my financiers as being normal, and indeed part of a strategy which had to first be aggressive before balancing itself out … At this point Parmalat was given the proposal of financing itself with bonds'. Tanzi said Chase Manhattan Bank, now part of JP Morgan Chase & Co., was the first to propose the bond strategy, adding it triggered 'an unbreakable chain of events'. JP Morgan Chase said it was confident its activities were appropriate and it is not one of four global banks involved in a separate Milan trial over Parmalat.

## Postscript

Parmalat managed to survive its bankruptcy and the disgrace of the Tanzi family and many

of its former executives, advisers and bankers. It has maintained a global presence in the dairy industry with 140 production facilities and 36,000 employees, and after completing a financial restructuring returned to be listed on the Milan Stock exchange in 2005.

In a further twist in August 2006 the Banca Popolare Italiana agreed to pay Parmalat €59.5 million ($76 million) to settle a lawsuit over the bank's role in the bankruptcy. Under Italian bankruptcy law Parmalat can sue its former lenders to unravel financial transactions carried out in the year leading up to bankruptcy, on the grounds the banks helped to prolong the fraud that brought the company down by easing the company's access to finance. Parmalat was seeking €7.5 billion in revocatory claims against 50 Italian and foreign banks. In June 2005 Morgan Stanley became the first foreign bank to settle when it paid €155 million, and Nextra an Italian asset management company owned by Crédit Agricole and Banca Intesa settled for €160 million.

## CONCLUSIONS

At Parmalat a controlling shareholder was able to exploit a system that lacks transparency and accountability. By December 2003 Parmalat already had a low score on the Institutional Shareholders Service Corporate Governance Quotient. The company appeared at the bottom of a list of 69 Italian companies rated by the proxy service. Throughout the 1990s Parmalat appeared a successful multinational company, with widely recognised consumer brands, and distribution channels around the globe. Beneath the surface of its marketing operation though, the company had abandoned its expansion strategy for a desperate and ill-conceived financial scheme to conceal its losses and preserve the controlling influence of the Tanzi family. Repeated fraudulent financial transactions at Parmalat were possible because of the affiliation between owners and directors, the independent directors' lack of expertise in financial and risk management,

and the corrupted entanglements of statutory auditors and investment bankers, prepared to allow high risk debt securities to be placed among retail investors.

## Questions

1 Examine the strengths and weaknesses of the Italian model of relationship based, insider corporate governance.
2 Investigate the complicity of Parmalat's auditors, bankers, analysts and regulators in the financial arrangements that led to the bankruptcy of the company.
3 Examine the effectiveness of the Italian corporate governance codes and compliance to these as revealed in the Parmalat case.
4 How successful is the reform process in corporate governance in Italy?
5 Compare and contrast the Parmalat financial scandal with the Enron collapse.

## REFERENCES

Adams, R. (2004) Enron to Parmalat: Now Europe Needs to Declare War on Fraud, *International Herald Tribune*, http://www.iht.com/articles/2004/01/14/edadams_ed3_.php

Arie, S. (2004) *Tanzi Offers Yachts to Repay Missing Millions* 5 January, http://www.guardian.co.uk/parmalat/story/0,14141,1116231,00.html

Bianchi, M., Bianco, M. and Enriques, L. (1999) *Pyramidal Groups and the Separation between Ownership and Control in Italy*, Working Paper ECG, http://papers.ssrn.com/sol3/papers.cfm?abstract_id=293882

Bianco, M. and Casavola, P. (1999) Italian Corporate Governance: Effects on Financial Structure and Firm Structure and Firm performance, *European Economic Review*, 43(4).

Di Staso, K.M. (2004) *Il Caso Parmalat*, Ceradi, Centro Di Ricerca Per il Diritto di Empresa, Libera Università Internazionale degli Studi Sociali, Rome.

*Economist* (2004) Turning Sour, 3 January, 8–9.

Ferrarini, G. and Guidici, P. (2005) *Financial Scandals and the Role of Private Enforcement*, European Corporate Governance, Working Paper 40, May.

Melis, A. (2000) Corporate Governance in Italy, *Corporate Governance: An International Review*, 8(4): 347–355.

Melis, A. (2004) On the Road of the Board of Statutory Auditors in Italian Listed Companies, *Corporate Governance: An International Review*, 12(1): 74–84.

*New York Times* (2003) Layers of Ownership Conceal Trouble in Italy, Tagliabue, J., http://www.nytimes.com/2003/12/30/business/worldbusiness/30parma.html, 30 December.

Parmalat (2004) http://www.parmalat.com, accessed 5 January.

Segato, L. (2006) A Comparative Analysis of Shareholder Protection in Italy and the United States, *Northwestern Journal of International Law and Business*, 26(2), ABI/INFORm Global, p. 373.

*Times* (2004) How It All Went Sour, Gumbel P., 21 November, http://www.time.com/time/europe/magazine/article/0,13005,901041129-785318,00.html

## Additional downloadable articles

Arie, Sophie (2004) Parmalat Dream Goes Sour *The Observer*, 4 January, http://observer.guardian.co.uk/business/story/0,6903,1115471,00.html

BBC (2003) *Q&A: Parmalat's troubles*, 27 December, http://news.bbc.co.uk/1/hi/business/3340641.stm

BBC (2004a) *Parmalat Bosses Play Blame Game*, 5 January, http://news.bbc.co.uk/1/hi/business/3368491.stm

BBC (2004b) *Parmalat Prompts Italy Reform Bid*, 16 January, http://news.bbc.co.uk/1/hi/business/3401785.stm

BBC (2004c) *Parmalat Lenders Reveal Exposure*, 17 January, http://news.bbc.co.uk/1/hi/business/3405193.stm

BBC (2004d) *Bank Chief Held in Parmalat Probe*, 19 January, http://news.bbc.co.uk/1/hi/business/3411357.stm

BBC (2004e) *Parmalat Crisis Hits Brazil's Dairy Industry*, 26 January, http://news.bbc.co.uk/1/hi/business/3429701.stm

BBC (2004f) *Parmalat Brazil Chief Forced Out*, 13 February, http://news.bbc.co.uk/1/hi/business/3485069.stm

BBC (2004g) *Parmalat Head's Family Arrested*, 17 February, http://news.bbc.co.uk/1/hi/business/3495565.stm

BBC (2004h) *EU Plans Tougher Auditing Rules*, 16 March, http://news.bbc.co.uk/1/hi/business/3517288.stm

BBC (2004i) *Bank Denies Any Parmalat Cover-up*, 1 April, http://news.bbc.co.uk/1/hi/business/3588283.stm

BBC (2004j) *Parmalat Probe Seeks Trial for 32*, 26 May, http://news.bbc.co.uk/1/hi/business/3749847.stm

Coffee, Jr., J.C. (2005) *A Theory of Corporate Scandals: Why the US and Europe Differ*, Columbia Law and Economics Working Paper, 274, March, http://papers.ssrn.com/sol3/papers.cfm?abstract_id=694581

CNN, http://edition.cnn.com/2006/BUSINESS/03/07/italy.parmalat.reut/

Edmondson, G. (2004) *How Parmalat Went Sour*, *Business Week Online*, 12 January, http://www.businessweek.com/magazine/content/04_02/b3865053_mz054.htm

Forbes, http://www.forbes.com/technology/feeds/afx/2006/03/14/afx2592611.html

Melis, A. (2004) *Corporate Governance Failures: To What Extent Is Parmalat a Particularly Italian Case?*, 30 September, http://papers.ssrn.com/sol3/papers.cfm?abstract_id=563223

Melis, G. and Melis, A. (2004) *Financial Reporting, Corporate Governance and Parmalat: Was it a Financial Reporting Failure?* http://papers.ssrn.com/sol3/papers.cfm?abstract_id=556575

Parmalat, http://www.parmalat.com/en/intro.html

Parmalat on Google News, http://news.google.com.au/news?hl=en&lr=&ie=UTF-8&oe=UTF-8&tab=wn&q=parmalat

Parmalat on Yahoo News, http://news.search.yahoo.com/search/news/?c=&p=parmalat

Parmalat entry on Wikipedia, http://en.wikipedia.org/wiki/Parmalat

Philly.com, http://www.philly.com/mld/inquirer/business/14042941.htm

Roberts, R.Y., Swanson, R.P. and Dinneen, J. (2004) *Spilt Milk: Parmalat and Sarbanes–Oxley Internal Controls Reporting*, http://www.ingentaconnect.com/content/pal/jdg/2004/00000001/00000003/art00003

Taub, Stephen (2004) *Parmalat Accounts on the Defensive*, *CFO.com*, 23 March, http://www.cfo.com/article/1,5309,12839%7C%7CT%7C741,00.html

# Case Study 6
# DaimlerChrysler

## EXECUTIVE SUMMARY

Daimler–Benz was the most distinguished car company in Europe. The company's decision to merge with the US Chrysler corporation in 1998 presented great cultural and governance obstacles. In many respects this was a coming together of European and US corporate governance in a hybrid corporation operating in the most competitive product market in the world. Negotiating the merger was a huge task, making the merged corporation into a commercial success was an even greater challenge:

> In 1998 Daimler–Benz and the Chrysler Corporation tied the knot. The newly created DaimlerChrysler [DCX] conglomerate was touted in the business world as a merger of equals with both companies retaining their unique and distinct identities. Soon after the merger the honeymoon period abruptly ended and the rancour began. Diametrically opposite management and cultural differences contributed to deep divisions which nearly scuttled the new relationship. Today, things are much different than they were in 1998; however it remains to be seen whether the long term partnership between the German and American automakers will outlast the deep, mutual distrust that prevailed for so many years.
>
> (Keegan 2005: 1)

Daimler indicating Chrysler was for sale early in 2007 signalled the partnership was failing.

## DAIMLER ORIGINS

A company which emerged during the industrial revolution, Daimler–Benz's survival into the 21st century as the luxury automaker, DaimlerChrysler, has been nothing short of remarkable. Its history can be divided into five parts:

### The growth of Daimler–Benz culminating in a golden era: 1890s–1930s

The two founders Gottlieb Daimler (1854–1900) and Carl Benz were auto inventors in their own right. Daimler worked and collaborated with innovators of the period and built the world's first motorcycle in 1885. He founded his motor company Daimler-Motoren-Gesellschaft in 1890 and launched the Mercedes car (named after the daughter of a Daimler dealer). At the same time Carl Benz (1844–1929) had established a company called Benz & Cie Rheinische Gasmotoren-Fabrik in 1882 which built internal combustion engines. In 1893, Benz unveiled his four-wheeled car called Victoria. Further, Benz, rather than Daimler, was alluded to as Henry Ford's German equivalent (Meyer-Larsen 2000: 37) though they did not share Ford's assembly line philosophy as cars remained the province of Germany's elite and wealthy. In 1926 both companies agreed to merge into Daimler–Benz AG, headquartered in Berlin.

## The war period and the occupation between 1935–1950

World War II had a dramatic effect on industrial companies in Germany, and like its rival, Volkswagen, Daimler–Benz would be tainted by its links to the Nazi regime.

Mercedes-Benz vehicle production at the Untertürkheim works was phased out in favour of war production. With the final assembly of the first vehicles in van, delivery, and ambulance versions, Daimler–Benz AG resumed post war production, with a total of 214 vehicles produced in 1946.

## National consolidation between 1950 and 1970

Daimler–Benz AG became the biggest German exporter of passenger cars and commercial vehicles. In 1954 it had a short stint in formula 1 racing but decided to withdraw a year later. Daimler–Benz expanded to Brazil and Australia.

New six-cylinder models, 220, 220 S and 220 SE, with tail fin bodies in which the safety cell developed by Béla Barényi was used for the first time in a car series gave Daimler–Benz its breakthrough to European market leader in the intermediate category.

## The experimentation era: 1980s–1990s

During the 1980s Daimler–Benz expanded into other sectors (such as aeronautics), which proved to be disastrous. It was during this period that Germany's corporate governance system came under scrutiny and questions were raised about the influence of German banks on company's strategy, especially Deutsche Bank which was the leading power on German supervisory boards. In the 1990s global consolidation in the auto industry made it seem imperative for the company to seek an international partner. Its willing partner became America's third largest auto company Chrysler.

## The new globalised era

### Operations Alpha, Beta and Gamma

Daimler–Benz entered the globalisation competition of the 1990s with some concerns. The luxury car market was a mature industry and Daimler–Benz had never capitalised on economies of scale in the way its American and Japanese rivals had relentlessly pursued, with an emphasis on quality rather than quantity. However, the Japanese maker Toyota was now threatening the niche at the luxury end of the market with its Lexus cars. Nevertheless, the Mercedes luxury marque was envied by the rest of the car industry, and unlike its closest luxury car rivals, Daimler–Benz was a financial powerhouse that could choose its partners selectively. For Daimler–Benz and its new CEO Jürgen Schrempp, it was better for the company to enter into a merger of choice before having to merge out of necessity.

Daimler–Benz consciously avoided merging with Japanese companies and fellow European companies. Daimler–Benz viewed the Japanese as being too strong, and any alliance with them would be unfavourable to Daimler–Benz. Japanese companies had a history of merging only if they were facing bankruptcy. Toyota was not interested in merging as it was already on the way to being the largest auto company in the world. With regard to potential European partners, Schrempp envisaged a global company and not a Eurocentric company. This left Daimler–Benz to concentrate on the three auto giants in America, calling its company strategy to merge with one of them, Operations Alpha, Beta and Gamma.

### Operation Alpha

A merger with General Motors (GM) came up but was never seriously considered as pragmatic. It was the biggest auto maker in the

world during the 1990s with an impressive line of cars and an extensive network of subsidiaries throughout developing and developed countries. However, it was also considered by far the most cumbersome, bureaucratic auto company around, with constant conflicts with its stakeholders. GM was undergoing an extensive reorganisation (Meyer-Larsen 2000: 69) that would take years to complete. As an organisation it was much larger and too structurally diverse from Daimler–Benz.

## Operation Beta

In recent years the Ford Motor Company had been in the shadow of GM, its bigger rival. It had always wanted to overtake GM and take the crown of world's biggest auto maker. Ford also had an extensive family history not dissimilar to Daimler–Benz and the Ford dynastic ties to the company continue today. Daimler–Benz and Ford shared the vision of becoming the number one company in the world. Some discussions ensued; however, sharing similar goals proved to be the proposal's undoing, since Ford believed itself capable of achieving number one, at least in America, without the help of an outsider. Naming rights also proved to be a thorny issue, Ford wanted to retain the Ford name, not change this to Ford–Daimler much less to Daimler–Ford.

## Operation Gamma

Chrysler Motor Corporation was established in 1925 by a former GM employee, Walter Chrysler. It survived the teething problems of the nascent automotive industry, and Chrysler's golden age was the 1950s with its family sedans. By the 1960s Chrysler faced declining sales and this was further compounded by the oil crisis of the 1970s. Up until this point Chrysler's lines of cars were composed of big inefficient gas-guzzlers that proved to be undesirable in a market filled with cheaper, more energy-efficient Japanese compact cars that were flooding into the American market at the time. By 1982 Chrysler was in crisis, and saving the company became a big political

issue. With accusations of the Chrysler rescue as a symbol of an American corporate welfare state, the charismatic former Ford president Lee Iacocca was brought in to revive the ailing company.

A year later and with an expanded portfolio that included small to medium cars, Chrysler showed its return to a healthier state by taking over the fourth largest auto company in America, the American Motors Corporation (AMC) from its French owner Renault. This strategy allowed Chrysler to build upon the Jeep brand, which was the forerunner of the sports utility vehicle (SUV) boom. By the 1990s, Chrysler was a company that had advanced adequately enough from its weak position in the early 1980s, yet was far from its golden age in the 1950s when it could rival GM in scope. Chrysler in the 1990s was the most innovative company of the big three and the most willing to take risks. It had a Swiss-born designer Robert Lutz who introduced innovative lines such as Viper and Neon, and the charismatic but fiery Iacocca was dramatically replaced by a GM manager Robert Eaton, who steadied the company during this period. On the surface, Chrysler was the corporate antithesis to Daimler–Benz. The American car maker was financially smaller, nimbler, had little presence in the European market, did not have a luxury car line and had larger economies of scale.

Yet Chrysler shared some core continental European qualities, most prominently a form of co-determination. Chrysler had a healthy respect for stakeholder values, especially amongst its workforce and unions (which bore the brunt of its restructuring during the 1980s), massive goodwill and unusually big financial reserves for an American company. The latter point was an issue that the largest and most vocal Chrysler shareholder Kirk Kerkorian wanted diminished in the form of higher dividends to its shareholders.

## The merger deal

By 1997 Chrysler was an attractive company and in a better shape than either GM or Ford. It was also leaner and more profitable

than Daimler–Benz. Despite the company's profitability, Daimler–Benz had reached a point of stagnancy as sales volumes were definitely too low compared to other car companies. While noted for its luxury, Schrempp found Daimler–Benz a little too provincial, and most certainly not the global company he envisaged. Diversifying into other areas had failed for Daimler–Benz and the company's foray into cheaper and less exclusive brands such as the A-Class and Smart cars did not prove a success in its home market (where VW was present), let alone in overseas markets (where a host of American and Japanese car makers had cornered the market). For Schrempp the way was clear – Daimler–Benz had the financial nous and the strategic inclination to broker a deal with Chrysler (Table C6.1).

Schrempp approached Eaton to discuss a possible joint venture in the emerging countries, and a year later in January 1998 at the Detroit Auto Show Schrempp told Eaton that 'he liked Chrysler a lot and suggested that maybe they should consider going all the way' (Seaman and Stodghill 1998). Eaton responded enthusiastically: 'I've been thinking about the same thing'. For Schrempp the transatlantic alliance crystallised his vision of a global Daimler brand. The merger was a question of mutual survival, but it also came out of mutual respect for each other's strengths and weaknesses. Daimler's strengths were in technology and market reach, while Chrysler's were in design and productivity. Though they complemented each other, in this partnership of equals it was Daimler that emerged on top.

## GERMAN CORPORATE GOVERNANCE

Germany is different from other countries in its corporate governance, as Schilling (2001) states, 'The German model is based on a strong consensus orientation with the idea that all the parties involved should sit around the table and sort things out among themselves' and in the past it was seen as 'the guideline for the management board in the direction of the company exclusively towards the best interest of the company'. As a result, German corporations have been perceived as relying more on teamwork than on individualistic charismatic managers, which allowed the management board of the company exclusive right to manage and represent the company and work independently of shareholder interests and supervision.

Key differences in the governance systems of Germany and the United States are at the board level in two aspects, German companies are governed by a two-tier structure that consists of the board of management and

| Date | Event |
| --- | --- |
| 1998 | |
| 12 January | Jürgen Schrempp and Robert Eaton meet at the Detroit Auto show with the former discussing possibilities of a merger |
| February to April | Formal discussions occur on the executive level and working teams from both companies meet to negotiate and discuss business combination |
| 6 May | Merger agreement signed |
| 9 May | Daimler's supervisory board agrees to merger |
| 23 July | European Commission approves the merger |
| 31 July | US Federal Trade Commission approves the merger |
| 18 September | 97.5% of Chrysler shareholders and 99.9 per cent of Daimler–Benz shareholders approve the merger |
| 12 November | DaimlerChrysler merger transaction closes |

Table C6.1 The DaimlerChrysler merger timeline.

the supervisory board of twenty members, by which, according to the German Co-Determination Act/Law of 1976, ten are elected by the shareholders and ten are elected by the employees including two union representatives. According to Schilling (2001) this leads 'to the weakening of supervisory board and strengthening of the management board'. Further, the management board is not subject to any instruction from any other body of the company and it is responsible for running the day to day operations of the company, whereas the supervisory board functions are essentially to appoint and control management (Neubauer *et al.* 2000). The largest proportion of the shares of the major German corporations were held until recently by other companies, and the direct influence of the private shareholder was very limited. Some changes have occurred in these structures with increased private investment in company shares (Schilling 2001).

## Market valuation

With access to larger and more liquid capital markets, the market capitalisation of Anglo-American corporations has tended to be considerably larger than for German corporations. For example Mannesmann was taken over through a share-swap by British-based Vodafone, that was riding the waves of high market valuations during the late 1990s technology boom. Arguably in the past, German companies have been undervalued and American companies often overvalued (Meyer-Larsen 2000: 21). Daimler–Benz was one of the few German companies listed on the New York Stock Exchange (NYSE) (initiated by the CEO predecessor of Schrempp, Edzard Reuter).

Daimler–Benz's listing on NYSE in 1993 boosted its market value and allowed its share price to be assessed with the same criteria as its future merger partner, in fact Daimler–Benz had a higher share price than Chrysler. After the companies merged in 1998, DaimlerChrysler was listed on NYSE with a ticker symbol of DCX. Proportionally 47 per cent of the shares were Chrysler's, while 53 per cent belonged to Daimler–Benz. The biggest shareholder of the merged company was still Deutsche Bank (previously the biggest shareholder at Daimler–Benz) at 12.7 per cent. Due to the bank's ill-fated influence on the strategic forays by Daimler into other industries, Deutsche Bank gradually reduced its ownership of German companies, including Daimler–Benz (in 1978 Deutsche Bank had 28 per cent share ownership of the company). Kirk Kerkorian, was left with 4.5 per cent of the newly merged company.

The NYSE listing clarified the financial relationship between the two companies and the main shareholders in the two companies had to adjust their financial relationship. In the past, Deutsche Bank's medium-to-long term investments in German corporations were made with the aim of helping rebuild the country after World War II. The stake Deutsche Bank had in Daimler–Benz was to help ensure its commercial viability for the betterment of the German economy. Now however, Deutsche Bank lessened its financial stake in DaimlerChrysler, in part due to the realisation that the Anglo-American market looked unfavourably on financial institution influence. On the other hand Chrysler shareholders realised that while this was a supposed merger of equals, the financially stronger company was Daimler–Benz.

## MERGING CULTURES

*The Daimler–Benz phenomenon is inseparable from its culture … any plan to merge with another company would have to factor it into the equation.*

*(Meyer-Larsen 2000: 50)*

The DaimlerChrysler boards and employee relationships have taken a hybrid German–American flavour. The merger was completed under German law, thus retaining the spirit of co-determination and two-tiered boards. The two-tiered nature of German boards, establishes a 'stronger monitoring rule' (Jackson 2003: 292), and a charismatic CEO or chair has

fewer opportunities to bulldoze his own criteria through the board than with unitary boards. After the merger, DaimlerChrysler established a unique concept – an independent 'chairperson's council' of non-executive directors that would satisfy requirements expected by the American authorities. The council is chaired by the chairperson of the management board (Schrempp) and was established to 'combine elements of both American and German corporate governance … and to meet the requirements of the various stakeholders' (DaimlerChrysler 2004).

## Executive compensation

It was in the area of executive compensation that the two companies most controversially diverged. While 'Germany … has considerably lower levels of compensation than the US [it also has] a very different corporate governance structure, characterised by concentrated firm ownership and a strong bank presence' (Elston and Goldberg 2003: 1392). Merging the two boards was not as straightforward as a merger between two companies in the same country, as the issue of 'executive compensation becomes a particularly important issue when a German firm merges with an American firm, such as in the case of the Daimler–Benz merger with Chrysler' (Elston and Goldberg 2003: 1392). Indeed Eaton was paid a great deal more during his tenure at Chrysler than Schrempp, who was running a bigger company. Historically, the banks have served as the monitors of executive compensation and, socially, co-determination with employees has been the barometer of whether a proposal might be won or lost.

When granting stock options for Daimler–Benz executives became an issue in 1995, non-executive employees protested, which brought about the introduction of employee share options for all Daimler employees (Jackson 2003: 293). Another instance of the German way of looking at industrial relations occurred in 1996 when Daimler–Benz moved towards reducing sick pay compensation with one of its metal unions. However, the other German car companies baulked as they wouldn't be able to afford the ensuing industrial unrest and Daimler backed down, as 'employer solidarity completely collapsed in the face of plant-level conflict' (Thelen and Kume 2003: 198). The rights of workers are further recognised in the European Works Council Directives on the formal rights of European workforces. Shareholders of DaimlerChrysler elect 50 per cent of the Supervisory Board while employees select the other half. In the US, employee participation is neither recognised nor encouraged, and the German union IG Metall offered one of its seats on the Aufsichtrat to the American union, United Auto Workers (UAW), as the UAW were not entitled to elect supervisory board representatives. In 2003 when the UAW was negotiating its work conditions for all three American-based companies, they first resolved negotiations with DaimlerChrysler, ahead of Ford and GM.

## The clash of cultures

'Mergers are tricky, the benefits and costs of proposed deals are not always obvious' (Myers 1976: 633). International mergers have to deal with differences in corporate culture, compensation policies, ownership structure and the legal environment. (Blǎsko et al. 2000: 100). The main obstacles to organisational fit that DaimlerChrysler faced were cultural and financial. The clash of corporate cultures between a nimble market oriented American company and a heavy engineering-based quality oriented German company was going to pose challenges not only for the workforce, unused to the capabilities of each other's different skills, but also to senior managers who had been used to a certain way of looking at things and reacting to the needs of their home markets. This issue was partly resolved when most of the Chrysler executives resigned and German managers took their places in America.

This symbol of how unequal the merger of equals proved to be was the financial challenge posed by compensation schemes. Daimler–Benz managers felt they were being underpaid with their salaries of hundreds of

thousands of euros, compared to their Chrysler counterparts who were paid salaries of millions of dollars. The situation was neatly reversed at plant level. The American labour force on lower wages with fewer entitlements cost about half of the total remuneration of the German workforce (Blăsko *et al.* 2000: 95).

## Merger synergies

The Chrysler board approved the merger because firstly there was substantial consolidation in the auto industry, and secondly the complementary quality of each other's strengths might strengthen the merged company (Blăsko *et al.* 2000: 81). Chrysler derived 93 per cent of its sales in America, while Daimler derived 63 per cent of sales from Europe (Blăsko *et al.* 2000: 81). The Daimler board approved the merger as it would strengthen its competitive position, improve financial liquidity, and provide the possibilities for short-term synergies in purchasing and distribution, and long term synergies in research and development, market and growth (Blăsko *et al.* 2000: 81). However, DaimlerChrysler suffered a financial setback immediately after the merger due to currency losses, poor sales and weak results on some car lines (Table C6.2), when share prices slid by more than 40 per cent from a high of €95.5 ($106) in 1999. There was some contest regarding the respective identity of the two brands: 'Daimler Chrysler jealously guards its Mercedes brand image: the last thing it wants is for consumers to perceive the luxury marque as just a more expensive Chrysler' (BusinessWeek 2002: 14).

However by 2003 the new Chrysler Viper range was marketed as 'crafted in Germany' and 'dreamed in America'. This was one of the more prominent and visible signs that the merger had come to fruition, from the research and development stage to the marketing stage. This was also an apt description of the confidence of the company five years on. DaimlerChrysler was the first automotive company with a genuinely global ownership structure (Blăsko *et al.* 2000: 92).

According to Meyer-Larsen (2000: 23) a company's management chooses three different ways of approaching a merger:

- *Laissez-faire* principle: where different cultures compete against one another until they ultimately blend.
- *Department* principle: when various divisions of the company taken over continue to work within their old cultural context.
- *Stalinist* principle: the stronger partner strictly forces its own culture onto the weaker one.

To a degree, all three principles were and remain present in the merged company. Firstly, the DaimlerChrysler culture has blended in a way so subtle that it could almost be missed. The Chrysler arm is becoming more sophisticated thanks to the superior German engineering under the hoods of Chrysler cars;

There's a Mercedes under your Chrysler bonnet

| | |
|---|---|
| Chrysler Crossfire: roadster/two seat coupés | First car jointly produced after the merger. Marketed as: dreamed in America, crafted in Germany. Designed by Chrysler with 40% of its components from Mercedes |
| Chrysler Pacifica: sports wagon | Rear suspension and axles from Mercedes |
| Chrysler Durango: SUV | Rear-wheel drive transmission from Mercedes |
| Chrysler Dodge and Concorde: sedans | Rear-wheel drive transmission and electronics from Mercedes |
| Chrysler Dakota: pick-up truck | 5-speed automatic Mercedes transmission |

Table C6.2 Merging DaimlerChrysler: product models.

while Daimler seems willing to take more risks. Secondly, principally operating in two countries whose financial, cultural and legal institutions carry exacting differences, the department principle is present in the labour relations in the two workforces. The German unions take a participative and more active role than their American counterparts. Negotiations between the company and the unions occur within the cultural and legal framework of each country. Thirdly, the Stalinist principle is present in the executive make-up of the company.

While the language used during the merger insisted that this was not a takeover, the actions by the financially stronger German partner immediately after the merger suggested otherwise. Most Chrysler senior managers left within 12 months after the completion of the merger, with their German counterparts replacing them in Detroit. The most vocal opponent of the merger and largest shareholder of Chrysler, Kirk Kerkorian, sued Daimler for misrepresentation of the takeover, and though he lost the case, in 2003 Daimler paid $300 million to settle a class-action lawsuit by American institutional investors over a similar accusation (Keeton 2003). Other companies managing global operations were even more assertive: 'The most successful global companies such as Nestlé, ABB, and GE have put their unambiguous imprint on all their operations by imposing one strong corporate culture with central management for the most critical functions' (Garten 1998).

## THE KEY PLAYER

### Chairman Jürgen Schrempp

Schrempp was recognised as the man behind Daimler's transformation, the dealmaker who became one of the most well-known global executives with the DaimlerChrysler merger. Schrempp didn't finish high school and become a mechanic apprentice. Meyer-Larsen observed 'Schrempp is one of the few top managers [in Daimler] who can take an ordinary diesel or auto engine apart and put it back together' (2000: 58). In 1974 Schrempp was

sent to South Africa to the company's customer service division, later becoming general manager. He became part of the Springbok mafia of German managers (most came from VW, BMW and the then Brown Boveri), so called because they were based in the closed market of South Africa, and would eventually return to command the head office in Germany.

Schrempp returned to Germany in 1987 and became the deputy manager of the board of directors. Daimler–Benz's strategic diversification into other areas saw him become chair of the aerospace arm of Daimler–Benz. This venture was something of a disaster since Daimler competed head-to-head with its own partner Airbus France, while it bought Fokker, not realising it was nearly bankrupt. The losses from the aerospace division (DM800 million in 1993) were only counterbalanced by the healthy growth in the auto business. For the most part the chair at the time, Edzard Reuter, was blamed for the aerospace debacle, and other misconceived diversifications. Ironically, Schrempp was rewarded for seeing it through when he succeeded Reuter as Daimler–Benz chair in May 1995. This recognition was cemented when he became a board member of the NYSE. The first year of Daimler–Benz under Schrempp was a record of sorts for the company. Fewer government defence contracts were issued (in most part due to the reunification of Germany and the weakening of the Russians), the aerospace arm went bankrupt after DM5.5 billion was funnelled into the division, and the company posted a then German company record loss of DM5.7 billion.

The most immediate strategic concern for Schrempp was to divest the company of ill-fated, poor-performing divisions, and to move away from the inherent influence of the banks. Starving the weak divisions of any funds, the first objective was soon realised. He was 'a striking example of a senior German manager that has marketed himself as an exemplar of a new breed of tough and entrepreneurial German executives' (O'Sullivan 1998: 40). Envious of colleagues in other auto companies in April 1996 Schrempp introduced a share

option incentive scheme for 170 of the company's senior executives. Clearly, Schrempp wanted to make shareholder interests the number one priority for the company, as this would directly benefit the executives and ensure a more robust approach in the event of a strategic merger. However, the non-executive employees of the company did not share Schrempp's vision. Dissent came from the IG Metall employee representative on the supervisory board stating the company's share price would assume overriding significance if the executives had large share options. Furthermore, job losses would be increased in attempts to get profits up so they would be reflected in the share price.

The move by Daimler–Benz towards a shareholder value system highlighted the changes that the German corporate governance system was undergoing. Shareholder value was objected to as it catered for a short-term vision, rather than the long-term capability of a firm. At the same time, a paradigm shift was occurring within the German banking system. Deutsche Bank, the stalwart of German finance, was also changing its behaviour towards funding home companies. From the Deutsche Bank quarter, Schrempp did not face the opposition to his shareholder value strategy that would have certainly occurred a decade earlier. It also helped Schrempp's cause that Deutsche Bank had introduced a similar share option scheme only a week earlier (*Financial Times*, 9 April 1996). In 2003 Schrempp in retrospect wryly noted the challenges he faced in putting this strategy to the forefront of his agenda: 'We have pushed this for the last 2 or 3 years. It has made me unpopular in Germany' (Simonian and Waters 2003). Daimler–Benz became one of the first German companies to transform into a hybrid company that had Anglo-American undertones.

## CORPORATE GOVERNANCE

### Post merger

The most important question is whether the merger was considered successful or not.

Christian Berggren offers a critical view of all merger activity, suggesting the motivations for mergers have more to do with executive ambitions and investment banks search for fee income, than any logic related to the development of the industry itself: 'When the DaimlerChrysler deal was announced, it was presented by *BusinessWeek* as a "marriage made in automotive heaven … if ever a merger had the potential for that elusive quality – synergy – this could be the one" and investors applauded by pushing Chrysler's shares up almost 20 per cent after the announcement' (Vlasic *et al.* 1998; Vlasic and Stertz 2000). Since then, share price and financial results have been on a long downhill slide. This is in line with market studies adopting a longer measurement period for the acquiring firm's stock performance which have demonstrated significant deterioration in 1–3 years after the merger (Scherer and Ross 1990: 169–170). It may be that the capital market reaction at the announcement date reflects positive expectations. Supported by massive public relations exercises from the actors involved in the deal – which are subsequently followed by disappointments as espoused 'synergies' do not materialise … Merger firms tend to underperform on the stock market in the three years after the merger [An] … explanation is that the market and management over-extrapolates the past performance of successful managers, and so called 'glamour firms' (2003: 3).

After struggling for some years after the merger, it appeared the DaimlerChrysler merger was at least a qualified success, as a stronger international car corporation emerged from the early hybrid form. However, if the objective was to create the world's greatest car corporation, this goal has not quite been achieved (Table C6.3).

Yet, the merger achieved what both companies needed – Daimler–Benz wanted security by accessing the American market, innovation and quantity, Chrysler wanted security by accessing the European market, quality and prestige. The merger reinvigorated the two companies in a way that would not have been possible had they remained separate.

| Daimler–Benz 1997 | 15th largest auto company in the world |
| | CEO: Jürgen Schrempp |
| | CEO salary (1997): 3 million DM |
| | 1997 Profit: $2.5b on $72b return |
| | 1997 Employees: 300,000 |
| Chrysler 1997 | 6th largest auto company in the world |
| | CEO: Robert Eaton |
| | CEO salary (1997): 20 million DM |
| | 1997 Profit: $4.6b on $61.1 return |
| | 1997 Employees: 121,0002 |
| Daimler Chrysler 2005 | 2nd largest auto company in the world |
| | CEO/Chair of the management board: Dr Dieter Zetsche |
| | Chair of the supervisory board: Hilmar Kopper (ex Deutsche Bank) |
| | 2002 CEO salary: $12 million |
| | 2005 Profit: euro 5,185 million |
| | 2005 Revenue: euro 149,776 million |
| | 2005 Employees: 382,000 |
| | 2003 Market capitalisation: $61.9 billion |

Table C6.3  Daimler–Benz vs. Chrysler.

The merger showed the establishment of a truly transatlantic global conglomerate a turning point, not only for fellow auto players keen to merge themselves, but also to German institutions. Deutsche Bank's hands-off approach showed its nationality as a German bank did not hold the same significance.

In one of a few instances in corporate history American shareholder-value business culture has had to sit alongside German stakeholder values. From the American point of view, there was unguarded joy in having the Daimler–Benz prestige. The then-president of the auto union, United Auto Workers, Stephen P. Yokich, exclaimed:

'We think it's good for Chrysler and our union'. Undoubtedly the relatively harmonious labour system of German co-determination was envied by those experienced in the sometime violently antagonistic style of American labour relations.

The aspirations of both companies may be encapsulated in this observation by an American worker: 'I just hope my stock goes up and I can buy a Mercedes with my Chrysler discount'!

(Seaman and Stodghill 1998)

## The future of the German corporate governance system

The DaimlerChrysler merger occurred in the context of an American share market with the internet economy surging beyond the rational limits of the industrial economy. In contrast, Germany was facing an economic crisis and a state of stagnancy. The crisis of faith occurred in its own corporate governance system as shareholder value reached Germany and became the ideology of key industrial leaders such as Schrempp. Mary O'Sullivan wrote on this

One of the most important lessons that the history of American corporate governance teaches us, is that in the face of unprecedented productive and financial challenges, 'organisation men' can be trained to be ardent proponents of shareholder value or any other mantra that justifies them lining their pockets … the biggest risk that the German system of corporate governance now faces, given the productive and financial challenges that it confronts, is that German labour and finance will insist on pursuing their own independent strategies to extract returns from

industrial enterprises. If this were to happen, German corporate governance would dissipate into a 'stakeholder economy' that undermines the foundations of organisational control.

(1998: 41)

DaimlerChrysler has experienced a major change in its shareholder body with a substantial dilution of traditional German holders and the addition of US institutional investors. The latter's presence rendered a substantial injection of US-style shareholder activism in the company. The DaimlerChrysler effect on German corporate law is impacting on other German companies. However, there remains a German national interest agenda whereby the existing institutional structures protect both entrenched insider interests and non-shareholder constituencies against the incursions of Anglo-American governance priorities. The DaimlerChrysler merger showed a genuine spirit of coexistence between different accounting and governance systems. Under the German system stakeholder values encompasses the interests of both the shareholders and employees. The DaimlerChrysler transaction may well establish a model for a German version of shareholder capitalism that would expose managers to a new level of capital market pressure to perform for shareholders, which would be far more disruptive of established patterns of governance and political economy.

### DaimlerChrysler today

DaimlerChrysler faced an even more competitive international automotive market from 2005 onwards. The combination of high oil prices leading customers to abandon larger fuel thirsty cars, and intensified overproduction as car companies increased their productivity when markets were expanding more slowly, left the industry in an enveloping crisis. The crisis was significantly worse in the United States where General Motors and Ford were faced with the nightmare of not only slipping further behind in the product

market compared to their more innovative Japanese and European competitors, but also the American companies had legacy problems from retirement and health benefits for their ageing workforces that they had not fully budgeted for. The share price of both General Motors and Ford hit rock bottom as losses mounted, and the prospects of earning their way out of the hole they were in diminished. Both General Motors and Ford resorted to the most massive voluntary redundancy schemes in the history of corporate America, involving tens of thousands of workers and multiple plant closures.

Against this grim market background the performance of DaimlerChrysler was not so bad. The company introduced significant restructuring and productivity initiatives to deal with serious problems from 2000 onwards in Detroit, and later in Germany, which reduced costs. DaimlerChrysler was successful in updating product lines in the United States, and new Chrysler models were regarded as more upmarket. Dieter Zetsche was rewarded for his five year effort at turning around Detroit, with the top job in Germany, 'You can see now that it clearly was a takeover, now that a Chrysler guy is running the show here in Stuttgart', he joked. It seemed as if DaimlerChrysler has exercised a vision of the potential of a global car corporation, leaving the two US rivals behind. But it was Toyota that had seized the role of leadership in the global car industry: with new hybrid electric/petrol cars, and continually improving quality and performance, by 2006 Toyota was becoming the largest and most profitable car company in the world. An astonishing indication of this was that the market capitalisation of Toyota in 2006 was greater than the market capitalisation of its three closest rivals, General Motors, Ford and DaimlerChrysler combined (Figure C6.1).

Faced with this competition from Toyota and the other Japanese manufacturers Honda and Nissan who were also doing comparatively well, following the US car manufacturers' example, all DaimlerChrysler could do was to embark on a further round of health benefit cuts and job cuts in the company. At the end of September 2005, the Board of

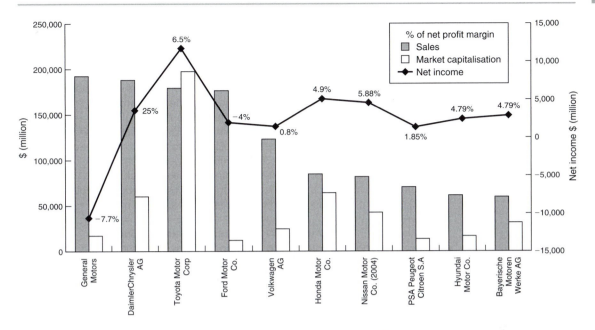

Top ten global car manufacturers' rank, by volume of sales.

Source: Compiled from respective company annual reports, Yahoo Finance, Reuters (2006).

Management approved a package of measures to be taken at the Mercedes car group aiming to reduce the workforce in Germany by 8,500 jobs. The staff reductions were to be achieved as a result of voluntary severance agreements over a period of twelve months, and were intended to increase the productivity of the Mercedes car group and help to secure the competitiveness of its facilities in Germany. As many European and Japanese manufacturers stake claims to the traditional Mercedes' hold on the high quality car market, it would be possible to conclude the effort involved in the merger with Chrysler was a mistake. A more realistic view though is that 'Without Daimler, Chrysler would be in liquidation; and without Chrysler, Mercedes would be confined to a limited future of narrowing horizons, as rivals encroached on the luxury car market' (*The Economist*, 30 March 2006).

One final irony as DaimlerChrysler faces up to an uncertain future is that its largest shareholder with a 7.2 per cent stake is the Emirate of Kuwait, followed by Deutsche Bank with 5 per cent, and the Emirate of Dubai with

| Germany | 47.5 |
| Other Europe | 26.7 |
| USA | 16.5 |
| Rest of the world | 9.3 |

Table C6.4 DaimlerChrysler shareholding, by region (%).

2 per cent of shares. In fact, the shareholding by region now represents the international aspirations of the company, though the implications of this for the future remain to be worked through (Table C6.4).

## Questions

1 'The DaimlerChrysler merger was a success'. Analyse critically.
2 Consider the argument that all international corporations are converging towards an Anglo-American model of corporate governance.

3 Examine how the introduction of a share-holder value orientation impacts upon the traditional practices of European corporations.

4 Compare the strengths and weaknesses of American shareholder value and German stakeholder values as guiding principles for management of corporations.

5 Investigate how the corporate governance of other international car companies might change as a result of further restructuring and consolidation of the industry.

## REFERENCES

Baums, Theodor (1998) *Corporate Contracting around Defective Regulations: the Daimler-Chrysler Case*, ECGI, http://papers.ssrn.com/sol3/papers.cfm?abstract_id=131730

Berggren, C. (2003) *Mergers, MNEs, and Innovation, Scandinavian Journal of Management*, www.eki.liu.se/content/1/c4/52/40/**berggren**_mergers_multinationals _and_innovation_pdf.pdf

Blăsko, M., Netter, J.M. and Sinkey Jr., J.F. (2000) Value Creation and Challenges of an International Transaction: The DaimlerChrysler Merger, *International Review of Financial Analysis*, 9(1): 77–102.

Burt, T. (2001) Daimler Brings in Council of Non-execs, *Financial Times*, 28 September. *Business Week* (2002) Daimler and Chrysler Have a Baby, 14 January, 36.

DaimlerChrysler website (2003) http://www.daimlerchrysler.com/, accessed 25 November.

DaimlerChrysler website (2006) http://www.daimlerchrysler.com/

Dinh, Viet D. (1999) *Co-determination and Corporate Governance in a Multinational corporation*, Georgetown University Law Center Business, Economics and Regulatory Law Working Paper, 169870, http://papers.ssrn.com/sol3/papers.cfm?abstract_id=169870

Elston, J.A. and L.G. Goldberg (2003) Executive Compensation and Agency Costs in Germany, *Journal of Banking and Finance*, 27: 1391–1410.

Garten, J.E. (1998) Daimler Has to Steer the Chrysler Merger, *Business Week*, 3587: 20.

Gordon, J.N. (2000) Pathways to Corporate Convergence? Two Steps on the Road to Share-holder Capitalism in Germany: Deutsche Telekom and DaimlerChrysler, *Columbia Journal of European Law*, Spring, 5: 219–241, http://papers.ssrn.com/sol3/papers.cfm?abstract_id=208508

Jackson, G. (2003) Corporate Governance in Germany and Japan: Liberalization Pressures and Responses during the 1990s, in K. Yamamura and W. Streeck (eds), *The End of Diversity? Prospects for German and Japanese Capitalism*. Ithaca: Cornell University Press, 261–305.

Keegan, M. (2005) *DaimlerChrysler Merger or Acquistion*, *Enzine*, http://ezinearticles.com/?DaimlerChrysler: -Merger-or-Acquisition?&id=89779

Keeton, Ann (2003) *DaimlerChrysler Loses Bid to Dismiss Merger Lawsuit*, DowJones Newswires in Yahoo!Finance, 21 November, http://biz.yahoo.com/djus/031121.1816001019_1.html

Liener, G. (1995) The Future of German Governance, *Corporate Board*, 16: 92.

Meyer-Larsen, W. (2000). *Germany, Inc.: The New German Juggernaut and Its Challenge to World Business*, New York: John Wiley and Sons.

Myers, S.C. (1976) *Modern Developments in Financial Management*, New York: Praeger.

Neubauer, F., Steger, U. and Rädler, G. (2000) The Daimler/Chrysler Merger: The involvement of the Boards, *Corporate Governance an International Review*, 8(4): 375–387.

O'Sullivan, M. (1998) *The Political Economy of Corporate Governance in Germany*, Working Paper, 226, February, INSEAD and Centre for Industrial Competitiveness, http://papers.ssrn.com

Scherer, F.M. and Ross, D. (1990) *Industrial Market Structure and Economic Performance*, Boston: Houghton Mifflin.

Schilling, F. (2001) Corporate Governance in Germany: The Move to Shareholder Value, *Corporate Governance: An International Review*, 9(3): 148–151.

Seaman, B. and Stodghill II, R. (1998) Here Comes the Road Test: The DaimlerChrysler deal, *Time*, 19(151): 66–70.

Simonian, H. and R. Waters (1998) The Different Corporate Cultures of Daimler-Benz and Chrysler Mean That Americans and Germans Cannot Work Together, *Financial Times*, 9 May.

Thelen, K. and Kume, I. (2003) Industrial Relations in Germany and Japan, in K. Yamamura and W. Streeck (eds), *The End of Diversity? Prospects for German and Japanese Capitalism*, New York: Cornell University Press, 183–211.

Vlasic, B. and Stertz, B.A. (2000) Taken for a Ride. New York: William Morrow.

Vlasic, B., Kerwin, K. and Woodruff, D. (1998) Daimler and Chrysler What the Deal Would Mean, *Buisness Week*, 18 May.

Walther, C. (1998) Letters to the Editor: No evidence That Anglo-Saxon Board Structure Is Better Set to Avoid Failure, *Financial Times*, 10 November.

Yahoo Finance (2003) http://finance.yahoo.com/q/ks?s=DCX, accessed 23 November.

# Case Study 7
# Vodafone–Mannesmann

## EXECUTIVE SUMMARY

The takeover of the German engineering and telecommunications multinational Mannesmann AG by the British-based Vodafone Airtouch Plc. in 2000 was a grievous shock to Germany's corporate culture. For the first time in the nation's corporate history a successful hostile foreign takeover bid was made on the open market for a leading German company. In fact the $195 billion (DM390 billion) takeover was the largest merger and takeover deal in the world. Vodafone was able to use the growing power of its stock market capitalisation in leveraging the takeover of the industrial giant Mannesmann (which had at the time 114,000 employees, DM40 billion in turnover, and was 109 years old). The newer and smaller Vodafone (with 12,600 employees, DM11 billion in turnover, and only 15 years old) dealt a crushing blow to German industrial pride (though of course for many years the British had been happily selling off manufacturing businesses to their German and Japanese counterparts, including almost the whole of the UK automotive industry). As a result of this apparent reversal of fortunes, German corporations came under insistent pressure to move on from their consensual stakeholder model of governance and control, to the equity market based Anglo-American model which pursued high share price valuations as the major source of leverage in global expansion and consolidation (Höpner and Jackson 2001).

## THE GERMAN CORPORATE GOVERNANCE SYSTEM

The German corporate governance system is derived from its social market economy which emphasises consensus in decision-making, and partnership between capital and labour. The company board structure in Germany is intended to reflect this consensus. In the Anglo-American model of a management board the system is unitary and consists of executive and outside directors. In Germany, the system is two-tiered with the existence of two boards: management and supervisory. The management board makes the executive decisions with significant input and influence from the supervisory board. It is enshrined in law that the supervisory board must have employee representatives. Typically, employee groups have 50 per cent representation on the supervisory board. The supervisory board also acts as the representative of the shareholder body.

Historically, German accounting and disclosure practices lack transparency. Companies have substantial discretion in the creation of hidden reserves and the valuation of assets. Generally assets are valued at book value leading to hidden valuation reserves for a potential buyer. Fifty per cent of profits can be dedicated to reserves, while liabilities may remain undisclosed. Until 1998 German companies were not required to disclose ownership stakes until they reached 25 per cent. (This is in contrast to the

declaration of ownership at 5 per cent stakes in the USA or 3 per cent in Britain.)

Due in part to the traumatic economic experiences of Germany in the 20th century, especially in its post-war re-industrialisation, the accounting rules favour long-term business conservatism.

In Germany share market valuations relative to real assets are lower than in Britain. British companies sustain higher share market valuations by generating higher earnings, while German corporations have higher sales turnover and are able to sustain nearly double the number of employees. Like other continental European countries industrial citizenship is highly regarded in Germany. The supervisory board represents *co-determination* between employers and employees on the future well-being of the company. Employee co-determination is important in the decision-making process and makes a significant impact as a long-term relational incentive in the company (Höpner and Jackson 2001).

While both German and Anglo-American investors share the same rate of return there are different distributional and strategic consequences for corporations (Höpner and Jackson 2001: 12). UK firms have higher share prices, requiring higher payments to investors to maintain their comparable returns to capital. German shareholders tolerate receiving lower returns on their investment, as marginal returns are usually favourable, and give fewer reasons for investors to defect. German corporations follow a 'low level' equilibrium of low earnings and low dividends, corresponding to lower share prices. Shareholders receive competitive rates of return as long as market capitalisation remains low due to ownership remaining concentrated among existing, stable shareholders.

## Attitudes towards equity markets

*Germany does not have a history of stock exchange culture ... It has an economy which is dominated by medium-sized companies and companies which are not quoted on the stock market. Historically, capital was extended to companies by the big banks rather than by the stock exchange. If you look at their balance sheets, what you see is far more bank debt than would be the case in Britain.*

*(unidentified German investment banker: Hooper and Gow 1999)*

Many Germans are known to harbour a degree of financial xenophobia towards Anglo-American 'predator' capitalism at odds with a system that prizes consensus (Hooper and Gow 1999). The German public is sceptical of the volatile equity culture of Anglo-American markets, viewing it as inherently risky and speculative. The US experience of hostile takeovers, bust-ups, poison pills, golden parachutes, corporate downsizing and shareholder value are considered ruthless cowboy tactics (Höpner and Jackson 2001). German management usually consists of people with strong engineering and industrial backgrounds, with financial specialists rarely becoming the leaders of the management board. The 'financial conception of corporate control' (Fligstein 1990) never became the dominant organisational paradigm in Germany, which emphasised collective responsibility for corporate decisions (Table C7.1).

## Mergers

Mergers in Germany are uncommon, apart from the years immediately following unification of East and West Germany in 1990. Mergers are generally negotiated on a friendly basis amongst large stakeholders, rather than through public tender offers and hostile bids (Höpner and Jackson 2001). Due to the traditional industrial strength of Germany in engineering and production, mergers are usually based on industrial logic aimed at industry rationalisation and realising economies of scale. In Germany mergers and takeovers are a complement to the internal organic growth of companies, rather than a substitute for this as in the US and UK market based systems.

| German model | Anglo-American model |
| --- | --- |
| Two tier system with supervisory board and management board. The former does not get directly involved in executive decisions, tending to influence decisions of the latter. The law requires employee representation on the supervisory board | Unitary system, Management board consisting of executive and outside directors. No employee membership |
| The supervisory board is interested in the well-being of staff and long term strength of business | Shareholder value is king. Board members aim to maximise share value during their tenure |
| Share market valuations are lower, dividends are lower | High market valuations generating higher earnings and dividends to maintain comparable returns to capital |
| Banks extend capital to companies | Capital extended to companies by market |
| Bank, blockholder or stakeholder oriented | Shareholder orientation among corporate management |
| Ownership is concentrated among non-financial corporations and banks | Ownership is concentrated among institutional and individual investors |
| Stakeholders have an inherent interest in the health of the company. Stakeholders actively monitor the management of their company | Individual investors have little control over the management of the company. Individual investors respond to poor performance by diversifying their portfolios and selling their shares |
| Thrive on long term relational incentives | Thrive on short to medium term relational incentives |
| Employee co-determination is important in the decision-making process | Employees are not important in the decision-making process on the company's future directions. Breaches of trust with employees are common |
| The market for corporate control is not important for governance functions among management | The market for control is important for governance functions among management |
| Capital is relatively illiquid | Capital is liquid |
| Assets are valued at book value leading to hidden valuation reserves | Assets are valued at market prices |
| Hostile takeovers are rare. Mannesmann was the first | Hostile mergers and acquisitions are normal |

Table C7.1 German and Anglo-American corporate governance models.

## MANNESMANN ORIGINS AND DEVELOPMENT

Throughout its history, Mannesmann was the personification of German engineering and industrial strength (Table C7.2). In 1885, the Mannesmann brothers Reinhard and Max invented a rolling process for seamless tubes production in the Rhineland region of Germany. Tubes production would be part of the company portfolio throughout its history. Mannesmann was officially incorporated in 1890 and joined the top ten corporations in Germany. The first half of the twentieth century saw the company's first period of expansion in Europe. After World War II, Mannesmann was liquidated by occupying powers into three subdivisions which recombined in 1955. This rebirth became an impetus for the company's second period of expansion for the next twenty years

| Year | Event |
| --- | --- |
| 1885 | Reinhard and Max Mannesmann invent a rolling process for seamless tubes production in Remscheid, Germany |
| 16 July 1890 | Mannesmann AG established with the incorporation of the German-Austrian Mannesmann Works AG. The new company joins the top ten corporations in the German empire |
| 1893 | The Mannesmann brothers resign from the board of directors after Deutsche Bank wrests control from the brothers |
| 1907 | Mannesmann shares trade on the German market |
| 1900–1945 | First period of expansion for the company, principally in Europe |
| 1945–1952 | Mannesmann AG liquidated by the occupying powers. The company is subdivided into three entities but recombine in 1955 |
| 1950s–1970s | Second period of expansion for the company in North and South America, and Central Asia |
| 1970 | Mannesmann and German metal works company, Thyssen Group AG, form an agreement that sees Mannesmann as the world's largest producer of tubes and pipes |
| 1970s–1990s | Mannesmann consolidates its position in the German coal, steel and iron industries. The company diversifies into machinery and plant construction, electrical and automotive industries and transform into a multinational corporation |
| 1984 | Vodafone Plc established |
| 1990 | Mannesmann celebrates its centenary |
| 1990s | The German telecommunications market is liberalised. Mannesmann expands into the telecommunications sector, with the licence to develop and operate the country's first private mobile phone network. Two-thirds of total investment during this decade is spent in the telecommunications arm. Mannesmann becomes a central player in European telecommunications |
| 1999 Annual report | Mannesmann: 130,000 employees €20.45 billion turnover P/E ratio of 56.1     Vodafone: 12,600 employees €5.62 billion turnover P/E ratio of 54.4 |
| May 1999 | Klaus Esser becomes chair of the management board |
| October 1999 | Esser announces spin-off of Mannesmann's core industrial business areas with a future specialisation solely on telecommunications. Mannesmann makes a takeover bid for Orange (UK) |
| November 1999 | Vodafone makes a friendly merger share swap offer of 43.7 Vodafone shares for 1 Mannesmann share. Mannesmann board rejects offer |
| December 1999 | Vodafone issues a share-swap-only hostile bid for Mannesmann AG for €180 billion at 53.7 Vodafone shares for 1 Mannesmann share |
| February 2000 | Vodafone Airtouch Plc takes over Mannesmann AG, successfully completing the first hostile bid for a German company. The industrial arm of Mannesmann is sold to Siemens AG |
| 2000 | The former industrial and traditional arms of Mannesmann are sold off to competitors, Bosch and Siemens. Orange is sold off to France Telecom |
| August 2001 | The final Mannesmann shareholders' meeting vote to replace company name with Vodafone |

Table C7.2 History of Mannesmann AG.

in North and South America, and Central Asia, transforming Mannesmann into a multinational corporation.

In 1970 Mannesmann and another German industrial company Thyssen formed an agreement that saw Mannesmann become the world's largest producer of tubes and pipes. From the 1970s to the 1980s Mannesmann consolidated its position in the German coal, steel and iron industries. During this period Mannesmann also diversified into machinery and plant construction, and the electrical and automotive industries. In 1990 Mannesmann celebrated its centenary coinciding with the liberalisation of the German telecommunications market. Mannesmann expanded into this sector after being granted the licence to develop and operate the country's private mobile phone network.

From 1990 to 1999 two-thirds of total company investment was funnelled into the telecommunications arm with purchases of other telecommunication companies in the European Union. By the beginning of 1999 Mannesmann was a central player in the European telecommunications industry with Vodafone, British Telecom, France Telecom, Dutch KPN and Deutsche Telecom, and telecommunications accounted for the largest share of turnover among Mannesmann's divisions (Höpner and Jackson 2001: 23). Though most of the company turnover and employees were in the engineering, automotive and pipes divisions of the company, with only 12 per cent of the employees the Mannesmann telecommunications division was delivering 68 per cent of the profit in 1998 (Table C7.3). In October 1999 two company strategies were announced:

■ Mannesmann would spin off its core industrial business area, with future specialisation concentrated on telecommunications.
■ Mannesmann issued a takeover bid for Orange a UK mobile phone company.

The following month Vodafone the pre-eminent mobile phone company and the biggest company in the UK, called for a friendly merger with Mannesmann. The German group rejected the offer and Vodafone issued a hostile bid for Mannesmann in December 1999.

By February 2000 Vodafone succeeded in taking over Mannesmann, completing the first hostile bid by a foreign company for a major German company. Mannesmann's core industrial arms were soon sold off to Siemens, Bosch and Salzgitter. Vodafone was left with Mannesmann's highly prized telecom business. Orange was sold off to France Telecom. A decade that began brightly for Mannesmann, closed with Mannesmann's demise and with it the loss of a significant part of German industrial history. This was the world's largest takeover, exceeding even the recent monster takeovers in the United States:

■ Vodafone–Mannesmann: $183bn;
■ AOL–TimeWarner: $181bn;

| Division | Sales | | Earnings | | Employees number | % |
|---|---|---|---|---|---|---|
| | Euros (million) | % | Euros (million) | % | | |
| Engineering | 6,602 | 35 | 229 | 16 | 45,503 | 40 |
| Automotive | 5,482 | 29 | 216 | 15 | 42,849 | 37 |
| Telecommunications | 4,654 | 24 | 982 | 68 | 14,081 | 12 |
| Tubes | 2,338 | 12 | 26 | 2 | 12,192 | 11 |
| Total | 19,076 | 100 | 1,453 | 100 | 114,625 | 100 |

Table C7.3 Mannesmann AG, 1998: sales, earnings and employment, by division.

Source: Adapted from Mannesmann AG Annual Report, 1998.

- MCI–WorldCom–Sprint: $127bn;
- Pfizer–Warner Lambert: $88bn;
- Exxon–Mobil: $86bn.

## MANNESMANN CORPORATE GOVERNANCE

### Management

The executive board was appointed for five-year terms by the supervisory board, though the executive board was appointed and could be dismissed with due cause by the supervisory board. In the final months of Mannesmann, Klaus Esser was the chair of the management board. Mannesmann received very good ratings for investor relations; however, even by German standards, Mannesmann's accounting practices were considered to lack transparency. One explanation of this was that Mannesmann was not capital market-oriented, and had few shareholder value-oriented performance criteria. Yet in 1999 Mannesmann accounted for one-tenth of the German share market (11.5 per cent of the DAX-30 index). Mannesmann shares were conservatively valued at €34 in 1996 but by February 2000 were valued at €300.

### Finance

In their 1999 Annual reports Mannesmann had €20.45 billion in turnover while Vodafone had €5.62 billion in turnover. Mannesmann had a price–earnings ratio of 56.1, and Vodafone 54.4. Mannesmann's price-to-book value ratio (PBR) was 1.4 in 1992, and 10.2 in 1999, while during the same period, Vodafone's PBR rose from 7.7 to 125.5. A reason why Mannesmann was less concerned with capital market performance metrics, was that traditionally German companies approached the banks for capital as opposed to going to the market. During the 1990s banks in Germany moved away from this form of relationship banking reorienting towards investment banking. Most German companies retained strong relations with a house (German) bank, but Mannesmann was unusual in this respect.

### Employees

Mannesmann had a strong history of industrial citizenship and co-determination (i.e. employee responsibility for the company), especially with employees in its core industrial business areas. This cooperative culture of the workplace is an asset in helping firms develop large reserves of internal flexibility, and employee support for incremental innovations in products and processes. Eighty per cent of the Mannesmann workforce was in the industrial arm (Hooper and Gow 1999). Mannesmann's Rhineland model of the social market economy saw strong incentives in employee investment and this model promoted high-skill internal labour markets that targeted market niches requiring a high level of skills and specialities. When Mannesmann began to develop its telecommunications business the massive transfer of investment to this area caused alienation and resentment in its traditional base. One union member from the traditional area said, 'billions were being spent on the acquisition of Orange, yet we had to fight for every hammer in the traditional business' (Höpner and Jackson 2001). Co-determination was not as developed in Mannesmann's new business, and the rate of unionism in the telecommunications business was low.

### Shareholders

Mannesmann had the most international ownership structure of any German company. For most of its life, share ownership was widely dispersed. After the Orange acquisition, the HK conglomerate had a 10.2 per cent share in Mannesmann. Forty per cent of Mannesmann shares were held by US and British institutional investors. Overall foreign investors held 60 per cent of Mannesmann shares (Table C7.4). In a sense it could be argued that Mannesmann had already

| Shareholder | Country of origin | % |
|---|---|---|
| Hutchison Whampoa | Hong Kong SAR | 10.2 |
| Capital Research & Management | USA | 2.8 |
| Schroder Investment Management | Germany | 2.1 |
| Janus Capital Corp. | USA | 1.8 |
| Templeton Investment Management | UK/Hong Kong | 1.8 |
| Deka Deutsche Kapitalgesellschaft | Germany | 1.8 |
| Deutsche Asset Management | Germany/USA/UK | 1.6 |
| Alliance Capital Management | USA | 1.5 |
| American Express Asset Management | USA | 1.1 |
| DWS Deutsche Gesellschaft für Wertpapiersparen | Germany | 1.0 |
| Fidelity Management & Research Co. | USA/UK | 0.9 |
| Foreign & Colonial Management | UK | 0.9 |
| Putnam Investment Management | USA | 0.7 |
| Commerzbank Investment Management | Germany | 0.7 |
| Dresdner Bank Investment Management | Germany | 0.7 |
| MFS Investment Management | USA | 0.7 |
| Union Investment Gesellschaft | Germany | 0.6 |
| Oppenheim Kapitalgesellschaft | Germany | 0.6 |
| UBS Brinson | Switzerland/Germany | 0.6 |
| Allianz Kapitalanlagegesellschaft | Germany | 0.6 |
| Robur Kapitalfervaltning | Sweden | 0.6 |
| Frankfurt Trust Investment Gesellschaft | Germany | 0.5 |
| Allfonds Bayerische Kapitalanlage | Germany | 0.5 |
| Universal-Investment-Gesellschaft | Germany | 0.5 |
| Mercury Asset Management | UK | 0.5 |
| Adig Allgemeine Deutsche Investment | Germany | 0.5 |
| Inka-Internationale KAG | Germany | 0.5 |
| Cumulative total, stakes of 1 per cent or more | 10 shareholders | 25.7 |
| Cumulative total, stakes of 0.5 per cent or more | 27 shareholders | 36.3 |
| Cumulative total, stakes of 0.1 per cent or more | 63 shareholders | 44.3 |
| Subtotal German institutional investors | | 13.1 |
| Subtotal UK/USA institutional investors | | 19.2 |

Table C7.4 Largest shareholders, 1999.

Source: Höpner and Jackson 2001: 26.

passed into foreign ownership, though it remained solidly under German management. Most domestic investors were from institutional banks while 7.5 per cent of Mannesmann shares were distributed amongst 130,000 Mannesmann employees. Most institutional investors held dispersed stakes (1 per cent or less) and lacked large stakes to exert control. Such stakes held little strategic incentives for holding shares (Höpner and Jackson 2001).

## THE TAKEOVER

*A landmark in Germany's momentous journey towards a different model of capitalism.*

*(Financial Times 2000)*

## Vodafone

In contrast to the century-long industrial heritage of Mannesmann, Vodafone was an

upstart enterprise, in part a result of the privatisation and liberalisation policies of the UK Thatcher government. Established in 1982 as an arm of a small electronics company to bid for the UK's first mobile phone licence, Vodafone grew astronomically during the worldwide telecommunications explosion of the 1990s. Prior to the takeover bid Vodafone and Mannesmann were publicly considered as alliance partners. The companies had joint stakes in different companies, though Vodafone was focused entirely on mobile networks. Vodafone held a large number of minority stakes in different telecommunication companies in 23 countries, and after the 1999 takeover of Airtouch (USA) Vodafone became the world's largest mobile phone provider.

Mannesmann also wanted to take advantage of the opportunities presented in the phenomenal and apparently unlimited growth in telecoms markets; however, the takeover of the UK mobile phone company Orange in October 1999 proved its undoing as 'this move threatened Vodafone's home market and rumours quickly spread that Vodafone might react by making a takeover bid for Mannesmann' (Höpner and Jackson 2001: 27). Vodafone's CEO Chris Gent in November 1999 offered a friendly merger with Mannesmann, arguing that the market value of the combined enterprise would exceed the value of the two separate companies. After the Mannesmann board rejected this offer Vodafone issued a hostile takeover bid the following month. Vodafone emphasised it was concerned by Mannesmann's takeover of Orange, condemning Mannesmann for failing to hold up its part of the unwritten alliance between them when Mannesmann became a competitor in Vodafone's home UK market.

### Public relations campaign

At this point a battle for shareholders' support began with extensive media campaigns launched for and against the takeover. Gent argued that far from being an expression of Wild West capitalism (now thriving in a hyper-speculative market), the takeover would help rationalise and develop the telecoms sector. Mannesmann countered that the telecommunications arena had considerable room for growth and Vodafone intervention would impede Mannesmann's strategic development. Vodafone responded that Mannesmann needed nurturing by Vodafone in order to succeed on a global scale (Höpner and Jackson 2001).

## MANNESMANN'S DEFENSIVE STRATEGY

Approximately 17 per cent of Mannesmann shares were in loyal hands, and the largest shareholder Hutchison Whampoa supported the management board. The many institutional investors who had small stakes in the company would decide the victor of the takeover attempt. For Esser and the board it was an uphill battle to convince institutional investors who judged the healthiness of an investment in a company by shareholder value, and who did not normally empathise with the long-term commitment of a German company to its stakeholders. To fend off Vodafone's bid the main defensive strategy pursued by Mannesmann management was to search for a 'white knight' who could repel the financial strength of Vodafone. For Mannesmann the targeted white knight came in the form of France's Vivendi with whom Esser announced partnership talks in January 2000. Vodafone's Gent immediately began negotiations with Vivendi as a possible buyer of Orange following the takeover battle, and soon after Vivendi announced a joint internet portal with Vodafone if the takeover succeeded. The white knight had joined the group of vultures circling the body of Mannesmann.

### Banks

While German banks played no role in Mannesmann's defence this was not the case with American investment banks, who were highly experienced in merger and acquisition

| Institutional banks advising Mannesmann | Institutional banks advising Vodafone |
| --- | --- |
| Morgan Stanley (advised Airtouch)<br>Merrill Lynch<br>J.P. Morgan | Goldman Sachs (advised Orange)<br>Warburg Dillon Read |

Table C7.5 The banks involved in the takeover bid.

Source: Adapted from Höpner and Jackson 2001.

deals from which they derived considerable fee income. American investment banks played significant advisory roles in the takeover bid (Table C7.5).

However, the credibility of the institutional bankers involved was undermined when it was revealed that Goldman Sachs had advised Orange in the merger with Mannesmann, while Morgan Stanley had advised Airtouch during its takeover by Vodafone. At one point, Mannesmann management petitioned a court to ban Goldman Sachs from further involvement in the takeover proceedings due to confidential Mannesmann papers Goldman Sachs would have accessed during its work for Mannesmann in the Orange takeover, but this request was turned down.

## Employees

As far as Mannesmann's employees were concerned Vodafone's objective in the takeover was Mannesmann's telecom business. With 80 per cent of jobs in Mannesman being in the non-telecom area, unions were concerned about the heavy job losses resulting from any consolidation process. The unions supported Mannesmann throughout the takeover; however, there was a feeling of having been failed by management. In the union view, management had not prepared an adequate strategy that addressed Mannesmann's diverging business areas. Mannesmann management had pursued the telecom business at the expense of the established engineering and manufacturing business Mannesmann was founded on.

## OTHER STAKEHOLDERS

### Public reaction

The German public's initial resentment at the hostile takeover by an British company soon turned into profound resignation. Discussion was dominated by the sobering fact that Vodafone was able to take over a German company five times its size due to its current market valuation. As *The Financial Times* pointed out, this Anglo-American valuation of companies by the market was a new form of capitalism that was alien to Germany. In this case, the market was largely composed of institutional investors who had little interest in the company and its social partners, except as to how it increased the return on their clients' investment portfolios. The local chamber of commerce demanded the national government institute laws preventing the break-up of corporations following hostile takeovers.

### Government

The political response underlined the nation's widespread suspicion of stock markets (Hooper and Gow 2000). Chancellor Schröder warned hostile takeovers threatened to destroy overnight the German co-deterministic corporate culture that had taken generations to develop. Concerns were raised about job losses and the flow-on effects the takeover and restructuring would have on supporting industries in the region. Most of the domestic Mannesmann employees were based in the heartland of the current ruling party. Some political parties railed

against such aggressive business tactics, while others noted Germany was on the losing side of this fundamental clash of corporate cultures. Germany increased demands from the EU to promote a more target-friendly law that would protect domestic firms in the event of hostile takeovers. For the present, it was hard to escape the conclusion that 'Rhenish capitalism becomes more Anglo-Saxon, and thus more unpleasant. Businesses will be less under the control of their supervisory boards and the banks, and more directly determined by the capital market; the voices of politicians and workers' delegates will be diminished, those of fund managers and analysts amplified. For company executives, hectic times have set in' (*Süddeutsche Zeitung* 2000).

## Shareholders

Perceived as a dynamic telecoms venture, Vodafone had a much greater market valuation than Mannesmann, and Vodafone could make a bid using only its inflated shares. Vodafone applied this financial market leverage using its shares as currency to give premiums to shareholders of Mannesman. Vodafone issued a share-swap only takeover bid of 53.7 Vodafone shares for 1 Mannesmann share. By mid-January 2000 it became clear a majority of shareholders would sell to Vodafone with foreign shareholders holding the majority of shares favouring Vodafone's takeover. (The shareholders who realised the immediate short-term gains were the biggest winners in the takeover. Mannesmann shares saw a 120 per cent rise in price or a gain of €100 million from October 1999 to February 2000.) An agreement was reached in early February between the two companies with the merged company having a 50.5 per cent/ 49.5 per cent ownership split in favour of Vodafone. The merged company was valued at €200 billion and became in 2000 – for a brief period at least – the fourth largest company in the world, and the world's largest telephone company:

- Microsoft: $532bn;
- GE: $445bn;
- Cisco Systems: $403bn;
- Vodafone: $365bn;
- NTT DoCoMo: $336bn;
- Intel: $334bn.

## Employees

After the white knight strategy failed, unions were informed of Vodafone's planned break-up of Mannesmann into legally separate corporations. Concern over job losses persisted, but once takeover was approved the employee representatives were resigned to 'accept the merger on this basis (of planned break-up)'. Financially, workers who had shares in the company did not play a decisive role as a 'notable portion of employee owners had already sold shares' (Höpner and Jackson 2001: 35). Labour representatives boycotted the shareholders' meeting immediately after takeover and abstained from voting in the February 2000 decision to approve the takeover. Distressed by the rapidity of the Mannesmann capitulation, German unions announced their plan for using pension funds and employee share ownership to promote employee-oriented corporate governance and their intention to have a voice in future investment decisions in other companies.

## Mannesmann management

Shareholder activists representing domestic and non-institutional investors accused Esser of letting Mannesmann shareholders down by not negotiating with Vodafone earlier, and by spending large amounts in the failed takeover defence against the interests of shareholders. Deep concerns were widespread in Germany regarding how the entrenched opposition of the Mannesmann management was suddenly replaced by acquiescence, and the influence that large severance payments agreed by the merged company for the Mannesmann management may have played in this sudden change of mind. Mannesmann CEO Klaus Esser received a severance payment of DM60 million, which was unheard of in Germany. Esser was accused of corruption

and of reaping financial rewards from the demise of the company.

## THE BREAK-UP OF MANNESMANN

Once Vodafone asserted its ownership over Mannesmann, Vodafone immediately set about dismantling the company according to industrial lines (see Figures C7.1 and C7.2).

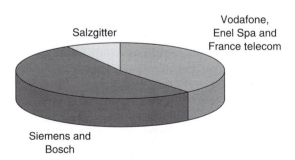

**Sales by area**

9% tubes and luxury watches

39% telecoms

52% Atecs engineering and automative

**Figure C7.1** Structure of Mannesmann, pre-takeover.

Source: Adapted from Höpner and Jackson (2001).

**Ownership by area**

Salzgitter

Vodafone, Enel Spa and France telecom

Siemens and Bosch

**Figure C7.2** Ownership structure of former Mannesmann units.

Source: Mannesmann archive website.

## Telecommunications

Infostrada was sold off to Enel Spa for €11 billion while Orange was sold off to France Telecom for €48 billion in May 2000. The unit that provoked the demise of Mannesmann did not last one year in the Mannesmann group of companies. Vodafone immediately realised a €60 billion profit from the undervalued Mannesmann telecommunications division, allowing it to concentrate on the remaining telecom units of Mannesmann/D2 and Omnitel.

## ATECS Division

The Automotive and Engineering Division (ATECS) was the main business of Mannesmann. It was Mannesmann's cash cow though its growth was nowhere as high as its telecommunications unit. ATECS had 90,000 employees worldwide, accounting for 70 per cent of Mannesmann employees and 53 per cent of its turnover. ATECS was sold off to Mannesmann's industrial rivals of Bosch and Siemens at €9.75 billion in April 2000. The ATECS division inside Siemens was broken up further. The German unions accused Vodafone's Gent of breaking his promise on job losses in the Mannesmann industrial divisions.

## Tubes

Tube production was the original product of Mannesmann and historically its core business, was sold off to Salzgitter AG for the symbolic price of one single deutschmark.

## REFLECTIONS ON A CORPORATE DEMISE

At the final shareholders' meeting of Mannesmann the shareholders voted unanimously to strike off Mannesmann from the new merged company name. Mannesmann was an anomaly in the new company, it once represented the best in German engineering, but now it had lost almost all of the elements that once made it a great business, and ceased to exist in the

new company. Striking off the Mannesmann name from the telecom business seemed the right thing to do in the circumstances, abandoning a century of industrial tradition for the promise of the new telecoms age.

## Problems within Mannesmann

Before the takeover of Mannesmann, vulnerabilities were emerging within the company. Mannesmann was already 'breaching its trust' with its employees as it continued to promote the telecommunications division at the expense of its industrial divisions in the last decade of the company's life. There was a lack of unity, and compared to other German companies, lower employee loyalty as Mannesmann's focus shifted from the industrial to telecommunications. The relatively weak support from the unions during the takeover was blamed on the previous lack of management support for industrial divisions and its unconvincing strategy on the strategic reorganisation of the increasingly diverging businesses of Mannesmann. Secondly, Mannesmann's management main defensive strategy during the takeover was singularly ill-conceived when it had a fragmented ownership structure and did not have majority support from non-management quarters. Using an unreliable partner such as Vivendi to fend off a tough opponent like Vodafone simply made

things worse for Mannesmann. Why Mannesmann management suddenly capitulated remained a mystery. It is possible Mannesmann was determined to become a focused telecommunications company, in which case the Vodafone takeover simply accelerated the process.

## German corporate culture

Before the Mannesmann takeover German companies in the 1990s acquired a series of British finance houses such as Morgan Grenfell and Kleinwort Benson, and engineering companies such as Rolls-Royce Motors and Rover Cars, and the political response to the Vodafone takeover was constrained by this precedent (Table C7.6). Some of Mannesmann's problems were unique such as its fragmented and international ownership, which indicates a slow subjection to Anglo-American ownership and governance structures, preceding the shock of the takeover. The reaction of domestic institutional investors though highlighted the willingness of at least one sector of German society to move towards a corporate culture where shareholder value is supreme.

The Mannesmann takeover demonstrated a profound inertia and deep resistance in Germany towards the global trend of emphasising the importance of shareholder value above

| UK company | Paid | Date | By German company |
|---|---|---|---|
| Thomas Cook | | Sept. 1999 | Preussaq |
| Morgan Grenfell | £844 million | 31 Jan. 1990 | Deutsche Bank |
| Keinwort Benson | £1 billion | Aug. 1995 | Dresdner RCM |
| Rover | £800 million | March 1995 | BMW |
| Rolls Royce | £470 million | | Volkswagen and BMW |
| Cornhill Insurance | £305 million | Jan. 1986 | Allianz |
| Lloyds Chemists | £684 million | Jan. 1997 | Gehe |
| One2one | £8.4 billion | Aug. 2006 | Deutsche Telekom |
| Freemans | £150 million | April 2006 | Otto Versand |

Table C7.6 Takeover of UK companies by German companies, 1986–2006.

all corporate objectives (Hooper and Gow 2000). The takeover proved to be a watershed in this sense of disquiet towards the apparently irresistible advance of the market system, and the loss of Mannesmann was a great psychological blow to the German industrial psyche. In consequence, at least one approach in Germany is developing a novel hybrid model of governance characterised by the institutionalised participation of labour within an increasingly open capital market (Höpner and Jackson 2001: 48).

## THE LONG AND BLOODY AFTERMATH OF THE TAKEOVER

It took six years for the events to fully unfold – which revealed there were darker dimensions to the Vodafone takeover of Mannesmann than suspected by the critics of the deal at the time. In many respects, the different fears of both the German and British opponents of the takeover were fully vindicated, with the announcement by Vodafone in February 2006 that its assets might be overvalued by as much as $48 billion, as revealed in the retrospective verdict of the *Financial Times*.

'Vodafone's epic battle for Mannesmann, sealed in February 2000, symbolised an era of record-breaking and gravity-defying deals, fuelled by inflated stock prices. The millennial merger frenzy began as a defensive response to the German company's surprise bid for Orange in October 1999. Vodafone felt it could not afford to see its dominance challenged so close to home and drew up audacious plans for a hostile response. As investor excitement grew, valuations climbed beyond anything that could be justified by current cash flow. Vodafone and its advisers brushed away such concerns with predictions of vast new revenue streams from video calls, TV downloads and online commerce. Only later did a second justification emerge: Vodafone began to argue that it did not matter that it had paid an inflated price, because it was paying with an inflated currency – its own shares. When the £112bn ($195bn) deal was completed, Vodafone was the fourth most valuable company in the

world. Yesterday's write down of assets, most of which were inherited from Mannesmann, was the clearest financial acknowledgement yet of just how overvalued the deal was' (27 February 2006).

## Vodafone's deconstruction

In fact Vodafone's share price began to collapse immediately the deal was done in 2000, and lost around 60 per cent of its value within two years with Vodafone's market capitalisation reduced by $200 billion. Vodafone's share price – the critical instrument by which it had seized control of Mannesmann – proved to be a massively inflated currency (Figure C7.3). It is true that during this period all of the large telecoms companies experienced a precipitous fall in their market capitalisation, as the market realised that the stunning claims of exponential growth in demand for mobile and data telecoms invented by WorldCom and enthusiastically supported by the self-aggrandising fantasies of most other telecoms executives were proved to be false. By this time the dramatic growth of the company achieved by the combination of successive acquisitions and rapid market growth in the mobile telephony sector which had fuelled the meteoric and massive rise in Vodafone's share price was long since over.

The hasty construction of the company often motivated by little more than aggressive executive ambition for growth and the spoils of war, was replaced by a prolonged and painful deconstruction of the company which could not manage its aspirations in a more competitive market with rapid technological advances which Vodafone failed to keep up with. Instead of contemplating the next vaulting acquisition, Vodafone degenerated into boardroom in-fighting as it failed to come to terms with new market and technological challenges. 'The boardroom at Vodafone is looking more like a faction-wracked politburo than the inner sanctum of one of the world's most admired companies. The mobile phone giant descended toward chaos last week as murky plots to undermine key executives were uncovered, and parried with retaliatory sackings and

**Figure C7.3** Vodafone–Mannesman historical stock prices, 1998–2006.

Source: LSE and NYSE Data 2006, http://www.vodafone.com/article/0,3029,CATEGORY_ID%253D411%2526LANGUAGE_ID%253D0%2526CONTENT_ID%253D231032,00.html

demands from nameless directors and share-holders for the ousting of the corporate old guard' (*Observer,* 12 March 2006).

Chris Gent faced a revolt by 30 per cent of Vodafone shareholders in July 2000 when awarded a £5 million cash bonus and 5 million in shares following the Mannesmann merger. With the company looking less certain about its future, he retired from Vodafone as CEO in December 2003, to be succeeded by Arun Sarin who had spent most of his career in the United States. At first Chris Gent retained the title of 'life president' of Vodafone, but this did not last, as Arun Sarin tried to redirect Vodafone: 'Sarin has to correct the problems left by Chris Gent. These are that Vodafone has not embraced convergence of technologies – broadband, information technology and TV, and it has not embraced the internet. So, while companies like BT are set to launch free internet TV services and Voice over Internet Protocol (VoIP) services this year, Vodafone has no

plans to follow. Voice and text revenues are going to fall, and 3G has not done well in the market best suited to it – Japan. Sarin has to come up with something. This is a power struggle between the management and the old guard who are at risk of being embarrassed because they did not face up to it' (*Observer,* 12 March 2006).

## Mannesmann directors on trial

The fate of the Mannesmann directors was much more humiliating. German prosecutors began investigations in 2001 that payments made to Mannesmann directors at the time of the takeover, totalling 120 million Deutschmarks ($56 million) were legal. Klaus Essen the Mannesmann CEO was targeted for his DM60 million severance pay. Vodafone responded to investigators that the company had no contract with Mannesmann directors

until they had agreed the merger. The allegations went to trial in Dusseldorf in 2004 with the state prosecutors calling for two year prison sentences for Deutsche Bank chair Josef Ackermann for his part in the Mannesmann bonuses as a member of the company supervisory board, and for a two and half year sentence for Klaus Esser, and three years for former chair Joachim Funk.

According to the BBC (21 January 2004), this was a clash of business cultures in deciding whether the money awarded to the Mannesmann directors was a bonus or a bribe. 'We have this fight between the German and the Anglo-American economic models', said Bernhard May from the German Economic Institute (DIW). 'We still have the model here in Germany that you're responsible for the whole company, including the people working there, while the American and maybe the British model is more that the CEO is responsible to the shareholders. Here you can see that selling Mannesmann took care of the shareholders while knowing that the workers would lose their jobs. The legal case against the directors was that they had committed *untreue* – or breach of fiduciary duty.

Kolla (2004: 4) outlines the case as:

On February 2, 2000, the day on which Esser and Christopher Gent, then CEO of Vodafone, concluded the takeover, Esser was awarded the €15 million appreciation award at the behest of Mannesmann's largest shareholder, Hong Kong based conglomerate Hutchison Whampoa. The compensation committee approved Esser's award on February 4, along with the other bonuses, which included a €3.1 million bonus for Joachim Funk that was suggested and voted upon by Funk himself. Irregularities in the approval process for the awards prompted a recall of the compensation committee and on February 28 they re-approved all the bonuses. By this time, Düsseldorf's public prosecutor had already received complaints concerning the legality of the awards, which eventually led to a public inquiry that culminated in the 2004 criminal trial.

All the defendants were found not guilty by the Dusseldorf court; however, the prosecutors appealed to the German Federal Court of Justice which in 2005 overruled the Dusseldorf district court's acquittal. Though Chris Gent appeared in the 2004 trial he refused to appear as a witness in the 2006 retrial of his Mannesmann colleagues. Ackerman and his defence team argued that big payouts to executives are common in the US and Britain, and are needed to motivate corporate leaders to take risks. Prosecutors contended that the payments were illegal because they were designed to persuade managers, and Esser in particular, to drop their resistance to Vodafone's bid after the long takeover battle.

A settlement finally came on 24 November 2006 with Ackermann, the chief executive of Deutsche Bank, agreeing to pay €3.2 million, or $4.2 million, as part of a settlement. Klaus Esser, the company's former chief executive agreed to pay €1.5 million. In return for the payments prosecutors agreed to drop charges of criminal breach of trust. Mark Landler writing in Germany for the *New York Times* concluded:

Through six years of investigations, a trial, an acquittal, and yet another trial, the Mannesmann case has come to symbolize the abiding resentment of many Germans for the sky-high executive compensation packages that are common in the United States, but still fairly unusual here. While this case is now almost certain to end without a conviction, legal experts said that the size of the financial penalties would make board members at other German companies think twice before giving top executives anything beyond the euros stipulated in their contracts.

(24 November 2006)

## Questions

1 Do you agree with Höpner and Jackson's claim that Anglo-American institutional investors were ultimately the reason behind Vodafone's takeover success?

2 'In Germany mergers and takeovers are a complement to internal organic growth of companies, rather than a substitute for this as in the US and UK market based systems'. Discuss.

3 Examine the reasons for the ineffective defensive tactics of Mannesmann, that allowed Vodafone to acquire a much larger company than itself.

4 Assess the future viability of the German model of corporate governance in the light of the Mannesmann takeover and subsequent events.

5 Are there any parallels between the use of inflated share prices in the late 1990s as an instrument of acquisition, with the use of low interest debt in the 2000s to achieve the same objective by private equity and hedge funds?

## REFERENCES

BBC News Archive (2000) *Vodafone v. Mannesmann*, http://news.bbc.co.uk/1/hi/business/621222.stm, news.bbc.co.uk/1/hi/ business/630293.stm

Berggren, C. (2003) Mergers, MNEs, and Innovation, *Scandinavian Journal of Management*, www.eki.liu.se/content/1/c4/52/40/**berggren**_mergers_multinationals_and_innovation_pdf.pdf

Black, Bernard S. (2000) The First International Merger Wave (and the Fifth and Last US Wave), *University of Miami Law Review*, 54: 799–818, SSRN: http://ssrn.com/abstract=231101

Cioffi, J.W. (2002) Restructuring 'Germany Inc': The Politics of Company and Takeover Reform in Germany and the European Union, *Law and Policy*, 24(4): 355–402.

European Industrial Relations Observatory (1999) *Vodafone's Hostile Takeover Bid for Mannesmann Highlights Debate on the German Capitalist Model*, http://www.eiro.eurofound.eu.int/1999/11/feature/de9911220f.html

Hooper, D. and Gow, D. (1999) *We're Talking Telephone Numbers*, Guardian Unlimited, 23 November, http://www.guardian.co.uk/g2/story/0,3604,252459,00.html

Höpner, M. and Jackson, G. (2001) *An Emerging Market for Corporate Control? The Mannessmann Takeover and German Corporate Governance*, Max Planck Institute: Cologne, http://papers.ssrn.com

Kolla, P. (2004) The Mannesmann Trial and the Role of the Courts, *German Law Journal*, 5(7).

Landler, M. (2006) *Deutsche Bank Executives to Pay Penalties in Settlement Over Bonuses*, New York Times, 24 November, http://www.iht.com/articles/2006/11/24/business/deutsche.php

Maier, S. (2006) A Close Look at the Mannesmann Trial, *German Law Journal*, 6(1).

Mannesmann (2003) *The Mannesmann Archive*, http://www.mannesmann-archiv.de

Plender, J. and Simonian, H. (2000) Whirlwinds of Change, *Financial Times* 4 February.

Register, http://www.theregister.co.uk/2001/11/06/vodafone_mannesmann_multimillion_payouts_not/

Schmid, F.A. and Wahrenburg, M. (2002) *Mergers and Acquisitions in Germany*, Working Paper 2002-027A, Federal Reserve Bank of St Louis, http://research.stlouisfed.org/wp/2002/2002-027.pdf

Tricker, R.I. (1994) *International Corporate Governance: Texts, Readings and Cases*, Singapore: Simon and Schuster.

# Asia Pacific Corporations

# Case Study 8
# James Hardie

## EXECUTIVE SUMMARY

James Hardie Industries was the most successful and well-established building materials company in Australia. In the 1990s increasing evidence emerged that many former employees and customers of its widely used asbestos products had contracted the killer lung disease mesothelioma. Instead of facing up to its corporate responsibilities, James Hardie dismissed the evidence, evaded accountability, and it appears attempted to abandon many of its victims by moving its company base to the Netherlands. The public exposure and present effort to remedy the corporate irresponsibility of James Hardie, is a dramatic test of the standards of business ethics and corporate governance in Australia.

Asbestos was used in the building industry throughout much of the twentieth century in the manufacture of sheeting and roofing, pipes and insulation materials, brake linings and other friction products. The release of its fibres can give rise to asbestosis, lung cancer, pleural diseases and mesothelioma. These diseases may take many years to manifest themselves, and a very slight exposure to asbestos fibres may lead to mesothelioma up to 40 years later, when the disease is often short, painful and fatal.

James Hardie ceased the manufacture of asbestos products finally in 1987, and the liabilities from that point began to be regarded as a 'legacy' issue, part of the 'rump' of the old company as the new company expanded its markets and horizons in Europe and the United States. This inhuman negligence of the company was roundly condemned by David Jackson, the Commissioner of the Special

Commission of Inquiry into this affair called by the New South Wales government: 'The notion that the holding company would make the cheapest provision thought "marketable" in respect of those liabilities so that it could go off to pursue its more lucrative interests insulated from those liabilities is singularly unattractive. Why should the victims and the public bear the cost not provided for?' (Jackson Report 2004: 13)

## ORIGINS OF JAMES HARDIE AND ASBESTOS MANUFACTURE

James Hardie Industries Limited (JHIL) and its wholly owned subsidiaries James Hardie & Coy Pty Ltd which manufactured and marketed asbestos products until 1987 and Jsekarb Pty Ltd which manufactured brake linings began manufacturing asbestos in 1916. Asbestos fibre was thought to be a 'wonder' product – it was strong, light and fireproof and was widely used in the manufacture of building products and insulation. Asbestos cement sheeting was the staple product of the post-World War II building boom in Australia where it was well suited due to its low cost, durability, and fire retarding qualities in a climate warm enough to require little additional insulation. Australia became one of the largest users of asbestos products in construction, shipping, motor vehicles and electrical and power generation plants. James Hardie developed into the largest building supplier in the country, and its growth was based so much on asbestos that until 1979 the stock exchange listed company was called James Hardie Asbestos, and the group's

imposing headquarters in Sydney was called Asbestos House.

The first indication of an association between asbestos and lung disease occurred in the medical journals in the 1930s. As early as 1957 a report by the Victorian State Health Department found 539 cases of lung damage and recommended that it was imperative that conditions improve in industries involving dust such as asbestos. By 1966 newspapers were carrying headlines such as 'Urgent Probe into New Killer Dust Disease' based on an article in the *British Journal of Industrial Medicine*. Though they knew of this growing evidence of the danger of its products, and by the end of the 1970s a total of 250 companies associated with asbestos were being sued in the United States, the James Hardie senior management took decades more to begin to face this reality and cease using these materials. Even very minimal exposure to asbestos fibre can cause pleural disease, asbestosis, lung cancer and/or mesothelioma, a painful disease of the lung cavity that is usually fatal. Those in control of the James Hardie companies knew, or ought to have known, of the dangers of asbestos and should have taken measures to guard against the risk of injury of their employees and customers. 'Hardie's workers were unaware of the risks to which they were exposed; Hardie failed in its duty to protect them and others exposed to like dangers through use of its products. A body of evidence indicates that it preferred engineering solutions that minimised commercial disruption to those that focused on the needs of workers and users themselves' (Redmond 2006: 22; Haigh 2006: 14–15). By negligently allowing both employees and consumers to be exposed to asbestos, JHIL and its subsidiaries were found responsible and legally liable to provide compensation to the victims of asbestos disease and/or their families, and a succession of cases were heard at the NSW Dust Diseases Tribunal in the 1970s and 1980s in which James Hardie was held liable.

When confronted by a rising number of James Hardie workers contracting these diseases and claiming compensation in the 1990s, the executive management of the company remained in denial. The company established the Medical Research and Compensation Foundation in 2001 to compensate victims, and declared: 'The Foundation will concentrate on managing its substantial assets for the benefit of claimants. Its establishment has effectively resolved James Hardie's asbestos liability and this will allow management to focus on growing the company for the benefit of shareholders' (Jackson Report 2004: 29). The company responsible for most of the cases was James Hardie Coy (renamed Amaca) as it was the primary manufacturing entity from 1937 to 1987. Because the disease can have a 40 year latency period (between exposure and the onset of illness) it was likely there would be many more successful cases brought against Amaca into the future. Potential claimants included not only past employees of James Hardie, but also carpenters and builders who used the building materials, as well as those unfortunate enough to live near the asbestos manufacturing factories or become exposed to the asbestos used in their homes. (The other major company involved for a time in asbestos manufacturing in Australia was CSR, which had extensive asbestos mining and milling operations in Western Australia, where because of low occupational safety standards there was enormous loss of life to asbestos related diseases.)

## NEW BUSINESS FRONTIERS

Despite this tragic history the James Hardie Group managed to build up a successful new business after abandoning asbestos. It acquired a US company that made a non-asbestos fibre cement, and steadily built up a considerable business in the house building industry in the United States. By the late 1990s James Hardie's Australian operations represented only 15 per cent of its global operations. However, the further development of its US business was starting to be held back by its asbestos liabilities in Australia. The company was finding it difficult to raise funds in the US due to investors' concerns over the potential cost of its history in asbestos (Jackson Report 2004: 2.7). Also, shareholders' returns

were being diminished by the tax implications of transferring revenues from the US to Australia.

The James Hardie Group (JHIL) needed to somehow contain or quantify its asbestos liabilities if it was to be able to grow the business, and it also needed to find a more tax-efficient method of transferring its US revenues back to Australia. A successful and efficient US business would also benefit asbestos victims because they could only be compensated if the company was continuing to produce sufficient profit to meet all its present liabilities, and sustain its development for the long term to meet future liabilities. JHIL identified several options for dealing with the difficult problem of its asbestos history (Jackson Report 2004: 11.7). The chosen option was to restructure the group so as to separate its current operating business from the Australian liabilities. This involved moving the operating assets to a tax-efficient Dutch company (JHNV) and then transferring James Hardie and Coy and Jsekarb (the companies with most of the asbestos liabilities) to an Australian holding company the Medical Research and Compensation Foundation (MRCF) that would act as a trust and manage the claims made against James Hardie and Coy and Jsekarb Pty Ltd.

There was an awareness that this process would have to be managed very carefully if it was not to rebound on James Hardie. Several companies in the US with similar asbestos issues had managed separation badly and ended up mired in litigation and hostile press. It was at this point James Hardie moved its corporate headquarters overseas, having put $293 million into the Foundation, and assuring the Supreme Court of NSW that a further $1.9 billion was available to fund the liabilities of the remaining James Hardie companies in Australia. Yet as the Foundation quickly exhausted the money available for compensation as the number of victims increased, James Hardie cancelled the access to the further $1.9 million in funds through its Australian subsidiaries. Although the separation apparently had been carried out without incident in 2001, James Hardie's misdeeds caught up with them in 2003/04 (Table C8.1).

## The scandal leading to a government inquiry

The scandal broke when in October 2003 the directors of MRCF announced publicly that the Foundation was severely under-funded. There was public outrage at the perception that the company had irresponsibly transferred its assets to the Netherlands leaving asbestos victims to suffer uncompensated in Australia.

| | |
|---|---|
| 1916 | JHIL starts manufacturing asbestos |
| 1937 | Coy becomes the manufacturing company |
| 1930s | Information becomes available on the dangers to health posed by asbestos |
| 1956 | First successful workers' compensation case for asbestos injury |
| 1960s | Information becomes available that asbestos is dangerous even at very low concentrations |
| 1985 | First successful common law case for asbestos injury (most others settled prior to verdict) |
| 1987 | Hardie ceases manufacturing asbestos products |
| 1989 | NSW Dust Diseases Tribunal created |
| 1990s | Operating and other assets are moved out of Coy into other Hardie Group companies |
| 1995 | Group fails at attempt to raise finance in USA |
| 2001 | Transfer of Coy from the Hardie Group to MRCF |
| | Movement of the Group holding company to the Netherlands |
| 2003 | MRCF indicates that it is under-funded |
| 2004 | Special Commission of Inquiry headed by David Jackson QC |
| 2005 | Funding arrangements agreed between Hardie and NSW Government |
| | Legal reforms proposed |

Table C8.1 James Hardie timeline.

Not only was this seen as morally wrong but financially it would mean that the cost of caring for the victims would fall upon the Australian government and its tax-payers. The foundation directors endeavoured to secure further substantial funds from James Hardie, but when this failed, the commission of inquiry was called. In February 2004 the NSW government set up a special commission headed by David Jackson QC to investigate the events leading to the under-funding of the MRCF and to make recommendations as to how the situation might be remedied. As the senior executives of the company were hauled in front of the inquiry the moral and legal fabrications the company had elaborately constructed, collapsed under public questioning. In one of the most withering interviews in the history of Australian broadcasting Kerry O'Brien on the *ABC 7-30 Report* asked Meredith Hellicar a long standing director if she had ever met one of the victims of the company. Admitting she had not, Hellicar in the interview seemed more concerned with the financial interests of shareholders. The actions of the company had become a political and legal scandal in the country, with both state and federal government determined to see the company live up to its obligations. The commission of inquiry fully exposed the moral bankruptcy of the company behind their sophisticated legal pretensions.

Through the long process of discussing restructuring models, Hardie's directors and managers were persistently advised that 'directors could not provide … more than that for which JHIL was legally responsible, without honestly believing that … what they were doing was of benefit to JHIL's shareholders'. When the foundation's funding had been clearly revealed as inadequate, the company justified its refusal to augment funding on the grounds that 'there can be no legal or other legitimate basis on which [JHIL] shareholders' funds can be used to provide additional funds to the Foundation and the duties of the company's directors preclude them from doing so' (Jackson Report 2004: 30.22). Like advice was earlier given that directors' duties would prevent provision for future claimants. Redmond (2006: 4) identifies three critical decisions made by James

Hardie directors which indicate the morally inhibiting influence of this constricted definition of directors' duties, and thrall of shareholder value:

- First, was the decision taken to cut the asbestos subsidiaries adrift without adequate funding to meet future claims.
- Second, even if the initial underfunding was unintentional, the foundation quickly informed Hardie of the inadequacy. Yet, for over three years, Hardie obdurately refused to supplement funding.
- Third, the decision to cut the potential funding lifeline for asbestos victims constituted by the partly paid shares in JHIL held by JHI NV. For this release of an obligation of $1.9 billion, JHIL received no advantage.

As Redmond concludes, 'Each of these decisions was driven by the interest of Hardie shareholders. What is missing in each is a concern for their effect upon those injured by past asbestos operations. That effect was profound and direct. The issues before directors and managers posed are seen in terms of the legal construction of the social reality of the situation, rather than in terms of their effect on individuals whose lives have been or will be painfully diminished by making or using the group's products. The human lives affected by the decisions are obscured from view, not part of the utility calculus except in so far as they may generate adverse governmental action. The legal imperatives of directors' duties and shareholder value, no less than those of separate personality and limited liability, conspired to obscure the human dimension of the problem. Their logic diminished the range of perspectives brought to the board table and displaced concern for the human consequences of the decisions' (2006: 5).

## THE RESTRUCTURING OF THE JAMES HARDIE GROUP

The inquiry was charged with examining the events leading to the separation of MRCF

from the James Hardie Group as well as the circumstances surrounding the separation process itself. It was asked to report on whether these events had contributed to the inability of the foundation to meet its asbestos liabilities. The restructuring involved a series of complex manoeuvres, the four key steps were as follows:

1 During the 1990s assets were transferred out of James Hardie and Coy into other group companies so that it was no longer an operating company.
2 In February 2001, James Hardie and Coy and Jsekarb Pty were separated from the main body of the James Hardie Group and placed in a foundation (MRCF).
3 In October 2001 the James Hardie Group was restructured such that its ultimate holding company was in the Netherlands not Australia.
4 In March 2003 JHIL was separated from the James Hardie Group and placed in another foundation (the ABN 60 Foundation).

## 1990s asset transfers out of James Hardie and Coy

During the late 1990s assets were moved out of James Hardie and Coy (the subsidiary with the largest exposure to asbestos liabilities) meaning that it was no longer able to earn profits in order to pay its liabilities. It was necessary for Commissioner Jackson to examine these transactions to see if any of them had been illegal or had contributed to the under-funding of MCRF. The key transactions were as follows (see Figure C8.1):

1 In 1995 James Hardie and Coy's core technology was sold to James Hardie Research Pty Ltd (JHR).
2 Between 1996 and 1997 significant dividends were paid from James Hardie and Coy to its shareholder JHIL. Also over the period 1990 to 1998 significant management fees were paid by James Hardie and Coy to JHIL.

Figure C8.1 The transfer of the assets of James Hardie & Coy and Jsekarb Pty.

3 In 1998 James Hardie and Coy sold:

(a) most of its plant and equipment to James Hardie Fibre Cement Pty Ltd;
(b) its trademarks to JHR; and
(c) its remaining assets (used to conduct the fibre cement business in Australia) to a new operating entity JHA, which was owned by a Dutch company JHNV.

After these transfer transactions James Hardie and Coy was left as a shell company, its assets consisting primarily of the proceeds of the various sales. The question for Jackson QC was whether there was anything suspicious behind these transfers. Had JHIL intended to avoid paying James Hardie Coy's asbestos liabilities by transferring these assets? His conclusion was that, for the most part, everything was above board. The 1995 sale of core technology 'occurred for perfectly sensible business reasons' (Jackson Report 2004: 1.29) and the 1998 asset sales had been at fair value (Jackson Report 2004: 1.29; 1.32). Although the 1998 transfers made the operating assets unavailable to asbestos claimants the company had 'quite adequate funds to pay its creditors as their debts fell due, and was doing so'. As for the significant dividends and management fees paid to JHIL, Jackson QC appeared to think they were borderline, i.e. there was a

chance, but not a good chance that they could be challenged successfully (Jackson Report 2004: 1.30–1.35). Overall however he considered that: 'The transfers of assets which took place within the James Hardie Group prior to February 2001 have not so far affected the ability of the Foundation to pay asbestos-related liabilities' (Jackson Report 2004: 1.36).

## February 2001: separation of James Hardie and Coy and Jsekarb Pty

The actual process of formally separating the bulk of the James Hardie Group's asbestos liabilities from its operating activities was authorised by the JHIL board on 15 February 2001. It involved setting up a new company, the Medical Research and Compensation Foundation (MRCF) as the ultimate parent of James Hardie and Coy and Jsekarb Pty (see Figure C8.2). After separation JHIL no longer owned either of those companies or their liabilities. To insure against the possibility of either James Hardie and Coy, Jsekarb Pty or asbestos victims trying to claim against JHIL in future an agreement was signed. It involved James Hardie and Coy and Jsekarb Pty agreeing (1) to indemnify JHIL in relation to any asbestos-related claims; and (2) not to make claims themselves against JHIL. The board of James Hardie and Coy when

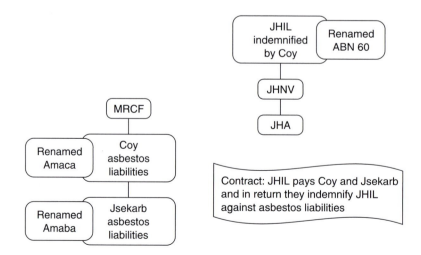

**Figure C8.2** James Hardie & Coy and Jsekarb Pty renamed and separated from James Hardie Group.

it made this agreement contained two directors from the James Hardie Group, who subsequently resigned from the James Hardie and Coy board. In return JHIL would make regular payments to James Hardie and Coy & Jsekarb Pty for a certain period into the future (Jackson Report 2004: 2.34). Also around this time the Group companies with asbestos liabilities were renamed James Hardie and Coy as Amaca; Jsekarb Pty as Amaba; and JHIL as ABN 60.

It was this process that left MRCF underfunded. James Hardie and Coy and Jsekarb Pty's assets (including the amounts to be paid by JHIL in return for the indemnity) amounted to about $293 million. The belief – if there was one – that this was enough to cover future claims, was based on an actuarial report (the Trowbridge report) which estimated James Hardie and Coy and Jsekarb Pty's asbestos liabilities at $286 million. In contrast, Commissioner Jackson considered that their asbestos liabilities would not be less than $1.5 billion (Jackson Report 2004: 1.6). It was how this huge under-funding was permitted to occur that became the focus of intense public concern.

## October 2001 scheme of arrangement

The next step in the separation process was to restructure the James Hardie Group into a Dutch holding company. The restructure was achieved by way of a scheme of arrangement approved by Justice Santow of the Supreme Court of New South Wales in accordance with section 411 of the *Corporations Act*. Rather than JHIL (with its asbestos history) being the parent of the group, Dutch JHI NV became the ultimate holding company (Figure C8.3). Shareholders swapped their shares in JHIL for shares in JHI NV. Thus JHI NV became the parent of both JHIL and JHNV (the company with the operating assets). An important aspect of the scheme was that JHI NV subscribed for partly paid shares in JHIL. This meant that if JHIL's funds ever became low in future (for example, in the event of successful litigation against it) the company would be able to call on JHI NV to pay the full price for the shares.

**Figure C8.3** Dutch Company JHI NV becomes holding company of group.

The main issue for Commissioner Jackson was whether relevant information had been withheld from Justice Santow which if disclosed, would have resulted in him refusing to approve the scheme. Although Jackson QC thought that there should have been disclosure of the fact that future cancellation of the partly paid shares was likely he was not sure it would have had a significant effect: 'Nor is it clear that if disclosure had been made, subsequent events would have turned out differently' (Jackson Report 2004: 25.91).

## March 2003 separation of JHIL

The final step in the separation process was to remove JHIL (now called ABN 60) from the James Hardie Group because it was the only remaining company with asbestos liabilities. It was offered to MRCF but on terms that were refused by the directors of MRCF. Instead it was transferred to a second foundation set up outside of the group, called the ABN 60 Foundation (Figure C8.4). As part of the process, the partly

Figure C8.4 JHIL removed from James Hardie group into ABN 60 Foundation.

sent to the stock exchange. This cancellation of a large potential source of funds was made when it was already realised there was a potential serious shortfall in Amaca's ability to meet its asbestos related liabilities, and earlier JHIL had informed the NSW court hearing that JHIL 'has access to capital of the group through the partly paid shares' (Jackson Report 2004: 25.21, 27.91; Redmond 2006: 28). Nevertheless, Commisioner Jackson concluded: 'On the evidence before me, I would not be prepared to find that the directors of ABN 60 breached their duty in canceling the partly paid shares, notwithstanding a lingering lack of enthusiasm for the commercial morality of the transaction'.

## The under-funding of the foundation

Much of the blame for the under-funding of the asbestos liabilities that were to be met by the foundation fell upon two of the James Hardie Group's senior executives, Peter Macdonald (managing director and chief executive officer) and Peter Shafron (senior vice-president finance & legal). Jackson found: 'In so far as Mr Macdonald and Mr Shafron are concerned, in my view they breached their duties as officers of JHIL by encouraging the Board to act on the Trowbridge report in forming a view that the Foundation would be "fully funded"' (2004: 24.82). The Trowbridge report was the key document relied upon by the board of JHIL in determining the funding that was provided to MRCF. It was also relied upon by the incoming board of MRCF in accepting that level of funding. Soon after the separation it became apparent that the Trowbridge report massively underestimated the amount that the fund would need to meet the asbestos liabilities. This was because the report had not been prepared for the purpose for which it was ultimately used. The report was simply an assessment of exposure to asbestos claims and was based on:

paid shares held by JHI NV were cancelled effectively depriving JHIL/ABN 60 of $1.9 billion of funds. Putting aside the issue of the partly paid shares, Commissioner Jackson did not consider this transaction to be significant: 'The creation of the ABN 60 Foundation considered separately from the Deed of Covenant, Indemnity and Access [an entirely advantageous transaction from ABN 60's point of view] had no impact on its financial position. It simply replaced one shareholder with another' (Jackson Report 2004: 27.121).

When it came to the partly paid shares he considered it to be another rather borderline transaction. Why did the directors of ABN 60 effectively give away $1.9 billion? They should have been acting in the best interests of ABN 60 but due to connections with the Dutch group they appeared not to have given 'real, independent consideration to the transaction'. The only two directors of JHIL were both executives of the Hardie group of companies, and JHI NV gave nothing of value in exchange for the transaction. Though a return was lodged with the corporate regulator, no notice was

- a model that resulted in a 'most likely' or 50 per cent chance of being accurate (unsuitable for a closed compensation fund);

- high rates of return for the companies' investments (too optimistic for a long-term fund); and
- low asbestos claim numbers which were not supported by the most recent data (because JHIL inexcusably did not provide this data to Trowbridge).

The key question was how such an unsuitable report had been relied upon – was it an innocent mistake or was it intentional? Jackson concluded, 'The evidence discussed so far makes it, to my mind, absolutely clear that JHIL, in permitting the incoming directors and outgoing directors to rely on the Trowbridge Report, engaged in conduct that was misleading and deceptive in contravention of s 52 of the Trade Practices Act, because that report was wholly unsuitable to be used for the purposes of assessing the likely life of the Foundation, and JHIL had no reasonable basis for implying that it was' (2004: 24.80).

This misleading and deceptive conduct included the issuing of a media release on 16 February 2001 containing the following important statement: 'The foundation has sufficient funds to meet all legitimate compensation claims anticipated from people injured by asbestos products that were manufactured in the past by two former subsidiaries of JHI' (Jackson Report 2004: 22.4). This was not true and officers of JHIL knew this. Why did they act in this hasty and deceiving manner? One of the key factors appears to be time pressure. In James Hardie there was a fear of a new Australian accounting standard ED 88 likely to come into force in 2001 which would require explicit disclosure of the size of the group's asbestos liabilities. It seems that both management and board were under great pressure to achieve separation by this deadline, whether the estimate of liability was accurate or not. As a result of the inquiry deliberations, at a very late stage JHI NV admitted that the foundation had been very seriously underfunded, and the commissioner found the value of likely asbestos claims in future years was about $1.5 billion, when the net assets of Amaca and the foundation were $180 million.

## JAMES HARDIE CAPITULATES

The very public scandal resulted in great harm to James Hardie's reputation, and to the reputations of its directors and executives. The company's share price suffered badly, with the possibility of more permanent damage if the affair was not quickly resolved (Figure C8.5). After release of the inquiry report in September 2004 both CEO Peter Macdonald and CFO Peter Shafron stood down from their positions, and shortly afterwards they both resigned. The New South Wales government delegated the Australian Council of Trade Unions to conduct negotiations with James Hardie concerning funding arrangements for the companies' future asbestos liabilities.

When negotiations stalled, the NSW government announced that it was drafting legislation to allow asbestos victims to claim compensation from JHI NV, wind back the 2001 restructuring and relocation to the Netherlands, and rescind the cancellation of the partly paid shares in JHIL. On 21 December 2004 James Hardie Industries NV signed Heads of Agreement with the NSW government, the Australian Council of Trade Unions and asbestos victims groups. 'The Heads of Agreement was an interim, non-binding agreement intended to be replaced with a binding and legally enforceable agreement in substantially similar terms. That Final Agreement was signed on 1 December 2005. It is undoubtedly the largest corporate settlement in Australia' (Redmond 2006: 31). The path-breaking agreement provided funding for the next forty years, which offered to meet future liabilities as fully as the company had the capacity to do:

> James Hardie will provide funding on a long-term basis to a Special Purpose Fund to compensate asbestos sufferers with claims against the former Hardie subsidiaries. The Fund will be substituted by legislation for the former asbestos subsidiaries as the entity responsible for James Hardie asbestos compensation. James Hardie will appoint a majority of the governing board of the Fund. At the start of each year James Hardie will ensure that the Fund has a two-year

**Figure C8.5** James Hardie's share price.

Source: ASX 2006, Yahoo Finance (2006).

rolling cash 'buffer' plus one year's contribution in advance, based on an annual actuarial assessment of expected claims for the next three years. The company's annual contribution is subject to a Cash Flow Percentage Cap, initially set at 35 per cent of James Hardie's net operating cash flow for the preceding year. There is provision for 'step down' of the Cash Flow Percentage Cap in five per cent increments if the company's previous four-year contribution is below the next five per cent level down; the step down may be reversed by reference to the same criterion. The final payment to the Fund will be made in 2045 although the New South Wales Government may extend this term. While it is not intended that there will be any cap on payments to individuals who establish their claim, no assurance is given that all claims will be met in view of the uncertainty as to the number of future claims, the quantum of future compensation awards and James Hardie's own financial performance over this period. The estimate

of future asbestos liabilities released with the Agreement is A$1.568bn discounted for net present value; the undiscounted estimate is A$3.306 billion.

(Redmond 2006: 31)

This agreement protects directors and executives of James Hardie from being sued for further compensation. However, it does not contain the immunities from prosecution by the corporate regulators ASIC that the James Hardie directors had held out for. Thus it is still possible that ASIC may bring civil or criminal proceedings against Hardie officers – Macdonald and Shafron being the most likely targets. The very fact that the $1.6 billion funding deal was eventually signed demonstrates the effect that public opinion has had on the company. Although the government threatened legislation the current state of the law does not actually require James Hardie to provide further funding. The agreement was a triumph of community and political pressure rather than legal enforcement. However, in a rather

sour note at the end of this singular strug-
gle between corporate good and evil, in which
good had apparently triumphed, the James
Hardie directors doubled their own director
fees, though the establishment of the new com-
pensation fund was delayed until late in 2006
while James Hardie negotiated for acceptable
tax concessions with the Australian taxation
office.

## WIDER CORPORATE GOVERNANCE IMPLICATIONS

If the boards of JHIL and MRCF had under-
stood the flawed basis of the Trowbridge report
they might not have relied upon it. If Trowbridge
and other professional advisers to the James
Hardie group had been given more accu-
rate and appropriate briefings from James
Hardie executives they may have presented
their advice very differently and thereby alerted
the board to the report's deficiencies. Corporate
governance structures are designed to reduce
the risk of such abuse by imposing account-
ability and control on executive management
through the board. Why did the JHIL board
fail to control officers such as Macdonald and
Shafron? Many of the directors of the James
Hardie entities involved in the scandal were
not independent. For example three of the four
incoming directors of MRCF had connections
with JHIL and thus may have placed too much
trust on the judgement of JHIL management.

Also the directors of James Hardie and Coy
included two executives of JHIL. Whilst James
Hardie and Coy was a wholly owned subsidiary
of JHIL this might not have mattered because
the directors were under a duty to act in the
best interests of the James Hardie and Coy's
shareholders, i.e. JHIL. However, as soon as
separation was on the agenda these directors
were faced with a significant conflict of inter-
est. If they had not had jobs at JHIL they may
not have agreed to the conditions of separa-
tion. In the circumstances they were extremely
likely to trust their colleagues at JHIL rather
than questioning the proposed restructure.

The inquiry report suggests that there may
have been a lack of understanding of the

basis of the Trowbridge report amongst Hardie
board members. It is questionable whether
the boards were capable of dealing with the
issue of the asbestos liabilities in terms of
their overall skill set and experience. There
should perhaps have been recognition of the
lack of knowledge of actuarial processes and
hence further inquiry and education on the sub-
ject, with access to independent consultants,
not simply those selected by the executives
of the company. The company separation pro-
posals were littered with risks which although
identified, did not seem to be systematically
managed and mitigated. The inquiry demon-
strates that key risks were often acknowledged
but swiftly forgotten or ignored in the hurry to
get the deals done. If a more formal risk man-
agement system had been in place, the key
issues would have been properly discussed
and analysed, perhaps leading to a different
outcome.

### Implications for corporate law

Perhaps the most striking point arising from
this case was that James Hardie had for the
most part acted legally. Even where actions
were potentially illegal there was likely to be
very little that could be gained from a law
suit. For example, it would be very difficult to
prove that misleading and deceptive conduct
described above had directly caused dam-
age that would otherwise not have occurred.
Commissioner Jackson commented: 'In short,
before Amaba and Amaca could increase their
funds by resort to litigation there would be many
hurdles to overcome. Probably too many' (2004:
24.85). The inquiry triggered much debate over
whether corporate law needs to be changed or
strengthened so as to prevent similar events
occurring in future. Two issues in particular
have arisen:

1 Should the long-standing doctrine of limited
liability be amended?
2 Should it be mandatory for companies to take
into account the interests of stakeholders
other than shareholders, such as employees
and consumers?

When considering legal reform it should not be forgotten that the MRCF was separated from the James Hardie group in February 2001, and since then corporate law has been strengthened to promote better governance of companies. In Australia the Corporate Law Economic Reform Programme: Policy Proposal Paper No. 9 (CLERP 9) has come into force and the Australian Stock Exchange has issued its Principles of Best Practice Corporate Governance. These reforms demanding greater disclosure and more independent boards may have remedied some of the weaknesses exposed in the James Hardie case, though could hardly have resolved the fundamental lack of integrity displayed. This question of integrity turns on fundamental aspects of corporate principles.

## Limited liability and the 'corporate veil'

A long established principle of corporate law is that a corporation is a separate entity from its shareholders. Hence, its assets are totally separate from those of its members or shareholders. This principle of limited liability was developed with the aim of encouraging people to invest in companies. Although the money they invested in a company was at risk if the company was sued, their personal assets would be safe.

In most circumstances this rule still has benefits today as otherwise people would be wary about investing in business enterprise. However, its purpose is questionable if not dubious where it is applied in the case of groups of companies. In these circumstances the protected shareholder is simply another company in the group and the rule allows assets to be moved around the group to avoid creditors including victims.

Because of the doctrine of limited liability, JHIL was always insulated from asbestos claims made against its subsidiary, James Hardie and Coy. The doctrine of limited liability was confirmed in James Hardie's favour in the case *James Hardie & Coy Pty Limited v. Putt* (1998). This is why JHIL's conduct in transferring money from James Hardie and Coy to itself

by way of dividends or management fees was suspect and subject to examination. It resulted in that money no longer being available to successful claimants against James Hardie and Coy. At the inquiry Jackson questioned whether the existing law on limited liability in corporate groups adequately reflected contemporary public expectations and standards. As a result the government has proposed that people negligently exposed to toxic products should be protected as a special class of creditor. This would help in protecting them not only from group restructuring but also in circumstances of insolvency. The proposals on long-tail liabilities released in October 2005 would:

- force companies to consider future victims on a winding up;
- impose significant penalties on executives who deliberately try to avoid the liability; and
- restrict transactions reducing the capital of a company facing a future mass claim.

## Corporate social responsibility

One of the explanations given by the Hardie directors for the path they chose to take was that they were legally bound to act in the best interests of JHIL's shareholders. They were advised that they needed: 'to be cognisant of the rights and interest of shareholders who could legitimately argue that it is not part of the business of the company to give money away to unproven potential creditors nor to lock up capital indefinitely' (Haigh 2006: 211). Presumably this advice was based upon the common law fiduciary duty of directors to act in the interests of 'the company as a whole' as well as their statutory duty under section 181 of the Australian Corporations Act 2001 to act 'in the best interests of the corporation'. These duties have generally been interpreted as requiring directors to consider the best interests of the company's shareholders. The debate is whether they preclude directors from also taking the interests of other stakeholders into account. The general answer appears to be that other stakeholders may be taken into

account but they do not have to be – the primary concern ought to be the economic welfare of the shareholders. It would have been open to the Hardie directors to argue that proper funding of the MCRF was in the long-term interests of the company; however, they were under no obligation to the victims to do so.

The Australian Federal Parliament in 2005/06 conducted two separate inquiries into corporate social responsibility prompted by the public outrage caused by the James Hardie affair. The Corporations and Markets Advisory Committee (CAMAC), and the Parliamentary Joint Committee (PJC) on Corporations and Financial Services both set up an inquiry into corporate responsibility. The PJC report issued in 2006 did not propose any fundamental change in Australian corporate law defining directors' duties in a more enlightened or pluralist way; however, the report did stress that the existing 2001 Corporations Act allowed directors to take into account other stakeholders' interests that impacted on the company, and encouraged companies to commit to greater social responsibility and to report on this. Perhaps the tragedy of the James Hardie legacy, will prove a stimulus for higher standards of corporate social responsibility in this country in the future.

## Questions

1 Is the current definition of directors' duties robust enough to readily encompass a socially responsible approach when confronted by human tragedy caused by corporate acts, or should further changes in the law be considered?

2 Would abolishing the doctrine of limited liability assist victims of the subsidiaries of companies organised in groups?

3 Do you think the government ought to require companies to report on issues of corporate social responsibility?

4 Is it possible for company directors to balance the interests of shareholders and stakeholders in an efficient and acceptable way?

5 What are the implications of James Hardie's company transfer to the Netherlands (with most of its operations and headquarters in the United States, and most of its shareholders in Australia) for the impact of the further internationalisation of corporations on their governance and regulation?

## REFERENCES

ASX Corporate Governance Council's *Principles of Good Corporate Governance and Best Practice Recommendations*, available at: http://www.asx.com.au/supervision/governance/index.htm

CAMAC Discussion Paper on Corporate Social Responsibility November 2005, http://www.camac.gov.au/

CAMAC Review on Long-tail liabilities, http://www.camac.gov.au/

Dunn, Edwina (2004) James Hardie: No Soul to Be Damned and No Body to Be Kicked, *The Sydney Law Review*, 27: 339.

Gideon, Haigh (2006) *Asbestos House: The Secret History of James Hardie Industries*, Melbourne: Scribe.

Jackson Report (2004) *Report of the Special Commission of Inquiry Into the Medical Research and Compensation Foundation* (James Hardie Affair), New South Wales, http://www.cabinet.nsw.gov.au/publications.html

*James Hardie & Coy Pty Limited v. Putt* (1998) 43 NSWLR 554.

NSW Dust Diseases Tribunal, which can be searched at http://www.austlii.edu.au/au/cases/nsw/NSWDDT/

Parliamentary Joint Committee on Corporations and Financial Services inquiry into corporate responsibility, http://www.aph.gov.au/senate/committee/corporations_ctte/corporate_responsibility/

Ramsey Ian, and Noakes David (2001) Piercing the Corporate Veil in Australia, *Company and Securities Law Journal*, 19: 250–271.

Redmond, Paul (2006) Supplementary Submission, Parliamentary Joint Committee on Corporations and Financial Services, Canberra: Commonwealth of Australia Government, http://www.aph.gov.au/senate/committee/corporations_ctte/corporate_responsibility/submissions/sub84a.pdf

# Case Study 9
# HIH Insurance Group

## EXECUTIVE SUMMARY

HIH the second largest general insurance company in Australia, and apparently an internationally successful enterprise, suddenly began haemorrhaging cash in 2000, and was bankrupt early the following year with devastating consequences for tens of thousands of policy holders. The Hon. Justice Neville Owen of the HIH Royal Commission succinctly stated the scale of this corporate tragedy: 'On 15 March 2001 the major companies in the HIH Insurance group were placed in provisional liquidation. The provisional liquidators were appointed, the magnitude of the HIH group's obligations began to emerge, and the journey towards oblivion proceeded. Formal winding-up orders were made on 27 August 2001 – the corporate equivalent of death. By then the deficiency of the group was estimated to be between $3.6 billion and $5.3 billion. If the ultimate shortfall is anywhere near the upper end of that range, the collapse of HIH will be the largest corporate failure Australia has endured to date' (HIH 2003a: xiii). As the Royal Commission into HIH's collapse met for 18 months from October 2001 to April 2003, the HIH story unfolded. Directors and executives of HIH were examined by the lawyers for the Commission, sometimes for days on end, and revealed a catalogue of neglect, indulgence and incompetence which represented a fascinating insight behind the corporate veil.

## ORIGINS AND GROWTH OF HIH INSURANCE GROUP

The origins of HIH may be traced back to 1968 when Ray Williams and Michael Payne formed an underwriting agency in Melbourne. As insurance brokers with Lloyd's of London they specialised in workers' compensation. Over the next two decades Williams and Payne diversified into underwriting other classes of insurance, including property, commercial, and professional indemnity. In 1989 CE Heath Underwriting Agencies became CE Heath International Holdings Limited, with Williams as principal executive. The partial float of CE Heath International Holdings (HIH) in 1992 saw the first foray by a general insurer into the Australian stock exchange. About 45 per cent of the issued capital was held by the public, 44 per cent by the UK based CE Heath plc and 11 per cent by the local CE Heath directors. Expansion into the UK was an early priority with the newly floated company, and operations commenced in August 1993 with the establishment of a subsidiary Heath International Holdings (UK) Limited under Payne as chief executive.

### The CIC acquisition

After 1995, the company embarked on a period of rapid growth achieved primarily through

acquisitions, which in turn brought significant changes in the company's investment and business strategies (Table C9.1). The first big acquisition was the CIC Insurance group for $154.2 million. The negotiations that led to the acquisition were initiated in 1993 by Colin Richardson of Hambros Corporate Finance, the Australian branch of Hambros Bank Ltd, which in turn held a substantial stake in CE Heath plc, and Richardson was involved in many of HIH's major transactions. The negotiations foundered but revived in 1994 when CIC and CE Heath carried out due diligence on each other. The subsequent report on CIC was signed off by Dominic Fodera, an Andersen partner, and the acquisition was completed in June 1995. The move lifted CE Heath's earnings and established it as a major force

in the Australian insurance industry, also providing a platform for future growth in Europe. HIH's reported revenue growth from 1994 to 2000 in an apparently impressive series of leaps until 2000 (Table C9.2).

The acquisition of CIC changed the size, nature and ownership of the CE Heath business. There were three parts to this transaction:

■ CIC Holdings sold CIC Insurance Limited to CE Heath. CIC Holdings, subsequently changed its name to Winterthur Holdings Australia Limited, and was a majority-owned subsidiary of the Swiss insurer, Winterthur Swiss Insurance Company.
■ The acquisition of CIC Insurance was funded by CE Heath issuing shares to Winterthur Australia.

| Geographical area | Year to December | | | | 18 months to June 1999 | Year to June 2000 |
|---|---|---|---|---|---|---|
| | 1994 | 1995 | 1996 | 1997 | | |
| Australia | 1,016.5 | 2,340.8 | 2,647.7 | 2,861.4 | 6,034.8 | 6,008.3 |
| United Kingdom | 62.8 | 111.3 | 132.4 | 377.9 | 625.0 | 949.0 |
| United States | 17.7 | 39.1 | 106.3 | 502.6 | 733.9 | 762.5 |
| New Zealand | 68.3 | 125.1 | 135.0 | 153.7 | 205.6 | 310.3 |
| Asia | 35.7 | 49.0 | 95.0 | 78.0 | 92.2 | 246.8 |
| Argentina | — | — | 10.5 | 13.1 | 33.9 | 50.2 |
| Total | 1,201.0 | 2,665.3 | 3,126.9 | 3,986.7 | 7,725.4 | 8,327.1 |

Table C9.1 HIH reported contributions to total assets, 1994–2000 (A$ million).
Source: HIH 2003a: 53.

| Geographical area | Year to December | | | | 18 months to June 1999 | Year to June 2000 |
|---|---|---|---|---|---|---|
| | 1994 | 1995 | 1996 | 1997 | | |
| Australia | 633.9 | 1,015.8 | 1,501.3 | 1,676.3 | 3,197.3 | 2,441.1 |
| United Kingdom | 30.1 | 90.4 | 113.5 | 266.2 | 664.2 | 1016.9 |
| United States | 79.8 | 83.7 | 114.4 | 244.9 | 736.4 | 488.8 |
| New Zealand | 25.9 | 51.7 | 68.1 | 88.0 | 187.7 | 286.0 |
| Asia | 12.3 | 27.3 | 46.8 | 59.9 | 150.3 | 197.8 |
| Argentina | — | — | 4.2 | 7.8 | 42.0 | 45.7 |
| Total | 782.0 | 1,268.9 | 1,848.3 | 2,343.1 | 4,977.9 | 4,476.3 |

Table C9.2 HIH reported contributions to consolidated revenue, 1994–2000 (A$ million).
Source: HIH 2003a: 53.

▨ The parent company of CE Heath, CE Heath plc, sold its entire shareholding in CE Heath to Winterthur Australia.

Within a short time Williams sold a portion of his own shareholding to Winterthur, and with the additional 3 per cent of shares obtained from Williams, Winterthur Australia became entitled to 51 per cent of the shares in CE Heath.

## Winterthur

A result of these transactions was that by 1995 Winterthur became the majority shareholder of CE Heath. Yet Winterthur agreed not to take control of the board, although it did retain the option. It chose instead to nominate only three members to join the existing seven directors, who were Erwin Heri, Willi Schurpf and Randolph Wein. Throughout this period CE Heath was audited by Andersen, as it had been since 1973, and in June 1995 Fodera, who until then was the auditor of CE Heath, was appointed group finance director of the company. In May 1997 he became a director of the company. In May 1996 the company changed its name to HIH Winterthur International Holdings Limited, and became the second largest general insurance underwriter in the Australian market. The company strengthened its position in the Australian market in May 1997 by acquiring the general insurance operations of Colonial Mutual General Insurance Company Limited in Australia and New Zealand. This allowed HIH Winterthur to position itself as the market leader in the provision of general insurance through banks and other financial institutions. HIH Winterthur and Colonial Mutual entered an agreement whereby all Colonial Mutual's insurance products would be underwritten by HIH Winterthur. A momentous change then occurred in the ownership of HIH:

> In August 1997 HIH Winterthur's principal shareholder, Winterthur, announced a proposed merger with Crédit Suisse. The board of HIH Winterthur expressed concern

that the merger might adversely affect its relationship with Winterthur – in particular, in terms of board control, the regulatory consequences in Australia, and the group's capacity to continue to expand overseas. Nevertheless, the merger of Winterthur and Crédit Suisse was finalised early in 1998, creating a major global company. Following a review of all the enlarged Crédit Suisse Winterthur group's operations – and in view of Winterthur's concerns about the management and direction of HIH – it was decided that the merged entity would focus on being a global financial services provider.

(HIH 2003a: 55)

## The public offering

The Swiss company announced that it proposed to sell all its shareholding in HIH Winterthur by way of a public offering. The offer at a final price of $2.58 was fully subscribed, the sale was completed in August 1998, and in October HIH Winterthur changed its name to HIH Insurance Ltd. In December Justin Gardener, a former managing partner of Andersen, joined the board, who had been the audit partner on CE Heath through the 1970s to the 1990s. The disposal of Winterthur's holding by a public offering profoundly changed HIH's shareholder base: in December 1997 there were 323 million HIH shares on issue, held by 5,265 shareholders, 3,750 of whom held less than 5,000 shares. By October 2000 there were 471 million shares on issue held by 29,973 shareholders, with around 18,000 shareholders, or 60 per cent, holding fewer than 5,000 shares. As the unsuspecting public poured into HIH, the better informed institutional investors began to have second thoughts: 'Another change was also evident following the Winterthur sale. This was the relatively small and declining institutional shareholder base. In March 1998 HIH's top 20 shareholders held about 83 per cent of all issued shares; by September 1999 the figure had fallen to 53 per cent and by October 2000 it was just 38 per cent' (HIH 2003a: 55).

## The FAI acquisition

HIH viewed FAI Insurance as a possible acquisition as a means to secure a major share of the Australian general insurance market. Among the problems of considering FAI for takeover were the difficulty in conducting any satisfactory due diligence combined with a reluctance to sell on the part of Rodney Adler who was the company's major shareholder. In September 1998 Adler changed his mind and after brief negotiations in September 1998 the board of what was still for a few weeks more HIH Winterthur decided to launch a takeover bid for FAI. The next day Adler offered approximately 15 per cent of FAI's capital for sale through the stock exchange at 75 cents per share. In the month preceding 23 September FAI shares had traded in the range of 42 to 53 cents. HIH acquired the 15 per cent stake and the same day announced a takeover bid for all the remaining shares of FAI. The takeover offer of one HIH share for every three FAI shares or one HIH share plus $2.25 cash for every six FAI shares, was not subject to any formal due diligence investigations by HIH into FAI. This did not take place because Rodney Adler refused to allow it, and HIH was too eager to make the acquisition to worry. After the takeover in early 1999, for $300 million, FAI became a wholly owned subsidiary of HIH, and in April 1999 Adler was appointed to the HIH board and was also engaged as a consultant (HIH 2003a: 56). One of the other unfortunate developments with Adler's arrival at HIH, was the accompanying influence of his unsavoury business colleague Brad Cooper, who proceeded to harass and eventually bribe HIH managers to release successive tranches of money amounting to millions of dollars he claimed he was owed as a result of various transactions he had conducted with FAI, bogus obligations that now HIH was persuaded to assume.

## OVERSEAS OPERATIONS

From the mid-1980s CE Heath gradually began to move into overseas markets and from the mid-1990s the company either expanded or made acquisitions in Hong Kong, Hawaii, Argentina, China, Thailand, Malaysia and the Philippines. However, the United States and the United Kingdom were the main focus. By the early 1990s Heath Cal was reporting rapid growth, but concern about legislative changes in California persuaded the board to sell Heath Cal in 1994 for $118.6 million. In 1997 HIH Winterthur re-entered the market by repurchasing Heath Cal, itself now known as CareAmerica Compensation and Liability Insurance Company. The price was $79.3 million, a substantial discount on the 1994 sale price, though the acquisition had been opposed by Winterthur, HIH Winterthur's majority shareholder. After the acquisition CareAmerica was renamed HIH America and the new entity moved to expand its operations and products in the United States. Ultimately returning to the US market proved a costly mistake as by November 2000 all remaining businesses there were put into run-off. Unfortunately the UK venture proved even more of a disaster than the US experience. In April 1994 a full licence was granted to HIH (UK) and from then on there was no need to seek approval from the Australian underwriting management as there was before. From 1994 the activities of the UK branch were expanded to include underwriting global insurance including reinsurance business, marine, property, travel and personal accident, professional indemnity, catastrophe, contingency, film finance and political risk (HIH 2003a: 57).

## Emerging problems

The UK operations were successful at first however problems emerged in 1996 as the Winterthur internal auditors raised concerns about the manner in which the London office was conducting its business. In particular, the auditors identified problems in provisioning data, the lack of a consistent underwriting approach and coherent business philosophy in relation to inwards reinsurance, and the insufficiency and poor quality of the financial information, and further

concerns about reinsurance being placed with companies that did not satisfy Swiss prudential requirements. In October 1996 Payne wrote to Williams and Fodera, alerting them to a PricewaterhouseCooper's review of the UK operations. The PWC report was critical of the underwriting by HIH (UK), of Payne's style of management, and of the lack of adequate controls. It warned that unless the account could be properly controlled it would have to be closed down or placed into run-off. Another audit report reviewing the inwards treaty reinsurance portfolio identified where business had expanded without the appropriate infrastructure and management controls.

In May 1997 the UK Department of Trade and Industry stepped in and asked for a detailed risk profile of the UK branch operations. An internal HIH (UK) report identified problems with the marine operations and significant losses. In October problems in the level of reserving in the UK operations were identified by PWC in a report highlighting significant differences between the recommended and actual carried reserve levels. Then in November an internal audit review concluded that the accounting operations and financial integrity of the UK branch were in an unacceptable state. Although problems were evident in the UK operations the Australian directors continued to focus on further expansion.

### The Cotesworth acquisition

A decision was made in 1998 to acquire the Cotesworth Group Limited which was the managing agent of four active Lloyd's syndicates, three of which wrote marine insurance. Under the deal, HIH provided the collateral for one of the Cotesworth companies to borrow money to invest in one of the Lloyd's syndicates. This was to create HIH's own corporate syndicate within the Lloyd's market in the United Kingdom that would enable the company eventually to write international insurance and reinsurance business through the Lloyd's licences. However, the contribution of the UK operation to the deterioration of HIH's reserves as at 31 December 1998

was assessed as approximately $300 million, the following year serious concerns surfaced in relation to substantial under-reserving in both HIH (UK) and Cotesworth. In January 1999 as a result of its acquisition of FAI, HIH became further exposed to losses in the UK market through earlier operations there by three FAI subsidiaries. The losses could not be sustained and in September 1999 HIH (UK) was put into run-off, and new business there was written through Cotesworth (HIH 2003a: 59).

### THE COLLAPSE OF HIH

The ambitious growth strategy adopted by HIH had a serious impact on the company's financial position (Table C9.3). The 1998–1999 annual report showed a substantial increase in the value of reported total assets and liabilities, but noted that these increases occurred in a commercial environment characterised by:

- weak premium rate returns;
- volatile investments; and
- a series of significant losses in overseas businesses.

Momentously, HIH reported an end-of-financial-year loss for the first time in its history. During 2000 HIH reported a significant deterioration in its profitability and capital base and the share price suffered. Difficulties in both the United Kingdom and the United States, together with the losses resulting from the acquisition of FAI were seen as contributing factors. The group's serious financial deterioration had by now become the subject of public attention through media and stockbrokers' reports. There were a number of negative reports relating to the company's management, particularly the management style of Williams, as well as HIH's business and investment practices. In 2000 the Australian Prudential Regulation Authority released drafts of proposed new prudential regulations. It was apparent to HIH management with its existing capital structure it would not be easy to meet these new requirements.

| Geographical area | Year to December | | | | 18 months to June 1999 | Year to June 2000 |
|---|---|---|---|---|---|---|
| | 1994 | 1995 | 1996 | 1997 | | |
| Australia | 11.5 | 57.6 | 77.3 | 67.9 | 78.4 | 152.5 |
| United Kingdom | 1.5 | 7.5 | 7.2 | 7.2 | (21.7) | (48.7) |
| United States | 7.9 | (2.6) | (5.9) | 9.4 | (20.5) | (45.4) |
| New Zealand | (0.7) | 9.0 | 8.8 | 9.5 | 17.4 | 7.2 |
| Asia | (1.4) | 1.6 | 4.8 | (2.4) | (5.4) | (11.9) |
| Argentina | — | — | (1.1) | (1.1) | 3.8 | 2.2 |
| Total | 18.8 | 73.1 | 91.1 | 90.5 | 52.0 | 55.9 |

Table C9.3 HIH reported contributions to operating profit before income tax (A$ million).

Source: HIH 2003a: 59.

HIH curtailed its growth strategy and announced a series of transactions with established insurers designed to provide substantial cash injections and consequent increases in cash reserves (HIH 2003a: 60).

## The Allianz joint venture

HIH entered a joint-venture arrangement with Allianz Australia Insurance Limited to come into effect in January 2001. HIH was to transfer a substantial part of its business including its personal lines and compulsory third party insurance products to the joint venture in which Allianz would hold a 51 per cent interest for a payment of $200 million. The announcement was accompanied by the disclosure that HIH's preliminary final result for the year to 30 June 2000 was a $42.1 million operating profit after tax. The market was alarmed and HIH's Standard & Poor's credit rating of A− was placed on 'Credit Watch: negative', and in the next few days HIH's share price fell from 99 cents to 53 cents, from which it never recovered.

Rather than shore up HIH's position, the stock market generally reacted with scepticism: the transactions were thought to offer temporary relief that would ultimately deprive HIH of its most profitable revenue. There was also considerable concern about the constitution of the HIH board, which was seen to have too many executive members; and concerning Williams's management performance. On 12 September 2000 a number of executive directors resigned, and Williams stood aside as chief executive and announced that he would resign as a director when the position of chief executive was filled, though he continued to play a role in HIH until January 2001. The board changes did not stem the widespread concerns, and in October 2000 HIH's banker Westpac called on the company to appoint Ernst & Young to review its financial position. Ernst & Young's draft report, presented to HIH a month later suggested the financial position of the company was 'delicately poised'. Williams resigned from the board on 15 December 2000 following Wein's appointment that day as the new chief executive (HIH 2003a: 61).

## The QBE joint venture

From January 2001 speculation grew about HIH's financial position, and intensified further when the company announced that its interim result to 31 December 2000 was likely to be a loss. This prompted Standard & Poor's to further downgrade five of HIH's core operating entities. Trading in HIH shares was temporarily suspended on 22 February, and Adler resigned from the board a few days later. ASIC began a formal investigation after being told the company's interim result was a loss of $378 million. HIH shares were again suspended from trading on 1 March 2001, by which time they had fallen

Figure C9.1 HIH's share price rise and decline, June 1992 to February 2001.

Source: HIH Royal Commission (2003) Vol. 1: *A Corporate Collapse and Its Lessons*, April, Commonwealth of Australia: Canberra, http://www.hihroyalcom.gov.au/finalreport/Chapter%204.HTML

to as low as 17.5 cents (Figure C9.1). Then APRA issued notices requiring HIH to 'show cause' why inspectors should not be appointed under the *Insurance Act 1973*.

Struggling for life, HIH entered a joint venture with QBE Insurance Ltd, whereby QBE in effect obtained 60 per cent of all HIH's corporate insurance on 6 March 2001. QBE also gained management control of the new joint venture. On the following day HIH effectively sold off its interest in all its former lines of retail business in the Allianz joint venture (Figure C9.2). HIH formally appointed KMPG to undertake a review of its financial position

and in the light of the results of that review the HIH board resolved on 15 March 2001 to appoint a provisional liquidator. On 27 August 2001 a further court order placed HIH and 17 companies in the group in official liquidation and appointed KPMG partners Anthony McGrath and Alexander Macintosh as joint liquidators.

### The response to the collapse

HIH's provisional liquidation had widespread and disastrous consequences for policyholders,

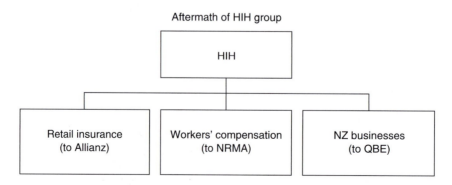

Figure C9.2 Sale of HIH principal assets, 2001.

in addition to the loss and hurt suffered by shareholders, other creditors and employees. Commonwealth, state and territory governments immediately came under pressure to provide assistance, and within weeks this was forthcoming. The states and territories undertook to meet most outstanding HIH builders' warranty and compulsory third party claims. Best estimates at 30 September 2002 were that total payouts for these lines could ultimately amount to about $1.444 billion, based on the following break-up: New South Wales, $902.6 million; Queensland, $453.4 million; Victoria, $78.2 million; Western Australia, $6.4 million; South Australia, $2.2 million; the Australian Capital Territory, $0.7 million; and Tasmania, $0.4 million.

On 17 May 2001 the Commonwealth announced its own scheme to help cases of 'genuine hardship'. The centrepiece was the formation of a non-profit, insurance industry-run company, HIH Claims Support Pty Ltd, to distribute the $640 million allocated by the Commonwealth to meet claims other than for workers' compensation and builders' warranty. The company began operating on 1 July 2001. As at the end of February 2003, the scheme had received more than 11,400 applications and had made payments on behalf of some 5,850 eligible claimants, for a total of approximately $195 million. Most claims arising from household, property, commercial and motor vehicle policies were paid. The majority of outstanding claims were from long-tail policies, including public liability and professional indemnity (HIH 2003a: 63).

## The impact of bankruptcy

Business failure in Australia is an uncommon phenomenon (Figures C9.3 and C9.4). The failure rate is less than four businesses per one thousand enterprises. Yet the impact of the HIH collapse was enormous: it slowed Australia's GDP rate by 0.5 per cent at a time when growth was 3 per cent, in effect directly diminishing by 16 per cent of Australia's economic growth. When HIH failed, a wide spectrum of the Australian community was greatly affected. Two million policyholders were with HIH, while 3,000 employees lost their jobs. Without insurance, an atmosphere of paralysis pervaded the community as HIH's failure was felt. Lawyers and doctors could not practise law or surgery without professional indemnity insurance. Community and sport events were cancelled as local councils were reluctant to hold events without cover. Further industry consolidation was accelerated by

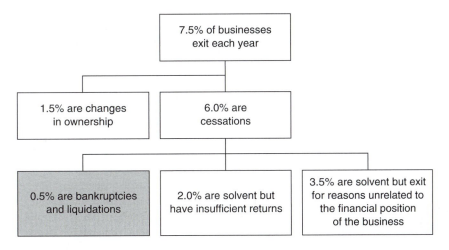

Figure C9.3 Causes of business exits in Australia.

Source: Adapted from Bickerdyke *et al.* (2000: XVIII).

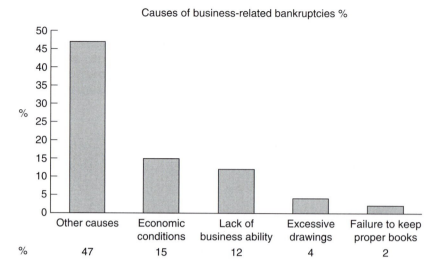

Figure C9.4  Causes of bankruptcies in Australia.

HIH's collapse as premiums rose. In 1998, the top 10 insurers owned 47 per cent of the market, by 2001, they owned 78 per cent.

## HIH OPERATIONAL, STRATEGIC AND GOVERNANCE PROBLEMS

HIH experienced a protracted and fundamental series of operational, strategic and governance weaknesses, that ultimately meant its demise was inevitable, a catalogue of business failures (Table C9.4):

1 Poor strategic sense, weak operational control, and corporate governance complacency was ingrained in HIH management. Dominated by one man, the board and chair were simply tools of the CEO, apparently powerless to prevent disastrous strategies.
2 In order to win business and expand its market share, HIH was systematically under provisioning on its insurance business, which meant it did not have the resources to meet claims when they fell due. This was a fundamental flaw in HIH's operations and undoubtedly in time would have caused a fatal collapse in the company, if mismanagement of acquisitions and strategy had not precipitated an earlier failure.

3 Pursuing a policy of reckless expansion (partly to conceal and compensate for its weak operational position) HIH made a critical takeover of fellow Australian insurer FAI without due diligence. FAI was overpriced: HIH paid A$290 million for a company whose book value was A$220 million and whose net assets amounted to only A$20 million. Even accounting for goodwill, HIH massively overpaid for FAI.
4 HIH expanded into the highly competitive markets of the USA and UK without the sufficient financial or strategic controls for such expansion. The expansions impacted the balance sheet and with the FAI acquisition, drained cash flow.
5 Re-entering the US market was a strategic disaster for HIH. The market environment in workers' compensation had changed, and eight of the top ten industry insurers collapsed. Enjoying complete autonomy from the Australian parent, HIH America also insured the Alaskan fishing fleet industry over claims for personal injury or death. As this was a specific area that its competitors would not handle, the gains might have been enormous, as might the losses. Unfortunately for HIH, the latter prevailed,

| Symptom | Reason |
| --- | --- |
| Decreasing profitability | A symptom of any number of causal factors |
| Decreasing sales | May be a consequence of an ineffective sales force or inappropriate product range |
| Increase in debt | Impacts on the requirement to service debt and reduces profitability. Impacts on cash flow requirements in reducing loans |
| Decrease in liquidity | Impacts on solvency |
| Reduction in dividends | Alteration in dividend policy could be symptomatic of the company not generating adequate cash flow |
| Unacceptable accounting practices | Inappropriate and unethical decisions are made |
| Poor management | Embraces all of the above |
| Poor systems | Weak internal controls, inappropriate and ill-functioning technology and support systems |
| Staff turnover | Inefficiencies with training and tasks not being performed on a timely basis |
| Declining market share | Market may react by downgrading the share and consequent price decline |
| Lack of strategic thinking | Untimely decisions being made with lost opportunities or costly consequences of ill-conceived strategic initiatives |

Table C9.4 Symptoms of business decline.

Source: Adapted from CCH 2001: 210.

and the failure of HIH America cost the company $500 million.

6 HIH UK had a profit of £2.3 million in 1997 but a year later, it made a loss of £9.3 million. Two years later the loss had risen to £27.7 million. HIH UK operations were impacted by the downturn in the marine and construction industries and had poor underwriting control (HIH 2003a: 41). HIH enthusiastically expected that the UK operations would recover, when overall, HIH lost A$1.7 billion in the UK venture: 'The UK operations were the largest single contributor to the collapse of HIH' (HIH 2003a: 35).

### The FAI debacle

FAI and HIH had many things in common: they were both general insurers and were dominated by leaders who liked to be seen to be dynamic but really possessed little strategic business sense. They shared the same recklessness in under-provisioning for insurance claims, and they had the same forgiving auditors: 'Williams took comfort from the fact that Andersen were the auditors of FAI'. (HIH 2003b: 203). On 23 September 1998, HIH launched a takeover bid for FAI at A$290 million. At the commission, it was revealed FAI's own investment bankers, Goldman Sachs had set FAI's net assets at A$20 million. The transaction to buy FAI went ahead without proper discussion and input from the other directors of the board who may have had doubts about the deal. Reliance on the auditors Andersen's, who worked for both companies was crucial.

Williams was committed to acquiring FAI, which coincidentally at the time of the takeover owned nearly 10 million shares of One.Tel – the other big corporate Australian corporate collapse. These shares were passed on to HIH, and at one point the company owned 25 million shares due to a bonus issue. By November 2000, 'the total of all realised and unrealised gains on the One.Tel holding was A$53.7 million, however HIH's remaining shareholding in One.Tel lost all value when One.Tel went into liquidation shortly afterwards'

(HIH 2003b: 245). In total FAI would cost HIH A$590 million with a net loss of A$145 million and FAI's impact on HIH's cash flow was such that it contributed to HIH's decision to later sell off its most profitable business to Allianz, just to extend its business life for a few weeks.

## Weaknesses in local operations

HIH's local operations did not fare much better than its overseas operations. HIH failed to 'build up capital reserves against unpredictable but inevitable large claims but chose to reinsure overseas against the possibility of large, exceptional payouts' (CCH 2001: 15). Indeed it was claimants who queried why they were not receiving payment for their claims that drew broad attention to how dire the financial situation had become at HIH. The local operations revealed problems with the company's budgets, reconciliations and computer systems. From 1997 onwards HIH failed to meet budget targets with senior management being 'aggressively optimistic'. By June 2000, 75 per cent of shareholders' equity was based on intangible assets with 50 per cent accounting for goodwill (in light of the optimistic appraisal of FAI). The budget was ineffective as a strategic planning tool with 'board members' reliance on budgets to exercise financial control over the actions of executive management, entirely misplaced' (HIH 2003a: xlv).

There was no formal process for regular, comprehensive reconciliation of the company's accounts with a number of unreconciled accounts dating from 1995. The introduction of a new electronic financial system in 1997, called GEN+ plagued daily operations with problems. As a result, the integrity of HIH's financial statements were 'questionable, inaccurate and incomplete' (HIH 2003a: xlv). The Ernst & Young team commissioned by WestPac to review HIH, encountered many constraints in their pursuit of information: lack of access to documents and people, complex issues, transactions requiring examination and lack of time, and as a result were not able to form an opinion on the solvency of HIH. Ernst &

Young could not ascertain the solvency of HIH because of the constraints cited above, while the board took this as absolving any doubts the company had regarding solvency issues. The board did not pursue any 'further work … on the question of solvency as a matter of urgency. [Yet] nothing was said by Ernst & Young that provided a reasonable justification for the board's inadequate response' (HIH 2003b: 568).

In the end, HIH stumbled unknowingly into bankruptcy. On 4 December 2000, Ernst & Young's final report was published and stated 'the overall position of the group is delicately poised … all strategies contain extreme risk … [and if] the decision was taken to cease operations today, it is our view that creditors would receive less than a full return' (HIH 2003b: 569). To outsiders, the response to the crisis in HIH was ambivalent: Standard & Poor's downgraded its rating for HIH while J.B. Were had a 'buy' on HIH as it reasoned the share price, at 17.5 cents, was a bargain. Meanwhile the industry regulator Australian Prudential Regulatory Authority (APRA) was reluctant to intervene due to its nascent role and its inexperience in appreciating the extent of the company's crisis. 'The month leading up to the provisional liquidation of HIH on 15 March 2001 was marked by a constant series of meetings at which the company and its bankers and advisers sought desperately to find a solution to the company's financial predicament' (HIH 2003b: 576). On 22 February, the Australian Stock Exchange halted trading on HIH shares after ASIC, served notice into trading that contravened 'HIH's obligation to disclose price sensitive information into the market' (HIH 2003b: 578). On 26 February, HIH released a net interim loss of more than A$250 million while Standard & Poor's further downgraded its rating for HIH. On 1 March, APRA finally issued a 'show cause' to HIH requesting why they should not appoint an inspector to HIH. In the ensuing 14 days, players within HIH made deals for a quick fire sale of the company as HIH's businesses were divested and sold off to its competitors as its share price collapsed.

## HIH'S DEEPLY FLAWED CORPORATE GOVERNANCE SYSTEM

The key to good corporate governance lies in substance, not form. It is about the way the directors of a company create and develop a model to fit the circumstances of the company and then test it periodically for its practical effectiveness' (HIH 2003a: 133). The fundamental notions of openness, integrity and accountability were lacking in the way corporate governance was practised within HIH. The board was dominated by a CEO who managed the affairs of the public company as if it was his very own private enterprise, while the chair took advantage of the honours of his office without exercising the responsibility or accountability that this position required. The CFO and auditors were pursuing their own agenda at the company's expense while the shareholders for the most part were 'apathetic' (HIH 2003a: 121). HIH's failure came at a time when its own industry regulator was mired with its own reorganisation and could not effectively monitor the entities it was supposed to be regulating, while the critical weakness within HIH was the failure of corporate governance and inadequacy of internal financial controls.

### Monitoring and control

The monitoring, control and auditing relationship of the four main parties of HIH involved the management, the board, the auditors and the shareholders, and were hopelessly conflicted (Figure C9.5):

1 The executive committee of HIH provided the internal audit, which was extensively relied upon by the auditors, Andersen. Information between these two parties was shared freely since the CFO was the former Andersen auditor, there was no independence, and conflicts of interest were rife.
2 Andersen's external audit was supplied to the board's audit committee, as their principal source of information along with internal audit prepared by the management.

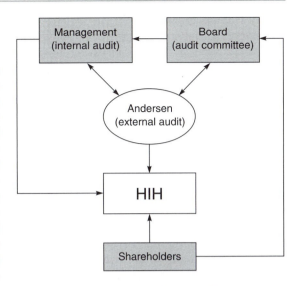

Figure C9.5 Conflicted auditing of HIH.

3 The board, which had no day-to-day control over the company, relied upon the external audit to monitor management.
4 The shareholders relied upon the board to monitor the management of the company.

### CEO Ray Williams

'You have accumulated around you fantastic, loyal, long-service yes-men, but they are all 1970s type managers with no view of the future' (Adler to Williams in Rennie 2001). Ray Williams was CEO of the various entities of HIH from 1968 until he resigned on 15 December 2000. Throughout his tenure, 'no one rivalled him in terms of authority and influence'. Despite the company having gone public, HIH was still treated by Williams as if it was a private firm in his old underwriting days: 'HIH was 'influenced strongly by senior management, and from which senior management benefits significantly [and has not transformed into] that of an ASX listed company run primarily in the interests of shareholders' (HIH 2003a: xxvi–xxvii). Williams was a successful founder but his judgement was increasingly faulty as time wore on: he

had not come to terms with the fact he was no longer the owner of the company, but a steward whose responsibility lay towards the many owners of the company. This attitude was borne out by Williams and his hand and influence were paramount in the messy operations overseas and the FAI acquisition. In 1999 the remuneration and allocation of bonuses amongst senior management was at his sole discretion, while 'the agenda for the board was controlled by management and not by the board' (HIH 2003a: xxxix). Williams' benevolent founder approach proved the single most important contributor to the failure of the company as company accountability, management performance, vision, and control were monopolised, while strategies and expenditure were a tangled result of his whims and prejudices.

## Chair

Geoffrey Cohen was the chair of the HIH board whose role was entirely ineffectual as he was presiding over a board made up of Williams' close friends, and there were no independent directors on the board as Corporate Governance International pointed out (Gluyas 2003). Cohen himself was an old Andersen partner and had a long association with Williams. Cohen also brought in other Andersen partners, including Dominic Fodera and Justin Gardener, with whom they shared the important managing and monitoring positions of the board (Table C9.4). Cohen failed to identify conflicts of interest and even when the Australian Shareholders' Association (ASA) criticised the company's relations with Andersen, Cohen believed that it was 'the responsibility of each of the directors to declare any conflict of interest they may have had'. The subsequent absence of disclosure of any such conflicts 'did not itself permit the chairman to assume there was no conflict of interest in a transaction' (HIH 2003a: xxxvii).

Cohen's relationship with Williams was subservient and Cohen was reluctant to rein in or criticise the CEO's actions. The board's agenda would be forwarded to Williams for his approval or comment. During the transaction to offload HIH's most profitable business to Allianz, Cohen 'took no step to ensure that non-executive directors' concerns about governance were dealt with in a proper manner at board level' (HIH 2003a: xxxvii). Notably, only one non-executive director, Neville Head, questioned the company's corporate governance procedures. He brought his concerns to Cohen who divulged this information to Williams. Williams did not agree with Head's concerns and so Head resigned from the HIH board in August 1999. Cohen failed to appreciate 'his role and duties as chairman of the board' (HIH 2003a: xxxviii).

## The auditors

Conflicts held by the Arthur Andersen-affiliated directors shone like beacons' (Gluyas 2003). Andersen's Audit Objectives and Procedures Manual (AOP) stated: 'The standards and policies are part of the glue that binds us together as one Firm, providing the consistently high quality of auditing service necessary to attract and retain clients. In an environment in which public and governmental attention is increasingly focused on the quality of auditors' work, adherence to standards is essential' (HIH 2003c: 69). Andersen became HIH's auditor in 1971 and as the auditing function matured, Andersen sought other ways to retain their client. Meanwhile there was mounting pressure from Andersen's overseas offices on the HIH audit team to increase their fees from the company by minimising the level of traditional audit work performed, 'in order to improve both the profitability of its retainer and its relationship with management' (HIH 2003c: 72).

By 2000, non-audit fees made up 48.96 per cent (or A$1.63 million) of the total fees billed by Andersen (Figure C9.6). Non-audit activities included advice on the acquisition of FAI, issue of preference shares, the Allianz transaction, the Winterthur sell-down, and the consultancy arrangements of Andersen personnel on the HIH team. The HIH audit team started cutting corners, relying extensively on

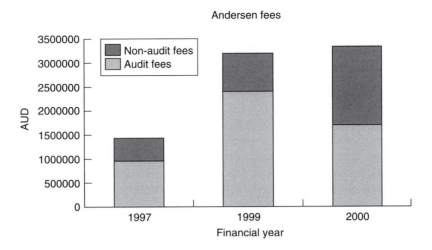

Andersen fees

Figure C9.6 Andersen's increasing non-audit fees.

Source: Adapted from HIH (2003: 86).

the internal audits provided by the company and having inexperienced engagement partners who would have not the capacity to thoroughly investigate HIH's books. At the time the integrity of HIH's risk control processes and financial statements were affected by the company's own computer problems. For the last two HIH audits Andersen did not evaluate them or confirm their adequacy even as Andersen's own assessment noted HIH a 'maximum risk client'. The presence of former Andersen partners on the board, as a result of the commonplace revolving door policy (the phenomenon where audit partners join to become senior financial executives of the client), ensured audits were passed and such 'risks were reduced to an acceptable level' (HIH 2003c: 73).

A few months before its collapse, in October 2000, some members of the audit team were of the view that 'Andersen probably ought not audit HIH any longer because of its aggressive accounting practices and the difficulty experienced by Andersen in resolving issues with management' (HIH 2003c: 73). The senior engagement partner, John Buttle, disagreed as Andersen had worked hard to get proper conclusions on the 2000 audit and 'Andersen's concern for its reputation would not have been a sufficient reasons for the ASIC (the regulatory watchdog) to approve its resignation' (HIH 2003c: 73). Senior Andersen personnel were aware of the risk associated with HIH (Table C9.5). In 2000 Terry Underwood the managing practice director noted HIH was Andersen Australia's second highest risk/profile client. 'By February 2001, HIH had become Andersen's number one risk audit client in Australia' (HIH 2003c: 75). In fact, Gardener was a member of HIH's audit team from 1973 to 1997 while Fodera was a senior member of the 2000 audit. For an

| Ex-Andersen partner | Role on HIH board |
|---|---|
| Geoffrey Cohen | Chair of the board |
| | Non-executive director |
| | Chair, then member of the audit committee |
| Dominic Fodera | Chief financial officer |
| | Executive director |
| Justin Gardener | Non-executive director |
| | Member, then chair of the audit committee |

Table C9.5 The influence of ex-Andersen auditors on HIH board.

audit to be effective, the 'auditor most be independent both in fact and in appearance'. Gardener's appointment to the HIH board created a split in the 1999 Andersen audit team as members Davies and Gooley raised concerns about the deterioration of financial reserves and the need to increase the independent members of the board's audit committee, without the knowledge of Williams: 'We were not satisfied that the audit committee properly understood the messages we were trying to impart'. The HIH–Andersen relationship briefly evolved suffered from 'one of the very best to absolute rock bottom' as Williams felt 'he was left out of the loop' and 'he should have been told as 'a matter of courtesy' (HIH 2003c: 91).

One member of the audit team, Davies, who was also a member of the Australian Accounting Standards Board (AASB), was replaced for the following year's audit. According to Justice Owen, Williams' reaction to Davies' 'was inappropriate' (HIH 2003c: 93) and that HIH had the tendency to 'shoot the messenger' if they did not like the message (HIH 2003c: 93), therefore Andersen was made aware. 'Andersen personnel who displeased HIH management might be removed from the audit ... thus giving rise to the perception that Andersen' independent audit of HIH was or could be compromised' (HIH 2003c: 93).

Andersen was directly responsible for the ensuing accounting errors:

- company goodwill represented 50 per cent of HIH's shareholder funds at 30 June 2000 (compared to rivals QBE and NRMA whose ratio of goodwill to shareholders' funds were 4.9 per cent and 0.4 per cent);
- there was no sufficient appropriate audit evidence as to the carrying value of the residual goodwill (HIH 2003c: 146);
- there was no appropriate audit evidence to carry the value of the goodwill of the FAI acquisition booked at A$275 million (HIH 2003c: 46);
- capitalisation of operating expenses;
- offset of the provision for deferred income tax against future income tax benefits attributable to tax losses.

- Andersen failed to notice the insolvency of HIH's subsidiaries.

Andersen and HIH had a strong relationship. Andersen was captivated by its client, while the client paid Andersen to get the 'right' results. Such was the incestuous relationship between HIH and Andersen, HIH's partners, Westpac and Allianz had to request different accounting firms, Ernst & Young and KPMG, to obtain the 'correct' information. Andersen placed profitability ahead of the integrity of the audit function and at the expense of their reputation.

## HIH ROYAL COMMISSION

The royal commission headed by Justice Neville Owen into the HIH collapse began 6 months after the provisional liquidation of the company on September 2001. There were 126 witnesses and 75 prepared written statements. While most were forthcoming, the commission had extraordinary difficulty in obtaining information from Andersen's offices overseas. 'The Commission encountered myriad difficulties in relation to the production of documents by Andersen. As the auditor of both FAI and HIH ... the response to this summons gave rise to extensive correspondence and meetings spanning many months' (HIH 2003a: 30) as the commission encountered difficulties in obtaining information on the HIH audit years, then the FAI 1998 audit, then the HIH-related documents in the UK and USA. 'The lack of cooperation from Andersen in the UK and US and the apparent inability of Andersen in HK to comply with the Commission's requests significantly curtailed the Commission's ability to investigate thoroughly matters related to HIH in those jurisdictions' (HIH 2003a: 32).

The commission addressed the following issues:

1 the extent to which actions of directors, employees, auditors, actuaries and advisers

contributed to HIH's failure or involved undesirable corporate practices;

2 whether those involved breached any laws and if criminal proceedings should be pursued;

3 the appropriateness of the manner in which powers were exercised under Commonwealth and state law;

4 adequacy of arrangements for regulation and supervision of general insurance at state and federal levels;

5 state insurance and tax regimes.

The commission highlighted the obligation a corporation such as HIH had to the community, as failure 'questioned the integrity of the market system itself' (HIH 2003a: xvi). Owen noted, 'The governance of a public company should be about stewardship. Those in control have a duty to act in the best interests of the company ... the law imposes duties and responsibilities on corporate officers and others such as auditors to ensure that problems that may adversely affect the solvency of a commercial entity are detected at an early stage. When problems of this nature are detected, corporate officers have a responsibility to take action' (HIH 2003a: xiii). In essence, 'HIH was mismanaged'. The stewards of the company lacked attention, lacked accountability and lacked integrity, and HIH executed a number of business decisions 'that were poorly conceived and even more poorly executed' (HIH 2003a: xvii).

Justice Owen absolved the regulatory body APRA of any serious responsibility, as they 'did not cause or contribute to the collapse of HIH'. Criticism of Andersen was severe as Owen recommended 'a mandatory period of four years following resignation from an audit firm before a former partner who was directly involved in the audit of a client can become a director of the client or take a senior management position with the client (HIH 2003a: lxvii) and ... a prohibition on any more than one former partner of an audit firm, at any time, being a director of or taking a senior management position with the client' (HIH 2003a: lxviii).

Owen recommended that Williams, Cohen, Adler, Fodera and other members of the HIH board face extensive civil penalties and criminal charges for the roles they played in the collapse of HIH: 'The board and management failed in their primary responsibilities in relations to the accounts of the company. The auditors failed to detect manifest deficiencies. They too must accept responsibility' (HIH 2003a).

**The prison sentences**

The disgraced former HIH director Rodney Adler lost his High Court bid to overturn his company directorship ban and fine of $450,000 over the collapse of the insurance giant. Adler had applied for special leave in the High Court to appeal against a 2002 NSW Supreme Court decision to ban him from holding a position of company director for 20 years, and fine him $450,000 over his role in HIH's demise. In a later criminal trial Rodney Adler was sentenced on 14 April 2005 to four and a half years jail, with a non-parole period of two and a half years. Adler's jail sentence came after pleading guilty on 16 February 2005 to four criminal charges, which included:

- two counts of disseminating information knowing it was false;
- one count of obtaining money by false or misleading statements;
- one count of being intentionally dishonest and failing to discharge his duties as a director in good faith and in the best interests of the company.

The judge, Justice John Dunford, said Adler's offences displayed 'an appalling lack of commercial morality.' The sentence was a lenient one, since the judge accepted the defendent's plea of mitigation, citing that he had not sold any of his own shares, or personally benefited from his actions. In the same month Adler also handed back his Order of Australia medal. He has since been disciplined for secretly conducting business affairs from jail.

Former HIH CEO Ray Williams pleaded guilty to three criminal charges arising from his management of the HIH group of companies in the three-year period 1998 to 2000:

- failing to properly exercise his director's duties;
- misleading investors in an annual report by overstating the HIH profit by $92 million; and
- omitting an important piece of information about the company in an attempt to raise money from the public.

He was sentenced to four-and-a-half years' jail with a non-parole period of two years and nine months.

ASIC laid criminal charges against Geoffrey Cohen, the former chair of HIH. ASIC alleged Cohen gave misleading information in the chair's address to shareholders at the HIH annual general meeting on 15 December 2000: it was alleged that at that meeting, Cohen made misleading statements about the joint venture between Allianz Australia Limited (Allianz) and HIH and these statements related to the effect of the joint venture on HIH's cashflow and the payment of $200 million by Allianz to HIH. Dominic Fodera, former chief financial officer of HIH Insurance Limited (HIH), pleaded not guilty to a criminal charge of authorising the issue of a prospectus from which there was a material omission, in the Supreme Court of New South Wales and was to go to trial commencing in February 2007.

Finally, a bit player in the HIH saga, Brad Cooper, was found guilty in the Supreme Court of New South Wales of six charges of corruptly giving a cash benefit to influence an agent of HIH Insurance Limited (HIH) under section 249B of the Crimes Act and was also found guilty of seven charges of publishing false or misleading statements with intent to obtain a financial advantage under section 178BB of the Crimes Act. Justice Bruce James of the NSW Supreme Court sentenced Cooper to eight years jail, and he will serve a minimum of five years before being eligible for parole on 30 October 2010.

## Questions

1 When private companies become publicly listed companies, there is a fundamental change in their responsibilities and accountability. Discuss in relation to how this change was managed at HIH.
2 Should the listing requirements for a public company include the training and development of directors in the governance requirements of a listed company?
3 Discuss the evolution of the auditing profession, and the recent regulatory constraints placed on auditors in the light of the HIH affair.
4 Examine the myth of the all-powerful CEO in the light of the evident failings of HIH's CEO. What can be done to alleviate the recurrence of this problem?
5 Discuss the role of institutional investors, regulators, the financial press and other external intermediaries in monitoring the activities of rogue companies such as HIH, before bankruptcy becomes inevitable.

## REFERENCES

Adams, M. (2005) *Are the HIH Sentences Enough*, *Risk Management Magazine*, http://www.riskmanagementmagazine.com.au/articles/2B/0C02F92B.asp?Type=125&Category=1241

Bickerdyke, I., Lattimore, R. and Madge, A. (2000) *Business Failure and Change: An Australian Perspective*, Productivity Commission Staff Research Paper. Ausinfo: Canberra.

CCH (2001) *Collapse incorporated: Tales, safeguards and responsibilities of corporate Australia*, Sydney: CCH Australia.

Gluyas, R. (2003) We Must Get Back to Basics on Governance, *The Australian*, 16 June.

HIH Insurance Limited, *deListed*, http://www.delisted.com.au/CompanyDisplay.aspx?id=3953

HIH Royal Commission (2003a) *A Corporate Collapse and Its Lessons*, vol. 1, April, Canberra: Commonwealth of Australia.

HIH Royal Commission (2003b) *Reasons, Circumstances and Responsibilities*, vol. 2, April, Canberra: Commonwealth of Australia.

HIH Royal Commission (2003c) *Reasons, Circumstances and Responsibilities*, vol. 3, April, Canberra: Commonwealth of Australia.

Main, A. (2003) *Other People's Money: The Complete Story of the Extraordinary Collapse of HIH*, Sydney: HarperCollins.

Rennie, P. (2001) What Adler Wrote to Williams, *Business Review Weekly*, 15 June.

Westfield, M. (2003) *HIH The Inside Story of Australia's Biggest Corporate Collapse*, Sydney: John Wiley.

# Case Study 10
# Nomura

## EXECUTIVE SUMMARY

This case study looks at the 1991 and 1997 scandals that occurred in Nomura, Japan's largest brokerage house. It also examines the Japanese business culture, the role Japan's Ministry of Finance played, the influence of the sokaiya (Japanese corporate racketeers) and the ramification of the scandals on Japanese corporate governance.

## NOMURA'S ORIGINS

Nomura is the largest investment house in Japan it opened as a backstreet Osaka bond house in 1925 although it had earlier beginnings in 1872. Prior to World War II the Nomura Zaibatsu was a closely linked web of financial businesses, with the Nomura Bank, eighth largest in Japan, holding the threads together. It was tenth of the 14 largest *zaibatsu* in the country. (The other *zaibatsu* were Mitsui, Mitsubishi, Sumitomo, Yasuda, Asano, Furukawa, Fuyo, Kawasaki, Nisso, Nichitsu, Okura, Riken and Shibusawa) (Case 1997: 247). World War II intervened and for a short while the firm's activities ceased. When the Americans left Japan, Nomura recouped its former business by single-handedly promoting the 'little man into the stock market, offering piggy banks to anyone who wanted to save and invest' (Friedland 1993: 83). Nomura expanded and strengthened during the Japanese industrial expansion from the 1960s to the 1980s. Nomura's international expansion coincided with Japan Inc.'s remarkable achievements worldwide, especially competing successfully with the industrial heartland of America during the 1980s. In 1998, 60 per cent of Japan's 2,300 listed companies were Nomura clients. Where Japanese corporations had a substantial presence, Nomura duly established subsidiaries to advise their clients. In 1987 Nomura unseated CS First Boston as the top global underwriter of Euromarket offerings, and in 1989 at the height of the Japanese economic bubble Nomura earned $3.7 billion in one financial year, a record in Japanese corporate history. In 1993 Nomura had over 5 million customers and employed 13,000 people in 28 countries. Nomura continues to be the number one financial brokerage house in Japan with a distribution network that foreign competitors would come up against repeatedly again every time they tried to enter the Japanese market. Today, Nomura is a *keiretsu,* which are more loosely linked than the old *zaibatsu,* but with cross-holdings, cross-directorships, inter-group trading and support and with a vast set of obligation, loyalty, and respect networks that lock members together (Case 1997: 247).

Nomura is also seen as the only non-western global competitor for financial groups. During the 1990s, Nomura's American and European subsidiaries evolved from being mere profitable boutique businesses to substantial contributors to the group's profits. In 1997, overseas operations contributed over 80 per cent of Nomura's profits as the Japanese economic downturn continued to harm its national operations.

At one point, Nomura was the world's number one investment firm though continuing woes in the home market have eroded this

| Firm name | Market capitalisation ($B) | Price to earnings ratio | Return on equity (%) | Price to book value |
|---|---|---|---|---|
| Morgan Stanley | 54 | 11.71 | 14.45 | 1.91 |
| Merrill Lynch & Co., Inc. | 51.4 | 12.44 | 16.88 | 1.63 |
| Goldman Sachs group | 45.9 | 10.34 | 19.87 | 1.78 |
| Lehman Brothers Holdings | 25.2 | 10.62 | 10.62 | 1.74 |
| Nomura Holdings Inc. | 24.1 | 27.54 | 5.17 | 1.393 |

Table C10.1 The top five investment firms in the world, as per May 2005.

Source: Compiled from Yahoo Finance 2006, http://biz.yahoo.com/p/brokermktd.html.

status and in 2004, it ranks fourth in terms of market capitalisation (Table C10.1).

## Nomura's corruption

When the governor of the Bank of Japan spiked the property asset price boom by raising the interest rate, the bubble finally burst in Japan at the start of the 1990s. Most believed this would be of short duration: how could a giant industrial power like Japan not bounce back? Instead this was the beginning of a disorientating decade-long recession for Japan that only began to be dispelled with signs of renewed growth and confidence in the period 2004–2006. During this intervening period Nomura was hit by not one scandal which most western firms would have found difficult to overcome, but by two. The fact that Nomura continues to exist today can be attributed to the resilience, unity and emphasis on social harmony inherent to Japanese cultural values, institutional practices and business relationships.

The first scandal for Nomura erupted in 1991 when it was revealed the firm had been compensating VIP clients (usually institutional clients and not retail customers) for losses incurred during the crash. The losses were incurred mainly on the investments in risky bonds for two US property projects. This favouritism was also present when Nomura admitted to excessively trading – ramping – the shares of the railway and leisure conglomerate Tokyu Corp, which Nomura was

underwriting (Friedland 1993: 83). It was also revealed that Nomura was laundering money incurred by illegal activities – Nomura was lending funds to members of the Japanese underworld (or yakuza). Nomura secured substantial holdings for Tokyu Corp shares for one of the underworld leaders, Susumu Ishii: 'Nomura had a dark, corrupt side' (Desmond 1998).

Beyond the iron triangle of politicians, bureaucrats and industrialists that contributed much to Japan's industrial development, the gangsters – the yakuza (the Japanese mafia) and the sokaiya (corporate racketeers) – were also taking a substantial interest. The latter were charged with keeping petty crime off the streets and they were duly compensated for their side of the social harmony bargain. This illicit relationship went unchallenged during the boom period but fell under great scrutiny during the long recession as symptomatic of the lack of transparency and legality of many Japanese business activities. The scandal of favouring institutional clients and employing Japanese gangsters was not limited to Nomura alone, but the firm's involvement was the biggest, and hence their reputation the most tarnished: 'Nomura is the one securities firm in Japan whose behaviour can reshape the market' (Sender 1993: 53). This scandal, like the second, was part of a wider banking malaise that was afflicting Japan. For example, Fuji Bank was revealed to have been forging certificates of deposit. In total, banking fraud was exposed at $5 billion while securities compensation

deals were revealed at $1.3 billion (Rowley 1991: 48).

The seriousness of the scandal was reflected with the resignations of Nomura's top two: chair Setsuya Tabuchi and president, Yoshihisa Tabuchi (unrelated). Both men were instrumental in the global expansion of Nomura. The new chair, Yukio Aida stated more in hope than in force, 'Nomura had been respected as one of Japan's top securities companies for 70 years. But over the last 2 or 3 years, although we didn't break the law, what we did was worse: we contravened the rules of society … The most important thing is to change the way that the securities business operates so that the Japanese stock market is allowed to function properly … Our task is to move it as close as possible to the Anglo-Saxon model' (Evans 1992: 50). The 1991 scandal exposed a systemic problem in the Japanese banking system that affected the rest of Japanese society and foreign investors. This scandal reinforced foreign investment criticisms that Japan lacked fairness and transparency in its capital markets: foreign operators and their clients were at a disadvantage when they operated in Japan. In response, CalPERS ordered the US-based Nomura Capital to suspend all trading with its parent company on behalf of the fund's account of $480 million when the scandal was exposed.

While a scandal of this size would have badly affected the reputation of any firm, and disturbed the firm for years to come, it seems business returned to normal at Nomura quite soon after. While some hoped for and anticipated a quick demise of Nomura: 'Nomura can no longer view itself as the ultimate arbiter of all matters financial, not only within Japan but also between Japan and the rest of the world' (Sender 1992: 49), this did not prove to be the case. Both of the Tabuchis were reinstated on the Nomura board in 1995, and there was no purge in Nomura. The relationship-oriented culture of Japan was fully demonstrated at Nomura – the incoming management were mentored by the Tabuchis – and out of respect for their elders, the new bosses at Nomura were unwilling to make dramatic changes, if any at all. The pace of business change in Japan was often described in the western media as *glacial,* and Nomura fully exemplified this. For some, this showed the sheer arrogance of Nomura; for others, this emphasised the resilience of a firm as big as Nomura.

The 1997 second scandal erupted for Nomura at the beginning of 1997 when information leaked out about the company's close ties with two sokaiya brothers and the circumstances surrounding Nomura's shareholder's meeting of 1995. In 1995 a sokaiya Ryuichi Koike threatened to disrupt Nomura's annual shareholder's meeting unless he was paid. At the time Nomura was in a vulnerable position having recorded poor results in 1994. There was also another item on the agenda – a vote that would allow the disgraced Tabuchis to return to the Nomura board. Again saving face was important for Nomura, and akin to most general meetings by Japanese corporations, Nomura meetings are scripted and last less than 15 minutes. Having awkward and unscripted questions during a general meeting meant that the company had not been paying their sokaiyas and was embarrassing. The president of Nomura, Hideo Sakamaki stated this paranoia when he revealed, 'I was always seized with fear, as if Koike was staring at me from the dark' (Alexander 1997). Ryuichi held 300,000 Nomura shares, a substantial amount that allowed him to make proposals at general meetings and wield a great deal of influence. The irony of this situation was that Nomura had 'loaned' him the money in order to buy Nomura shares. To guarantee his silence during the general meeting and to allow resolutions to pass through the meetings quietly without any objections, Nomura paid Ryuichi $400,000. Ryuichi kept his silence and the Nomura managers were able to gain the shareholder approval of the return of the Tabuchis to the board 'without embarrassing accusations about impropriety' (Mainichi 1999). The payment to Ryuichi might have been overlooked, and indeed for 2 years it was, had there not been other circumstances in play.

Ryutaro Hashimoto who had been Japan's finance minister when the first Nomura

scandal broke, was now Japanese prime minister. He never forgot the humiliation he suffered as finance minister when Yoshihisa Tabuchi revealed the ministry knew about the compensation deals in 1991. Secondly, Nomura was under surveillance since the 1995 vote returning the two Tabuchis. Thirdly and this was the catalyst to the 1997 exposé, the Ministry's surveillance of Nomura bore fruit when it was revealed two Nomura managing directors at Nomura, Nobutaka Fujikura and Shimpei Matsuki, had paid for the real estate company owned by Ryuichi Koike's brother, Yoshinori. This payment was funded by profits from unauthorised trading of shares and warrants at Nomura. In March 1997 the 16 directors (including the two Tabuchis) and the president of Nomura resigned when this scandal broke.

When Ryuichi Koike was arrested he revealed that over the course of his dealings with Nomura, he had received $50 million in unwarranted trading profits. This was a fraction of the amount he extorted from Dai-Ichi Kangyo Bank, some $300 million in illegal loans. He also alleged that that Nikko, Daiko and Yamaichi Securities made illegal discretionary stock deals for him. In 1997 Nomura still was the world's biggest securities house. After this second scandal, this position was rapidly lost. As the scandal was broadcast, Nomura's own subsidiaries, such as Nomura Investment Management, publicly stated they would not be doing any deals with the parent company. Nomura customers were also filing shareholder lawsuits, an uncommon phenomenon in Japan. On 2 May a Nomura shareholder (a company), filed a lawsuit for the reimbursement of the amount paid to Yoshinori Koike's property project. The second shareholder lawsuit (an individual) requested several million yen in compensation for the scandal. Unlike the first scandal when most customers of Nomura stayed with the firm, once bitten-twice shy, the company's VIP clients were prompted to take their business elsewhere. Nomura was blackballed by its regular customers – Japan's pension fund managers and corporations. The boycott of trading with Nomura was more prolonged and lasted longer than during the first

scandal and saw a huge drop in the firm's profits.

## THE COMPANY CULTURE

Nomura's culture combined the norms of Japanese business and the traits of a stock-broking firm. Nomura was committed to life-time employment. Directors of Nomura have been lifelong company men, and those holding the roles of chair and president held in great esteem. Indeed the affiliation a Nomura employee had to his firm (as inevitably most Nomura employees are men) lasted beyond retirement. The elders of Nomura who contributed greatly to the firm usually took an advisory role after the term of their directorships had ended. Some have likened joining Nomura to joining a cult: 'It was like a religious group. If you had reservations, it was better to leave' (Sender 1993: 50). Nomura employees exuded 'an unsubtle mixture of hubris and muscle. And that hubris was always by swaggering self-confidence' (Friedland 1993: 82). As with Matsushita and other major Japanese enterprises, the social harmony of the firm was valued above all, and the firm did not take too kindly to those who showed independence and displayed too much initiative. Unlike other Japanese securities firms such as Yamaichi Securities few arguments were heard at Nomura: 'We became placement robots' (Sender 1993: 51).

The ambition and arrogance fostered by internal competition is best exemplified by the sales force at Nomura. In this aspect Nomura did not diverge from other Wall Street financial firms. As the number one securities firm in Japan, the fear of losing this spot was considerable: 'The Nomura ethos represented a triumph of the poor man's mentality – the get-rich-quick desire of someone who has known poverty and dreads its return' (Sender 1993: 51). 'The sales force of Nomura had a reputation of "rough-and-tumble sales tactics and top executives" perks' (Friedland 1993: 83). Similar to western financial institutions that face deep divisions between their research and sales forces,

the sales division at Nomura would discourage independent research as this 'distracted [them] from getting behind the shares of the day'. While illegal in some countries, the sales people at Nomura would pressure the traders 'to lose Nomura money in order to get the best price and resultant commission from a corporate client' (Desmond 1998). When Albert Alletzhauser an American who used to work as a Tokyo stockbroker, wrote a book called *The House of Nomura* which was rather critical of the company, Nomura brought a libel action against Alletzhauser and tried to prevent its publication in Japan. (Preventing the publication was successful for Nomura until the 1991 scandal erupted and Japanese publishers sought the publishing rights as the book received widespread publicity as an accurate indictment of Nomura.) 'Nomura was the Godzilla of the capital markets, breaking its competitors' grasp over clients through predatory pricing and the power of its Japanese distribution network' (Friedland 1993: 83).

## THE KEY PLAYERS

### The role of the regulators

The government regulators in this saga reflected the frequent experience of other government regulators of capital markets – institutional bias and regulatory capture. Before resigning Yoshihisa Tabuchi announced the the Ministry of Finance knew what was happening at Nomura, 'the Ministry knew and implicitly condoned the firm's practice of compensating its best clients' (Sender 1992: 52). In a society that clung on the values of saving face, this made Tabuchi rather unpopular with the establishment and the then Finance Minister, Ryutaro Hashimoto. There was not one single regulatory body that oversaw the financial market in Japan; rather, they were distended groups within the Ministry of Finance and the laws at the time relied on the good faith of players rather than prescriptive legislation on proper market behaviour. As a result of the scandal, the Securities Supervisory

Board was set up in response. Despite calls for a US SEC-style body, the SSB was not self-regulatory nor did it have much power. 'In that sense it's a typically Japanese organisation' (Evans 1992: 51).

## CORPORATE GOVERNANCE

### Japanese corporate governance environment

Anglo-Saxon corporate governance 'will never find popularity in Japan' although elements of the system are finding their way into Japan (Aronson 2003). Many reforms in the Commercial Code occurred because the Japanese felt they were being left behind as the Anglo-American markets surged at the same time the Japanese economy lay in the doldrums. The mantra to Americanise corporate Japan never found great support within Japanese institutions and in the post-Enron era the Japanese were satisfied that their cautious approach towards radical implementation of American-style corporate governance edicts were justified. The main difference between the corporate governance systems of Japan and America is that the former have powerful stakeholders and the latter have powerful shareholders. Japan like other non-Anglo-Saxon countries was alarmed by the massive salary packages and stock options American corporate executives received during the 1990s and continue to receive. For example, directors at Toyota would receive less than a quarter of the payments their GM colleagues would receive.

For Japan, corporate governance is seen as a way to improve transparency inside these almost medieval corporations:

> Japanese are still cautious, and regard how the form of corporate governance relates to business performance or has other economic benefits is unproven. They also doubt the existence of any particular optimal form of corporate governance and the wisdom of legally imposing a particular set of practices on Japanese corporations.

Despite widespread acknowledgement of the necessity for change, some Japanese still believe that the emphasis should instead be on greater transparency and disclosure regardless of the particular institutional arrangements relating to corporate governance.

(Aronson 2003)

## The ties that bind

A main role corporate governance could play in Japan would be to provide governance mechanisms that emphasise transparency, accountability and disclosure to concerned stakeholders. Empowering the stakeholders and disempowering the hold of the sokaiya would be a unique Japanese goal as no other industrialised country faces the systemic hold of criminal syndicates. The sokaiya are blamed for Japan's weak corporate governance system. A corporation tainted by sokaiya connections will dismiss executives, but these are replaced with executives who have similar networks. Japanese corporate governance for the most part relies on networks of long-term shareholders, who possess a latent ability to control the company. For most corporations, the sokaiya are part of that network. In a perverse way the 1997 Nomura scandal was in one sense a sign of the developing pressure for openness, resulting from pressure from the media, equity markets and government for greater corporate disclosure, with the result that for the first time the shady connections of Japanese corporations with the sokaiya are becoming exposed.

After the scandals at Nomura, companies are under growing pressure to improve the way their annual meetings are conducted and to make them more meaningful and substantive (Hiroshi 1997). 'There is a growing sense abroad that buying the influence of sokaiya, for whatever domestic reason, must not be condoned' (Hiroshi 1997: 13). In November 1996, the Japanese Supreme Court ruled it was inappropriate for employee shareholders to take front row seats in advance of the meeting. While this decision may seem absurd (why would a court rule on the seating arrangements of a meeting?), the front row seats are usually occupied by the sokaiya, thus this directive is aimed at diminishing their influence to disrupt meetings:

Japanese companies stand at a crossroads. If they continue to allow the rampage of sokaiya, a symbol of non-transparency in Japan's corporate system, foreign distrust in corporate Japan will never go away … The question for Japanese companies is whether they will be able to cut their ties to sokaiya and build a management system that is truly oriented toward shareholder interests … the challenge for Japan's corporate executives is clear enough: Change the way annual meetings are held and eliminate collusion with sokaiya. Unless and until this is done, the peculiar custom of holding their annual meetings all on the same day will remain a permanent feature of Japan's corporate culture.

(Hiroshi 1997: 14–15)

## Domestic shareholders

Similar to other industrial countries, small Japanese shareholders do not have much influence. In Anglo-Saxon countries the influential shareholders are the institutional investors who hold large blocks of the company's shares. In Japan the influential shareholders are other corporations in an arrangement called cross-shareholding between companies, whereby the majority interests in a corporation is normally held by big corporate shareholders that support the management, such as banks, clients, members of the *keiretsu* business groups and the sokaiya (Hiroshi 1997). Theoretically Japanese shareholders have more say in the corporations: in the USA, the only way shareholders can show their displeasure at companies is through the election of directors. In Japan shareholder approval is required for electing directors and statutory directors and approving executive compensation, balance sheets, profit and loss statements, and appropriation of retained earnings.

Companies cannot even pay taxes nor conduct routine business activities unless they receive shareholder approval. This does not happen in practice because backroom deals are made with the cross-shareholders (Hiroshi 1997). The president and chair of a company have the real powers in selecting directors and auditors, so they effectively control the company. Nevertheless, such powers are available for Japanese shareholders should they wish to invoke them.

## Foreign shareholders

Foreign shareholders are usually sourced from two groups: Japanese corporations who have a substantial foreign shareholder presence, and stakeholders of Japanese subsidiaries in countries who have sophisticated procedures in place when dealing with corporate malfeasance. In the first Nomura scandal, it was CalPERS who exercised its shareholder influence by filing a lawsuit, a practice that is the norm in the USA. In the second Nomura scandal, local Japanese shareholders filed lawsuits while foreign shareholders boycotted the company. The use of lawsuits to recover and compensate moneys lost and loss of trust is unusual in corporate Japan. Aronson notes

> shareholder suits depart from normal corporate decision-making and try to strike a balance between affording directors sufficient discretion to make business decisions and providing directors with an incentive for good faith performance of their fiduciary duties. The fear of abuse of derivative litigation is probably even stronger in Japan than elsewhere due perhaps to the past role of sokaiya racketeers in extorting money from corporate management and a general reluctance to place substantial liability on individual directors who, in most cases are merely employees who have risen through the ranks.
>
> (2003)

For a country unused to seeking legal redress for wrongs committed, lawsuits by foreigners are a powerful tool to force change in Japan's corporate governance system.

In the celebrated Daiwa Bank case an employee of a New York subsidiary of Daiwa Bank, concealed losses of $377 million. Daiwa initially kept silent about the losses and publicly withheld the information for five weeks. When it was finally reported US bank regulators realised the matter was more serious than first thought and the loss in fact, was $1.1 billion. Daiwa pleaded guilty in 1996 over this concealment and paid a criminal fine of $340 million. What was special about this case was the failure by the Japanese parent to save face, hush up the incident and hide the problem from the US authorities. This case also revealed the failure of Japan's Finance Ministry to disclose relevant information to US authorities. The Daiwa case provoked changes in the banking, if not the corporate governance, system of Japan. Problems with Japan's internal controls and statutory compliance were highlighted, and policies and procedures to prevent and detect employee wrongdoing were enacted. Aronson declares the case provides 'a milestone or dividing line demarcating traditional behaviour of banks, and an increased emphasis on law in Japanese corporate governance as exemplified by the court's emphasis on the legal duties of directors' (2003). This case also highlighted an underlying trend towards the increasing role of foreign intervention in the formal legal system of Japanese corporate governance.

## Overhauling the commercial code

For fifty years Japan's commercial code was relatively unchanged. It suited both government and business that the code would be as indeterminate and advisory as possible, as opposed to being determinate and prescriptive. For most of these fifty years, the code lay as the background to the exponentially expanding and influential Japan Inc. However, the economic malaise that hit Japan in the 1990s and the scandals at Nomura and elsewhere made it clear that the code had to change to reflect current practices.

Major commercial code amendments 1993–2002

| 1993 | Fixing fee of ¥8200 for shareholder derivative suits |
|------|------|
| | Introducing a board of statutory auditors (kansayakukai) |
| | Reducing shareholder threshold to demand inspection of records |
| 1994 | Deregulating limitations on repurchase of shares (1) |
| 1997 | Introducing stock option system (deregulating limitations on repurchase of shares (2)) |
| | Simplifying merger procedures |
| 1998 | Deregulating limitations on repurchase of shares (3) |
| 1999 | Creating share exchange system |
| 2000 | Creating company spin-off system |
| 2001 | Lifting ban on treasury stock |
| | Creating new stock acquisition right system (shin kabu yoyaku ken) |
| | Expanding the authority of statutory auditors |
| | Authorising limitations on managers' liability |
| 2002 | Creating an option to form committees on board of directors in lieu of the statutory auditor system |

Table C10.2 Major commercial code amendments, 1993–2002.

Source: Adapted from Gilson and Milhaupt 2004.

Weak disclosure laws and lax accounting standards allowed the management of corporations to hide damaging news from investors and prevent the disclosure of sokaiya pay-offs. Regulators abetted these companies in hiding their losses as well. Shareholders failed to demand accurate corporation information and cross-shareholding arrangements allowing undesirable influence by these corporations over the financial markets.

The major changes in the code (outlined in Table C10.2) called for the establishment of three board committees: audit, nominating and compensation, similar to American reforms. The changes also called for the separation of directors and officers, bypassing two important German-inspired features of Japanese corporate law (the representative director and statutory auditor). Directors serving on the audit committee would replace the statutory auditors. The board is also obliged to take action to establish overall policies for internal controls and compliance with the law (Gilson and Milhaupt 2004; Milhaupt 2003). To a great extent, the code amendments were influenced by the American reforms, despite American boards not being esteemed as exemplars of good behaviour.

### Ministry of Finance

'Nomura's fate is also bound up with the future of Japan itself' (Desmond 1998). The Ministry of Finance was the government body overlooking the regulation of the securities market and its players. Like most government bodies it fostered close relationships with major industry players, and its closeness to Nomura ensured that the ministry's role in dealing with this errant company was severely scrutinised. After two major scandals at Nomura the ministry has reluctantly moved towards introducing Anglo-Saxon inspired reforms in the regulation of the securities market. The following details the reaction and reforms made by the ministry in the two Nomura scandals.

### First Nomura scandal

After the economic bubble burst in Japan, there was a great deal of concern the ministry would be inclined to liberalise the Japanese local market, especially in the fixed commissions system, and encourage foreign companies to stimulate economic growth. This was ironically called 'Wimbledonisation': Why Wimbledon?

Well, the tennis tournament is held in the United Kingdom but no British player has won it for many years. Among Japan's financial services sector the fear was that they would soon be dominated by American players such as Merrill Lynch, Goldman Sachs and Morgan Stanley, hence the loss of the local market to foreign players. The further irony was the markets were indeed liberalised but not before the subsequent scandals. The first scandal proved to be a catalyst in policy changes towards opening the local market. This was a form of punishment to the local players who had misbehaved so badly in 1991. In hindsight, a senior ministry official noted 'We should have controlled the [securities] industry more tightly' (Sender 1993: 50). The 1991 scandal was more widespread than the ministry feared: while it sometimes turned a blind eye towards minor transactions involving compensation deals, the size of the obligations incurred by brokers to compensate for losses of favoured clients shocked the ministry. The players were digging themselves a bigger hole by compensating these clients, transferring the liabilities to the vast majority of Japanese, and thus prolonging the economic recession of Japan. The scandal exposed an 'unholy side to alliances between financial bureaucrats and financiers, revealing them to be ties of self interest that sometimes operate at the expense of the public interest' (Rowley 1991: 48).

The scandal also exposed senior ministry bureaucrats being offered plum jobs in the securities industry after retirement and a list of 229 people who benefited from compensation agreements which included the names of half a dozen prominent Japanese politicians.

With Tabuchi dragging the ministry into the Nomura scandal, the ministry saw fit not only to save face but to show that the Nomura tail was not wagging the ministry dog. Thus by 1991 standards the penalties imposed including a six-week trading ban on Nomura were severe and showed the ministry was capable of punishing 'Nomura, its long-time ally in controlling Japan's capital markets, along with other securities houses' (Rowley 1991: 48). The scandal prompted a new resolve in the ministry – the ministry would no longer tolerate the practice of brokerage houses paying compensation for losses incurred by clients. (In one inscrutable twist to the story foreign brokers believed that the Japanese security houses arranged for the ministry to 'punish' them, so they might disown their traditional responsibility to compensate their big clients, as the market had fallen 55 per cent over the last year and they could no longer honour payments that ran into the hundreds of billions of dollars (*Sunday Times* 14 July 1991). Within the ministry, the implementation of this new resolve was initially dismissed; after all the ministry is 'legislator, executive and judiciary rolled into one' (Rowley 1991: 49). It had a department called the Securities Bureau, which did not have the resources nor the inclination to regulate the players in the industry in the manner of the SEC. There was a great deal of pressure on the ministry to let go some of its powers so that a new body would be able to regulate the securities industry instead of merely giving administrative guidance.

According to Aronson (2003), 'administrative guidance, utilised in conjunction with industrial policy, is largely responsible for the widespread view that Japan has a "unique" culturally based administrative system'. The ministry now realised that administrative guidance alone did not hold the same weight as it did during the industrial expansion of Japan in the 1960s. As a direct result of the scandal, the ministry set up the Securities and Exchange Surveillance Commission (SESC) which has criminal investigative powers. On the other hand the ministry's response, and that of parliament the diet, did not serve to alter significantly behaviour amongst the securities players. An inquiry into the securities scandal proved to be a disappointment. Lower house members were upset that Nomura executives were afflicted with the same memory lapses as their western counterparts, failing to recall, at the very least, involvement of crime syndicates in the firm.

## Second Nomura scandal

The ministry was quick to retaliate against this second Nomura transgression: the nascent

SESC initiated actions against Nomura having informed the firm in December 1996 they were 'under suspicion of having illegally paid trading profits to sokaiya racketeers and that some of its executives were believed to be involved in shady dealings' (Hayabusa 1997). Government prosecutors charged Nomura officials with conspiracy and violating the Commercial Code (which banned dealing with the *sokaiya*) and the Securities and Exchange Act (which prohibited compensation for investment losses). Furthermore the Japanese government banned Nomura from trading its own account and underwriting government bonds for the last five months of 1997 (Desmond 1998). The prosecution was highly symbolic as 1997 was the start of the stock market boom for America and Ishizuka posits that the government cracked down because there was an undercurrent of fear that Japanese 'business leaders are being left behind in the global economy. Fair, free and global are the buzzwords of financial deregulation, without which Japan's financial industry is considered doomed' (1997: 20).

The scandal contributed to the prolonged recession and Prime Minister Hashimoto, who saw Nomura's 1997 scandal as personally insulting, was concerned at what 'kind of reaction Japan's financial markets would get from the international community' (Starr 1997). Furthermore, the behaviour of Nomura was an affront to the Japanese people: 'Those who promised never to repeat wrongdoings did the same again, and covertly. This has damaged the securities industry as a whole' (Spindle *et al.* 1997). Due to the loss of trust in the local players the second scandal was another impetus for deregulation that had begun in the country in the early 1990s. In 1997 Japan liberalised its $2 trillion pension fund market. In 1999 Japan abolished the long term separation of commercial, trust and long term credit banks, commissions were deregulated and this gave the opportunity for international money managers to enter Japan with huge windfalls in mutual funds.

The Nomura scandal represented a further humiliation for Japan and signalled to the rest of the world that the corruption in Japanese businesses began at the top – an image that the Japanese government of the time did not need to see fostered: it was a great public embarrassment that the leader of a leading Japanese corporation had been implicated in such a serious scandal. Despite the ministry's quick action against Nomura, one anomaly existed – Nomura was a victim of extortion, the punishment handed to Nomura surpassed that given to the extortionist. The impression was and is that the corporate crooks were far more severely punished than the crooks themselves.

## The sokaiya

The yakuza is the Japanese mafia. The sokaiya are corporate extortionists and racketeers. Both are part of the Japanese social and business landscape. The paths of these two do cross and interchange but it is the sokaiya who strike fear in corporate Japan. Most Japanese firms are vulnerable to the sokaiya. Big industrial firms, such as Kirin Brewery and Sony, which have struck fear in other countries' markets, in turn fear the sokaiya. The sokaiya extorts money from Japanese companies by hiring racketeers to keep other shareholders in line at meetings. If the sokaiya aren't paid, the racketeers would publicise supposed 'personal' scandals at meetings that are trivial by American standards but in face-saving Japan, are considered fatal (Desmond 1998).

Corporate executives rather than stand up to the sokaiya, would pay off their extortionists to save their faces, and so the cycle continued. Thus, 'Once a company turns to a sokaiya, it becomes easy prey for years of blackmail over the relationship' (Ishizuka 1997: 18). In the 1990s there were four yakuza-related killings of Japanese managers. In an infamous case, the managing director of Fuji Film was murdered outside his home when he was spearheading a company campaign against corporate extortion (Martin 1997). In 1981, a policy survey showed there were 6,800 sokaiya in 500 separate groups extorting $400 million annually (Sase 2003: 28). In 1994 there were

20,000 reported cases of corporate shake-downs by sokaiya. In 1997 Japan's National Police Agency estimated there were more than 1,200 major companies approached by the sokaiya seeking 'donations', 'subscriptions to non-existent magazines' or 'Mafia-style protection payments' (Martin 1997). Four hundred of these companies paid $8 million each, while other corporations who have a long history of ties with the sokaiya, such as Nomura, paid many times over that amount annually.

To counter this, most Japanese corporations hold their annual general meetings on the same day and with the same start time so the resources of the sokaiya racketeers would be stretched. This meant a decrease in the sokaiya's bargaining power and an emphasis on selectivity, a chosen few firms would be cracked down heavily by the sokaiya on that day. According to Tokyo police, a record number of 2,308 company annual general meetings were held on Friday 27 June 1997 starting at 10 am. This was an increase of 67 from the previous year. While 10,000 police attended these meetings the police still identified 13 major criminal groups and more than 5,000 racketeer shareholders in attendance (Martin 1997).

The 1982 amendment to the Commercial Code made sokaiya practices illegal, but in practice the sokaiya participation is rife. The sokaiya is a Japanese economic institution. The prevalence of the sokaiya is so brazen that various sokaiya directories have been published. In Nomura's case, its successes and downfalls are intimately linked to its long, historical association with the sokaiya (Table C10.3). In the 1960s, Nomura's powerful chair, Minoru Segawa, was associated with the yakuza boss, Yoshio Kodama. Kodama was involved with the downfall of the then Prime Minister, Kakuei Tanaka, who admitted to receiving pay-offs when the American company, Lockheed, tried to enter the Japanese market. In turn, Kodama mentored sokaiya Rikiya Kijima, a publishing company president. Kijima's publications would be subscribed to

| Yakuza/sokaiya | Political/business link |
| --- | --- |
| Yoshio Kodama (yakuza; mentored Kijima) | 1960s Nomura boss Minoru Segawa |
| | 1970s Lockheed payoff involving then Japanese prime minister Kakuei Tanaka |
| Rikiya Kijima (sokaiya, publisher; mentored Ryuichi Koike) | 1991 Nomura president Yoshihisa Tabuchi |
| | 1991 Nomura chair Setsuya Tabuchi |
| Susumi Ishii (yakuza) [Involved in 1991 scandal] | 1991 Nomura president Yoshihisa Tabuchi (presided over Nomura glory days in 1989) |
| | 1991 Nomura chair Setsuya Tabuchi |
| Shitetsu Kamimori (sokaiya, publisher; introduced Koike to Nomura executives) | Various Nomura executives |
| Ryuichi Koike (sokaiya) | 1995–7 Nomura adviser Yoshihisa Tabuchi and Setsuya Tabuchi (returned to board) |
| Yoshinori Koike (sokaiya) (involved in 1997 scandal) | 1997 Nomura president Hideo Sakamaki |
| | 1997 Nomura Managing directors Shimpei Matsuki and Nobutaka Fujikura |
| | 1997 Nomura general affairs official in charge of shareholder's meetings Osamu Fijita |

Table C10.3 The underworld players and the Nomura players.

Source: Adapted from Reuters 1997.

by Nomura. Amongst the Nomura elite, Kijima was an influential and highly regarded man and he mentored Ryuichi Koike. It was because of the Kijima connection that Nomura was never able to fend off Koike. One Nomura branch manager solemnly noted, 'The sokaiya, as well as crooked politicians and bureaucrats, are so deeply rooted in this company that they cannot be easily dismissed' (Desmond 1998).

The anomaly in Japanese law is that the penalties for blackmail are minor compared to compensation for losses. While Koike was arrested over this affair, some sokaiya members who were arrested for blackmail were fined $100,000 and handed three-month jail sentences, which was small punishment compared to the lavish amounts of money and extravagant lifestyle they were able to extort in the sokaiya business. Nomura suffered a loss of reputation, trust, confidence and investment as a result of its relationship with criminal gangs. The sokaiya is part of the moral hazard of doing business in Japan. 'The sokaiya thrive in an atmosphere of secrecy. Greater transparency and fuller disclosure are desperately needed to insure shareholder democracy ... Accountability as Western management understands it, is still virtually non-existence in corporate and bureaucratic Japan. This is why the current trend toward Western-style corporate governance is both so difficult and so important for the future of corporate Japan' (Tsukimura in Martin 1997).

## Reforms in Nomura

In 1998, Nomura's profits had shrunk to $320 million as a direct result of the boycotts against the firm. Internationally, Nomura's reputation took quite a battering beyond the events that happened in Japan. In Australia, Nomura was accused by the ASX of misleading and deceptive conduct when Nomura's London arm manipulated the Australian currency in the foreign exchange market. The issue of insider succession was attributed as one of the main causes as to why Nomura failed miserably to implement any reforms within the organisation after the 1991 scandal. The successor to the disgraced president of Nomura was Juinichi Ujiie. He was chosen because he spent most of his career outside Japan in the American operations of Nomura. One former Nomura executive, Yoshio Terasawa, stated 'If it were not for the scandals, Ujiie would never have made CEO. He thinks and acts like an American. This is going to be an interesting case for Japan' (Desmond 1998). Ujiie was untainted by the sokaiya connections that had plagued his predecessors. The first thing Ujiie did was to cut the ties that bounded the company to the sokaiya. He cancelled 700 journal publication subscriptions that were owned by the sokaiya, and in April 1998 he sacked 11 of the 34 board members who were cronies of Sakamaki.

Amendments in the Commercial Code on the role of auditors in the intervening years have helped Ujiie diversify the Nomura board. The amendments allowed Nomura to appoint outside directors including one of 'the best known Japanese attorneys in the area of corporate law and governance practices' (Aronson 2003). Ujiie also took the radical step in Japan of transforming Nomura from having seniority-based payment and relationship-oriented promotions, towards implementing an incentive-based payment and performance-oriented promotion: '[I hope to] gradually increase Anglo-American style compensation systems in areas where the labour market is very transparent' (Desmond 1998). By June 2004 the reforms seemed to have largely succeeded and Nomura survived: revenues at Nomura reached $10 billion, a marked change from the figure six years before, and Nomura's share price has recovered somewhat though it will probably never reach again the heights of the late 1980s (Figure C10.1).

As for the sokaiya, the company feared retaliation from its ex-underworld connections (Desmond 1998) and 24-hour bodyguards were hired for Ujiie. Perhaps it is safe to say that the publicity the sokaiya had in the Nomura scandals and the high profile implementation of the reforms, have made it difficult for the underworld to target Ujiie. Ujiie oversaw one

Figure C10.1 Nomura share price.

Source: Bigcharts/Marketwatch

of the most publicised reorganisations to ever occur in a Japanese company and has survived to become Nomura chair in 2004. It is fair to say that Nomura has survived one of the more prominent examples of cultural transformation in the Japanese financial services sector. From being one of the most homogenous boards in Japan, full of inside connections and internal promotions, Nomura's board in 2004 is relatively radical in its structure and representation compared to its peers (Table C10.4).

## Nomura trials

The two managing directors were charged with violating securities laws while Sakamaki was arrested. The second Nomura scandal threatened to engulf the rest of the Japanese finance industry as the 1991 scandal did. However, the impact was isolated to the biggest securities firms in Japan (which controlled 30 per cent of the deals on the Tokyo Stock Exchange): Nomura, Daiwa Securities, Nikko Securities, Yamaichi Securities, and one bank, Dai-Ichi Kangyo. In January 1999 the Tokyo District Court handed down guilty verdicts on the charge of sokaiya payoffs, to Nomura the firm, and three of its former executives (Mainichi 1999).

The court also found the complicit behaviour of ministry officials who were wined, dined and wooed by the people they were regulating. The court stated that the large payoffs to the Koike brothers allowed the extortionists to expand their activities. Not only did this damage the trust investors and the general public had placed in the securities market, but it also tarnished Japan's international

| Nomura Holdings | |
| --- | --- |
| Foreign ownership (%) | 28.97 (NYSE-listed ADRs) |
| No. of board directors | 11 |
| No. of outside directors | 4 (36) |
| No. of nomination committee directors | 3 |
| No. of nomination committee outside directors | 2 (67) |
| No. of audit committee directors | 3 |
| No. of audit committee outside directors | 2 (67) |
| No. of compensation committee directors | 3 |
| No. of compensation committee outside directors | 2 (67) |
| No. of officers | 27 |
| No. of executive directors | 4 (15) |

Table C10.4 The board structure of Nomura Holdings.

Source: Adapted from Gilson and Milhaupt (2004: 45–47).

reputation (Mainichi 1999). Despite the strong condemnation by the court, the verdict did not leave everyone satisfied. Nomura still has 10,000 VIP accounts and clients which include politicians and senior bureaucrats who receive preferential treatment. Nomura executives who were involved in both scandals received or retained plum jobs. A former Nomura auditor Kiichiro Iwasaki, heads Nomura Finance. Yoshikazu Kitsuda a president of Nomura finance who resigned over the massive and shady sales of Tokyu, heads another company, Nippon Mutual Securities Company. An executive director who resigned over the scandal Nobuo Nakazawa, has an executive director post with another brokerage company, Kokusai Securities (Nikkei 1997).

The Nomura scandal did not widely taint nor disgrace the careers of the people involved. For some the scandal had the opposite effect. For the ordinary investor, the feeling that the corruption, the root cause of the scandal, still lingers on. Both scandals badly affected the firm's reputation but its size and network provided counterweights. However, Nomura tarnished the image of Japanese business, 'The spectacle of yet another Nomura scandal has left many Japanese jaded. They look at this and say, 'Oh yeah, Nomura again?' (Snyder 1998)

## Questions

1 Is the association of established business with criminal elements a uniquely Japanese phenomenon?.
2 A strong stakeholder system as the one present in Japan still retains many corporate governance weaknesses. Discuss.
3 Compare and contrast the strengths and weaknesses of the Japanese corporate governance with the Anglo-American corporate governance system.
4 What do you see are the respective roles of government and business in Japan?
5 Clarke and Bostock (1994) noted the strengths of Japanese corporate governance were characterised by a long-term industrial strategy, stable capital and major overseas investment in emerging markets, but let down by the weaknesses of financial speculation, secretive governance procedures and weak accountability. Assess the contemporary relevance and accuracy of this statement.

## REFERENCES

Alexander, J. (1997) Case Study: Nomura Securities, *Corporate Governance: An International Review*, 5(4): 247–252, http://www.blackwell-synergy.com/links/doi/10.1111/1467-8683.00069/abs/

Aronson, B.E. (2003) Reconsidering the Importance of Law in Japanese Corporate Governance: Evidence from the Daiwa Bank Shareholder Derivative Case, *Cornell International Law Journal*, 36, Spring.

Desmond, E.W. (1998) An Ex-champ Battles Back, *Fortune*, 137(11): 187–192.

Evans, G. (1992) Six Men at the Eye of the Storm, *Euromoney*, August, 50–56.

Fackler, M. and D. Macintyre (1997) The Who's Who of Japanese Racketeers, *Hindu Business Line*, 7 July.

Friedland, J. (1993) Nomura's New Look, *Far Eastern Economic Review*, 23 September, 82–84.

Gilson, R.J. and Milhaupt, C.J. (2004) *Choice as Regulatory Reform: The Case of Japanese Corporate Governance*, http://www.isnie.org/ISNIE04/Papers/milhaupt.pdf

Hayabusa, N. (1997) The Question Is Whether Nomura Can Change: The Old Order of the Company Has Remained Unchanged, *Asahi Shimbun*, 15 May.

Hiroshi, O. (1997) The Sokaiya's Grip on Corporate Japan, *Japan Quarterly*, 1 July, 44(3).

Ishizuka, M. (1997) Japanese Firms' Sokaiya Ties Run Deep, *Asian Business*, August, 18–20.

*Mainichi Daily News* (1999) Nomura Verdict, 24 January.

Martin, N.A. (1997) Bowing to Pressure, *Barron's*, 11 August, 19–20.

Milhaupt, C.J. (2003) *A Lost Decade for Japanese Corporate Governance Reform*, Working Paper, 234, Centre for Law and Economic Studies, Columbia Law School.

Nikkei English News (1997) Disgraced Nomura Execs Get Plum Posts, 10 May.

Pascale, R.T. and A.G. Athos (1986) *The Art of Japanese Management*, London: Penguin Business.

Reuters (1997) Nomura's Yoshihisa Tabuchi Says Never Met Koike, 5 June.

Rowley, A. (1991) Ministry of Myopia, *Far Eastern Economic Review*, 12 September, 48–50.

Sase, Takao (2003) *The Irresponsible Japanese Top Management under the Cross-Shareholding Arrangement*. Occasional Paper, 50, Centre on Japanese Economy and Business, Columbia Business School, January.

Sender, H. (1992) The Humbling of Nomura, *Institutional Investor*, February, 49–53.

Starr, P. (1997) Recasts with the Finance Ministry's Move, Agence France-Press, 5 June.

Snyder, J. (1998) Japan's Nomura Embroiled in Scandal – Again, Reuters, 14 January.

## Additional downloadable articles

BBC News on Nomura, http://newssearch.bbc.co.uk/cgi-bin/search/results.pl?scope=newsifs&tab=news&q=nomura+scandal

Bremner, B. (1997) A Big Stink Speeds Up Tokyo's Big Bang, *BusinessWeek*, http://www.businessweek.com/1997/27/b3534163.htm

Bremner, B. (2003) Nomura's Comeback, *Businessweek*, 7 April, http://www.businessweek.com/magazine/content/03_14/b3827134_mz035.htm

CNN Money (1997) Nomura Head May Resign, 7 March, http://money.cnn.com/1997/03/07/companies/nomura_pkg/

Foreign Press Center (1997) *Ex-president of Nomura Securities Arrested*, 16 June, http://www.fpcj.jp/e/shiryo/jb/j9717.html

Healy, Tim (1997) Containing the Damage: Nomura Securities Reels from a Trading Scandal, 21 March, http://www.asiaweek.com/asiaweek/97/0321/biz4.html

Hills, Ben (1998) The Financial Monster That Tried to Eat Australia, *Sydney Morning Herald*, 11 December, http://www.globalpolicy.org/socecon/bwi-wto/normura.htm

Nomura, http://www.nomuraholdings.com/investor/cg/

Nomura entry on Wikipedia, http://en.wikipedia.org/wiki/Nomura

# Appendix 1
# Corporate Governance Websites

## ACADEMIC

Canadian Corporate Governance Institute, Alberta
http://www.bus.ualberta.ca/ccgi/
Centre for Corporate and Commercial Law, Cambridge
http://cccl.law.cam.ac.uk/
Centre for Corporate Governance, UTS
http://www.ccg.uts.edu.au
Centre for Corporate Governance Research – University of Birmingham,
http://www.bham.ac.uk/page.asp?section=00010001000900010000500040003
Center for Corporate Governance, Dartmouth
http://mba.tuck.dartmouth.edu/ccg
Centre for Corporate Governance and Performance, Yale
http://yccg.som.yale.edu/
Centre for Corporate Law and Securities Regulation, Melbourne
http://cclsr.law.unimelb.edu.au/
Centre for Leadership and Change Management, Wharton
http://leadership.wharton.upenn.edu/governance/index.shtml
Centro di Ricerca per il Diritto d'Impresa, LUISS Guido Carli
http://www.luiss.it/ricerca/centri/ceradi/
Corporate Governance Initiative, HBS
http://www.corpgov.hbs.edu/
Corporate Governance Project, Canberra
http://www.blis.canberra.edu.au/corpgov-aps/

## BUSINESS

American Institute of Certified Public Accountants
http://aicpa.org/
American Association of Bank Directors
http://www.aabd.org/
Australian Institute of Company Directors
http://www.companydirectors.com.au
Association of Superannuation Funds of Australia Limited (ASFA)
http://www.asfa.asn.au
Australian Council of Super Investors Inc. (ACSI)
http://www.acsi.org.au
Australian Institute of Superannuation Trustees (AIST)
http://www.aist.asn.au
Business Council of Australia
http://www.bca.com.au
Business Roundtable: Corporate Governance
http://www.businessroundtable.org
Centre for International Private Enterprise
http://www.cipe.org/
European Corporate Governance Service
http://www.ecgs.net/
Institute of Chartered Accountants in England and Wales
http://www.icaew.co.uk/
International Chamber of Commerce
http://www.iccwbo.org/
Investments and Financial Services Association Limited (IFSA)
http://www.ifsa.com.au/

Investor Responsibility Research Centre
http://www.irrc.org/index.html
Institutional Shareholder Services
http://www.issproxy.com
UK Institute of Chartered Secretaries and Administrators
http://www.icsa.org.uk/
UK Institute of Directors
http://www.iod.com
US National Association of Directors
http://www.nacdonline.org/
Value Alliance
http://www.thevaluealliance.com
World Economic Forum
http://www.weforum.org

## GOVERNMENT

Australian Securities and Investments Commission
http://www.asic.gov.au
Bank for International Settlements
http://www.bis.org/index.htm
European Central Bank
http://www.ecb.int/home/html/index.en.html
European Commission
http://europa.eu.int/comm/internal_market/company/index_en.htm
European Court of Auditors
http://www.eca.eu.int/
European Ombudsman
http://www.euro-ombudsman.eu.int/home/en/default.htm
H.K. Securities and Futures Commission
http://www.sfc.hk/sfc/html/EN/
Japanese Financial Services Agency
http://www.fsa.go.jp/indexe.html
OECD Corporate Governance
http://www.oecd.org/topic/0,2686,en_2649_37439_1_1_1_1_37439,00.html
Sarbanes–Oxley Act
http://www.legalarchiver.org/soa.htm
Singapore Monetary Authority
http://www.mas.gov.sg
UK Disqualified Directors Register
http://www.companieshouse.gov.uk/ddir/
UK Financial Services Authority
http://www.fsa.gov.uk/

UNCTAD
http://www.unctad.org/
US Department of Justice
http://www.usdoj.gov/
US Federal Reserve Board
http://www.federalreserve.gov/
US Securities and Exchange Commission
http://www.sec.gov/index.htm

## OTHER RESEARCH AND POLICY INSTITUTIONS

Asian Corporate Governance Association
http://www.acga-asia.org/index.cfm
Asian Centre for Corporate Governance
http://www.asiancentre.org/
Australian Stock Exchange
http://www.asx.com.au
Brookings Institution: Corporate Governance
http://www.brook.edu/gs/research/areas/corporate/corporate_hp.htm
California Public Employees' Retirement System
http://www.calpers.ca.gov/
Cato Institute
http://www.cato.org/current/corporate-governance/
Centre for Economic Policy Research
http://www.cepr.org/
Club of Florence
http://www.cof-cg.org/about/index.php
Commonwealth Association of Corporate Governance
http://www.cacg-inc.com/index.html
Corporate Governance, Japan
http://www.rieti.go.jp/cgj/en/index.htm
Corporate Governance Network
http://www.corpgov.net/
Corporate Library
http://www.thecorporatelibrary.com
Encycogov
http://www.encycogov.com/
European Corporate Governance Forum
http://ec.europa.eu/internal_market/company/ecgforum/index_en.htm
European Corporate Governance Institute
http://www.ecgi.org
European Corporate Governance Training Network
http://www.ecgtn.org/

Global Corporate Governance Forum, World Bank Group
http://www.gcgf.org/
Global Reporting Initiative
http://www.globalreporting.org
Governance Metrics International
http://www.gmiratings.com
International Business Ethics Institute
http://www.business-ethics.org
International Corporate Governance Network
http://www.icgn.org
International Organization of Securities Commissions
http://www.iosco.org
National Association of Pension Funds, UK
http://www.napf.co.uk/
NASDAQ
http://www.nasdaq.com
New York Stock Exchange
http://www.nyse.com
Organisation for Economic Co-operation and Development
http://www.oecd.org
Securities Industry Research Centre of Asia Pacific
http://www.sirca.org.au/
TIAA-CREF
http://www.tiaa-cref.org/
UK Universities Superannuation Scheme (USS)
http://www.usshq.co.uk
World Bank – Private Sector Development (Corporate Governance)
http://rru.worldbank.org/Themes/CorporateGovernance/
World Bank Institute – Private Sector Development (Corporate Governance and Corporate Social Responsibility)
http://www.worldbank.org/wbi/corpgov
World Federation of Exchanges
http://www.world-exchanges.org/

## OTHER STAKEHOLDERS

Business for Social Responsibility
http://www.bsr.org
Business Leaders' Initiative on Human Rights
http://www.blihr.org/human.htm

Centre for Social and Environmental Accounting Research
http://www.ceres.org/
CorpWatch
http://www.corpwatch.org/
European Social Investment Forum
http://www.eurosif.org/
Executive Paywatch
http://www.aflcio.org/corporateamerica/paywatch
Investor Responsibility Research Center
http://www.irrc.org
IT Governance Institute
http://www.itgi.org/
Pension Research Council
http://prc.wharton.upenn.edu/prc/prc.html
Proxy Matters
http://www.proxymatters.com/
Social Funds
http://www.socialfunds.com
Transparency International
http://www.transparency.org/
United for a Fair Economy
http://www.faireconomy.org/
US Social Investment Forum
http://www.socialinvest.org/
World Business Council for Sustainable Development
http://www.wbcsd.org/
World Environment Foundation
http://www.wef.org.uk/

## JOURNALS AND ONLINE PUBLICATIONS

Corporate Board Member
http://www.boardmember.com/
Corporate Governance – An International Review
http://www.blackwellpublishing.com/journal.asp?ref=0964-8410
Corporate Governance – International Journal of Business in Society
http://www.emeraldinsight.com/Insight/viewContainer.do?containerType=JOURNAL&containerId=12183
Directors and Boards
http://www.directorsandboards.com/
ECGI Working Papers
http://www.ecgi.org/wp/index.php
Financial Times
http://news.ft.com/businesslife/governance

Google Scholar
http://scholar.google.com/scholar?q=
%22corporate+governance%22&ie=UTF-8&oe=
UTF-8&hl=en
Governance UK
http://www.governance.co.uk/index.htm
International Journal of Auditing
http://www.blackwellpublishing.com/journal.asp?
ref=1090-6738&site=1
OECD Principles
http://www.oecd.org/document/56/
0,2340,en_2649_34813_31530865_1_1_1_1,00.
html
REPEC
http://repec.org/
Social Science Research Network
http://papers.
ssrn.com
Wikipedia
http://en.wikipedia.org/wiki/
Corporate_governance
Wikipedia: List of Companies
http://en.
wikipedia.org/wiki/List_of_companies

## CORPORATE LINKS

### Argentina

Aerolineas Argentinas
http://www.aerolineas.com.ar/ar/index.asp?
pais=ar&idi=en&secc=1&subs=1&tipo=A
FaSinPat
http://www.fasinpat.com.ar/

### Australia

ABC Learning Centres
http://www.childcare.
com.au/investor/overview.htm
AMP
http://www.amp.com.au/group/2column/
0,2445,CH8463%255FNI74096%255FSI3,00.html
ANZ
http://www.anz.com/australia/aboutanz/
corporateinformation/corpgovpolicy/
Aristocrat
http://www.aristocrat.com.au/

Babcock & Brown
http://www.
babcockbrown.com
BHP Billiton
http://www.bhpbilliton.com/bb/
aboutUs/governance.jsp
Commonwealth Bank
http://shareholders.
commbank.com.au/group_display/
0,1922,NI2221%255FCH2221,00.html
Fosters
http://www.fosters.com.au/about/
governance.htm
James Hardie
http://www.ir.jameshardie.com.au/
default.jsp?xcid=38
Perpetual
http://www.perpetual.com.au/
shareholder_centre/corporate_responsibility.
htm
Qantas
http://www.qantas.com.au/info/about/
corporateGovernance
QBE
http://www.qbe.com/Version_2/investors/html/
investors/QBE_investors_corporategovernance.
html
Macquarie Bank
http://www.macquarie.com.au/au/about_
macquarie/corporate_governance.htm
NAB
http://www.nabgroup.com/0,,33874,00.html
Rio Tinto
http://www.riotinto.com/investor/
information/corpGovernance.aspx
Telstra
http://www.telstra.com.au/abouttelstra/
corp/governance.cfm
Westpac
http://www.westpac.com.au

### Brazil

Banco Bradesco
http://www.bradesco.com.br/ir/
Banco Do Brasil
http://www.bb.com.br/appbb/
portal/ri/eng/MenuEstCorp.jsp

Petrobras
http://www2.petrobras.com.br/Petrobras/ingles/
visao/vis_index.htm

## Canada

Alcan
http://www.alcan.com/web/publishing.nsf/
Content/Investors+-+Corporate+Governance
Bombardier
http://www.bombardier.com/en/
0_0/0_0_1_7/0_0_1_7_7/0_0_1_7_7.jsp
CanWest
http://www.canwestglobal.com/
corp_governance.html
George Weston
http://www.weston.ca/en/
inv_governance.html
Manulife
http://www.manulife.com/corporate/corporate2.
nsf/Public/corporategovernance.html
Royal Bank of Canada
http://www.rbc.com/governance/index.html

## Chile

Codelco
http://www.codelco.com/la_corporacion/
fr_corporacion.html

## China

Bank of China (Hong Kong) Ltd
http://www.bochk.com/web/common/
multi_section.xml?section=about&level_2=
corporate_governance&fldr_id=30246
China First Automotive Works
http://www.faw.com/webcontent/aboutfaw.jsp
China Life Insurance
http://www.chinalife.com.cn/
China Mobile Communications
http://www.chinamobile.com/ENGLISH/index.
html
China National Petroleum
http://www.cnpc.com.cn/english/gsgk/gsjj.htm
China Telecommunications
http://www.chinatelecom.com.cn

Hutchison Whampoa
http://www.hutchison-whampoa.com/eng/about/
csr/csr.htm
Industrial & Commercial Bank of China
http://www.icbc.com.cn/e_about/index.
jsp?column=About+Us%3EAnnual+Report
Lenovo
http://www.pc.ibm.com/ww/lenovo/
investor_relations.html
Shanghai Baosteel Group
http://www.baosteel.com/english_n/
e02introduction_n/0201.htm
Sinopec
http://english.sinopec.com/en-ir/en-governance/
index.shtml

## Denmark

Bang & Olufsen
http://www.bang-olufsen.com/web2/investors/
Moller-Maersk
http://www.maersk.com
Danske Bank
http://www.danskebank.com/Link/
corporategovernance

## Finland

Nokia
http://www.nokia.com/A402704

## France

Alcatel
http://www.alcatel.com/apropos/values/
governance/
Airbus/EADS
http://www.eads.net/web/lang/ en/1024/content/
OF00000000400004/6/03/31000036.html
AXA
http://www.axa.com/en/governance/
BNP Paribas
http://www.bnpparibas.com/en/
group/board.asp
Carrefour
http://www.carrefour.com/english/
groupecarrefour/gouvernementEnt.jsp

Crédit Agricole
http://www.credit-agricole-sa.fr/
rubrique.php3?id_rubrique=342
Electricité de France
http://www.edf.fr/75125i/Homecom/
Shareholders/Group/Corporategovernance.html
France Telecom
http://www.francetelecom.com/en/group/
development/governance/
Gaz de France
http://www.gazdefrance.com/
Groupe Danone
http://www.danone.com/wps/portal/jump/
DanoneCorporateIntl.Finance.
Highlights.GovCorporate
L'Oréal
http://www.loreal.com/
LVMH
http://www.lvmh.com/comfi/pg_gouv.
asp?rub=8&srub=2
Michelin
http://www.michelin.com/corporate/front/
templates/affich.jsp?codeRubrique=
7&lang=EN
Peugeot
http://www.psa-peugeot-citroen.com/en/
psa_espace/corporate_governance_f42.php
Renault
http://www.renault.com/renault_com/en/main/
20_FINANCE/Gouvernement_ d_entreprise/
Sanofi-Aventis
http://en.sanofi-aventis.com/
investors/enterprise_government/
p_administration_council.asp
Suez
http://www.suez.com/groupe/english/
organisation/index.php
Total
http://www.total.com/en/group/
corporate_social_responsibility
Vivendi
http://finance.vivendiuniversal.com/finance/
group_overview/corpo-gove-00.htm

## Germany

Allianz
http://www.allianz.com/azcom/dp/cda/
0,,80824-44,00.html

BASF
http://corporate.basf.com/en/
investor/cg/
Bayer
http://www.bayer.com/about-bayer/
corporate-governance/page698.htm
Bertelsmann
http://www.bertelsmann.com/
BMW
http://www.bmwgroup.com/e/nav/
index.html?
http://www.bmwgroup.com/e/
0_0_www_bmwgroup_com/
verantwortung/leitbild_nachhaltigkeit/
leitlinien.html
CommerzBank
http://www.commerzbank.com/aktionaere/
governance/index.html
DaimlerChrysler
http://www.daimlerchrysler.com/dccom/
0,,0-5-58355-1-58551-1-0-0-0-0-0-
243-7155-0-0-0-0-0-0-0,00.html
Deutsche Bahn
http://www.db.de/site/bahn/en/db__group/
investor__relations/corporate__governance/
corporate__governance.html
Deutsche Bank
http://www.db.com/en/content/company/
corporate_governance.htm
Deutsche Telekom
http://www.telekom3.de/en-p/inve/8-co/1-co/
home/corporate-governance-code-
ar,templateId=_2Fdt_2Fweb_2Fstruct_
2FContent.jsp.html
E.ON
http://www.eon.com/en/investoren/
939.jsp
KarstadtQuelle
http://www.karstadtquelle.com/
englisch/konzern/2904.asp
Munich Re
http://www.munichre.com/pages/05/
corporate_governance/default_en.aspx
SAP
http://www.sap.com/company/governance/
index.epx
Siemens
http://www.siemens.com/index.jsp?
sdc_p=ft6ml1s4uo1330857i1052305pcz2&sdc_
bcpath=1229196.s_7,&

ThyssenKrupp
http://www.thyssenkrupp.com/
en/investor/corporate-governance.html
Volkswagen
http://www.volkswagen-ir.de/
Corporate_Governance.286.2.html

## India

Bharat Gears
http://www.bharatgears.com/company/
govern.html
Bharat Petroleum
http://www.bharatpetroleum.
com/corporate/code_of_conduct.asp?from=corp
Hindustan Petroleum
http://hindustanpetroleum.
com/hp.aspx
Indian Oil
http://www.iocl.com/
initiatives_corporate.aspx
Mittal Steel
http://www.mittalsteel.com/
Investor+Relations/Corporate+Governance/

## Italy

Assicurazioni Generali
http://www.generali.com/generalicom/
sezione.do?idItem=120243&idSezione=120242
Benetton
http://press.benettongroup.com/ben_en/
about/
Bulgari
http://production.investis.com/bulgari/
frameset/
Eni
http://www.eni.it/eniit/eni/print.do?lang=
en&sessionId=11464410&RID=@2sXDV|0?
xoidcmWopk&showPrintButton=false&
contestualize=false&menu=false&layout=
la_compagnia
Fiat
http://www.fiatgroup.com/main.php?w=
OSUK7ONA8Q84S94RMZ3L
Telecom Italia
http://www.telecomitalia.it/opa/eng/
ir_corporate.html

## Japan

Hitachi
http://www.hitachi.com/csr/group/
management/index.html
Mitsubishi UFJ Financial Group
http://www.
mufg.jp/english/profile/governance/
Mitsui Fudosan
http://www.mitsuifudosan.co.jp/
english/home/corporate_governance.html
NTT Docomo
http://www.nttdocomo.co.jp/
Panasonic
http://panasonic.co.jp/csr/
Sony
http://www.sony.net/SonyInfo/IR/
governance.html
Sumitomo
http://www.sumitomocorp.co.jp/
english/company_e/governance/index.shtml
Toyota
http://www.toyota.co.jp/en/ir/

## Luxembourg

Arcelor
http://www.arcelor.com/index.php?lang=en&
page=231

## Mexico

Pemex
http://www.pemex.com/index.cfm?
action=content&sectionID=11&catID=117

## Netherlands

ABN AMRO
http://www.abnamro.com/com/ir/
corp_gov.jsp
Fortis
http://www.fortis.com/Governance/index.asp
Heineken
http://www.heinekeninternational.com/
governance/index.jsp

ING Group
http://www.ing.com/group/showdoc.jsp?docid=
074059_EN&menopt=cog
Rabobank
http://www.rabobank.com/content/rabobank/
CorporateGovernance.jsp
Royal Philips Electronics
http://www.philips.
com/about/company/corporategovernance/
index.html
Royal Ahold
http://www.ahold.com/index.aspx?id=484
TNT
http://group.tnt.com/corporategovernance/

## New Zealand

Fonterra
http://www.fonterra.com/content/
corporategovernance/boardoffonterra/
default.jsp
Telecom NZ
http://www.telecom.co.nz/stream/
0,3898,202679-1547,00.html

## Norway

Norsk Hydro
http://www.hydro.com/en/about/
corp_governance/index.html
Statoil
http://www.statoil.com/fin/svg03595.
NSF/UNID/
91219B556C4ABAEFC12570AC00480E9B?
OpenDocument

## Philippines

Ayala
http://www.ayala.com.ph/about/
corpgov.asp
San Miguel
http://www.sanmiguel.com.ph/
SM
http://www.smprime.com

## Russia

Gazprom
http://eng.gazpromquestions.ru/page19.shtml
LukOil
http://www.lukoil.com/static_6_5id_298_.html
Yukos
http://www.yukos.com/New_IR/
Corporate_governance_charter.asp
UES of Russia
http://rao-ues.rustocks.com/
index.phtml/eng/CGCode

## Saudi Arabia

Al Rajhi Bank
http://www.alrajhibank.com.sa/
EN/HeaderNav/About_US/
Sabic
http://www.sabic.com/sabic-www/
index_Overview.htm
Saudi Aramco
http://www.saudiaramco.com/

## Singapore

Flextronics
http://www.flextronics.com/
Singapore Air
http://www.singaporeair.com/saa/
en_UK/content/company_info/responsibility/
corporategovernance.jsp
SingTel
http://home.singtel.com/about_singtel/
corporate_governance/corporate_
governance.asp
Temasek Holdings
http://www.temasekholdings.com.sg/

## South Africa

De Beers
http://www.debeersgroup.com/
NedBank
http://www.nedbankgroup.co.za/
content/main/corporate_gov.asp
SAB Miller
http://www.sabmiller.com/

South African Airways
http://ww4.flysaa.com/en/en_content_frameset.
html?contents=/about_saa/company_
information/za_message_from_the_ceo_
content.html

## South Korea

Daewoo
http://www.daewoo.com/english/
company/vision.jsp
Hyundai
http://worldwide.hyundai-motor.com/
LG
http://www.lge.com/
Samsung
http://www.samsung.com/
AboutSAMSUNG/ELECTRONICSGLOBAL/
InvestorRelations/CorporateGovernance/
CEOMessage/index.htm

## Spain

BBVA
http://ws1.grupobbva.com/TLBB/tlbb/jsp/ing/
gobcorpo/index.jsp
BSCH
http://www.gruposantander.com/pagina/indice/
0,,416_3_2,00.html
Endesa
http://www.endesa.es/Portal/es/
gobierno_corporativo/estructura_gobierno/
Principios_gobierno_corporativo.htm
Gamesa
http://www.gamesa.es/
Repsol YPF
http://www.repsolypf.com/eng/
todosobrerepsolypf/accionistaseinversores/
gobiernocorporativo/gobiernocorporativo.asp?
FormatoID=4503&PaginaID=53020&Nivel=2
Telefonica
http://www.telefonica.es/investors/

## Sweden

Ericsson
http://www.ericsson.com/ericsson/corpinfo/
corp_governance/index.shtml

Electrolux
http://www.electrolux.com/node31.aspx
SCA
http://www.sca.com/about/cg_corporate.asp

## Switzerland

ABB
http://www.abb.com/global/abbzh/abbzh252.nsf/
0/2ff55ab29cc587c5c1256f9c005171c1?
OpenDocument
Nestlé
http://www.ir.nestle.com/Nestle_Overview/
Corporate_Responsibility/
Corporate+Responsibility.htm
Novartis
http://www.novartis.com/
about_novartis/en/leadership_governance.shtml
Roche
http://www.roche.com/
UBS
http://www.ubs.com/1/e/about/cg/overview.
html

## Taiwan

ACER
http://global.acer.com/about/investor/
reports.htm
Foxconn - Hon Hai Precision Industry
http://www.foxconn.com/about/
introduction.asp

## Thailand

PTT
http://www.pttplc.com/en/ptt_core.asp?
page=ir_go

## Turkey

Koc Holding
http://www.koc.com.tr/User/InvestorInfo.
aspx?LANGUAGE_CODE=EN#

## UAE

Emirates
http://www.ekgroup.com/AnnualReports/
Index.asp
First Gulf Bank
http://www.fgb.ae/

## UK

BP
http://www.bp.com/subsection.do?
categoryId=9002180&contentId=7014793
GlaxoSmithKline
http://www.gsk.com/about/corp-gov-ethics.htm
HSBC
http://www.hsbc.com/hsbc/
investor_centre/corporate-governance
RBS
http://www.rbs.com/corporate03.asp?id=
CORPORATE_RESPONSIBILITY/
CORPORATE_GOVERNANCE
Royal Dutch Shell
http://www.shell.com/home/investor-en/html/
iwgen/company_information/
corporate_governance/dir_corporate_
governance.html
Unilever
http://www.unilever.com/ourcompany/
investorcentre/corp_governance/
Vodafone
http://www.vodafone.com/section_article/
0,3035,CATEGORY_ID%
253D302%2526LANGUAGE_ID%253D0%
2526CONTENT_ID%253D230702,00.html

## USA

Altria
http://www.altria.com/about_altria/
1_5_corporategovernance.asp
Amazon
http://phx.corporate-ir.net/phoenix.zhtml?c=
97664&p=irol-govHighlights
Berkshire Hathaway
http://www.berkshirehathaway.com/govern/
govern.html

Boeing
http://www.boeing.com/corp_gov/
Citigroup
http://www.citigroup.com/citigroup/
corporategovernance/
Disney
http://corporate.disney.go.com/corporate/
governance.html
eBay
http://investor.ebay.com
Exxon-Mobil
http://www.exxonmobil.com/Corporate/
InvestorInfo/ Corp_II_Governance.asp
General Electric
http://www.ge.com/en/company/investor/
corp_governance.htm
General Motors
http://www.gm.com/company/
investor_information/corp_gov/
Google
http://investor.google.com/conduct.html
IBM
http://www.ibm.com/investor/corpgovernance/
index.phtml
Intel
http://www.intel.com/intel/finance/corp_gov.
htm
Johnson & Johnson
http://www.investor.jnj.com/governance/
index.cfm?textOnly=false
Microsoft
http://www.microsoft.com/msft/governance/
guidelines.mspx
News Corporation
http://www.newscorp.com/corp_gov/
index.html
Wal-Mart
http://investor.walmartstores.com/phoenix.
zhtml?c=112761&p=
irol-govhighlights

## Venezuela

Petroleos de Venezuela
http://www.pdv.com/index.php?tpl=interface.
en/design/readmenuprinc.tpl.
html&newsid_temas=11

# Appendix 2
# Regional and Country Codes and Reports

## UNITED STATES

(Figure 4.1)

### US federal statutes

Glass Banking Act (1932).
Glass Steagall Act (1932).
Securities Act (1933).
Securities Exchange Act (1934).
Public Utility Holding Company Act (1935).
Securities Act (1935).
Social Security Act (1935).
Wagner Act (1935).
Investment Advisers Act (1940).
Investment Compact Act (1940).
Trust Indenture Act (1940).
Taft Harley Act (1947).
Bank Holding Company Act (1956).
Landrum-Griffin Act (1959).
Employment Retirement Income Security Act (1974).
Foreign Corrupt Practices Act (1977).
Gramm Leach Billey Act (1999).
Sarbanes–Oxley Act (2002).

## UK

(Figure 4.3)

Cadbury, A. (1992) *The Committee on the Financial Aspects of Corporate Governance* (Cadbury Report), London: Gee and Company.
*The Committee on Corporate Governance* (1998) (Hampel Report), London: Gee and Company.

Department of Trade and Industry (2001) *Modern Company Law Review*, London: DTI.
Department of Trade and Industry (2003) *Co-ordinating Group on Audit and Accounting Issues (CGAA) Report*, London: DTI.
Department of Trade and Industry (2003) *Review of the Regulatory Regime of the Accountancy Profession: Legislative Proposals*, London: DTI.
Department of Trade and Industry (2003) *Review of the Role and Effectiveness of Non-executive Directors* (Higgs Report), London: DTI.
European Commission (2003) *Modernising Company Law and Corporate Governance in the European Union: A Plan To Move Forward* (Jaap Winter Report), Brussels: EC.
Financial Reporting Council (2003) *Audit Committees Combined Code Guidance* (Smith Report), London: FRC.
Financial Reporting Council (2003) *The Combined Code on Corporate Governance*, London: FRC.
Greenbury, R. (1995) *Directors' Remuneration: Report of a Study Group by Sir Richard Greenbury* (Greenbury Report), London: Gee and Company.
HM Treasury (2001) *Institutional Investment in the UK* (Myners Report), London: HM Treasury.
Institute of Chartered Accountants in England and Wales (1999) *Internal Control: Guidance for Directors on the Combined Code* (Turnbull Report), London: ICAEW.
Institutional Shareholders Committee (2002) *Statement of Principles on Shareholder Activism*, London: Investment Management Association.
London Stock Exchange (1998) *Combined Code*, London: LSE.
Royal Society of Arts (1992) *Tomorrow's Company Inquiry*, London: RSA.

## Statutes

UK Company Law Reform Act (2006).
US Sarbanes–Oxley Act (2002).

## AUSTRALIA

### (Figure 4.5)

ACSI (2003) *Corporate Governance Guidelines for Superannuation and Fund Trustees and Corporations*, Australian Council of Super Investors Inc.

AIMA (1995) *Guide and Statement of Recommended Practice*, Sydney: Investment and Financial Services Association.

ASX Corporate Governance Council (2003) *Principles of Good Corporate Governance and Best Practice Recommendations*, Sydney: Australian Stock Exchange.

Bosch, H. (1995) *Corporate Practices and Conduct* 3rd edn (Bosch Report), Sydney: Australian Institute of Company Directors.

Hilmer, F. (1993; 1998) *Strictly Boardroom: Improving Governance to Enhance Company Performance* (Report of the Independent Working Party into Corporate Governance), Melbourne: Business Library.

IFSA (1999) *Corporate Governance: A Guide to Investment Managers and Corporations*, Sydney: Investment and Financial Services Association.

IFSA (2002) *Corporate Governance: A Guide to Investment Managers and Corporations* (Blue Book), Sydney: Investment and Financial Services Association.

NSW Audit Office (1997) *Corporate Governance*, vol. 1: *In Principle* (Performance Audit Report), Sydney: NSW Government.

NSW Audit Office (1997) *Corporate Governance* vol. 2: *In Practice* (Performance Audit Report), Sydney: NSW Government.

NSW Audit Office (1998) *On Board: Guide to Better Practice for Public Sector Governing and Advisory Boards*, Sydney: NSW Government.

Owen, N. (2003) *The HIH Royal Commission Report*, Canberra: Commonwealth of Australia.

Psaros, J. and Seamer, M. (2002) *Horwath Corporate Governance Report*, Newcastle: University of Newcastle.

SAI Global (2003) *Governance Guidelines*, Sydney: SAI.

## Statutes

Australian Company Law Reform program (Audit Reform and Corporate Disclosure) Act (2004) known as CLERP 9.
US Sarbanes–Oxley Act (2002).

## EUROPE

### (Figure 5.3)

AFG (1998; 2001; 2004) *Recommandations sur le gouvernement d'enterprise*, Paris: Association Française de la Gestion Financière.

Aldama y Miñon, E. (2003) *Report by the Special Commission to Foster Transparency and Security in the Markets and in Listed Companies* (Aldama Report), Madrid: Government of Spain.

Asbrink, E. (2004) *Swedish Code of Corporate Governance: Report of the Code Group*, Stockholm: Swedish Government.

Baums, T. (2001) *German Government Panel on Corporate Governance*, Berlin: Government of Germany.

Böckli, P. (2002) *Swiss Code of Best Practice for Corporate Governance*, Zurich: Swiss Business Federation.

Borsa Italiana (1999) *Code of Conduct Report by the Committee for the Corporate Governance of Listed Companies* (Preda Code), Rome: Borsa Italiana.

Cadbury, A. (1992) *The Committee on the Financial Aspects of Corporate Governance* (Cadbury Report), London: Gee and Company.

CNFP and AFEP (1995) *The Boards of Directors of Listed Companies in France* (Vienot Report I), Paris: Conseil National du Patrona Français and Association Française des Enterprises Privées.

Cromme, G. (2002; 2003; 2005; 2006) *German Corporate Governance Code* (Cromme Code), Düsseldorf: Government Commission on the German Corporate Governance Code.

CSE (2001) *Recommendations for Corporate Governance in Denmark* (Nørby Committee), Copenhagen: Copenhagen Stock Exchange.

CSE (2003) *Report on Corporate Governance in Denmark*, Copenhagen: Copenhagen Stock Exchange.

EC (2003 ) *Modernising Company Law and Enhancing Corporate Governance*, Brussels: European Commission.

ICA (2004) *Principles of Good Corporate Governance: Spain*, Madrid: Instituto de Consejeros-Administradores.

Lippens, M. (2004) *Belgian Code on Corporate Governance*, Brussels: Corporate Governance Committee.

Norwegian Shareholders' Association *et al.* (2004) *The Norwegian Code of Practice for Corporate Governance*, Oslo: Norwegian Shareholders Association, Norwegian Institute of Public Accountants, Institutional Investor Forum, Norwegian Financial Services Association, Norwegian Society of Financial Analysts, Confederation of Norwegian Business and Industry, Norwegian Association of Private Pension Funds, Oslo Børs & Norwegian Mutual Fund Association.

OECD (1999; 2004) *Principles of Corporate Governance*, Paris: OECD.

Olivencia Ruiz, M. (1998) *El Gobierno de las Sociedades Cotizadas* (Olivencia Report), Madrid: Ministry of Economy and Finance.

Tabaksblat, M. (2003) *The Dutch Corporate Governance Code* (Tabaksblat Code), The Hague: Corporate Governance Committee.

Vienot, M. (1999) *Recommendations of the Committee on Corporate Governance* (Vienot Report II), Paris: Association Française des Enterprises Privées & Mouvement des Enterprises de France.

## European statute

Italian Legislative Decree no. 58 (1998) Consolidated Law on Financial Intermediation (known as the Draghi Reform).

## ASIA PACIFIC

## (Figure 6.4)

Berli, K.M. (2000) *Report of the Kumar Mangalam Birla Committee on Corporate Governance*, Mumbai: Securities and Exchange Board of India.

Council on Corporate Disclosure and Governance (2005) *Code of Corporate Governance*, Singapore: Ministry of Finance.

CSRC (2001) *Code of Corporate Governance for Listed Companies in China*, Beijing: China Securities Regulatory Commission.

NCCG (2001) *Indonesian Code for Good Corporate Governance*, Jakarta: National Committee on Corporate Governance.

Securities Commission (2000) *Malaysian Code on Corporate Governance*, Kuala Lumpur: Securities Commission.

SEC (2002) *Philippine Code of Corporate Governance*, Manila: Securities and Exchange Commission.

SEHK (2004) *Hong Kong Code on Corporate Governance*, Hong Kong: Stock Exchange of Hong Kong.

SET (1999; 2004) *Code of Best Practice for Directors of Listed Companies*, Bangkok: Stock Exchange of Thailand.

TSE (2004) *Principles of Corporate Governance for Listed Companies*, Tokyo: Tokyo Stock Exchange.

## INTERNATIONAL CODES REFERENCES

## (Figure 7.5)

ACGA (2000) *Building Stronger Boards and Companies in Asia*, Singapore: Asian Corporate Governance Association.

ADB (2003) *Corporate Governance Principles for Business Enterprises*, Manila: Asian Development Bank.

APEC and Pacific Economic Co-operation Council (2001) *Guidelines for Good Corporate Governance Practice*, Singapore: PECC.

Business Roundtable (2005) *Principles of Corporate Governance*, Washington, DC: Business Roundtable.

CACG (1999) *CACG Guidelines: Principles for Corporate Governance in the the Commonwealth*, London: Commonwealth Association for Corporate Governance.

EBRD (1999) *Corporate Governance: Foundation for Capital Flows*, London: European Bank for Reconstruction and Development.

EC (2003) *Corporate Governance: Modernising Company Law and Enhancing Corporate Governance*, Brussels: European Commission.

ICGN (2005) *Statement on Global Corporate Governance Principles*, London: International Corporate Governance Network.

NYSE (2003) *Corporate Governance Rules*, New York: New York Stock Exchange.

OECD (2005) *Guidelines on Corporate Governance of State-owned Enterprises*, Paris: Organisation for Economic Cooperation and Development.

OECD (2006) *Corporate Governance of Non-Listed Companies in Emerging Markets*, Paris: OECD.

UN Economic Commission for Africa (2002) *Guidelines for Enhancing Good Economic and Corporate Governance in Africa*, May, Addis Ababa: UNECA.

World Bank (2000) *Corporate Governance: A Framework for Implementation*, Washington DC: World Bank Group.

# REFERENCES

AccountAbility (2005) *Stakeholder Engagement Standard*, London: AccountAbility.

Aglietta, M. and Breton, R. (2001) Financial Systems, Corporate Control and Capital Accumulation, *Economy and Society*, 30(4): 433–466.

Aglietta, M. and A. Rebérioux (2005) *Corporate Governance Adrift: A Critique of Shareholder Value*, Cheltenham: Edward Elgar.

Aguilera, R. (2005) Corporate Governance and Director Accountability: an Institutional Comparative Perspective, *British Journal of Management*, 16: S39–S53.

Aguilera, R. V. and A. Cuervo-Cazurra (2004) Codes of Good Governance Worldwide: What is the Trigger?, *Organization Studies* 25(3): 415–443.

Aguilera, R. and Jackson, G. (2003) The Cross-national Diversity of Corporate Governance: Dimensions and Determinants, *Academy of Management Review*, 28(3): 447–465.

Aguirre, G.J. (2003) The Enron Decision: Closing the Fraud-Free Zone On Errant Gatekeepers? *Delaware Journal of Corporate Law*, 28: 447–511.

Ahmadjian C.L. and Okumura, A. (2006) Corporate Governance in Japan, in C.A. Mallin (ed.) *Handbook of International Corporate Governance*, Cheltenham: Edward Elgar, 130–150.

Ahrens, J. (2002) *Governance and Economic Development: A Comparative Institutional Approach*, Cheltenham: Edward Elgar.

Al-Hawamdeh, A. M. M. and Snaith, I. A. N. (2005) Is 'Private Briefing' Illegal in the United Kingdom?, *Corporate Governance: An International Review*, 13: 489–504.

Alchian, A. and Demsetz, H. (1972) Production, Information Costs, and Economic Organisation, *American Economic Review*, 62, 777–795.

Alexander, L. (2000) *Corporate Governance and Cross-border Mergers*, New York: Conference Board.

Ali, P. and Greogriou, G.N. (2006) *International Corporate Governance after Sarbanes–Oxley*, New York: Wiley Finance.

Ali, P., Stapledon, G. and Gold, M. (2003) *Corporate Governance and Investment Fiduciaries*, Sydney: Thomson Lawbook Company.

Allen, F. and Herring, R. (2001) *Banking Regulation versus Securities Market Regulation, 01.29*, Financial Institutions Centre, Wharton Business School.

Allen, F. and Sherer, P. (1995) The Design and Redesign of Organizational Form, in, E.H. Bowman and B. Kogut (eds), *Redesigning the Firm*, New York: Oxford University Press, 183–196.

Amable, B. (2000) Institutional Complementarity and Diversity of Social Systems of Innovation and Production, *Review of International Political Economy*, 7(4): 645–87.

American Law Institute (1994) *Principles of Corporate Governance: Analysis and Recommendations*, vol. 1, Philadelphia: American Law Institute Publishers.

AMP Capital Investors (2005) *Financial Payback from Environmental & Social Factors*, Sydney: AMP.

AMP Capital Investors (2006a) *Corporate Governance: Mid-Year Update*, Sydney: AMP, 1–8.

AMP Capital Investors (2006b) *Corporate Governance: Why Bother? Corporate Governance Report*, Sydney: AMP.

AMP Henderson Global Investors (2003) *SRI Team Position Papers*, Sydney: AMP Henderson Global Investors.

Andrews, K.R. (1981) Replaying the Board's Role in Formulating Strategy, *Harvard Business Review*, 59(3):18–26.

Anonymous (2001) *Board Diversity needs Improving: Companies Turn Equal Access into a Free-For-All Investor Relations Business*, 8 January, 1.

Aoki, M. (1990) *Information, Incentives and Bargaining in the Japanese Economy: A Micro-theory of the Japanese Economy*, Cambribge: Cambridge University Press.

Aoki, M. (2001) *Towards a Comparative Institutional Analysis*, Boston: MIT Press.

Aoki, Masahiko and Masahiro Okuno (1996) *Keizai Shisutemu No Hikaku Seido Bunseki* [Comparative Institutional Analysis of Economy], Tokyo University Press.

Apreda, R. (2003) *The Semantics of Governance: The Common Thread Running through Corporate, Public and Global Governance*, Working Paper Series, 245, November. University of CEMA, Argentina.

Association of British Insurers (2004) Risk, Returns and Responsibility, London: Association of British Insurers, www.abi.org.uk

ASX Corporate Governance Council (2003) *Principles of Good Corporate Governance and Best Practice Recommendations*, Sydney: Australian Stock Exchange.

Australian Councils of Super Investors (2005) *Corporate Social Responsibility: Guidance for Investors*, Discussion Paper, September, Sydney: ACSI.

Backman, M. (1999) *Asian Eclipse: Exposing the Dark Side of Business in Asia*, Singapore: John Wiley.

Bagley, C.E. (2002) *Managers and the Legal Environment*, Cincinnati: Thomson Learning.

Bajaj, M., Mazumdar, S.C. and Sarin, A. (2000) *Securities Class Action Settlements: An Empirical Analysis*, SSRN Paper Collection Series, http://www.ssrn.com/paper.taf?abstract_id=25802

Bakan, J. (2004) *The Corporation*, London: Constable.

Banks, E. (2004) *Corporate Governance: Financial Responsibility, Controls and Ethics*, New York: Palgrave Macmillan.

Barry, P. (1990) *The Rise and Fall of Alan Bond*, Melbourne: Bantam.

Bauer, R. and Guenster, N. (2003) *Good Corporate Governance Pays Off: Well-Governed Companies Perform Better on the Stock Market*, Working Paper, University of Maastricht, April.

Baums, T. (1998a) *Corporate Governance in Germany: System and Current Developments*, http://papers.ssrn.com/sol3/papers.cfm? abstract_id =158038.

Baums, T. (1998b) Shareholder Representation and Proxy Voting in the European Union: A Comparative Study in K.J. Hopt, H. Kanda. M.J. Roe, E. Wymeersch and S. Prigge (eds), *Comparative Corporate Governance: The State of the Art and Emerging Research*, Oxford: Oxford University Press, 545–64.

Baxt, R. (1976) The Duties of Directors of Public Companies: The Realities of Commercial Life, the Contradictions of the Law, and the Need for Reform, *Australian Business Law Review*, 4: 289.

Baysinger, B.D. and Butler, H. (1985) Corporate Governance and the Board of Directors: Performance Effects of Changes in Board Composition, *Journal of Law, Economics, and Organizations*, 1: 101–124.

Bebchuk, L.A. (2005a) The Case for Increasing Shareholder Power, *Harvard Law Review*, 118(3): 833–914.

Bebchuk, L. (2005b) *The Myth of the Shareholder Franchise*, Harvard Law School, National Bureau of Economic Research, October, http://papers.ssrn.com/sol3/papers. cfm?abstract_id=829804

Bebchuk, L.A. and Fried, J.M. (2003) Executive Compensation as an Agency Problem, *Journal of Economic Perspectives*, 17(3): 71–92.

Bebchuk, L.A. and Fried, J.M. (2005) *Pay Without Performance: Overview of the Issues*, Harvard Law School Discussion Paper, 528, Harvard University.

Bebchuk, L.A. and Grinstein, Y. (2005a) *The Growth of Executive Pay, Harvard Law School*, Discussion Paper, 510, Harvard University.

Bebchuk, L.A. and Grinstein, Y. (2005b) *Firm Expansion and CEO Pay*, Harvard Law School, Discussion Paper, 533, Harvard University.

Bebchuk, L.A. and Roe, M.J. (2004). A Theory of Path Dependence in Corporate Governance and Ownership, in J. Gordon and M. Roe (eds), *Convergence and Persistence of Corporate Governance Systems*, Cambridge: Cambridge University Press.

Bebchuk, L, Cohen, A. and Ferrell, A. (2004) *What Matters in Corporate Governance*, Harvard Law School Discussion Paper, 491, http://papers.ssrn.com/sol3/papers.cfm?abstract_id=593423

Becht, M. (1997) *Strong Blockholders, Weak Owners and the Need for European Mandatory Disclosure*, European Corporate Governance Network: Executive Report, http://www.ecgi.org/research/control_europe/documents/eu.pdf

Becht, M., Bolton, P. and Röell, A. (2002) *Corporate Governance and Control*, Working Paper Series in Finance, 02/2002, European Corporate Governance Institute.

Bell, S. (2002) *Economic Governance and Institutional Dynamics*, Oxford: Oxford University Press.

Bendell, J. (2004) *Barricades and Boardrooms: A Contemporary History of the Corporate Accountability Movement*, Geneva, United Nations Research Institute for Social Development, www.unrisd.org

Bendell, J. and Shah, R. (2002) Lifeworth 2002, *Annual Review of Corporate Responsibility*, January–March.

Benn, S. and Dunphy, D. (2006) *Corporate Governance and Sustainability*, London and New York: Routledge.

Bennet, M. and James, P. (1998) *The Green Bottom Line: Environmental Accounting for Management – Current Practices and Future Trends*, Sheffield: Greenleaf Publishing.

Bennis, W. (2001) Corporate Boards *Executive Excellence*, 18: 7–8.

Berle, A.A. (1930) Corporations and the public investor, *American Economic Review*, 20(1): 54–71.

Berle, A.A. (1931) Corporate Powers as Powers in Trust, *Harvard Law Review*, 44: 1049.

Berle, A.A. (1935) For Whom Corporate Managers are Trustees: A Note, *Harvard Law Review*, 45: 1365.

Berle, A.A. (1955) *The 20th Century Capitalist Revolution*, New York: Harcourt Brace.

Berle, A.A. and Means, G.C. (1933) *The Modern Corporation and Private Property*, Commerce Clearing House.

Beyer, J. and Hassel, A. (2002) The Effects of Convergence: Internationalisation and the Changing Distribution of Net Value Added in Large German Firms, *Economy and Society*, 31(3): 309–32.

Bhagat, S. (2002) *Econometrics of Corporate Governance Studies*, Cambridge, MA: MIT.

Bhagat, S. and B. Black (2000) *Board Independence and Long-term firm Performance*, Law and Economics Working Paper, 185, Stanford Law School.

Bhasa, M.P. (2004) Global Corporate Governance: Debates and Challenges. Corporate Governance, *International Journal of Business in Society*, 4(2): 5–17.

BHP Billiton (2006) *Board Governance*, Melbourne: BHP Billiton.

Biancha, M., Bianco, M., Enriques, L. (1997) *Ownership, Pyramidal Groups and Separation between Ownership and Control in Italy*, Brussels European Corporate Governance Network.

Bianco, M. and Casavola, P. (1999) Italian Corporate Governance: Effects on Financial Structure and Firm Performance, *European Economic Review*, 43: 1057–1069.

Bielefeld, S., Higginson, S., Jackson, J. and Ricketts, A. (2004) Directors' Duties to the Company and Minority Shareholder Environmental Activism, *Company and Securities Law Journal*, 28: 40.

Bingham, K. (2000) *International Corporate Governance: A Management Report on the Rise of Global Governance*, London: Gee Publishing.

Black, B. (2000) *Political Determinants of Corporate Governance*, Oxford: Oxford University Press.

Black, B. (2001) The Legal and Institutional Preconditions for Strong Securities Markets, *UCLA Law Review*, 48(4): 781–858.

Black, B. and Coffee, J. (1994), Hail Britannia? Institutional Investor Behaviour Under Limited Regulation, *Michigan Law Review*, 92: 1999–2087.

Blair, M.M. (1995) *Ownership and Control: Rethinking Corporate Governance for the 21st Century*, Washington, DC: Brookings Institute.

Blair, M.M. (1996) *Wealth Creation and Wealth Sharing: A Colloquium on Corporate Governance and Human Capital*, Washington DC: Brookings Institute.

Blair, M.M. (2003) Director's Duties in a Post-Enron World, *Wake Forest Law Review*, 38: 885–910.

Blair, M.M. (2004) The Neglected Benefits of the Corporate Form: Entity Status and the Separation of Asset Ownership from Control, in A. Grandori (ed.), *Corporate Governance and Firm Organisation: Microfoundations and Structural Forms*, Oxford: Oxford University Press, 45–66.

Blair, M.M. and L.A. Stout (1999) A Team Production Theory of Corporate Law, *Virginia Law Review*, 85(2): 247–328.

Blair, M. and Stout, L. (2001) Director Accountability and the Mediating Role of the Corporate Board, *Washington University Law Quarterly*, 79: 403.

Blumberg, J., Korsvold, A., and Blum, G. (1996) *Environmental Performance and Shareholder Value*, Geneva: World Business Council for Sustainable Development.

Blume, M.E., Keim, D.B. and Patel, Sandeep A. (1991) Returns and Volatility of Low-Grade Bonds, 1977–1989, *Journal of Finance*, 46(1): 49–74.

Bockli, P. (1998) Switzerland, in A.R. Pinto and G. Visentini (eds), *The Legal Basis of Corporate Governance in Publicly Held Corporations: A Comparative Approach*, The Hague: Kluwer, 195–218.

Bogle, J.C. (2005). *The Battle for the Soul of Capitalism*, New Haven, CT: Yale University Press.

Boisot, M. and Child, J. (1996) From Fiefs to Clans: Explaining China's Economic Order, *Administrative Science Quarterly*, 41, 614–25.

Bomann-Larsen, L. and Wigen, O. (2004) *Responsibility in World Business: Managing Harmful Side Effects of Corporate Activity*, Tokyo: United Nations University Press.

Bonaglia, F., de Macedo, J.B. and M. Bussolo (2001) *How Globalization Improves Governance*, CEPR Working Paper, London.

Boone, C., De Brabander, B. and Hellemans, J. (2000) CEO Locus of Control and Small Firm Performance, *Organization Studies*, 21: 641–646.

Bosch, H. (2002) The Changing Face of Corporate Governance, *University of New South Wales Law Journal*, 25(2): 270–293.

Boyer, R. (2005). From Shareholder Value to CEO Power: The Paradox of the 1990s, *Competition and Change*, 9(1): 7.

Bradley, M., Schipani C.A., Sundaram, A.K., and Walsh, J.P. (1999) The Purposes and Accountability of the Corporation in Contemporary Society: Corporate Governance at a Crossroads, *Law and Contemporary Problems*, 62(3): 9–86.

Braithwaite, J. and Drahos, P. (2000) *Global Business Regulation*, Cambridge: Cambridge University Press.

Brancato, C.K. (1997) *Institutional Investors and Corporate Governance: Best Practices for Increasing Corporate Value*, Chicago: Irwin Publishers.

Branson, D. (2001) The Very Uncertain Prospects of Convergence in Corporate Governance, *Cornell International Law Journal*, 34, 321–361.

Branson, D. (2003) Enron – When All Systems Fail: Creative Destruction or Roadmap to Corporate Governance Reform?, *Villanova Law Review*, 48: 989.

Branson, D. (2004) The Very Uncertain Prospects for Global Convergence in Corporate Governance, in, T. Clarke, *Theories of Corporate Governance, London:* Routledge, 259–286.

Bratton, W. (2001) Berle and Means Reconsidered at the Century's Turn, *Journal of Corporation Law*, 26(3): 737–70, reproduced in T. Clarke (ed.), *Corporate Governance: Critical Perspectives in Business and Management*, vol. 1, *The Genesis of Corporate Governance*, London: Routledge.

Bratton, W. (2002) Enron and the Dark Side of Shareholder Value, *Tulane Law Review*, 76: 1275–1361.

Bratton, W. (2003) Enron, Sarbanes–Oxley, and Accounting: Rules Versus Principles Versus Rents, *Villanova Law Review*, 48(4), http:// papers.ssrn.com/sol3/papers.cfm?abstract_id=399120

Bratton, W.W. and McCahery, J.A. (1999) Comparative Corporate Governance and the Theory of the Firm: The Case Against Global Cross Reference, *Columbia Journal of Transnational Law*, 38, 213–297.

Bratton, W. and McCahery, J. (2002) *Comparative Corporate Governance and Barriers to Global Cross Reference in Corporate Governance Regimes: Convergence and Diversity*, Oxford: Oxford University Press, 23–55.

Breedon, R.C. (2003) *Restoring Trust*, Report on Corporate Governance for the Future of MCI, Inc., to the Hon. Jed. S. Rakoff, the United States District Court, for the Southern District of New York.

Brennan, G. (2002) Law Values and Charity, *Australian Law Journal*, 76: 492.

Brennan, M.J. (2004) *How Did It Happen?* Anderson Graduate School of Management & Finance, Paper 4-04, University of California, Los Angeles.

Brickley, K.F. (2003) From Enron to WorldCom and beyond: Life and Crime after Sarbanes–Oxley, *Washington University Law Quarterly*, 81.

Brill, H., Brill, J.A. and Feigenbaum, (2000) *Investing With Your Values: Making Money and Making a Difference*, Gabriola Island, Canada: New Society Publishers.

Brountas, P.P. (2004) *Boardroom Excellence: A Commonsense Perspective on Corporate Governance*, San Francisco, CA: Jossey-Bass.

Bruntland Commission (1987) *Our Common Future*, Oxford: Oxford University Press.

Buira, A. (2005) *Reforming the Governance of the IMF and the World Bank*, London: Anthem Press.

Burritt, R., Hahn, T., Schaltegger, S. (2002) Towards a Comprehensive Framework for Environmental Management Accounting: Links Between Business Actors and Environmental Management Accounting Tools, *Australian Accounting Review*, 12(2): 39–50.

Bush, Tim (2005) Divided by Common Language: Where Economics Meets the Law–US vs Non-US Reporting Models, London: Institute of Chartered Accountants of England and Wales (ICAEW).

Business Council of Australia (2001) *Towards Sustainable Development: How Leading Australian*

and Global Corporations Are Contributing to Sustainable Development, May, Sydney: BCA.

Business Roundtable (1997) Statement on Corporate Governance, Washington DC: Business Roundtable.

Business Sector Advisory Group on Corporate Governance (1998) Corporate Governance: Improving Competitiveness and Access to Capital in Global Markets, Paris: OECD.

Cabot, L. (1976) Penn Central, Harvard Business Review.

Cadbury, A. (1992) Report of the Committee on the Financial Aspects of Corporate Governance, London: Gee & Co.

Cadbury, A. (2000) World Bank, Corporate Governance: A Framework for Implementation (Foreword), Washington: World Bank.

Cadbury, A. (2002) Corporate Governance and Chairmanship, Oxford: Oxford University Press.

Cadbury, A. and Millstein, I.M. (2005) The New Agenda for ICGN, Discussion Paper, 1, London: International Corporate Governance Network.

Calder, F. and Culverwell, M. (2005) Following up the World Summit on Sustainable Development Commitments on Corporate Social Responsibility, Royal Institute of International Affairs, London: Chatham House.

Camejo, P. (2002) The SRI Advantage: Why Socially Responsible Investing Has Outperformed Financially, Gabriola Island, Canada: New Society Publishers.

Canadian Democracy and Corporate Accountability Commission (2001) An Overview of Issues, Toronto: Canadian Democracy and Corporate Accountability Commission, 49 pp.

Canadian Democracy and Corporate Accountability Commission, (2002) The New Balance Sheet: Corporate Profits and Responsibility in the 21st Century, Final Report, January, Toronto: Canadian Democracy and Corporate Accountability Commission, 51 pp.

Carbon Trust (2005) A Climate for Change: A Trustee's Guide to Understanding and Addressing Climate Risk, www.thecarbontrust.co.uk

Carlsson, R.H. (2001) Ownership and Value Creation: Strategic Corporate Governance in the New Economy, Chichester: Wiley.

Carson, T.L. (2003) Self-Interest and Business Ethics: Lessons of the Recent Corporate Scandals, Journal of Business Ethics, 43: 389.

Carter, C.C. and Lorsch, J.W. (2004) Back to the Drawing Board: Designing Corporate Boards for a Complex World, Cambridge, MA: Harvard Business School Press.

Carver, J. (2002) Corporate Boards That Create Value: Governing Company Performance from the Boardroom, San Francisco: Jossey Bass.

Cascio, W.F. (2004) Board Governance: A Social System Perspective, Academy of Management Executive, 18(1): 97–100.

Catanach, A.H. and Rhoades, S.C. (2003) Enron: A Financial Reporting Failure?, Villanova Law Review, 48(4): 1057.

Caufield, C. (1997) Masters of Illusion: The World Bank and the Poverty of Nations, London: Pan Books.

Centre for European Policy Studies (CEPS) (1995) Corporate Governance in Europe, Brussels: Centre for European Policy Studies, June.

Cernat, L. (2004) The Emerging European Corporate Governance Model: Anglo-Saxon, Continental or Still the Century of Diversity?, Journal of European Public Policy, 11(1): 147–166.

Certified General Accountants Association of Canada (2005) Measuring Up: A study on Corporate Sustainability Reporting in Canada, Vancouver: CGA.

CFA Institute Centre for Financial Market Integrity (2006) Breaking the Short-term Cycle, New York: CFA Institute Business Roundtable for Corporate Ethics.

Chaganti, R., Mahajan, V. and Sharma, S. (1985) Corporate board size, composition and corporate failures in the retailing industry, Journal of Management Studies, 22: 400–416.

Chakrabarti Rajesh (2005) Corporate Governance in India: Evolution and Challenges, 17 January, SSRN: http://ssrn.com/abstract=649857

Chaney, P.L. and Philipich, K.L. (2002) Shredded Reputation: The Cost of Audit Failure, Journal of Accounting Research, 40(4): 1221–1245.

Charkham, J. (2005) Keeping Better Company, Oxford: Oxford University Press.

Charkham, J. and Simpson, A. (1999) Fair Shares: The Future of Shareholder Power and Responsibility, Oxford: Oxford University Press.

Cheffins, B.R. (2000) Corporate Governance Reform: Britain as an Exporter: Corporate Governance and the Reform of Company Law, Hume Papers on Public Policy, 8(1): 11–28.

Cheffins, B.R. (2001a) History and the Global Corporate Governance Revolution: The UK Perspective, Business History, 43(4): 87–118.

Cheffins, B.R. (2001b) Law, Economics and the UK's System of Corporate Governance: Lessons from History, Journal of Corporate Law Studies, 1: 71–89.

Chew, Jr., D.H. and Gillan, S.L. (eds) (2005) *Corporate Governance at the Crossroads: a Book of Readings*, Boston, MA: McGraw Hill.

Christian Aid (2004) *Behind the Mask: The Real Face of Corporate Social Responsibility*, London: Christian Aid.

Chung, C.-N. (2004) Institutional Transition and Cultural Inheritance: Network Ownership and Corporate Control of Business Groups in Taiwan, 1970s–1990s, *International Sociology*, 19(1): 25–50.

Cioffi, J.W. ( 2000) Governing Globalization? The State, Law, and Structural Change in Corporate Governance, *Journal of Law and Society*, 27(4): 572–600.

Cioffi, J. and Cohen, S.S. (2000) The Advantages of Forwardness: The State, Law, and Corporate Governance in an Age of Globalization, in S. Cohen and G. Boyd (eds), *Globalization and Corporate Governance: Strategic and Long Range Planning Issues*, Cheltenham, UK and Northhampton, MA: Matthew Elgar, 307–349.

Claessens, S. (2004) *Corporate Governance and Development, Global Corporate Governance Forum*, Washington, DC: World Bank.

Claessens, S. and Fan, J.P.H (2002) Corporate Governance in Asia, *International Review of Finance*, 3(2): 71–103.

Claessens, S., Djankov, S. and Lang, L.H.P. (2000) The Separation of Ownership and Control in East Asian Corporations, *Journal of Financial Economics*, 58(1): 81–112.

Clark, M. (1916; 2005) The Changing Basis of Economic Responsibility, *Journal of Political Economy*, 24(3): 13–19; also in T. Clarke (ed.), *Corporate Governance Critical Perspectives on Business and Management*, London: Routledge, 2005, 45–60.

Clarke, F., Dean, G. and Oliver, K. (2003) *Corporate Collapse*, Cambridge: Cambridge University Press.

Clarke, M. (2004) Hamstrung or Properly Calibrated? Federalism and the Appropriate Role of Government in the Post-Sarbanes–Oxley World, *International Journal of Disclosure and Governance*, 1(4): 385–412.

Clarke, T. (1998) The Stakeholder Corporation: A Business Philosophy for the Information Age, *Long Range Planning*, 31(2): 182–194.

Clarke, T. (2000) Haemorrhaging Tigers: The Power of International Financial Markets and the Weaknesses of Asian Modes of Corporate Governance, *Corporate Governance: An International Review*, 8(2): 101–116.

Clarke, T. (2004a) Cycles of Crisis and Regulation: The Enduring Agency and Stewardship Problems of Corporate Governance, *Corporate Governance: An International Review*, 12(2): 153–161.

Clarke, T. (2004b) *Theories of Corporate Governance*, London: Routledge.

Clarke, T. (2005) *Corporate Governance: Critical Perspectives in Business and Management*, vol. 1: *The Genesis of Corporate Governance*, vol. 2: *Anglo-American Corporate Governance*, vol. 3: *European Corporate Governance*, vol. 4: *Asian Corporate Governance*, vol. 5: *Contemporary Developments in Corporate Governance*, London: Routledge.

Clarke, T. and Bostock, R. (1994) International Corporate Governance: Convergence and Diversity, in, T. Clarke and E. Monkhouse, *Rethinking the Company*, London: Financial Times Pitman.

Clarke, T. and Clegg, S. (2000) *Changing Paradigms: The Transformation of Management Knowledge for the 21st Century*, London: HarperCollins Business.

Clarke, T. and dela Rama, M. (2003) The Impact of Socially Responsible Investment on Corporate Social Responsibility, in D. Crowther and L. Rayman-Bacchus (eds), *Perspectives on Corporate Social Responsibility*, Aldershot: Ashgate.

Clarke, T. and dela Rama, M. (2006) *Corporate Governance and Globalisation*, London: Sage.

Clarke, T. and Monkhouse, E. (1994) *Rethinking the Company*, London: Financial Times Pitman.

Clarke, T. and Yuxing, D. (1998) Corporate Governance in China: Explosive Growth and New Patterns of Ownership, *Long Range Planning – International Journal of Strategic Management*, Pergamon, 31(2): pp 239–251.

Clarkson, M.B.E. (1995) A Stakeholder Framework for Analysing and Evaluating Corporate Social Performance, *Academy of Management Review*, 20: 92–117.

Clearfield, A.M. (2005) With Friends Like These, Who Needs Enemies? The Structure of the Investment Industry and Its Reluctance to Exercise Governance Oversight, *Corporate Governance: An International Review*, 13(2): 114–121.

Coase, R. (1937) The Nature of the Firm, *Economica*, 4.

Cochran, P.L., Wood, R.A. and T.B. Jones (1985) The Composition of Boards of Directors and Incidence of Golden Parachutes, *Academy of Management Journal*, 28: 664–671.

Coffee, J. (2001) The Rise of Dispersed Ownership: The Role of the Law in the Separation of Ownership and Control, *Yale Law Journal*, 111(1).

Coffee, J. (2002a) Convergence and Its Critics: What are the Preconditions to the Separation of Ownership and Control?, in J.A. McCahery, P. Moerland, T. Raaijmakers and L. Renneboog (eds) *Corporate Governance Regimes: Convergence and Diversity*, Oxford: Oxford University Press.

Coffee, J. (2002b) Understanding Enron: It's about the Gatekeepers, Stupid, *Business Lawyer*, 57(4): 1403.

Cohen, A. and Brodsky, D. (2004) The US Sarbanes–Oxley Act of 2002: What Audit Committees of Non-US Issuers Need to Know, *International Journal of Disclosure and Governance*, 1(4): 313–23.

Cohen, B. (1997) *The Edge of Chaos: Financial Booms, Bubbles, and Chaos*, London: Wiley.

Cohen, S.S. and Boyd, G. (2000) *Corporate Governance and Globalization: Long Range Planning Issues*, Cheltenham: Edward Elgar.

Coles, D. and Green, D. (2002) *Just Pensions: Do UK Pension Funds Invest Responsibly?*, www.justpensions.org

Commission of the European Countries (2001) *European Governancel*, a white paper, Brussels: EC.

Commission of the European Communities (2002) *Corporate Social Responsibility: A Business Contribution to Sustainable Development*, Communication from the Commission, COM (2002) 347 Final, Brussels.

Commission of the European Communities (2003) *Modernising Company Law and Enhancing Corporate Governance in the European Union – A Plan to Move Forward*, Communication from the Commission to the Council and the European Parliament, Brussels, 21 May 2003, COM (2003) 284 final.

Commission on Global Governance (1995) *Our Global Neighbourhood*, New York: Oxford University Press.

Committee on Public Finance, (2002) *Corporate Social Responsibility and Socially Responsible Investment*, Consultation Paper, Assemblée Nationale, Québec, Secrétariat des commissions, May.

Company Law Review Steering Group (CLR) (2000) *Modern Company Law for a Competitive Economy: Developing The Framework*, London: Department of Trade and Industry.

Confederation of Indian Industry (1998) *The Draft Report of the Committee on Corporate Governance*, New Delhi: Confederation of Indian Industry.

Confederation of Indian Industry (CII) (2004) *Concept Paper on Companies Bill 2004: CII's Views*, www.ciionline.org

Conference Board (1996) *The Corporate Board: A Growing Role in Strategic Assessment*, New York: Conference Board.

Conger, J.A. (2001) *Corporate Boards: Strategies that Add Value At the Top*, San Francisco: Jossey Bass.

Consumers' Association (2001) *Profits at the Consumers' Expense*, Policy Report, London: Consumers' Association.

Consumers' Association (2004) *Memorandum to the Treasury Committee on Restoring Confidence in Long-Term Savings*, London: Consumers' Association.

Conyon, M. (2000) Discussion of the Increasing Use of Non-executive Directors: Its Impact on UK Board Structure and Governance Arrangements, *Journal of Business Finance and Accounting*, 27: 1343–1348.

Cooke, C.A. (1950) *Corporation, Trust and Company*, Manchester: Manchester University Press.

Coombes, P. and Watson, M. (2000) Three Surveys on Corporate Governance, *McKinsey Quarterly*, McKinsey Corporation, 4: 74–77.

Co-operative Insurance (2002) *Sustainability Pays*, www.forumforthefuture.org.uk/publications/default.asp?pubid=16

Core, J.E., Guay, W. and Larcker, D.F. (2003) Executive Equity Compensation and Incentives: A Survey, *Economic Policy Review*, April: 1–64.

Corfield, A. (1998) The Stakeholder Theory and its Future in Australian Corporate Governance: A Preliminary Analysis, *Bond Law Review*, 10: 213.

Cornelius, P. (2005) Good Corporate Practices in Poor Corporate Governance Systems: Some Evidence from the Global Competitiveness Report, Corporate Governance: *International Journal of Business in Society*, 5(3): 12–23.

Cornelius, P. and Kogut, B. (eds) (2003) *Corporate Governance and Capital Flows in a Global Economy*, New York: Oxford University Press.

Cornford, A. *Internationally Agreed Principles for Corporate Governance and the Enron Case*, UNCTAD, http://www.g24.org/acorngva.pdf

Corporate Responsibility Coalition (2005) *Corporate Social Responsibility in the Finance Sector in Europe*, London: Corporate Responsibility Coalition (CORE).

Corporation of London, *Financing the Future: The London Principles*, www.cityoflondon.gov.uk/living_environment/sustainability/sustainable_finance.htm

Corporations and Markets Advisory Committee (2005) *Corporate Social Responsibility*, Discussion Paper, Sydney: Australian Government.

Correia da Silva, L., Goergen, M. and Renneboog, L. (2004) *Dividend Policy and Corporate Governance*, Oxford: Oxford University Press.

CPA Australia (2005) *Sustainability Reporting: Practices, Performance and Potential*, Melbourne: CPA Australia.

Crédit Suisse First Boston Report (2005) European Wholesale Markets: Hedge Funds and Investment Banks, *Equity Research*, 4–5, 9 March.

Crutchley, C.E., Hudson, C.D. and Jensen, M.R.H. (1998) The Shareholder Wealth Effects of CalPERS Activism, *Financial Services Review*, 7(1): 1–10.

Cruver, B. (2002) *Anatomy of Greed, The Unshredded Truth from an Enron Insider*, New York: Carroll and Graf.

CSR Wire: *The Corporate Social Responsibility Newswire Service*, http://www.csrwire.com/csr/index.mpl?arg=all

Culp, C. and Niskanen, W. (eds) (2002) *Corporate Aftershock*, Hoboken, NJ: John Wiley & Sons.

Cutler, T. (2004) The Wages of Capital: The Rise and Rise of Corporate Governance, *Competition and Change*, 8(1): 65–83.

Daily, C.M., Dalton, D.R., and Cannella, A.C. ( 2003) Corporate Governance: Decades of Dialogue and Data, *Academy of Management Review*, 28(3): 371–382.

Dalton, C.M. and Dalton D.R. (2005) Boards of Directors: Utilising Empirical Evidence in Developing Practical Prescriptions, *British Journal of Management*, 16: 91–97.

Dalton, D.R., Daily, C.M., Ellstrand, A.E. and Johnson, J.L. (1998) Meta-analytical reviews of board composition, leadership structure, and financial performance, *Strategic Management Journal*, 19: 269–290.

Davies, A. (1999) *A Strategic Approach to Corporate Governance*, Aldershot: Gower.

Davies, P. (2000) Board Structure in the UK and Germany: Convergence or Continuing Divergence?, *International and Comparative Law Journal*, 2.

Davies, P. (2005) Enlightened Shareholder Value and the New Responsibilities, W.E. Hearn Lecture at the University of Melbourne Law School, 4 October.

Davis, E.P. (2000) *Implications of the Growth of Institutional Investors for the Financial Sectors*, Discussion Paper PI-0001, Pensions Institute, Birkbeck College, University of London, http://www.pensions-institute.org/

Davis, E.P. (1996) *The Role of Institutional Investors in the Evolution of Financial Structure and Behaviour*, in The Future of the Financial System, Proceedings of a Conference Held in the Reserve Bank of Australia, Sydney, and Financial Markets Group Special Paper, 89, London School of Economics.

Davis, E.P. (2002) *Institutional Investors, Corporate Governance, and the Peformance of the Corporate Sector*, Middlesex, UK: Brunel University.

Davis, E.P. and Steil, B. (2000) *Institutional Investors*, Boston: MIT Press.

Davis, E.P. and Steil, B. (2001) *Institutional Investments*, Cambridge, MA: MIT Press.

Davis, G.F. (1991) Agents without Principles? The Spread of the Poison Pill through the Intercorporate Network, *Administrative Science Quarterly*, 36(4): 583–613.

Davis, G.F. and Useem, M. (2002) Top Management, Company Directors and Corporate Control, in A. Pettigrew, H. Thomas and R. Whittington (eds), *Handbook of Strategy and Management*, London: Sage.

Davis, J.H., Schoorman, F.D., Donaldson, L. (1997) Toward a Stewardship Theory of Management, *The Academy of Management Review*, 22(1): 20–47.

De Trenck, C., Cartledge, S., Daswani, A., Katz, C., and Sakmar, D. (1998) *Red Chips and the Globalisation of China's Enterprises*, Hong Kong: Asia 2000 Ltd.

Deakin, S. (2003) After Enron: An Age of Enlightenment?, *Organisation*, 10(3): 583–587.

Deakin, S. (2005) The Coming Transformation of Shareholder Value, *Corporate Governance: An International Review*, 13(1): 11–18.

Deakin, S. and Hughes, A. (1997) *Enterprise and Community: New Directions in Corporate Governance*, Oxford: Blackwell.

Deakin, S. and Konzelmann, S.J. (2004) Learning From Enron, *Corporate Governance: An International Review*, 12(2): 134–142.

Deakin, S. and Slinger, G. (1997) Hostile Takeovers, Corporate Law, and the Theory of the Firm, *Journal of Law and Society*, 24(1): 124–151.

Delhaise, P.F. (1998) *Asia In Crisis: The Implosion of the Banking and Finance Systems*, Singapore: John Wiley.

Della Sala, V. (2004) The Italian Model of Capitalism: On the Road between Globalization and

Europeanization?, *Journal of European Public Policy*, 11(6): 1041–1057.

Demb, A. and Neubauer, F.F. (1992) *The Corporate Board: Confronting the Paradoxes*, Oxford: Oxford University Press.

Demirag, I.S. (1998) *Corporate Governance, Accountability and Pressures to Perform: An International Study*, Stamford, CT: JAI Press.

Demirag, I. and O'Brien, J. (2004) Conflicting and Conflating Interests in the Regulation and Governance of the Financial Markets in the United States, *Journal of Corporate Citizenship*, 15: 111–119.

Denis, D. and McConnell, J. (eds) (2005) *Governance: An International Perspective*, London: Edward Elgar.

Dennis, D. and Sarin, A. (1999) Ownership and Board Structure in Publicly Traded Corporations, *Journal of Financial Economics*, 52: 187–224.

Department of the Environment and Heritage, (2003) *The Materiality of Environmental Risk to Australia's Finance Sector*, Canberra: Commonwealth of Australia, www.deh.gov.au/industry/finance/publications/index.html

Department of the Environment and Heritage (2003) *The State of Public Environmental Reporting in Corporate Australia*, Canberra: Commonwealth of Australia, www.deh.gov.au/industry/finance/publications/index.html

Department of the Environment and Heritage (2003) *Triple Bottom Line Reporting in Australia – A Guide to Reporting Against Environmental Indicators, Canberra: Commonwealth of Australia* www.deh.gov.au/industry/finance/publications/index.html

Department of the Environment and Heritage (2004) Triple Bottom Line Report: Our Environment, *Social and Economic Performance*, September, Australia.

Department of Trade and Industry (DTI) (2000a) *Modern Company Law for A Competitive Economy: Developing the Framework, a Consultation Document from the Company Law Review Steering Group*, London: HMSO.

Department of Trade and Industry (DTI) (2000b) *Corporate Governance, Board Structure and Accountability*, ESRC Centre for Business Research, University of Cambridge.

Department of Trade and Industry (DTI) (2003) *Rewards for Failure*, London: DTI.

Dew-Becker, I. and Gordon, R.J. (2005) *Where Did the Productivity Growth Go? Inflation Dynamics and the Distribution of Income*, Washington, DC: Brookings Panel on Economic Activity.

Dewing, I.P. and Russell, P.O. (2004) Accounting, Auditing and Corporate Governance of European Listed Companies: EU Policy Developments Before and After Enron, *Journal of Common Market Studies*, 42(2): 289.

Digby, Q. and Watterson, L. (2004) *Pursuing Profit, Productivity and Philanthropy: The Legal Obligations Facing Corporate Australia, Keeping Good Companies*, June, Sydney: Chartered Secretaries Australia.

Di Maggio, P.J. and Powell, W.W. (1983) The Iron Cage Revisited: Institutional Isomorphism and Collective Rationality in Organisational Fields, *American Sociological Review*, 48: 147–160.

Dignam, A. and Galanis, M. (1999) Governing the World: The Development of the OECD's Corporate Governance Principles, *European Business Law Review*, 10(9/10): 396–407.

Dimma, W.A. (2002) *On the Board: Best Practices in Corporate Governance,* Toronto: Wiley.

Dine, J. and Rider, B. (2006) *The Governance of Corporate Groups*, Cambridge: Cambridge University Press.

Dion, M. (1998) *Investissements Ethiques et Régie d'Entreprise, Entre la Mondialisation et la Mythologie, Médiaspaul, Coll. Interpellations*, Montréal, 100 pp.

Doane, D. (2005) The Myth of CSR, Stanford Social Innovation Review, *Stanford University Graduate School of Business*, fall: 23–29.

Dodd, E.M. (1932; 2005) For Whom Are Corporate Managers Trustees?, *Harvard Law Review*, 45: 1145; in; T. Clarke (ed.), *Corporate Governance Critical Perspectives on Business and Management*, London: Routledge, 2005, 61–75.

Donahue, J.D. and Nye, Jr., J.S. (eds) (2001) *Governance amid Bigger, Better Markets, Washington*, DC: Brookings Institution Press.

Donaldson, L. (1990) The Ethereal Hand: Organisational Economics and Management Theory, *Academy of Management Review*, 15(3): 369–381.

Donaldson, L. and Davis, J.H. (1991) Agency Theory or Stewardship Theory: CEO Governance and Shareholder Returns, *Australian Journal of Management*, 16: 49–64.

Donaldson, T. and Preston, L. (1995) The Stakeholder Theory of the Corporation: Concepts, Evidence, Implications, *Academy of Management Review*, 20: 65–91.

Donaldson, W.H. (2005) Speech to 2005 CFA Institute Annual Conference, U.S. Securities and Exchange Commission, 8 May.

Dore, R. (2000) *Stock Market Capitalism: Welfare Capitalism*, Oxford: Oxford University Press.

Dore, R. (2002) Will Global Capitalism Be Anglo-Saxon Capitalism?, *Asian Business & Management*, 1(1): 9–18.

Downes, G.R. (1999) *Institutional Investors and Corporate Behavior*, Washington: AEI Press.

Drobetz, W., Schillhofer, A. and Zimmerman, H. (2004) Corporate Governance and Expected Stock Returns: Evidence From Germany, *European Financial Management*, 10(2): 267–293.

Dunphy, D., Griffiths, A. and Benn, S. (2003) *Organizational Change for Corporate Sustainability*, London: Routledge.

Easterbrook, F.H. (1997) International Corporate Differences: Markets or Law?, *Journal of Applied Corporate Finance*, 9(4): 23–30.

EAU (2003) *China's Industrial Rise: East Asia's Challenge*, Economic Analytical Unit, Department of Foreign Affairs and Trade, Canberra: Australian Government.

Eden, L. and Dobson, W. (2005) *Governance, Multinationals and Growth*, Cheltenham: Edward Elgar.

Eichenwald, K. (2005) *Conspiracy of Fools*, New York: Broadway.

Eisenberg, T. and Macey, J.R. (2004) Was Arthur Andersen Different? An Empirical Investigation of Major Accounting Firm Audits of Large Clients, *Journal of Empirical Legal Studies*, 1(2): 263.

Eisenhardt, K.M. (1988) Agency and Institutional Theory Explanations: The Case of Retail Sales Compensation, *Academy of Management Journal*, 31: 488–511.

Eisenhardt, K.M. (1989) Agency Theory: An Assessment and Review, *Academy of Management Review*, 14: 57–74.

EIU (2005) *The Importance of Corporate Responsibility*, White Paper, London: Economist Intelligence Unit Ltd.

Elkington, J. (1997) *Cannibals with Forks: The Triple Bottom Line of 21st Century Business*, Oxford: Capstone Publishing Limited.

Elson, C.M. and Gyves, C.M. (2003) The Enron Failure and Corporate Governance Reform, *Wake Forest Law Review*, 38: 855–884.

Enriques, L. (2003) Bad Apples, Bad Oranges: A Comment from Old Europe on Post-Enron Corporate Governance Reform, *Wake Forest Law Review*, 38: 911–34.

Entine, J. (2003) The Myth Of Social Investing: A Critique of Its Practice and Consequences for Corporate Social Performance Research, *Organization & Environment*, 16(3): 352–368.

Environmental Resources Management, (2000) *ERM Survey of UK Pension Funds*, June, 4 pp.

Epstein, E.M. (1987) The Corporate Social Policy Process and the Process of Corporate Governance, *American Business Law Journal*, 25: 361–383.

The Equator Principles: *A Framework for Banks to Manage Environmental and Social Issues in Project Financing*, www.equator-principles.com

Ernst & Young (2002) *Corporate Social Responsibility of Global Companies*, New York: Ernst & Young.

Erturk, I., Froud, J., Johal, S. and Williams, K. (2004) Corporate Governance and Disappointment, *Review of International Political Economy*, 11(4): 677–713.

Ethical Investment Association (EIA) (2002) *Socially Responsible Investment in Australia: 2002*, www.eia.org.au

Estrin, S. (2002) Corporate Governance and Privatization: Lessons from Transition Economies, *Journal of African Economies*, 1(1): 105–110.

European Commission (2001) *Developing a European Framework for Corporate Social Responsibility*, Green Paper, Brussels: European Union.

European Commission (2002a) *Communication Concerning Corporate Social Responsibility: A Business Contribution to Sustainable Development*, Brussels: European Union.

European Commission (2002b) *Corporate Social Responsibility: A Business Contribution to Sustainable Development*, Brussels: European Union.

European Commission (2003a) *Corporate Social Responsibility: A Business Contribution to Sustainable Development*, Brussels: European Union.

European Commission (2003b) *EU Multistakeholder Forum on Corporate Social Responsibility*, Brussels: European Union.

European Commission (2004a) *Corporate Social Responsibility: National Public Policies in the European Union*, Brussels: European Union.

European Commission (2004b) *Directive on Minimum Transparency Requirements for Listed Companies*, European Commission.

European Commission (2005a) *Company Law & Corporate Governance*, http://www.europa.eu.int/comm/internal_market/company/index_en.htm

European Commission (2005b) Consultation and Hearing on Future Priorities for the Action Plan

on Modernising Company Law and Enhancing Corporate Governance in the European Union, Summary Report, Directorate General for Internal Market and Services, Brussels: European Commission 2005.

European Commission (2005c) *The EU Economy 2005 Review: Rising International Integration – Opportunities and Challenges*, Commission of the European Communities, Director General Economic and Financial Affairs.

Eurosif (2006) *Active Share Ownership in Europe*, European Social Investment Forum, European Handbook.

Faccio, M. and Lang, M. (2002) The Ultimate Ownership of Western European Corporations, *Journal of Financial Economics*, 65: 365–395.

Fama, E. and Jensen, M.C. (1985) Separation of Ownership and Control, *Journal of Law and Economics*, 26: 301–26.

Farrar, J. (2001) *Corporate Governance in Australia and New Zealand*, Oxford University Press, Melbourne.

Fayers, C., Cocklin, C. and Homes, D. (2000) Environmental Considerations in the Decisions of Australian Investment Professionals, *Journal of Environmental Assessment Policy Management*, 2(2).

FEE (2003) *Financial Reporting and Auditing Aspects of Corporate Governance*, Discussion Paper, July, Brussels: Federation des Experts Comptables Europeens.

Feldman, S., Soyka, P. and Ameer, P. (1997) Does a Firm's Environmental Performance Result in a Higher Stock Price?, *Journal of Investing*, winter: 87–97.

Felton, F., Hudnut, A. and van Heeckeren, J. (1996) Putting a Value on Board Governance, *McKinsey Quarterly*, 170–174.

Ferlie, E.F., Ashburner, L. and Fitzgerald, L. (1994) The Non-executive Director and the Board: Some Evidence from the NHS, unpublished paper, Centre for Corporate Strategy and Change: University of Warwick.

Ferlie, E., Pettigrew, A., Ashburner, L. and Fitzgerald, L. (1996) *The New Public Management in Action*, Oxford: Oxford University Press.

Financial Reporting Council (2006) Combined Code on Corporate Governance, London: Financial Reporting Council.

Finkelstein, S. and Mooney, A.C. (2003) Not the Usual Suspects: How to Use Board Process to Make Boards Better, *Academy of Management Executive*, 17(2): 101–113.

Fisher, L. (2001) Informed and On-message, *Accountancy*, 127: 46–47.

Fitzgerald, R. and Abe, E. (eds) (2004) *The Development of Corporate Governance in Japan and Britain*, Aldershot: Ashgate.

Fliaster, A. and Marr, R. (2001) Change of the insider-oriented corporate governance in Japan and Germany: between Americanisation and tradition, *Journal of Change Management*, 1(3): 242–256.

Fligstein, N. and Freeland, R. (1995) Theoretical and Comparative Perspectives on Corporate Organization, *Annual Review of Sociology*, 21.

Foley & Lardner (2006a) *The Cost of Being Public in the Era of Sarbanes–Oxley*, Boston: Foley & Lardner.

Foley & Lardner (2006b) *The Impact of Sarbanes–Oxley on Private and Non-Profit Companies*, Boston: Foley & Lardner.

Forbes, D.P. and Milliken, F.J. (1999) Cognition and Corporate Governance: Understanding Boards of Directors as Strategic Decision-Making Groups, *Academy of Management Review*, 24(3): 489–505.

Ford, H.A.J. (2001) *Ford's Principles of Corporations Law*, 10th Ed., Sydney: Butterworths.

Fosberg, R.H. (2001) CEO Replacement and Compensation around Dividend Omissions, *Corporate Governance*, 9: 25–33.

Fraser, S. (2005) *Wall Street: A Cultural History*, London: Faber and Faber.

FRC (1998) Combined Code on Corporate Governance, London: Financial Reporting Council.

FRC (2003) *Combined Code on Corporate Governance*, London: Financial Reporting Council.

FRC (2005) *Revised Guidance on Internal Controls*, London: Financial Reporting Council.

FRC (2006b) *Review of the 2003 Combined Code: The Findings of the Review*, January 2006, London: Financial Reporting Council.

Freeman, R.E (1994) The Politics of Stakeholder Theory: Some Future Directions, *Business Ethics Quarterly*, 4: 409–422.

Freeman, R.E. and Reed, W.M. (1990) Corporate Governance: A Stakeholder Interpretation, *Journal of Behavioural Economics*, 19(4): 337–360.

Frentrop, P.M.L. (2003) *A History of Corporate Governance 1602-2002*, Brussels: Deminor.

Freshfields Bruckhaus Deringer (2005a) *The World Bank is Not Enough: Equator Principles Survey 2005*, part 1: *The Banks*, London: Freshfields Bruckhaus Deringer.

Freshfields Bruckhaus Deringer (2005b) *A Legal Framework for the Integration of Environmental,*

*Social and Governance Issues into Institutional Investment*, October, London: Freshfields Bruckhaus Deringer.

Friedman, M. (1962) *Capitalism and Freedom*, Chicago: Chicago University Press.

Froud, J., Haslam, C., Johal, S. and Williams, K. (2000) Shareholder Value and Financialisation, *Economy and Society*, 29(1): 80–110.

Fruin, W.M. (1992) *The Japanese Enterprise System: Competitive and Cooperative Structures*, Oxford: Oxford University Press.

Fujita, T., Kanai, T., Teranishi, K., Yamamoto, Y. and Nikko Citigroup (2004) The Global Environment and Socially Responsible Investment: Environmental Technologies Fuelling Zones of Growth, in *The Materiality of Social, Environmental and Governance Issues to Equity Pricing*, Geneva: UNEP, 33–37.

Fukuyama, F. (1996) *Trust: The Social Values and the Creation of Property*, New York: Free Press.

Fuller, J. and Jensen, M.C. (2002) Just Say No to Wall Street: Courageous CEOs are Putting a Stop to the Earning Game and We Will All Be Better Off for It, *Journal of Applied Corporate Finance*, 14(4): 41–46.

Galbraith, J.K. (1955) *The Great Crash*, London: Hamish Hamilton.

Galbraith, J.K. (2004) *The Economics of Innocent Fraud*, London: Allen Lane.

Gandossy, R. and Sonnenfield, J. (eds) (2005) *Leadership and Governance from the Inside Out*, Hoboken: John Wiley & Sons.

Garratt, B. (2003) The Learning Board, 6[th] International Conference on Corporate Governance and Board Leadership, Henley: Henley Management College.

Garz, H., Kudszus, V., Volk, C. and West, L.B. A.G. (2004) Insurance and Sustainability: Playing with Fire in *The Materiality of Social, Environmental and Governance Issues to Equity Pricing*, Geneva: UNEP, 47–50.

Gasparino, C. (2005) *Blood on the Street*, New York: Free Press.

Gauthier, C. (2005) Measuring Corporate Social and Environmental Performance: The Extended Life Cycle Assessment, *Journal of Business Ethics*, 59: 199–206.

Geisst, C. (1997) *Wall Street: A History*, New York: Oxford University Press.

Geithner, T. (2004) Hedge Funds and Their Implications for the Financial System – Keynote Speech; National Conference on the Securities Industry, presented by AICPA and Financial Management Division of the Securities Industry Association, New York City.

General Accounting Office (2003) *Investment Banks: The Role of Firms and Their Analysts with Enron and Global Crossing*, GAO-03511, Washington, DC: GAO.

Gill, A. (2001) *Corporate Governance in Emerging Markets*, Hong Kong: Crédit Lyonnais Securities Asia.

Gillan, S.L. and Starks, L.T. (2003) Corporate Governance, Corporate Ownership, and the Role of Institutional Investors: A Global Perspective, *Journal of Applied Finance*, 13(2): 4–22.

Gilles, V., Wright, A., Amusategui, L., Cipelletti, M. and UBS (2004) European Emissions Trading Scheme in *The Materiality of Social, Environmental and Governance Issues to Equity Pricing*, Geneva: UNEP, 41–46.

Gilson, R.J. (2006) Catalysing Corporate Governance: The US System in the 1980s and 1990s, Melbourne Law School, 24 February.

Gilson, R.J. and Kraakman H. (1991) Reinventing the Outside Director: An Agenda for Institutional Investors, *Stanford Law Review*, 43: 863.

Glass, Lewis and Co (2006) *Getting It Wrong the First Time*, San Francisco: Glass, Lewis and Co., 2 March.

Glassman, C.A. (2006) Internal Controls Over Financial Reporting – Putting Sarbanes–Oxley Section 404 in Perspective, U.S. Securities and Exchange Commission, Twelfth Annual CFO Summit, Tampa, Florida, 8 May.

Global Reporting Initiative, (2000) *Sustainability Reporting Guidelines on Economic, Environmental, and Social Performance*, June, 54 pp.

Global Reporting Initiative (GRI) (2002) *Sustainability Reporting Guidelines*, Amsterdam: GRI, www.globalreporting.org

Gobert, J. and Punch, M. (2003) *Rethinking Corporate Crime*, London: Butterworths.

Goergen, M. (1998) *Corporate Governance and Financial Performance: A Study of German and UK Initial Public Offerings*, Cheltenham: Edward Elgar.

Goldman Sachs JB Were (2006) *Good Corporate Governance = Good Investment Returns*, Melbourne: Goldman Sachs JB Were.

Goldstein, A. (2000a) Corporate Governance and Regulation in Privatised Utilities: Telecommunications in Four European Countries, *Business and Politics*, 2(2): 189–223.

Goldstein, D. (2000b) Hostile Takeovers as Corporate Governance? Evidence from the 1980s, *Review of Political Economy*, 12(4): 381–402.

Gompers, P., Ishii, J. and Metrick, A. (2003) Corporate Governance and Equity Prices, *Quarterly Journal of Economics*, 118(1): 107–55.

Goncharov, I., Werner, J.R. and Zimmermann, J. (2006) Does Compliance with the German Corporate Governance Code Have an Impact on Stock Valuation? An Empirical Analysis, *Corporate Governance: An International Review*, 14(5): 432–445.

Goodstein, J., Gautam, K. and W. Boeker (1991) Turbulence at the Top: A New Perspective on Governance Structure Changes and Strategic Change, *Academy of Management Journal*, 34: 306–330.

Gordon, J.N. (2002) What Enron Means for the Management and Control of the Modern Business Corporation: Some Initial Reflections, *University of Chicago Law Review*, 69: 1233–1250.

Gordon, J.N. and Roe, M.J. (2004) *Convergence and Persistence in Corporate Governance*, Cambridge: Cambridge University Press.

Gorton, G. and Schmid, F. (1996) *Universal Banking and the Performance of German Corporations*, NBER Working Paper, 5453.

Goswami, O. (2001) The Tide Turns Gradually: Corporate Governance In India, paper presented to policy dialogue meeting on corporate governance in developing countries and emerging economies, Organisation for Economic Cooperation and Development, Paris.

Governance Metrics International Inc. (2003) *GMI Ratings on Australia's ASX50*.

Gower, L.C. (1956) Some Contrasts Between British and American Corporation Law, *Harvard Law Review*, 69(8): 1369–1402.

Goyer, M. (2001) Corporate Governance and the Innovation System in France 1985–2000, *Industry and Innovation* 8(2): 135–158.

Graham, J.R., Harvey, C.R. and Rajgopal, S. (2005) The Economic Implications of Corporate Financial Reporting, *Journal of Accounting and Economics*, 40(3): 73.

Grandmont, R., Grant, G., Silva, F. and Deutsche Bank (2004) Beyond the Numbers – Corporate Governance: Implications for Investors, in *the Materiality of Social, Environmental and Governance Issues to Equity Pricing*, 17–18, Geneva: UNEP.

Grandori, A. (2006) *Corporate Governance and Firm Organization: Micro-foundations and Structural Forms*, Oxford: Oxford University Press.

Gray, R. (1996) Reporting for Sustainable Development, in R. Welford and R. Starkey (eds), *Business and the Environment*, London: Earthscan.

Greenspan, A. (2002) Corporate Governance, Stern School of Business, New York University, New York, 26 March, http://www.federalreserve.gov/boarddocs/speeches/2002/200203262/default.htm

Gregg, P., Machin, S. and Szymanski, S. (1993) The Disappearing Relationship Between Directors' Pay and Corporate Performance, *British Journal of Industrial Relations*, 31(1): 1–9.

Gregory, H. (2000) Globalisation of Corporate Governance. *Global Counsel*, September/October, New York: Weil, Gotshal and Manges.

Gregory, H. (2002) *Comparison of Key Board-related Aspects of Sarbanes-Oxley and the NYSE and NASDAQ Corporate Governance Proposed Listing Standards*, New York: Weil, Gotshal and Manges.

Gregory, H. and Pollack, J.G. (2002) Corporate Social Responsibility, *Global Counsel*, March, 41–55, www.practicallaw.com/global

Grindle, M.S. (2004) Good Enough Governance: Poverty Reduction and Reform in Developing Countries. *Governance: An International Journal of Policy, Administration and Institutions*, October, 17(4): 525–548.

Group of 100 Incorporated (G100) (2003) *Sustainability: A Guide to Triple Bottom Line Reporting*, www.group100.com.au

Guerard, J.B. (1997) Is There a Cost to Being Socially Responsible in Investing?, *Journal of Investing*, summer: 40–45.

Gugler, K. (ed.) (2001) *Corporate Governance and Economic Performance*, Oxford: Oxford University Press.

Gugler, K., Mueller, D.C. and Yurtoglu, B.B. (2004) Corporate Governance and Globalization, *Oxford Review of Economic Policy*, 20(1): 129–156.

Halabi, Y. (2004) The Expansion of Global Governance into the Third World: Altruism, Realism, or Constructivism?, *International Studies Review*, 6(1): 21–48.

Hale, K. (2003) Corporate Law and Stakeholders: Moving Beyond Stakeholder Statutes, *Arizona Law Review*, 45: 823.

Hall, B.J. (2003) Six Challenges in Designing Equity Based Pay, *Journal of Applied Corporate Finance*, 15(3): 21–33.

Hall, P. and Soskice, D. (2001) *Varieties of Capitalism*, New York: Oxford University Press.

Hamilton, D.S. and Quinlan, J.P. (2005) *Deep Integration: How Transatlantic Markets are Leading Globalisation*, Brussels, Centre for European Policy Studies.

Hamilton, S., Jo, H., and Statman, M., (1993) Doing Well While Doing Good? The Investment Performance of Socially Responsible Mutual Funds, *Financial Analysts Journal*, November–December: 62–6.

Hampel Committee (1998) *Report of the Committee on Corporate Governance*, London: Gee.

Hancock, E. (2005) Corporate Risk of Liability for Global Climate Change and the SEC Disclosure Dilemma, *Georgetown International Environmental Law Review*, 233: 249.

Hansmann, H. and Kraakman, R. (2001) The End of History for Corporate Law, *Georgetown Law Journal*, 89: 439.

Harvey-Jones, J. (1998) *Making it Happen*, London: Collins.

Hawken, P., Lovins, A.B. and Lovins, L.H. (1999) *Natural Capital: The Next Industrial Revolution*, London: Earthscan.

Hawley, J.P. and Williams, A.T. (2000) *The Rise of Fiduciary Capitalism: How Institutional Investors Can Make Corporate America More Democratic*, Philadelphia: University of Pennsylvania Press.

Hayes, R.H. and Abernathy W.J. (1980) Managing Our Way to Economic Decline, *Harvard Business Review*, 60: 71–79.

Healy, J. (2003) *Corporate Governance and Wealth Creation in New Zealand*, Palmerston, New Zealand: Dunmore Press.

Healy, P.M. & Palepu, K.G. (2003) The Fall of Enron, *Journal of Economic Perspectives*, 17(3): 3–26.

Heinrich, R.P. (2002) *Complementarities in Corporate Governance*, Berlin and New York: Springer.

Held, D. (2003) Executive to Cosmopolitan Multilaterism, in Held, D. and Koenig-Archbugi, M. (2003) *Taming Globalisation: Frontiers of Governance*, Cambridge: Polity Press.

Held, D. and McGrew, A. (eds) (2002) *Governing Globalization*, Cambridge: Polity Press.

Hellman, T. (2001) *IPOs, Acquisitions and the Use of Convertible Securities in Venture Capital*, SSRN Paper Collection Series, http://www.ssrn.com/paper.taf?abstract_id=25760

Hendy, J. (2005) Beyond Self-Interest: Agency Theory and the Board in a Satisficing World, *British Journal of Management*, 16: S55–S63.

Henke, J.W. (1986) Involving the Directors in Strategic Planning, *Journal of Business Strategy*, 7: 87–95.

Henwood, D. (1997) *Wall Street*, London: Verso.

Hermalin, B. and M. Weisbach, 2003, Boards of Directors as an Endogenously Determined Institution: A Survey of the Economic Literature, *Federal Reserve Bank of New York Economic Policy Review* 9: 7–26.

Herman, E. (1981) *Corporate Control, Corporate Power*, New York: Cambridge University Press.

Higgs Report (2003) *Review of the Role and Effectiveness of Non-Executive Directors*, London: Department of Trade and Industry.

HIH Royal Commission (2003) *The Failure of HIH Insurance*, Canberra: Australian Government.

Hillman, A.J. and Daziel, T. (2003) Boards of Directors and Firm Performance: Integrating Agency and Resource Dependence Perspectives, *Academy of Management Review*, 28(3): 383–396.

Hillman, A.J., Cannella, A.A. & Paetzold, R.L. (2000) The resource dependence role of corporate directors: strategic adaptation of board composition in response to environmental change, *Journal of Management Studies*, 37: 235–254.

Hilmer, F. (1998) *Strictly Boardroom: Improving Governance to Enhance Company Performance*, Melbourne: Information Australia.

Hilmer, F.G. and Tricker, R.I. (1994) *An Effective Board: Corporate Governance for Directors*, London: Director Books.

Ho, S.S.M. and Wong, K.S. (2001) A Study of Corporate Disclosure Practice and Effectiveness in Hong Kong, *Journal of International Financial Management and Accounting*, 12: 75–102.

Hofstede, G. (2004) Business Goals and Corporate Governance, *Asian Pacific Business Review*, 10(3–4): 292–301.

Hogan, W.P. (1997) Corporate Governance Lessons from Barings, *ABACUS*, 33(1): 1–23.

Holderness, C.G. (2003) A Survey of Blockholders and Corporate Control, *Economic Policy Review*, 9(1): 51–64.

Holderness, C.G., Kroszner, R.S. and Sheehan, D.P. (1999) Were the Good Old Days That Good? Changes in Managerial Stock Ownership and the Great Depression, *Journal of Finance*, 54: 435–69.

Holdsworth, W.S. (1908) *A History of English Law*, vol. 3, London: Methuen; Sweet and Maxwell.

Holmstrom, B. (1999) Managerial Incentive Problems – A Dynamic Perspective, The Review of Economic Studies, 66: 169–182.

Hood, C., Rothstein, H. and Baldwin, R. (2004) *The Government of Risk*, Oxford: Oxford University Press.

Hopt, K. (1984) New Ways in Corporate Governance: European Experiments with Labour Representation on Corporate Boards, *Michigan Law Review*, 82: 1388–63.

Horrigan, B. (2002) Fault Lines in the Intersection between Corporate Governance and Social Responsibility, *University of New South Wales Law Journal*, 25: 515.

Hoshi, T., Kashyap, A. and Scharfstein, D. (1991) Corporate Structure, Liquidity, and Investment: Evidence from Japanese Industrial Groups, *Quarterly Journal of Business and Economics*, 106(1): 33–60.

Hosking, D.M. (1996) Negotiated Order, in, N. Nicholson (ed.), *Encyclopaedic Dictionary of Organisational Behaviour*, Oxford: Blackwell Business.

Hosono, K., Tomiyama, M. and Miyagawa, T. (2004). Corporate governance and research and development: evidence from Japan. *Economics of Innovation and New Technology*, 13(2): 141–146.

Hossain, M., Prevost, A.K. and Rao, R.P. (2001) SSRN Paper Collection Series, http://www.ssrn.com/paper.taf?abstract_id=2524603.

House Committee on Financial Services (2003) *Rebuilding Investor Confidence, Protecting US Capital Markets: The Sarbanes-Oxley Act – The First Year*, Washington DC: HCFS US Congress.

Howell, M. (2003) *Predators and Profits*, Upper Saddle River, NJ: Reuters Prentice Hall.

Huffington, A. (2003) *Pigs at the Trough, How Corporate Greed and Political Corruption Are Undermining America*, New York: Crown.

Hurt, C. (2003) Counselor, Gatekeeper, Shareholder, Thief: Why Attorneys Who Invest in Their Clients in a Post-Enron World are "Selling Out" Not "Buying In", *Ohio State Law Journal*, 64: 897–956.

Huse, M. (2005) Accountability and Creating Accountability: a Framework for Exploring Behavioural Perspectives of Corporate Governance, *British Journal of Management* 16(s1): S65–S79.

Huse, M. and Gabrielsson, J. (2004) Context, Behavior and Evolution: Challenges in Research on Boards and Governance, *International Studies of Management and Organization*, 34(2): 11–36.

Husted, B.W. and Allen, D.B. (2000) Is It Ethical to Use Ethics as Strategy?, *Journal of Business Ethics*, 27(1–2): 21–31.

Hutton, W. (2001) *Putting Back the P in Plc: Public Companies and a New Corporate Citizenship*, London: Industrial Society.

Hutton, W. (2005) The Shape of Things to Come, *Director*, January, London: Institute of Directors.

Hyuk-Rae, K., Oh, I., Paik, Y. and Yoneyama, S. (2004) Recasting East Asian Economic Governance: An Institutional Perspective, *Asian Business and Management*, 3(3): 281–307.

ICAEW (2005) *Pressure Points: Contrasting US and UK Securities Markets*, London: Institute of Chartered Accountants of England and Wales.

IMF (1998) *Hedge Funds and Financial Market Dynamics*, Occasional Paper 166, Washington: International Monetary Fund.

IMF (2006) *World Economic Outlook: Financial Systems and Economic Cycles*, Washington: International Monetary Fund.

Institute of Chartered Accountants in Australia (ICAA) (2003) *Environmental Management Accounting*, Melbourne: ICAA.

Institute for Sustainable Futures (2005) *Mainstreaming SRI: A Role for Government*, Institute for Sustainable Futures, University of Technology, Sydney.

Ito, T. and Krueger, A.O. (2004) *Governance, Regulation, and Privatization in the Asia-Pacific Region*, Chicago: University of Chicago Press.

Iu, J. and Batten, J. (2001) The Implementation of OECD Corporate Governance Principles in Post-Crisis Asia, *Journal of Corporate Citizenship*, 4: 47–62.

IUCN, UNEP and WWF. (1991) Caring for the Earth. A Strategy for Sustainable Living, Gland, Switzerland, 228 pp.

Jack, A. (1995) Corporate Revolution, *Financial Times*, 14 July.

Jackson, D.F. (2004) *Report of the Special Commission of Inquiry into the Medical Research and Compensation Foundation (James Hardie Affair)*, Canberra: New South Wales Government.

Jacoby, S.M. (2002) Corporate Governance in Comparative Perspective: Prospects for Convergence, *Comparative Labor Law & Policy Journal*, 22(1): 5–28.

Jacoby, S.M. (2004) *The Embedded Corporation: Corporate Governance and Employment Relations in Japan and the US*, Princeton: Princeton University Press.

Jayasuriya, K. and Rosser, A. (2001) Economic Orthodoxy and the East Asian Crisis, *Third World Quarterly*, 22(3): 381–396.

Jensen, M.C. (1986). Agency Costs of Free Cash Flow, Corporate Finance, and Takeovers, *American Economic Review*, 76(2): 323–329.

Jensen, M.C. (1994) Self-interest, Altruism, Incentives and Agency Theory, *Journal of Applied Corporate Finance*, Summer: 40–55.

Jensen, M.C. and Meckling, W.H. (1976) Theory of the Firm, Managerial Behaviour, Agency Costs and Ownership Structure, *Journal of Financial Economics*, October: 305–360.

Jensen, M.C. and Meckling, W.H. (1994) The Nature of Man, *Journal of Applied Corporate Finance*, 7(2): 4–19.

Jensen, M. and Murphy, K.J. (1990) Performance Pay and Top Management Incentives, *Journal of Political Economy*, April: 225–265.

Jesover, F. and Kirkpatrick, G. (2005) The Revised OECD Principles of Corporate Governance and their Relevance to Non-OECD Countries, *Corporate Governance: An International Review*, 13(2): 127–136.

JETRO (2005) *Focus: Japan Enters New Phase of its Economic Recovery*, New York: JETRO, 9 September.

Jin, L. (2001) *CEO Compensation, Diversification, and Incentives*, SSRN Paper Collection Series, http://www.ssrn.com/paper.taf?abstract_id= 25426

Johnson, J., Daily, C. and Ellestrand, A.E. (1996) Boards of Directors: A Review and Research Agenda, *Journal of Management*, 22(3): 409–439.

Johnstone, S. (1995) Managerial Dominance of Japan's Major Corporations, *Journal of Management*, 21(2): 192–209.

Jones, T.M. (1995) Instrumental Stakeholder Theory: A Synthesis of Ethics and Economics, *Academy of Management Review*, 20(2): 404–437.

Jordan, C. (1999) *Corporate Governance in Asia and the Asian Financial Crisis, OECD and Korea Development Institute Conference in Asia: A Comparative Perspective*, Seoul 3–5 March, Paris: OECD.

Judge, W.Q. and C.P. Zeithaml (1992) Institutional and Strategic Choice Perspectives on Board Involvement in the Strategic Decision Process, *Academy of Management Journal*, 35: 766–794.

Jurgens, U., Lung, Y., Volpato, G. and Frigant, V. (2002) The Arrival of Shareholder Value in the European Auto Industry: A Case Study Comparison of Four Car Makers, *Competition and Change*, 6(1): 61–80.

Jurgens, U., Naumann, K., and Rupp, J. (2000) Shareholder Value in an Adverse Environment: The German Case, *Economy and Society*, 29(1): 54–79.

Kaen, F.R. (2003) *A Blueprint for Corporate Governance: Strategy, Accountability, and the Preservation of Shareholder Value*, New York: AMACOM.

Kar, P. (2001) Corporate Governance in India, in *Corporate Governance in Asia: A Comparative Perspective*, Paris: Organisation of Economic Cooperation and Development.

Kaswell, S.J. and Johnson, M.C. (2004) Regulatory Reform Redux: Corporate Governance and the New York Stock Exchange, *Journal of Investment Compliance*, 4(4): 62–72.

Kaufmann, D. (2003) *Rethinking Governance, Empirical Lessons Challenge Orthodoxy*. Washington, DC: World Bank.

Kaufmann, A. and Englander, E.J. (1993) Kohlberg Kravis Roberts & Co. and the Restructuring of American Capitalism, *Business History Review*, 67: 52–97.

Kay, J. and Silberton, A. (1995) Corporate Governance, *National Institute Economic Review*, August: 84–97.

Keasey, K., Thompson, S. and Wright, M. (eds) (1999) *Corporate Governance*, Cheltenham: Edward Elgar.

Keasey, K. and Wright, M. (eds) (1997) *Corporate Governance: Responsibilities, Risks, and Remuneration*, Chichester: Wiley.

Kell, G. (2005) The Global Compact: Selected Experiences and Reflections, *Journal of Business Ethics*, 59(1): 69–79.

Kendall, N. (1998) *Real-world Corporate Governance: A Programme for Profit-enhancing Stewardship*, London: Pitman.

Kennedy School of Government Corporate Responsibility Initiative (2004) Leadership, Accountability and Partnership: Critical Trends and Issues in Corporate Social Responsibility, Report of Launch Event 4 March, Harvard University.

Kesner, I.F. (1987) Directors' Stock Ownership and Organizational Performance: An Investigation of Fortune 500 Companies, *Journal of Management*, 13: 499–508.

Kesner, I.F., Victor, B. and Lamont, B.T. (1986) Board Composition and the Commission of Illegal Acts: An Investigation of Fortune 500 Companies, *Academy of Management Journal*, 29: 789–799.

Keynes, J.M. (1936) *The General Theory of Employment, Interest and Money*, New York: Harcourt, Brace and Company, 154–155.

Khanna, T., Kogan, J. and Palepu, K. (2006) Globalisation and Similarities in Corporate Governance: A Cross-Country Analysis, *Review of Economics and Statistics*, 88(1): 69–90.

Khatri, N., Tsang, E.W.K. and Begley, T.M. (2006) Cronyism: A Cross-cultural Analysis, *Journal of International Business Studies*, 37(1): 61–75.

Khurana, R. (2002) *Searching for a Corporate Saviour: The Irrational Quest for Charismatic CEOs*, Princeton, NJ: Princeton University Press.

Kiel, G. and Nicholson, G. (2003) *Boards That Work: A New Guide for Directors*, Sydney: McGraw-Hill.

Kim, B., Prescott, J.E. and Kim, S.M. (2005) Differentiated Governance of Foreign Subsidiaries in Transnational Corporations: An Agency Theory Perspective, *Journal of International Management*, 11(1): 43–66.

Kimber, D., Lipton, P. and O'Neill, G. (2005) Corporate Governance in the Asia Pacific Region: A Selective Review of Developments in Australia, China, India and Singapore, *Asia Pacific Journal of Human Resources*, 43(2): 180–197.

Kindleberger, C. (2000) *Manias, Panics and Crashes*, Hoboken: John Wiley & Sons.

Klein, A. (2000) *Audit Committee, Board of Director Characteristics, and Earnings Management*, SSRN Paper Collection Series, http://www.ssrn.com/paper.taf?abstract_id=246674

Klein, E. and Du Plessis, J. (2005) Corporate Donations, the Best Interest of the Company and the Proper Purpose Doctrine, *University of NSW Law Journal*, 28: 69.

Kobrin, S.J. (2002) Economic Governance in an Electronically Networked Global Economy, in R.H. Bruce and T.J. Biersteker, *The Emergence of Private Authority in Global Governance*, New York: Cambridge University Press.

Kono, T. (1992) *Long Range Planning of Japanese Corporations*, Berlin: Walter de Gruyter.

Kooiman, J. (1993) *Modern Governance*, London: Sage.

Kooiman, J. (2000) Societal Governance, in J. Pierre (ed.), *Debating Governance*, Oxford: Oxford University Press, 138–166.

Kosnik, R. (1987) Greenmail: A Study of Board Performance in Corporate Governance, *Administrative Science Quarterly*, 32, 163–85.

KPMG (2005a) *International Survey of Corporate Responsibility Reporting*, June, KPMG, www.kpmg.com

KPMG (2005b) *The State of Sustainability Reporting in Australia*, Sydney: KPMG, CAER and Deni Green Consulting Services.

Kreander, N., Gray, R., Power, D., and Sinclair, C., (2000) *Evaluating the Performance of Ethical and Non-Ethical Funds: A Matched Pair Analysis*, University of Glasgow, Working Paper, July.

Kruger, J., Levy, D. and Egan, D. (2003) A Neo-Gramscian Approach to Corporate Political Strategy: Conflict and Accommodation in the Climate Change Negotiations, *Journal of Management Studies*, 40(4): 803–829.

Krugman, P. (1996) *Pop Internationalism*, London: IMF Press.

Kuhndt, M., Tuncer, B., Andersen, K. and Liedtke, C. (2004) *Responsible Corporate Governance*, Wuppertal Paper, 19, Wuppertal Institute on Globalisation.

Kulpa, A.M. and Long, B. (2006) The Wolf in Shareholder's Clothing: Hedge Funds' Use of Cooperative Game Theory and Voting Structures to Exploit Corporate Control and Governance, *University of California Davis Business Law Journal*, 6(4): 1 January.

Kurtz, L. (1997a) The Impact of Social Screening on Growth-oriented Investment Strategies, *Journal of Performance Measurement*, spring: 67–71.

Kurtz, L. (1997b) No Effect, or No Net Effects? Studies on Socially Responsible Investing, *Journal of Investing*, winter: 37–49.

Kytle, B. and Ruggie, J. (2005) *Corporate Social Responsibility as Risk Management: A Model for Multinationals*, Boston: Kennedy School of Government.

La Porta, R. (2000) Investor Protection and Corporate Governance, *Journal of Financial Economics* 58(1): 3–27.

La Porta, R., F. Lopez-de-Silanes, Shleifer, A. and Vishny, R. (2000) Investor Protection and Corporate Governance. *Journal of Financial Economics*, 58(1): 3–27.

La Porta, R., Lopez-de-Silanes, F. and Shleifer, Al. (1999) Corporate Ownership Around the World, *Journal of Finance*, 54(2): 471–517.

La Porta, R., Lopez-De-Silanes, F. *et al.* (2002) Investor Protection and Corporate Valuation, *Journal of Finance*, 57(3): 1147–1170.

La Porta, R., Lopez-de-Silanes, F. *et al.* (1998) Law and Finance, *Journal of Political Economy*, 106(6): 1113–1155.

Lamba, A. and Stapledon, G. (2001) *The Determinants of Corporate Ownership Structure: Australian Evidence*, Public Law and Legal Theory Working Paper, 20, Faculty of Law, University of Melbourne, http://papers.ssrn.com/sol3/papers.cfm?abstract_id=279015

Lane, C. (2003). Changes in Corporate Governance of German Corporations: Convergence to the Anglo-American Model? *Competition and Change*, 7(2): 79–100.

Lane, C. (2004) Globalization and the German Model of Capitalism: Erosion or Survival? *British Journal of Sociology*, 51(2): 207–234.

Langevoort, D.C. (2003) Managing the Expectations Gap in Investor Protection: The SEC and the Post-Enron Reform Agenda, *Villanova Law Review*, 48(4): 1139.

Lannoo, K. (1999) A European Perspective on Corporate Governance, *Journal of Common Market Studies*, 37(2): 269–94.

Lawrence, J. and Stapledon, G. (1996) *Corporate Governance in the Top 100: An Empirical Study of the Top 100 Companies' Board of Directors*, Centre for Corporate Law and Securities Regulation, University of Melbourne.

Lazonick, W. (1992) Controlling the Market for Corporate Control: The Historical Significance of Managerial Capitalism, *Industrial and Corporate Change*, 1(3): 445–488.

Lazonick, W. (2001) Public and Corporate Governance: The Institutional Foundations of the Market Economy, *Economic Survey of Europe*, 2: 59–76.

Lazonick, W. (2002) *American Corporate Economy*, vol. 1: *Critical Perspectives on Business and Management*, London: Routledge.

Lazonick, W. and O'Sullivan, M. (2000) *Perspectives on Corporate Governance, Innovation and Economic Performance*, Fontainebleau: INSEAD.

Lazonick, W. and O'Sullivan, M. (2002) *Corporate Governance and Sustainable Prosperity*, New York: Palgrave.

Learmont, S. (2002a) *Corporate Governance: What Can Be Learned from Japan?* Oxford: Oxford University Press.

Learmont, S. (2002b) *Theorising Corporate Governance: New Organisational Alternatives, ESRC Centre for Business Research*, University of Cambridge, Working Paper, 237.

Leblanc, R. and Gillies, J. (2005) *Inside the Boardroom*, New York: Wiley.

Letendre, L. (2004) The Dynamics of the Boardroom, *Academy of Management Executive*, 18(1): 97–100.

Levitt, A. (2002) *Take on the Street*, New York: Pantheon Books.

Levy, D.L. and Prakash, A. (2003) Bargains Old and New: Multinational Corporations in Global Governance, *Business and Politics*, 5(2): 131–150.

Licht, A. (2001) The Mother of All Path Dependencies: Towards a Cross-cultural Theory of Corporate Governance Systems, *Delaware Journal of Corporate Law*, 26: 147–209.

Licht, A. (2003) *The Maximands of Corporate Governance: A Theory of Values and Cognitive Style*, European Corporate Governance Institute, Law Working Paper, 16, ECGI.

Lindblom, C. (2001) *The Market System,* New Haven, CT: Yale University Press.

Lingle, C. (1997) *The Rise and Decline of the Asian Century*, Hong Kong: Asia 2000 Ltd.

Linklaters (2005) *The Matrix: An Overview of Corporate Governance*, London: Linklaters.

Lipton, M. and Lorsch, J. (1991) A New Compact for Owners and Directors, *Harvard Business Review*, July–August, 141–143.

Logsdon, J.M. and Wood, D.J. (2005) Global Business Citizenship and Voluntary Codes of Ethical Conduct, *Journal of Business Ethics*, 59: 55–67.

Lomborg, B. (2004) *Global Crises, Global Solutions*, Cambridge: Cambridge University Press.

Lorsch, J. (1995) Empowering the Board, *Harvard Business Review*, 73(1): 107–117.

Lorsch, J. and MacIver, E. (1989) *Pawns or Potentates: The Reality of America's Corporate Boards*, Boston, MA: Harvard Business School Press.

Lowestein, R. (2004) *Origins of the Crash*, New York: Penguin.

Luis, C. (2005) People v. Profits: A False Dichotomy?, *University of California Davis, Business Law Journal*, 5(6).

Lynall, M.D., Golden, B.R. and Hillman, A.J. (2003) Board Composition from Adolescence to Maturity: A Multi-theoretic View, *Academy of Management Review*, 28(3): 416–431.

MacAvoy, P.W. and Millstein, I.M. (2004) *The Recurrent Crisis in Corporate Governance*, Stanford, CA: Stanford Business Books.

Mace, M.L. (1971) *Directors: Myth and Reality*, Boston, MA: Harvard University Press.

Maher, M. and Anderson, T. (2000) Corporate Governance: Effects on Firm Performance and Economic Growth, in L.J. Renneboog *et al.* (eds), *Convergence and Diversity of Corporate Governance Regimes and Capital Markets*, Oxford: Oxford University Press.

Malik, O. (2003) *Broadbandits*, Chichester: John Wiley & Sons.

Mallin, C. (2004) *Corporate Governance*, Oxford: Oxford University Press.

Manifest (2004) *Milestones in UK Corporate Governance*, London: Manifest Proxy Voting Agency.

Marens, R. and Wicks, A. (1999) Getting Real: Stakeholder Theory, Managerial Practice, and the General Irrelevance of Fiduciary Duties Owed to Shareholders, *Business Ethics Quarterly*, 9(2): 273–293.

Marginson, D. and L. McAulay (2005) *Exploring the Debate on Short-termism: A Theoretical and Empirical Analysis*, Manchester: Manchester School of Management.

Mathieu, E. (2000) Response of UK Pension Funds to the SRI Disclosure Regulation, London: UK Social Investment Forum, October, 50 pp.

Mayer, C.P. (1988) New Issues in Corporate Finance, *European Economic Review*, 32: 1167–1183.

Mayes, D. and Wood, G. (eds) (2005) *The Structure of Financial Regulation*, London: Routledge.

Mays, S. (2003) *Corporate Sustainability: An Investor Perspective*, Canberra: Department of Environment and Heritage, Commonwealth of Australia.

McCahery, J.A., Moerland, P. *et al.* (2002) *Corporate Governance Regimes: Convergence and Diversity*, Oxford, Oxford University Press.

McCahery, J.A. and Vermeulen, P.M. (2005) Does the European Company Prevent the Delaware Effect, *European Law Journal*, 11(6): 785–801.

McCarthy, D.J. and Puffer, S.M. (2002) Russia's Corporate Governance Scorecard in the Enron Era, *Organisational Dynamics*, 31(1): 19–34.

McClintick, D. (2006) How Harvard Lost Russia, *Institutional Investor*, 40(1): 62–90.

McConvill, J. and Joy, M. (2003) The Interaction of Directors' Duties and Sustainable Development in Australia: Setting Off on the Uncharted Road, *Melbourne University Law Review*, 27: 116.

McDonnell, B.H. (2002) Convergence in Corporate Governance: Possible, But Not Desirable, *Villanova Law Review*, 47(2): 341–386.

McDonough, W.J. (2005) *Corporate Board Elections and Internal Controls*, 27 September, Federal Reserve Bank of New York.

McGrew, A. (2000) Power Shift: From National Government to Global Governance? in, D. Held, *A Globalising World? Culture, Economics, Politics*, London: Routledge.

McKague, K. and Cragg, W. (2005) Compendium of Ethics Codes and Instruments of Corporate Responsibility, September, Schulich Business School, York University, Canada.

McKinsey (2000a) *McKinsey Investor Opinion Survey*, June, New York: McKinsey Company.

McKinsey (2000b) Three Surveys on Corporate Governance, *McKinsey Quarterly*, 4: 73–77.

MacLean, B. and Elkind, P. (2003) *The Smartest Guys in the Room*. New York: Penguin Viking.

McLeod, R. H. and Garnaut, R. (1998) *East Asia in Crisis: From Being a Miracle To Needing One*, London: Routledge.

McNulty, T. and A. Pettigrew (1999) Strategists on the Board, *Organization Studies*, 20: 47–74.

McNulty, T. Roberts, J. and Stiles, P. (2003) *Creating Accountability Within the Boardroom: The Work of the Effective Non-Executive Director*, Research Report, Higgs Inquiry, London: Department of Trade and Industry.

McNulty, T., Roberts, J. and Stiles, P. (2005) Undertaking Governance Reform and Research: Further Reflections on the Higgs Review, *British Journal of Management*, 16: S99–S107.

Means, G.C. (1931; 2005) The Separation of Ownership and Control in American Industry, *Quarterly Journal of Economics*, 46(1): 68–100, in T. Clarke, *Corporate Governance: Critical Perspectives in Business and Management*, vol. I. *The Genesis of Corporate Governance*, London: Routledge, 2005.

Mehran, H. (1995) Executive Compensation Structure, Ownership, and Firm Performance, *Journal of Financial Economics*, 38(2): 163–84.

Melis, A. (2000) Corporate Governance in Italy, *Corporate Governance*, 8(4): 347–355.

Melis, A. (2004) On the Role of the Board of Statutory Auditors in Italian-listed Companies. *Corporate Governance*, 12(1): 74–84.

Millar, C., Eldomiaty, T., Choi, C. and Hilton, B. (2005) Corporate Governance and Institutional Transparency in Emerging Markets, *Journal of Business Ethics*, 59(1–2): 163–174.

Mills, C. Wright (1971) *The Power Elite*, New York: Oxford University Press.

Millstein, I. (1998) *The Evolution of Corporate Governance in the United States*, Davos: World Economic Forum.

Millstein, I.M. (2001) The Evolution of Corporate Governance in the United States – Briefly Told, *Forum for US_EU Legal-Economic Affairs*, Rome, Italy, September 12–15: 1–22.

Millstein, I.A. and MacAvoy, P.W. (1998) The Active Board of Directors and Performance of the Large Publicly Traded Corporation, *Columbia Law Review*, 98: 1283–1321.

Minerals Council of Australia (2004) *Enduring Value: The Australian Minerals Industry Framework for Sustainable Development*, Melbourne: MCA.

Mitchell, L.A. (2001) *Corporate Irresponsibility: America's Newest Export*, New Haven, CT: Yale University Press.

Mizruchi, M.S. (1983) Who Controls Whom? An Examination of the Relation Between Management and Boards of Directors in Large American Corporations, *Academy of Management Review*, 8: 426–35.

Moerland, P.W. (1995). Corporate Ownership and Control Structures: An International Comparison, *Review of Industrial Organization*, 10(4): 443–464.

Monas-Beecher, E. (2003) Corporate Governance in the Wake of Enron: An Examination of the Audit Committee Solution, *Journal of Business Law*, 205.

Monks, R. (1998) *The Emperor's Nightingale: Restoring the Integrity of the Corporation*, Oxford: Captstone.

Monks, R. and Minow, N. (1991) *Power and Accountability*, New York: HarperCollins.

Monks, R. and Minow, N. (2001) *Corporate Governance*, Oxford: Blackwell Publishing.

Monks, R., Miller, A. and Cook, J. (2004) Shareholder Activism on Environmental Issues: A Study of Proposals at Large US Corporations 2000–2003, *Natural Resources Forum*, 28: 317–330.

Montgomery, C. and Kaufman, R. (2003) The Board's Missing Link, *Harvard Business Review*, March: 26–33.

Morck, R. (ed.) (2000) *Concentrated Corporate Ownership*, Chicago: University of Chicago Press.

Morck, R. (2006) *A History of Corporate Governance around the World: Family Business Groups to Professional Managers*, Washington, DC: NBER.

Morin, F. (2000) A Transformation in the French Model of Shareholding and Management, *Economy and Society*, 29(1): 36–53.

Munari, F. and Sobrero, M. (2003) Corporate Governance and Innovation, in M. Calderini, P. Garrone, and M. Sobrero (eds), *Corporate Governance, Market Structure and Innovation*, Cheltenham: Edward Elgar.

Murphy, D. (2004) *The Structure of Regulatory Competition*. Oxford: Oxford University Press.

Myners Report (2004) *Myners Principles For Institutional Investment Decision-making: Review of Progress*, London: HM Treasury.

Myners, P. (2005) *Progress One Year On, Report to the Shareholders Voting Working Group*, London: Department of Trade and Industry.

Nadler, P. (2000) Issues in Corporate Governance, *Secured Lender*, 56: 60–66.

Najam, A. (2000) World Business Council for Sustainable Development: The Greening of Business or a Greenwash?, *Yearbook of International Cooperation on Environment and Development 1999/2000*.

Nelson, B. (2006) *Law and Ethics in Global Business: Integrating Corporate Governance into Business Decisions*, London: Routledge.

Nelson, J. (2005) Does Good Corporate Governance Really Work? More Evidence from CalPERS, *Journal of Asset Management*, 6(4): 274–287.

Nestor, S. and Thompson, J.K (2000) *Corporate Governance Patterns in OECD Economies: Is Convergence Under Way?*, Discussion Paper, Paris: OECD.

Neubauer, F.-F. (1998) *The Family Business: Its Governance for Sustainability*, New York: Routledge.

Neumann, S. and Egan, M. (1999) Between German and Anglo-Saxon Capitalism: The Czech Financial Markets in Transition, *New Political Economy*, 4(2): 173–194.

Niederhoffer, V. (1999) *The Education of a Speculator*, New York: Wiley.

Nodoushani, O. and Nodoushani, P.A. (1999) The Debate on Corporate Governance: An Historical Analysis of Berle and Means Contributions, *Journal of Behavioral and Applied Management*, 1(1): 55–64.

Noe, T.H. (2002). Investor Activism and Financial Market Structure, *Review of Financial Studies*, 15(1): 289–318.

Nofsinger, J. and Kim, K. (2003) *Infectious Greed*, Upper Saddle River, NJ: FT Prentice Hall.

Nölke, A. (2003) Private International Norms in Global Economic Governance: Coordination Service Firms and Corporate Governance, Working Papers Political Science No. 06/2003. Studies in the Transnational Political Economy of Corporate Governance 2, Amsterdam.

Nooteboom, B. (2002) *Trust: Forms, Foundations, Functions, Failures and Figures*, Cheltenham: Edward Elgar.

Norburn, D. and Grinyer, P. (1974) Directors without Direction, *Journal of General Management*, 1: 30–39.

Nystrom, P.C. and Starbuck, W.H. (1984) To Avoid Crises, Unlearn, *Organisational Dynamics*, 13, 53–65.

O'Brien, J. (2003) *Wall Street on Trial*, Chichester: John Wiley & Sons.

O'Brien, J. (2004a) Beyond Compliance: Testing the Limits of Reforming the Governance of Wall Street, *International Journal of Business Governance and Ethics*, 1(2/3): 162–174.

O'Brien, J. (2004b) Ethics Probity and the Changing Governance of Wall Street: Cure or Remission, *Public Integrity*, 7(1): 43–56.

O'Brien, J. (ed.) (2005) *Governing the Corporation, Regulation and Corporate Governance in an Age of Scandal and Global Markets*, Chichester: John Wiley.

O'Brien, P.K. (2003) *The Governance of Globalization: The Political Economy of Anglo–American Hegemony 1793-2003*, CESIFO Working Paper, 1023, September, University of Munich.

O'Brien, W.J. (1998) *The Soul of Corporate Leadership: Guidelines for Values-centered Governance*, Waltham, MA: Pegasus.

O'Loughlin, J. and Thamotheram, R. (2006) *Enhanced Analytics for a New Generation of Investor*, Liverpool: Universities Superannuation Scheme Ltd.

O'Neal, D. and Thomas, H. (1995) Director Networks/Director Selection: The Board's Strategic Role, *European Management Journal*, 13: 79–90.

O'Sullivan, M.A. (2000a) Corporate Governance and Globalization, *Annals of the American Academy of Political and Social Science*, 570(1): 153–172.

O'Sullivan, M.A. (2000b) The Innovative Enterprise and Corporate Governance, *Cambridge Journal of Economics*, 24: 393–416.

O'Sullivan, M.A. (2001) *Contests for Corporate Control: Corporate Governance and Economic Performance in the United States and Germany*, London: Oxford University Press.

OECD (1976; 2000) *Guidelines for Multinational Enterprises*, Paris: OECD.

OECD (1995a) Financial Markets and Corporate Governance, *Financial Market Trends*, 62, November, Paris: OECD.

OECD (1995b) OECD Economic Surveys – Germany, Paris: OECD.

OECD (1996) OECD Economic Surveys – Japan, Paris: Organisation for Economic Co-operation and Development.

OECD (1997) OECD Economic Surveys – France, Paris: OECD.

OECD (1998a) *Corporate Governance: Improving Competitiveness and Access to Capital in Global Markets, A Report to the OECD by the Business Sector Advisory Group on Corporate Governance*, Paris: OECD.

OECD (1998b) *Economic Outlook*, 64, Paris: OECD.

OECD (1999) *Principles of Corporate Governance*, Paris: OECD.

OECD (2001a) *Corporate Governance in OECD Member Countries: Recent Developments and Trends, OECD Steering Group on Corporate Governance*, 26–27 April, Paris: OECD.

OECD, (2001b) *Corporate Responsibility: Private Initiatives and Public Goals*, Paris OECD, 112 pp.

OECD (2001c) *Institutional Investors Statistical Yearbook*, Paris: OECD.

OECD (2001d) *The New Economy: Beyond the Hype: The OECD Growth Project*, Paris: OECD.

OECD (2003) *White Paper on Corporate Governance in Asia*, Paris: OECD.

OECD (2004a) *Principles of Corporate Governance*, Paris: OECD.

OECD, (2004b) *Corporate Governance: A Survey of OECD Countries*, Paris: OECD.

OECD (2004c) *Survey of Corporate Governance Developments in OECD Countries*, Paris: OECD.

OECD (2004d) *Survey of Governance Trends in OECD Countries*, Paris: OECD.

OECD (2005a) *OECD Guidelines for Insurers' Governance*, Paris: OECD, http://www.oecd.org/dataoecd/19/10/34799740.pdf

OECD (2005b) *OECD Guidelines for Pension Fund Governance*, Paris: OECD, http://www.oecd.org/dataoecd/18/52/34799965.pdf

OECD (2005c) *Pension Markets in Focus, Newsletter*, December, 2, http://www.oecd.org/dataoecd/44/18/35836532.pdf

OECD (2005e) *Modernising Government*, Paris: OECD.

OECD (2006) Highlights of Recent Trends in Financial Markets, *Financial Market Trends*, 90: 9–31, Paris: OECD.

OECD Watch (2005) *Five Years On: A Review of the OECD Guidelines and National Contact Points*, Amsterdam: Centre for Research on Multinational Corporations.

Oman, C., Fries, S. and Buiter, W. (2005) Corporate Governance in Developing, Transition and Emerging-market Economies, *OECD Policy Insight*, 3, Paris: OECD.

Ong, D.M. (2001) The Impact of Environmental Law on Corporate Governance: International and Comparative Perspectives, *European Journal of International Law*, 12(4): 685–726.

Osano, H. & Tachibanaki, T. (eds) (2001) *Banking, Capital Markets, and Corporate Governance*, New York: Palgrave.

Pahl, R.E. and Winkler, J.T. (1974) The Economic Elite: Theory and Practice, in P.J. Stanworth, and A. Giddens (eds) *Elite and Power in British Society*, Cambridge: Cambridge University Press, 103–128.

Parkinson, J. (1994) *Corporate Power and Responsibility: Issues in the Theory of Company Law*, Oxford: Clarendon Press.

Parkinson, J. (2000) Corporate Governance: The Company Law Review and Questions of 'Scope', *Hume Papers on Public Policy*, 30–53.

Parkinson, J., Gamble, A. and Kelly, G. (eds) (2000) *The Political Economy of the Company*, Oxford: Hart Publishing.

PCAOB (2005) *An Audit of Internal Control Over Financial Reporting Performed in Conjunction with an Audit of Financial Statements, Policy Statement Regarding Implementation of Auditing Standard Number 2*, Washington: Public Company Accounting Oversight Board.

Pearce, J.A. and Zahra, S.A. (1991) The Relative Power of CEOs and Boards of Directors: Associations with Corporate Performance, *Strategic Management Journal*, 12: 135–153.

Pedersen, T. and Thomsen, S. (1999) Economic and Systemic Explanations of Ownership Concentration among Europe's Largest Companies, *International Journal of Economics and Business*, 6(3): 367–381.

Perotti, E.C. and von Thadden, E.L. (2006) Corporate Governance and the Distribution of Wealth: A Political Economy Perspective, *Journal of Institutional and Theoretical Economics*, 162(1): 204–217.

Pettigrew, A. (1992) On Studying Managerial Elites, *Strategic Management Journal*, 13: 163–182.

Pettigrew, A. (1997) What is Processual Analysis?, *Scandinavian Management Journal*, 13: 337–348.

Pettigrew, A.M. and McNulty, T. (1995) Power and Influence in and around the Boardroom, *Human Relations*, 8: 845–873.

Pettigrew, A. and McNulty, T. (1998) Control and Creativity in the Boardroom, in D.C. Hambrick, D.A. Nadley and M.L Tushman (eds) *Navigating Change: How CEOs, Top Teams and Boards Steer Transformation*, Cambridge: Harvard Business School Press, 226–255.

Pfeffer, J. (1972) Size and Composition of Corporate Boards of Directors: The Organization and Its Environment, *Administrative Science Quarterly*, 17: 218–229.

Pfeffer, J. (1973) Size, Composition and Function of Hospital Boards of Directors: A Study of Organization–Environment Linkage, *Administrative Science Quarterly*, 18: 349–364.

Pierce, C. and Waring, K. (2005) *The Handbook of International Corporate Governance*, London: Kogan Page.

Pinto, A.R. (2005) Globalization and the Study of Comparative Corporate Governance, *Wisconsin International Law Journal*, 23(3): 477–504.

Piore, M.J. (2004) *Innovation, the Missing Dimension*, Cambridge, MA: Harvard University Press.

Porter, M. (1990) *Competitive Advantage of Nations*, New York: Free Press.

Porter, M.E. (1992) Capital Disadvantage: America's Failing Capital Investment System, *Harvard Business Review*, 70(5): 65–82.

Pleon (2005) *Accounting for Good: The Global Stakeholder Report*, Berlin: Pleon.

Porter, M. (1992) Capital Disadvantage: America's Failing Capital Investment System, *Harvard Business Review*, September–October: 65–82.

Portnoy, F. (1999) *Fiasco: The Inside Story of a Wall Street Trader*, New York: Penguin.

Portnoy, F. (2003) *Infectious Greed*, London: Profile Books.

Post, J.E. (2002) *Redefining the Corporation: Stakeholder Management and Organisational Wealth*, Stanford, CA: Stanford Business Books.

Post, J.E., Preston, L.E. and Sachs, S. (2003) Managing the Extended Enterprise: The New Stakeholder View, *California Management Review*, 45(1): 6–28.

Pound, J. (1992) Beyond Takeovers: Politics Comes to Corporate Control, *Harvard Business Review*, 83–93.

Pound, J. (1995) The Promise of the Governed Corporation, *Harvard Business Review*, 73(2): 89–98.

Powell, W.W., (1990) Neither Market Nor Hierarchy: Network Forms of Organisation, in, B. Staw and L.L. Cummings (eds), *Research in Organisational Behaviour*, Greenwich, CT: JAI Press.

PriceWaterhouseCoopers (PwC) (2001) *The Role of Australia's Financial Sector in Sustainability*, Report Prepared for Environment Australia, Canberra.

PriceWaterhouseCoopers (2004) *Findings of UK Pension Scheme Governance Survey*, London: PriceWaterhouseCoopers.

Prin, N. (2005) *Other People's Money*, New York: New Press.

Provan, J.G. (1980) Board power and organizational effectiveness among human service agencies, *Academy of Management Journal*, 23: 221–236.

Prowse, S. (1998) Corporate Governance in East Asia: A Framework for Analysis, Managing Capital Flows: National and International Dimensions, Conference, 15–16 June, Bangkok.

Puri, P. and Larsen, J. (2004) *Corporate Governance and Securities Regulation in the 21st Century*, Markham, ON: LexisNexisButterworths.

Pye, A. (2002) The Changing Power of 'Explanations': Directors, Academics and their Sensemaking from 1989 to 2000, *Journal of Management Studies*, 39(7): 907–925.

Pye, A. and Camm, G. (2003) Non-Executive Directors: Moving beyond the 'One-size-fits-all' View, *Journal of General Management*, 28(3): 52–70.

Pye, A. and Pettigrew, A. (2005) Studying Board Context, Process and Dynamics: Some Challenges for the Future, *British Journal of Management*, 16: S27–S38.

Quere, M. (2004) National Systems of Innovation and National Systems of Corporate Governance: A Missing Link?, *Economics of Innovation and New Technology*, 13(1): 77–90.

Qi, D., Wu, W., and Zhang, H. (2000) Shareholding Structure and Corporate Performance of

Partially Privatized Firms: Evidence from Listed Chinese Companies, *Pacific Basin Finance Journal*, 587–6101.

Radygin, A. and Malginov, G. (2004) *The Russian Experience, Policy Dialogue on Corporate Governance in China*, OECD and Shanghai Stock Exchange.

Raghunaandan, K., Sankaraguruswamy, S. and Whisenant, J.S. (2001) *The Information Content of Internal Control related Matters Noted During and Audit in Form 8-K Filings of Auditor Realignments and Relation to Auditor Resignations*, SSRN Paper Collection Series, http://www.ssrn.com/paper.taf?abstract_id=25981.

Rajan, R.G. and Zingales, L. (2000) The Governance of the New Enterprise in X. Vives (ed.), *Corporate Governance*, Cambridge: Cambridge University Press, 201–227.

Rajan, R. and Zingales, L. (2003) The Great Reversals: The Politics of Financial Development in the Twentieth Century, *Journal of Financial Economics*, 5: 5–50.

Rajgopal, S., Venkatachalam, M. and Kotha, S. (2000) *Managerial Actions, Stock Returns, and Earnings: The Case of Business-to-Business Internet Firms*, SSRN Paper Collection Series, http://www.ssrn.com/paper.taf?abstract_id=25791

Rashad Abdel-Khalik, A. (2002) Reforming Corporate Governance Post Enron: Shareholders' Board of Trustees and the Auditor, *Journal of Accounting and Public Policy*, 21: 97–103.

Reberioux, A. (2000) European Style of Corporate Governance At the Crossroads: The Role of Worker Involvement, *Journal of Common Market Studies*, 40(1): 113–34.

Redding, G. (2004) The Conditional Relevance of Corporate Governance Advice in the Context of Asian Business Systems, *Asia Pacific Business Review*, 10(3–4): 272–291.

Redmond, P. (2005) *Companies and Securities Law: Commentary and Materials*, Thomson Lawbook, Sydney: LBC.

Redmond, P. (2005) *Submission Parliamentary Joint Committee on Corporations and Financial Services Inquiry into Corporate Responsibility*, Canberra: Commonwealth of Australia.

Reed, D. (2002) Corporate Governance Reforms in Developing Countries, *Journal of Business Ethics*, 37(3): 223–247.

Reed, D. and Mukherjee, S. (2004) *Corporate Governance, Economic Reforms & Development: The Indian Experience*, Oxford: Oxford University Press.

Reid, A.S. (2003) The Internationalisation of Corporate Governance Codes of Conduct, *Business Law Review*, October: 233–238.

Renneboog, L. (2000) Ownership, Managerial Control and the Governance of Companies Listed on the Brussels Stock Exchange, *Journal of Banking and Finance*, 24: 1959–1995.

Rhoades, D.L., Rechner, P.L. and Sundaramurthy, C. (2000) Board Composition and Financial Performance: A Meta-analysis of the Influence of Outsider Directors, *Journal of Managerial Issues,* 12(1): 76–91.

Rhodes, M. and Apepdoorn, B. van (1998) Capital Unbound? The Transformation of European Corporate Governance, *Journal of European Public Policy*, 5(3): 406–427.

Roberts, J., McNulty, T. and Stiles, P. (2005) Beyond Agency Conceptions of the Work of the Non-Executive Director: Creating Accountability in the Boardroom, *British Journal of Management*, 16: S5–S26.

Roche, J. (2005) *Corporate Governance in Asia*, London: Routledge.

Roe, M.J. (1994) *Strong Managers, Weak Owners: The Political Roots of American Corporate Finance*, Princeton, NJ: Princeton University Press.

Roe, M.J. (2005a) The Inevitable Instability of American Corporate Governance, in J. Lorsch, L. Berlowitz, and A. Zelleke (eds), *Restoring Trust in American Business*, Cambridge, MA: MIT Press.

Roe, M.J. (2005b) Regulatory Competition in Making Corporate Law in the United States – and its Limits, *Oxford Review of Economic Policy*, 21(2): 232–242.

Rogerson, P. (1999) Open Season, *The Accountant*, April: 16.

Romano, R. (2002) Less is More: Making Institutional Investor Activism a Valuable Mechanism for Corporate Governance, in McCahery, J.A., Moerland, P., Raaijmkaer, T. and Renneboog, L. (eds) *Corporate Governance Regimes: Convergence and Diversity*, Oxford University Press.

Romano, R. (2004) *The Sarbanes-Oxley Act and the Making of Quack Corporate Governance*, European Corporate Governance Institute Finance Working Paper, 52/2004.

Rosenstein, J. (1987) Why Don't US Boards Get More Involved in Strategy?, *Long Range Planning*, 20(3): 20–34.

Rosser, A. (2003) Coalitions, Convergence and Corporate Governance Reform in Indonesia, *Third World Quarterly*, 24(2): 319–337.

Rossouw, G.J. and van Vuuren, L.J. (2003) Modes of Managing Morality: A Descriptive Model of Strategies for Managing Ethics, *Journal of Business Ethics*, 46(4): 389–402.

Rubach, M.J. (1999) *Institutional Shareholder Activism: The Changing Face of Corporate Ownership*, New York: Garland.

Russell Reynolds (2000) *Corporate Governance in the New Economy – International Survey of Institutional Investors*, Russell Reynolds.

Russo, M.V. and Fouts, P.A. (1997) A Resource-Based Perspective on Corporate Environmental Performance and Profitability, *Academy of Management Journal*, 40(3): 534–59.

Rwegasira, K. (2000) Corporate Governance in Emerging Capital Markets, Whither Africa?, *Corporate Governance an International Review*, 8(3): 258–267.

Rybczynski, T. (1997a) The Development of European Capital Markets, in J. Revell (ed.), *The Changing Face of European Banks and Securities Markets*, London: Macmillan.

Rybczynski, T. (1997b) *The Recent Evolution of Financial Systems*, New York, St Martin's Press, S: 3–15.

SAM (2003) *Climate Change the Next Major Challenge, SAM Insight 2/03*, Zurich: Sustainable Asset Management.

Samuel, C. (1996) *Stock Market and Investment: The Governance Role of the Market*, Washington DC: World Bank.

Sarkar, J. and Sarkar, S. (2000) Large Shareholder Activism in Corporate Governance in Developing Countries: Evidence from India, *International Review of Finance*, 1(3): 161–194.

Sarra, J. (ed.) (2005) *Corporate Governance in Global Capital Markets*, Vancouver: UBC Press.

Sauer, D.A. (1997) The Impact of Social-Responsibility Screens on Investment Performance: Evidence from the Domini 400 Social Index and Domini Equity Mutual Fund, *Review of Financial Economics*, 6(2): 137–49.

Schipani, C.A. and Fort, T.L. (2003) Adapting Corporate Governance for Sustainable Peace, *Vanderbilt Journal of Transnational Law*, 36: 377–426.

Schmidt, R. (1975) Does Board Composition Really Make a Difference?, *Conference Board Record*, 129(1): 38–41.

Schmidt, R. (1977) The Board of Directors and Financial Interests, *Academy of Management Journal*, 20: 677–682.

Schrage, M. (2004) What's a Director to Do?, *STRATEGY+BUSINESS*, 7 September, McLean, VA: Booz Allen Hamilton.

Schroder, M. (2003) *Socially Responsible Investments in Germany, Switzerland and the United States: An Analysis of Investment Funds and Indices*, Mannheim: Centre for European Economic Research.

Schumpeter, J.A. (1939) *Business Cycles*, New York: McGraw Hill.

Schwalbach, J. (ed.) (2001) *Corporate Governance: Essays in Honor of Horst Albach*, Berlin: Springer.

Schwartz, M. (2002) A Code of Ethics for Corporate Codes of Ethics, *Journal of Business Ethics*, 41(1/2): 27–45.

Scott, C. (2000) Accountability in the Regulatory State, *Journal of Law and Society*, 27(1): 38–60.

Scott, J.P. (1997) *Corporate Business and Capitalist Classes*, Oxford: Oxford University Press.

SEC (2003) *Implications of the Growth of Hedge Funds*, Washington: Securities and Exchange Commission.

SEC (2005) *Roundtable Discussion on Implementation of Internal Control Reporting Provisions*, Washington: United States Securities and Exchange Commission, 13 April.

Segal, G. and Goodman, D.S.G. (2000) *Towards Recovery in Pacific Asia*, London: Routledge.

Segura, R. (1998). Spain, *International Financial Law Review*, April, special supplement: 51.

Seligman, J. (2003) *The Transformation of Wall Street: A History of the Securities and Exchange Commission and Modern Corporate Finance*, New York: Aspen.

Sethi, S.P. (2003) *Setting Global Standards, Guidelines for Creating Codes of Conduct in Multinational Corporations*, London: John Wiley & Sons.

Shafer, W.E., Morris, R.E. and Ketchand, A.A. (2001) The Effects of Formal Sanctions on Auditor Independence, *Journal of Accountancy*, 191: 104.

Shiller, R.J. (2000) *Irrational Exuberance*, Princeton, NJ: Princeton University Press.

Shleifer, A. and Vishny, R.W. (1997) A Survey of Corporate Governance, *Journal of Finance*, 52: 737–783.

Sidak, J.G. (2003) The Failure of Good Intentions: The WorldCom Fraud and the Collapse of American Telecommunications after Deregulation, *Yale Journal of Regulation*, 20(2): 207–67.

Siebert, H. (2004) Germany's Capital Market and Corporate Governance, Kiel Working Paper No. 1206, Kiel Institute for World Economics, Kiel, Germany.

Sifonis, J.G. (1996) *Corporation on a Tightrope: Balancing Leadership, Governance, and Technology in an Age of Complexity*, Oxford: Oxford University Press.

Simpson, S. (2002) *Corporate Crime, Law and Social Control*, Cambridge: Cambridge University Press.

Skeel, D. (2005) *Icarus in the Boardroom*, New York: Oxford University Press.

Smith, A. (1976) *An Inquiry Into the Nature and Causes of the Wealth of Nations* (1776), Chicago: University of Chicago Press.

Smith, N.C. (1990) *Morality and the Market: Consumer Pressure for Corporate Accountability*, London: Routledge.

Social Investment Forum (1997) Report on Responsible Investing Trends in the United States, Washington, DC: Social Investment Forum Research Program.

Social Investment Forum Industry (2001) *Report on Socially Responsible Investing Trends in the United States*, Washington, DC: Social Investment Forum Research Program.

Soederberg, S. (2003) The Promotion of 'Anglo-American' Corporate Governance in the South: Who Benefits from the New International Standard?, *Third World Quarterly*, 24(1): 7–27.

Solomon, J. and Solomon, A. (2004) *Corporate Governance and Accountability*, Chichester: John Wiley & Sons.

Solomon, J.F., Solomon, A. and Norton, S.D. (2002) Socially Responsible Investing in the UK: Drivers and Current Issues, *Journal of General Management*, 27(3): 1–13.

Sommer, A.A. (1980) Corporate Governance: Its Impact on the Profession, *Journal of Accountancy*, July: 52–60.

Soros, G. (1998) *The Crisis of Global Capitalism*, London: Little Brown and Company.

Sparkes, R. (2002) *Socially Responsible Investment: A Global Revolution*, London: Wiley Europe.

Sparkes, R. and Cowton, C.J. (2004) The Maturing of Socially Responsible Investment: A Review of the Developing Link with Corporate Social Responsibility, *Journal of Business Ethics*, 52(1): 45–57.

Spira, L.F. (2002) *The Audit Committee: Performing Corporate Governance*, Boston: Kluwer Academic Publishers.

Stapledon, G. (1996) Disincentives to Activism by Institutional Investors in Listed Australian Companies, *Sydney Law Review*, 18(152): 175–188.

Stapledon, G. (1996) *Institutional Shareholders and Corporate Governance*, Oxford University Press.

Stapledon, G. (1998) Australian Sharemarket Ownership, in G. Walker (ed.), *Securities Regulation in Australia and New Zealand*, North Ryde, NSW: LBC Information Services.

Statman, M. (2000) Socially Responsible Mutual Funds, *Financial Analysts' Journal*, May/June: 30–39.

Steane, P.D. and Christie, M. (2001) Nonprofit Boards in Australia: A Distinctive Governance, *Corporate Governance*, 9: 48–58.

Steger, U. (ed) (2004) *Mastering Global Corporate Governance*, Hoboken, NJ: Wiley.

Steinberg, R.M. and Pojunis, D. (2000) Corporate Governance: The New Frontier, *Internal Auditor*, 57: 34–39.

Stiglitz, J. (2002) *Globalization & Its Discontents*, New York: Norton.

Stiglitz, J. (2003a) Globalisation, Technology and Asian Development, *Asian Development Review*, 20(2): 1–18.

Stiglitz, J. (2003b) *The Roaring Nineties*, New York: Norton.

Stiles, P. and B. Taylor (2002) *Boards at Work: How Directors View Their Roles and Responsibilities*, Oxford: Oxford University Press.

Stout, L. (2003) *The Mechanisms of Market Inefficiency: An Introduction to the New Finance*, Research Paper, 03-23, UCLA Law School.

Streeck, W. (2001) *The Transformation of Corporate Organization in Europe: An Overview*, Cologne: Max Planck Institute, MPIFG Working Paper, 01/8.

Strine, L. (2002) Derivative Impact: Some Early Reflections on the Corporation Law Implications of the Enron Debacle, *Business Lawyer*, 57(4): 1371–1402.

Sullivan, R. and Mackenzie, C. (2006) *Responsible Investment*, Sheffield: Greenleaf Publishing.

Sundaramurthy, C. and Lewis, M. (2003) Control and Collaboration: Paradoxes of Governance, *Academy of Management Review*, 28(3): 397–415.

SustainAbility (2001) *Buried Treasure: Uncovering the Business Case for Corporate Sustainability*, UNEP/SustainAbility.

SustainAbility Ltd/UNEP (2002) *Trust Us: The Global Reporters 2002 Survey of Corporate Sustainability Reporting*, SustainAbility Ltd/UNEP, www.sustainability.com

SustainAbility (2005) *The Changing Landscape of Liability: A Director's Guide to Trends in Corporate Environmental, Social and Economic Liability*, London: SustainAbility.

Swanson, C.B. (1996) Corporate Governance: Sliding Seamlessly into the Twenty-First Century, *Journal of Corporation Law*, 21: 417–456.

Swartz, M. and Watkins, S. (2003) *Power Failure: The Inside Story of the Collapse of Enron*, New York: Doubleday.

Sykes, A. (1994) Proposals for a Reformed System of Corporate Governance to Achieve Internationally Competitive Long-Term Performance, in N.H. Dimsdale and M. Prvezer (eds), *Capital Markets and Corporate Governance*, Oxford: Oxford University Press.

Sykes, T. (1996) *The Bold Riders: Behind Australia's Corporate Collapses*, Sydney: Allen and Unwin.

Taggart, R.A. (1986) Have US Corporations Grown Financially Weak?, in B.M. Friedman (ed.), *Financing Corporate Capital Formation*, Chicago: University of Chicago Press.

Tanimoto, K. (2004) Changes in the Market Society and Corporate Social Responsibility, *Asian Business and Management*, 3(2): 151–172.

Taylor, B. (2001) From Corporate Governance to Corporate Entrepreneurship, *Journal of Change Management*, 2(2): 128–147.

Taylor, B. (2003a) Corporate Governance: The Crisis, Investor's Losses, and the Decline in Public Trust, *Corporate Governance: An International Review*, 11(3): 155–163.

Taylor, B. (2003b) The Crisis in Corporate Governance, *Corporate Governance: An International Review*, 11(3): 155–63.

Taylor, B. (2004) Leading the Boardroom Revolution, *Corporate Governance: An International Review*, 12(4): 415–425.

Teck Corp Ltd v. Millar (1973) *Delaware Law Review*, 33, (3d).

Tenev, S., Zhang, C. and Brefort, L. (2002) *Corporate Governance and Enterprise Reform in China: Building the Institutions of Modern Markets*, Washington: World Bank.

Thomas, C.W. (2002) The Rise and Fall of Enron, *Journal of Accountancy*, 193(4): 41–54.

Thomsen, S. (2003) The Convergence of Corporate Governance Systems and European and Anglo-American Standards, *European Business Organisation Law Review*, Cambridge University Press, 4: 31–50.

Thomsen, S. (2005) Corporate Governance as a Determinant of Corporate Values, *Corporate Governance: International Journal of Business in Society*, 5(4): 10–27.

TIAA-CREF (2001) *Institute Paper*, TIAA-CREF Pension Fund, November.

Tonge, A., Greer, L. and Lawton, A. (20XX) The Enron Story: You Can Fool Some of the People Some of the Time…, *Business Ethics: A European Review*, 12(1): 4.

Triantis, G.G. (2001) *Financial Contract Design in the World of Venture Capital*, John M. Olin Law & Economics Working Paper, 115, Chicago.

Tricker, R.I. (1984) *Corporate Governance*, Aldershot: Gower.

Tricker, R.I. (1994) *International Corporate Governance*, Singapore: Prentice Hall.

Tricker, R.I. (1994a) Editorial, *Corporate Governance: An International Review*, 2(2–3).

Tricker, R.I. (2000) *Corporate Governance: The History of Management Thought*, London: Ashgate Publishing.

Turnbull, S. (1997) Corporate Governance: Its Scope, Concerns and Theories, *Corporate Governance: An International Review*, 5(4): 180–205.

Turner, P. (1991) Capital Flows in the 1980s: A Survey of Major Trends, *BIS Economic Papers No. 30*, Basle, Bank for International Settlements.

Tyson Report (2003) *Recruitment and Development of Non-Executive Directors*, London Business School, Department of Trade and Industry.

UBS Warburg (2001) *Sustainability Investment*, UBS Warburg, August.

UK Department for Environment, Food and Rural Affairs (2005) *Environmental Key Performance Indicators: Reporting Guidelines for UK Business*, London: DEFRA.

UK Department of Trade and Industry (2001) *Business and Society: Developing Corporate Social Responsibility in the UK*, London: DTI, March, 18 pp.

UK Social Investment Forum (2001) www.uksif.org/home/welcome/content.shtml

UN (1992) *Rio Declaration on Environment and Development*, Geneva: UN.

UN (2000) *Global Compact*, Geneva: UN.

UNCTAD (2002) *Trans National Corporations and Export Competitiveness*, World Investment Report, Geneva: United Nations Conference on Trade and Development.

UNCTAD (2004) *Development and Globalisation: Facts and Figures*, Geneva: UN.

UNCTAD (2005) *Trade and Development Report 2005: New Features of Global Interdependence*, Geneva: UNCTAD.

UNCTAD (2006) *Guidance on Good Practices in Corporate Governance Disclosure*, Geneva: UNEP.

UNEP Finance Initiative (2002a) *Climate Change and the Financial Services Industry*, Geneva: UNEP.

UNEP Finance Initiative (2002b) *Financing for Sustainable Development*, Geneva: UNEP.

UNEP Finance Initiative (2002c) *Financing Sustainable Energy Directory: A Listing of Lenders and Investors*, Geneva: UNEP.

UNEP Finance Initiative (2002d) *Foreign Direct Investment: Financing Sustainability*, Geneva: UNEP.

UNEP Finance Initiative (2002e) *Industry as a Partner for Sustainable Development: Finance and Insurance*, Geneva: UNEP.

UNEP Finance Initiative (2002f) *Sustainable Venture Finance*, Geneva: UNEP.

UNEP Finance Initiative (2003a) *Environmental Disclosure in Financial Statements*, Geneva: UNEP.

UNEP Finance Initiative (2003b) *Mainstreaming Sustainable Investment*, Geneva: UNEP.

UNEP Finance Initiative (2003c) *Risk, the Environment, and the Role of the Insurance Industry*, Geneva: UNEP.

UNEP Finance Initiative (2004d) *Generation Lost: Young Financial Analysts and Environmental, Social and Governance Issues*, Geneva: UNEP.

UNEP Finance Initiative (2004a) *The Materiality of Social, Environmental and Governance Issues to Equity Pricing*, Geneva: UNEP.

UNEP Finance Initiative (2004b) *Implementing Responsible Investment*, Geneva: UNEP.

UNEP Finance Initiative (2004c) *Values to Value: A Global Dialogue on Sustainable Finance*, Geneva: UNEP.

UNEP Finance Initiative (2005a) *CEO Briefing on the Future of Climate Change Policy: The Financial Sector Perspective*, Geneva: UNEP.

UNEP Finance Initiative (2005b) *A Legal Framework for the Integration of Environmental, Social and Governance Issues into Institutional Investment*, October, Geneva: UNEP.

UNEP (2006) *Show Me the Money: Lining Environmental, Social and Governance Issues to Company Value*, Geneva: UNEP Financial Initiative Asset Management Working Group.

Unerman, J. and O'Dwyer, B. (2004) Enron, WorldCom, Andersen *et al.*: A Challenge to Modernity, *Critical Perspectives on Accounting*, 15: 971–993.

United States Environmental Protection Agency (EPA) (1995) *An Introduction to Environmental Accounting as a Business Management Tool: Key Concepts and Terms*, Washington, DC: EPA.

United States Environmental Protection Agency (EPA) (2000) *The Lean and Green Supply Chain: A Practical Guide for Materials and Supply Chain Managers to Reduce Costs and Improve Financial Performance*, Washington, DC: EPA.

U.S. Environmental Protection Agency (US EPA) (2000) *Green Dividends? The Relationship between Firms' Environmental Performance and Financial Performance*, www.epa.gov/ocempage

US Senate (2002) The Role of the Board of Directors in Enron's Collapse, Committee on Governmental Affairs, Washington: US Senate.

USC Marshall School of Business/Heidrick and Struggles (2006) *Corporate Board Survey*, University of Southern California.

Useem, M. (1984) *The Inner Circle: Large Corporations and the Rise of Political Activity in the US and UK*, New York: Oxford University Press.

Useem, M. (1996) *Investor Capitalism: How Money Managers are Changing the Face of Corporate America*, New York: Basic Books.

Useem, M. and Zelleke, Z. (2006) Oversight and Delegation in Corporate Governance: Deciding What the Board Should Decide, *Corporate Governance: An International Review*, 14(1): 2–22.

Van den Berghe, L. (1999) *International Standardisation of Good Corporate Governance: Best Practices for the Board of Directors*, Boston: Kluwer.

Van den Berghe, L. (2002) *Corporate Governance in a Globalising World: Convergence or Divergence? A European Perspective*, Boston: Kluwer.

Van der Velden, B. and Hepkema, S. (1998). The Netherlands, *International Financial Law Review*, April, (special supplement): 41.

Vance, S.C. (1955) *Functional Control and Corporate Performance in Large Scale Industrial Enterprise*, Amherst, MA: University of Massachusetts.

Vance, S.C. (1964) *Boards of Directors: Structure and Performance*, Eugene, OR: University of Oregon Press.

Varallo, G.V. and Rollo, R.P. (2001) Corporate Governance: Developments in Shareholders' Meetings: New Delaware Legislation and the ABA Handbook, *Insights: The Corporate & Securities Law Advisor*, 15: 9.

Velayutham, S. and Perera, M.H.B. (2004) The Influence of Emotions and Culture on Accountability and Governance, *Corporate Governance: International Journal of Business in Society*, 4(1): 52–64.

Vienot, M. (1995) *Le Conseil d'Administration des Societes Cotes*, Rapport du Comite Conjoint, Paris: CNPF-AFEP (Vienot I).

Vinten, G. (1998) Corporate Governance: A UK/USA Comparison, *Credit Control*, 19(6): 18–24.

Visentini, G. (1997) Compatibility and Competition between American and European Corporate Governance: Which Model of Capitalism?, *Brooklyn Journal of International Law*, 23(3): 833–852.

Vitols, S. (2001) Frankfurt's Neuer Markt and the IPO Explosion: Is Germany on the Road to Silicon Valley?, *Economy and Society*, 30(4): 553–64.

Vogel, D. (2005) *The Market for Virtue: The Potential and Limits of Corporate Social Responsibility*, Washington, DC: Brookings Institute.

Von Tunzelmann, N. (2001) *Historical Coevolution of Governance and Technology: The Future of Innovation Studies*, Eindhoven University of Technology, The Netherlands, 20–23 September.

Waddock, S. (2003) Myths and Realities of Social Investing, *Organization & Environment*, 16(3): 369–380.

Waddock, S. (2004) Creating Corporate Accountability: Foundation Principles to Make Corporate Citizenship Real, *Journal of Business Ethics*, 50: 1–15.

Waddock, S.A. and Graves, S.B. (1997) The Corporate Social Performance-Financial Performance Link, *Strategic Management Journal*, 18(4): 303–319.

Walsh, J.P. and Seward, J.K. (1990) On the Efficiency of Internal and External Corporate Control Mechanisms, *Academy of Management Review*, 15(3): 421–458.

Wedderburn, W. (1985) Southey Memorial Lecture 1984: The Social Responsibility of Companies, *Melbourne University Law Review*, 15: 4.

Weil, Gotshal and Manges (2002) *Comparative Study of Corporate Governance Codes Relevant to the European Union and Its Member States, Final Report and Annexes*, New York: Weil, Gotshal and Manges.

Weinstein, B.L (1997) Welcome to the New Economy, *Perspectives*, 12(2): 1–4.

Wei Shen (2005) Improve Board Effectiveness: The Need for Incentives, *British Journal of Management*, 16: S81–S89.

Weisbach, M.S. and Hermalin, B.E. (2000) *Boards of Directors as an Endogenously Determined Institution: A Survey of the Economic Literature*, SSRN Working Paper Series, http://papersn.ssrn.com/paper.taf?ABSTRACT_ID=233111

Welford, R. (2002) Globalisation, Corporate Social Responsibility and Human Rights, *Corporate Social Responsibility and Environmental Management*, 9(1): 1–7.

Wells, H. (2002) The Cycles of Corporate Social Responsibility: An Historical Retrospective for the Twenty-First Century, *Kansas Law Review*, 51: 77.

Westphal, J.D. (1998) Board Games: How CEOs Adapt to Increases in Structural Board Independence from Management, *Administrative Science Quarterly*, 43: 511–537.

Westphal, J.D. (1999) Collaboration in the Boardroom: Behavioral and Performance Consequences of CEO-Board Social Ties, *Academy of Management Journal*, 42(1): 7–24.

Westphal J.D. and Khanna, P. (2003) Keeping Directors in Line: Social Distancing as a Control Mechanism in the Corporate Elite, *Administrative Science Quarterly*, 48(3): 361–398.

Westphal, J.D. and Zajac, E.J. (1995) Defections From the Inner Circle: Social Exchange, Reciprocity and the Diffusion of Board Independence in US Corporations, *Academy of Management Best Papers Proceedings*, 281–5.

Wheeler, D. (1997) *The Stakeholder Corporation: The Body Shop Blueprint for Maximizing Stakeholder Value*, London: Pitman.

Wheeler, S. (2002) *Corporations and the Third Way*, Oxford: Hart Publishing.

Whelan, C. and McBarnet, D. (1997) *Creative Accounting and the Cross Eyed Javelin*, Chichester: John Wiley & Sons.

Widen, W.H. (2003) Enron at the Margin, *Business Lawyer*, 58(3): 961–1002.

Williams, C. (2002) Symposium: Corporations Theory and Corporate Governance Law. Corporate Social Responsibility in an Era of Economic Globalisation, *University of California Davis Law Review*, 35: 705.

Williamson, O.E. (1975) *Markets and Hierarchies: Analysis and Anti-Trust Implications*, New York: Free Press.

Williamson, O.E. (1979) Transaction-Cost Economics: The Governance of Contractual Relations, *Journal of Law and Economics*, 22: 233–261.

Williamson, O.E. (1985) *The Economic Institutions of Capitalism*, New York: Free Press.

Williamson, O.E. (1996) *Mechanisms of Governance*, New York: Oxford University Press.

Williamson, O.E. (1998) Corporate Finance and Corporate Governance, *Journal of Finance*, 63(3): 567–591.

Williamson, O.E. (1998). The Institutions of Governance. *American Economic Review* 88(2): 75–79.

Willis, C. (2005) *The I Hate Corporate America Reader: How Big Companies from McDonald's to Microsoft Are Destroying Our Way of Life*, New York: Thunder's Mouth Press.

Wilson, A.C. and Campbell, W.M. (2003) Enron Exposed: Why It Took So Long, *Business and Economic Review*, 49(6).

Woidtke, T. (2002). Agents Watching Agents? Evidence from Pension Fund Ownership and Firm Value, *Journal of Financial Economics*, 63(1): 99–131.

Wolf, M. (2002) Why It Is So Hard to Fix the Flaws of Modern Capitalism, *Financial Times*, 20 November.

World Bank (2000) *Corporate Governance: A Framework for Implementation*, Washington: World Bank.

World Bank Group (1993) *The East Asian Miracle: Economic Growth and Public Policy*, Oxford: Oxford University Press.

World Bank Group (1996) *From Plan to Market: World Development Report 1996*, Oxford: Oxford University Press.

World Bank Group (1997) *The State in a Changing World: World Development Report 1997*, Oxford: Oxford University Press.

World Bank Group (2002a) *Public Sector Roles in Strengthening Corporate Social Responsibility: A Baseline Study*, Washington, DC: WBG.

World Bank Group (2002b) *The State of Corporate Governance: Experience From Country Assessments*, Policy Research Working Paper, Corporate Governance Unit, Washington, DC: WBG.

World Bank Group (2003) *Strengthening Implementation of Corporate Social Responsibility in Global Supply Chains*, October, Washington, DC: WBG.

World Bank Group (2004) *Public Sector Roles in Strengthening Corporate Social Responsibility: Taking Stock*, Washington, DC: WBG.

World Business Council for Sustainable Development (2002) *Corporate Social Responsibility: The WBCSD's Journey*, WBCSD.

World Business Council for Sustainable Development (2004) *Running the Risk*, WBCSD.

World Commission on the Social Dimension of Globalisation, *A Fair Globalisation: Creating Opportunities for All*, Geneva: International Labour Office, 2004.

World Economic Forum (2005) *Mainstreaming Responsible Investment*, World Economic Forum.

World Federation (2004) *Annual Report and Statistics*, Paris: World Federation of Stock Exchanges.

World Federation of Exchanges (2005) Annual Report and Statistics.

World Resources Institute, United Nations Environment Programme, and the World Business Council for Sustainable Development, Tomorrow's Markets – Global Trends and Their Implications for Business (2002) Washington, DC: World Resources Institute.

Wymeersch, E. (1996) Corporate Governance after the Investment Services Directive, Part 2, *European Financial Services Law*, 3: 130–141.

Xu, X.N. and Wang, Y. (1999) Ownership Structure and Corporate Governance in Chinese Stock Companies, *China Economic Review*, 10:75–98.

Yan, Y. (2005) *Foreign Investment & Corporate Governance in China*, London: Palgrave Macmillan.

Yasui, T. (1999) Corporate Governance in Japan, *Corporate Governance in Asia: A Comparative Perspective*, Seoul, 3–5 March, OECD/Korean Development Institute.

Yeung, K. (2004) *Securing Compliance: A Principled Approach*, Oxford: Hart Publishing.

Young, M.R. (ed.) (2002) *Accounting Irregularities and Financial Fraud: A Corporate Governance Guide*, New York: Aspen Law & Business.

Young, R. (1997) *Restructuring Europe: An Investor's View*, Goldman Sachs International.

Young, S. (2000) The Increasing Use of Non-executive Directors: Its Impact on UK Board Structure and Governance Arrangements, *Journal of Business Finance & Accounting*, 27: 1311–1342.

Zadek, S. (2004) The Path to Corporate Responsibility, *Harvard Business Review*, December, Boston: HBR.

Zahra, S. A. (1996) Governance, Ownership, and Corporate Entrepreneurship: The Moderating Impact of Industry Technological Opportunities, *Academy of Management Journal*, 39: 1713–1735.

Zahra, S.A., Neubaum, D.O. and Huse, M. (2000) Entrepreneurship in Medium-sized Companies: Exploring the Effects of Ownership and Governance Systems, *Journal of Management*, 26(5): 947–976.

Zahra, S.A. and Pearce, J.A. (1989) Boards of Directors and Corporate Financial Performance: A Review and Integrative Model, *Journal of Management*, 15: 291–344.

Zahra, S.A. and Pierce, J.A. (1990) Determinants of Board Directors' Strategic Involvement, *European Management Journal*, 8(2):164–173.

Zahra, S.A. and W.W. Stanton (1988) The Implications of Board of Directors' Composition for

Corporate Strategy and Performance, *International Journal of Management*, 5(2): 229–236.

Zajac, E.J. and Westphal, J.D. (1996) Director Reputation, CEO-Board Power, and the Dynamics of Board Interlocks, *Administrative Science Quarterly*, 41: 507–29.

Zeff, S. (2003) How the US Accounting Profession Got Where It Is Today, *Accounting Horizons* 17(4): 67–286.

Zeitlin, M. (1974) Corporate Ownership and Control: The Large Corporation and the Capitalist Class, *American Journal of Sociology*, 79: 1073–119.

# INDEX

accountability 5, 39–40, 50, 60, 274

Accounts Modernisation Directive (EU) 284

Ackerman, Josef 416

Acton, Lord 81

Adelphia Communications 107, 153, 328–9

Adia, Yukio 454

Adler, Rodney 437, 439, 445, 449

agency theory 23–6, 29–31, 58, 87, 92, 127

Aglietta, M. 88, 100

agriculture 274

Aguilera, R. 70

Ahmadijan, C.L. 214

Ahold see Royal Ahold

Aldama Report (2003) 178

Allen, Jamie 225

Alletzhauser, Albert 456

American Corporate Counsel Association 155

American Law Institute 38

AMP Capital Investments 32, 122–4

Anglo-American system of corporate governance 9, 11, 100–1, 129–69; myth of 162–5

Aoki, M. 97

Argus, Don 38

Arie, S. 380–1

Aronson, B.E. 456–60

Arthur Andersen (accountancy firm) 42–4, 107, 315, 320, 325–6, 329, 342–5, 443–9

Asahi Life Socially Responsible Investment 289

Asia Pacific countries, corporate governance system in 104, 109,

200–27; development of codes for 219–21; and growth 204–5; reform of 207–19; weaknesses of mechanisms and institutions 202–4

Asian boards of directors 48, 203, 209–10

Asian Corporate Governance Association 225

Asian Development Bank 14

Asian financial crisis (1997–8) 14, 85, 106, 114, 201, 205–7

Asian Roundtable on Corporate Governance 222

Association of British Insurers 119, 289, 296

Astra-Zeneca 115

AT&T 335

audit committees 50–1

auditability 303

auditor capture 325

Australia 64, 126–7, 144–9, 158–9, 167–8, 281, 284, 298–9, 310

*Australian Financial Review* 154, 329

Australian Stock Exchange (ASX) 38, 45, 56–7, 168–9, 432, 444, 463

Bagley, C.E. 36

Baker, James 322

Bangladesh 204

Bank of America 187, 380, 382, 385

Bank of Credit and Commerce International (BCCI) 140

Bank of Italy 384

bank finance 171–3, 211, 409–10

banks, influence of 93–4, 97

Barényi, Béla 389

Barry, Paul 146

Baums, T. 97

Baums Report (2001) 178

Bebchuk, L.A. 47, 75–9, 98, 106, 121, 123

Belgium 175, 179

Belnick, Mark 357, 359

Bendell, J. 303

Benz, Carl 388

Berggren, Christian 396

Berle, A.A. 4–5, 9, 87–92, 281

Berlin Initiative Group 64

Beyer, J. 193–4

BHP Billiton 38, 40

Bianco, M. 375

Biemond, Hendrik Jan 370–1

Blair, M.M. 29, 68–9

blockholder systems of company ownership 96–7

boards of directors 7–8, 24, 29–30; accountability of and value creation by 45–8, 67–9, 104; *active* and *passive* 40–2, 66, 82; in Asia 48, 203, 209–10; best practice for 56–8; changing role of 48–50; design of 49; functions and duties of 33–8, 131, 164; powers reserved for 39; process research on 58–9; reform of 50–3, 82; relationships with chief executive officers 38–40; role in monitoring and strategy 59–60, 65–7; size and composition of 35, 209, 211; structure of 174; variations between countries 48–9

Bobbitt, Max 344

Bockli, P. 142

Bogle, John C. 108, 125–6
Boisot, M. 216
Bond, Alan 146
Bondi, Enrico 380, 382
Bosch, Henry 146
Brabbs, Steven 345
Bratton, W. 88, 96
Breeden, Richard C. 17, 44–5, 61–2, 80, 331, 344, 347–8
Breen, Edward D. 360–1
Brennan, M.J. 15
British Telecom (BT) 115
Broad Market Social Index (BMSI) 300
Brundtland Commission 272
bubbles 3–4, 14–15
'bullet-dodging' 79
Bush, George (senior) 79, 322
Bush, George W. 321–2, 325
Bush, Tim 162
business association, forms of 6–8
business cycles 11–13
business judgement rule 36–7
Business Roundtable 36, 137, 155
BusinessWeek 154, 394, 396
Buttle, John 447

Cabot, Louis 41
Cadbury, Sir Adrian 2, 8, 13, 35, 55, 66–8, 80, 111, 122, 127, 140
Cadbury Report (1992) and Code 2, 13, 22, 38, 41, 50, 53, 55, 65, 68, 104, 111–12, 140–3, 175, 179, 284, 376
California Pension Fund (CalPERs) 46
Calvert Social Index 300
Cannella, A. 24, 26, 29
Capellas, Michael 348
capital markets 11, 31, 46, 89–93
car industry 194–5
Carbon Disclosure Project 269
Carbon Trust 287
Carrefour 266
Carter, C.C. 33, 40–1, 49, 57–8
Carter, William 371
Casavola, P. 375
Cendant 19
Certified General Accountants Association of Canada 272
CFA Institute 117–18
chairs of company boards 53–5
Chakrabarti, Rajesh 217–18

Charkham, J. 121–2
Chase Manhattan Bank 385
Chaucer, Geoffrey 2
Cheffins, B.R. 92–3, 131, 144, 172–3
Cheney, Dick 322
Chicago School of law and economics 149
chief executive officers (CEOs): accountability of 39–40; end of dominance of 80–1; powers of 29, 69–71, 108, 138, 159; relations with boards of directors 38–40; remuneration of 18–21, 35, 72–9, 108, 157
Child, J. 216
China 202–5, 214–17, 220–1
Chrysler, Walter 390
Chryler Corporation 388–96
Cicero 2
CIMA 46
Cisco 15
Citigroup 157, 326
City of London 139–40
civil law systems 91–2, 286
Claessens, S. 95, 109, 201–3, 223
Clark, Maurice 279–81
Clarke, T. 11, 177
classified board provision 72
Clearfield, A.M. 119–21
climate change 267, 287
CNN Money 19
Coase, Ronald 26
codetermination 88–9
Coffee, J. 9, 92
Cohen, Geoffrey 446, 449–50
Coles, D. 296
Combined Code on Corporate Governance (UK) 37, 50–1, 54–7, 60, 65, 143–4, 165; revision of 166
common law jurisdictions 36, 88, 91–2, 286
community development financial institutions 295
community investing 291
company law, European 173–4, 192
Company Law Reform Bill (UK, 2005) 36, 283
Company Law Review (UK, 1998–2001) 166, 282–4
ConAgra 357
conflicts of interest 63–4

Connell, Laurie 146
Consumers Association 125
Cooke, C.A. 3
Cooper, Brad 437, 450
Cooper, Cynthia 338, 342–5
Core, J.E. 77
corporate governance: advisers on 121; American approach to 90–1; broad view of 31; compliance-driven 57; control mechanisms for 104–6; and corporate performance 22–3, 45–8, 119–20, 127, 309; crisis in 14–22, 106–9; definitions of 1–2, 45; dispersed-ownership and concentrated-ownership forms of 87; dissonance between theory and practice in 8; diversity in 8–11, 176–80; failures of 14, 32, 187–8; globalisation of 11; institutional involvement in 120–4; international 112; of investment institutions 124–8; lifecycles of 7–8, 12–13; long-standing defects in 17; market-based system of 129–31; market for control of 98–100; models of 48; origins of 3–6, 85–8; outsider and insider systems of 9–10, 30–1, 83–5, 101, 107, 129–30, 144, 170; paradigms of 93–5; principles-based 162; reasons for recent interest in 1; reform of 17–18, 122–3, 188–92; regimes of 83–5, 100; relationship-based approaches to 85, 170–1, 200–1; rules-based 162, 200; and sustainability 23; theoretical perspectives on 25–30; in transitional economies 197–9
corporate governance resolutions 293–5
Corporate Monitor arrangements 347
corporate social responsibility 267–305; future prospects 304; integrity of 269–71; legitimacy of 279–88; reporting on 303; significance and impact of 267–9; and socially-responsible investment 288–91, 302
Council of Institutional Investors 295

Council of Institutional
   Shareholders 138
Countrywide 19
Cox, Christopher 79
Cragnotti, Sergio 381
creative accounting 63, 109
Credit Suisse First Boston 115
Cromme Code 178
Czech Republic 198

Daily, C.M. 24, 26
Daimler, Gottlieb 388
Daimler-Benz 181
DaimlerChrysler 32, 193, 309,
   388–400
Daiwa Bank 458
Dalton, C.M. 41, 58
Dalton, D.R. 24, 26, 41, 58
Davies, P. 282
Davis, E.P. 93–4, 98
Davis, G. 71, 138
Davis, J.H. 26
de Ruiter, Henny 367, 371
de Vries, Peter 371
Deakin, S. 150
debt: *direct* control by means of
   93–4; *market* control by means
   of 94
del Soldato, Luciano 381
dela Rama, M. 11
Delaware 4, 36–7, 72, 87, 124,
   133–5, 155–6
Delaware opinion 111
delegation 39
Deloitte & Touche 367, 383, 385
Demb, A. 34, 180–1
democratic processes 274; *see
   also* shareholder democracy
Denmark 178
Department of Trade and
   Industry (UK) 78, 119,
   166–7, 438
deregulation 211, 315–16, 332
Desmond, E.W. 456, 459
Deutsche Bank 48, 198, 268, 389,
   392, 396–9
Deutsche Telecom 335
Dew-Becker, I. 76
Dick, Melvin 343–5
Dignam, A. 145–6
directors of companies 29;
   changing role of 48–50;
   definition of 36; duties of 36–7,

283–4; remuneration of 78,
   142–3
disclosure issues 7, 13, 64–5, 89,
   104, 130–1, 174, 208
Disney case (2005) 123
Doane, Deborah 270
Dodd, E.M. 281
Domino 400 Social Index
   (DSI) 300
Donaldson, L. 26
Donaldson, William H. 18, 113,
   117, 157, 161
Dore, R. 212
Dow Jones Sustainability Index
   (DJSI) 269, 290, 301
Draghi Reform (Italy, 1998)
   176–8, 376
Dreazen, Y.J. 345
Dresdner Kleinwort
   Wasserstein enskip268
Drexel Burnham Lambert
   137–8, 315
Dunford, John 449
Dutch East India Company 3
Dynergy 319–20, 326

earnings guidance 118
earnings misstatements 21–2, 160
Easterbrook, F.H. 92
Eaton, Robert 390–3
Ebbers, Bernard 44–5, 62, 81,
   153, 331–40, 344–5, 348, 357
E.Capital Partners 302
economic impact, definition of
   272–3
*The Economist* 384, 399
Economist Intelligence Unit (EIU)
   277–9
ecosystems 273–4
education, financial 118
*efficient capital markets*
   hypothesis 119
Egan, M. 198
Eisenberg, D. 346
Elston, J.A. 393
emissions control 273
employee representation 174
energy supplies 273
Enron 14–17, 35, 42–4, 50, 61,
   81–3, 107, 152–6, 162, 165, 167,
   187, 309, 315–29, 342, 354
entrenchment index 47

environmental, social and
   governance (ESG) issues 268,
   271, 285–8
environmental costs 23, 275
environmental impact, definition
   of 272–3
environmental reporting 277
Environmental Resources
   Management 296
Equator Principles 269
equity: *direct* control by means of
   94–5; *market* control by means
   of 94; ownership structures 83
Ernst & Young 439, 444, 448
Erturk, I. 78
*esprit de corps* of company boards
   70–1
Esser, Klaus 407–16
Ethibel Sustainability Index
   (ESI) 301
Ethical Investment
   Association 289
Euronext 197
Europe, international role of
   196–7
European Commission 176,
   188–91, 196–7, 272,
   288–9, 384
European style of corporate
   governance 109, 170–99;
   convergence in 179–93;
   development of codes for
   175–81; failures of 187; reform
   of 177, 188–92; transformation
   of systems 181–7
European Sustainable and
   Responsible Investment Forum
   (Eurosif) 197, 288
European Union 17, 173, 284
expansion capital 116
externalisation of costs 23

family-owned companies 85, 195,
   201–2
family relationships 109
Fan, J.P.H. 202–3
Fastow, Andrew 42, 315–18,
   324–9
Federal Communications
   Commission 332, 335, 343
Federal Trade Commission 366
Federation des Experts
   Compatables Européens 190
Ferraris, Alberto 381

Fiat 195
fiduciary duties 5, 88–9, 281, 286
financial engineering 137
Financial Executives
  International 161
Financial Reporting Council (UK)
  37, 51, 56–7, 62–3, 166
*Financial Times* 15, 115, 408, 410
*financialisation* of business
  activity 151
Finkelstein, S. 49
Fodera, Dominic 435, 438, 446,
  449–50
Fokker 395
Ford Motors 98, 390, 398
foreign direct investment (FDI)
  196–7
*Fortune* magazine 153
Fox, L. 320–5
France 83, 90, 96, 173–6, 185–6,
  289; corporate governance
  system in 103–4
France Telecom 335, 406
Freshfields Bruckhaus Deringer
  286–7
Fried, J.M. 75–9, 106
Friedland, J. 455–6
FTSE4Good indices 300–3
Fuji Bank 453–4
Fujikura, Nobutaka 455
fund managers 121
Funk, Joachim 416

Galanis, M. 145–6
Gardener, Justin 446, 448
Garratt, Bob 60–1, 80
Garten, J.E. 395
Gelithner, Timothy F. 114
General Electric 15
General Motors 41, 98,
  389–90, 398
Gent, Chris 409, 415–16
Germany 48, 64, 83, 89–90, 93,
  96–9, 178, 193–5; corporate
  culture 413–14; corporate
  governance system in 101–3,
  391–3, 397–8, 402–4;
  distribution of share
  ownership 171
Gilbertson, Brian 38
Gillies, J. 40
Gilson, R.J. 136
Gimein, M. 333
Glass, Lewis & Co. 21–2, 160

Glass-Steagall Act 91, 131
Global Crossing 17, 50, 107,
  335, 341
Global Reporting Initiative 269,
  272–3, 279, 303
globalisation 11, 29, 31
Gobbi, Oliviero 302
Goldberg, L.G. 393
Goldman Sachs 22, 268, 340,
  410, 443
Goldstein, A. 194
Gompers, P. 47
good faith 36–7
Goodyear, Chip 38
Gorbachov, Mikhail 323
Gordon, J.N. 156
Gordon, R.J. 76
Gorreri, Franco 382
Gorton, G. 97
'governance effect' on share
  prices 119
Governance Metrics International
  47, 145, 279
Gower, C. 3–4, 188, 265
Goyer, M. 185–6
Gramm, Wendy 322
Gramm-Leach-Billey Act 131
Grant Thornton 383, 385
Grasso, Dick 156–7
Green, D. 296
Greenbury Report (1995) 142–3
Greenspan, Alan 15, 113–14, 152,
  157, 323
Grinstein, Y. 77–8
Grubman, Jack 341–2, 345

Hall, Brian J. 81
Hall, P. 185
Hamel, Gary 326–7
Hampel Report (1998) 143
Hanbo Steel 205
harmonisation of corporate
  governance systems 192–3
Harvey-Jones, Sir John 65, 70
Hashimoto, Ryutaro 454–6, 461
Hassel, A. 193–4
HCA Inc. 117
Head, Neville 446
Healey, Joseph 148
health conditions 273
HealthSouth 354
hedge funds 113–16, 309
Heijn, Albert 365
Heins-Bunde, Joachim 183–4

Hellicar, Meredith 424
Hendy, J. 25
Heri, Erwin 436
Hermalin, B. 58
Hermes (pension fund) 22, 46,
  167, 214, 297
Higgs Report (2003) 56, 58, 60,
  143–4, 165
'high-performing Asian
  economies' (HPAEs) 204
HIH Insurance Group 126,
  158–9, 167, 310, 434–50
Hillman, A.J. 29
Hilmer, Fred 34
Hinkley, Robert 304
Hiroshi, O. 457
Hogg, Sarah 34, 65
Holderness, C.G. 77
Holdsworth, W.S. 3
Holmstrom, B. 328
Holton, G. 317
Hong Kong 204, 220–1
Höpner, M. 409, 411
Hosking, D.M. 48
hostile takeovers 71–2,
  136–7, 195
House Committee on Financial
  Services 17
HSBC 268
Hutton, Will 35

IAC/Interactive 19
IG Metall 393, 396
incentive pay 106–8, 118
incorporation of companies,
  decisions on 6–7
India 205, 217–21
Indonesia 204, 219–20
initial public offerings 7
innovation, aspects of 273
inside ownership of firms 77
insider trading 64, 79, 208
Institute of Chartered
  Accountants of England and
  Wales 162
Institute of Chartered
  Accountants of Scotland 46
Institute for a Fair Economy 77
*institutional complementarity* thesis
  192–3
institutional investors 85–6, 92–4,
  129–31, 138, 165; governance
  and regulatory relationships of
  128; increasing importance of

109–18; monitoring by 120; new era for 118–28
Institutional Investors Research Centre 47
Institutional Shareholders Services Corporate Governance Quotient 53
institutional theory 29
Intel 15
intellectual capital 30
internal controls 62–3, 100
International Accounting Standards Board 65
International Finance Corporation 269
International Financial Reporting Standards 65
International Monetary Fund (IMF) 107, 204–7
Investment Advisers Act (US, 1940) 133
Investment Company Act (US, 1940) 91, 133
investment indices, social and environmental 299–302
investment institutions, governance of 124–8
Investor Responsibility Research Centre 155
'irrational exuberance' 152
Italy 96, 103, 172–8, 186–7
Iwasaki, Kiichiro 465

Jackson, David (and Jackson Report, 2004) 421–9
Jackson, G. 392, 409, 411
Jacoby, S.M. 9, 113, 212
James, Bruce 450
James Hardie Industries 285, 301, 421–33
Japan 49, 93, 96–7, 202–5, 209–14, 220–1; corporate governance system in 104
Japanese External Trade Organisation (JETO) 212–14
Jensen, M.C. 23–4, 77
Jesovar, F. 8
Johnstone, S. 209
JP Morgan Chase 326
judgement, exercise of 34
junk bonds 94, 104, 126, 138
Jurgens, U. 193
JustPensions survey 296–8

Kaiser, Mark P. 371
Kaplan, S.N. 328
Kaufman, R. 164
Keegan, M. 388
keiretsu system 97, 209, 212
Kellett, Stiles 340
Kennedy School of Government 272
Kerkorian, Kirk 390, 392, 395
Keynes, John Maynard 13
Khanna, P. 71
Kijima, Riyika 462–3
Kimber, D. 219
Kinder, Richard 323
Kirin Brewery 461
Kirkpatrick, G. 8
Kitsuda, Yoshikazu 465
KLD Research and Analytics 300
knowledge-based theory of the firm 30
Kodama, Yoshio 462
Kohlberg Kravis Roberts & Co. (KKR) 117, 137
Koike, Ryuichi 454, 463–4
Koike, Yoshimori 455, 464
Kolla, P. 416
Korea, Republic of 200, 204
Kozlowski, Denis 78, 354–61
KPMG 276–7, 343–4, 440, 448
Krugman, Paul 152
Kulpa, A.M. 115
Kume, I. 393
Kyoto Protocol 269, 302

labour law 88
Lamba, A. 146
Landler, Mark 416
Lane, Christel 193
Lannoo, K. 176
La Porta, R. 91–2, 95
Large Cap Social Index (LCSI) 300
Lavella, L. 356
'law matters' thesis 91
Law Society 46
Lay, Kenneth 42–3, 315–16, 320–9
Lazard Frères 340
Lazonick, W. 72, 75, 95, 126
leadership, corporate 118
Leblanc, R. 40
Lee, Timothy 371
legal personalities of corporations 68

leveraged buy-outs (LBOs) 116–17, 137, 309
leveraging 94–5
liability, legal and moral 284–5
life insurance companies 110–12
limited liability 6–7, 23, 68, 432
Lingle, C. 205
Lipper (rating agency) 289–90
Lipton, M. 138
listed companies 7–8; number of 97, 209
London Stock Exchange 104, 139, 142
Long Term Capital Management (LTCM) 114
Long, B. 115
Lorsch, J. 33, 40–1, 49, 57–8, 131, 138
Lutz, Robert 390

MacAvoy, P.W. 47
McCahery, J.A. 96, 134
McCarthy, D.J. 198
McChessney, R. 332
Macdonald, Peter 428–30
McDonnell, B.H. 9
McDonough, William J. 14, 72, 74, 114, 161–2
Mace, M.L. 29
McGrath, Anthony 440
McGuire, William W. 82
Macintosh, Alexander 440
MacIver, E. 131
McKinsey & Co. 46, 320–1, 326–7
McNulty, T. 34, 50, 55, 59, 66, 82
majority shareholders, control by 95–8, 100
Makihara, B. Minoru 31
Malaysia 200, 204, 219–20
Malginov, G. 198–9
management boards 64
management buy-outs (MBOs) 116, 137
managerial capitalism 135
managerialist theory 29, 71
Mannesmann, Reinhard and Max 404
Mannesmann (company) 98, 309, 392, 404–16
Maremont, M. 355, 360
Mark, Rebecca 323–4
mark-to-market accounting 317

market capitalisation of stock exchanges 97, 207, 226
Martin, N.A. 462
Matsuki, Shimpei 455
Maxwell Communications Corporation 140
May, Bernhard 416
Mays, S. 280
MCI Communications 16, 80, 348–9
Means, G.C. 4–5, 9, 87–92, 281
Meckling, W.H. 23–4
Mehran, H. 77
Melis, A. 186, 377–8
Mercedes 398–9
Mercer Investment Consulting 287
mergers 191–2, 214, 403
Merrill Lynch 326
Metcalfe's law 152
Meurs, Michael 188, 365, 368–72
Meyer-Larsen, W. 392–5
Microsoft 15
Milken, Michael 137–8
Miller, James 371
Millstein, I.M. 8, 13, 35, 47, 66–7, 80, 91, 111, 122, 127, 135, 137, 151
Minnow, N. 122, 150
minority shareholders 7–8
misselling 125–6
Mitchell, L.A. 23, 267, 271
Moberg, Anders 369–72
mobility patterns 274
Modern Company Law Review (UK) 46, 166–7, 282, 289
modern prudent investor rule 286
Modernising Company Law and Enhancing Corporate Governance (EU Directive, 2006) 176, 190–2
Moinho Pacifico 385
Money Magazine 341
Monks, R. 122
Montgomery, C. 164
Mooney, A.C. 49
Morgan Stanley 386
Morley (fund managers) 290
Mosbacher, Robert 322
multinational corporations 11
Murphy, K.J. 77
mutual funds market 125
Myers, David 338–40, 344–5, 348
Myers, S.C. 393

Myners, Paul (and Myners Report, 2001) 122–3, 144, 166

Nakazawa, Nobuo 465
National Association of Corporate Directors (US) 155
National Association of Pension Funds (UK) 167
National Association of Securities Dealers (US) 342
natural capital 273–4
Naumann, K. 193
Netherlands, the 175, 179
network theory 29
Neubauer, F.F. 34, 180–1
Neumann, S. 198
new institutional economics 26
New York Stock Exchange (NYSE) 156–7
New Zealand 144–5, 148–9
newly industrialised economies (NIEs) 204
Nextra 386
Nikko Fund 289
Nissay Asset Management 214
Nokia 32
nomination committees 50–3
Nomura 310, 452–65
Nonaka, Tomoyo 213
non-executive directors 24, 30, 40, 50–1, 55–6, 59, 104, 131, 165
Norby Report (2001) 178
Norman, Tony 348
Normand, Troy 344–5
Norway 179
Novartis 115
NTT 335
nutrition and malnutrition 273

O'Brien, Kerry 424
Okamura, A. 214
Olimpia 186–7
Olivencia Report (1998) 178
One-Tel 158–60, 167, 443
operating and financial reviews (OFRs), extension of 289
Oreu, Eduardo 371
Organisation for Economic Cooperation and Development (OECD) 2, 9–14, 46–9, 64–5, 96, 107, 109, 119, 127–8, 131, 181, 185, 201–3, 221–3, 269,

334–5; Principles of Corporate Governance 37
O'Sullivan, Mary 395, 397
over-disclosure 355
Owen, Neville 159, 434, 448–9
ownership of companies: active and passive types of 5; advantages of concentration in 97; in Japan 210; separation from control 4–5, 9, 87–8, 92; subdivision of 4–5
Oxley, Michael G. 17

Paetzold, R.L. 29
Parmalat 16, 109, 187, 309, 365, 374–86
partnerships 3–7
path dependence 98
pay of business executives 35, 72–9, 82, 95, 108, 118, 122; linked to performance 106–8
Payne, Michael 434, 438
Penn Central 41, 136
pension funds 110–13, 119, 125–7, 167, 171–2, 287, 295–8, 345–6
performance measures, corporate 119
perpetual succession 7
Peters Code (1997) 175
Pettigrew, A. 25, 45, 47, 58–9
Pfizer 15
Philippines, the 220–1
Pillmore, E.M. 360–1
'poison pills' 72, 137–8
'politics matters' thesis 91
Polly Peck 140
Porter, M.E. 150–1, 185
Powers, William 42
Powers Report (2002) 326, 328
Preda Code (Italy, 2002) 178, 376–7
PriceWaterhouseCoopers (PWC) 359, 438
principal-agent relationships 23–4, 31, 83, 87, 127
private companies 7
private equity firms 116–17, 309
Provera, Marco Tronchetti 186–7
Prowse, S. 206–7
Public Company Accounting Oversight Board (PCAOB) 161–2

Public Company Accounting Reform and Investor Protection Act (2002) see Sarbanes-Oxley Act
Public Utility Holding Company Act (US, 1935) 133
Puffer, S.M. 198
Pye, A. 25, 45, 58–9

Qwest 50, 335

Radygin, A. 198–9
Rainmaker Research 119
Ramos, Charles E. 156
Rathenau, Walther 5
Rebérioux, A. 88, 100
Redmond, Paul 6, 68, 271, 282–3, 424, 429–30
regulation 13, 18, 88–90, 109, 208; of corporate governance 104 see also deregulation; self-regulation
regulatory capture 343
Relational Investors 46
remuneration committees 51, 78
Renault 390
reputational intermediaries 105–6
Resnick, Michael 371
resource dependence theory 29
responsibility, social and environmental 31
retained earnings 95
Reuter, Edzard 392, 395
revenue recognition 160
Rich, Jodie 159
Richardson, Colin 435
Rigas, John 153
Rio Tinto 298
Ripley, A. 344
risk management 60–4
RJR Nabisco 117
Roberts, Bert 345
Roberts, J. 34, 50, 55, 59, 66, 82
Roe, Mark 91, 97–8, 134–5
Roosevelt, F.D. 131
Rowley, A. 460
Rowley, Coleen 344
Royal Ahold 32, 109, 187–8, 309, 365–72
Royal Institute for International Affairs 271
Rupp, J. 193
Russia 198–9
Rybczynski, T. 93

Rynecki, D. 356
Ryöppönen, Hannu 371–2

Saab 98
Sakamaki, Hideo 454
Salomon Smith Barney (SSB) 341
Sanchez, Jose 371
Santow J 427
Sanyo 213
Sara Lee (company) 367
Sarbanes, Paul 17
Sarbanes–Oxley Act (2002) 17–18, 35, 42, 50, 58, 65, 81, 83–5, 107–8, 117, 154–6, 160, 165, 190, 328; costs of implementation 161–2
Sarin, Arun 415
Schilling, F. 391–2
Schmid, F. 97
Schoorman, F.D. 26
Schrage, M. 35–6
Schrempp, Jürgen 389–96
Schröder, Gerhard 410
Schurpf, Willi 436
screening of portfolios 291–2
Seaman, B. 391
Securities Acts (US) 6, 132–5
Securities and Exchange Commission (SEC) 16, 18, 42, 89–91, 115–16, 132–6, 154–5, 329, 335, 347, 355–60, 368, 371
Securities Investor Protection Act (US, 1970) 133
Segato, L. 375
Segawa, Minoru 462
self-interest, managerial 24–5
self-regulation 13, 18, 91–2
Sender, H. 456, 460
shadow directors 222
Shafron, Peter 428–30
Shah, R. 303
share option schemes 18, 70, 78–82, 106, 108, 150, 210
shareholder activism 122–3, 293
shareholder advocacy 291–3
shareholder democracy 191
shareholder primacy 68–9, 281
shareholder rights 5, 68–9, 72, 94, 130–1, 174
shareholder theory of the firm 150
shareholder value ideology 9, 23, 83, 127, 138, 149–58, 193–6, 210, 279–82

'shark repellents' 72, 137–8
Shiller, Robert 15
short-termism 117–18
Sidak, J.G. 331–2, 343
Sidgmore, John 333, 340, 345–8
Siebert, H. 181–2
Siemens 193
Simpson, A. 121–2
Singapore 204, 220–1
Skase, Christopher 146
Skilling, Jeffrey 42, 315–26, 329
Smith, Adam 4
social capital theory 30
social impact, definition of 273
Social Investment Forum 288–9, 293, 298
social responsibility resolutions 293–5
socially-responsible investment 289–99; and corporate social responsibility 288–91, 302
societal costs 275
SOCRATES database 300
sokaiya 454, 461–3
sole tradership 7
Solomon, D. 345
Sonnenfeld, J.A. 360
Sony 211–14, 461
Soskice, D. 185
South Sea Bubble 3–4
Spain 175, 178
Sparkes, R. 289
special purpose entities (SPEs) 317–20, 325–6
special purpose vehicles (SPVs) 187
Spitzer, Eliot 18, 125, 156–7
'spring-loading' 79
Sprint Corporation 17
stakeholders 9, 23–6, 167, 202, 279–81; internal and external 29
Stapledon, G. 146
Starr, P. 461
Steil, B. 98
Stern, C. 342, 348
Stern Review (2006) 267
stewardship theory 26–7, 30
Stiglitz, Joseph 198
Stiles, P. 24, 29–30, 33–4, 50, 55, 59, 66–7, 82
stock markets, control of companies by 100
stock options see share options

Stodghill, R. 391
Stout, L. 68–9
Stringer, Howard 213–14
Sullivan, Scott 337–40,
  344–5, 348
Sumitomo Bank 212
supermajority provision 72
supervisory boards 48–9, 64, 174,
  182–5
sustainability: of the firm 23, 30;
  social and environmental
  269–73, 277
Sustainable Asset Management
  Group 274–5
Swanson, C.B. 92–3, 131
Swartz, Mark 356, 359
Sweden 179
Switzerland 178
Sykes, T. 145
Symonds, W.C. 356, 360

Tabuchi, Setsuya 454–5
Tabuchi, Yoshihisa 454–6
Taiwan 204
takeover bids 71–2, 92, 94,
  98–100, 136–8, 195, 208
Tanaka, Kakuei 462
Tanaka, Wataru 214
Tanzi, Calisto (and Tanzi family)
  187, 374–86
taxation 7
Taylor, B. 15, 24, 29–30, 33, 66–7
Teck Corp Ltd v. Millar case 281
Telecom Italia 186–7
Terasawa, Yoshio 463
Thailand 200, 204–5, 219–20
Thelen, K. 393
Thomsen, Linda C. 371
3i 34, 65
Thurlow, Edward 68
Tokyo Stock Exchange 211
Tonna, Fausto 378, 381, 385
Toriihara, M. 215
total factor productivity
  (TFP) 204
Toyota 389, 398, 456
transaction cost theory 26, 29–30
transitional economies 197–9
transparency 106–7, 118,
  297, 303
Transparency Directive (EU) 65

Tricker, R.I. 30, 34
Trowbridge Report (2004) 428–31
trust 30
Trust Indenture Act (US,
  1939) 133
Turnbull Report (1999) 144
Tyco 16, 32, 50, 78, 81–2, 107,
  309, 328–9, 354–61
Tyson Report (2003) 165

UBS 268
Ujiie, Juinichi 463
Underwood, Terry 447
unitary boards 48–9
United Nations Conference on
  Trade and Development
  (UNCTAD) 65
United Nations Environment
  Program (UNEP) 23, 268, 285–7
United Nations Global
  Compact 269
United States Justice Department
  367, 371
United States Supreme Court 329
United Auto Workers 393
UnitedHealth Group 82
Universities Superannuation
  Scheme 297–8
urbanisation 274
Useem, Michael 70, 360

Valero Energy 19
van der Hoeven, Cees 188,
  365–72
Vasella, Daniel 115
venture capital 116
Verizon Communications 348–9
Vermeulen, P.M. 134
Verschoor, C.C. 359–60
Viconti, Paola 381
Vienot Reports (1995, 1999) 90,
  175–6
Vinson, Betty 348
Vinson & Elkins (law firm) 315,
  325–6
Vinten, G. 142
vision, managerial 69–70
Vitols, S. 182
Vivendi 32, 409
Vodafone 98, 115, 309, 335, 392,
  406–16

Vogel, David 269–70
Volkswagen 195
Volvo 98
voting rights and voting systems
  96, 122–4, 130
Vuursteen, Karel 371

Wall Street crash (1929) 91, 106,
  131, 135
Wall Street rule 120
Wal-Mart 366
Walsh, Frank 356
water supplies 274
Watkins, Sherron 319–20,
  323–8, 344
Webb Report (2003) 156
Wei Shen 70–1
Wein, Randolph 436, 439
Weingarten, Reid 357
Weisbach, M. 58
Westphal, J.D. 30, 71
Will, Sandy 157
Williams, Ray 434, 438–9, 443–50
Williamson, O.E. 26, 93
Winter Report (2002) 189–90
Wolf, M. 17
Wolfensohn, James 1
World Bank 1–2, 14–17, 107, 204,
  207, 217, 269, 272, 316
World Business Council for
  Sustainable Development
  269, 272
World Federation of
  Exchanges 269
World Health Organisation 303
WorldCom 35, 44–5, 50, 61–2,
  80–2, 107, 153–4, 309, 315,
  328–54, 414
Wyman, Bill 41

Yahoo 19
Yates, Burford 348
Yokich, Stephen P. 397

Zajac, E.J. 30
Zelleke, Z. 70
Zetsche, Dieter 398
Zhender, Egon 40
Zini, Gianpaolo 383, 385

eBooks – at www.eBookstore.tandf.co.uk

# A library at your fingertips!

eBooks are electronic versions of printed books. You can store them on your PC/laptop or browse them online.

They have advantages for anyone needing rapid access to a wide variety of published, copyright information.

eBooks can help your research by enabling you to bookmark chapters, annotate text and use instant searches to find specific words or phrases. Several eBook files would fit on even a small laptop or PDA.

**NEW:** Save money by eSubscribing: cheap, online access to any eBook for as long as you need it.

## Annual subscription packages

We now offer special low-cost bulk subscriptions to packages of eBooks in certain subject areas. These are available to libraries or to individuals.

For more information please contact webmaster.ebooks@tandf.co.uk

We're continually developing the eBook concept, so keep up to date by visiting the website.

## www.eBookstore.tandf.co.uk